ANN GOLDSTEIN AND ANNE RORIMER

RECONSIDERING THE OBJECT OF ART:
1965-1975 *With essays by Lucy R. Lippard, Stephen Melville, and Jeff Wall*

The Museum of Contemporary Art, Los Angeles

The MIT Press, Cambridge, Massachusetts, and London, England

This publication accompanies the exhibition "1965-1975: Reconsidering the Object of Art," organized by Ann Goldstein and Anne Rorimer and presented at The Museum of Contemporary Art, Los Angeles, 15 October 1995-4 February 1996.

"1965-1975: Reconsidering the Object of Art" is part of the reopening of MOCA at the Temporary Contemporary, sponsored by Philip Morris Companies Inc.

The exhibition is also made possible by the generous support of The Capital Group, Inc., Gilbert Friesen, Jay and Donatella Chiat, and the National Endowment for the Arts, a federal agency.

Library of Congress Cataloguing-in-Publication Data
Goldstein, Ann.
    Reconsidering the object of art : 1965-1975 / Ann Goldstein, Anne Rorimer ; with essays by Lucy R. Lippard, Stephen Melville, Jeff Wall.
        p.   cm.
    Exhibition presented at the Museum of Contemporary Art, Los Angeles, 15 October 1995-4 February 1996.
    Includes bibliographical references.
    ISBN 0-262-57111-0 (pbk. : alk. paper)
    1. Conceptual art--Exhibitions.
    2. Art. Modern--20th century--Exhibitions.   I. Rorimer, Anne. II. Museum of Contemporary Art (Los Angeles, Calif.) III. Title.
N6494.C63G66 1995
700--dc20   95-31848
                CIP

EDITED BY **RUSSELL FERGUSON AND JOHN ALAN FARMER** | DESIGNED BY **LORRAINE WILD, BETH ELLIOTT AND SUSAN PARR—REVERB, LOS ANGELES** | PRINTED AND BOUND BY **DRUKKERIJ ROSBEEK BV, THE NETHERLANDS** | DISTRIBUTED BY **THE MIT PRESS,** 55 Hayward Street, Cambridge, Massachusetts 02142

Cover, **DANIEL BUREN** , photo/souvenir of BUS BENCHES (1970/82). Third Street and San Vicente Boulevard, October 1982. Postcard. A work in situ consisting of fifty bus benches, located throughout Los Angeles, silkscreened with 8.7 cm (3 1/2 in.) white and colored vertical stripes. Courtesy the artist.

Half-title and frontispiece, **JOHN BALDESSARI**, CREMATION PROJECT (details) (1970). Courtesy the artist.

CONTENTS

ARTISTS IN THE EXHIBITION

Vito Acconci
Bas Jan Ader
Giovanni Anselmo
Eleanor Antin
Art & Language
Michael Asher
David Askevold
John Baldessari
Robert Barry
Lothar Baumgarten
Bernd and Hilla Becher
Mel Bochner
Marcel Broodthaers
Stanley Brouwn
Daniel Buren
Victor Burgin
André Cadere
James Coleman
Hanne Darboven
Jan Dibbets
Peter Downsbrough
Ger van Elk
Morgan Fisher
Gilbert & George
Dan Graham
Hans Haacke
Douglas Huebler
Joan Jonas
Stephen J. Kaltenbach
On Kawara
John Knight
Joseph Kosuth
Christine Kozlov
David Lamelas
William Leavitt
Sol LeWitt
Richard Long
Tom Marioni
Gordon Matta-Clark
N.E. Thing Co.
Bruce Nauman
Maria Nordman
Dennis Oppenheim
Blinky Palermo
Giulio Paolini
Adrian Piper
Yvonne Rainer
Allen Ruppersberg
Edward Ruscha
Robert Smithson
Michael Snow
Niele Toroni
William Wegman
Lawrence Weiner
Ian Wilson

RICHARD KOSHALEK

PREFACE: BUILDING A CONTEMPORARY TRADITION

With the long-awaited reopening of the Temporary Contemporary, a landmark has returned to Los Angeles and the international art community, and The Museum of Contemporary Art is again able to present a comprehensive program fully utilizing the distinctive spaces of its two extraordinary buildings. Prior to the interim closure of the Temporary Contemporary in 1992 — at the request of the City of Los Angeles and the developer of a large-scale construction project that was subsequently cancelled — the museum had established an unparalleled record of original exhibitions and performance programs. Highlights include "The First Show: Painting and Sculpture from Eight Collections 1940-1980" (1983), "Dan Flavin: Monuments for V. Tatlin" (1984), "Blueprints of Modern Living: History and Legacy of the Case Study Houses" (1989), "Ellen Sebastian: Sanctified" (1990), and "Helter Skelter: L.A. Art in the 1990s" (1992), to name just a few. In addition, the Temporary Contemporary was the site of the first presentation of works from MOCA's rapidly growing permanent collection.

Now, with a new 99-year lease from the City of Los Angeles in place, we continue building on that tradition. It is highly appropriate that our first exhibition in the reopened Temporary Contemporary is "1965-1975: Reconsidering the Object of Art," the first historical examination of a period in art that ever since has exercised a powerful influence on the practice and production of art, and on the public's engagement with its ideas and issues. MOCA has a long record of support for the work of many of the artists included in the exhibition, and, indeed, about one third of the artists in the exhibition have been active in California, fifteen of them in Los Angeles. The museum has been the site of major exhibitions by Allen Ruppersberg (1985), Bruce Nauman (1988 and 1994), Marcel Broodthaers (1989), and John Baldessari (1990), as well as projects by Michael Asher (1983), Maria Nordman (1983 and 1984), and Douglas Huebler (1984). "1965-1975: Reconsidering the Object of Art" has been organized by Ann Goldstein, Curator at The Museum of Contemporary Art, and Anne Rorimer, a noted scholar and independent curator. Their collaboration dates back to the presentation at MOCA of "A Forest of Signs: Art in the Crisis of Representation" in 1989, an exhibition that was in large part devoted to work influenced by the artists in the current exhibition. Both curators deserve our great admiration and gratitude for their dedicated commitment to this exhibition. We also give our thanks to all the artists, and to the lenders who have generously made their work available.

To mark the re-opening of the Temporary Contemporary, we are also happy to present ACTION OCCUPATION by Elizabeth Streb and her company, Ringside, a project that celebrates the art of movement, as did our very first program twelve years before, "Available Light," by Lucinda Childs, John Adams, and Frank O. Gehry. Both ACTION OCCUPATION and "Available Light" were specifically commissioned for the Temporary Contemporary, and both celebrated the body interacting with the building's spaces. The Temporary Contemporary is a unique environment — a stage for performances that transcend traditional boundaries and — equally important — a platform on which to set forth nothing less than the evolution of contemporary art. Thus we are proud to present alongside "1965-1975: Reconsidering the Object of Art," "Images of an Era," presenting superb examples of MOCA's permanent collection from 1940 to 1975. This year-long presentation is a stunning tribute to the generosity and vision of many noted collectors, among them Rita and Taft Schreiber, Barry Lowen, Beatrice and Philip Gersh, and Marcia Simon Weisman. It includes major works by Jasper Johns, Willem de Kooning, Mark Rothko, and Arshile Gorky, among many others.

The organization and presentation of acquisitions and exhibition programs of this scope require the dedicated efforts of many individuals. We are especially grateful to our Board of Trustees and the leadership provided by David Laventhol as Chairman, John C. Cushman III as President, Gilbert B. Friesen as Program Committee Chairman, and Audrey M. Irmas as Acquisitions Committee Chairman. They are building on the tradition of leadership that sprang full-blown into place at MOCA's founding in 1979 with the guiding efforts of Eli Broad, William Norris, W. F. Kieschnick, Frederick M. Nicholas, and Lenore S. Greenberg, all of whom have served as our Chairmen and Presidents at different times in MOCA's history.

As part of the reopening of MOCA at the Temporary Contemporary, "1965-1975: Reconsidering the Object of Art" is sponsored by Philip Morris Companies Inc. The exhibition is also made possible by the generous support of The Capital Group, Inc., Gilbert Friesen, Jay and Donatella Chiat, and the National Endowment for the Arts, a federal agency. From all of us, our deepest appreciation.

In closing, I welcome you back to a new era of programming at the Temporary Contemporary, and continuation of a tradition of excitement and engagement at all levels — in our programs, in educational activities, and in accessibility — that we hope will yield new insights into the arts and the issues they reflect in our lives. We look forward to having you with us.

LENDERS TO THE EXHIBITION

Vito Acconci
Bas Jan Ader Estate
Gallery Paule Anglim,
  San Francisco
Giovanni Anselmo
Michael Asher
David Askevold
Robert Barry
Lothar Baumgarten
Mel Bochner
The Eli and Edythe L. Broad
  Collection
Daniel Buren
Victor Burgin
Eileen and Michael Cohen
James Coleman
Paula Cooper Gallery,
  New York
Jane Crawford
Daled Collection
Anny de Decker and
  Bernd Lohaus
Anthony d'Offay Gallery,
  London
Peter Downsbrough
Morgan Fisher
Galerie Liliane & Michel
  Durand-Dessert, Paris
Thomas Erben
Eric Fabre
Ronald Feldman Fine Arts,
  New York
FER Collection
Maria Gilissen
Barbara Gladstone Gallery,
  New York
Marian Goodman Gallery,
  New York
Dan Graham
The Grinstein Family
Solomon R. Guggenheim
  Museum, New York
Solomon R. Guggenheim
  Museum, New York, Panza
  Collection, Extended Loan
Hans Haacke
Heithoff Family Collection
Herbert Collection, Ghent,
  Belgium
Rhona Hoffman Gallery,
  Chicago
Douglas Huebler
Joan Jonas
Stephen J. Kaltenbach
On Kawara
John Knight
Joseph Kosuth
Kunstmuseum, Bonn
Yvon Lambert
Margo Leavin Gallery,
  Los Angeles
Sol LeWitt
Lucy R. Lippard
Lisson Gallery, London
Tom Marioni
Gordon Matta-Clark Trust
Milwaukee Art Museum
Museum of Contemporary Art,
  San Diego
The Museum of Modern Art,
  New York

Museum moderner Kunst,
  Stiftung Ludwig, Vienna
N. E. Thing Co.
National Gallery of Canada,
  Ottawa
John Natsoulas Gallery,
  Davis, California
Bruce Nauman
Maria Nordman
Dennis Oppenheim
Patrick Painter Editions,
  Inc., Vancouver and
  Hong Kong
Public Freehold
Yvonne Rainer
Craig Robins
Edward Ruscha
Robert Shapazian
The Siegelaub Collection &
  Archives
Estate of Robert Smithson
Holly Solomon Gallery,
  New York
Ileana Sonnabend
Sonnabend Gallery, New York
Stuart and Judy Spence
Gian Enzo Sperone
Sperone Westwater, New York
Stedelijk Museum, Amsterdam
Stedelijk Van Abbemuseum,
  Eindhoven, The Netherlands
Norah and Norman Stone
Tate Gallery, London
Niele Toroni
Ian and Charlotte Townsend-
  Gault
University of British
  Columbia, Morris and
  Helen Belkin Art Gallery,
  Vancouver
The Dorothy and Herbert
  Vogel Collection
Councilman Joel Wachs
John Weber Gallery, New York
William Wegman
Alice Zimmerman Weiner
Jack and Nell Wendler
Michael Werner Gallery,
  New York and Cologne
Angela Westwater
and anonymous lenders

ANN GOLDSTEIN AND ANNE RORIMER

ACKNOWLEDGMENTS When we made the commitment to initiate and pursue this exhibition in October 1990, we never imagined how deeply we would be able to plunge into this most pivotal period of contemporary art history. Five years later, we can reflect back upon the process of organizing such a complex project, the great opportunities it offered, and the many unexpected directions it took—not the least of which was seeing the initial list of twenty-five artists that we drew up at our first meeting grow to include more than twice that number.

This project has been dependent on the tremendous efforts of numerous individuals who have contributed enormously to its planning, development, and realization. We extend our deepest gratitude to the artists in the exhibition, whose work has been its inspiration, and for their generous participation and enthusiasm that has sustained us throughout its development. This publication is enriched by the contributions of our guest authors Lucy R. Lippard, Stephen Melville, and Jeff Wall, all of whom have offered unique and invaluable insights into the work and the framework of the period.

This exhibition would not have been possible without the tremendous support from those who have funded it, as well as the commitment and generosity of the lenders who have shared with us the most important works of this period. We also extend our sincerest gratitude to the museums, galleries, libraries, archives, and other collections and institutions that provided generous assistance to our staff.

We are grateful for the support of MOCA's Board of Trustees and staff throughout the progress of this project. We are deeply indebted to MOCA's Director Richard Koshalek for his unwavering support of this ambitious and complex project and the encouragement to develop it to its fullest potential. Paul Schimmel, Chief Curator, has been a supporter of this project from its inception. We wish to thank Kathleen S.

Bartels, Director of Administration, and Erica Clark, Director of Development, for their constant involvement and valued counsel throughout the various facets of administration and funding, respectively.

This project could not have been realized without the extraordinary efforts and expertise of Stacia Payne, Curatorial Assistant, whose commitment, initiative, and unparalleled organizational abilities contributed to every aspect of it. Her contributions cannot be underestimated. Similarly, Susan L. Jenkins, Research Assistant, has devoted over three years to tireless efforts in all phases of its research and organization. Her work has greatly enriched the scholarship of this project, including the very extensive exhibition chronology and bibliography of the period that will help to facilitate further exploration of this subject.

This extensive publication was conceived in close collaboration with Russell Ferguson, Editor, who contributed enormously to its content, and whose understanding of a myriad of complexities and priorities made it possible for all involved to participate in its realization. This publication could not have been completed without the intelligence, sensitivity, and indefatigable efforts of John Alan Farmer, Assistant Editor, who brought utmost care and commitment to every detail of its production. Our research was also supplemented by the contributions of Curatorial Interns Angelene Taccini and Birgit Plinke, as well as those of early interns Susanne Riedel and Rikki Cox. We also wish to extend our gratitude to the other members of MOCA's curatorial staff—Curators Kerry Brougher, Julie Lazar, and Elizabeth A. T. Smith, Exhibition Coordinator Alma Ruiz, Curatorial Assistants Colette Dartnall and Brent Zerger, Assistant to the Chief Curator Diane Aldrich, and Curatorial Secretary Virginia Edwards—for their support and friendship. Former Curatorial Assistant Susan Colletta and Assistant Editor Sherri Schottlaender worked with us to initiate this project.

Lorraine Wild, Beth Elliott and Susan Parr/ReVerb, Los Angeles, provided the design of this book, and we are grateful not only for the thoughtfulness and beauty of their work but also for their tremendous care and patience throughout the process.

The design and installation of the exhibition has been made possible through the extraordinary expertise of John Bowsher, Exhibition Production Manager, who, having worked on every exhibition in the Museum's history, is a critical partner in all of our projects. David Bradshaw, Media Arts Technical Manager, has aptly overseen the countless complexities of the technical components of this project, and Eric Magnuson, Chief Preparator, and Staff Preparators Jang Park, Valerie West, Barry Grady, Jeremy Goff, and Jay Dunn, have, as always, worked with tremendous care and effort to bring it to fruition. The enormous efforts of Portland McCormick, Assistant Registrar, as well as Robert Hollister, Registrar, can certainly attest that Conceptual art is certainly full of objects.

We are particularly appreciative of the sustained efforts of June Scott, Grants Officer, which brought us critical funding. We also wish to extend our thanks to Jack Wiant, Chief Financial Officer, and Jay Myres, Controller, who have helped us face the challenges of our budget.

9

Kim Kanatani, Acting Director of Education, Education staff member Kathleen Johnson, and Art Talks Coordinator Caroline Blackburn have worked closely with the artists to develop and implement innovative Education programs to open up this exhibition to a greater public awareness. In addition, the efforts of Dawn Setzer, Assistant Director of Communications, Media Relations, have directed a successful link with the media.

For their contributions to this project we also wish to thank Randall Murphy, Facilities and Operations Director; Sharla Barrett, Manager Special Events, Visitor Services; Beth Gruenberg, Special Events Associate; Sylvia Hohri, Assistant Director of Communications, Community Relations; Kim Franklin, Personnel Manager; Margaret Steele, Campaign Manager; Leslie Marcus, Assistant Director of Development, Support Programs and Government Relations; Ron Goorahoo, Chief Engineer; Cecil Widdifield, Manager of Retail Operations; Cindy Estes, Designer; Assistant Chief of Security Frank Munoz; and Patricia Cross, Receptionist.

In addition, we are grateful to MOCA's former Associate Director Sherri Geldin, for her critical support of this project in its earlier development and her invaluable friendship.

This exhibition has greatly benefited from the generous friendship and counsel of Coosje van Bruggen and Claes Oldenburg, and the active interest of Gilbert Friesen and Gianna Carotenuto. In addition, we offer our appreciation to Frederik Leen. Finally, we extend very special thanks to Cora Rosevear, John Vinci, and Christopher Williams.

It is our pleasure to extend our sincere gratitude to the many other individuals who, in numerous ways, have made invaluable contributions: *Alexander Alberro, Bruce J. Altschuler, Carl Andre, Terry Atkinson, Julie Barry, David Bellman, Cindy Bernard, Justine Birbil, Marja Bloem, Laura Bloom, Thomas Borgmann, Wendy Brandow, Marie-Puck Broodthaers, Kathan Brown, Patricia Brundage, Susan Brundage, Benjamin H. D. Buchloh, Elaine Budin, Lynda Bunting, Chantal Buren, Christine Burgin, Jacklyn Burns, Eugenia P. Butler, John Caldwell, Gisela Capitain, Anne M. Carley, Leo Castelli, Germano Celant, Piet Coessens, Jim Cohan, Sadie Coles, Lynne Cooke, Paula Cooper, Claire Copley, Jef Cornelis, Michael Corris, Jane Crawford, Douglas Crimp, Susan Cross, Amada Cruz, Kaatje Cusse, Herman Daled and Sylvia Goldschmidt, Nicole Daled, Kim Davenport, Jan Debbaut, David Deitcher, Colin de Land, Chris Dercon, Wilhemina Dibbets, Courtney Graham Donnell, Liliane and Michel Durand-Dessert, Cliff Einstein, Ronald Feldman, Konrad Fischer, Peter Fischer, Isi and Laurence Fiszman, Mark Francis, Richard Francis and Tamar Burchell, James Fraser, Rudi Fuchs, Lance Fung, Monica Furmanski, Yves and Danielle Gevaert, Susanne Ghez, Bill Giamela, Jon Gibson, Maria Gilissen, Claude Gintz and Judith Aminoff, Barbara Gladstone, Hal Glicksman and Marianne Duganne Glicksman, Elyse Goldberg, Paula Goldman, Felix Gonzalez-Torres, Marian Goodman, Jay Gorney, Nigel Greenwood, Elyse and Stanley Grinstein, Madeleine Grynsztejn, Catherine Gudis, Linda Haacke, John Hanhardt, Charles Harrison, Pat Hearn, Michelle Heithoff, Josef Helfenstein, Ydessa Hendeles, Steve Henry, Anton and Annick Herbert, Jean-Noël Herlin, Joanne Heyler, Robert Hobbs, Rhona Hoffman, Antonio Homem, Roni Horn, Stephanie Weinschel Huebler, Grita Insam, Linda Johnson, Hiroko Kawara, Andrea Keller Miller, Mike Kelley, Colleen A. Kelly, Jule Kewenig, Andrea Kirsh, Judith Russi-Kirshner, Kasper König, Barbara Kruger, Katherine Laing,*

Cornelia Lauf, Françoise Lambert, Yvon Lambert, Louise Lawler, Margo Leavin, Constance Lewallen, Carol LeWitt, David Leiber, Steven Leiber, Werner Lippert, Thomas Locher, Nicholas Logsdail, Barbara London, Kynaston McShine, Bartomeu Marí-Gustinet, Mary Jo Marks, Lisa Martin, Dorine Mignot, Robert C. Morgan, Caroline Nathusius, Juliet Myers, Joyce Nereaux, Albert Oehlen, Patrick Painter, Janet Passehl, Birgit Pelzer, Clive Phillpot, David Platzker, Amy Plumb, Evelyne Pomey, Pat Poncy, Alan Power, Stephen Prina, Martin Prinzhorn, Rebecca Quaytman, Lawrence Rinder, Christina Ritchie, Randall Rogers, Susan Rosenfeld, Mark Rosenthal, Bonnie Rubenstein, Alan Rutenberg, Anthony Sansotta, Michelle Saylor, Susan Bates Schlotterbeck, Christoph Schreier, Allan Sekula, Robert Shapazian, Nick Scheidy, Seth Siegelaub, Natasha Sigmund, Susanna Singer, Howard Singerman, Cindy Smith, Dirk Snauwaert, Holly Solomon, Abigail Solomon-Godeau, Mary Solt, Ileana Sonnabend, Stuart and Judy Spence, Sally Stein, Ellen Steinberg, Charles F. Stuckey, Mary Suzor, Micheline Szwajcer, Lucien Terras, Mayo Thompson, Dalmas Toroni, Herbert and Dorothy Vogel, Joel Wachs, Ian Wallace, Frazer Ward, Scott Watson, John Weber, Alice Z. Weiner, John Welchman, Jennifer Wells, Jack and Nell Wendler, Angela Westwater, Toby Wilcox, Luce Wilson, Pam Wilson, Helene Winer, Amy Wolf, Monika Wullfers, Donald Young.

ANN GOLDSTEIN AND ANNE RORIMER

INTRODUCTION The richness and diversity of aesthetic activity between 1965 and 1975 has played a significant role in determining the present course of art. During this period, many artists engaged with and challenged the shared language and conventions of modernism to re-evaluate, and in the process change, the formal, ontological, and functional parameters of art.

The work of most of the artists represented in this exhibition has come to be classified under the heading of Conceptual art, a term that at first was used along with other, more specific labels such as Idea Art, Earth Art or Land Art, Body Art, Arte Povera, Serial Art, etc. Over the past three decades, the word "Conceptual" has assumed many meanings, from defining a precise historical period that set parameters around very specific practices that critically engaged the idea of art and how meaning is produced, to an all-encompassing category made up of disparate bodies of work from the mid-1960s to the present that do not answer to traditional forms or trajectories of specific mediums such as painting, sculpture, photography, or film. The association of Conceptual art with the primacy of the idea, in some cases to the point of the elimination of a physical art object, does represent a key strategy. The "dematerialization of the art object," as Lucy R. Lippard has described this practice in her invaluable resource book on the period of 1966-72, *Six Years*, describes a critical break with the autonomous work of art. While these new works were often not dematerialized in a literal sense, they were nevertheless no longer contained within the object. Instead, it became a point of reference and question.

Still, for better or for worse, the word "Conceptual," with all its inadequacies, has stuck; it provides an umbrella under which to look for common historical and thematic denominators that might be applied to the analysis of a variety of works that have sought to reject or disregard the traditional physical art object. The intent of this exhibition is not to define a term, and in fact, certain artists in this exhibition would either reject the label or be incorrectly categorized depending on its definition. Thus, rather than devote our efforts to a process of terminological definition, we have attempted instead to engage directly with the works of art, and to encourage an examination of the broad range of practices that can be associated with the process of reconsidering the art object, and the objective of art.

In the interest of formulating new approaches to aesthetic production, the artists in this exhibition, each in their own way, have struggled to resist formulaic modes of working. At the halfway point of the 1960s, major works had been realized that explicitly and literally defined themselves in some elemental and radical way as sculpture or as painting—the former with regard to questions of volume and space, the latter with those of planarity and illusionism—in order to explicitly embody and address their own condition as objects within one of these categories. During the same years, a number of artists, in the interest of finding alternatives to what they saw as art's distance from everyday life, took a different route of aesthetic inquiry. Like Allan Kaprow, Claes Oldenburg, and the many other individuals who participated in the organization of Happenings or in the international Fluxus movement, artists of the slightly later period who have been identified with Conceptualism similarly sought, literally and figuratively, to take art, as an unquestioned object of contemplation and value, down from its pedestal. They accomplished this by questioning conventional methods of representation rather than through acts of deliberate irreverence. If Fluxus artists sought, in many different ways, to renegotiate relationships between art and life, it might be said that Conceptual artists amplified that ongoing dialogue by giving non-art, vernacular conventions a greater voice within the work itself, in an attempt to ground it using a vocabulary of everyday terms.

The most salient characteristic of this exhibition is the absence of painting on canvas (with some notable exceptions) as well as of materially defined, three-dimensional sculptures. The exhibition is marked instead by works that utilize language, photography, publications, video, film, and performance, and/or that take account of their own physical context to make a critique of the institutional premises that condition experience in the process of signification. Making use of non-art forms and systems drawn from the conventions of everyday life, and of diverse disciplines such as anthropology, philosophy, and literature, the resulting works were pointedly removed from the traditional object of art.

All the artists in the exhibition have endeavored to ensure the self-criticality of their work by foregrounding crucial factors contributing to its formation, presentation, and reception. They have been able to address issues pertaining to authorship on the one hand and of context on the other. In the process of addressing such issues, they have created works that challenge traditional divisions between object, viewer, and surroundings. As a thematic corollary, their works often allude to their own commodity status, as enhanced by the value attributed to authorial originality, mastery, and authenticity, and to rarity and preciousness.

The most famous artist's statement of the early 1960s may have been that of Frank Stella, who maintained that in his painting there is nothing there "besides the paint on the canvas" and that "only what can be seen there is there."[1] Douglas Huebler's frequently quoted statement speaks in a new vein for the second half of the decade: "The world is full of objects, more or less interesting; I do not wish to add anymore." Huebler went on to say: "I prefer, simply, to state the existence of things in terms of time and/or place."[2] With these remarks, he drew renewed attention to the world of external reality.

The period between 1965 and 1975 includes the work of numerous artists working in a broad range of heterogeneous and overlapping practices. This exhibition examines the work of fifty-five individual artists or collectives whose work had emerged by the end of the 1960s. Focusing specifically on artists in the United States, Canada, and Western Europe, the intention of this exhibition is to explore work that engaged in a shared dialogue and critique of conventions. The initial phase of Conceptual art can be characterized by its studied dismantling of, and ultimate break with, the Western tradition of modernism. The self-referentiality of Minimalism becomes in Conceptual art a self-examination of the machinery of a work of art. Numerous new questions are raised through this work: what is the function of a work of art? How is its meaning constructed? Where and when does the work exist? Why does it take the form it does? To whom is it addressed?

The works in this exhibition have been chosen to represent a broadly-defined cross-section of historically related endeavors. There is no attempt at an all-inclusive temporal narrative, nor of any overview of individual careers. It is hoped, however, that it will attest to the goals, both shared and separate, of the generation of artists who paved the way for the more recent developments to be seen in the work of a younger generation. While this period is still dominated by the work of men, the work of the women in the exhibition was particularly important in raising crucial questions about the authority and function of cultural representations—a critical contribution to current practices that have more directly engaged issues of race, gender, and sexuality. This period in art, so pivotal in its introduction of a new approach to the conception, production, and experience of works of art, is key to an appropriate understanding of post-modernism and the work of the "post-Conceptual" generation of artists that emerged in the mid-to-late 1970s and early 1980s. The work of the past two decades has also increasingly relied on strategies established in the late 1960s involving the use of non-art systems, documentation, contextual and/or site-specific installations, and more generally, the abnegation of the object's autonomous position in relation to physical, social, political, or historical realities. Along with other artists from the period of the late 1960s, the artists shown here have led the way methodologically to further areas of thematic investigation, confrontation, and concern.

It is important to note that this work was conceived and produced in the tumultuous period of the sixties (and as Lucy Lippard describes in her text, many of the artists in this exhibition were participants in the activism of the period)—a context characterized by the assassinations of President John F. Kennedy, Malcolm X, Martin Luther King, Robert Kennedy (which was itself preceded by one day with the shooting of Andy Warhol), a period that saw the escalation and conclusion of the war in southeast Asia, Richard Nixon's presidency, culminating in the Watergate scandal, the student protests of May 1968 in Paris, and the 1970 murder of the students protesting the Vietnam war at Kent State, as well as the continued struggles for civil rights, and the emergence of feminism. At this time, all aspects of tradition and authority in culture were called into question, including art. While some of the work in this exhibition makes specific references to the socio-political context in which it was made, the work overall reflects the challenge to authority and tradition that characterized the activities of younger people during this period.

A great many artists were active participants in this movement. All of the individual artists who made significant contributions to this radical change in art making, with its worldwide repercussions, could not be accommodated in a single exhibition. It is hoped, therefore, that the works by those who are included will speak for the scope of the innovation that occurred internationally within this historical time frame, and for the shared, but differently manifested, ideas that were at stake. This project is intended to provide a foundation for further historical examination of this most pivotal period of contemporary art, a history still relatively misunderstood and highly contested—particularly in the United States. It is a history that requires and deserves substantive reflection, reconsideration, expansion, and revision. We hope that this exhibition will be followed by further such inquiries.

Notes

1. Frank Stella, quoted in Bruce Glaser, "Questions to Stella and Judd," in Gregory Battcock, ed., *Minimal Art: A Critical Anthology* (New York: E. P. Dutton and Co., 1968), 157-158.

2. Douglas Huebler, in Ursula Meyer, *Conceptual Art* (New York: E. P. Dutton and Co., 1972), 137.

LUCY R. LIPPARD

ESCAPE ATTEMPTS

Conceptual Artists are mystics rather than rationalists. They leap to conclusions that logic cannot reach. . . . Illogical judgements lead to new experience. Sol LeWitt, 1969 [1] *(I. A Biased History)* The era of Conceptual art—which was also the era of Vietnam, the Women's Movement, and the counter-culture—was a real free-for-all, and the democratic implications of that phrase are fully appropriate, if never realized. "Imagine," John Lennon exhorted us. And the power of imagination was at the core of even the stodgiest attempts to escape from "cultural confinement," as Robert Smithson put it, from the sacrosanct ivory walls and heroic, patriarchal mythologies with which the 1960s opened.

On a practical level, Conceptual artists offered a clear-eyed look at what and where art itself was supposed to be; at the utopian extreme, some tried to visualize a new world and the art that would reflect it. Conceptual art (or "ultra-conceptual art," as I first called it, in order to distinguish it from Minimal painting and sculpture, earthworks, performances, and other grand-scale endeavors which appeared in the early sixties as abnormally cerebral) was all over the place in style and content, but materially quite specific. In 1973, I compiled *Six Years: The Dematerialization of the Art Object from 1966 to 1972*, a book "focused on so-called conceptual or information or idea art with mentions of such vaguely designated areas as minimal, antiform, systems, earth, or process art"; the initial manuscript was about twice the size of that which was finally published. Looking back through it I am re-amazed by the richness and diversity of the genre(s). Unfettered by object status, Conceptual artists were free to let their imaginations run rampant. With hindsight it is clear that they could have run further, but in the late sixties art world, Conceptual art was the only race in town.

Conceptual art, for me, means work in which the idea is paramount and the material form is secondary, lightweight, ephemeral, cheap, unpretentious, and/or "dematerialized." Sol LeWitt distinguished between conceptual art "with a small c" (e.g., his own work, in which the material forms were often conventional, although generated by a paramount idea) and Conceptual art "with a capital C" (more or less what I have described above, but also, I suppose, anything by anyone who wanted to belong to a movement). This has not kept commentators over the years from calling virtually anything in unconventional mediums "Conceptual art."

There has been a lot of bickering about what Conceptual art is/was; who began it; who did what when with it; what its goals, philosophy, and politics were and might have been. I was there, but I don't trust my memory. I don't trust anyone else's either. And I trust even less the authoritative overviews by those who were not there. So I'm going to quote myself a lot here, because I knew more about it then than I do now, despite the advantages of hindsight.

Adrian Piper
CATALYSIS IV (1970-71)
Documentation of street performance, New York.
Courtesy John Weber Gallery, New York.

The times were chaotic and so were our lives. We have each invented our own history, and they don't always mesh; but such messy compost is the source of all versions of the past. Conceptual artists, perhaps more concerned with intellectual distinctions in representation and relationships than those who rely on the object as vehicle/receptacle, have offered posterity a particularly tangled account. My own version is inevitably tempered by my feminist and left politics. Almost thirty years later my memories have merged with my own subsequent life and learnings and leanings. As I reconstitute the threads that drew me into the center of what came to be Conceptual art, I'll try to arm you with the necessary grain of salt, to provide a context, within the ferment of the times, for the personal prejudices and viewpoints that follow. I'm not a theoretician. This is an occasionally critical memoir of a small group of young artists' attempts to escape from the frame-and-pedestal syndrome in which art found itself by the mid-1960s.

When the decade began I was a free-lance researcher, translator, indexer, bibliographer, and would-be writer in New York. I began to publish regularly in 1964. The mid-to-late sixties were one of the most exciting times of my life on every level: I began to make a living from free-lance writing (at almost the exact moment my son was born). I curated my first exhibition, gave my first lectures, published my first two books, began to travel, wrote some fiction, got unmarried, got politicized. Conceptual art was an integral part of the whole process. I came to it, as did most of my artist colleagues, through what came to be called Minimalism. But we converged from very different directions and eventually went off again in others.

The word Minimal suggests a tabula rasa—or rather the failed attempt at a clean slate, a utopian wish of the times that never came true but was important for the goals and desires it provoked. It was and still is an idea that appeals to me, though not for its reality quotient. In graduate school I had written a long paper about a tabula rasa swept clean by the Zen monk's broom and Dada's vitriolic humor. I saw materialist echoes of these impossible longings in the paintings of Robert Ryman and Ad Reinhardt. From 1960 to 1967, I lived with Ryman, who was never called a Minimalist in those days because the roots of his white paintings from the late fifties were in Abstract Expressionism; he was "discovered" around 1967 through the advent of the messier "process art" and was included in a surprising number of "Conceptual art" shows, although the term is really inappropriate for his obsession with paint

and surface, light and space. We lived on Avenue A and Avenue D and then on the Bowery. Sol LeWitt was a close friend of ours, and my major intellectual influence at the time. (We had all worked at The Museum of Modern Art in the late fifties. Ryman was a guard; LeWitt was at the night desk; I was a page in the library.)

On and around the Bowery, an art community formed that included LeWitt, Ray Donarski, Robert Mangold, Sylvia Plimack Mangold, Frank Lincoln Viner, Tom Doyle, and Eva Hesse. My own history of Conceptual art is particularly entwined with that studio community, and with LeWitt's work and writings; through him, around 1965-66, I met or saw the work of Dan Graham, Robert Smithson, Hanne Darboven, Art & Language, Hilla and Bernd Becher, Joseph Kosuth, and Mel Bochner.

Around 1964-65, Kynaston McShine and I had begun work at The Museum of Modern Art on what became the "Primary Structures" exhibition he curated for The Jewish Museum in 1966. That year I also wrote the catalogue for The Jewish Museum's retrospective of Ad Reinhardt, the reluctant hero of one branch of what was to become Conceptual art. Joseph Kosuth's storefront Museum of Normal Art was "dedicated" to him. Around the same time, I met Carl Andre, whose poetic detours around art-as-art made him a cantankerous part of the Conceptual community in spite of himself; he never liked or sympathized with the products, although he hung out with the artists. Donald Judd was also a powerful figure, an obdurately blunt artist and writer who was a model for many younger artists. And Robert Morris, elusive and virtually styleless, was the progenitor of many soon-to-be "seminal" concepts.

In 1967, John Chandler and I wrote the article on "The Dematerialization of Art" that was published in the February 1968 *Art International*, in which we saw "ultra-conceptual art" emerging from two directions: art as idea and art as action. In late 1967, I went to Vancouver and found that Iain and Ingrid (then Elaine) Baxter (the N. E. Thing Co.) and others there were on a wavelength totally unconnected yet totally similar to that of many New York friends. This and later encounters in Europe confirmed my belief in "ideas in the air"—"the spontaneous appearance of similar work totally unknown to the artists that can be explained only as energy generated by [well-known, common] sources and by the wholly unrelated art against which all the potentially 'conceptual' artists were commonly reacting," as I once described the phenomenon.

The question of sources has since become a sore point. Marcel Duchamp was the obvious art-historical source, but in fact most of the artists did not find his work all that interesting. The most obvious exceptions, perhaps, were the European-connected Fluxus artists; around 1960 Henry Flynt coined the term "concept art," but few of the artists with whom I was involved knew about it, and in any case it was a different kind of "concept"—less formal, less rooted in the subversion of art-world assumptions and art-as-commodity. As responsible critics we had to mention Duchamp as a precedent, but the new art in New York came from closer to home: Reinhardt's writings, Jasper Johns's and Robert Morris's work, and Ed Ruscha's deadpan photo-books, among others. Duchampian "claiming," however, was an occasional strategy: the N. E. Thing Co. categorized its work as ACT (Aesthetically Claimed Things) or ART (Aesthetically Rejected Things); Robert Huot, Marjorie Strider, and Stephen Kaltenbach all did pieces that "selected" art-like objects from real life in the city.

Iain Baxter and Seth Siegelaub with "March" stamp and "March" on mirror, N. E. Thing Co.'s contribution to "One Month" (also known as "March 1969"), various locations throughout the world, 1-31 March 1969, organized by Seth Siegelaub. Courtesy The Siegelaub Collection & Archives. Photo N. E. Thing Co.

The four participating artists in "January 5-31, 1969," rented office space at 44 East 52nd Street, New York, organized by Seth Siegelaub. Left to right: Robert Barry, Douglas Huebler, Joseph Kosuth, and Lawrence Weiner. Courtesy The Siegelaub Collection & Archives. Photo Seth Siegelaub.

In my own experience, the second branch of access to what became Conceptual art was a jurying trip to Argentina in 1968. I returned belatedly radicalized by contact with artists there, especially the Rosario Group, whose mixture of conceptual and political ideas was a revelation. In Latin America I was trying to organize a "suitcase exhibition" of dematerialized art that would be taken from country to country by "idea artists" using free airline tickets. When I got back to New York, I met Seth Siegelaub, who had begun to reinvent the role of the "art dealer" as distributor extraordinaire through his work with Lawrence Weiner, Douglas Huebler, Robert Barry, and Joseph Kosuth. Siegelaub's strategy of bypassing the art world with exhibitions that took place outside of galleries and/or New York and/or were united in publications that were art rather than merely *about* art dovetailed with my own notions of a dematerialized art that would be free of art-world commodity status. A practical man, unencumbered at the time by addiction to ideology or esthetics, Siegelaub went right ahead and did what had to be done to create international models for an alternative art network.

On my return from Latin America I was also asked to co-curate (with painter Robert Huot and political organizer Ron Wolin) an exhibition of important Minimal artworks against the Vietnam war, as a benefit for Student Mobilization and the opening show at Paula Cooper's new Prince Street space. (It

included LeWitt's first public wall drawing.) In January 1969 the Art Workers Coalition (AWC) was formed on a platform of artists' rights which was soon expanded into opposition to the Vietnam war. (Anti-racism and then anti-sexism were soon added to the anti-war agenda.) The AWC provided a framework and an organizational relationship for artists who were mixing art and politics that attracted a number of "Conceptual artists." Kosuth designed a fake membership card for entrance to The Museum of Modern Art—one of our major targets—with AWC rubberstamped in red across it. Andre was the resident Marxist. Smithson, Judd, and Richard Serra were skeptical, non-participating presences. The Guerrilla Art Action Group (GAAG), consisting at that time of Jean Toche, Jon Hendricks, Poppy Johnson, and Silvianna, was a major force in the AWC's Action Committee, though maintaining its own identity. While GAAG's almost Dada letters to President Nixon ("Eat What You Kill") and other world leaders were in the spirit of the general "conceptual movement," their blood-and-guts performance style and their connections to Europe, via Fluxus and Destruction Art, separated them from the cooler, Minimal art-oriented Conceptual mainstream.

> *Concept art is not so much an art movement or vein as it is a position or world-view, a focus for activity.*   Ken Friedman, formerly head of Fluxus West, San Diego, 1971 (258)

Installation view, opening exhibition of Paula Cooper Gallery,
New York (benefit for Student Mobilization Committee to End
the War in Vietnam), October 1968. Courtesy Paula Cooper
Gallery, New York. Photo Walter Russell.

*Guerrilla Art Action Group (Jean Toche, Jon Hendricks, Poppy Johnson,
and Silvianna)*
BLOOD BATH (A CALL FOR THE IMMEDIATE RESIGNATION OF ALL THE ROCKE-
FELLERS FROM THE BOARD OF TRUSTEES OF THE MUSEUM OF MODERN ART,
NEW YORK, 10/18 NOVEMBER 1969
Documentation of action. Courtesy Jon Hendricks, New York.
Photo © Ka Kwong Hui.

So "Conceptual art"—or at least the branch of it in which I was involved—was very much a product of, or fellow traveler with, the political ferment of the times, even if that spirit had arrived belatedly in the art world. (A small group of artists, including Rudolph Baranik, Leon Golub, Nancy Spero, and Judd had been organizing against the war for several years by then. Even earlier, Reinhardt had also spoken out and demonstrated against intervention in Vietnam, but the Reinhardtian attitude remained that art was art and politics were politics and that when artists were activists they were acting as artist citizens rather than as esthetic arbiters.) The strategies with which we futilely schemed to overthrow the cultural establishment reflected those of the larger political Movement, but the most effective visual antiwar imagery of the period came from outside the art world, from popular/political culture.

For me, Conceptual art offered a bridge between the verbal and the visual. (I was writing abstract, conceptual "fiction" then; at one point I tried alternating pictorial and verbal "paragraphs" in a narrative; nobody got it.) By 1967, although I had only been publishing art criticism for a few years, I was very aware of the limitations of the genre. I never liked the term critic. Having learned all I knew about art in the studios, I identified with artists and never saw myself as their adversary. Conceptual art, with its transformation of the studio into a study, brought art itself closer to my own activities. There was a period when I saw myself as a writer-collaborator with the artists, and now and then I was invited by artists to play that part. If art could be anything at all that the artist chose to do, I reasoned, then so could criticism be whatever the writer chose to do. When I was accused of becoming an artist, I replied that I was just doing criticism, even if it took unexpected forms. I organized my first exhibition ("Eccentric Abstraction") at the Fischbach Gallery in 1966, when critics rarely curated, and considered it, too, just another kind of "criticism." (At the height of my conceptually hybrid phase, Kynaston McShine asked me to write a text for The Museum of Modern Art's Duchamp catalogue. I constructed it of "readymades" chosen by a "random system" from the dictionary, and to my amazement, they used it.)

I also applied the conceptual freedom principle to the organization of a series of four exhibitions which began in 1969 at the Seattle Art Museum's World's Fair annex. They included wall works, earthworks, and sculptural pieces as well as more idea-oriented pieces. Three aspects (or influences) of Conceptual art were incorporated in these shows: the titles ("557,087" in Seattle) were the current populations of the cities; the catalogues were randomly arranged packs of index cards; and with a team of helpers, I executed (or tried to) most of the outdoor works myself, according to the artists' instructions. This was determined as much by economic limitations as by theory; we couldn't afford plane fare for the artists.

When the show went to Vancouver, it acquired a new title ("955,000"), additional cards, a bibliography, and many new works, which were shown in two indoor locations (the Vancouver Art Gallery and the Student Union at the University of British Columbia) and all

Seattle Installation
1) Reading room (Ruscha, Kawara, Darboven, etc.)
2) Latham, Perreault, (Bollinger)

over the city. My texts in the card catalogues included aphorisms, lists, and quotes and were mixed in, unsequentially, with the artists' cards. The idea was that the reader could discard whatever s/he found uninteresting. Among my cards:

> *Deliberately low-keyed art often resembles ruins, like neolithic rather than classical monuments, amalgams of past and future, remains of something "more," vestiges of some unknown venture. The ghost of content continues to hover over the most obdurately abstract art. The more open, or ambiguous, the experience offered, the more the viewer is forced to depend upon his [sic] own perceptions.* (112)

The third version, in 1970, was a more strictly conceptual and portable exhibition that originated at the Centro de Arte y Comunicación in Buenos Aires as "2,972,453"; it included only artists not in the first two versions: among others, Siah Armajani, Stanley Brouwn, Gilbert & George, and Victor Burgin. The fourth version, in 1973, was "C. 7,500"—an international women's Conceptual show that began at the California Institute of the Arts in Valencia, California, and traveled to seven venues, ending in London. It included Renate Altenrath, Laurie Anderson, Eleanor Antin, Jacki Apple, Alice Aycock, Jennifer Bartlett, Hanne Darboven, Agnes Denes, Doree Dunlap, Nancy Holt, Poppy Johnson, Nancy Kitchel, Christine Kozlov, Suzanne Kuffler, Pat Lasch, Bernadette Mayer, Christiane Möbus, Rita Myers, Renee Nahum, N. E. Thing Co., Ulrike Nolden, Adrian Piper, Judith Stein, Athena Tacha, Mierle Laderman Ukeles, and Martha Wilson. I list all these names here, as I said on a catalogue card at the time, "by way of an exasperated reply on my own part to those who say 'there are no women making conceptual art.' For the record, there are a great many more than could be exhibited here."

The inexpensive, ephemeral, unintimidating character of the Conceptual mediums themselves (video, performance, photography, narrative, text, actions) encouraged women to participate, to move through this crack in the art world's walls. With the public introduction of younger women artists into Conceptual art, a number of new subjects and approaches appeared: narrative, role-playing, guise and disguise, body and beauty issues; a focus on fragmentation, interrelationships, autobiography, performance, daily life, and, of course, on feminist politics. The role of women artists and critics in the Conceptual art flurry of the mid-sixties was (unbeknownst to us at the time) similar to that of women on the Left. We were slowly emerging from the kitchens and bedrooms, off the easels, out of the woodwork, whether the men were ready or not—and for the most part they weren't. But even lip service was a welcome change. By 1970, thanks to the liberal-to-left politics assumed by many male artists, a certain (unprecedented) amount of support for the feminist program was forthcoming. Several men helped us (but knew enough to stay out of the decision-making) when the Ad Hoc Women Artists Committee (an offshoot of the AWC) launched its offensive on the Whitney Annual exhibition. The "anonymous" core group of women faked a Whitney press release stating that there would be fifty percent women (and fifty percent of them "non-white") in the show, then forged invitations to the opening and set up a generator and projector to show women's slides on the outside walls of the museum while a sit-in was staged inside. The FBI came in search of the culprits.

One of the reasons we were successful in forcing the Whitney to include four times as many women as before in that year's sculpture show was the establishment of the Women's Art Registry, initiated in angry response to the "There-are-no-women-who . . ." (make large sculpture, Conceptual art, kinetic art, etc., etc.) syndrome. As a freelance writer I was unaware of personal gender discrimination (it's hard to know what jobs you don't get), but it was easy enough to perceive when it came to women artists, who were virtually invisible in the mid-sixties, with a very few exceptions: Lee Bontecou, Carolee Schneemann,

following pages:

Lee Lozano
DIALOGUE PIECE (begun 21 April 1969)
Documentation in notebook of a series of actions. Courtesy Barry Rosen & Jaap van Liere Modern & Contemporary Art, New York.

Daniel Buren
UNTITLED, (1968)
Photo/souvenir: a work in situ. View of green-and-white paper on signboards carried by "sandwich men," Paris.
Photo Bernard Boyer.

"557,087." Seattle Art Museum Pavilion, Seattle Art Museum, 5 September–5 October 1969. Index card from the catalogue.

~~Be careful & sometimes another dog approaches~~

IT WAS A CONGENIAL MEETING & WAS ONLY OCCASIONALLY BROKEN
BY SMALL FARTS..... SCREW, THE WEEKLY SEX REVIEW.

DIALOGUE PIECE (STARTED APRIL 21, 69) OR ~~VERBALL~~ **VERBALL**

CALL (OR WRITE) [SPEAK TO] PEOPLE FOR THE <u>SPECIFIC</u> PURPOSE
OF INVITING THEM TO YR LOFT FOR A DIALOGUE.
<u>IN PROCESS</u> FOR THE <u>REST</u> OF "LIFE."

APRIL 21, 69 - CALL MOOSE (ROBT MORRIS). LEAVE NAME & NUMBER
       WITH HIS ANSWERING SERVICE.

MAY 11, 69 - CALL WALTER DE MARIA. LEAVE NAME ONLY WITH A.S.

MAY 13, 69 - CALL WALTER DE MARIA. LEAVE NAME & NO. WITH A.S.

MAY 14, 69 - CALL JAP (JASPER JOHNS) AT CASTELLI GALLERY.
     LEAVE NAME & NO. WITH DAVID WHITE WHO PROMISES
     TO GET MESSAGE TO JAP ALTHO JAP IS "VERY BUSY &
     IN & OUT OF TOWN THIS WEEK."

MAY 19, 69 - CALL POONSIE (LARRY POONS). HE ANSWERS PHONE,
     WE MAKE A DATE FOR MAY 21 (WED), 4 P.M.

<u>NOTE</u>: START ~~RECORDING OF~~ [WRITE-UP OF] PIECE WHEN YOU HAVE MADE
THE FIRST "CONTACT." SO FAR THE PEOPLE CALLED
ARE THOSE WITH WHOM A DIALOGUE HAS ALREADY
BEEN STARTED IN THE "PAST", A DIALOGUE ~~WHICH~~
MIGHT BE INTERESTING TO "PURSUE."

MAY 16, 69 - MOOSE RET'NS MY CALL. WE MAKE DATE FOR MAY 17 (SAT), 5 P.M.

MAY 17, 69 - MOOSE VISITS, THEN WE GO TO HIS CRIB, TURN ON & HAVE
    A GREAT DIALOGUE, THAT IS, A LONG INTENSE TALK WITHOUT
    TOO MUCH TENSION DURING WHICH WE EXCHANGE MANY IDEAS.

<u>NOTE</u>: THE PURPOSE OF THIS PIECE IS TO ~~TALK TO~~ [HAVE A DIALOGUE WITH AS MANY] PEOPLE, [AS POSS.]
NOT TO MAKE A PIECE. ANY PERSONAL INFORMATION EX-
CHANGED DURING DIALOGUE WILL BE PROTECTED BY MY
CONFIDENCE. IF ANYONE WISHES IDEAS TO BE PASSED ON ~~TO
OTHER PEOPLE~~ I SHALL COMPLY, AS MUCH AS POSS.

MAY 18 - CALL JOHN GIORNO, LEAVE NAME & NO. W/A.S.

" - CALL CLAUS OLDENBURG. SPEAK TO PATTY WHO WILL PASS MESSAGE ON
    TO CLAUS WHEN HE GETS BACK TO N.Y. IN 2 WKS.

" - CALL YVONNE RAINER. WE MAKE DATE FOR SUN, MAY 25, [ILLEG]

" - [CALL] MY MOTHER, WHO IS ILL. SHE IS HAVING FIRST DRUG EXPERIENCE
    & I INVITE HER TO HAVE DIALOGUE BY LONG-DIST. PHONE.

" - ATTEND OPENING OF LUCY'S SHOW AT PAULA COOPER'S. SPEAK
    TO AT LEAST 13 PEOPLE WHOM I'LL CALL FOR A DIALOGUE.

~~NOTE: "DIALOGUE" = AN EXCHANGE BETWEEN 2 PEOPLE,
THE FORM OF WHICH NEED NOT BE LIMITED TO VERBAL.~~

VERBALL — GIVES SOME INDICATION.

VERBALL — DEFINITION OF "DIALOGUE" REMAINS OPEN.

NOTE: DEFINITION OF "DIALOGUE" REMAINS OPEN.

and Jo Baer being practically the only ones around my age; the others were older, second-generation Abstract Expressionists. A brilliant horde was waiting in the wings.

In terms of actual Conceptual art, the major female figure in New York in the 1960s was Lee Lozano, who had shown her huge industrial/organic paintings at Dick Bellamy's cutting-edge Green Gallery. She was making extraordinary and eccentric art-as-life Conceptual works in the late sixties: a "general strike piece," an "I Ching piece," a "dialogue piece," a "grass piece," and "infofictions." "Seek the

extremes," she said, "That's where all the action is." (When the Women's Movement began, Lozano made the equally eccentric decision never to associate with women.)

Yoko Ono, who had participated in Fluxus since the early 1960s, continued her independent proto-Conceptual work. In 1969 Agnes Denes began her DIALECTIC TRIANGULATION: A VISUAL PHILOSOPHY, involving rice, trees, and haiku as well as mathematical diagrams. Martha Wilson, still a student at the Nova Scotia College of Art and Design, began her examinations of gender and role playing that evolved into performance and continue today in her "impersonations" of Nancy Reagan, Tipper Gore, and other friends of the arts. Christine Kozlov, who was also very young, was Joseph Kosuth's collaborator in the Museum of Normal Art and other enterprises and did her own rigorously "rejective" work. Yvonne Rainer's drastic alterations of modern dance were also very influential. On the West Coast, Eleanor Antin pursued the whimsical, narrative vein that was to lead her to neo-theatrical performance and filmmaking, especially with her cinematic 100 BOOTS postcards (1971), in which pairs of rubber boots wandered out of the gallery to explore the real world, traveling through the U. S. mails.

By the end of the decade Adrian Piper (also very young then) had made a series of mapping pieces and intellectual actions that explored philosophical/spatial concepts, somewhat reminiscent of LeWitt and Huebler. By 1970 she had launched into her own totally original identity works—the Catalysis series, in which she recreated or destroyed her own image/identity in bizarre public activities. Conceptual art has continued to be the basis of much important postmodern feminist work, from Piper, Antin, Martha Rosler (who was making photo-text pieces in Los Angeles in 1970), Suzanne Lacy, Susan Hiller, and Mary Kelly to Barbara Kruger, Jenny Holzer, and Lorna Simpson, among others.

(II. Outside the frame)   For years people have been concerned with what goes on inside *the frame. Maybe there's something going on* outside *the frame that could be considered an artistic idea.*   Robert Barry, 1968 (40)

*Ideas alone can be works of art; they are in a chain of development that may
eventually find some form. All ideas need not be made physical. . . . The words of
one artist to another may induce an idea chain, if they share the same concept.*
Sol LeWitt, 1969 (75)

*I was beginning to suspect that information could be interesting in its own right
and need not be visual as in Cubist, etc. art.*   John Baldessari, 1969 (14)

Although Conceptual art emerged from Minimalism, its basic principles were very different, stressing the
acceptively open-ended in contrast to Minimalism's rejectively self-contained. If Minimalism formally
expressed "less is more," Conceptual art was about saying more with less. It represented an opening up
after Minimalism closed down on expressionist and Pop excesses. As Robert Huot said in a 1977 billboard piece: "Less Is More, But It's Not Enough."

I'm often asked by younger students of the period why I talk about Conceptual art in political terms
when, looking back, most of it seems supremely apolitical. Part of the answer is relative. With a few
exceptions, the art was apolitical, but in an art world that still idolized Clement Greenberg (who in turn
publicly abhorred Pop and Minimal art), that denied even the presence of political concerns, and offered
little or no political education or analysis, Conceptual artists, most of whom were then in their twenties
and thirties, looked and sounded like radicals. Now, with a few exceptions, their art looks timid and dis-
connected in comparison to the political activism of the sixties and the activist art of the late seventies
and eighties, much of which is Conceptually aligned. The prime exceptions were GAAG and the work of
the Uruguayan expatriate Luis Camnitzer.

Writing from a consciousness almost non-existent in the American art world, Camnitzer wrote in
1970 that despite the fact that so many people in the world were starving to death, "artists continue to
produce full-belly art." He mused about why the phrase "Colonial Art" was art-historically positive, and
applied only to the past, because "In reality it happens in the present, and with benevolence it is called
'international style'" (168-169). In perhaps the most inspired political Conceptual artwork, ORDERS & CO.
(Camnitzer) sent a letter to Pacheco Areco, president of Uruguay in 1971, ordering him to do things he
could not help doing, so as to expose the dictator to dictatorship: "The 5th of November you will simu-
late normal walking but you will be conscious that for this day Orders & Co. have taken possession of
every third step you take. It is not necessary for you to obsess yourself with this."

Around the same time, Hans Haacke wrote:

*Information presented at the right time and in the right place can potentially be
very powerful. It can affect the general social fabric. . . . The working premise is to
think in terms of systems: the production of systems, the interference with and the
exposure of existing systems. . . . Systems can be physical, biological, or social.* [2]

One could argue that art is rarely in the right place, but Haacke's statement was sharpened when
his 1971 exhibition of systems was canceled by the Guggenheim Museum (his champion, curator Edward
Fry, was also fired). The offending piece was "social," a thoroughly-researched work on actual absentee
landlords, with whom the Guggenheim apparently shared an intense class-identification. Censorship
sent Haacke's art in a more political direction, his "museum-quality" resistance eventually providing a
bridge between Conceptualism, activism, and postmodernism.

Eleanor Antin
100 BOOTS ON THE JOB (15 February 1972, 12:15 p.m.)
Signal Hill, California. Courtesy Ronald Feldman Fine Arts,
New York.

Adrian Piper
CATALYSIS IV (1970-71)
Documentation of street performance, New York.
Courtesy John Weber Gallery, New York.

However, it was usually the form rather than the content of Conceptual art that carried a political message. The frame was there to be broken out of. Anti-establishment fervor in the 1960s focused on the de-mythologization and de-commodification of art, on the need for an independent (or "alternative") art that could not be bought and sold by the greedy sector that owned everything that was exploiting the world and promoting the Vietnam war. "The artists who are trying to do non-object art are introducing a drastic solution to the problems of artists being bought and sold so easily, along with their art. . . . The people who buy a work of art they can't hang up or have in their garden are less interested in possession. They are patrons rather than collectors," I said in 1969. (Now that's utopian . . .)

It was also becoming clear how authorship and ownership were intertwined. In Paris, in 1967, Daniel Buren (whose first striped works had been made in 1966), Olivier Mosset, and Niele Toroni invited reviewers to make or claim their paintings: "In order to discuss a forgery," wrote the critic Michel Claura, "one must refer to an original. In the case of Buren, Mosset, Toroni, where is the original work?" (32). In Holland, in 1968, Jan Dibbets, who had stopped painting in 1967, said: "Sell my work? To sell isn't part of the art. Maybe there will be people idiotic enough to buy what they could make themselves. So much the worse for them" (59). Carl Andre said of his outdoor line of hay bales at Windham College in Vermont in 1968 (another Siegelaub enterprise) that it "is going to break down and gradually disappear. But since I'm not making a piece of sculpture for sale . . . it never enters the property state" (47). This attack

on the notion of originality, "the artist's touch," and the competitive aspects of individual style constituted an attack on the genius theory, the hitherto most cherished aspect of patriarchal, ruling-class art.

Some Conceptualists took a page from Pop (imagery and techniques) and Minimalism (fabrication out of the artist's hands) by assuming an "industrial" approach. Ruscha had said, early on, that his photographic artist's books were not "to house a collection of art photographs—they are technical data like industrial photography" (12). He eliminated text so the photos would become "neutral." There was a cult of "neutrality" in Minimalism, applied not only to the execution of objects but to the ferocious erasure of emotion and conventional notions of beauty. (Morris's 1963 CARD FILE and STATEMENT OF ESTHETIC WITHDRAWAL were precedents.) In 1967, LeWitt said "The idea becomes a machine that makes the art" (28). Bochner curated an exhibition of "working drawings" at the School of Visual Arts, which included "non-art" as well as businesslike art diagrams. Andre explained his work, based on "particles" of material, in Marxist terms. Dennis Oppenheim did two large-scale earthworks that were about (and resulted in) wheat production. In Germany, Hilla and Bernd Becher were offering a new framework for documentary photography with their frontal, unmodulated images of industrial sites. And in England John Latham initiated the Artists Placement Group (APG), which placed artists in "real world" work-places. Frequently perceptible beneath the surface of such statements was the need to identify art with respectable work, and on a more superficial level, with the working class.

A related notion, also designed to avoid the isolation of art from the "ordinary" world, was a new angle on style and authorship, which led to post-Dada appropriation. Reviewing "557,087" in *Artforum*, Peter Plagens suggested that "There is a total style to the show, a style so pervasive as to suggest that Lucy Lippard is in fact the artist and that her medium is other artists" (111). Of course a critic's medium is always artists; critics are the original appropriators. Conceptual artists followed the Dadas into this territory. Starting from their Duchampian notion of "claiming," appropriation in the 1960s became more political as art-world artists borrowed John Heartfield's classic poster-makers' technique of co-opting media and other familiar images for new and often satirical ends (the "corrected billboard" of the later 1970s expanded this idea). Information and systems were seen as fair game, in the public domain. The appropriation of other artists' works or words, sometimes mutually agreed-upon as a kind of collaboration, was another Conceptual strategy. A combative attitude toward art as individual product was also implied, in line with the general sixties appeal of the collective act. Barthelme took on the alter ego James Robert Steelrails; a pseudonymous Arthur R. Rose (a multiple pun, perhaps, on Rrose Sélavy, Barbara Rose, Art, Author/ity, etc.) interviewed artists; I quoted the mythical Latvan (later Latvana) Greene. In 1969, the Italian artist Salvo appropriated the letters of Leonardo da Vinci to Ludivoco il Moro. In 1970, Eduardo Costa mocked the art world's first-come-first-served bias in A PIECE THAT IS ESSENTIAL-LY THE SAME AS A PIECE MADE BY ANY OF THE FIRST CONCEPTUAL ARTISTS, DATED TWO YEARS EARLIER THAN THE ORIGINAL AND SIGNED BY SOMEBODY ELSE.

In ROBERT BARRY PRESENTS A WORK BY IAN WILSON (July 1970), the work was *Ian Wilson*, a fragment of the elusive "Oral Communication," which Wilson once described as taking "the object or the idea of oral communication out of its natural context" and putting it in an art context, by speaking it, at which point "it became a concept" (180).

In another work from this series of "presentations" of others' work, Barry kidnapped three of my card catalogues and a review as the total contents of his 1971 Paris exhibition. In one particularly convoluted interchange, I wrote something about all this mutual appropriation, much enjoying the twists and turns on art, plagiarism, and criticism encountered, and my text became simultaneously part of two different artworks—by Douglas Huebler and David Lamelas. "It's all just a matter of what to call it?"

I asked rhetorically. "Does that matter?" (188). (I still wonder and I still try to blur the boundaries between art and everything else as much as possible.) This is as close as Conceptual art came to the meaningful play of Dada, and these were, actually, political questions that affected the whole conception of what art was and what art could do.

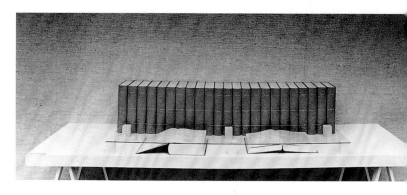

> *The root word "image" need not be used only to mean representation (in the sense of one thing referring to something other than itself). To re-present can be defined as the shift in referential frames of the viewer from the space of events to the space of statements or vice versa. Imagining (as opposed to imaging) is not a pictorial pre-occupation. Imagination is a projection, the exteriorizing of ideas about the nature of things seen. It re-produces that which is initially without product.*
>
> Mel Bochner, 1970. (167)

For artists looking to restructure perception and the process/product relationship of art, information and systems replaced traditional formal concerns of composition, color, technique, and physical presence. Systems were laid over life the way a rectangular format is laid over the seen in paintings, for focus. Lists, diagrams, measurements, neutral descriptions, and much counting were the most common vehicles for the preoccupation with repetition, the introduction of daily life and work routines, philosophical positivism, and pragmatism. There was a fascination with huge numbers (Mario Merz's pseudo-mathematical Fibonacci series, Barry's ONE BILLION DOTS (1969), Kawara's ONE MIL-LION YEARS (1969)), and with dictionaries, thesauruses, libraries, the mechanical aspects of language, permutations (LeWitt and Darboven), the regular, and the minute (for example, Ian Murray's 1971 TWENTY WAVES IN A ROW). Lists of words were equally popular, e.g. Barry's 1969 piece that included its own "refinement" as it progressed at least into 1971, which began: "It is whole, determined, sufficient, individual, known, complete, revealed, accessible, manifest, effected, effectual, directed, dependent" (250).

Austerity took precedence over hedonism, even to the point of deliberate "boredom" (sanctified by Minimalism as an alternative to frenetic expressionist individualism and crowd-pleasing Pop). There was a decidedly puritanical cast to much Conceptual art, as well as a fascination with pseudo-scientific data and neo-philosophical gobbledygook. One elegant precedent was Graham's MARCH 31, 1966, which listed distances from "1,000,000,000,000,000,000,000,000.00000000 miles to edge of known universe" through celestial, geographic, then local sectors to the artist's typewriter and glasses to ".00000098 miles to cornea from retinal wall" (14). Donald Burgy's 1968 Rock series combined this impetus with the notion of context and took it to an almost absurd extreme, documenting "selected physical aspects of a rock; its location in, and its conditions of, time and space," including weather maps, electron microscopy, X-ray photographs, spectrographic and petrographic analysis. "The scale of this information extends, in time," said Burgy, "from the geologic to the present moment; and, in size of matter, from the continen-

tal to the atomic" (51). Sometimes a certain wit was involved, as in Dibbets's manipulations of perspective so that non-rectangles appeared rectangular; he did this on walls, on the ground, and, in 1968, on television, showing a tractor furrowing ground with perspective corrections matching the rectangular frame of the TV screen.

The emphasis on process also led to art-as-life, life-as-art pieces, like Lozano's, Piper's, and Gilbert & George's living sculptures, and especially Mierle Laderman Ukeles's "Maintenance Art" series, which began in 1969. In 1971, as Haacke's real-estate piece was being censored, Allan Kaprow published his influential text on "the education of the un-artist," and Christopher Cook executed a grand-scale "art-as-life" work by assuming the directorship of the Institute of Contemporary Art in Boston as a year-long piece. In performance, conceptualized improvisation played a similar role, as in Vito Acconci's "following" piece, or his ZONE (1971), in which he tried to keep a cat confined in a taped square for half an hour, blocking its moves by walking, no hands. The later work of Linda Montano, Lynn Hershman, and Tehching Hsieh inherited and extended this legacy.

Communication (but not community) and distribution (but not accessibility) were inherent in Conceptual art. Although the forms pointed toward democratic outreach, the content did not. However rebellious the escape attempts, most of the work remained art-referential, and neither economic nor esthetic ties to the art world were fully severed (though at times we liked to think they were hanging by a thread). Contact with a broader audience was vague and undeveloped.

Surprisingly little thought was given in the United States (as far as I know) to education, especially within or as alternatives to the existing institutions. In 1967, Amsterdam artists Dibbets, Ger van Elk, and Lucassen began the short-lived "International Institute for the Reeducation of Artists." The most powerful model was Joseph Beuys, who said in 1969:

> To be a teacher is my greatest work of art. The rest is the waste product, a
> demonstration. . . . Objects aren't very important for me any more. . . . I am try-
> ing to reaffirm the concept of art and creativity in the face of Marxist doctrine. . . .
> For me the formation of the thought is already sculpture. (121-122)

Verbal strategies enabled Conceptual art to be political through verbal strategies, but not populist. Communication between people was subordinate to communication about communication. "Whereas it took years to get a work to Europe or California [from New York]," said Siegelaub, "now it takes a telephone call. These are significant differences. The idea of swift communication implies that no one has anything" (126). In the era of faxes, this seems quaint, but at the time the adoption of telex technology by N. E. Thing Co. and Haacke seemed daringly "beyond art."

Occasionally the content seemed relatively accessible, as in James Collins's Introduction Pieces of 1970-71, in which he introduced two total strangers in a public place, photographed them shaking hands, then asked them to sign an "affidavit" on the transaction. However, there was also a "semiotic" component to these works that effectively academicized them: "That the message functioned *disjunctively* culturally was employed as a device to re-align the recipients' relationship to the message, as a theoretical construct" (226).

Robert Barry
ONE BILLION DOTS (1971)
Twenty-five volumes. Photo courtesy The Getty Center for the
History of Art and the Humanities, Santa Monica, California.

On Kawara
ONE MILLION YEARS (1969)
Index card from catalogue for "557,087."

Mierle Laderman Ukeles
WASHING, TRACKS, MAINTENANCE (1973)
From the Maintenance Art Performance series. Documentation of
performance at the Wadsworth Atheneum, Hartford, Connecticut.
Courtesy Ronald Feldman Fine Arts, New York.

For the most part communication was perceived as distribution, and it was in this area that populist desires were raised but unfulfilled. Distribution was often built into the piece. Weiner offered the most classic and concise examination of this issue in the stipulations for "ownership" (or for avoiding ownership) that accompanied all of his works:

> *1. The artist may construct the piece.*
>
> *2. The piece may be fabricated.*
>
> *3. The piece need not be built.*
>
> *Each being equal and consistent with the intent of the artist, the decision as to condition rests with the receiver upon the occasion of receivership.* (73-74)

Since novelty was the fuel for the conventional art market, and novelty depended upon speed and change, Conceptual artists gloried in speeding past the cumbersome established process of museum-sponsored exhibitions and catalogues by means of mail art, rapidly edited and published books of art, and other small-is-better strategies. "Some artists now think it's absurd to fill up their studios with objects that won't be sold, and are trying to get their art communicated as rapidly as it is made. They're thinking out ways to make art what they'd like it to be in spite of the devouring speed syndrome it's made in. That speed has not only to be taken into consideration, but to be utilized," I told Ursula Meyer in 1969; "the new dematerialized art . . . provides a way of getting the power structure out of New York and spreading it around to wherever an artist feels like being at the time. Much art now is transported by the artist, or *in* the artist himself [sic], rather than by watered-down, belated circulating exhibitions or by existing information networks" (7-8).

> *Communication relates to art three ways: (1) Artists knowing what other artists are doing. (2) The art community knowing what artists are doing. (3) The world knowing what artists are doing. . . . It's my concern to make it known to multitudes. [The most suitable means are] books and catalogues.*
> Seth Siegelaub, 1969 (124)

One of the things we often speculated about in the late sixties was the role of the art magazine. In an era of proposed projects, photo-text works, and artists' books, the periodical could be the ideal vehicle

for art itself rather than merely for reproduction, commentary, and promotion. At one point I recall brainstorming with friends about a parasite magazine, each "issue" of which would appear noted as such in a different "host" magazine each month. The idea was to give readers first-hand rather than second-hand information about art. (Kosuth, Piper, and Ian Wilson published works as "ads" in newspapers at the time; in the 1980s this strategy was revived by Haacke and Group Material.)

In 1970, Siegelaub, with the enthusiastic support of editor Peter Townsend, took over an issue of the then lively British journal *Studio International* and made it a kind of magazine exhibition with six "curators" (critics David Antin, Germano Celant, Michel Claura, Charles Harrison, Hans Strelow, and myself). We were each given eight pages and could fill them however we liked, with whatever artists we liked, doing whatever they liked. Claura chose only Buren, who striped his pages in yellow and white; Strelow chose Dibbets and Darboven; the rest of us chose eight artists with a page each. My "show" was a round robin. I asked each artist to provide a "situation" within which the next artist was to work, so the works created one cumulative, circular piece. (For example: Weiner to Kawara: "Dear On Kawara, I must apologize but the only situation I can bring myself to impose upon you would be my hopes for your having a good day. Fond Regards, Lawrence Weiner." Kawara replied with a telegram: I AM STILL ALIVE, sent to LeWitt, who responded by making a list of seventy-four permutations of that phrase.)

Decentralization and internationalism were major aspects of the prevailing distribution theories. This sounds odd now, when the "art world" extends to most of the western world (though "global" is still out of reach, "Magiciens de la terre" and the Bienal de La Habana notwithstanding). In the sixties, however, New York was resting in a self-imposed, and self-satisfied, isolation, having taken the title of world art capital from Paris in the late fifties. At the same time, the political struggles of the sixties were forging new bonds among the youth of the world. (The Parisian Situationists, though rarely mentioned in the Conceptual art literature, paralleled its goals in many ways, although the French focus on media and spectacle was far more politically sophisticated.)

The easily portable, easily communicated forms of Conceptual art made it possible for artists working out of the major art centers to participate in the early stages of new ideas. Huebler, for instance, one of the most imaginative and broad-ranging early Conceptualists, lived in Bradford, Massachusetts. They could also carry their work with them as they moved around the country or world. When artists travel more, I argued at the time—not to sightsee, but to get their work out—they take with them the ambience, stimulus, and energy of the milieu in which the work was made (New York was still implied as the prime source of that energy): "People are exposed directly to the art and to the ideas behind it in a more realistic, informal situation." (This was before the "visiting artist" lecture series became an American academic institution; with the artists' slide registry, which came out of the Women's Movement, such series transformed the American art student's education and voided the curatorial excuse, "there are no good artists out there.") Spirits were high. In a de-commodified "idea art," some of us (or was it just me?) thought we had in our hands the weapon that would transform the art world into a democratic institution.

Joseph Kosuth
I. EXISTENCE (ART AS IDEA AS IDEA) and
VI. TIME (ART AS IDEA AS IDEA) (1968)
Installation view, "January 5–31, 1969," rented office space at 44 East 52nd Street, New York. Courtesy The Siegelaub Collection & Archives. Photo Seth Siegelaub.

Projects by *On Kawara* and *Sol LeWitt* for Lucy R. Lippard's contribution to "July–August 1970," an exhibition organized by Seth Siegelaub and presented in *Studio International* 180, no. 924 (July–August 1970): 1–48.

By the end of the decade, connections had been made between "idea artists" and their supporters around the United States and in England, Italy, France, Germany, Holland, Argentina, and Canada (Vancouver and Halifax in particular). By 1970 Australia (the Inhibodress group in Sydney) and Yugoslavia (the OHO group) had also kicked in. We began to see that Europe was more fertile ground than the United States for these new networks and means of dissemination. As younger American artists were invited to Europe, younger European artists began to show up in New York independently, making contact with their peers, cooking up inexpensive but expansive international "projects" unaffiliated with the commercial gallery system; French was the lingua franca, as few then spoke good English. The generous government funding in Europe (and more curatorial sympathy on the intellectual/political level) and, in Germany, the Kunsthalle system made more and quicker experimentation possible. The New York art world was so full of itself that it didn't need to pay much attention to the Conceptual gnats nipping at its fat flanks. The British critic Charles Harrison pointed out that in the late 1960s, Paris and the various European cities were in the position that New York was around 1939: a gallery and museum structure existed, but it was so dull and irrelevant to new art that there was a feeling that it could be bypassed. "Whereas in New York," I said, "the present gallery-money-power structure is so strong that it's going to be very difficult to find a viable alternative to it" (8).

Kynaston McShine's fully international "Information" show at The Museum of Modern Art in the summer of 1970 was an unexpected exception. Born of an art-oriented interest in systems and information theory, and then transformed by the national rage attending Kent State and Cambodia, it became a state-of-the-art exhibition unlike anything else that cautious and usually unadventurous institution had attempted to date. The handsome catalogue looked like a Conceptual artist's book, with its informal "typewritten" text and wild range of non-art imagery from anthropology to computer science, and an eclectic, interdisciplinary reading list. I am listed in the table of contents with the artists because of the weird critical text I contributed (from Spain, where I was writing a novel deeply influenced by Conceptual art), and elsewhere as a "critic" (in quotation marks). Many of the artists might have preferred the quotation-marks treatment too, as a way of distancing themselves from predictable roles. Another departure for the time: films, videos, books, and John Giorno's Dial-A-Poem were among the exhibits. Adrian Piper's contribution was a series of notebooks filled with blank pages in which the viewers were

requested to write, draw, or otherwise indicate any response suggested by this situation (this statement, the blank notebook and pen, the museum context, your immediate state of mind, etc.)

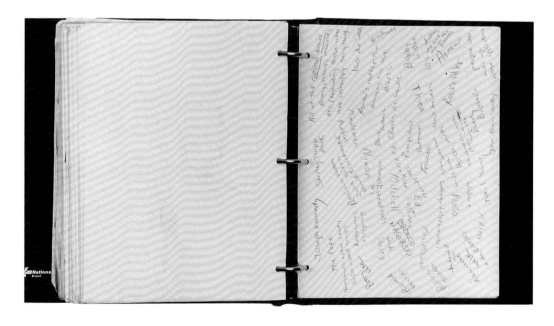

Adrian Piper
CONTEXT #7 (1970)
Seven three-ring binders filled with blank pages written and drawn on by visitors to "Information," The Museum of Modern Art, New York, 2 July–20 September 1970. Each binder, 3 x 11 3/4 x 10 1/2 in. (7.6 x 29.8 x 26.7 cm) (closed); each page, 11 x 8 1/2 in. (27.9 x 21.6 cm). Courtesy John Weber Gallery, New York.

Installation view, "Information," The Museum of Modern Art, New York, 2 July–20 September 1970. Photo © 1995 The Museum of Modern Art, New York.

(III. The Charm of Life Itself) At its most inventive, it has the mystery and charm of life itself. It is the toughness of art that is lacking. Amy Goldin on Conceptual art, 1969 (104) Inevitably, the issue of Conceptual art as "not art," "non-art," and "anti-art" was raised in the face of all these typed and xeroxed pages, blurry photographs, and radical (sometimes preposterous or pretentious) gestures. Barthelme (who later gave up his cantankerous forays into "visual" art to become a well-known novelist) rejected the notion of [art] by refusing to say the word:

> *I do not agree that by putting something into an   context one admits to making   . . . . I do not like the word   . I do not like the body of work defined by the word   . What I do like is the notion production. I produce in order to pass the time. (60)*

It was sometimes a question of who was an artist and to what extent art is style. The late Australian artist Ian Burn, who was an early member of Art & Language, stated the anti-style position of many Conceptualists when he said in 1968: "Presentation is a problem because it can easily become a form in itself, and this can be misleading. I would always opt for the most neutral format, one that doesn't interfere with or distort the information" (37).

> *There is something about void and emptiness which I am personally very concerned with. I guess I can't get it out of my system. Just emptiness. Nothing seems to me the most potent thing in the world.* Robert Barry, 1968 (40)

One of the suggested solutions was a tabula rasa. In 1970, John Baldessari cremated all his art dated May 1953 to March 1966, thereby giving himself a fresh start. Kozlov showed an empty film reel, and made rejection itself her art form, conceptualizing pieces and then rejecting them, freeing herself from execution while remaining an artist. In England, Keith Arnatt titled a work IS IT POSSIBLE FOR ME TO DO NOTHING AS MY CONTRIBUTION TO THIS EXHIBITION? and mused on "Art as an Act of Omission." In Australia, Peter Kennedy made a ten-minute piece that transferred bandages from a microphone onto a camera, forming a doubly muted transition between silence and invisibility.

In 1969 I organized an exhibition at the Paula Cooper Gallery, a benefit for the Art Workers Coalition, in which the symptoms of dematerialization were well advanced: an (apparently) "empty" room contained Haacke's AIR CURRENTS (a small fan), Barry's invisible MAGNETIC FIELD, Weiner's

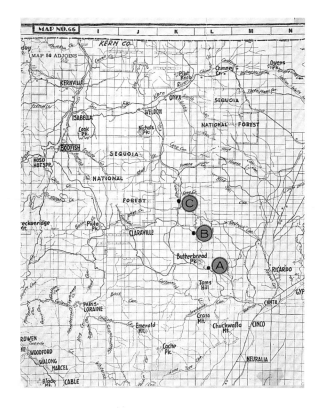

Location Piece #13
Kern County, California

On June 3, 1969 three 1/2 gallon sealed plastic containers of distilled spring water were buried in the 'high desert' approximately 20 miles north of Mojave, California. Any traveler in the area who is in need of water and able to locate any one of the containers is invited to disinter it and use the contents.

Three photographs, California Section Map No. 66 and a general map of California pinpoint the locations and join, altogether, with this statement to constitute the form of this piece.

June, 1969   *Douglas Huebler*

MINUTE PIT IN THE WALL FROM ONE AIR-RIFLE SHOT, Wilson's "Oral Communication," a "secret" by Kaltenbach, a small black blip painted on the wall by Richard Artschwager, Huot's "existing shadows," and a tiny cable wire piece by Andre on the floor. The smallest room was, by contrast, crammed with printed matter—photo, text, xerox, and otherwise shrunken art.

This was a relatively conservative statement. Barry rejected the closed claustrophobic spaces of the gallery system by closing the gallery for one of his shows. Buren sealed off the entrance to a gallery space in Milan with his trademark white-and-one-color striped fabric, "opening" and "closing" the show in one move. In Argentina, Graciela Carnevale welcomed opening visitors to a totally empty room; the door was hermetically sealed without their knowing it: "The piece involved closing access and exits, and the unknown reactions of the visitors. After more than an hour, the 'prisoners' broke the glass window and 'escaped'" (49).

Such escape attempts were in fact being made by the artists rather than by the audiences. In this case the audience was forced to act out the artists' desires—to break out of the system. Much of this discussion had to do with boundaries—those imposed by conventional art definitions and contexts, and those chosen by the artists to make points about the new, autonomous lines they were drawing. "All legitimate art deals with limits," said Smithson. "Fraudulent art feels that it has no limits" (90). Some, like Huebler and Oppenheim, focused on the redistribution of site or place, although the more abstract notions of space and context usually prevailed over local specificity.

> *The more successful work from the minimal syndrome rejected itself, allowing the*
> *viewer a one-to one confrontation with pure limit or bounds. This displacement*
> *or sensory pressures from object to place will prove to be the major contribution*
> *of minimalist art.* Dennis Oppenheim, 1969 (80-81)

Huebler "dematerialized" place (or space) in his many map pieces, which in a quintessentially "Conceptual" manner disregarded time and space limitations, and in works like one from 1970, which consisted of a vertical line drawn on a sheet of paper with the line below it reading: "the line above is rotating on its axis at a speed of one revolution each day." Bochner, who made a series of works delineating interior architectural measurements, wrote the same year: "A fundamental assumption in much recent past art was that things have stable properties, i.e. boundaries. . . . Boundaries, however, are only the fabrication of our desire to detect them" (166). Applying the idea to a social context, Baldessari executed a "ghetto boundary" piece with George Nicolaidis for "557,087" in Seattle in 1969 which, although intended as a consciousness-raising device, would probably be perceived as racist today: they affixed small silver and black labels to telephone poles or street signs along the boundary of an African-American neighborhood.

> *I'm beginning to believe that one of the last frontiers left for radical gestures is*
> *the imagination.* David Wojnarowicz, 1989 [3]

Even in 1969, as we were imagining our heads off and, to some extent, out into the world, I suspected that "the art world is probably going to be able to absorb conceptual art as another 'movement' and not pay too much attention to it. The art establishment depends so greatly on objects which can be bought and sold that I don't expect it to do much about an art that is opposed to the prevailing systems" (7-8). (This remains true today—art that is too specific, that names names, about politics, or place, or anything else, is not marketable until it is abstracted, generalized, defused.) By 1974, I was writing with some disillusion in the "Postface" of *Six Years:* "Hopes that 'conceptual art' would be able to avoid the general

Douglas Huebler
Detail from LOCATION PIECE #13 (KERN COUNTY, CALIFORNIA) (1969).
Three color photographs, California Section Map No. 66, general map of California, and statement. Each photograph, two at 10 x 8 in. (25.4 x 20.3 cm) and one at 8 x 10 in. (20.3 x 25.4 cm); section map, 10 3/8 x 8 1/2 in. (26.4 x 21.6 cm); general map, 25 x 14 in. (63.5 x 35.6 cm); statement, 11 x 8 1/2 in. (27.9 x 21.6 cm). Collection the artist. Photos Paula Goldman.

commercialization, the destructively 'progressive' approach of modernism were for the most part unfounded. It seemed in 1969 . . . that no one, not even a public greedy for novelty, would actually pay money, or much of it, for a xerox sheet referring to an event past or never directly perceived, a group of photographs documenting an ephemeral situation or condition, a project for work never to be completed, words spoken but not recorded; it seemed that these artists would therefore be forcibly freed from the tyranny of a commodity status and market-orientation. Three years later, the major conceptualists are selling work for substantial sums here and in Europe; they are represented by (and still more unexpected—showing in) the world's most prestigious galleries. Clearly, whatever minor revolutions in communication have been achieved by the process of dematerializing the object . . . , art and artist in a capitalist society remain luxuries" (263).

Yet, with a longer view, it is also clear that the Conceptual artists set up a model that remains flexible enough to be useful today, totally aside from the pompous and flippant manners in which it has sometimes been used in the art context. Out of that decade from 1966 to 1975 came a flock of

JOHN BALDESSARI
GEORGE NICOLAIDIS

June 17, 1931
September 6, 1939

National City, California
Jersey City, New Jersey

Title: Ghetto Boundary Project

Date: First Version April 6, 1969

■ ■ ■ BOUNDARY ■ ■ ■

A SECTION OF A CITY, ESPECIALLY A THICKLY POPU-
LATED AREA INHABITED BY MINORITY GROUPS OFTEN
AS A RESULT OF SOCIAL OR ECONOMIC RESTRICTIONS.

Description: Two thousand ghetto boundary stickers were affixed to telephone poles, street signs, etc. along the fifteen mile boundary on the ghetto in southeast San Diego. Boundary location was supplied by the San Diego Planning Commission. Project can be done wherever there is a ghetto. Number of stickers used varies with size of ghetto.

cooperative galleries (55 Mercer and A. I. R. being the notable survivors), a tide of artists' books (which led to the formation in 1976 of Printed Matter and the Franklin Furnace Archive), another activist artists' organization led by former Conceptualists (Artists Meeting for Cultural Change) after the AWC faded with the Vietnam war, and an international performance art and video network. Activist and ecological/site-specific work that had its beginnings in the 1960s in Conceptual-related projects has seen a revival in the 1980s and 1990s; the much-maligned Whitney Biennial of 1993 featured more-and-less "political" art that recalled its Conceptual sources; and feminist activists like the Guerrilla Girls and the Women's Action Coalition (WAC) also renewed 1960s and early 1970s concerns with women's representation in the media, daily life, and role playing/gender-bending.

Perhaps most important, Conceptualists indicated that the most exciting "art" might still be buried in social energies not yet recognized as art. The process of discovering the boundaries didn't stop with Conceptual art: These energies are still out there, waiting for artists to plug into them, potential fuel for the expansion of what "art" can mean. The escape was temporary. Art was recaptured and sent back to its white cell, but parole is always a possibility.

Notes

1. Sol LeWitt, "Sentences on Conceptual Art," in Lucy R. Lippard, *Six Years: The Dematerialization of the Art Object from 1966 to 1972* (New York: Praeger, 1973), 75. Page numbers for further references to *Six Years* are cited in parentheses within the text.

2. Jeanne Siegel, "An Interview with Hans Haacke," *Arts Magazine* 45, no. 7 (May 1971): 21.

3. David Wojnarowicz, "Post Cards from America: X-Rays from Hell," in *Witnesses: Against Our Vanishing*, exh. cat. (New York: Artists Space, 1989), 10.

John Baldessari and George Nicolaidis
GHETTO BOUNDARY PROJECT, 6 April 1969 (first version).
Index card from catalogue for "557,087."

Lisa Kahane
WAC WOMEN UNITE! (1992)
Photograph of outdoor slide presentation and speak-out orga-
nized by the Women's Action Coalition in protest of the 1992
Republican Convention in Houston.

ANN GOLDSTEIN AND ANNE RORIMER

ARTISTS IN THE EXHIBITION

VITO ACCONCI

(b. 24 January 1940, Bronx, New York; lives in Brooklyn, New York)

In the late 1960s, Vito Acconci abandoned the creation of poetry works that dealt with the page as a performance space. As a poet, he had viewed the page as an area in which to act, and in his "Notes on Poetry," he defined words as props for movement and the page as a thing, a container, a map, and a field for movement.[1] His last works of poetry, done "in a poetry context," as he has observed, "were 'poetry events': the occasion was a poetry reading—I used props (an audio recorder, the walls of the room or the chairs in that room)—the attempt was not to read from a page but to read the room." Alternatively, his "first pieces, in an art context, were ways to get [himself] off the page and into real space."[2]

In his shift from poetry to visual art, Acconci ultimately replaced his former arena of activity, the space of the page, with the space of the gallery. This shift from the use of the page to a consideration of the exhibition space was marked by a fertile and experimental period of activity commencing in 1969. At this time, the artist established his performative manner of working, which revolved around his own physical and psychological being as highlighted by self-imposed activities of different kinds. These activities proposed a new definition of the material object by erasing traditional lines between an artist and his or her audience, a thing and a temporal event, and a work of art and its existence within a spatial and/or social context.

Acconci's early works attest to the diversity of his means and the rationale for his methods. Some pieces involving motions and actions carried out against urban or landscape backgrounds were recorded photographically, although many other works, such as SERVICE AREA (1970) or PROXIMITY PIECE (1970), were realized within the framework of temporary exhibitions. In the former, Acconci used his space in The Museum of Modern Art's "Information" exhibition as a place to have his mail delivered. In this way, he linked the traditional exhibition space with spaces and systems normally only associated with public service.

PROXIMITY PIECE, which "took place" in the exhibition "Software: Information Technology: Its Meaning for Art," presented at The Jewish Museum in New York in 1970, required that Acconci be present at the exhibition for its duration. He would randomly choose a viewer whom he did not know personally to stand close or next to until that viewer moved to another part of the room. In this performative way, in real time and place, Acconci carved out his own space within the exhibition as a whole, instead of displaying a physical object. Additionally, he identified the process of viewing with the process of making the work and thus set the stage for later works that overtly made reference to others and explicitly brought the viewing subject into the parameters of the work.

In installation pieces of the early 1970s, Acconci was audibly, if not always visibly, present. The sound of his voice penetrated the exhibition space as he verbally engaged with the visitor in order "to make my space and viewer space come together, more coincident with each other." By the second half of the 1970s, Acconci had further realized that a work, as well, "could use gallery space as a kind of model for an overall cultural space."[3] Although the artist dismissed himself as a live presence within works after 1974, he continued to be an active presence by means of tapes that serve to convey his image and/or carry his voice from point to point within a particular installation. In his performance/installation pieces, Acconci's utterances served to demarcate the physical gallery space as a space for mental interaction between the viewing subject, the artist, and the resulting work of art. — AR

Notes

1. Vito Acconci, in *Vito Acconci: A Retrospective: 1969 to 1980*, exh. cat. (Chicago: Museum of Contemporary Art, 1980), 10.

2. Vito Acconci, "Notes on My Photographs, 1969-1970," in *Vito Acconci: Photographic Works 1969-1970*, exh. cat. (Chicago: Rhona Hoffman Gallery, New York: Brooke Alexander, and Geneva: Galerie Eric Franck, 1988), unpag.

3. Vito Acconci, in Martin Kunz, "Interview with Vito Acconci about the Development of His Work Since 1966," in *Vito Acconci*, exh. cat. (Lucerne: Kunstmuseum Luzern, 1978), unpag.

PROXIMITY PIECE
Activity. Varying times over fifty-two days. Realized for "Software: Information Technology: Its Meaning for Art," The Jewish Museum, New York, 16 September–8 November 1970.

Standing near a person and intruding on his/her personal space.

During the exhibition, sometime each day, I wander through the museum and pick out, at random, a visitor to one of the exhibits: I'm standing beside that person, or behind, closer than the accustomed distance—I crowd the person until he/she moves away, or until he/she moves me out of the way.

(Attached to the wall, in the midst of the other exhibits, a 3" x 5" index-card notes the activity and describes it as above; the card might or might not be noticed by a viewer passing by.)

44

SERVICE AREA
Installation/activity. 72 x 36 x 36 in. (193.0 x 91.4 x 91.4 cm); three months,
varying days, varying times each day. Realized for "Information," The Museum of
Modern Art, New York, 2 July–20 September 1970.

During the exhibition, my mail is forwarded by the post office to the museum. My space in the museum functions as my mailbox.

Whenever I need mail, want mail, I go to the museum to get it.

BAS JAN ADER

(b. 19 April 1942, Winschoten, The Netherlands; last seen 9 July 1975, Cape Cod, Massachusetts)

In 1963 Dutch-born Bas Jan Ader came to Southern California. From 1969, when he completed his studies at Claremont Graduate School in Claremont, California, until his disappearance in 1975, Ader produced a significant body of work, including films, videotapes, photographs, installations, and performances exploring "the search for the understanding and structuring of life in its totality."[1]

In this work Ader sought to engage and challenge the ideal of the heroic master through the themes of falling and failing, playing off of the similarity between the two words and their meanings.[2] Using the tools of beauty, vulnerability, and melodrama with a cool detachment and a self-mocking criticality, these works are characterized by mysterious and elusive double meanings that evoke sincere pathos, yet elicit a consciousness of the manipulative and cliched sentimentality that the artist employs.

The evocation of vulnerability and the act of falling were literally joined in LIGHT VULNERABLE OBJECTS THREATENED BY EIGHT CEMENT BRICKS (1970), an installation/performance consisting of cinder blocks suspended by ropes over such fragile objects as potted flowers, a string of lights, pillows, a pile of eggs,

FAREWELL TO FARAWAY FRIENDS (1971)
Color photograph. 19 5/8 x 23 5/8 in. (50 x 60 cm).
Collection Bas Jan Ader Estate, Courtesy Patrick
Painter Editions, Inc., Vancouver/Hong Kong.

46

a photograph, and a cake in a box. Rather than leave the objects in a state of potential doom, Ader eventually cut the ropes and released the blocks onto them; most were destroyed in the process.

The "falling" works continued in a series of films and photographs. In his film FALL I, LOS ANGELES (1970), Ader attempts to sit in a chair on the rooftop of his home in Claremont. Unsuccessful, he falls off. In FALL II, AMSTERDAM (1970), he rides a bicycle along the bank of a canal and then suddenly into the water. Both films are silent, black and white, and just a few seconds in length. In addition, each ends abruptly at the moment of impact, purposefully leaving the aftermath unknown. Ader's own comments on this group of works reflect his use of self-deprecation: "I'm making a subdued work. On the film I silently state everything which has to do with falling. It's a large task which demands a great deal of difficult thinking. It's going to be poignant. I like that. I'm a Dutch Master." [3] In such 1971 works as ON THE ROAD TO A NEW NEO PLASTICISM WESTKAPELLE HOLLAND, Ader literally grapples with the formal elements of the history of Neo-Plasticism, launched by the twentieth-century Dutch master Piet Mondrian, futilely falling under its weight.

In 1970-71, Ader made a series of works, including a photograph, a postcard, and two films titled I'M TOO SAD TO TELL YOU. The second and only extant version of the film shows Ader breaking down in tears. While he gave no explanation for the work, his notes show an outline of reference points: "Descend, Roger van der Weyden/Giovanni Bellini, tears exhaustion tears/Picasso Guernica." [4] Resistant to specific interpretation and difficult to categorize, Ader's works were, at the time, described in the terms of the "body art" of the period. His response to such categorization was typically elusive: "I do not make body sculpture, body art, or body works. When I fell off the roof of my house, or into a canal, it was because gravity made itself master over me. When I cried it was because of extreme grief." [5]

In 1972, Ader presented at Art & Project in Amsterdam a performance titled THE BOY WHO FELL OVER NIAGARA FALLS. Sitting in a comfortable chair within a domestic setup, he read a text from *Readers' Digest* as he periodically sipped water from his glass. He finished the text as he finished his water. As Paul Andriesse has observed, "The drinking of the water was a kind of mini-waterfall, while the gradually emptying glass functioned as an hourglass." [6]

Ader's interest in Mondrian was again manifested in two related works, a set of untitled photographs and a color videotape,

PRIMARY TIME (both 1974). In these works, he translated Mondrian's theory of Neo-Plasticism into flower arrangements. Dressed in black, he carefully arranged, re-mixed, and re-arranged red, blue, and yellow carnations, slowly shifting them into monochromatic arrangements.

At the time of his disappearance in 1975, Ader was in the process of making IN SEARCH OF THE MIRACULOUS. This work was initially manifested in 1973 as IN SEARCH OF THE MIRACULOUS (ONE NIGHT IN LOS ANGELES), a series of eighteen black-and-white photographs of the artist walking alone in Los Angeles, with a transcription of the lyrics of the Coasters' song "Searchin'" handwritten along the bottom of each. The second version was conceived as a three-part work, commencing with an exhibition at Claire Copley Gallery in Los Angeles, continuing with the artist's voyage in a sailboat from Cape Cod to Falmouth, England, and concluding with an exhibition at the Groniger Museum in Groningen, The Netherlands. The Claire Copley exhibition, which included the 1973 photographic version of the piece, opened with a performance by a choir singing sea songs, which was documented and shown as a slide projection/sound installation. On 9 July 1975 Ader set sail for England, a trip that was estimated to take sixty to ninety days. Radio contact with him ceased after three weeks, and the following spring his boat was found off the coast of Ireland. His body was never recovered. — AG

Notes

1. Paul Andriesse, "Bas Jan Ader, an artist in search of the miraculous," in *Bas Jan Ader: Kunstenaar/Artist*, exh. cat. (Amsterdam: Stedelijk Museum, 1988), 72. The author wishes to acknowledge the importance of this book.

2. It has been suggested that Ader's interest in the hero and master stems from his own life experiences (his father was a celebrated World War II hero who helped Dutch Jews hide from the Germans and was ultimately imprisoned and executed for his activities). In "Quotations of Bas Jan Ader/Comments by William Leavitt," in *Bas Jan Ader*, 70-71, Ader's friend William Leavitt cites this history as an important influence on the artist's life and career:

> [H]e had a corresponding attraction to the imperfect, the broken, the mistaken, and the misunderstood. That his father died a martyred hero in World War II had something to do with this. His father was the absolute ideal that existed powerfully in his imagination, but there was however, no balancing image of a fallible human being by which he could gauge himself, and he therefore could only participate with a handicap in the natural process of the son striving to surpass the father.

3. Cited in Andriesse, "Bas Jan Ader," 75.

4. Cited in ibid., 76.

5. Cited in "Rumbles," *Avalanche* (New York), no. 2 (Winter 1971): 3.

6. Andriesse, "Bas Jan Ader," 79.

yeh I've been searchin'

Oh yeh, Searchin' everywhich way

Searchin' everywhich way

but I'm like that Northwest Mounty

Well now I I have to swim a river
you know I will

Oh yeh searchin' my goodness

IN SEARCH OF THE MIRACULOUS (ONE NIGHT IN LOS ANGELES) (1973)
Eighteen black-and-white photographs with handwritten text in white ink. Each,
8 x 10 in. (20.3 x 25.4 cm). Private Collection, London.

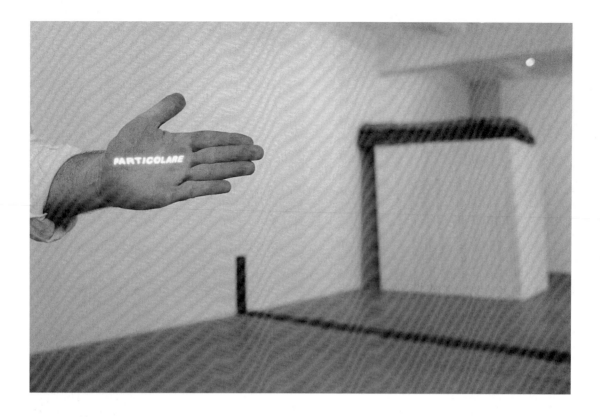

GIOVANNI ANSELMO

(b. 5 August 1934,
Borgo Franco d'Ivrea,
Italy; lives in Turin)

In 1969 Giovanni Anselmo wrote that what interested him was "the world, things, life—situations involving energy." He further noted that it is important not to "crystalize" these situations.[1] Anselmo's concern with conveying essentials without resorting to absolutes unites his sculpture of the second half of the 1960s with his installations of the early 1970s. The idea of an abstract energy emanates from three-dimensional objects such as SENZA TITOLO (Untitled, 1968) and TORSIONE (Contortion, 1968), insofar as the sculptures, in a sense, are in a state of performing. The first consists of a modestly scaled, upright, rectangular granite block resembling a pedestal. A separate, but matching, cube of stone is attached by a wire to the main form in order to sandwich a leafy head of lettuce. The attempted integration of an organic material and a non-living stone acknowledges the artist's desire to question traditional sculptural form in order to identify the sculpture with reality more closely, if not to bring it to life literally. TORSIONE, as its title suggests, presents a state of having been, and of being, wound up. An iron bar, suspended from a tightly twisted, fustian cloth, hangs on the wall. This work thereby embodies the process of making a sculpture that displays the way in which it is a function of its own materiality.

Anselmo's use of slide projection follows from works that speak about the invisible in relation to the visible and that radically break with more traditional approaches to sculpture. Subtly calling attention to the architectural surrounds with which they merge, Anselmo's projection pieces, such as PARTICOLARE (Detail, 1972), supercede the materiality of a singular object without sacrificing attention to the physicality of reality more generally. PAR-TICOLARE, in particular, animates the location it occupies when the Italian word "particolare" is projected onto the various components of the exhibition area from projectors dispersed throughout the space. A variable number of projected "details" label the floor, the wall, and the ceiling, as well as other architectural details, such as vents, moldings, or radiators. These small, illuminated words identify the components of the work's setting and display the room as the ineffable sum of its parts. They articulate, while also tying together, the entire physical context of the exhibited work. In this way, the work itself meshes with the reality it defines through a single word—a detail from linguistic usage. In short, language participates directly with/in its place of display so as to conjoin the formal/verbal content of the work with its exhibition context.

In related works from the beginning of the 1970s, Anselmo projected other single words or parts of words onto the surfaces of objects or directly onto the surface of the wall as in INFINITO (Infinite, 1971); INVISIBLE (Invisible, 1971), with its projection of the word "visibile"; and TUTTO (All, 1971), with its projection of "tut." In these works Anselmo singled out an all-encompassing word that linguistically directs viewers to a consideration of the relationship between conceiving and perceiving. If the invisible can be addressed, it cannot be seen any more than the infinite can be understood but not materially shown. Nor can "all" be all-inclusive. — AR

Notes

1. Giovanni Anselmo, in *Giovanni Anselmo*, exh. cat. (Paris: Galerie Sonnabend, 1969), unpag. This passage comprises the first paragraph of a longer statement by the artist that reads: "Moi, le monde, les choses, la vie—nous sommes des situations d'energie. L'essentiel est de ne pas cristaliser ces situations: de les maintenir ouvertes et vivantes en tant que fonctions de la vie."

PARTICOLARE (Detail, 1972/77)
Installation view, "Europe in the Seventies: Aspects of Recent Art," Art
Institute of Chicago, 8 October–27 November 1977. Photo Rusty Culp

PARTICOLARE (Detail, 1972/92)
Installation view, "Giovanni Anselmo," Marian Goodman Gallery, New York,
7 March–4 April 1992. Courtesy Marian Goodman Gallery, New York.

ELEANOR ANTIN

(b. 27 February 1935,
New York City;
lives in Del Mar,
California)

Eleanor Antin's work combines and reflects the diversity of studies and activities in which she has engaged: art, writing, theater, philosophy, painting, and poetry. Since the mid-1960s, her work in sculpture, photography, video, installation, and performance has explored and questioned the nature of identity and representation, reality and fiction, biography and autobiography, and objectivity and objectification through the process of self-reflection and transformation. As Kim Levin has written, her work of the late 1960s and early 1970s assumed an alternative position relative to Conceptual art:

> While substituting historical fictions for Conceptualist facts, Eleanor Antin is commenting on society's pretensions as well as art's. After insisting on all the quirks and illusions and narrative possibilities of the personal, the intimate, the psychological, artists are expanding their investigations to include the social, political and moral responsibilities of that self, and Eleanor Antin was one of the first to delve into the interactions between the private self and the public world.[1]

Examining the interactions between how individuals are self-defined and how they are culturally formed and represented, many of Antin's early works are biographical. From 1965 to 1968 Antin produced BLOOD OF A POET BOX, a green box containing one hundred glass slides with specimens taken over a three-year period of the blood of one hundred poets. Like Marcel Duchamp's LA MARIEE MISE A NU PAR SES CELIBATAIRES, MEME (BOITE VERTE) (The Bride Stripped Bare by Her Bachelors, Even [Green Box], 1934), this work is comprised of a collection of specimens; its title derives from the title of Jean Cocteau's film LE SANG D'UN POETE (1931). In an interview with Cindy Nemser in 1982, Antin commented on her choice to represent the artist with blood: "You could read the names of the poets with these smears of blood on a slide. If you thought there was a relation between the blood and the name there was one; if you didn't, there wasn't."[2]

At the same time she was working on BLOOD OF A POET BOX, Antin started to make sculptures from consumer goods that functioned as biographical portraits of fictional and real people: "I built up an image of a person, real or fictional, from the semantics of appropriately chosen consumer goods."[3] In CALIFORNIA LIVES, first shown at the Gain Ground Gallery in 1970, Antin portrayed twelve people, women and men, some real and some fictional. Becoming increasingly involved in feminism, she produced PORTRAITS OF EIGHT NEW YORK WOMEN, first shown in 1971 at the Chelsea Hotel in New York. In this work Antin made portraits of various women in the art world, including the artists Carolee Schneeman and Yvonne Rainer, the poet Hannah Weiner, the critic Amy Goldin, and Lynn Traiger, a publicist for a New York museum. Describing the consumer sculptures, Antin has remarked: "Those works told stories, delineated characters, acted as stage sets, crossed and confused genres, were political and sociological."[4]

In the early 1970s, Antin began to explore narrative structure. Conceived in 1971, 100 BOOTS, which she has described as a picaresque novel, comprises fifty-one postcards sent to a mailing list of approximately one thousand people over a period of two and a half years, starting on 15 March 1971. The postcards follow the adventures of one hundred rubber boots—Antin's "hero"—as they travel on a journey that takes them from a conventional life in the suburbs to joblessness, war, and finally an exhibition entitled "Projects: 100 Boots by Eleanor Antin (Northwest/Far West)," which was presented from 30 May to 8 July 1973 at The Museum of Modern Art in New York. Distributed through the mail, the postcards were sent at intervals according to the "internal necessities of the narrative," playing with time by compressing or expanding it according to the boots' actions.[5]

Following 100 BOOTS, Antin began to explore autobiography, moving from physical to psychological transformations. CARVING: A TRADITIONAL SCULPTURE (1972) is comprised of 148 black-and-white photographs depicting Antin's ten-pound weight loss over a period of thirty-six days. Each day Antin was photographed naked before a door in four views: front, rear, and right and left profile. Attempting to "carve" her body into "an esthetic Greek sculpture," she represented the barely perceivable, incremental, day-to-day changes of her image and identity.[6] As Jonathan Crary has written, "[a]lthough this project does draw our attention to what is not there, to the spaces and time between what is shown, Antin is more preoccupied here with the transformation of the subject than with its absence. And CARVING, with its careful monitoring of changes in her physical self, seems to lead directly into works in which her identity is transformed."[7]

Antin further developed her examination of self in her first videotape, REPRESENTATIONAL PAINTING (1972), in which, using the video monitor as a mirror, she attempts to transform herself into someone else by putting on makeup. Moving from exterior transformations of her body and image, in 1973 Antin began to make works that examine and play with the psychological self and the construction of autobiography through four self-personas she created: the King, the Ballerina, the Black Movie Star, and the Nurse. Antin commented on this transition:

> When I started moving out of those more plausible or expectable transformations like dieting, putting on street make-up, or changing my regular artist's self into a more bourgeois image, all these things we do all the time, I moved into perfectly plausible but less expected and perhaps more exotic transformations. I got interested in the transformational nature of the self and the possibilities of defining my limits, such as age, sex, space, time, talent, what have you, all the things that restrict our possibilities.[8] — AG

Notes

1. Kim Levin, "The Angel of Mercy and the Fiction of History," in *The Angel of Mercy*, exh. cat. (La Jolla: La Jolla Museum of Contemporary Art, 1977), unpag.

2. Eleanor Antin in Cindy Nemser, "Eleanor Antin," in *Art Talk: Conversations with 12 Women Artists* (New York: Charles Scribner's Sons, 1975), 278.

3. Eleanor Antin, "Out of the Box," *The Art Gallery Magazine* (Ivoryton, Conntecticut) 15, no. 9 (June 1972): 26.

4. Eleanor Antin in Dinah Portner, "Interview with Eleanor Antin," *Journal* (Los Angeles), no. 26 (February-March 1980): 34.

5. Antin in Nemser, "Eleanor Antin," 269.

6. Ibid., 280.

7. Jonathan Crary, "Eleanor Antin: A Post Modern Itinerary," in *The Angel of Mercy*, unpag.

8. Antin in Nemser, "Eleanor Antin," 284.

BLOOD OF A POET BOX (1965-68)
Box with one hundred glass slides of poets' blood specimens. 11 1/2 x 7 3/4 x
1 1/2 in. (29.2 x 19.7 x 3.8 cm). Courtesy Ronald Feldman Fine Arts, New York.
Photo Peter Moore

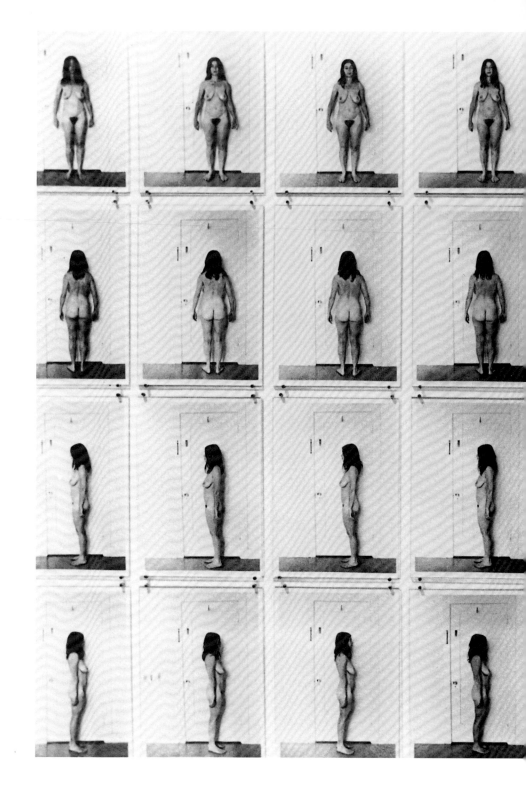

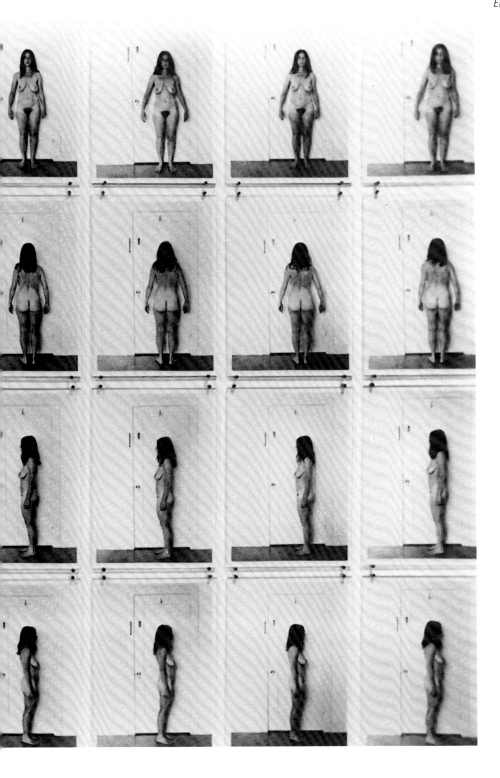

CARVING: A TRADITIONAL SCULPTURE (detail) (1972)
148 black-and-white photographs and text panel. Each photograph, 7 x 5 in.
(17.8 x 12.7 cm); text panel, 15 1/2 x 10 1/4 in. (39.4 x 26.0 cm).
Courtesy Ronald Feldman Fine Arts, New York.

ART & LANGUAGE

(Terry Atkinson, b. 1939, Barnsley, Yorkshire, England; David Bainbridge, b. 1941, Barnsley, Yorkshire, England; Michael Baldwin, b. 1945, Chipping Norton, Oxfordshire, England; Harold Hurrell, b. 1940, Barnsley, Yorkshire, England)

Art & Language is the name of a shifting collaboration among artists that has undergone many changes over the years. It was founded in England in 1968 by Terry Atkinson, David Bainbridge, Michael Baldwin, and Harold Hurrell. By late 1969, Art & Language's activities included the publication of the journal *Art-Language*, for which Joseph Kosuth was briefly the American editor. The name was derived from the journal, which itself had been generated from conversations among the founders dating back to 1966. In 1971, Ian Burn and Mel Ramsden merged their New York-based Society for Theoretical Art and Analyses with Art & Language. The history of the group throughout the early and mid-1970s is marked by the expansion and contraction of its membership on both sides of the Atlantic, as later chronicled by the art historian, critic, and editor, Charles Harrison—himself an Art & Language proponent and collaborator since 1971.[1] The artistic work of Art & Language has been carried on since the end of 1976 by Baldwin and Ramsden in Great Britain. Harrison continues to maintain his original literary and conversational association.

In the late 1960s and early 1970s, the artists of Art & Language dealt with questions surrounding art production and reception in a common quest to liberate art making from the then conventionally non-linguistic modes of painting and sculpture. As Harrison has written,

It became gradually if unevenly possible to conceive a breaking down of those hierarchies which had served absolutely to distinguish the critical from the aesthetic and art from language. It was under these conditions that a practice such as Art & Language was to represent could feasibly emerge as a first-order practice of art.[2]

The artists of Art & Language assumed a critical and sometimes combative position in relation to the culturally-established modernist views of art critics such as Clement Greenberg and Michael Fried. Their aesthetic practice grew out of their respective, initial concerns with "matters of linguistic/'pictorial' referentiality" and resulted in their analysis of texts.[3] The intricacies and complexities of the process of inquiry, in which they involved themselves *as artists*, were made dramatically manifest in the Indexes realized in the years between 1972 and 1974.

The first of these Indexes, INDEX 01 (1972), was shown in Kassel at Documenta 5. As an installation, it includes eight metal file cabinets set on four grey blocks. Forty-eight different drawers—six per cabinet—contain writings published in the journal *Art-Language*, as well as unpublished texts by Art & Language members. Hinged one on top of the other within each drawer, these texts are arranged in alphabetical and sub-alphabetical sequences according to the order of their completion and the nature of their completeness. The entirety of the surrounding walls, furthermore, is papered with the results of their system for indexing approximately 350 textual citations. This system makes use of the symbols '+,' '-,' and 'T' to signify compatibility, incompatibility, or lack of relational value. In this way, the codified results of Art & Language's critical investigations are made manifest as an intricate web of cross-referenced relationships. Searching authorship as a communal endeavor founded on textual analysis, the INDEX effactually redefines the traditional object of contemplation by raising the process of contemplation to the level of constructive thought. It thereby encompasses the work of art within the order of its own aesthetic business. — AR

Notes

1. See Charles Harrison, *Essays on Art & Language* (Oxford: Basil Blackwell, 1991).

2. Charles Harrison, "Art & Language: Some Conditions and Concerns of the First Ten Years," in *Art & Language: The Paintings*, exh. cat. (Brussels: Société des Expositions du Palais des Beaux-Arts, 1987), 6.

3. Michael Baldwin and Mel Ramsden in letter to the author, 22 March 1995.

INDEX 01 (1972)
Eight file cabinets, forty-eight photostats, and one text in frame. Each cabinet, 9 x 11 3/8 x 24 5/8 in. (23 x 29 x 62.5 cm); text, 29 1/2 x 20 7/8 in. (75 x 53 cm). Private collection. TOP: Installation view, "L'art conceptuel, une perspective," Musée d'Art Moderne de la Ville de Paris, 22 November–18 February 1989. BOTTOM: Installation view, Documenta 5, Neue Galerie and Museum Fridericianum, Kassel, 30 June–8 October 1972.

MICHAEL ASHER

(b. 15 July 1943, Los Angeles; lives in Los Angeles)

Since the late 1960s, Michael Asher's work has offered a sustained critique of the institutions that present and represent works of art: museums, commercial galleries, and alternative exhibition spaces. All of his works are derived from the architectural, historical, and social specificity of their respective sites. Addressing the conditions that structure and define these sites, Asher intervenes in given situations by subtly altering or shifting aspects of their structures. As a result, he draws attention to previously unapparent or unarticulated aspects of them. As Benjamin H. D. Buchloh has written,

> Asher's work committed itself to the development of a practice of situational aesthetics that insisted on a critical refusal to provide an existing apparatus with legitimizing aesthetic information, while at the same time revealing, if not changing, the existing conditions of the apparatus.[1]

In 1966-67, in response to the illusionistic materiality of painting and the fundamental forms of Minimalist sculpture of the mid-1960s, Asher developed a group of pressured air works that resisted the autonomy of the art object—contributing to the basis of a contextual practice. These vertical columns or planes of accelerated air produced by off-the-shelf air blowers were initially developed and installed in a garage adjacent to his apartment. The first exhibited air work was produced for "The Appearing/Disappearing Image/Object" at the Newport Harbor Art Museum in Newport Beach, California, in 1969. In that work, Asher used air blowers to produce a planar body of air that extended across the passageway just inside the entrance to the museum's gallery, where it was encountered by visitors. A subsequent work, produced for the Whitney Museum of American Art's 1969 exhibition, "Anti-Illusion: Procedures/Materials," consisted of a planar body of pressured air extending five feet across an eight by eight-foot passageway between two galleries. Visitors could encounter the work while passing through the space, although they could also bypass it by walking through the three feet to the left of the airflow. This piece was conceived within the overall context of the exhibition, which included the work of twenty-two artists, including Carl Andre, Eva Hesse, Robert Ryman, Richard Serra, and Joel Shapiro. As Asher wrote,

> The works in this group show ranged from such expressively solid sculptural pieces as Richard Serra's HOUSE OF CARDS to the extreme subtlety of my laminar airflow. Understanding the potential for comparative analysis of different works and their possible interrelationship within an exhibition, I decided to reduce the velocity of the airflow to a minimum.[2]

In 1973, for an exhibition at the Lisson Gallery in London—his first in a commercial gallery—Asher cut a 1/4-inch wide by 1 1/2-inch deep architectural reveal into the walls of the basement at their intersection with the floor, thus producing the appearance that the walls and floor were physically separated. As he has written, this work involved the subtraction, rather than the addition, of material to the space:

> The creation of a pictorial or sculptural sign traditionally involves the addition of materials to an initial support until some sort of resolution is brought about. The work at the Lisson Gallery reversed this process by creating a mark or sign through a process of material subtraction, in which existing materials were withdrawn from the architectural support.[3]

Asher further explored the process of removal in a work made for an exhibition later that year at Galleria Toselli in Milan, in which he had the walls of the exhibition space sandblasted, thus removing several layers of white paint to expose the brown plaster surface of the walls and ceiling. Through the strategy of removal, this work examined the separation between the refined space of the gallery and vernacular architecture. As Asher observed,

> In this work, a large exhibition space had been totally stripped of all the conventional coatings that had built up over the years on its display surface. The brown plaster surfaces resembled the common, indigenous outdoor plaster walls of the community. The previously concealed plaster essentially brought inside an outdoor material, disclosing a relationship between the gallery and its surroundings.[4]

In 1974, for an exhibition at Claire Copley Gallery in Los Angeles, Asher developed another work that involved the removal of an aspect of the architecture. A partition wall separating the exhibition space in the front of the gallery from the office/utility/storage space in the back was removed. As a result, the two areas, previously distinguished from one another, were joined into one. Both the symbolic and functional distinctions between the two spaces were erased, for visitors were able to view the gallery personnel in the actual exhibition space. This work specifically implicated Asher's own practice of institutional critique within the commercial gallery system:

> What came under scrutiny in the Claire Copley work was the question of whether a work of art whose discourse disclosed the system of economic reproduction could possibly, at the same time, engender that economic reproduction for itself. Just as the work served as a model of how the gallery operated, it also served as a model for its own economic reproduction.[5] — AG

Notes

1. Benjamin H. D. Buchloh, "Editor's Note," in Michael Asher, *Writings 1973-1983 on Works 1969-1979*, ed. Buchloh (Halifax: The Press of the Nova Scotia College of Art and Design and Los Angeles: The Museum of Contemporary Art, 1983), vii.

2. Asher, *Writings*, 8. For the current exhibition, Asher has conceived an air work adapted from these early works, which, because of their context-specific nature, cannot be reconstructed. The work, developed for a specific space at MOCA's Temporary Contemporary, consists of a column of accelerated air situated immediately adjacent and parallel to an existing structural column. The flow of air is perceptible by a spectator passing through it. In this work, Asher subtly annotates the architecture and the path of a visitor through the space.

3. Ibid., 81.

4. Ibid., 89.

5. Ibid., 100.

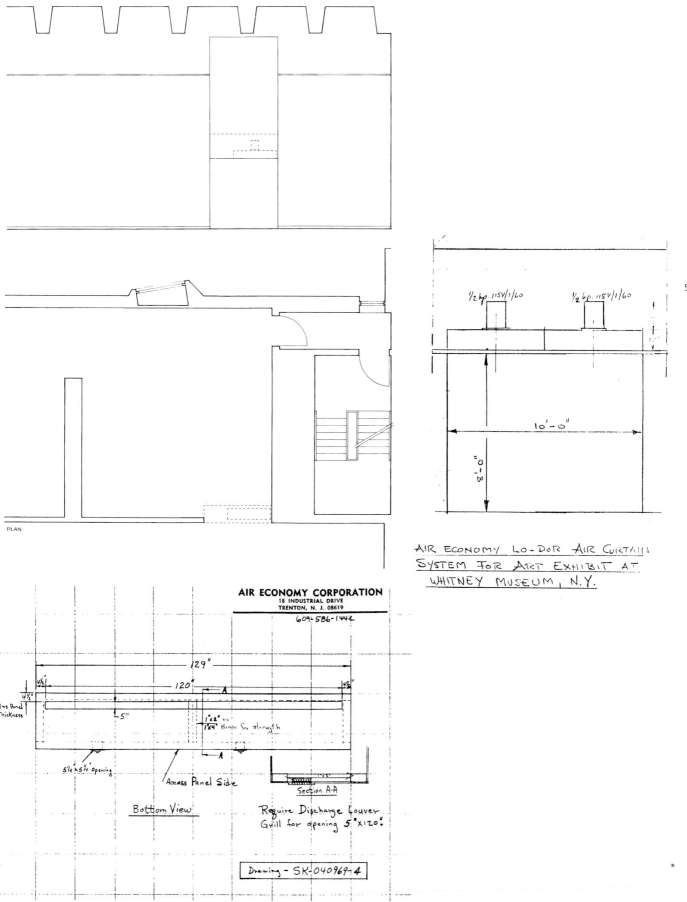

AIR ECONOMY LO-DOR AIR CURTAIN
SYSTEM FOR ART EXHIBIT AT
WHITNEY MUSEUM, N.Y.

AIR ECONOMY CORPORATION
18 INDUSTRIAL DRIVE
TRENTON, N. J. 08619

609-586-1442

PLAN

½ hp. 115V/1/60   ½ hp. 115V/1/60

10'-0"

8'-0"

129"

120"

4½"   4½"

Plus Panel
Thickness

5"

1"x2" or
1"x4" Brace for strength

5¼"x5¼" opening

Access Panel Side

Section A·A

Bottom View

Require Discharge Louver
Grill for opening 5"x120"

Drawing - SK-040969-4

Project for "Anti-Illusion: Procedures/Materials," Whitney Museum of American
Art, New York, 19 May–6 July 1969. Preliminary construction plans for air-
curtain installation, designed by Air Economy Corporation. TOP LEFT: Elevation
drawing for the installation in the exhibition area (drawing by Lawrence
Kenny); MIDDLE LEFT: Ground plan of the exhibition area within which the air
installation was placed (drawing by Lawrence Kenny); MIDDLE RIGHT: Section of
installation; BOTTOM: Bottom view.

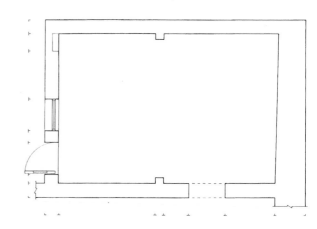

Groundplan of exhibition space.

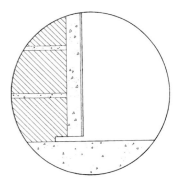

60

Project for Lisson Gallery, London, 24 August–16 September 1973. TOP: Ground
plan of exhibition and detail of wall and architectural reveal;
BOTTOM: Installation view, south wall.

Project for Galleria Toselli, Milan, 13 September–8 October 1973.
Viewing east in installation. Photo Giorgio Colombo.

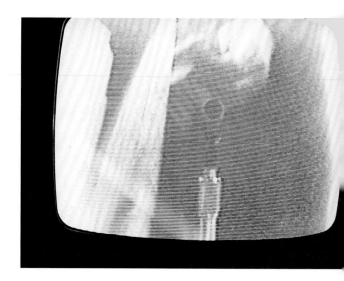

DAVID ASKEVOLD

(b. 30 March 1940, Conrad, Montana; lives in Halifax, Nova Scotia)

Since the late 1960s, David Askevold has employed in his work the systematic structures and procedures of games, propositions, and narratives. Yet, while he structures his work in conventional linear systems, matrices, and tropes, Askevold's methodology is associative and suggestive rather than conclusive, as meaning is rendered subjective, ambiguous, and shifting. As Frederick Dolan has written, "The space of the daydream, the fantasy, the slip of the tongue: what was for psychoanalysis the marker of an underlying, predictable process becomes for us an entrance to a different and irrational, prelogical dimension."[1]

Many of Askevold's early works, such as THREE SPOT GAME (1968), SHOOT DON'T SHOOT (A SUM ZERO GAME MATRIX) (1970), and TAMING EXPANSION (1971), are structured as a game or proposition that appears to employ straightforward procedures of hypothetical analysis and documentation. For example, the elusive photographic images of a shootout in SHOOT DON'T SHOOT are joined with a diagram in the form of a multiplication table that suggests the four possible consequences of the acts to which the title alludes: "Death for Both, Life for One, Death for One, Life for Both." Constructing a narrative within documentary form, TAMING EXPANSION describes an event in New Mexico, staged for filming, in which six actors attempt to tame six rattlesnakes in the center of a circle. When one of the actors is bitten by a snake, the event is disrupted and postponed. The form of the work constitutes a storyboard incorporating a lithograph of the descriptive text and a diagram of the circle of snakes, with an accompanying photograph of the site. In both of these works, documentation is indistinguishable from fiction as the trope of the game is destabilized by the life and death consequences of the actions.

FILL (1970)
Videotape: 8 min., b/w, sound.

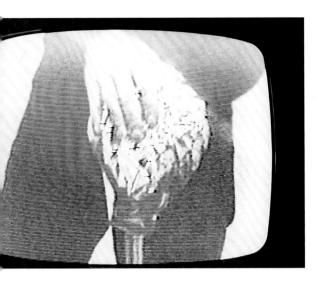

In his film and video works of the early 1970s, Askevold continued to undermine the authority of logical forms and literal interpretation. In his videotape FILL (1970), he wraps a microphone with sheets of aluminum foil until the screen is filled, and then unwraps it piece by piece. The sound of the crumpling aluminum produced by every move is increasingly inconsonant with the image—as the image of foil expands, the sound of its making is increasingly muffled. In LEARNING ABOUT CARS & CHOCOLATES (1973), Askevold sits in a window and gazes down on the street below. The structure of the work links two otherwise unrelated activities: with each car that passes, Askevold picks up and tastes a chocolate and describes both the car and the flavor of the sweet, accelerating or slowing his pace in coordination with the speed and frequency of the passing cars. The tape concludes when he finishes tasting the chocolates.

THE AMBIT: NINE CLAUSES AND THEIR ALLOCATIONS (1975-76), one of Askevold's most important works, moves away from the logical structure of the earlier pieces. Originally commissioned as a text for a series of articles by artists on culture, THE AMBIT comprises nine photographic panels or "clauses," each divided into four sections. Peggy Gale has written that "the more [Askevold] worked over the necessarily vague areas implied by the assignment, the more he became interested in discussing a fictitious but complete 'culture' of his own."[2] Finding their form and content in light, shadow, and reflection, the images and texts that constitute this culture are elusive, indirect, and often unidentifiable. The texts in the lower left and right corners of each panel are dated; those on the left are all dated November-December 1975, while those on the right shift in time. As Askevold has written, these temporal and perceptual shifts undermine the linear narrative form of the work:

The Ambit, (sphere of influence—circumference/surrounding) is a self legislative enactment to sum up a given body of acts/works, as if that body might act as a prognosis to determine its continuum. Advancement takes place when the primary agent simply produces its terms and the receptive party/agent reacts by recording its reactions. The active participation by this receiver negates or reaffirms the validity of this body.
The Right Side: mumbling to the self—over-riding dialogues.
The Left Side: legislative—the agent which attempts to re-direct the right side through affirmation and negation....The active participation by the right side naturally negates or re-affirms the validity of the left side legislative body. Phrases are read as conditioned units and their various parts and attributes are not to be separated into fragments to be re-assembled to form complete meanings.[3]

Subjective and objective, psychological and parapsychological, and hovering between fact and fiction, Askevold's works offer visual and verbal references that elicit a range of interpretations from the viewer. As the artist has written, "There is never one invariable meaning although there is a preferred range for reading implied. It is difficult to say that the interpretation of something and that something itself must be independent of interpretation if the interpretive process is not to fall itself into arbitrariness."[4]—AG

Notes

1. Frederick Dolan, "For David Askevold: A Note for an Essay," *David Askevold*, exh. cat. (Eindhoven: Stedelijk Van Abbemuseum, 1981), 3.

2. Peggy Gale, "Earlier Askevold," in *David Askevold*, 29.

3. David Askevold, "Notes on the Ambit, An Introduction," in *David Askevold*, 5.

4. David Askevold, "Notes for Explanation and Attitude," in *Video* (Toronto: Art Metropole, 1975).

64

LEARNING ABOUT CARS & CHOCOLATES (1973)
Videotape: 30 min., b/w, sound.

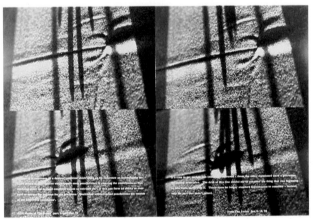

THE AMBIT: NINE CLAUSES AND THEIR ALLOCATIONS (detail) (1975-76)
Nine color photographs with text. Each, 40 x 60 in. (101.6 x 152.4 cm).
Stedelijk Van Abbemuseum, Eindhoven.

JOHN BALDESSARI

(b. 17 June 1931,
National City,
California; lives in
Santa Monica,
California)

In his paintings, photographs, films, videotapes, books, and texts, John Baldessari has, since the mid-1960s, challenged the conventions of these media to address the construction of meaning through the interactions of words and images. Having initially studied art history at Berkeley, Baldessari turned to painting, studying in San Diego and, briefly, in Los Angeles at Chouinard and Otis Art Institutes in the late 1950s. While living and working in National City, California, Baldessari began to make paintings that drew from photographic source materials and incorporated fragments of discarded billboards. After the mid-1960s Baldessari broke with the traditional trajectory and conception of painting with a series of text and photo-text canvases produced by means of sign painters and photomechanical processes—in which the canvas became the sole conventional painting or art signifier. As he wrote in 1981,

> By late 65 I was finished with painting and by early 66 had begun these pieces. I was weary of doing relational painting and began wondering if straight information would serve. I sought to use language not as a visual element but as something to read. That is, a notebook entry about painting could replace the painting. And visual data less as pleasing artistically than as documentation, as in a store catalogue or police photograph.
>
> For the most part, these pieces are on a standard size canvas. Most are white or grey, though a few were done in pastel colors (stock wall color). Many of the photos used were originally taken for non-art use, some were taken to violate then current photographic norms, and others were taken pointing the camera out the window while driving. I was attempting to make something that didn't emanate art signals. The only art signal I wanted was the canvas.
>
> Important was that I was the strategist. Someone else built and primed the canvases and took them to the sign painter, the texts are quotations from art books, and the sign painter was instructed not to attempt to make attractive artful lettering but to letter the information in the most simple way.[1]

The first of these works, completed in 1967 and 1968, is dated 26 April 1967—the day Baldessari paid the sign painter for the production of texts.[2] The photographic sources of these works include snapshots by Baldessari and others, as well as reproductions of existing images from art magazines, children's books, and instructional manuals. As Baldessari has stated, "Rauschenberg had done overlaps of paint and screened photographic images, one over the other onto the canvas in a transfer method he had invented himself. But I wanted to be less artful than Rauschenberg and Warhol: this is a photograph, here's a text. That's it. And I thought, because they're done on canvas, they might be equated with art."[3]

Among Baldessari's photo-text works are THE SPECTATOR IS COMPELLED... (1967-68) and THIS IS NOT TO BE LOOKED AT (1968). Coosje van Bruggen has described the structure of the former as follows:

> Baldessari is seen from the back looking down the street in a pose that illustrates the pictorial convention of establishing an eye level. In fact, the composition of the picture is taken from a manual by Ernest R. Norling, Perspective Made Easy, which illustrates eye level by showing an artist seen from behind standing on train tracks. The title of Baldessari's work, however, intimates that he or she should ignore any didactic purpose: why not just stare directly down the road into the middle of the picture for no reason at all.[4]

In the latter, the title, a translation of NO SE PUEDE MIRAR, the title of a work from Francisco Goya's series of etchings, Los desastres de la guerra (The Disasters of War, 1820/63), is paired with an image of the cover of the November 1966 issue of Artforum, which features Frank Stella's painting UNION III (1966).[5] This pairing constructs a critique of the formalism and literalism of high modernist painting, including reference to the statements of Frank Stella, which include the oft-quoted phrase, "What you see is what you see."

The texts for Baldessari's text-only canvases are derived from a variety of sources. Those for A WORK WITH ONLY ONE PROPERTY (1967-68), COMPOSING ON A CANVAS, (1967-68), and PAINTING FOR KUBLER (1967-68) are drawn from such sources as art history books and manuals on making art and photography. In a series of three canvases he used the major contemporary painting critics of that moment—Clement Greenberg, Barbara Rose, and Max Kozloff. The representational aspect of painting is also critiqued in A PAINTING THAT IS ITS OWN DOCUMENTATION (1968), which literally incorporates into its form its exhibition history from its first public presentation in the artist's first one-person exhibition in Los Angeles at Molly Barnes Gallery in 1968, to the present.

In addition to the photo-text and text canvases in this exhibition, Baldessari included two illuminated moving message works that eliminate the canvas altogether by using commercial

THE SPECTATOR IS COMPELLED
TO LOOK DIRECTLY DOWN THE
ROAD AND INTO THE MIDDLE OF
THE PICTURE.

advertising technology to display definitions of perception, isocephaly, and viewpoint. For example, the text for LIGHTED MOVING MESSAGE: ISOCEPHALY (1968) reads: "Isocephaly—a style of composition characteristic of the classical period—especially in relation to Greek in which the figures in a composition are so arranged that they are all of the same height; as for instance in a frieze."

In the summer of 1970, Baldessari joined the faculty at the California Institute of the Arts in Valencia and moved from National City to Santa Monica, California. Just prior to the move, he completed CREMATION PROJECT (1970), in which, in a desire to perform a ritual "house-cleaning" of his studio (a former movie theater owned by his father), he cremated the paintings he had produced before the photo-text and text canvases. He publicly registered this act on 10 August 1970 in the *San Diego Union*: "Notice is hereby given that all works of art done by the undersigned between May 1953 and March 1966 in his possession as of July 24, 1970 were cremated on July 24, 1970 in San Diego, California." [6]

That September the ashes and other documentation of the project were included in the historic group exhibition, "Software: Information Technology: Its Meaning for Art," organized by Jack Burnham for The Jewish Museum in New York. — AG

Notes

1. John Baldessari, statement in *John Baldessari*, exh. cat. (Eindhoven: Stedelijk Van Abbemuseum and Essen: Museum Folkwang, 1981), 6.

2. Coosje van Bruggen, *John Baldessari*, exh. cat. (Los Angeles: The Museum of Contemporary Art and New York: Rizzoli, 1990), 29.

3. John Baldessari in ibid.

4. Ibid., 32.

5. UNION III, which is in the permanent collection of The Museum of Contemporary Art, will be included in "Images of an Era," an exhibition of the collection at the Temporary Contemporary that will be on view simultaneously with "1965-1975: Reconsidering the Object of Art." When this work was reproduced on the cover of *Artforum*, it accompanied Michael Fried's seminal essay "Shape as Form: Frank Stella's New Paintings," which, along with Clement Greenberg's "Modernist Painting," served to consolidate the formalist interpretation of high modernism.

6. Cited in van Bruggen, *John Baldessari*, 56.

THE SPECTATOR IS COMPELLED... (1967-68)
Acrylic and photoemulsion on canvas. 59 x 45 in. (149.9 x 114.3 cm).
Collection Robert Shapazian, Los Angeles. Photo Paula Goldman.

COMPOSING ON A CANVAS.

STUDY THE COMPOSITION OF PAINTINGS. ASK YOURSELF QUESTIONS WHEN STANDING IN FRONT OF A WELL COMPOSED PICTURE. WHAT FORMAT IS USED ? WHAT IS THE PROPORTION OF HEIGHT TO WIDTH ? WHAT IS THE CENTRAL OBJECT ? WHERE IS IT SITUATED ? HOW IS IT RELATED TO THE FORMAT ? WHAT ARE THE MAIN DIRECTIONAL FORCES ? THE MINOR ONES ? HOW ARE THE SHADES OF DARK AND LIGHT DISTRIBUTED ? WHERE ARE THE DARK SPOTS CONCENTRATED ? THE LIGHT SPOTS ? HOW ARE THE EDGES OF THE PICTURE DRAWN INTO THE PICTURE ITSELF ? ANSWER THESE QUESTIONS FOR YOURSELF WHILE LOOKING AT A FAIRLY UNCOM - PLICATED PICTURE.

COMPOSING ON A CANVAS (1967-68)
Acrylic on canvas. 114 x 96 in. (289.6 x 243.8 cm). Museum of
Contemporary Art, San Diego, Gift of the Artist.

CLEMENT GREENBERG

ESTHETIC JUDGMENTS ARE GIVEN AND CONTAINED IN THE IMMEDIATE EXPERIENCE OF ART. THEY COINCIDE WITH IT; THEY ARE NOT ARRIVED AT AFTERWARDS THROUGH REFLECTION OR THOUGHT. ESTHETIC JUDGMENTS ARE ALSO INVOLUNTARY; YOU CAN NO MORE CHOOSE WHETHER OR NOT TO LIKE A WORK OF ART THAN YOU CAN CHOOSE TO HAVE SUGAR TASTE SWEET OR LEMONS SOUR. (WHETHER OR NOT ESTHETIC JUDGMENTS ARE HONESTLY REPORTED IS ANOTHER MATTER.)

CLEMENT GREENBERG (1967-68)
Acrylic on canvas. 65 x 57 in. (165.1 x 144.8 cm).
Collection Craig Robins, Miami Beach.

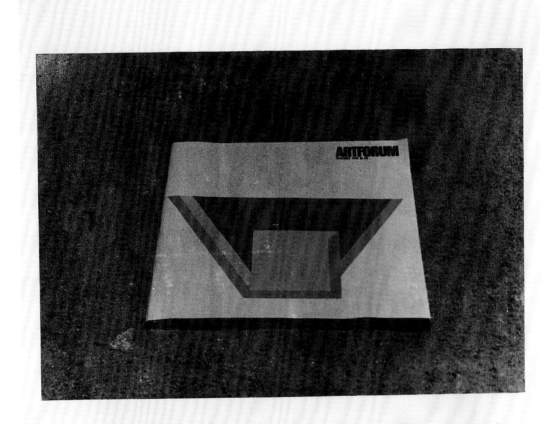

THIS IS NOT TO BE LOOKED AT.

THIS IS NOT TO BE LOOKED AT (1968)
Acrylic and photoemulsion on canvas. 59 x 45 in. (149.9 x 114.3 cm).
Collection Councilman Joel Wachs, Los Angeles.

ROBERT BARRY

(b. 9 March 1936, New York City; lives in New Jersey)

Early in his career, Robert Barry noted his interest in what might be going on outside of the frame of painting. In 1968 he said: "There is something about void and emptiness which I am personally very concerned with....*Nothing* seems to me the most potent thing in the world."[1] His works since that time have explored ways of escaping the previously known physical limits of the art object in order to express the unknown or unperceived. Pursuant to the development of his Word Drawings of the mid-1970s, which feature isolated words or phrases disposed on paper or, as of 1978, on walls or other architectural surfaces, Barry explored a number of different avenues toward defining the usually unseen space around objects, rather than producing objects that would visibly insert themselves into and occupy space. Major nonvisible works from this early period include the CARRIER WAVE, RADIATION, and INERT GAS pieces. The artist's radical decision to work with materials such as carrier waves of different frequencies, ultrasonic sound, microwaves, electromagnetic energy fields, radioactive substances, and inert gases enabled him to produce pieces that could be materially accounted for, but not seen by the naked eye.

A number of Barry's nonmaterial works realized through the use of language probed the exhibition space as an area for aesthetic activity without proffering literal objects for display. His INTERVIEW PIECE (1969) was to be found only in the catalogue for "Prospect 69," an exhibition held at the Kunsthalle Düsseldorf in 1969. In this work, the artist, in an interview with himself, responds to his questions with immediate reference to the work itself. Although it cannot be shown as a material entity, the work is an actuality inasmuch as it stimulates thinking about art.

Several other pieces further indicate the various methods Barry employed at the time toward an examination of the nature of art activity in its dependence on invisible systems for communicating thoughts that originate with the artist. His CLOSED GALLERY (1969) consists of the cards mailed to announce a series of exhibitions in galleries in the United States and Europe. Uncustomarily, however, the mailers state that for the duration of the exhibitions "the gallery will be closed." With no object to see and with no exhibition area to enter physically, Barry stimulated thought about the spaces for showing art as entities possessing both concrete and abstract properties in and of themselves. Alternatively, his MARCUSE PIECE (1970-71), realized in half a dozen different spaces, was written directly on the wall of the gallery in pencil and read: "Some places to which we can come, and for a while, 'be free to think about what we are going to do.' (Marcuse)." Barry specifically prompted viewers to ponder those spaces that promote mental creativity by leading to the production of objects of thought and, by extension, to objects of art.

TELEPATHIC PIECE (1969), included in the "Simon Fraser Exhibition," presented at the Centre for Communications and the Arts at Simon Fraser University in Burnaby, British Columbia, in 1969, appeared only as a bracketed statement in the catalogue:

[During the Exhibition I will try to communicate telepathically a work of art, the nature of which is a series of thoughts that are not applicable to language or image.][2]

Foregrounding the underlying ingredients of art making—communication and thinking—the work abnegates the need for tangible materiality while proposing the possible existence of a purely mental space.

Other works of these early years, which Barry initially typed on index cards and subsequently realized as slide projections, exist simply as verbal statements. These statements are open to an infinite number of readings, which individual readers may supply on their own, should they so choose. All the statements begin with the indefinite pronoun "it"; and although they are definitions of a sort, they are never "definitive." Whatever the "it" may be remains unknown. Avoiding the description of anything specific, these works acknowledge the artist as the catalyst for engendering inquiry and for creating an actual, if abstract, space for viewer participation. — AR

Notes

1. Robert Barry, tape-recording of symposium held on 8 February 1968 in conjunction with the exhibition "Carl Andre, Robert Barry, Lawrence Weiner," presented at Bradford Junior College, Bradford, Massachusetts. Cited in Lucy R. Lippard, *Six Years: The Dematerialization of the Art Object from 1966 to 1972* (New York: Praeger, 1973), 40.

2. Robert Barry, in *Catalogue for the Exhibition*, exh. cat. (Burnaby, British Columbia: Centre for Communications and the Arts, Simon Fraser University, 1969), unpag. In the "Presentation" section of the catalogue, Barry wrote: "At the conclusion of the exhibition (June 19, 1969), the information about the work of art was made known in this catalogue."

Artist's studio being occupied simultaneously by carrier wave pieces, 1969

Robert Barry

RADIATION PIECE

Cesium 137   0.51 MEV Beta-Energy

March 6, 1969   H. L. 30 Years

RADIATION PIECE, CESIUM 137 (1969)
Cesium. Solomon R. Guggenheim Museum, New York, Panza Collection, Extended
Loan. Photo courtesy The Getty Center for the History of Art and the
Humanities, Santa Monica, California.

Inert Gas Series: <u>Krypton</u>, from a measured volume to indefinite
expansion. On March 3, 1969 in Beverly Hills California one liter
of Krypton was returned to the atmosphere.

R.BARRY '69

INERT GAS SERIES: KRYPTON (1969)
(From a measured volume to indefinite expansion. On March 3, 1969 in
Beverly Hills, California, one liter of Krypton was returned to the
atmosphere.) Documentation: three color photographs and typewritten
texts. Overall, 11 3/4 x 15 3/4 in. (30 x 40 cm) (framed).
FER Collection Laupheim, Germany.

TELEPATHIC PIECE (1969)
Pages from catalogue for "Simon Fraser Exhibition," Centre for Communications
and the Arts, Simon Fraser University, Burnaby, British Columbia, 19 May–19 June
1969. Offset on paper. Each page, 9 x 6 in. (22.9 x 15.2 cm). Courtesy the
artist and Holly Solomon Gallery, New York. Photo Paula Goldman.

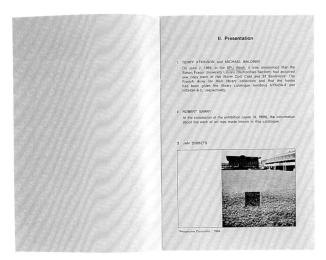
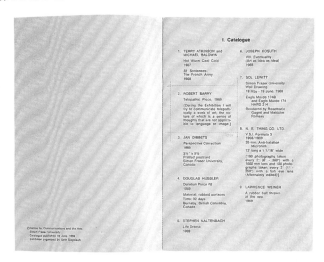

ROBERT BARRY

MARCH 10 THROUGH MARCH 21
THE GALLERY WILL BE CLOSED

EUGENIA BUTLER   615 N. LA CIENEGA BLVD.
LOS ANGELES, CA. 90069

CLOSED GALLERY (detail) (1969)
Four announcement cards. 13 3/4 x 33 1/4 in. (34.9 x 84.5 cm). The Dorothy and
Herbert Vogel Collection. Photo Paula Goldman.

LOTHAR BAUMGARTEN

(b. 1944, Rheinsberg, Germany; Lives in Berlin and New York City)

While still a student at the Staatliche Kunst-akademie in Düsseldorf, Lothar Baumgarten had begun to develop strategies for undermining the commercial aspect of art and of investing his work with a social point of reference. His variously colored sculptures of 1968, the Pyramids, were made in direct response to the commercialism he experienced at the Cologne Art Fair of 1967. They consisted of pure pigment shaped into pyramidal forms that disintegrated into powdery dust when touched. These works eventually fell apart after several months and, in essence, privileged perishability over portability and the temporal over the timeless.

With the aim of subverting the commercial viability of art, Baumgarten explored various means for realizing works that embodied their own temporality and took into account the metaphorical possibilities of diverse modes of representation, including photography, language, and the juxtaposition of objects not otherwise related to each other, which he termed "manipulated reality." In these early works, as well as in later ones that conjoin linguistic elements with their architectural context, Baumgarten has often inscribed references to other lands and peoples within the boundaries of his practice. Primarily, however, he has sought to convey the concept of ephemerality with respect to the works themselves, which avoid taking the form of static or fixed objects and respond to the changing conditions of nature and society.

EINE REISE ODER "MIT DER MS REMSCHEID AUF DEM AMAZONAS": DER BERICHT EINER REISE UNTER DEN STERNEN DES KÜHLSCHRANKS (A Voyage or "With the MS Remscheid on the Amazon": The Account of a Voyage under the Stars of the Refrigerator, 1968-70) is a twelve-and-a-half minute slide projection with a metaphoric dimension. The work is comprised of photographs and texts. The former were taken by the artist (often of his own previously made ephemeral works) or were appropriated from one of three sources: Robert Lehman-Nitsche's DIE SAMMLUNG BOGGIANI: INDIANERTYPEN AUS DEM CENTRALEN SÜDAMERIKA (The Boggiani Collection: Types of Indians of Central South America [Buenos Aires, 1904]) and Theodor Koch-Grünberg's ZWEI JAHRE UNTER DEN INDIANERN: REISEN IN NORDWEST-BRASILIEN, 1903/05 (Two Years among the Indians: Travels in Northwest Brazil, 1903/05 [Berlin, 1905]) and VOM ROROIMA ZUM ORINOCO: ERGEBNISSE EINER REISE IN NORD-BRASILIEN UND VENEZUELA IN DEN JAHREN 1911-1913 (From Roroima to Orinoco: Results of a Voyage in Northern Brazil and Venezuela in the Years 1911-1913 [Berlin, 1917-28]). Textual excerpts from these early twentieth-century ethnographic accounts are interspersed with, and shown in contrast to, the black-and-white and color photographs to heighten the experience of viewing different aspects of anthropological field work.

EINE REISE may be considered on a number of different, interconnecting levels. Although it may be seen simply as a voyage in actual viewing time from the first slide to the last—as a "passage" from one visual point to the next—it also represents anthropological exploration and serves as a reportage into the psyche of things. As a totality, it is a multi-layered work that covers a vast amount of territory: from the objects, including the Pyramids, installed in Baumgarten's studio (or in his refrigerator), to foreign places inhabited by nomadic peoples, to the overarching, ungraspable cosmos. Made manifest through the mechanical procedure of projected images, EINE REISE is made possible by, and reflects on, photographic and linguistic representation, which serve to guide the mental processes of projecting thoughts to other times, places, and societies through the channels of the imagination.

In PROJEKTION (Projection, 1971), a projected image and real objects are fused together in life-size scale. Like a window set into the architecture and affected by the constantly changing daylight, this work similarly deals with temporality and illusionistic representation, giving precedence to the former and inverting the latter. As opposed to the material permanence of a traditional work, Baumgarten's projection vanishes with the flick of a switch at the same time as it allows natural light to be a part of the work. PROJEKTION conjoins a photographed wall of Baumgarten's kitchen in 1968, where a number of his works of that period were realized, with actual objects that include several early works, as well as photographs. They are affixed to the actual wall of the exhibition space onto which the image of the kitchen wall is projected. The photographs represent a variety of images relating to nature, culture, and architecture. In this way, real and represented objects are similarly absorbed into the projected image. Actual objects and photographed objects, thus choreographed as a group of diverse elements, merge in a single image and participate inseparably on the equalizing surface of the wall. The scene presented, furthermore, relates to and revises the theme of the artist's studio—a traditional subject in painting. — AR

74

PROJEKTION (Projection) (1971)
Projection of one slide combined with real objects. 118 x 197 in. (300 x 500
cm). Stedelijk Van Abbemuseum, Eindhoven. Installation view, "Lothar Baumgarten:
Antwerpen," Wide White Space, Antwerp, 4-25 February 1974.

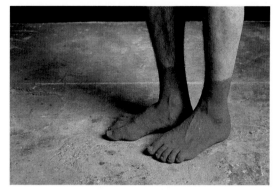

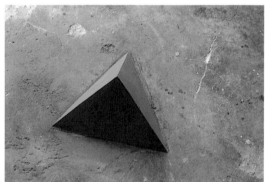

EINE REISE ODER "MIT DER MS REMSCHEID AUF DEM AMAZONAS": DER BERICHT EINER REISE
UNTER DEN STERNEN DES KÜHLSCHRANKS (A Voyage or "With the MS Remscheid on the
Amazon": The Account of a Voyage under the Stars of the Refrigerator) (1968–70)
Projection of eighty-one slides. Projected image, 35 x 24 in. (90 x 60 cm).
Collection the artist and Marian Goodman Gallery, New York.

BERND AND HILLA BECHER

(Bernd Becher, b. 20 August 1931, Siegen, Germany; Hilla Becher, b. 2 September 1934, Potsdam, Germany; began working together in 1959; both live in Düsseldorf)

Bernd and Hilla Becher began to photograph industrial architecture in 1959. In 1956, Bernd Becher, then a painter, had made his first photographs of industrial buildings as potential subjects for his works. His collaboration with Hilla Wobeser began while they were both studying photography at the Staatliche Kunstakademie in Düsseldorf. Their subjects have included blast furnaces, cooling towers, silos, grain elevators, gas tanks, preparation plants, mineheads, and water towers in Germany, Holland, Belgium, England, Scotland, France, Luxembourg, and the United States.

The Bechers' ongoing project is centered upon the collection of information according to a specific set of guidelines that provide an understanding of the form and function of industrial structures. The photographs they produce as the primary component of this project join together the genres of documentary and portrait photography with architecture and sculpture. An early book of their photographs, *Anonyme Skulpturen: Eine Typologie technischer Bauten* (Anonymous Sculpture: A Typology of Technical Constructions, 1970), gave a label, "anonymous sculptures," to their photographs. This term placed their work outside of the conventional history of photography, which, when they began

their project, still rigidly distinguished documentary practices from art photography. Collapsing the distinctions between these two modes, the Bechers' photographs simultaneously have use-value not only for an art audience, but for industrial archaeologists, historians, engineers, and administrators, among others, as well.

While the Bechers' photographs reflect historically on the archaeology of a site and the passage into obsolescence of a landscape formed by the Industrial Revolution, their project is, as R. H. Fuchs has written, not romantic, but

characterized by a cool, objective vision—and what is especially important is that the Bechers developed this vision at a time when architecture-historians considered the study of civil engineering constructions beneath their dignity, and industrial archaeology was still primarily concerned with technological advances. [1]

Through the use of several constants and constraints, including an absence of human figures, even tonality, lowered horizon lines, undramatic lighting, clarity of detail, and precise camera angles and points of view, the Bechers have established a consistent "grammar" to comprehend industrial structures. [2] Their subjects are classified typologically according to function, shape, material, and viewpoint. [3] In this respect, their work is historically linked to the projects of August Sander, Albert Renger-Patzsch, and Karl Blossfeldt, German photographers of the 1920s and

1930s known for the typological organization or cataloguing of their subjects.

Within each typological series, the Bechers compose their photographs in groupings of up to nine. In addition, they make a written record of their subjects, including the size, dates, and details of construction. They have commented on their work:

The groups of photographs are more about similarities than distinctions. The group is decided by the family to which each image belongs. By looking at the photographs simultaneously, you store the knowledge of an ideal type, which can be used the next time. You see the aspects which remain the same so you understand a little more about the function of the structure. Our selections are obvious but it has taken us many years to realise they are obvious. When you first see a group of cooling towers there are perhaps five different ways to form them into relationships: shape, size, materials, date and area. But as the collection expanded these categories became very crude. Within each group there are the same distinctions and more. It is not our selection that is important but what the structures teach us about themselves. [4] — AG

Notes

1. R. H. Fuchs, "Bernd and Hilla Becher," in *Bernd und Hilla Becher*, exh. cat. (Eindhoven: Stedelijk Van Abbemuseum, 1981), unpag. (English translation inserted into catalogue).

2. Bernd and Hilla Becher, in Lynda Morris, "Introduction," in *Bernd and Hilla Becher*, exh. cat. (London: The Arts Council of Great Britain, 1974), unpag.

3. See Carl Andre, "A Note on Bernhard and Hilla Becher," *Artforum* 11, no. 4 (December 1972): 59.

4. Bernd and Hilla Becher, in Morris, "Introduction," *Becher*, unpag.

TYPOLOGY OF WATER TOWERS (detail) 1972)
Six suites of nine photographs each. Each photograph, 15 3/4 x 11 3/4 in.
(40 x 29.8 cm; overall, 52 1/8 x 40 1/16 in. (132.4 x 101.8 cm). The Eli
and Edythe L. Broad Collection.

MEL BOCHNER

(b. 23 August 1940, Pittsburgh; lives in New York City)

As of the mid-to-late 1960s, Mel Bochner began to turn a number of previously held attitudes toward aesthetic production inside out. His WORKING DRAWINGS AND OTHER VISIBLE THINGS ON PAPER NOT NECESSARILY MEANT TO BE VIEWED AS ART (1966) functioned as a curated exhibition, which the artist had been invited to organize at the School of Visual Arts in New York, where he was an instructor. The works "not necessarily meant to be viewed as art"—such as a preliminary sketch for a work or a shopping receipt for materials—were in part provided by other artists and also include pages from books related to disciplines other than art, such as math and science. Conceived on the one hand as a straightforward display of diverse procedural documents, the exhibition was, on the other, a work by Bochner himself.

For the realization of this early work-cum-exhibition, Bochner photocopied and compiled the individual drawings in loose-leaf notebooks, as opposed to matting and framing them separately. Having thus consolidated a variety of items pertaining to processes of thought, he installed the notebooks on pedestals, thereby ironically treating them as if they were traditional sculptures—that is, as "volumes" containing information. In this early instance, Bochner already had sought to feature the procedural aspect of art production over the finished product and to foreground the mental activity behind the physical materialization of any work of art.

To such ends, he anticipated concerns of the period pertaining to the redefinition of a work of art whose value issues from its authenticity as an original because its author has had a direct "hand" in its creation. The drawings of WORKING DRAWINGS are not by the artist himself and, as photocopies, are not "the real thing" but reproductions. This work, furthermore, not only took the form of books, as opposed to paintings or sculptures, but that of an exhibition as opposed to a simple object. It thus thematically acknowledged the authority of the art-exhibition context to validate non-art objects chosen by an artist as art.

At the outset of his career, Bochner focused on forging relationships between theory and practice, knowledge and experience, and numerical and linguistic systems and visible reality. Ultimately, his interests centered on his "desire for an art that did not add anything to the furniture of the world."[1] His particular methods of formulation, in and of themselves, determined the form of works such as the MEASUREMENT ROOMS, A THEORY OF PAINTING (1969-70), LANGUAGE IS NOT TRANSPARENT (1970), and AXIOM OF INDIFFERENCE (1973).

The MEASUREMENT ROOMS fuse the numerical fact of measurement with the actuality of existing walls that define a room and, significantly, redefine the conventional notion of art as an object placed within a room. Using 1/2-inch black tape, the artist demarcated the distances of given wall segments of an entire room and stated their exact lengths in feet and inches. He thereby divided the existing empty space into spatial intervals on an abstract, mental level, yet left the room undivided and whole as an "object" of perception and experience. The exhibition space itself, once the artist has measured and delineated it with thin, black lines of tape, itself becomes the work of art, rather than the

MEASUREMENT ROOM (1969)
Black tape and Letraset on wall. Dimensions determined by installation.
Installation view, "Measured Room Series – 48 Inch Long Longitudinal Projection," Galerie Heiner Friedrich, Munich, 1969.

container for it. Viewers of a Measurement Room observe a three-dimensional blueprint of the real space in which they stand and, in this way, literally assume a central position within the material confines of a work in which nothing has been materially changed.

For his contribution to the exhibition "Language IV," presented at the Dwan Gallery in New York in June 1970, Bochner wrote in white chalk on a black wall the phrase "Language is Not Transparent." This statement speaks for the skepticism of the period regarding language's once-assumed transparency and operates within the framework of art on different levels. On one, it transformed the work in the exhibition into language, while, on another, it self-reflexively used language to comment on the relationship of language to observable reality. No more than pictorial representation, Bochner's piece implies, can language offer a window onto reality without also being recognized as possessing an independent reality of its own.

AXIOM OF INDIFFERENCE (1973) explicitly demonstrates the discrepancy between saying and seeing, at the same time that it offers a new interpretation of sculpture. Although this work supplies evidence of the interior/exterior condition of a sculptural, three-dimensional object, it paradoxically negates its own material mass. It consists of small, flat objects (pennies) placed by the artist in different sets of relationships to squares in different configurations created by masking-tape adhered to the floor.[2] The work proves the indifference, as its title suggests, of language to observable facts. The two may coincide, just as much as they need not, which the artist demonstrates with respect to the location of the pennies vis-à-vis statements written on the masking tape boundaries of the squares. The statements respectively maintain: "Some are in," "Some are not in," "All are in," and "All are not in." Bochner considers this work to be a summation of many of his ideas, its main issue being "the problematization of the naively accepted relationship between language and experience."[3] As he has further elaborated, AXIOM OF INDIFFERENCE

*revolves around references and how we define them. To
what do these statements refer? What is their level of
specificity or generality? Is it only the relationship of
pennies to tape? Or is it pennies to tape to wall? Or to
the whole gallery space? Or to the world outside?
Where does one draw the boundaries? Each viewer
must construct his/her own set of references, or frames
with which to think about the complex overlapping levels of [this work]. But each viewer's 'frame of reference'
must be different. And it is this realization which
reveals the central subject of the piece: It is axiomatic
that the facts themselves will always remain indifferent
to any interpretation.*[4]

Through the simultaneous confrontation and integration of verbal and visual information Bochner constructed an alternative to sculpture in the round at the same time that he directly referred, without deferring, to its traditional spatial boundaries. — AR

Notes

1. Mel Bochner, in "Mel Bochner," *Data* (Milan) 2, no. 2 (February 1972): 64.

2. See Bruce Boice, "Mel Bochner: The Axiom of Indifference," *Arts Magazine* 47, no. 6 (April 1973): 66-68.

3. Mel Bochner, letter to the author, June 1995.

4. Ibid.

WORKING DRAWINGS AND OTHER VISIBLE THINGS ON PAPER
NOT NECESSARILY MEANT TO BE VIEWED AS ART (1966)
Four notebooks, each filled with one hundred photocopies, displayed on
four sculpture pedestals. Each notebook, 11 5/8 x 10 3/4 x 3 7/8 in.
(29.8 x 27.9 x 10.1 cm); each pedestal, 35 3/4 x 24 3/4 x 11 7/8 in.
(91.4 x 63.5 x 30.48 cm). Installation view, Visual Arts Gallery, School
of Visual Arts, New York, 2-23 December 1966.

84

AXIOM OF INDIFFERENCE: EAST SIDE AND WEST SIDE (1973)
Ink on masking tape and pennies on floor. Each square, 12 x 12 in.
(30.5 x 30.5 cm). Courtesy the artist.

MARCEL BROODTHAERS

(b. 28 January 1924, Saint-Gilles [or Brussels], Belgium; d. 28 January 1976, Cologne)

Marcel Broodthaers's diverse work includes books, films, and prints, as well as installations centered on the subject of the museum, that challenge traditional relationships between the object of art and the systems of its presentation and reception, with an eye to the situation of the work in its broader cultural framework. From 1964, when he formally announced his decision to abandon the writing of poetry in favor of the creation of objects and images, until his death in 1976, Broodthaers never ceased to be motivated by the idea that "it is perhaps possible to find an authentic means of calling into question art, its circulation, etc." [1]

UN JARDIN D'HIVER (A Winter Garden, 1974) was originally conceived for a group exhibition at the Palais des Beaux-Arts in Brussels. [2] Allocated a room of its own, this work consists of a composite arrangement of items brought together in a poetic ensemble: potted palm trees, folding garden chairs, six framed black-and-white, enlarged reproductions of nineteenth-century English engravings, a rolled-up red carpet, and a video monitor and camera on a pedestal that, in black and white, records the room within its purview and visitors passing in front of its eye. Two old-fashioned, wooden table vitrines, placed along the side of one wall, contain the original, colored bookplates and the opened catalogue pages designed by the artist for the Brussels exhibition, as well as a copy of the original invitation card. Significantly, the engravings, taken from a book of natural history, represent six different species of mammals, birds, and insects, which have been separately grouped in their appropriate categories. The engravings illustrate camels, elephants, falcons, peacocks, beetles, and bees, didactically portraying the varying types of beast according to each animal's respective classification.

Modeled on the palm court, which at one time graced many a European bourgeois interior as a reminder of more sunny, exotic, and essentially inaccessible tropical climes, UN JARDIN D'HIVER deals with various levels of fiction through the accumulation of real objects. These objects run the gamut from live plants, to reproductions of living creatures encased in vitrines, to reproductions of these reproductions secured within frames on the wall. The theme of captivity and its corollary, decontextualization, resonate throughout. The blown-up engravings equally suggest the capturing of other lands in the process of colonization and the capturing of an image in the creation of an illusion. While the rolled-up red carpet hints nostalgically at social pomp and circumstance, the video camera self-reflexively presents the room and its visitors on the monitor. The monitor thereby grounds the installation in its reality as art although, paradoxically, UN JARDIN D'HIVER puts the viability and veracity of traditional, isolated objects of display in question through the artificiality of its own decor. Moreover, this decor bears pointed reference to the animal kingdom whose "subjects," imprisoned within their frames on the wall, metaphorically allude to the many forms taken by commercially motivated acts of relocation and domination.

If the video monitor anchors the work within the framework of its own context, the pages from the accompanying exhibition catalogue on view in one of the vitrines refer to the domain of language and typography. Using the phrase "The Art of Fine Printing" to demonstrate numerous typefaces, scripts, and fonts, Broodthaers allied the installation with the realm of language. [3] His desire to give the word a visual status equal to that of the image is one of the primary, underlying themes of his oeuvre. Language, as a system of representation and reality unto itself, delivers art from the deception wrought by pictures. — AR

Notes

1. Marcel Broodthaers, "Ten Thousand Francs Reward," *October*, no. 42 (Spring 1987) [special issue published as a book entitled *Marcel Broodthaers: Writings, Interviews, Photographs*, ed. Benjamin H. D. Buchloh], 46.

2. "Carl Andre, Marcel Broodthaers, Daniel Buren, Victor Burgin, Gilbert & George, On Kawara, Richard Long, Gerhard Richter," presented at the Palais des Beaux-Arts in Brussels, 9 January-3 February 1974.

3. For a full explication of the meaning of the catalogue pages as well as the text on the invitation card, see Yves Gevaert, "Un jardin d'hiver: Un «bibelot d'inanité sonore»," in *Marcel Broodthaers: Oeuvre graphique: Essais* (Geneva: Centre genevois de gravure contemporaine, 1991), 81-94.

UN JARDIN D'HIVER (A WINTER GARDEN) (1974)
Room installation. Dimensions variable with installation.
Courtesy Michael Werner Gallery, New York and Cologne.

DANIEL BUREN

(b. 25 March 1938, Boulogne-Billancourt, France; lives and works in situ)

Since 1967 Daniel Buren has worked in situ—that is, with direct reference to a given location or situation. Probably the first artist to adopt this Latin phrase, now used extensively to describe pieces done on site, he associates it with all of his works. Initially desiring to strip painting of any and all illusionistic reference or expressive characteristics so that it might function purely as a sign of itself, Buren arrived at the decision in 1965 to reduce the pictorial content of his work to the repetition of alternating white and colored vertical bands 8.7 cm (about 3½ in.) in width. He realized that he did not have to paint the bands himself but could order mechanically-printed material to suit his particular needs. Commercially-obtained, prefabricated material with vertical stripes—intended to be as neutral a (de)sign as possible—thus serves to free the artist from the constraints of a canvas's framing edge or an allotted exhibition space. The placement of striped material governs the form and meaning of each work by Buren, who chose to direct his concerns away from the canvas field in order to examine and expose the work of art's affiliation with its external surroundings. Having dispensed with the canvas as an arena for exclusive activity, he has explored and visually highlighted its contextual frame of reference in numerous works over the years. "Right from the start," Buren has asserted, "I have always tried to show that indeed a thing never exists in itself." [1]

Works by Buren participate in the given, non-art reality while concurrently commenting on the authority of the museum or gallery whose delegated exhibition spaces they often circumvent. BUS BENCHES (1970/82/95) exemplifies the way in which Buren's works are an integral part of their context, be this an architectural one or, as in this work, an economic and social one. Buren first realized this work in 1970 when he silkscreened numerous bus benches in Los Angeles with blue and white vertical stripes. He realized the work again in 1982, this time publishing a postcard with an image of a bus stop at the corner of San Vicente Boulevard and Third Street on one side and with his name, the work's title, and a listing of fifty-one bus bench locations on the other. Elyse and Stanley Grinstein sponsored both manifestations of the work.

Buren labelled the work by placing an anonymous announcement in a daily newspaper that stated where the striped benches could be seen. He did not identify himself as the author of the work, since the idea of anonymity functioned as a significant aspect of a work in which painting in its most basic form was interposed as a sign with all manner of other, overtly commercial signs. By using the advertising space on bus benches, Buren created a work that was interwoven with the urban fabric. As opposed to being a static object, his work fused art and everyday reality. It featured a wide spectrum of points from which it, as a work, might "transport" viewers—along with a diversity of non-art travellers—who could enjoy the brightly colored, decorated benches throughout the city, while directing them beyond the previously established confines of art.

A similarly anonymous work, realized in Paris in 1968, is comparable with the Los Angeles piece. For this early work, Buren pasted approximately two hundred rectangular sheets of green-and-white-striped paper to many of the billboards found throughout Paris and its suburbs. He placed the striped rectangles randomly over or beside advertisements of every kind, juxtaposing them with the commercial statements and images already there. In speaking of this work, Buren emphasized that he accomplished it anonymously and without permission, that is "without invitation, and without commercial support and without a gallery." [2] The work materialized quite literally "without," and thus "outside of," the usual framework of artistic activity. Neither contained within the edges of a frame like a painting on canvas, nor shown as part of the conventional exhibition system, it was inserted instead into the context of everyday, outdoor advertising display. Buren thereby produced a work that had no designated author and communicated no inherent message. Moreover, glued beside and over all manner of advertisements, the striped rectangles, viewed as works of art, ironically did not possess any institutional or economic "backing" of their own.

Through his deliberate negation of museum or gallery auspices, in the BUS BENCHES, as well as in the billboards, Buren challenged then accepted methods of both making and exhibiting art in order to re-evaluate the interrelated roles of authorship, content, and presentation in the creation of aesthetic meaning. Twenty-five years later, BUS BENCHES may be viewed within the framework of an historical exhibition. At this point in time, with hindsight and in retrospect, it questions the relationship between the interior confines of a museum exhibition space and the advertising "space available" filled by a work of art that is outside of, yet nonetheless connected with, an institutional context. Such questions may be asked and examined for the very reason that they first were addressed by the artist himself from within his own oeuvre. — AR

Notes

1. Daniel Buren, "On the Autonomy of the Work of Art," in *Daniel Buren: Around "Ponctuations"*, exh. cat. (Lyon: Le Nouveau Musée, 1980), unpag.

2. Daniel Buren, cited in R. H. Fuchs, ed., *Discordance/Coherence*, exh. cat. (Eindhoven: Stedelijk Van Abbemuseum, 1976), 4.

UNTITLED (1968)
Photo/souvenir: a work in situ. Installation view of green and white papers pasted
on two hundred billboards in Paris and its suburbs (detail). Photo the artist.

92

UNTITLED (1969)
Photo/souvenir: a work in situ. Installation view (interior and exterior),
"Daniel Buren," Wide White Space, Antwerp, 17 January–6 February 1969.
Photo the artist.

VICTOR BURGIN

(b. 24 July 1941,
Sheffield, England;
lives in San Francisco)

Victor Burgin's work of the late 1960s demonstrates a concern with the space of the gallery, as opposed to the creation of autonomous objects to be set within it. However, ALL CRITERIA... (1970) was designed to be valid wherever it might be encountered. Typeset propositions, whether papered on the wall or printed in a journal or catalogue, invite spectators to peruse whatever space they find themselves in according to the supplied criteria. These criteria, left general and all-encompassing, involve the interaction between individuals, events, and things. For example, number five of the fourteen elements that comprise the work states: "ALL CRITERIA BY WHICH YOU MIGHT ASCRIBE INDIVIDUALITY TO THINGS OTHER THAN OBJECTS." The open-ended nature of the statements entrusts the spectator with the responsibility for filling in specifics.

PERFORMATIVE/NARRATIVE (1971) juxtaposes multiple texts with what at first may appear to be a single photograph of an office setting shown sixteen times but is in fact a series of different photographs of permutations of binary states of the same object: a desk (drawer open or closed), a chair (under the desk or away from it), a reading lamp (on or off), and a file folder (open or closed). A series of binary digits (e.g., 0101) appears in each section of the work and reflects the changed state of the objects photographed. Two parallel texts accompany the photographs. One, in narrative form, speaks of events which might have taken place in the office. These narrative fragments also obey binary conditions, which are put forth in the introductory text preceding each sequence and reflected in the same binary numbers that refer to the photgraphs. The other sequence of texts, each consisting of four simple propositions, obeys the same binary logic. (For example, the final sequence of numbers, "0000," corresponds to propositions that begin "not..., not..., not..., not...."). This sequence asks viewers to consider all the criteria upon which their knowledge is based.

Whereas language has the capacity to scour all representational eventualities, a photograph runs the risk of misrepresentation both because of what it omits or cannot encompass and also because of the quantity of information it includes. Burgin has pointed out that "the photographic image can carry a large number of different meanings," which generally are controlled by its juxtaposition with a verbal text.[1] PERFORMATIVE/NARRATIVE anticipates his subsequent exploration of textual and verbal relationships in connection with advertising. At this stage, drawing on his engagement with structuralism and semiotics, he specifically illustrated the way in which photography, as an all-pervasive, if not all-telling, visual presence in the social landscape, "performs" in association with the verbal permutations of an accompanying text.

"Art," Burgin has written, "can be useful in so far as it helps to maintain 'openness' in a society by engendering a flexibility of linguistic forms in that society."[2] A work of 1973, VI marks another step in his thinking. Here, the same photograph is repeated in tandem with a changing text. VI includes more explicitly socially-oriented subject matter than PERFORMATIVE/NARRATIVE. The photograph, taken from a British mail-order catalogue, presents an "image" of a typical British nuclear family. The captions under each photograph, written by Burgin, and the accompanying individual statements deal directly with dominant social values and beliefs in order to question, if not completely undermine, the seemingly straightforward nature of the photographs.

By mid-decade, Burgin was making use of feminist and psychoanalytical criticism in his reading of how photographs and language are used in Western culture. Having at first enlisted photography and language in the interest of presenting conditions rather than objects, Burgin now pitted these two representational systems, as used in the commercial media, against each other to expose their ability to belie their own factual appearance. A tripartite work of 1975, SENSATION/CONTRADICTION/LOGIC, in which Burgin juxtaposed texts and images he extracted and recombined from advertisements, may be seen, like VI, as an anticipation of the appropriation methods used by artists throughout the 1980s. — AR

Notes

1. Victor Burgin, "Art, Common Sense and Photography," *Camerawork* 3 (July 1976): 2.

2. Victor Burgin, "Commentary Part I," *Work and Commentary* (London: Latimer New Dimensions Limited, 1973), unpag.

ALL CRITERIA... (1970)
Courtesy the artist, John Weber Gallery, New York,
and Galerie Liliane & Michel Durand-Dessert, Paris.

1

ALL CRITERIA BY WHICH YOU MIGHT
DECIDE THAT ANY SERIES OF BODILY
ACTS, DIRECTLY KNOWN TO YOU AT
ANY MOMENT PREVIOUS TO THE
PRESENT MOMENT, CONSTITUTES A
DISCRETE EVENT

2

ALL CRITERIA BY WHICH YOU MIGHT
ASSESS THE SIMILARITY OF ANY ONE
EVENT TO ANY OTHER EVENT

3

ANY SERIES OF SIMILAR EVENTS
DIRECTLY KNOWN TO YOU PREVIOUSLY
TO THE PRESENT MOMENT

4

ANY OBJECT WITHIN 3 WHICH YOU
KNOW TO BE THE SAME INDIVIDUAL
THROUGHOUT 3 AND TOWARDS
WHICH ANY BODILY ACTS WERE
DIRECTED

5

ALL CRITERIA BY WHICH YOU MIGHT
ASCRIBE INDIVIDUALITY TO THINGS
OTHER THAN OBJECTS

6

ALL INDIVIDUALS WITHIN 3 OTHER
THAN OBJECTS

7

A HYPOTHETICAL EVENT IN SERIES
WITH 3 OCCURRING LATER THAN THE
PRESENT MOMENT

8

AN OBJECT WITHIN 7 WHICH IS THE
SAME INDIVIDUAL AS 4

9

ALL HYPOTHETICAL INDIVIDUALS
WITHIN 7 OTHER THAN OBJECTS

10

ALL INDIVIDUALS WHICH ARE BOTH
MEMBERS OF 9 AND OF 6

11

ANY OBJECT DIRECTLY KNOWN TO YOU
AT THE PRESENT MOMENT TOWARDS
WHICH ANY BODILY ACT IS DIRECTED

12

ALL INDIVIDUALS DIRECTLY KNOWN TO
YOU AT THE PRESENT MOMENT OTHER
THAN OBJECTS

13

THE SUBSTITUTION OF 11 FOR 8 AND
FOR 4

14

THE SUBSTITUTION OF 12 FOR 9 AND
FOR 6

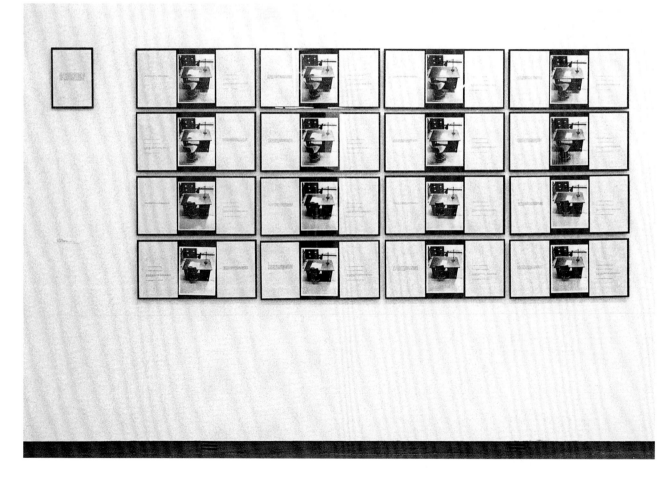

PERFORMATIVE/NARRATIVE (1971)
Black and white photographs and printed text in sixteen parts. Each, 18 x 34
in. (45.7 x 86.4 cm). Courtesy the artist, John Weber Gallery, New York,
and Galerie Liliane & Michel Durand-Dessert, Paris.

TOP: Detail. BOTTOM: Installation view, "Master Works of Conceptual Art,"
Galerie Paul Maenz, Cologne, 8 October-12 November 1983.

VI (1973)
Offset lithography and printed text in ten parts. Each, 18 x 24 in.
(45.7 x 86.4 cm). Courtesy the artist, John Weber Gallery, New York, and
Galerie Liliane & Michel Durand—Dessert, Paris. TOP: Installation view,
Stedelijk Van Abbemuseum, Eindhoven, 1977. Photo Hans Biezen. BOTTOM: detail.

ANDRE CADERE

(b. 20 May 1934, Warsaw; d. 2 August 1978, Paris)

For eight years, from 1970 until his death at the age of forty-four in 1978, Romanian artist André Cadere developed an artistic and discursive practice centered upon the circulation of his BARRES DE BOIS ROND (Round Bars of Wood). Cadere was born in Warsaw in 1934 to a Romanian mother and a French father. After World War II, his family moved to Romania, where he attended the Academy of Bucharest. In 1967, Cadere moved to Paris, where he was influenced by Op art, as well as by Minimalist and Conceptual art, which were then becoming more visible in the city in part through the activities of Galerie Yvon Lambert. As Cornelia Lauf has observed, Cadere assimilated both tendencies by merging "his somewhat psychedelic formal vocabulary with the institutional critique provided by Conceptual artists."[1]

From 1969 to 1972, Cadere produced painted round pieces of wood glued on a flat surface and shown on the floor and later on pedestals.[2] He conceived of the BARRES DE BOIS ROND in 1970 and fully realized his conception by 1972. The bars consist of cylinders (the diameter of each being equal to its height) painted with two coats of enamel and then assembled with wooden dowels and glue. Their heights range from approximately one foot to six feet and are derived from permutations of a given system of colors: primary (red, yellow, blue), secondary (orange, purple, green), and black and white. Each bar includes a unique error made by switching two segments; no two are the same.

Cadere displayed the first bar publicly in an exhibition of the work of Niele Toroni at Galerie Yvon Lambert in 1970.[3] In "Six Pages by Paris Artists," published in the March 1973 issue of *Studio International*, he contributed a photograph of himself holding a bar and the following statement: "This work is exhibited in all places where it is seen: through any museum, placed in any exhibition by any artist, shown anywhere (street, underground, supermarket...)." According to the accompanying biographical notes, this contribution was his "first exhibition of an official character."[4] Cadere's unofficial "exhibitions" took place as he carried his bars in the street and into the exhibitions of other artists at galleries and museums in cities throughout Europe, including such major international exhibitions as Documenta and the Venice Biennale. These activities or "displacements" served to circulate his work outside of the existing institutional structure of art. As he stated in a 1974 lecture,

A round bar of wood is materially a small thing and cannot physically disturb ordinary works of art. The fight takes place on an ideological level, and the aggression and violence are part of the arsenal employed by those who are powerful. But to emphasize the independence of the work, it is important to show outside art enclaves—in the streets, subways, restaurants, everywhere—a possibility because the presence of the wall is not necessary.[5]

Until 1975, Cadere's work was met with "indifference or hostility."[6] Following that date his exhibitions became increasingly official. Shortly before his death, in a letter to Yvon Lambert, Cadere summarized his a [aesthetic] esthetic strategy:

1) It is obvious that a round bar of wood can be exhibited anywhere, without patron or client, a special location, or an express authorization. At the same time, such a place does not depend on any private or public wall; it requires no nails, no glue, color matching or any other system of installation.

View of exhibition at Kunsthalle Düsseldorf in 1976 with one of the BARRES DE BOIS ROND in situ. Courtesy Galerie Yvon Lambert, Paris. Photo Jens Bode.

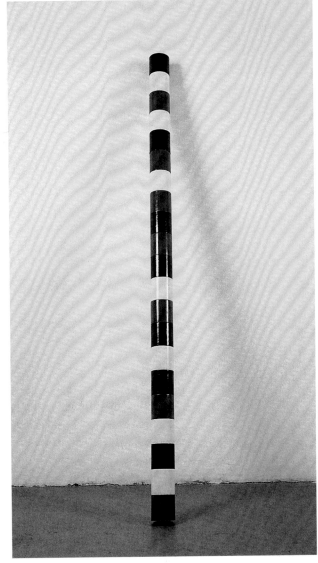

2) However, the very same work can be hung on a wall—including a gallery wall—and fixed or set up in any number of ways in the place traditionally assigned to "classical" works. For it is important that this "classical" power should not marginalize my pieces, isolating them in something like an "avant-garde" zone.

3) Since one can present them in a classical fashion, one should also be able to show them in this way, according to their own possibilities and precisely to slough off any "revolutionary idealism." We shouldn't assume that they are outside of the galleries or against someone or other. ...I show my pieces towards and against everyone and everything, my sole aim being the pieces themselves.[7] — AG

Notes

1. Cornelia Lauf, "A Tactic of the Margins," in *André Cadere: All Walks of Life*, exh. cat. (New York: The Institute for Contemporary Art, P.S. 1 Museum), 116.

2. Bernard Marcelis, "André Cadere: The Strategy of Displacement," in *André Cadere*, 44.

3. Marcelis, "André Cadere," 43.

4. "Six Pages by Paris Artists," *Studio International* 185, no. 953 (March 1973): 120, 118

5. André Cadere, "Presentation of a Work/Utilization of a Work," in *André Cadere*, 34, 36.

6. Marcelis, "André Cadere," 44.

7. André Cadere, "Letters to Yvon Lambert," in *André Cadere*, 22.

BARRE DE BOIS ROND (Round Bar of Wood)
Twenty-one painted wooden segments. Height: 77 1/4 in. (198 cm); diam.:
3 3/4 in. (9.5 cm). Courtesy Galerie Liliane & Michel Durand-Dessert, Paris.
Photo Adam Rezepka.

JAMES COLEMAN

(b. 1941, Ireland;
lives in Dublin, Ireland)

James Coleman emerged as an artist in the late 1960s, when he broke with traditional forms through his use of photography, slide projections, audiotape, video, film, and performed works questioning the mechanisms of representation and the production of meaning. His early work, through 1972, explores the relationships among time, memory, and perception and incorporates increasingly complex psychological elements that directly engage the viewer.

Writing about Coleman's work of the early 1970s, Jean Fisher observed that he "redirects our attention not only to what we experience, but to how we are experiencing it. This severs our habits of seeing, making us aware of our active role in perception and the means by which objects acquire meaning."[1] In a key work from this period, FLASH PIECE, presented at Studio Marconi in Milan in 1970, three-minute sequences of blue and yellow lights were flashed against the gallery wall. While the length of the flashing cycles remained constant, that of the intervals between them differed, yet appeared the same to the viewer. As Anne Rorimer has written, "the significance of this work lies in the way it drew attention to the viewer's sense of time insofar as time as measured and time as experienced did not coincide."[2]

In PROJECTIONS (1958/71), Coleman constructed a visual representation of the experience of time, place, and memory. A pastel drawing of a tree in the landscape, made by the artist when he was seventeen, is illuminated by a spotlight and hung next to two Super-8 film projections—one a recent view of the actual landscape depicted in the drawing (the tree now felled), the other focusing upon the tree stump. The passage of time is thus represented through three different visual means—from the scene portrayed in the drawing, to the later changes in the land-

scape and the rings that mark the age of the stump visible in the films. This is also echoed by the time-based manner of the work's presentation.

This examination of perception and identity through various points of view is crystallized in SLIDE PIECE (1972-73), which marks a significant shift in Coleman's engagement with images and sound to elicit the contingencies of identity and meaning that he would continue to explore in his later work. SLIDE PIECE consists of the projection of a series of color slides, each bearing the same image of an early morning street scene in Milan showing a deserted square with a gasoline station, leafless tree, and buildings in the background. Coleman showed this image to various individuals who were asked to describe and interpret it. Their different responses form the texts that are recited by a single speaker on a synchronized audiotape. With the projection of each identical image, a different description is heard. The point of view of the spectator is central to the work. As Anne Rorimer has noted, "By means of diverse 'views' gathered together with respect to a single image, SLIDE PIECE underscores the way in which each spectator's verbal representation of the provided visual image differed. The work thereby includes the viewing process within its content, making subjective outlook the object of its inquiry."[3] This single image elicits a multitude of interpretations and is an ongoing work in which the constellation of viewpoints increases as Coleman continues to add further descriptions. — AG

Notes

1. Jean Fisher, "James Coleman," in *James Coleman*, exh. cat. (Dublin: The Douglas Hyde Gallery, Trinity College, 1982), 10.

2. Anne Rorimer, "James Coleman 1970-1985," in *James Coleman: Selected Works*, exh. cat. (Chicago: The Renaissance Society at The University of Chicago and London: Institute of Contemporary Arts, 1985), 8.

3. Anne Rorimer, "Michael Asher and James Coleman at Artists Space," in *Michael Asher/James Coleman*, exh. cat. (New York: Artists Space, 1988), 8.

SLIDE PIECE (1972-73)
Projected images with synchronized audio narration. Courtesy the artist.
Photo courtesy Marian Goodman Gallery, New York.

HANNE DARBOVEN

(b. 29 April 1941, Munich; lives in Hamburg)

Born in Munich and raised in Hamburg, where she currently lives, Hanne Darboven, after a brief career as a pianist, studied at the Hochschule für bildende Kunst in Hamburg. Following art school, she came to New York in 1965, where she lived on and off for several years.

Darboven describes her activity as "writing": "I both write and draw...because 'no more words' is a writing process, it's not a drawing process. The writing fills the space as a drawing would. It turns out to be esthetic, but that wasn't my first aim."[1] Darboven's "writing" chronicles existence and evokes the passage of time: a day, a month, a year, a century, a lifetime. She develops her work through the calendar, using dates, numbers, and mathematical operations as the basis of her quantifications of time. Hundreds of sheets of paper can comprise a single work, representing a period of days or a century, complete with an index, which is an integral aspect of the work. As Coosje van Bruggen has written, "Darboven's constructs of time stretch it, shorten it, and occupy it."[2] Her use of the calendar and specific references that range from the personal to literary, musical, scientific, or historical sources serve to "personify time," and her wave-like script that fills the pages reduces the act of handwriting to a sign of its essential expression and rhythm.[3] Like On Kawara's Today series of date paintings, Adrian Piper's graphic analyses of her point of view in the Hypothesis series, or Christine Kozlov's representation of the years of her existence through a parallel bibliography in her NEUROLOGICAL COMPILATION, Darboven's systematic approach to time reflects the proof and flux of one's passage through it. Her process incorporates not only a reference to time but bears its mark as she crosses out the word "heute" (today) when that day has passed. As she wrote in February 1968, "[a] system became necessary: how else could I in a concentrated way find something of interest which lends itself to a continuation? My systems are numerical concepts, which work in terms of progressions and/or reductions akin to musical themes and variations....In this moment I know about what I did. What I am doing, what will happen further, I shall see."[4]

Lucy R. Lippard has observed that Darboven uses a consistent mathematical system to structure her work: "The armature is provided by simple, but highly flexible number systems. Yet the content does not concern mathematics so much as the process of

24 GESÄNGE—B. FORM (24 Songs–B. Form, 1974)
Ink on paper. 120 parts: 48 at 50 5/8 x 12 in. (128.6 x 30.5 cm); 72 at
17 x 70 3/8 in. (43.2 x 178.8 cm). Stedelijk Museum, Amsterdam.

continuation—a process which takes time to do, which takes time as one of its subjects, and which takes from time (the calendar) its numerical foundations."[5] Darboven's work process extends from the addition of the numbers that quantify a date in European form (day/month/year) to determine the base number or "K" (for Konstruktion) that is the foundation of each work. In her system each number is separated and added together.

The form and structure of many of Darboven's works have musical connotations, and her numbers have at times been translated into musical notes, including scores that have been performed. Two monumental related works, 24 GESÄNGE—A FORM (24 Songs—A Form) and 24 GESÄNGE—B FORM (24 Songs—B Form,) (both 1974), constitute a major early project in which Darboven's numerical computations are systematically developed into the notes of the musical scale. Writing about these works, Klaus Honnef described her method:

> The artist develops a specific method, by which she translates the numerical constructions of her works into musical notations. The number 2 stands for the note f, 3 for g, 4 for a, etc. All compound numbers are, on the analogy of the numerical construction, expressed in two

notes, an interval: Accordingly, 11 = e-e, 12 = e-f, 13 = e-g, etc. The numbers containing o come out as two broken chords, fundamental chord and four-six-chord, and are treated as a unit.[6]

24 GESÄNGE—B FORM is a large-scale work comprising 576 individual parts composed into 120 framed panels. In this work, the expansive form—physically enveloping the spectator—constructs a structure, like architecture, that accommodates and expresses the experience of the temporal aspect of music. — AG

Notes

1. Hanne Darboven, in Coosje van Bruggen, "Afterword: Today Crossed Out," in *Hanne Darboven: Primitive Zeit/Urhrzeit, Primitive Time/Clock Time*, exh. cat. (Philadelphia: Goldie Paley Gallery, Moore College of Art and Design, 1990), 4.

2. van Bruggen, "Afterword," 3.

3. Ibid., 4.

4. Hanne Darboven, in "Artists on Their Art," *Art International* 12, no. 4 (20 April 1968): 55.

5. Lucy R. Lippard, "Hanne Darboven: Deep in Numbers," *Artforum* 12, no. 2 (October 1973): 35.

6. Klaus Honnef, "Art Encyclopedias of Culture: Klaus Honnef on Hanne Darboven," in *Hanne Darboven: Primitive Zeit/Uhrzeit*, 11.

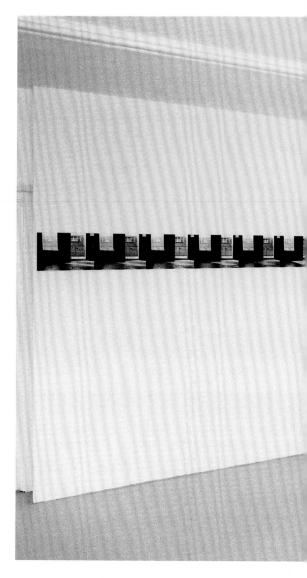

JAN DIBBETS

(b. 9 May 1941, Weert, The Netherlands; lives in Amsterdam)

Since 1967, Jan Dibbets's work has included sculptural interventions into the landscape, photography, film, video, and audio. Often using nature as his object, he has consistently investigated the physical realities and ambiguities of perception and the mechanics of representation "to develop a way of seeing."[1] As Barbara M. Reise observed, his work explores "the paradoxical nature of illusion and reality immediately and directly perceived. Thus, the reality of a seemingly 'natural' visual observation is counter-posed by a physical or conceptual reality."[2]

Dibbets began his career as an abstract painter whose influences included Giotto, Vermeer, Pieter Saenredam, and Mondrian. His last paintings are serial, geometric works constructed in space to engage changing viewpoints. In 1967 Dibbets attended St. Martin's School of Art in London for six months, where he met Richard Long, Barry Flanagan, Hamish Fulton, and Gilbert & George. He subsequently began to make sculptural interventions into the landscape, such as GRASS SQUARE (1967), a trapezoidal shape cut into grass so that it would appear to be a square when photographed, and GRASS ROLL, a square of grass cut out of the ground and rolled into a cylinder. Working with nature and natural processes, these early works incorporate their *perceived* reality. In a related work, Dibbets divided a field bordering twenty kilometers of the railroad tracks from Amsterdam to Hilversum into squares. The regularity of the squares marked a contrast with the changing landscape in which they were set, which was visible to passengers in the train.

Although most critics associated these early works with Earth or Land art,[3] Reise separated Dibbets from this movement:

Throughout his work, Dibbets's attitude to Nature has a dispassionate objectivity about it which is far from the associative empathy and historicity of artists like Richard Long, Hamish Fulton, Gilbert & George—or even Michael Heizer and Robert Smithson. With Dibbets, Nature is observed, modified for some specific times, but left and accepted as a fact which is "other." An extension of this is that factual nature is phenomenologically distanced by its representation through such man-made apertures as windows, microphones and amplifiers, camera lenses and projectors, and the human eye—which themselves are treated as "factually" as the phenomena perceived.[4]

While photographing his land-based works, Dibbets developed the concept for his Perspective Corrections, a series of approximately forty works produced between September 1967 and late 1969. The Perspective Corrections consist of trapezoidal forms—outlined in white rope on grass, taped on the floor, drawn on a wall, or inscribed into the sand at the beach—designed so as to appear to be perfect squares from the viewpoint of the camera.

The resulting squares appear to hover above the ground, parallel to, and, in effect, joining with the surface of the photograph. Shown with the diagrams that reveal the process of their production, these works cancel out "one illusion with another, thereby making the photographic plan visible."[5]

Reise described Dibbets's work as dealing with the elements of earth, air, fire, and water, as well as with movement, time, and light.[6] Reflecting the latter concerns is SHADOWS TAPED OFF A WALL (1969), in which Dibbets marked the movement of the sun by tracing in tape the outlines of the shadows cast on the walls, ceiling, and floor of a gallery in the Museum Haus Lange in Krefeld, Germany. He elaborated upon the sequential nature of this work in THE SHADOWS IN MY STUDIO (1969), which records the process of time through a systematic record of the changes of light and shadow on the artist's studio floor shot from a fixed point of view looking toward the open window and door. This work comprises thirty-four images photographed ten minutes apart between 8:40 a.m. and 2:10 p.m. and has been arranged in a grid with an accompanying diagram and as a single line that stretches, like a strip of film, across the wall. Working simultaneously with time, light, and movement, THE SHADOWS IN MY STUDIO is "a linear condensation of time. It makes time visible as moving light. It gives form, or rather imposes a rhythmical form of equal repetitive movements, to a process that would otherwise never be visible with such a degree of concentration."[7] — AG

Notes

1. M. M. M. Vos, "On Photography and the Art of Jan Dibbets," in *Jan Dibbets*, exh. cat. (Minneapolis: Walker Art Center, 1987), 14.

2. Barbara M. Reise, "Notes[1] on Jan Dibbets's[2] Contemporary[3] Nature[4] of Realistic[5] Classicism[6] in the Dutch[7] Tradition[8]," *Studio International* 183, no. 945 (June 1972): 253. This text, which takes the form of footnotes to its title, parallels Dibbets's working practice of emphasizing the mechanics of constructing a representation and is a critical interpretation of the artist's work.

3. One of the earliest group exhibitions that included the work of Dibbets was "Earth Art," presented at the Andrew Dickson White Museum of Art at Cornell University in Ithaca, New York, 11 February-16 March 1969. An interview with Dibbets by Willoughby Sharp, which appears in *Avalanche* (New York), no. 1 (Fall 1970): 34-39, was conducted on the occasion of his participation in this exhibition.

4. Reise, "Notes,[1]" 252.

5. Vos, "On Photography," 19.

6. Reise, "Notes,[1]" 252.

7. R. H. Fuchs, "The Eye Framed and Unframed," in *Jan Dibbets*, 53.

THE SHADOWS IN MY STUDIO AS THEY WERE AT 27-7-69 FROM 8:40-14.10 PHOTOGRAPHED EVERY 10 MINUTES (1969)
Thirty-four black-and-white photographs mounted on cardboard.
9 1/8 x 407 1/2 in. (23.2 x 1035 cm). Herbert Collection, Ghent.

PETER DOWNSBROUGH

(b. 8 September 1940, New York City; Lives in Brussels and New York City)

Peter Downsbrough's work of the late 1960s established his ongoing interest in the conditions of place and displacement, location and dislocation, and difference as generated through the literal intersection of architecture and language. In his early work, Downsbrough developed modest physical interventions that marked a place spatially, whether in the landscape or on a sheet of paper. In 1970 he began to work with the conceit of two vertical parallel lines of differing heights. These forms have been manifested as wooden rods, metal pipes, and neon tubes. His lines are thin (approximately two centimeters in diameter) and are always located eight centimeters apart. When installed indoors, one is hung from the ceiling, and the other is mounted parallel to its counterpart on the floor. Because the floor element is always taller than the ceiling element, their lengths cannot simply be added together to recover a single line whose length equals the distance from the floor to the ceiling. Rather, the two lines must be considered in relation to each other and to the surrounding space.

In 1972 Downsbrough published his first artist's book, NOTES ON LOCATION, which he originally composed in 1968/69. In this book, he lists such terms as place, location, structure, vertical, horizontal, zone, interior, exterior, up, down, inside, and outside.[1] These terms of description are relative and relational, rather than standard signifiers of measurement and analysis.

Since 1972, Downsbrough has used the form of the book to produce and distribute his work. In the eight he published between 1972 and 1975, he constructed a series of permutations derived from the concept of two parallel lines. Some of these books include photographs of works manifested in public spaces. For example, TWO PIPES, FOURTEEN LOCATIONS (1974) includes photographs of two parallel vertical pipes of heights up to six meters installed in various locations. The pipes are seen in relation to one another, as well as to their sites. The clarity of their apparently perfect perpendicularity to the ground unsettles the surrounding image by overlaying one set of relationships on another.

Downsbrough's works are markers that define the intersections between the conditions and experience of their construction and perception. Rather than describing a situation, they concretize, fragment, and intervene in the process and conditions of representation. They do not delineate a place but the conditions of place. — AG

Notes

1. Peter Downsbrough, NOTES ON LOCATION (New York: The Vanishing Rotating Triangle, 1972).

CHALK SQUARE (13 December 1968)
Red powdered chalk on snow. 8 x 8 ft. (244 x 244 cm). Etna, New Hampshire.
Photo © Peter Downsbrough.

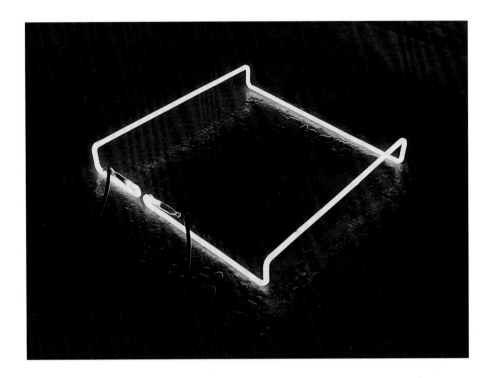

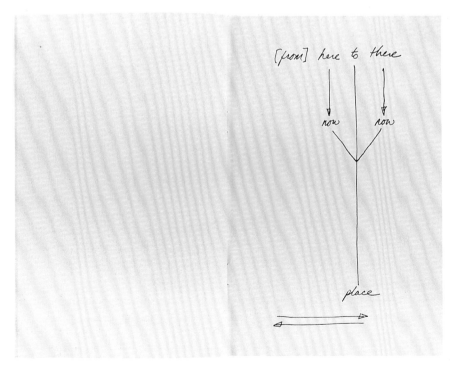

Page spread from NOTES ON LOCATION (New York: The Vanishing
Rotating Triangle, 1972). Photo Paula Goldman.

UNTITLED (1969)
Neon. Approx. 12 x 12 in. (30.5 x 30.5 cm).
Photo © Peter Downsbrough.

7'/5' (1971-72). Two wooden dowels. Heights: 7 ft. (2.13 m) and 5 ft. (152 cm);
diam.: 1 in. (2.5 cm). Studio view. Photo © Peter Downsbrough.

1.60 M (detail) (1972)
Heights: 17.9 ft. (5.5 m) and 62.4 in. (160 cm). Two black metal pipes.
Daled Collection, Brussels. Photo © Peter Downsbrough.

"19' | 13'. Windham College, Putney, Vermont, U.S.A."
From TWO PIPES, FOURTEEN LOCATIONS (New York: Norman Fisher, 1974).
Photo Paula Goldman.

GER VAN ELK

(b. 9 March 1941, Amsterdam; lives in Amsterdam)

Ger van Elk has stated that he has consistently aimed "to present a work of art from which you can distill all sorts of facets and double meanings."[1] Van Elk has worked in a number of different ways, with an eye turned toward the artifice of art in its capacity to manipulate reality. Early three-dimensional installations, such as WELL POLISHED FLOOR PIECE (1969), anticipate two-dimensional works that use photographic means to play with perceptions and expectations about reality. For the realization of this work, a section of the exhibition floor is given a glossy sheen. By virtue of this fact, the artist, in effect, demonstrates his ability to intervene into ordinary reality and to influence the way in which it is experienced.

Works such as PAUL KLEE—UM DEN FISCH, 1926 (1970), THE ROSE MORE BEAUTIFUL THAN ART, BUT DIFFICULT, THEREFORE ART IS SPLENDID (1972), and The Adieu series deal with painting as real on one level, yet give evidence of its fictional relationship to reality on another. In the first work, van Elk brings the painted subject matter of Klee's well-known painting to life, so to speak, by enacting the eating of the depicted fish in a sequence of projected images. THE ROSE, similarly utilizing slides as a point of reference to reality, creates an inseparable melding of actuality and artificiality through the projection of a hand onto the surface of a framed watercolor of a vase of roses. The hand, appearing to move, is ostensibly rearranging the flowers. Once again, the artist deliberately (con)fuses fact and fiction at the same time that the subject matter of the work indirectly comments on compositional placement as a component of traditional painting.

THE ADIEU, III (1974) is one of five paintings consisting of gouache and ink applied to a color photograph. The works belonging to this series are not rectangular, as are conventional paintings; instead, each is contained within a differently proportioned trapezoidal frame. Within the framed format of THE ADIEU, III, a painting reminiscent of a seventeenth-century Dutch landscape is presented on an easel before a curtained, stage-like setting. The landscape painting has been tipped forward as if to counter the picture plane and break through its impenetrable barrier of flatness. From within the landscape, a small human figure waves, bidding farewell to the traditional rectangular painting.

Through his use of photography in conjunction with gouache and ink, van Elk succeeds in simultaneously pointing to and playing with the artificiality of a work of art as something staged. If the literal content of The Adieu series is the depiction of a painting within a painting on a proscenium, its underlying thematic content must be interpreted "in view of" the fictional nature of painted perspective. While the trapezoidal frame reinforces the idea that a painting is an object in its own right, the depicted scene speaks about the fact that art is a fictional construct. — AR

Notes

1. Ger van Elk, cited in R. H. Fuchs, "On Semantics, Ger van Elk, Structure and Other Difficult Terms," in Ger van Elk, exh. cat. (Amsterdam: Stedelijk Museum, 1974), 54.

PAUL KLEE — UM DEN FISCH, 1926 (1970)
Nine color slides projected on table with white tablecloth (ed. 4).
Stedelijk Museum, Amsterdam.

THE ROSE MORE BEAUTIFUL THAN ART, BUT DIFFICULT, THEREFORE ART IS SPLENDID (1972)
Color slides projected on framed watercolor on paper. Collection Liliane and
Michel Durand-Dessert, Paris.

THE ADIEU, III (1974)
Gouache and ink on color photograph mounted on aluminum. 39 1/8 x 36 3/8 in. (99.2 x
92.3 cm). The Museum of Modern Art, New York, Hedwig van Amerigen Foundation Fund,
1975. Photograph © The Museum of Modern Art, New York.

MORGAN FISHER

(b. 13 June 1942,
Washington, D.C.; lives
in Santa Monica,
California)

In describing his early interest in filmmaking in the mid-1960s, Morgan Fisher cites as "a golden moment" an issue of *Film Culture* in which stills from Jack Smith's independent film FLAMING CREATURES (1962) and Sam Fuller's Hollywood movie THE NAKED KISS (1964) were represented on equal terms: "The unifying idea was that of being an artist in film, no matter where."[1] In his films since 1968, Fisher has attempted to maintain that "unifying idea" of an artist in film through a practice that deliberately engages and is produced with standard commercial materials, equipment, and techniques of production to "illuminate and criticize industry practice itself."[2] His work establishes a discourse on representation that uses the means of production as the means of critique.

Fisher's titles/subjects are standard film terms directly stated: THE DIRECTOR AND HIS ACTOR LOOK AT FOOTAGE SHOWING PREPARATIONS FOR AN UNMADE FILM (2) (1968), PHI PHENOMENON (1968), SCREENING ROOM (1968), PRODUCTION STILLS (1970), PICTURE AND SOUND RUSHES (1973), and CUE ROLLS (1974). These films meticulously replicate every detail of commercial production. A standard-length, 400-foot role of 16mm film often determines the length of the films, which are conceived and produced as single, continuous, un-edited shots. In addition, standard industry equipment, such as Mitchell cameras and soundstages, are used. Straightforward and materially consistent, Fisher's films also have a slow, deadpan quality that is a product of the contradictions and the carefully managed play of complexities inherent to the subject/object relationship they construct.

For example, in PRODUCTION STILLS, Fisher uses the production of stills as the film's subject and object. This film begins with a white screen and the sounds of people speaking. A flash of light then fills the screen, and soon two hands enter the frame with a photograph, which they pin to the white backdrop. The photograph shows the setup of filmic/photographic production, and

as we experience another flash of light and a new photograph is pinned up to replace the previous one, it becomes clear that we are watching the production of the stills of the film we are watching, each new image giving us a different shot of the production team. Scott MacDonald writes about Fisher's overlapping of means with end:

> Normally, production stills are taken while a film is being shot, as an aid in marketing the finished film: they are a means to an end. In Fisher's film the making and presentation of the production stills is the end, and moments of motion picture illusion—the hands entering the image, the apparent use of sync sound, the making of the film itself—are means for getting the stills mounted so that we can examine them.[3]

PRODUCTION STILLS is full of contradictions and overstatements of technique: though it is shot in color, the stills are in black and white; though it is produced with a studio camera and shot on a soundstage, neither are technically necessary. As Fisher has stated, it is "an industry production of a non-industry film. It's a deliberate underutilization of the equipment."[4]

In SCREENING ROOM (1968), Fisher incorporates not only the means of production, but also the means of presentation. The film is "site-specific" and is especially produced for each different screening location. SCREENING ROOM begins with the camera moving into the theater wherein a filmless projector illuminates the screen (and the surrounding space) with white light. The camera then zooms into the "image" on the screen, ultimately conjoining the image on the screen with the image portrayed. It literally becomes an image of itself, playing with aspects of cinematic representation and illusion. As Fisher has stated, "What's on the screen of the film we're watching is still an image, but no longer an illusional one, or at least no longer illusional in the usual sense, in that it's no longer an image of someplace else."[5] The film closes the gap between what is represented and what is "real"—creating a situation wherein they no longer can be visually distinguished—thus playing with their apparent autonomy. Fisher concludes: "Perhaps what the film presents is the illusion that the displacements disappear, creating the illusion that there is no illusion, since the demonstration depends on some of the very effects of representation that the film is doing its best to rid itself of."[6] —AG

Notes

1. Scott MacDonald, "Morgan Fisher: An Interview," *Film Quarterly* (Berkeley, California) 40, no. 3 (Spring 1987): 25.

2. Ibid., 30.

3. Scott MacDonald, "Putting All Your Eggs in One Basket," *Afterimage* (Rochester, New York) 16, no. 8 (March 1989): 14.

4. MacDonald, "Morgan Fisher," 30.

5. Letter to the author, 16 November 1993.

6. Ibid.

PHI PHENOMENON (1968)
Still from film (16mm, 11 mins.; b/w, silent).

THE DIRECTOR AND HIS ACTOR LOOK AT FOOTAGE SHOWING PREPARATIONS
FOR AN UNMADE FILM (2) (1968)
Still from film (16mm, 15 min., b/w, sound).

PICTURE AND SOUND RUSHES (1973)
Still from film (16mm, 11 min., b/w, sound).

118

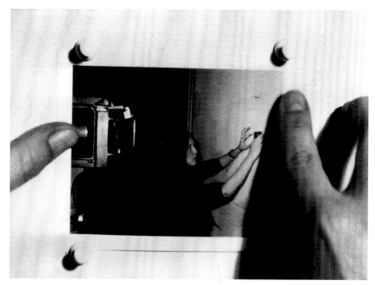

PRODUCTION STILLS (1970)
Stills from film (16mm, 11 min., color, sound).

SCREENING ROOM (1968/70)
Still from film (16mm, 4 min., b/w, silent. State for 1409
Melnitz Hall, University of California, Los Angeles).

GILBERT & GEORGE

(Gilbert, b. 1943,
Dolomites, Italy;
George, b. 1942, Devon,
England; met in 1967 at
St. Martin's School of
Art, London; both
live in London)

Gilbert & George met during their studies at St. Martin's School of Art in London. Declaring themselves to be living sculptures, they consider everything they make to be sculpture, including "living sculpture pieces, object-sculptures, lecture sculptures, magazine sculptures, postal sculptures, book sculptures, a film they consider a living sculpture, and the sculptures they call photo-pieces."[1] Barbara M. Reise summarized their work in 1971:

> Gilbert & George present Gilbert & George—as well as calling cards, block-printed broadsheets, hand-written invitations, meals, meetings, enormous charcoaled images on paper, song and dance routines, individually dedicated limericks and long discursive printed prose, recordings, and series of over-life-sized oil paintings as sculpture, as physical art. They make it, conceive it, structure it all and present it in lecture-halls, art-schools, municipal museums, pubs, newspapers, commercial avant-garde galleries, music festivals, through the postal system, and in their very own clean and well-painted sitting-room gallery 'Art for All.'[2]

As Reise also observed, Gilbert & George were unified as subject and object, artist and artwork.[3]

Dating back to 1969, the living sculptures include the SINGING SCULPTURE, in which the artists, wearing bronze metallic makeup on their faces, stood upon a table that served as a pedestal, as a tape of the English music-hall song "Underneath the Arches," was played multiple times; they silently sang and danced and then exchanged their vaudeville-like glove and cane with each rewind of the tape. Reise observed that the double SINGING SCULPTURE (1969) was presented at a rock concert inside London's Lyceum and outdoors during the National Jazz and Pop Festival in Sussex "among groups like The Who and 20,000 sprawling youth; the contrast of these crowds with the two business-suited metallic-headed figures shuffling robot-like in the spotlight was as important as the audial difference between the Sounds of the 'Seventies with the hand-wound victrola strains of the 1920s gently sad and nostalgic vaudeville ballad Underneath the Arches."[4]

The Nature Photo-Pieces (1971) are Gilbert & George's first photo-pieces. The works of one early 1970s consist of multiple images of the artists in irregularly formed arrangements that represent multiple and simultaneous points of view. The images, often manipulated in terms of double-exposure, camera movement, solarization, cropping, repetition, or placement, express different states of being. In the case of the forty-seven works produced for the exhibitions "The Evening Before the Morning After" (1972), "Any Port in a Storm" (1972), "New Decorative Works" (1973), and "Modern Rubbish" (1973), they represent the artists in various states of inebriation. SMASHED (1972) comprises ten photographs of Gilbert & George standing at a bar. All the photographs derive from the same source image, manipulated by variations in cropping and printing. Toppling over each other in an irregular form on the wall, they evoke the state of drunkenness. Similarly, RAINING GIN (1973), comprised of forty-four small photographs derived from the same image of the artists and a drinking glass, breaks out of a grid-like arrangement. The assembly of disembodied and disorienting fragments of images unsettles their overall composition. — AG

Notes

1. Carter Ratcliff, "Gilbert and George: The Fabric of Their World," in *Gilbert & George: The Complete Pictures* (New York: Rizzoli, 1986), ix.

2. Barbara M. Reise, "Presenting Gilbert & George, the Living Sculptures," *Art News* 70, no. 7 (November 1971): 62.

3. Ibid., 63.

4. Ibid., 64.

THE SINGING SCULPTURE (1970)
Photo courtesy Anthony d'Offay Gallery, London.

122

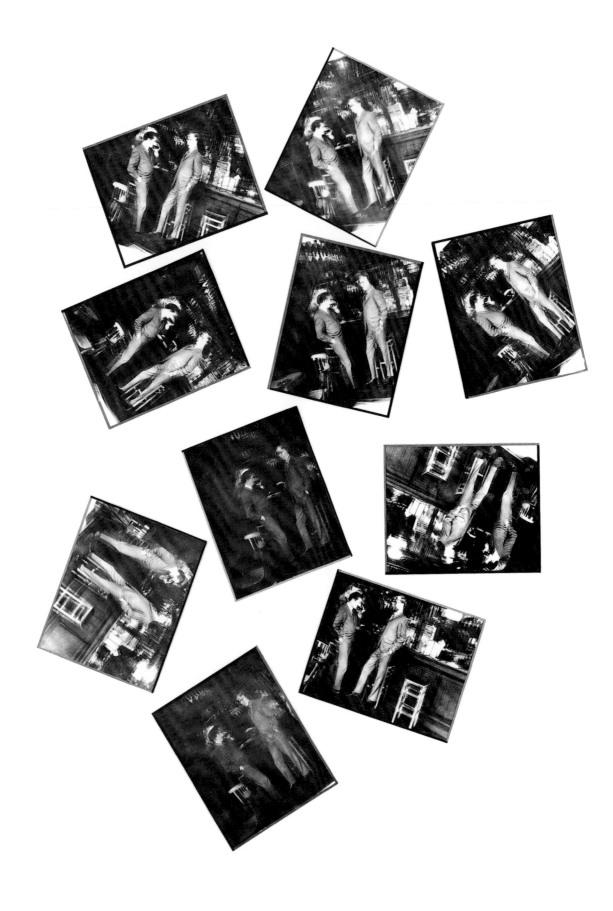

SMASHED (1972)
Ten black-and-white photographs. Overall, 75 x 52 in. (190.5 x 132.1 cm).
Collection Ileana Sonnabend, New York.

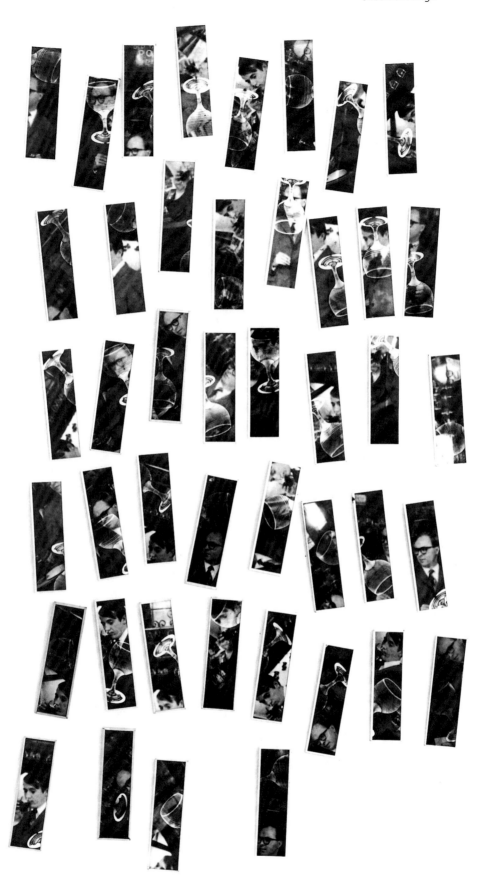

RAINING GIN (1973)
Forty-four black-and-white photographs. Overall, 78 x 45 in. (198.1 x 114.3 cm).
Courtesy Sonnabend Gallery, New York.

DAN GRAHAM

(b. 31 March 1942, Urbana, Illinois; lives in New York City) From his earliest magazine pieces to his recent architectural Pavilion/Sculptures, Dan Graham has continuously initiated aesthetic strategies for overcoming the barrier between the viewing subject and the object viewed. In his radical re-evaluation of sculpture, he has sought to eliminate the traditional separations between work, spectator, and environment.

Bridging the gap between the concerns attributed solely to sculpture and those attributed to other media, Graham has channelled his ideas about sculpture through his engagement with other disciplines, including performance, film, video, and architecture. His early performances explored methods for encompassing the audience within the temporal and thematic content of the work itself. To similar ends, the films he produced between 1969 and 1974 self-referentially foreground the actual filming process and the immediate viewing process as the crucial aspect of the work's own subject matter. Furthermore, because of its ability to collapse spatial and temporal boundaries, video has also served Graham in a range of provocative endeavors. In recent years, he has focused his attention on outdoor Pavilion/Sculptures, various structures made of transparent, reflective, and mirrored glass.

As early as the mid-1960s, Graham sought to challenge the art object's claim to autonomy, noting that works of art depend as much on an economic support system as they do on physical walls. Having directed an art gallery from 1964 to 1965, Graham early on experienced the economic contingencies that circumscribed the idealized space of the "white cube."[1] As he has written, "after the gallery failed I began experimenting myself with art works which could be read as a reaction against the gallery experience, but also as a response to contradictions I discerned in gallery artists."[2] His magazine pieces, which he pursued until 1969, are crucial in this regard. Each of these works, in one way or another, was motivated by his wish to question the indomitable commodification of works of art. Having come to the idea of using publications as an exhibition forum, Graham placed his first works in magazines rather than in museums or galleries. Taking form both in and on the page, each of these works is bound to and in its place of display. Neither unique nor saleable as isolated objects, they depend on the immediacy of a magazine's circulation rather than on the traditional concept of art's timelessness.

The works in this exhibition suggest the various ways in which the magazine pieces function in direct, self-referential relationship to their given page (SCHEMA, 1966), in relation to advertising (FIGURATIVE, 1965), as an advertisement as well as a work (DETUMESCENCE, 1966), as a formal grid based on research by the artist (SIDE EFFECT/COMMON DRUG, 1966–67), or as a photo-essay (HOMES FOR AMERICA, 1966–67). The process of buying and selling is literally averted in the "handling" of these works by virtue of their placement in magazines. At the same time, works such as DETUMESCENCE and HOMES FOR AMERICA address the commercial underpinnings of the social system with respect to the social psyche more generally. If the former draws attention to a lacuna resulting from society's tendency to romanticize, the latter points to the way in which language colors what is seen. Graham's work thereby alludes to realities that may easily and otherwise be overlooked. — AR

Notes

1. See Brian O'Doherty, *Inside the White Cube: The Ideology of the Gallery Space* (San Francisco: Lapis Press, 1986).

2. See Dan Graham, "My Works for Magazine Pages: 'A History of Conceptual Art,'" in *Dan Graham*, exh. cat. (Perth: The Art Gallery of Western Australia, 1985), 8.

```
A   02.53
A   02.34
A   00.98
A   01.42
A   00.65
A   00.80
A   00.27
A   00.39
A   00.53
A   00.53
A   00.41
A   00.49
A   00.25
A   00.49
A   00.43
A   00.59
A   00.26
A   00.25
A   00.65
A   01.18
A   00.42
A   00.69
A   00.48
A   00.39
A   00.29
A   00.29
A   00.35
A   00.34
A   00.24
A   00.39
A   00.47
A   00.79
A   00.47
A   00.29
A   00.40
A   00.33
A   00.83
A   01.25
A   01.03
A   00.11
A   00.41
A   00.20
A   00.44
A   00.02
```

Scheme for Magazine Page 'Advertisment' — 1965

Dan Graham

FIGURATIVE (1965)
Cash register receipt and variant published in *Harper's Bazaar,* March 1965, 90.
Herbert Collection, Ghent, Belgium.

Homes for America

D. GRAHAM

Belleplain
Brooklawn
Colonia
Colonia Manor
Fair Haven
Fair Lawn
Greenfields Village
Green Village
Plainsboro
Pleasant Grove
Pleasant Plains
Sunset Hill Garden

Garden City
Garden City Park
Greenlawn
Island Park
Levitown
Middleville
New City Park
Pine Lawn
Plainview
Plandome Manor
Pleasantside
Pleasantville

Large-scale 'tract' housing 'developments' constitute the new city. They are located everywhere. They are not particularly bound to existing communities; they fail to develop either regional characteristics or separate identity. These 'projects' date from the end of World War II when in southern California speculators or 'operative' builders adapted mass production techniques to quickly build many houses for the defense workers over-concentrated there. This 'California Method' consisted simply of determining in advance the exact amount and lengths of pieces of lumber and multiplying them by the number of standardized houses to be built. A cutting yard was set up near the site of the project to saw rough lumber into those sizes. By mass buying, greater use of machines and factory produced parts, assembly line standardization, multiple units were easily fabricated.

"The Serenade" - Cape Coral unit, Fla.

Each house in a development is a lightly constructed 'shell' although this fact is often concealed by fake (half-stone) brick walls. Shells can be added or subtracted easily. The standard unit is a box or a series of boxes, sometimes contemptuously called 'pillboxes.' When the box has a sharply oblique roof it is called a Cape Cod. When it is longer than wide it is a 'ranch.' A

Two Entrance Doorways, 'Two Home Homes', Jersey City, N.J.

two-story house is usually called 'colonial.' If it consists of contiguous boxes with one slightly higher elevation it is a 'split level.' Such stylistic differentiation is advantageous to the basic structure (with the possible exception of the split level whose plan simplifies construction on discontinuous ground levels).

There is a recent trend toward 'two home homes' which are two boxes split by adjoining walls and having separate entrances. The left and right hand units are mirror reproductions of each other. Often sold as private units are strings of apartment-like, quasi-discrete cells formed by subdividing laterally an extended rectangular parallelopiped into as many as ten or twelve separate dwellings.

Developers usually build large groups of individual homes sharing similar floor plans and whose overall grouping possesses a discrete flow plan. Regional shopping centers and industrial parks are sometimes integrated as well into the general scheme. Each development is sectioned into blocked-out areas containing a series of identical or sequentially related types of houses all of which have uniform or staggered set-backs and land plots.

Set-back, Jersey City, New Jersey

The logic relating each sectioned part to the entire plan follows a systematic plan. A development contains a limited, set number of house models. For instance, Cape Coral, a Florida project, advertises eight different models:

A The Sonata
B The Concerto
C The Overture
D The Ballet
E The Prelude
F The Serenade
G The Noctune
H The Rhapsody

Center Court, Entrances, Development, Jersey City, N.J.

In addition, there is a choice of eight exterior colors:
1 White
2 Moonstone Grey
3 Nickle

LAWN GREEN

4 Seafoam Green
5 Lawn Green
6 Bamboo
7 Coral Pink
8 Colonial Red

As the color series usually varies independently of the model series, a block of eight houses utilizing four models and four colors might have forty-eight times forty-eight or 2,304 possible arrangements.

Dan Graham

Housing Development, rear view, Bayonne, New Jersey

Housing Development, front view, Bayonne, New Jersey

Interior of Model Home, Staten Island, N.Y.

Each block of houses is a self-contained sequence — there is no development — selected from the possible acceptable arrangements. As an example, if a section was to contain eight houses of which four model types were to be used, any of these permutational possibilities could be used:

Bedroom of Model Home, S.I., N.Y.

AABBCCDD	ABCDABCD
AABBDDCC	ABDCABDC
AACCBBDD	ACBDACBD
AACCDDBB	ACDBACDB
AADDCCBB	ADBCADBC
AADDBBCC	ADCBADCB
BBAADDCC	BACDBACD
BBCCAADD	BCADBCAD
BBCCDDAA	BCDABCDA
BBDDAACC	BDACBDAC
BBDDCCAA	BDCABDCA
CCAABBDD	CABDCABD
CCAADDBB	CADBCADB
CCBBDDAA	CBADCBAD
CCBBAADD	CBDACBDA
CCDDAABB	CDABCDAB
CCDDBBAA	CDBACDBA
DDAABBCC	DACBDACB
DDAACCBB	DABCDABC
DDBBAACC	DBACDBAC
DDBBCCAA	DBCADBCA
DDCCAABB	DCABDCAB
DDCCBBAA	DCBADCBA

Basement Door, House, New Jersey

'Discount Store', Sweeten on Rocks, New Jersey

The 8 color variables were equally distributed among the house exteriors. The first buyers were more likely to have obtained their first choice in color. Family units had to make a choice based on the available colors which also took account of both husband and wife's likes and dislikes. Adult male and female color likes and dislikes were compared in a survey of the homeowners:

'Like'

Male	Female
Skyway	Skyway Blue
Colonial Red	Lawn Green
Patio White	Nickle
Yellow Chiffon	Colonial Red
Lawn Green	Yellow Chiffon
Nickle	Patio White
Fawn	Moonstone Grey
Moonstone Grey	Fawn

Two Family Units, Staten Island, N.Y.

'Dislike'

Male	Female
Lawn Green	Patio White
Colonial Red	Fawn
Patio White	Colonial Red
Moonstone Grey	Moonstone Grey
Fawn	Yellow Chiffon
Yellow Chiffon	Lawn Green
Nickle	Skyway blue
Skyway Blue	Nickle

Car Hop, Jersey City, N.J.

A given development might use, perhaps, *four* of these possibilities as an arbitrary scheme for different sectors; then select four from another scheme which utilizes the remaining four unused models and colors; then select four from another scheme which utilizes all eight models and eight colors; then four from another scheme which utilizes a single model and all eight colors (or four or two colors); and finally utilize that single scheme for one model and one color. This serial logic might follow consistently until, at the edges, it is abruptly terminated by pre-existent highways, bowling alleys, shopping plazas, car hops, discount houses, lumber yards or factories.

'Split-Level', 'Two Home Houses', Jersey City, N.J.

'Ground-Level', 'Two Home Houses', Jersey City, N.J.

Although there is perhaps some aesthetic precedence in the row houses which are indigenous to many older cities along the east coast, and built with uniform façades and set-backs early this century, housing developments as an architectural phenomenon seem peculiarly gratuitous. They exist apart from prior standards of 'good' architecture. They were not built to satisfy individual needs or tastes. The owner is completely tangential to the product's completion. His home isn't really possessable in the old sense; it wasn't designed to 'last for generations'; and outside of its immediate 'here and now' context it is useless, designed to be thrown away. Both architecture and craftsmanship as values are subverted by the dependence on simplified and easily duplicated techniques of fabrication and standardized modular plans. Contingencies such as mass production technology and land use economics make the final decisions, denying the architect his former 'unique' role. Developments stand in an altered relationship to their environment. Designed to fill in 'dead' land areas, the houses needn't adapt to or attempt to withstand Nature. There is no organic unity connecting the land site and the home. Both are without roots — separate parts in a larger, predetermined, synthetic order.

Kitchen Trays, 'Discount House', New Jersey

ARTS MAGAZINE/December 1966-January 1967

Dan Graham

127

HANS HAACKE

(b. 12 August 1936, Cologne; lives in New York City)

By means of texts and images, Hans Haacke seeks to penetrate the contemporary social environment and especially the various hidden systems that drive it. In many of his works, he juxtaposes textual and/or photographic information so as to display assembled facts and expose dissembled images that veil contradictions within society. Haacke approaches his work somewhat like a social scientist gathering empirical data.[1] Since 1969, when he began conducting polls of visitors to exhibitions, he has created works of art that depend on the acquisition of factual material and its presentation in a straightforward manner. Haacke's poll pieces, executed over a period of several years for museum and gallery exhibitions in which he was invited to participate, define an early interest in pinpointing certain kinds of information. During a one-person exhibition at the Howard Wise Gallery in New York in 1969, he tabulated the birthplaces and current residences of the visitors, having asked them to put red and blue pins, respectively, on maps of Manhattan and the five boroughs of New York City.[2] The resulting accumulation of demographic data determined the form of the piece, which foregrounds its viewers' "backgrounds" within its own framework.

For a slightly later work of 1971, Haacke applied this fact-finding approach to an inquiry into the politically-charged relationships among individuals, geographical location, and housing. SHAPOLSKY ET AL. MANHATTAN REAL ESTATE HOLDINGS, A REAL-TIME SOCIAL SYSTEM, AS OF MAY 1, 1971 (1971) comprises two enlarged maps (showing the Lower East Side and Harlem), in addition to 142 black-and-white photographs of building facades or empty lots, framed above typed data sheets. The accompanying typed pages give the address of the property concerned, its block and lot number, size, and building code, as well as the corporation or individual holding title, with address and names of officers, date of acquisition, prior owner, mortgage, and assessed tax value—information found in public records. Also included are six charts of business transactions connected with the ownership of the buildings. The work is an exhaustive, sweeping survey of one family's real-estate holdings in lower-income neighborhoods of New York City. It brings the particulars of a situation together under one roof that, until systematically compiled, would otherwise have remained hidden and disregarded. Thus laid out on the wall and framed as an aggregate of separate but connected units, the piece as a whole opens the door to speculation, not on the value of real estate, but on the "real" value, in broader terms, of extremely lim-

ited private ownership. Facts, made visually concrete by Haacke's method of analysis, contribute to a greater understanding of the factors at work in the economic and social sphere.

The slightly later works, MANET-PROJEKT '74 (1974) and SEURAT'S "LES POSEUSES" (SMALL VERSION), 1888-1975 (1975), are about the commodification of works of art. The subject of MANET-PROJEKT '74 is a painting by Manet entitled BUNCH OF ASPARAGUS (1880), now in the Ludwig Museum in Cologne; LES POSEUSES (SMALL VERSION) by Seurat was recently bequeathed to the Philadelphia Museum of Art. Both pieces by Haacke document the provenance of the paintings in question and provide detailed biographical information on their owners, displayed within individually-framed panels. Haacke thus ties in each painting's history with the lives of its successive owners—nine, besides Manet, in the case of the former and thirteen in the latter—who have shared in the determination of its fate. The recorded events pertaining to the history of the paintings, inextricably linked with the lives and social affiliations of their possessors, express to what extent external conditions control their separate destinies. In these two works, Haacke poignantly emphasizes that the intrinsic qualities of the paintings have no real bearing on, or control of, their commodity status and their value as personal property. He makes clear that the autonomy of the artwork, paradoxically, leads to its subjugation by economic and social forces. As he affirmed in an interview, "the social forces that have an effect on the art world naturally are the same forces that affect everything else in the country, and in the world. The art world is not an isolated entity."[3] Through his work, Haacke seeks to make "direct reference to these 'outside' determinants."[4] He thereby alludes to the interconnections between art and society and the interactions between institutions of power, including those devoted to art. — AR

Notes

1. For a discussion of this aspect of Haacke's work, see Howard S. Becker and John Walton, "Social Science and the Work of Hans Haacke," in *Hans Haacke: Framing and Being Framed: 7 Works 1970-75* (Halifax: The Press of the Nova Scotia College of Art and Design and New York: New York University Press, 1975), 145-153.

2. See "Catalogue of Works: 1969-1986," in *Hans Haacke: Unfinished Business*, ed. Brian Wallis, exh. cat. (New York: The New Museum of Contemporary Art and Cambridge: The MIT Press, 1986) for complete information on this and the following works discussed.

3. Hans Haacke, "Interview by Robin White," *View* (Oakland, California) 1, no. 6 (November 1978): 12.

4. Ibid.

SHAPOLSKY ET AL. MANHATTAN REAL ESTATE HOLDINGS, A REAL-TIME SOCIAL SYSTEM, AS OF MAY 1, 1971, (1971)
Two maps, 142 black-and-white photographs with typewritten data sheets framed in 23 sets of 6 per frame and 1 set of 4 per frame, 6 charts, and explanatory panel (ed. 2). Maps: each, 24 x 20 in. (61.0 x 50.8 cm); photographs and data sheets: each, 20 x 7 1/2 in. (50.8 x 19.1 cm) (framed sets, 23 at 21 x 43 1/2 [53.3 x 110.5 cm] and 1 at 21 1/2 x 30 in. [54.6 x 76.2 cm]; charts: each, 24 x 20 in. (61.0 x 25.4 cm); panel, 24 x 20 in. (61.0 x 50.8 cm). Collection the artist. Installation view, Venice Biennale, 1978. Photo courtesy the artist and John Weber Gallery, New York.

St., NYC
President('63)
resident('64)
to Real Estate

t Foundation,
NYC,

9-1963, due
ssionaries
onvention,
r bldgs.)

75 000.- (includ-

214 E 3 St.
Block 385   lot 11
5 story walk-up old law tenement

Owned by Harpmel Realty Inc., 608 E 11 St., NYC
Contracts signed by Harry J. Shapolsky, President('63
                     Martin Shapolsky, President('64)
Principal Harry J. Shapolsky(according to Real Estate
Directory of Manhattan)

Acquired 8-21-1963 from John the Baptist Foundation,
c/o The Bank of New York, 48 Wall St., NYC,
for $237 600.- (also 7 other bldgs.)

$150 000.- mortgage at 6% interest, 8-19-1963, due
8-19-1968, held by The Ministers and Missionaries
Benefit Board of the American Baptist Convention,
475 Riverside Drive, NYC (also on 7 other bldgs.)

Assessed land value $25 000.- , total $75 000.- (incl
ing 212 and 216 E 3 St.) (1971)

SHAPOLSKY ET AL. MANHATTAN REAL ESTATE HOLDINGS, A REAL-TIME SOCIAL SYSTEM, AS OF
MAY 1, 1971, (1971)
Detail of photographs with typewritten data sheets.

E 3 St.
ck 385 Lot 11
tory walk-up old law tenement

ed by Harpmel Realty Inc., 608 E 11 St., NYC
tracts signed by Harry J. Shapolsky, President('63)
                    Martin Shapolsky, President('64)

ncipal Harry J. Shapolsky(according to Real Estate
ectory of Manhattan)

uired 8-21-1963 from John the Baptist Foundation,
   The Bank of New York, 48 Wall St., NYC
 $237 600.-(also 7 other bldgs.)

0 000.- mortgage at 6% interest, 8-19-1963, due
9-1968, held by The Ministers and Missionaries
efit Board of the American Baptist Convention,
   Riverside Drive, NYC (also on 7 other bldgs.)

essed land value $25 000.-, total $75 000.- (includ-
 212-14 E 3 St.) (1971)

228 E 3 St.
Block 385 Lot 19
24 x 105' 5 story walk-up old law tenement

Owned by Harpmel Realty Inc.   608 E 11 St.   NYC
Contracts signed by Harry J. Shapolsky, President('63)
                    Martin Shapolsky, President('64)

Acquired from John The Baptist Foundation
c/o The Bank of New York, 48 Wall St. NYC
for $237 000.- (also 5 other properties) , 8-21-1963

$150 000.- mortgage (also on 5 other properties) at 6%
interest as of 8-19-1963 due 8-19-1968
held by The Ministers and Missionaries Benefit Board of
The American Baptist Convention, 475 Riverside Dr. NYC

Assessed land value $8 000.- total $28 000.-(1971)

292 E 3 St.
Block 372 1
22 x 105' 5

Owned by Br
Contracts s:

Principal H:
Directory o

Acquired 10-
475 Riversi

$55 000.- m
The Ministe
American Ba
(also on 31

Assessed la

DOUGLAS HUEBLER

(b. 27 October 1924, Ann Arbor, Michigan; lives in Truro, Massachusetts)

From his historically important one-person exhibition in November 1968 organized by Seth Siegelaub, until the end of the 1970s, when he again shifted his manner of working, Douglas Huebler has used language and photography in conjunction. His numerous "Location," "Duration," and "Variable" works, realized over the period of a decade, rely on the complimentary systems of photographic representation and linguistic statement. Photographs with, or in lieu of, other forms of documentation accompany the artist's signed, typewritten statements that structure the work as a whole. Huebler includes multiple photographs to illustrate the information conveyed in the text, and thereby presents an alternative to the singularly enframed painted or photographic image. In his work, the ensemble of photographs supplement language; each photograph alone presents just one of a myriad possible points of reference to the real world, as opposed to presenting a single, aesthetically chosen view. Snapshots document what the statements recapitulate as the artist's scheme for mapping the parameters of the work. In tandem with his use of photography as a "duplicating device," as he has termed it, Huebler's written statements serve as a straightforward notation of procedures that exempt the artist from imbuing his art with personal markings or hierarchical compositional form. Functioning as co-dependent representational systems, language and photography steer the viewer toward possibilities for seeing disparate and otherwise unperceivable facets of reality from more than one angle at once. Furthermore, they eradicate the distinction between a consolidated object and the space that surrounds it—a result not achievable through traditional approaches to sculpture.

The November 1968 exhibition was both a starting and a turning point in Huebler's career. Unlike the sculptures he presented in "Primary Structures: Younger American and British Sculptors," presented in 1966 at The Jewish Museum in New York, his works in the Siegelaub exhibition did not assume three-dimensional form.

So-called Drawings, begun in 1968, pointedly address the power of language to dictate the nature of perception. The texts for the twenty-five drawings published in the XEROXBOOK (an exhibition in catalogue form only organized/published by Seth Siegelaub and John W. Wendler in December 1968), for example, serve as a caption or subtitle to describe the point/points—or line/lines, as the case may be—shown above them. The first and second drawings self-reflectively state what they represent: "An 8 1/2" x 11" Sheet of Paper"; "A Point Located in the Exact Center of an 8 1/2" x 11" Xerox Paper." Ensuing wordings are more provocative, such as: "A and B Represent Points Located 1,000,000,000 Miles Behind the Picture Plane." The Drawings engage viewers in skeptical thought by means of statements that tell them what they are seeing, whether it be empirically verifiable or not. They, therefore, demand the reconsideration "of the experience of any phenomenon after it has been processed by language."[1]

The typed and signed statements in Huebler's VARIABLE PIECE #101, WEST GERMANY (1973) exemplify the way in which language serves to bind together the images comprising his photographic works. Ten different facial expressions of the artist Bernd Becher have been arbitrarily matched with ten words that denote ten professions or social types. The accompanying statement explains the procedure Huebler followed for engendering the work, while the piece as a whole concerns the manner in which language accords meaning to visual fact. The work, in this case, demonstrates language's ability to dominate phenomena and to foster stereotypical thought. "I'm speaking against the irresponsibility of language," Huebler has said of his primary interest "in freeing nature from the imposition of language, mythology and literature."[2] — AR

Notes

1. Conversation with the author, June 1994.

2. Michael Auping, "Talking with Douglas Huebler," LAICA Journal (Los Angeles), no. 15 (July-August 1977): 38.

132

UNTITLED (1969)
Courtesy the artist, Collection Gian Enzo Sperone, Turin.

THIS SURFACE CONSTITUTES A DRAWING THAT WILL BE COMPLETED AFTER ITS PERCIPIENT HAS:
LOOKED AT IT
BREATHED TOWARD IT
READ THESE WORDS
FORGOTTEN THEM.

Variable Piece #101
West Germany

On December 17, 1972 a photograph was made of Bernd Becher at the instant almost exactly after he had been made to "look like" a priest, a criminal, a lover, an old man, a policeman, an artist, "Bernd Becher," a philosopher, a spy and a nice guy ... in that order.

To make it almost impossible for Becher to remember his own "faces" more than two months were allowed to pass before prints of the photographs were sent to him; the photographs were numbered differently from the original sequence and Becher was asked to make the "correct" associations with the given verbal terms.

His choices were:

1 Bernd Becher	6 Policeman
2 Nice Guy	7 Priest
3 Spy	8 Philosopher
4 Old Man	9 Criminal
5 Artist	10 Lover

Ten photographs and this statement join together to constitute the final form of this piece.

March, 1973

VARIABLE PIECE #101, WEST GERMANY (1973)
Ten black-and-white photographs and statement. Each photograph, 6 1/2 x 4 1/2 in.
(16.5 x 11.4 cm); statement, 11 x 8 1/2 in. (27.9 x 21.6 cm); overall, 32 x 38 in.
(81.3 x 96.5 cm). Collection the artist.

JOAN JONAS

(b. 13 July 1936, New York City; lives in New York City)

Since the late 1960s, Joan Jonas has explored the psychology of perception through works that include performance, film, video, and sound—often in combination. Jonas did not come to performance as a dancer or as a student of dance, but from a background in art history and sculpture. Influenced by the dance performances at the Judson Church in New York in the mid-1960s, she later studied dance with Trisha Brown, Deborah Hay, Steve Paxton, and Yvonne Rainer. By 1968 Jonas had begun to use performance in her work to engage directly in the construction and perception of illusional space:

While I was studying art history I looked carefully at the space of painting, films, and sculpture—how illusions are created within a framed space, and how to deal with a real physical space with depth and distance. When I switched from sculpture to performance I just went to a space and looked at it. I would imagine how it would look to an audience, what they would be looking at, how they would perceive the ambiguities and illusions of the space.... I also began with a prop such as a mirror, a cone, a TV, a story. [1]

With her MIRROR PIECES of 1968-71, Jonas began to use mirrors in her performances. Reflecting and fragmenting the bodies of the

performers who carried them, as well as the bodies of the specta-tors in the audience, these works broke down the conventional dis-tinctions between illusion and reflection, spectator and performer, activity and passivity, and looking and being looked at. Bruce Ferguson has described the effect of these works on the viewer:

> As a symptom of the excessive space hidden by the
> 'truth' of structuralism's either/or, Joan Jonas' mirror
> is the postmodern paradigm's paradigm; a simple, con-
> founding mode of dramatic skepticism which utterly dis-
> places, excavates and disconjuncts the passivity that
> presides over the modernist gaze which sees for a muse-
> ological, judicial and theological eye. [2]

In addition, Douglas Crimp has likened Jonas's use of mirrors to Velazquez's LAS MENINAS:

> [T]he audience, seeing itself reflected in the performance
> space, became an image of participation without actually
> moving from its privileged position. This subject/object
> dichotomy is one of the many metaphors Jonas has
> achieved through the manipulation of spatial perception.
> Velazquez's Las Meninas—the masterpiece of the mirror
> as metaphor for the complexities of spatial illusionism—is
> invoked and restated in terms of literal space. [3]

Jonas powerfully turned the mirror toward her own body in the performance MIRROR CHECK (1970). Standing naked before an audience, she held a round mirror in her hand and examined her body in circular motions moving down from her face. She held the mirror so as to obscure the reflected image from the audience, whose members sat approximately twenty feet from her and were thus able to see only her self-inspection, not what she herself saw. In this work, Jonas self-consciously worked within and against the conventional distinctions between the viewer and the viewed. As Howard Junker observed, "[s]he was both the model in a life class—a typical female role—and the artist preparing for a self-por-trait. She was Narcissus, the emblem of the '70s, using a speculum in the political act of self-examination." [4]

The mirror was ultimately joined with the closed-circuit and taped video image as the key elements of Jonas's work. As she has written,

> My own thinking and production has focused on issues
> of space—ways of dislocating it, attenuating it, flatten-
> ing it, turning it inside out, always attempting to
> explore it without ever giving to myself or to others the
> permission to penetrate it. I have returned again and
> again to a specific set of formal/material metaphors
> with which to shape this space. The two most important
> of these are the mirror—with its capacity to interrupt
> and therefore to fragment deep space and its property
> of disorientation through left-right reversal—and the
> transmission of signals through a dislocating medium,
> such as very deep landscape that creates delays and
> relays of the signal, or the video feedback, which both
> dislocates and fragments the signal. [5]

In her early works using video, Jonas further explored this interest in dislocation and fragmentation by making the view-er aware of the processes that maintain and challenge the integri-ty of the video image. In VERTICAL ROLL (1972) she used that con-dition of a television image out of register and in perpetual motion to construct a videotape that incorporates and plays with the altered image. Like her work with mirrors, she attempted to recon-cile the fractured image through her activities (clapping, jumping, marching) into a coherent and credible rhythm of sound and image. Writing on VERTICAL ROLL, Rosalind Krauss has observed:

> [T]he grammar of the camera is eroded by the dislocat-
> ing grip of the roll....[T]he illusion this creates is one of
> a continuous dissolve through time and space. The
> monitor, as an instrument, seems to be winding into
> itself a ribbon of experience, like a fishing line being
> taken up upon a reel, or like magnetic tape being
> wound upon a spool. The motion of continuous dissolve
> becomes, then, a metaphor for the physical reality not
> only of the scan-lines of the video raster, but of the phys-
> ical reality of the tape deck, whose reels objectify a finite
> amount of time. [6]

Continuing to explore narcissism and voyeurism, Jonas developed the persona of "Organic Honey." In ORGANIC HONEY'S VISUAL TELEPATHY and ORGANIC HONEY'S VERTICAL ROLL (both 1972), she first used live performers, projected film and videotapes, closed-cir-cuit video images, sound, drawings, props, and costumes. These works use props as archetypal symbols employed by Organic Honey to explore the construction and transformation of her identity and image. They also incorporate closed-circuit live feeds, as well as videotapes of earlier works such as MIRROR CHECK and VERTICAL ROLL and Richard Serra's videotape ANXIOUS AUTOMATION (1972). In addition, Jonas produced drawings during the performances while looking into a monitor, rather than at the sheet of paper. She has described the impetus of her video performance work:

> ORGANIC HONEY'S VISUAL TELEPATHY evolved as I found
> myself continually investigating my own image in the
> monitor of my video machine. I then bought a mask of a
> doll's face, which transformed me into an erotic seduc-
> tress. I named this TV persona Organic Honey. I became
> increasingly obsessed with following the process of my
> own theatricality, as my images fluctuated between the
> narcissistic and a more abstract representation. The risk
> was to become too submerged in solipsistic gestures. In
> exploring the possibilities of female imagery, thinking
> always of a magic show, I attempted to fashion a dia-
> logue between my different disguises and the fantasies
> they suggested. [7] – AG

Notes

1. Joan Jonas, "Closing Statement," in *Joan Jonas: Scripts and Descriptions, 1968-1982*, ed. Douglas Crimp (Berkeley: University Art Museum and Eindhoven: Stedelijk Van Abbemuseum, 1983), 137.

2. Bruce Ferguson, "AmerefierycontemplationonthesagaofJoanJonas," in *Joan Jonas: Works 1968-1994*, exh. cat. (Amsterdam: Stedelijk Museum, 1994), 17.

3. Douglas Crimp, "Joan Jonas's Performance Works," *Studio International* (London) 192, no. 982 (July-August 1976): 10.

4. Howard Junker, "Joan Jonas: The Mirror Staged," *Art in America* 69, no. 2 (February 1981): 90.

5. Joan Jonas (with Rosalind E. Krauss), "Seven Years," *The Drama Review* (New York) 19, no. 1 (March 1975): 13.

6. Rosalind E. Krauss, "Video: The Aesthetics of Narcissism," *October*, no. 1 (Spring 1976): 61.

7. Jonas, "Closing Statement," 137.

MIRROR CHECK (1970)
This performance presented as part of ORGANIC HONEY'S VISUAL TELEPATHY,
Ace Gallery, Los Angeles, 1972. Photo Roberta Neiman.

ORGANIC HONEY'S VISUAL TELEPATHY (1972)
This performance presented at Lo Guidice Gallery, New York, 1972. Performed by
Suzanne Harris, Joan Jonas, Kate Parker, and Linda Patton. Photo Peter Moore.

Joan Jonas

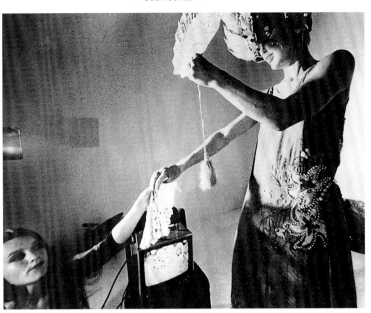

ORGANIC HONEY'S VISUAL TELEPATHY (1972)
This performance presented at Ace Gallery, Los Angeles, 1972. Photo Larry Bell.

ORGANIC HONEY'S VERTICAL ROLL (1972)
This performance presented at "Festival d'automne," Musée Galleria, Paris, 1973.
Performed by Joan Jonas; camera by Babette Mangolte; sound by Kurt Munkacsi.

STEPHEN J. KALTENBACH

(b. 5 May 1940, Battle
Creek, Michigan;
lives in Sacramento,
California)

In 1966-67, while he was studying at the University of California, Davis, Stephen J. Kaltenbach proposed a number of Room Constructions, one of which was exhibited at the Whitney Museum of American Art in New York in 1969. In the interest of paring down the elements of his work in Minimalist fashion—short of allowing the work to disappear—he built simple, enterable shapes. As he has remarked, the Room Constructions are "not living rooms...designed for human comfort," but specifically presented obstacles to those who entered them.[1] Significantly, Kaltenbach covered each confrontational shape with "a traditional interior finishing material so that it would become part of the room."[2] Early on, therefore, he sought to counter expectations about the formal qualities of an object and its function as a work of art.

In ensuing works from 1967 to 1970, when he was based in New York, Kaltenbach further attempted to deter viewers from worn-out paths of thinking. In these pieces, he sought to lend greater validity to works of art as social stimuli as opposed to objects of material value. Pieces such as the Time Capsules, Sidewalk Plaques, *Artforum* Ads, Graffiti, and SLANT STEP suggest the nature of Kaltenbach's aesthetic concerns and the great variety of his activity.

The Time Capsules (1967-69) were given by the artist to individuals in the art world, such as Barbara Rose and Bruce Nauman, and to institutions such as The Museum of Modern Art in New York. They are sealed until the date specified on the outside of the capsule, at which point the material inside (whether information and/or things) becomes known. The Capsules defy the traditional "handling" of art insofar as they are not meant to be commercially viable. Moreover, they invert the idea that art is "timeless." Once the work's literal contents are revealed, its thematic content (the act of concealment) is negated.

The bronze Sidewalk Plaques were conceived for placement in city pavements. They enabled Kaltenbach to remain anonymous and, tangentially, to make an object that was not a conventional commodity. Each plaque bears a different word in raised relief: "blood," "fire," "air," "bone," and "water." By positioning these single word elements in the street, Kaltenbach integrated his work with the quotidian reality of the city. The Sidewalk Plaques provided a new option for sculpture in that they were not designed to be shown on a pedestal within a museum or gallery

situation. Concluding, however, that they ultimately only "brought the museum out into the street and [that] they identified what was going on as an art work," Kaltenbach subsequently sought other methods for discarding conventions that determine the recognizability of art as such.[3]

His KISS (GRAFFITI STAMP: LIPS OF THE ARTIST) (1968) relates both to advertising and to the anonymity of the artist. Kaltenbach carried onto the New York subway a rubber stamp with an image he designed of lips. He stamped the image onto a ubiquitous poster for Fruit of the Loom stockings, placing it beside the brand name and on the thigh of the model pictured. In this way, he made his own mark without revealing that the image was his or, for that matter, any artist's.

The advertisements Kaltenbach placed in *Artforum* in 1968 and 1969 present another alternative to the installation of three-dimensional objects inside or outside the museum. The first advertisement, consisting of the phrase "Art Works," appeared in *Artforum* in November 1968. The second, which was published in the December issue, is a lozenge shape based upon the "blp," an oval shape that the artist Richard Artschwager constructed or spray-painted in various sites throughout the late 1960s—including museums and galleries, as well as the street—as a kind of graffito. Enigmatically inscribed with the name "Johnny Appleseed," this advertisement reflects Kaltenbach's interest in transforming the meaning of another artist's work through appropriation, recontextualization, and the addition of new information to it. The third advertisement, published in January 1969, is a photograph of a sculpture of the word "ART" wrapped as a package and repeatedly labelled "ART"; the fact that the work is wrapped conceals the identity of the work and of the word. Finally, the other

"ART WORKS" (1968)
From Sidewalk Plaque series. Cast bronze plaque to be set in concrete. 5 x 8 1/8 x 5/8 in. (12.7 x 20.6 x 1.6 cm). Collection the artist.

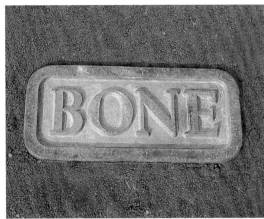

advertisments are succinct and sometimes suggestive statements such as "You Are Me" that offered a forum for a provocative incursion into the weightiness of critical dogma found in art magazines and for further challenging accepted "high" art notions as well. [4]

  Kaltenbach's work EXPOSE YOUR SELF was first realized for the exhibition "Between Man and Matter: Tokyo Biennale '70," presented at the Tokyo Metropolitan Art Gallery in May 1970. The piece consisted of the three words "Expose Your Self" stenciled onto the four walls of a room in seven different languages in a sequence chosen by the museum. Kaltenbach recreated the piece for "Information," presented at The Museum of Modern Art in the summer of 1970. He had intended to have the phrase stenciled in the same manner in public restrooms throughout the city of New York before the opening of the exhibition. However, the phrase was ultimately only stenciled in a restroom in the museum. Inside the museum, the work questioned assumptions about the nature of an artwork by slyly urging viewers to open their minds to what might appear as artless art. Outside the institutional context, it functioned purely as graffiti, as opposed to a work by an artist's hand. — AR

Notes

1. Stephen J. Kaltenbach, in Cindy Nemser, "An Interview with Stephen Kaltenbach," *Artforum* 9, no. 3 (November 1970): 48.

2. Ibid.

3. Ibid., 52.

4. They are: "Tell a lie," 7, no. 6 (February 1969): 71; "Start a rumor," 7, no. 7 (March 1969): 96; "Perpetrate a hoax," 7, no. 8 (April 1969): 80; "Build a reputation," 7, no. 9 (May 1969): 73; "Become a legend," 7, no. 10 (Summer 1969): 11; "Teach Art," 8, no. 1 (September 1969): 69; "Smoke," 8, no. 2 (October 1969): 79; "Trip.," 8, no. 3 (November 1969): 85; "You are me," 8, no. 4 (December 1969): 75.

"FLESH" (1968)
From Sidewalk Plaque series. Cast bronze plaque to be set in concrete. 4 x 10 1/2 x 1/4 in. (10.2 x 26.7 x 0.6 cm). Courtesy the artist and John Natsoulas Gallery, Davis, California.

"BONE" (1968)
From Sidewalk Plaque series. Cast bronze plaque to be set in concrete. 4 x 9 x 1/4 in. (10.2 x 22.9 x 0.6 cm). Courtesy the artist and John Natsoulas Gallery, Davis, California.

"ART" (1969)
From the *Artforum* Ads series. Offset on paper. Page size, 10 1/2 x 10 1/2 in.
(26.7 x 26.7 cm); image size, 5 3/8 x 10 1/2 in. (13.7 x 26.7 cm). Published in
Artforum 7, no. 5 (January 1969): 15.

142

Time capsule for Bruce Nauman (1968)
Stainless steel cylinder. Collection Bruce Nauman.

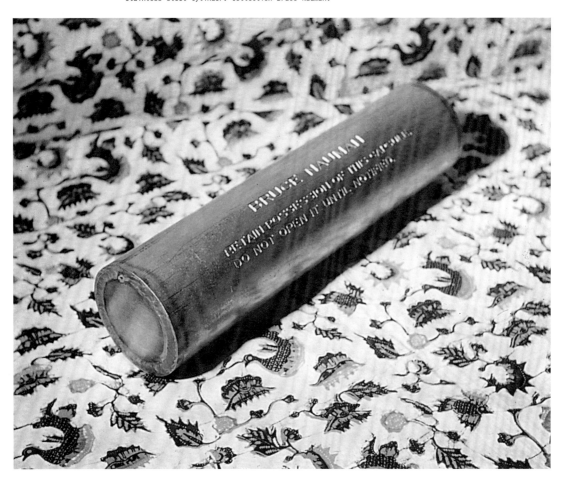

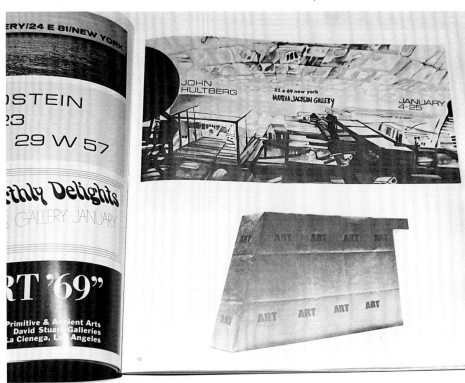

"ART WORKS" (1968)
From the *Artforum* Ads series. Offset on paper. Page size, 10 1/2 x 10 1/2 in.
(26.7 x 26.7 cm); image size, 2 1/4 x 4 3/8 in. (5.7 x 11.1 cm).
Published in *Artforum* 7, no. 3 (November 1968):72.

ON KAWARA

(15 October 1995: 22,940 days)

On Kawara's TITLE (1965), a three-panel, magenta painting, anticipates the well-known date paintings he began on 4 January 1966. Foreshadowing the date paintings, TITLE proclaims its own, physical presence as an abstract message concerning painting: an object ("one thing") whose creation is necessarily "located" in time ("1965") and "takes place" in history ("Vietnam"). Each date painting belongs to the TODAY series, which the artist considers a single, ongoing work that will be completed at the end of his lifetime. In contrast to the postcards, telegrams, and books that constitute another significant part of Kawara's oeuvre, the TODAY series takes the form of traditional painting by preserving the conventions of two-dimensionality and rectilinearity, but redefines it with respect to representational imagery.

Each of Kawara's paintings represents a single day—the one designated by the actual date on which the work was made. Letters, numerals, and punctuation marks, scaled to the size of the canvas, are placed laterally across its center. Although they give the impression of having been stenciled, the letters of the month, rendered in capitals and abbreviated when necessary, along with the numbers of the day and year are in fact skillfully drawn by hand in white upon a dark background. The subjectively-chosen typeface subtly varies among the paintings and is not determined by an objectively definable rationale or system. The backgrounds of the earliest works in the series are cerulean blue or red; later ones tend to gravitate toward dark grey-browns, grey-greens, or blues that verge on, but are never, black. Kawara applies four or five layers of paint to the background of each canvas and uses an additional six or seven layers of paint for the date. He obtains a rich matte surface but effaces all traces of brushwork. Always horizontal in format, the TODAY paintings may be one of eight predetermined sizes. Aside from the fact that a work must be started and completed on the actual day of its date, the artist does not impose a preconceived system of production. When they are small, as many as three paintings may be created in a day; on other days none may be painted.

The significance of these paintings lies in the fact that they depict not only a date, but also their *own* date. If, historically, paintings have been fixed in time by a date on the front or back of the canvas, the date itself for Kawara becomes the subject of the painting and the sole embodiment of the work's figurative imagery. Letters and numbers, which may be perceived as independent objects, allow an otherwise immaterial date to assume material form. The date paintings succeed in turning abstract, temporal measurement into the concrete reality of painting, since numbers and letters function as forms and symbols simultaneously. By virtue of existing as a date represented by means of language, each painting asserts that *it* is "present," although its date, perforce, refers to a time already past.

CODE (1965) achieves the same literal and factual quality as the date paintings. The text of a narrative (in this case, love stories) is translated into horizontal lines comprised of interconnected, colored markings, which resemble a kind of generic script, onto sheets of writing paper. The question as to what constitutes meaning—the verbal or the visual—underlies these drawings, in which color symbols, signaling art, have been substituted for linguistic symbols, signaling language.

CODE implies that the verbal and the visual are mutually implicated in concealing and revealing each other. Similarly, in Kawara's Today series language, a socially-shared code for communication, mediates between abstract signification and the non-illusionistic, self-referential, and material presence of painting.

Kawara's art is not limited to paintings and drawings. His "I got up at" postcards (sent between 1968 and 1979), his "I am still alive" telegrams (sent intermittently since 1970), and the books ONE MILLION YEARS-PAST (1971) and ONE MILLION YEARS-FUTURE (1981), as well as series entitled I Read (1966-), I Met (1968-79), and I Went (1968-79), represent the immaterial passage of time in concrete, material terms. They position themselves—and by extension, the viewer—in relation to the artist's own, ultimately finite lifeline, insofar as this is invisibly inscribed against the background of spatial and temporal infinity. — AR

144

ONE MILLION YEARS—PAST (1971)
Ten volumes. Each approx. 12 x 9 x 3 in. (30 x 23.5 x 8 cm). Photo courtesy
The Getty Center for the History of Art and the Humanities, Santa Monica,
California.

CODE (1965)
Collection Keiji Usami. Photo Mamoru Takahashi.

TITLE (1965)
Liquitex on canvas. Three panels: two at 46 1/2 x 51 1/2 in. (118.1 x
130.8 cm); one at 51 1/2 x 63 in. (130.8 x 160.0 cm). Collection the artist.

JOHN KNIGHT

(b. 26 March 1945, Hollywood; lives in New York City)

John Knight has employed a plurality of representational means since the late 1960s to generate a dialogue between a work of art and its site. Soon after he completed his undergraduate studies at California State College, Los Angeles, he installed two works at the school's Fine Arts Gallery that employed an early manifestation of closed-circuit video. [1] The installations were shown in two phases during December 1969 and January 1970. During the first phase, Knight placed a video monitor in one corner of the room in order to display a different, adjacent corner of the same room. For the second phase, he presented on a monitor set in the center of the exhibition space an image in real time of the Home Economics classroom, which was located down the hall from the gallery.

Referring to these works as "Displacements" and "Replacements", with the aim of producing a number of variations, Knight was interested in video's capacity to register information relayed simultaneously from one location to another. In both of these works the image is a function of the work's site of display. In Knight's hands, video thus served to convey aspects of a work's otherwise unobservable context within its own representational purview.

If Knight's early video works united the object of art with its environment, ensuing works similarly resulted from his search for ways in which to connect the object with its surroundings. For example, ONE INCH TO A FOOT (1971), exhibited in 1973 at the Riko Mizuno Gallery in Los Angeles, integrates the verbal and graphic elements of the title's statement with the exhibition space: the words "one inch to a foot" (with obvious reference to the symbolic scale notations on architectural plans) are etched in one-inch high Helvetica letters on the glass plate of a floor-mounted, standard overhead projector and illuminate the wall onto which they are projected as one-foot high letters. In this work, Knight succeeded in fusing language, light, and architecture, since words literally articulate their spatial confines as both representational fact and abstract figuration. Just as the meaning of the phrase "one inch to a foot" coincides with the reality of the letter sizes etched on the glass projector plate and projected on the wall, the letters themselves may be experienced as elegantly designed objects set within the framing architecture in which the work is situated. ONE INCH TO A FOOT may be shifted from one exhibition space to another, but it is nonetheless always conjoined in signlike fashion with its place of presentation.

Whereas the video pieces linked the work of art to its architectural environment by means of an image viewed in the reality of the moment, language, as used in ONE INCH TO A FOOT, offered Knight another option from that of video because of its applicability to the combined production of meaning and "graphic" imagery, along with its incorporation of the principles of design in the fashioning of lettering. Having relied primarily on language during the first half of the 1970s, Knight subsequently investigated representational systems—including but not confined to language—in conjunction with art and non-art support systems. Founded on his initial interest in registering the work's site of display, Knight's aesthetic concerns led him to a questioning of the dividing line between high and low art. In this regard, his work anticipated the burgeoning involvement with popular culture on the part of a following generation of artists. — AR

Notes

1. Other works did not materialize beyond the proposal stage because of the expense of renting equipment. In these years, video was still in its unwieldy infancy.

One of two closed-circuit video installations exhibited at the Fine Arts Gallery, California State College, Los Angeles, December 1969.

ONE INCH TO A FOOT (1971)
Installation view, "John Knight," Riko Mizuno Gallery, Los Angeles, 16 October–10 November 1973.

JOSEPH KOSUTH

(b. 31 January 1945, Toledo, Ohio; lives in New York City)

For Joseph Kosuth the signifying process itself is the subject and object of inquiry. "Being an artist now," the artist maintained in a discussion in 1969, "means to question the nature of art." [1] In order to clarify further the self-reflexive character of art's meaning system, Kosuth at this time underscored the representational potential for language that might function independently of a canvas. Like harbingers of the 1970s, Kosuth's early works thematically announce a radical break from categorized adherence to traditional concepts of medium.

In a broadcast interview in 1970, Kosuth stated that he first used language in 1965 in conjunction with a large sheet of glass leaning against the wall. [2] On an accompanying label the title stated ANY FIVE FOOT SHEET OF GLASS TO LEAN AGAINST ANY WALL. As a first, but major, step toward severing his work from traditional association with the painted canvas, Kosuth's use of "see-through" glass (normally used to protect an enframed, painted image) shifted representational responsibility from figurative or abstract imagery to language, at the same time as it eliminated the need for a canvas.

Subsequently, Kosuth merged the abstraction of words with the concrete objects they identified within the material confines of the work. That is, he melded the work and its label into an inextricable whole that left no doubt as to what was being shown. CLEAR SQUARE GLASS LEANING (1965) not only consists of what its title describes—four square sheets of glass propped on the floor against the wall—but the four words are lettered, one per sheet, directly on the glass. Additionally during this early period, Kosuth employed neon to create phrases that, like signs, reflect what they specify. "Five Words in Blue Neon," in effect, advertises what is literally on display in the work FIVE WORDS IN BLUE NEON (1965). Pieces such as this and others illuminate the way in which meaning may be produced independently from the auratic presence emanating from nonlinguistic objects whose materiality remains associated with and thematically attached to signs of personal touch, such as the brushstroke in the process of forming/composing a work.

The tripartite works of Kosuth, in which an everyday, useful object—such as a chair, broom, lamp, hammer, clock, etc.—along with a photograph and a photographic enlargement of an existing dictionary definition of the object prefigure his Art as Idea as Idea series (1966-68). The objects, like Marcel Duchamp's Readymades, are functional objects chosen by the artist for use within the context of art. They stand on their own, materially untransformed. Not part of a painted or traditional sculptural context, they are bracketed by their mechanically-reproduced image and by their linguistic definition. Having been extracted from the "real" world of use and re-placed to function within the work of art, the objects re-present themselves. Kosuth thereby represented the idea of representation per se through photographic and/or linguistic means. As the combination of three equal parts, a photograph, an object, and a text, these works are statements of fact, not simply about external reality, but about the means to register it.

Works subtitled Art as Idea as Idea are comprised of photographically enlarged definitions found in and extracted from dictionaries. In these works, language asserts itself as exactly that which it describes, and, without the inclusion of an actual object, allows for a range of abstract subject matter such, as "nothing," "normal," or "meaning," to present itself. On the most literal, superficial, and *surface* level, the typeface of the particular dictionary definition presents a concrete image: printed words arranged in rows. However, because of the capacity of language to be what it *is* and what it *is about* simultaneously, the meaning embodied in the definition succeeds in lending "depth" to the work without falling into any form of pictorial illusionism. As Kosuth has explained,

I felt I had found a way to make art without formal components being confused for an expressionist composition. The expression was in the idea, not the form—the forms were only a device in the service of the idea. [3]

Kosuth's appropriation of dictionary definitions bestowed a new autonomy on the use of language within the context of visual art through the substitution of linguistic definition for pictorial depiction. By means of the photostats Kosuth was able to free the work of art from its former dependence on painted imagery or on subject matter outside of the material reality of the work. The photostated definitions bring into relief, so to speak, the idea that art is about ideas, which, in turn, are about art and does not specifically pertain to emotive subject matter or technical skill and virtuosity.

Following upon the photostats of dictionary definitions belonging to THE FIRST INVESTIGATION, in which the art object has shed its formal, compositional attributes along with the signs of virtuosity, THE SECOND INVESTIGATION (1968-69), proposed a clash between art and non-art systems and contexts. In his noted essay of 1969, "Art after Philosophy," Kosuth maintained that "a work of art is a kind of *proposition* presented within the context of art as a comment on art." [4] It was this reasoning that permitted him in THE SECOND INVESTIGATION to go outside of the art context to locate his work in the world. As he wrote in 1974, such works initiated "an increased shift of focus from the 'unbelievable' object to what was believable and real: the context. Objects or

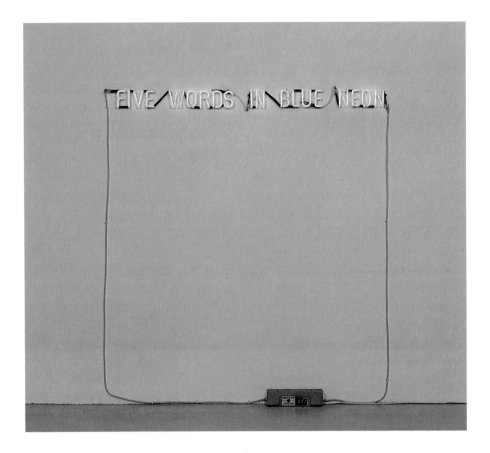

forms employed became more articulations of context than simply and dumbly objects of perception in themselves."[5] To realize THE SECOND INVESTIGATION, Kosuth anonymously published sections from the "Synopsis of Categories," found in Roget's Thesaurus, in the advertising spaces of public media from different countries, such as billboards, handbills, advertising, and newspapers. The "Synopsis of Categories" lays out hierarchies of linguistic taxonomy that have been absorbed into a published public context in which, categorically by themselves, their meaning is put in question. As part of an artwork, however, they hold their own within the artist's meaning system.

A few years later, Kosuth further expanded his aesthetic vocabulary. From the wealth of textual material to be found in and extracted from the dictionary, he turned his attention to the world of textual material at large and to a consideration of working with reading "material" shown in/as reading rooms. His later INVESTIGATIONS alter the ambience and expectations that envelop and fill exhibition spaces generally. — AR

Notes

1. Joseph Kosuth, in Arthur R. Rose [pseud.], "Four Interviews with Barry, Huebler, Kosuth, Weiner." *Arts Magazine* 43, no. 4 (February 1969): 23.

2. Joseph Kosuth, in Jeanne Siegel, "Art as Idea as Idea: An Interview with Jeanne Siegel," in *Art after Philosophy and After: Collected Writings, 1966-1990* (Cambridge: The MIT Press, 1991), 49.

3. Ibid., 50.

4. Joseph Kosuth, "Art after Philosophy," in *Art after Philosophy and After*, 19-20.

5. Joseph Kosuth, "(Notes) on an 'Anthropologized' Art," in *Art after Philosophy and After*, 99.

FIVE WORDS IN BLUE NEON (1965)
3 7/8 x 41 3/4 in. (10 x 106 cm). Blue neon tubing. Herbert Collection, Ghent.

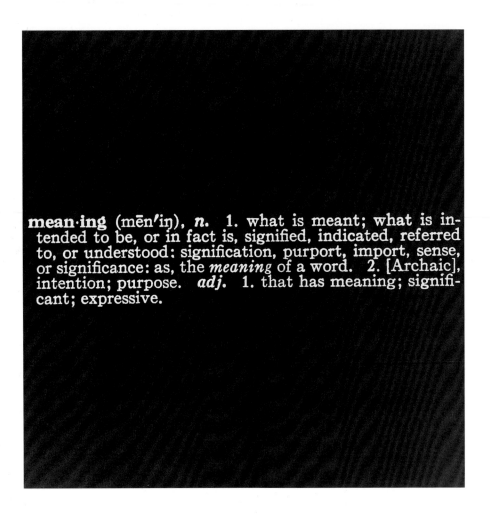

152

TITLED (ART AS IDEA AS IDEA) (1967)
Photostat on paper mounted on wood, 47 x 47 in. (119.4 x 119.4 cm). The Menil
Collection, Houston. Photo Hickey-Robertson, Houston.

THE SECOND INVESTIGATION (1968)
Advertisements placed in newspapers for the exhibition "When Attitudes Become
Form: Works — Concepts — Processes — Situations — Information: Live in Your
Head," Kunsthalle, Bern, 22 MArch-27 April 1969.

INFORMATION ROOM (THE THIRD INVESTIGATION) (1969)
For the exhibition "Conceptual Art and Conceptual Aspects," The New York
Cultural Center, New York, 10 April–25 August 1970. Photo Jay Cantor.

CHRISTINE KOZLOV

(b. 6 December 1945,
New York City; lives
in London)

In the mid-1960s, Christine Kozlov began to make information the basis and vehicle of her artistic production.

Her works subject standard forms of documentation and communication, such as films, audiotapes, photographs, texts, telegrams, and announcement cards, to the processes of compilation and analysis, comparison and cross-reference. Often working in response to a specific given or self-determined situation, Kozlov characteristically cross-references one set of information with another unlikely or seemingly incompatible one. Her projects question what can and cannot be quantified or proven, making self-referentiality and reflectivity central elements of her work.

Kozlov's early Sound Structures of 1965, shown in the exhibition "Non-Anthropomorphic Art by Four Young Artists: Joseph Kosuth, Christine Kozlov, Michael Rinaldi, Ernest Rossi" at the Lannis Gallery in New York in 1967, graphically represent the occurrence, location, and duration of different constant and/or overlapping sounds. Presenting photocopies of drawings, rather than the drawings themselves, Kozlov downplayed the hand-drawn qualities of the originals, as well as the importance of originality itself. These works are, as the artist wrote in her exhibition statement, "concerned with symmetry, asymmetry, progression, or with their own intrinsic development."[1]

Kozlov's NO TITLE (BLACK FILM #1) (1965), a film that documents black objects, is itself black and is shown as an object in its canister. Her later NO TITLE (TRANSPARENT FILM #2) (1967), comprising white film leader, is also shown in its canister. These works were thus conceived to document, represent, and constitute their subjects and material qualities as film, without being screened. Kozlov's work of the later 1960s includes quantifications or analyses of her daily activities. For example, 271 BLANK SHEETS OF PAPER CORRESPONDING TO 271 DAYS OF CONCEPTS REJECTED (1968), a work that is literally self-described, quantifies her activities through a standard form of writing; but rather than diaristically documenting her artistic progress, Kozlov represents the results of her activity with blank pages. Similarly, EATING PIECE (FIGURATIVE WORK #1) (1969) chronicles everything Kozlov ate each day from 20 February to 12 June 1969, and SELF-PORTRAITS (1968) is a series of daily photo booth self-portraits shown in a binder, each representing the artist front-side-side-front.

In 1966 Kozlov began NEUROLOGICAL COMPILATION (C. 1967), a set of binders that comprises a list she compiled of titles of articles on brain research. Although she intended to work back through the years from the inception of the project to her birth,

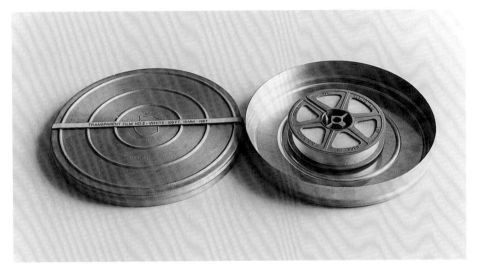

she ultimately concluded after ten years were represented; each volume is devoted to one year. The articles' titles—such as "Catecholamine containing neurons in the cockroach brain," "Fatty acid composition of normal mink tissues," or "Changes in brain norepinephrine after decapitation"—are, in effect, indexed to the artist's life.

The strategy of overlaying one system on another is also used in INFORMATION DRIFT (1968). In this work Kozlov combined radio broadcasts of news bulletins on the shootings of Andy Warhol and Robert Kennedy, which occurred just one day apart. The material is presented through description, rather than through the actual recordings. Later, in INFORMATION: NO THEORY (1970), a tape recorder with a continuous loop tape records the sounds audible in the exhibition space, only to erase them and record new sounds every two minutes. This work is described in Kozlov's four-point statement:

1. The recorder is equipped with a continuous loop tape.

2. The recorder will be set at record. All the sounds audible in the room will be recorded.

3. The nature of the loop tape necessitates that new information erases old information. The "life" of the information, that is, the time it takes for the information to go from "new" to "old" is the time it takes the tape to make one complete cycle.

4. Proof of the existence of the information does in fact not exist in actuality, but is based on probability.[2]

— AG

Notes

1. Christine Kozlov, in "Non-Anthropomorphic Art by Four Young Artists: Joseph Kosuth, Christine Kozlov, Michael Rinaldi, Ernest Rossi," exh. brochure (New York: Lannis Gallery, 1967), unpag.

2. Christine Kozlov, cited in Lucy R. Lippard, ed. *Six Years: The Dematerialization of the Art Object from 1966 to 1972* (New York: Praeger, 1973), 80.

NO TITLE (BLACK FILM #1) (1965)
Film in canister. Canister: 3 3/4 in. (9.5 cm) diam. Private collection. Photo Jay Cantor.

NO TITLE (TRANSPARENT FILM #2) (1967)
Leader tape in canister. Canister: 7 in. (17.8 cm) diam. Private collection. Photo Jay Cantor.

271 BLANK SHEETS OF PAPER CORRESPONDING
TO 271 DAYS OF CONCEPTS REJECTED.

FEBRUARY, 1968 – OCTOBER, 1968

271 SHEETS OF BLANK PAPER CORRESPONDING TO 271 DAYS OF CONCEPTS REJECTED (1968)
Sheets of blank paper with typewritten top sheet. 11 x 8 1/2 x 1 in.
(27.9 x 21.6 x 2.5 cm). Private collection. Photo Jay Cantor.

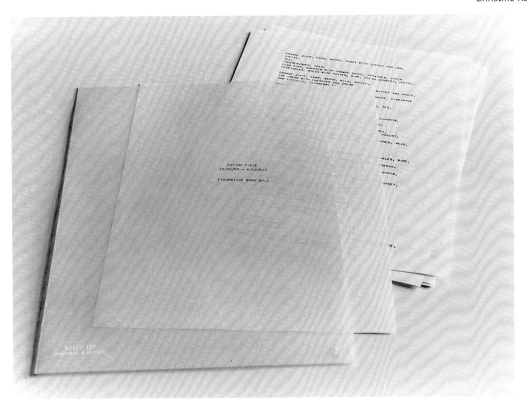

EATING PIECE (FIGURATIVE WORK #1) (1969)
Twelve typewritten sheets of paper. 11 x 8 1/2 in. (27.9 x 21.6 cm).
Collection Eric Fabre, Paris. Photo Jay Cantor.

A MOSTLY RED PAINTING

A MOSTLY PAINTING (RED) (1969)
Acrylic on canvas. 9 1/4 x 12 1/8 in. (23.5 x 30.6 cm).
Private collection. Photo Shirley O'Loughlin.

DAVID LAMELAS

(b. 12 December 1946, Buenos Aires; lives in New York City)

Born in Buenos Aires, David Lamelas moved to London in 1968 for post-graduate study at St. Martins School of Art, to Los Angeles in the mid-1970s, and then to New York, where he has lived since the late 1980s. The various locales in which he has lived and worked have significantly influenced his artistic production. As he has written, "it is important to think of my work in reference to a particular *time* and *place* in which the work has been produced; I work as a response to the conditions of life in which I function at a particular moment and location." [1]

On the evolution of Lamelas's early work in Argentina, Lynda Morris has written:

> A predominant interest was in the similarity of thought represented in disciplines as diverse as philosophy, psychology, literature and the visual arts. This interest provided an analytical background which approached the problems then presented by minimal art. Through the isolation of technical forms from any external content the work suggested a non-descriptive and non-physical art form. [2]

Lamelas's work soon evolved into an analysis of information, addressing a particular subject with respect to the circumstances of its social and political context. Representing Argentina at the 1968 Venice Biennale, Lamelas produced a work titled OFFICE OF INFORMATION ABOUT THE VIETNAM WAR AT THREE LEVELS: THE VISUAL IMAGE, TEXT, AND AUDIO. He arranged an office space with a desk, telex machine, and chairs on a grey platform, all behind a glass partition that "separated the real world from the information space." [3] The telex relayed information about the Vietnam war from a news agency in Rome, which was taped and then read over a microphone to the spectators. Lamelas thus transformed the pavilion into a newsroom, making an architectural space an informational one to emphasize the symbolic and political dimensions of the national pavilion. Although the work was not intended as a personal statement about the Vietnam war, it challenged the notion that art should be distinct from politics. [4]

After the Biennale, film became the major focus of Lamelas's work. His first film, STUDY OF RELATIONSHIPS BETWEEN INNER AND OUTER SPACE (1968-69), produced by the Camden Arts Centre in London, moves from an examination of the Centre itself out into the city. The film's documentary form is used toward an institutional critique that directly connects an art institution

158

OFFICE OF INFORMATION ABOUT THE VIETNAM WAR AT THREE LEVELS: THE VISUAL IMAGE, TEXT, AND AUDIO (1968)
Installation view, Venice Biennale, 1968.

with its broader socio-political context. Rather than showing works of art, the film features employees of the Centre, including a curator, gallery attendant, and custodian, who describe their jobs. It concludes with interviews with passersby about the current event of the day—the May 1969 launching of the Apollo 10 mission and the prospect of the first man landing on the moon—which included the question, "Would you be surprised if the first man on the moon turned out to be a black man?"

In FILM SCRIPT (THE MANIPULATION OF MEANING) (1972), Lamelas examined how information is constructed and represented—and how meaning is ultimately manipulated. This work consists of the projection of a short, silent, Super-8 film and three 35mm slide sequences. The ten-minute film appears to be an actual scene from a commercial movie, but is in fact a fictional one of Lamelas's invention. Inspired by the feature film SUNDAY, BLOODY SUNDAY (1971), Lamelas adopted the genre of the Hitchcockian thriller without specific quotation. Filmed with a stationary camera at the Nigel Greenwood Gallery in London, the scene shows simple actions: a woman walks into the space, she answers the phone, a glass breaks. Accompanying the film are three slide projections, each showing stills of the same action in the film, but in an altered form. From one projection to the next, the information is increasingly restructured, repeated, reversed, or deleted, each time in relationship to the previous projection. Conjoining linguistic structure with the techniques and conventions of documentary and theatrical film, Lamelas breaks down the conventions of narrative form as he constructs and deconstructs the distinctions between fiction and reality.

While Lamelas's early films were intended to be screened in a gallery or museum setting, rather than in a cinema, THE DESERT PEOPLE (1974) was intended for a theatrical context. A critique of ethnographic film, THE DESERT PEOPLE combines the documentary form with the genre of the "road movie." It focuses upon five people—four Anglos and one Native American—recalling their experiences living with the Papago Indians of the Southwestern United States. The film's narrative moves back and forth between shots of the subjects in a car, either on their way from or to the Papago reservation. When all of the recollections are concluded, the car suddenly plunges off a cliff. Discussing this work, Rosetta Brooks has observed that "[t]he subject-matter of all the conversations is cultural differences (between the visitors and the Indians) and yet the narrative precludes the imposition of one cultural form (the documentary) onto another society (the tribe)."[5] — AG

Notes

1. David Lamelas, in *Contemporary Artists*, ed. Colin Naylor (Chicago: St. James Press, 1989), 535.

2. Lynda Morris, "David Lamelas: An Introduction to the Structural Development," *Studio International* (London) 187, no. 962 (January 1974): 44.

3. Conversation with the artist, 24 November 1993.

4. Lamelas has recalled that his reference to Vietnam did not please the cultural officials and that he ultimately saw his work re-titled in the exhibition catalogue as NEWS INFORMATION ABOUT A SELECTED SUBJECT. Ibid.

5. Rosetta Brooks, "David Lamelas," *Studio International* (London) 190, no. 977 (September-October 1975): 162.

THE DESERT PEOPLE (1974)
Stills from film (16mm, 49 min., color, sound).

WILLIAM LEAVITT

(b. 27 November 1941, Washington, D.C.; lives in Los Angeles)

William Leavitt describes his work in terms of an interest in a "distilled narrative."[1] Since 1969, his installations, photographic works, drawings, performances, videotapes, and films have employed ordinary fragments of popular culture and vernacular architecture as both props and signifiers within a generic narrative structure, in many cases modeled on 1960s soap operas and Hollywood B-movies. Leavitt takes into account the significance of every aspect of his works, including their location, lighting, atmosphere, props, actors, and costumes. As Thomas Lawson has written, "[i]t has been his practice to isolate a circumscribed group of features—the set, a few props, a potentially emotional situation—and circle them, refining his presentation as he clarifies his ideas, seeking ever greater economy and elegance of means."[2] Incorporating the "seams" or unfinished edges, rather than obscuring the artifice, of his constructions, Leavitt typically makes visible the process by which he takes apart an image. The resulting works are cohesive, yet quietly unnatural.

Interested in the often arbitrary nature of how symbols are assigned, Leavitt creates his own through this process of elimination and relocation. On the function of melodrama in his work, Lawson has written:

> What Leavitt is doing, in effect, is to isolate elements of the subtext of any Hollywood movie, those spaces and objects and gestures invested with an ambiguous psychological content, the elements which serve to carry the audience along with the story on an almost subliminal level. It is this subtext which generates the anxiety which can only be assuaged by finding out what happens next.[3]

The culture and atmosphere of Los Angeles has played a significant role in Leavitt's interest in the play between illusion and reality. In 1988 the artist wrote:

> When I first came to California I visited a back lot of a movie studio and I loved the deception of going up to one of those perfect houses and opening the door and seeing that there was nothing but canvas and 2 x 4's holding it up. I thought that was spectacular: all the bricks were made of composition board. It's built, not totally illusion, but something that is necessarily constructed. Maybe what I'm interested in is the edge between illusion and how it's supported—maybe that could also be the edge of the tract homes: here is this nice community—organized, everything is fine, green lawns, but just a few hundred yards away is this desert and wilderness again. If there is a rift between the two, one can go from one to the other and see both. But in order to have a true picture, one would have to hold both of them in mind.[4]

CALIFORNIA PATIO, an installation first shown in an exhibition organized by Helene Winer for the Pomona College Gallery in Claremont, California, in 1972, consists of a free-standing wall with a sliding-glass door behind opened brocade curtains. Visible through the slightly opened door is an evening scene of a flagstone patio with illuminated "Malibu" outdoor garden lights in the surrounding artificial plants. In contrast to an illusional diorama-like scene, the free-standing installation is located at an angle adjacent to one of the existing gallery walls so that one may walk

around to view the patio on the other side, thus comprehending the artifice of the work, which is accompanied by a text that describes much more than is physically present in the installation, thereby "setting the scene" and further conditioning its meaning and animating its silent stillness with additional allusions. Like a storyboard, the text catalyzes more images, which are familiar but not wholly specific, and emphasizes the directness of the installation's set-like artificiality. Winer contrasted it with photography:

> The scene is very believable and rich in associations. Instead of the isolation and displacement establishing a surreal aura, the piece succeeds in allowing a direct rapport and involvement with the proposition. We are obliged to consider a scene, encountered often in its ordinary context, and one which obviously requires the viewer's response for completion. Leavitt has provided a setting and a mood, with no apparent critical intent. The potential of the scene is of honest unmanipulated information. Unlike a photographic likeness, what appears to be a faithful reproduction is actually arrived at through careful deletions of specific details.[5]

Leavitt's work often evolves through various media, elaborating upon a specific scenario through different forms and building a vocabulary of symbolic objects or images that frequently populate different works. PAINTED IMAGE (1972) is a framed portrait of a "Shane"-like, Hollywood-studio dog painted by Leavitt that rests upon a free-standing painting easel. Taken out of context, this generic dog—like an actor—is open to characterization by the spectator.

Leavitt's first performance, THE SILK (1975), a drama in five scenes, evolved from a 1974 photographic work entitled THE TROPICS, as well as from an unrealized treatment for a film, THE LURE OF SILK, of the same year. THE TROPICS, first shown at Art & Project in Amsterdam in October 1974, consists of three black-and-white photographs framed together in a single horizontal line and includes images of a painting of a leopard, a close-up of a woman's neck adorned by a string of pearls, and tropical plants illuminated at night. Like CALIFORNIA PATIO, THE TROPICS is accompanied by a text, in this case describing a woman receiving a pearl necklace from a man in a modern apartment with a painting of a "South American jungle cat" over the sofa and a sliding glass door open to a garden of tropical plants illuminated by colored lights. The performance THE SILK substitutes a city view for the tropical garden, a painting of an orchid for the leopard, and a silk dress for the pearls and, like his earlier works, constructs its narrative through the assembly of disparate fragments. — AG

163

Notes

1. Conversation with the artist, 22 February 1995.

2. Thomas Lawson, "Every Picture Tells a Story, Don't It?," *Real Life Magazine* (New York), no. 2 (October 1979): 11.

3. Ibid.

4. William Leavitt, in *The Pasadena Armory Show 1989*, exh. cat. (Pasadena, California: The Fellows of Contemporary Art and The Armory Center for the Arts, 1989), 50.

5. Helene Winer, "Introduction," in *Bas Jan Ader, William Leavitt, Ger van Elk*, exh. cat. (Claremont, California: Pomona College Art Gallery, Montgomery Art Center, 1972), unpag.

THE TROPICS (1974)
Three black-and-white photographs (ed. 3). 16 x 60 in. (40.6 x 152.4 cm).
Private Collection.

It is evening in the backyard and garden of a contemporary hillside home in Southern California. There is a swimming pool, a flagstone patio, a redwood fence, some lawn and the usual tropical landscaping of succulents, ferns, leafy plants, and flowering shrubs. The beauty of the scene is most evident at this time of day when the combination of lighted pool, soft garden lights, black sky and the lights of surrounding homes comes into play.

On this particular evening a small cocktail party is being held on the patio adjoining the house. The guests are all close friends of the host and hostess. Their presence adds the elements of motion and sound to the setting; the men standing near the edge of the patio engaged in relaxed conversation, while the women sit in a loose circle of garden chairs arranged on the lawn. Now the hostess comes out through the sliding glass door to announce that a light buffet supper is ready inside.

CALIFORNIA PATIO, (1972)
Mixed-media. Dimensions variable. Courtesy Margo Leavin Gallery, Los Angeles.

SOL LEWITT

(b. 9 September 1928,
Hartford, Connecticut;
lives in Chester,
Connecticut)

Sol LeWitt's famed "Paragraphs on Conceptual Art," which he wrote for *Artforum* in 1967, codifies on a theoretical level the major principles of art as he and many of his generation perceived them. They also have served to define the ground rules for his own practice. Of particular note is the passage that explicates a significant aspect of his manner of working:

> To work with a plan that is pre-set is one way of avoiding subjectivity. It also obviates the necessity of designing each work in turn. The plan would design the work. . . . [The] fewer decisions made in the course of completing the work, the better.[1]

LeWitt made his first wall drawing for a group exhibition at the Paula Cooper Gallery in New York in October 1968. For the artist, "[t]he wall is understood as an absolute space, like the page of a book. One is public, the other private."[2] The wall presents a context for the expression of ideas that are "read" differently from those in a book because of their scale. In 1969 LeWitt arrived at the idea of making "a total drawing environment" by treating "the whole room as a complete entity—as one idea."[3] Since then, he has realized numerous wall drawings in exhibition spaces throughout the world. LeWitt's use of predetermined systems for generating lines and shape allows any one of his wall drawings to be realized on any chosen wall or within any exhibition space. By way of example, a pen-and-ink drawing of 1973 sets forth one of a number of basic series: ALL COMBINATIONS OF ARCS FROM CORNERS AND SIDES, STRAIGHT LINES, NOT-STRAIGHT LINES, AND BROKEN LINES. "No matter how many times the piece is done it is always different visually if done on walls of differing sizes,"[4] according to the artist.

The superimposed configuration of linear elements, adapted to the chosen space, interlocks with the existing spatial support.

The Location Drawings stipulate exactly how and where the elements of each work are to be sited and situated. For example, the text for one of a series of five Location pieces entitled LOCATION OF TWO LINES, first exhibited at the L'Attico Gallery in Rome in 1973, reads:

> A line from the center of the wall to a point halfway between the center of the wall and the midpoint of the right side; and a line equal in length to that of the first line, drawn from the midpoint of the first line toward the lower left corner. [5]

As the artist has explained, "Lines, points, figures, etc., are located in these spaces by words. The words are the paths to the understanding of the location of the point. The points are verified by the words." [6] The verbal elements of such works remain crucial to the drawing since the work as a whole relies on the linguistic directives that make it manifest as a visual experience. LeWitt's incorporation of language into a predetermined plan serves to bring about the fusion of two-dimensional form and background support. — AR

Notes

1. Sol LeWitt, "Paragraphs on Conceptual Art," *Artforum* 5, no. 10 (Summer 1967): 80.

2. Sol LeWitt, in *Sol LeWitt*, exh. cat. (New York: The Museum of Modern Art, 1978), 139.

3. Bernice Rose, "Sol LeWitt and Drawing," in *Sol LeWitt*, 32.

4. Ibid., 130.

5. Catalogue entry no. 181, in *Sol LeWitt Wall Drawings: 1968-1984*, exh. cat. (Amsterdam: Stedelijk Museum, Eindhoven: Stedelijk Van Abbemuseum, and Hartford: Wadsworth Athenaeum, 1984), 171.

6. Sol LeWitt, in *Sol LeWitt*, 139.

WALL DRAWING #146. ALL TWO-PART COMBINATIONS OF BLUE ARCS FROM CORNERS AND SIDES, AND BLUE STRAIGHT, NOT STRAIGHT AND BROKEN LINES (September 1972)
Blue crayon on wall. Solomon R. Guggenheim Museum, New York, Panza Collection, Gift, 1992. Photo © Giorgio Colombo, Milan.

RICHARD LONG
(b. 2 June 1945, Bristol, England; lives in Bristol)

Since the mid-1960s, Richard Long has made sculptures, photographs, maps, texts, and books based upon his solitary walks through various landscapes around the world. As he has stated, he considers all these media integral to his practice: "A sculpture, a map, a text, a photograph; all the forms of my work are equal and complementary. The knowledge of my actions, in whatever form, is the art. My art is the essence of my experience, not a representation of it."[1] Integrating the act of walking with the production of sculpture, Long synthesizes the abstract and contingent aspects of duration, distance, location, and subjective experience in his work.

While studying at the West of England College of Art in Bristol in the early 1960s, Long made his first outdoor work, A SNOWBALL TRACK (1964). While studying at St. Martin's School of Art in London, he produced his first walking work, A LINE MADE BY WALKING (1967), which he created on a field of grass.[2] The forms of Long's sculptures—circles, squares, spirals, and lines—reflect the abstract signs and geometric forms of Minimalism. He literally integrates these forms with the landscape, in some cases superimposing a form onto a site, such as the X-shape created on

a field of daisies in ENGLAND 1968 (1968), which Long selected specifically for its potential contrast of black and white.[3]

Some of Long's subsequent works have been produced by collecting, transporting, and assembling materials from the sites of his walks, such as stones or wood, to other locations, such as a museum or gallery; these works index both the original site and its resulting displacement. However, many of his works are site-specific and ephemeral; and the only record of their existence in the landscape is often through photographs and maps that describe and document the artist's activities.

Early in his career, Long began to use photography not only as a form of documentation but also to destabilize the relationship between physical and photographic reality. UNTITLED–ENGLAND (1967), for example, comprises two photographs. The first shows a circle on a field of grass outlined by a black rectangle that appears to have been drawn on top of the photograph. However, the second disturbs the photographic illusion of the first through a shift in the viewpoint of the camera/spectator that reveals the black rectangle to be, like the circle, an actual object in the field. With this critique of pictorial illusionism, Long calls into question the truth-value of the photograph as document.

BEN NEVIS HITCH-HIKE (1967) is Long's first work to join photographs with a map. It reflects a six-day journey by walking and hitchhiking in April 1967 from London to the summit of Ben Nevis and back. Each day Long took two photographs at 11 a.m.— one by pointing the camera straight up, the other by pointing it straight down. Together with a map that indicates the six locations photographed, these pictures do not portray their sites conventionally, but rather represent a passage through space and time. In 5 FIFTEEN MINUTE EVEN WALKS ON DARTMOOR, MOORLAND, MARSH, WOODS, ROAD (27 March 1971), a map and text comprise the entire work. Each line of the text designates one of the walks and is different in length, due to the nature of each of the terrains—moorland, marsh, woods, and road—he covered. — AG

Notes

1. Richard Long, as cited in "Richard Long: Books, Prints, Printed Matter," exh. brochure (New York: The New York Public Library, 1994), unpag.

2. Robert C. Morgan, "Richard Long's Poststructural Encounters," *Arts Magazine* 61, no. 6 (February 1987): 76.

3. Richard Long, "Fragments of a Conversation I," in *Richard Long: Walking in Circles*, exh. cat. (London: Hayward Gallery, 1991), 44.

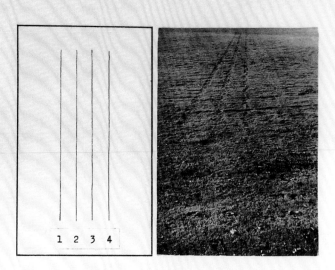

2½ MILE WALK SCULPTURE   RICHARD LONG 1969

Line 1 55 yards Walked 32 times Total distance 1 mile
Line 2 55 yards Walked 24 times Total distance ¾ mile
Line 3 55 yards Walked 16 times Total distance ½ mile
Line 4 55 yards Walked 8 times   Total distance ¼ mile

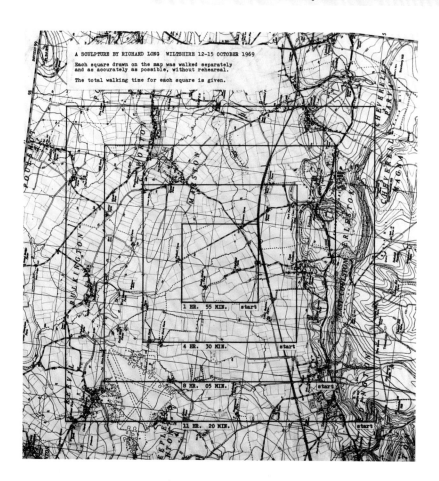

A SCULPTURE BY RICHARD LONG WILTSHIRE 12–15 OCTOBER 1969
Each square drawn on the map was walked separately
and as accurately as possible, without rehearsal.

The total walking time for each square is given.

A 2 1/2 MILE WALK SCULPTURE (1969)
Black-and-white photograph and text on paper. 7 x 8 in. (18 x 20 cm). Solomon R. Guggenheim Museum,
New York, Panza Collection, 1991. Photo © Gian Sinigalia, Milan.

WILTSHIRE (1969)
Map with text. 14 x 13 in. (35 x 33 cm). Solomon R. Guggenheim Museum,
New York, Panza Collection, 1991. Photo © Gian Sinigalia, Milan.

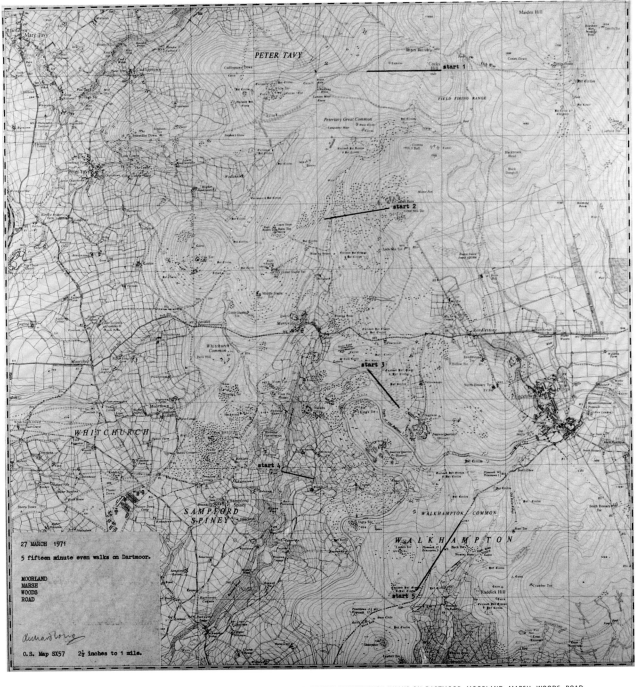

5 FIFTEEN MINUTE EVEN WALKS ON DARTMOOR, MOORLAND, MARSH, WOODS, ROAD
(27 March 1971)
Map and typewritten text. 16 x 16 in. (40.6 x 40.6 cm). Collection Angela
Westwater, New York, Courtesy Sperone Westwater, New York. Photo Bevan Davies.

TOM MARIONI

(b. 21 May 1937,
Cincinnati; lives in San
Francisco)

Born and raised in Cincinnati, Tom Marioni moved to San Francisco in 1959, following his studies in commercial and fine art at the Cincinnati Art Academy. In 1968 a one-person exhibition of his sculptures was presented at the Richmond Art Center, in Richmond, California. Shortly thereafter, Marioni was hired as the center's curator, a post he held until 1971. As curator, he presented new or unfamiliar work in such exhibitions as "Invisible Painting and Sculpture," "The Return of Abstract Expressionism," "Acid Painters of San Francisco," and "California Girls."

During this period, Marioni decided to exhibit his own work under the fictitious name Allan Fish; when Marioni left his job at the Richmond Art Center, Fish ceased to exist. As he saw his artwork become increasingly dematerialized, he began to view his work as a curator as a sculptural activity in itself by realizing his sculptural concerns through the organization of thematic exhibitions. In 1978 Marioni reflected on the influence on his work of his experience as a curator:

> When I went to work as a curator in '68 I thought of sculpture in terms of, at most, an environment, a single room; but after working as a curator, I thought on a much larger scale. I was concerned with all elements of an exhibition, with the publicity, with the arrangements, with the catalogue—even with aspects that reached outside the space itself. And maybe I would never have had that awareness if I hadn't gotten that job as a curator.[1]

In February 1970 Marioni founded the Museum of Conceptual Art (MOCA) in San Francisco. A "large-scale social and public work of art," MOCA functioned as a museum with a membership and a collection that presented social actions and "situational art."[2] When he founded MOCA, Marioni defined Conceptual art as "idea oriented situations not directed at the production of static objects."[3] The museum's early exhibitions comprised performances and screenings by such artists as Vito Acconci, Joseph Beuys, Chris Burden, Paul Cotton, Terry Fox, Dan Graham, Paul Kos, Linda Montano, Dennis Oppenheim, Bonnie Sherk, and Barbara Smith. Its opening event on 22 March 1970 was an evening of films by sculptors that was followed later that year by an exhibition entitled "Sound Sculpture As," which featured actions by nine artists including Marioni himself under the name of Allan Fish.[4] The museum's permanent collection included documentation in the form of photographs, films, and videotapes, as well as physical residues or changes to the site's architecture, of the activities it presented.

Marioni recalls the founding of MOCA as an attempt to create situations for the realization of a certain type of work:

> When I started MOCA in early 1970, it was underground, because it dealt with something that no one else was doing. ...I mean, there weren't other places that were providing a situation for this kind of art. So, because of where it was, and the style of it, and the name of it, and nature of it, and the esoteric and ephemeral quality of it, it was an underground museum.[5]

In September 1970 Marioni organized THE ACT OF DRINKING BEER WITH FRIENDS IS THE HIGHEST FORM OF ART at the Oakland Art Museum. On a Monday afternoon when the museum was closed to the public, he invited a small group of his friends to join him at the museum to drink beer. The activity of drinking beer and talking with friends comprised the work; the debris (empty beer cans, cigarette butts, melted ice, etc.) was exhibited for one month and constituted a record of the event. Since that original event and exhibition at the Oakland Art Museum, Marioni has recreated this work numerous times, redesigning it to fit each

new situation. For example, every Wednesday during 1973-74, free beer was made available at MOCA from a refrigerator with the words "FREE BEER" printed on its door. During that time, videotapes by artists were shown in the gallery and the empty beer bottles were collected on shelves. In 1976, Wednesday afternoon meetings called "Cafe Society" were started at Breen's under MOCA's auspices; after Breen's closed in 1979, Cafe Society continued next door at Jerry and Johnny's Bar. In that year the San Francisco Museum of Modern Art presented MOCA during a six-week exhibition. Free Anchor Steam beer was again available in an installation illuminated by yellow lights that also included a table with chairs, a framed poster, and shelves to collect the empty bottles. Although MOCA closed in 1984, Cafe Society continues in the Archive of MOCA, established in Marioni's studio in 1990. Marioni has described his concept of "cafe society" as "drunken parties where ideas are born." [6] "There's a German word for it, 'Stammtisch.' 'Tisch' is table and 'stamm' is a tree-trunk, in this case, a trunk that has branches going out like a family. Hans (Haacke) told me that word. So, it's a place, a particular table, where similar people gather." [7] — AG

Notes

1. Tom Marioni, in Robin White, *View* (Oakland, California) 1, no. 5 (October 1978): 8.

2. White, *View*, 16.

3. Statement by the artist, 1979.

4. Marioni, under his own name, continued to work with sound as a sculpture material throughout the 1970s when he was well-known as a performance artist. At the same time, he began developing his work with drawing and with installation art, his primary focus today.

5. Marioni in White, *View*, 4-5.

6. Ibid., 3.

7. Ibid., 4.

Sculptural work commemorating beer drunk by artists on Wednesday afternoons at the Museum of Conceptual Art, San Francisco (1973–74). Empty beer bottles on shelves. Courtesy the artist. Photo Paul Hoffman.

GORDON MATTA-CLARK

(b. 22 June 1943, New York; added mother's surname, Clark, to his in 1971; d. 27 August 1978, New York City)

Gordon Matta-Clark's work developed as an active dialogue with and against architecture, altering and transforming buildings by literally slicing into and dissecting them. The son of the Surrealist artist Roberto Matta, Matta-Clark graduated with a B.A. in architecture from Cornell University in 1968 and had a brief yet influential career that ended with his untimely death in 1978 at the age of thirty-five.

While at Cornell, Matta-Clark assisted Dennis Oppenheim in the creation of two projects for the "Earth Art" exhibition organized by Willoughby Sharp for the university's Andrew Dickson White Museum of Art in 1969. That year he also moved to New York, where his early work included cooking and alchemical projects, such as PHOTO FRY (1969), in which he literally fried photographs in a pan of grease—an early example of his ongoing interest in processes of transformation. In 1970 Matta-Clark became involved in 112 Greene Street, the seminal alternative gallery space founded by the artist Jeffrey Lew. In 1971 he created a series of works in the space, including CHERRY TREE, in which he excavated a hole in the basement floor and planted a tree that died after three months, marking the work's completion. Other works from this period include WINTER GARDEN: MUSHROOM AND WAISTBOTTLE RECYCLONING CENTER, which involved the cultivation of mushrooms in the basement, and TIME WELL, in which Matta-Clark entombed a jar of fermenting fruits and cherry pits in the hole remaining from CHERRY TREE within a chimney pipe covered by a concrete slab, its seams filled with lead. The process of filling in and covering the hole did not, however, obliterate the history of the space, but literally outlined it, separating it from the surrounding floor.

In 1971 Matta-Clark co-founded (with Carol Goodden, Suzanne Harris, Tina Girouard, and Rachel Lew) Food, a cooperative restaurant at the corner of Prince and Wooster Streets in Soho. Conceived as both an artwork and a functioning restaurant, Food was, among other things, the site of performances involving artists as guest chefs. It also provided a meeting place for the "Anarchitecture" group, a loose coalition of artists including Matta-Clark, Laurie Anderson, Tina Girouard, Suzanne Harris, Jene Highstein, Jeffrey Lew, Ree Morton, Richard Nonas, and George Trakas. Matta-Clark's notion of "anarchitecture" has been described as "an anarchistic approach to architecture, marked physically by a breaking down of convention through a process of 'undoing' or 'destructuring,' rather than creating a structure—and philosophically by a revolutionary approach that sought to reveal and later alleviate societal problems through art."[1]

Matta-Clark's major "cuttings" of abandoned buildings began in 1972-73 with the BRONX FLOORS. In these works he focused on ordinary, vernacular architecture, choosing his sites by "the degree to which my intervention can transform the structure into an act of communication."[2] In his essay on the artist, Dan Graham wrote that his "aim can be viewed as a form of urban 'ecology'; his approach is not to build with expensive materials, but to make architectural statements by removing in order to reveal existing, historical aspects of vernacular, ordinary buildings. Thus, the capitalist exhaustion of marketable material in the name of progress is reversed."[3] Matta-Clark himself articulated the social directions he saw for his work:

> By undoing a building there are many aspects of the social conditions against which I am gesturing: first, to open a state of enclosure which had been preconditioned not only by physical necessity but by the industry that profligates suburban and urban boxes as a context for insuring a passive, isolated consumer—a virtually captive audience. The fact that some of the buildings I have dealt with are in Black ghettos reinforces some of this thinking, although I would not make a total distinction between the imprisonment of the poor and the remarkably subtle self-containerization of higher socio-economic neighborhoods. The question is a reaction to an ever less viable state of privacy, private property, and isolation.[4]

In his most ambitious work, SPLITTING (1974), Matta-Clark made use of a wooden house in Englewood, New Jersey, that was to be demolished by its owners, Horace and Holly Solomon. For this project he divided the house in half by incising two parallel cuts one inch apart and removed the material between them. The house was then literally split apart by the removal of a section of the foundation on one side, which tilted it back. In addition to splitting the house, Matta-Clark cut out the four top corners on the second floor. The house/sculpture was on view from June through August of 1974 and the corner fragments were later exhibited at Holly Solomon Gallery in New York. In addition, Matta-Clark's photographs of the transformed spaces were assembled into collages that evoke a sculptural presence. — AG

Notes

1. Mary Jane Jacob, "Introduction and Acknowledgments," in *Gordon Matta-Clark: A Retrospective,* exh. cat. (Chicago: Museum of Contemporary Art, Chicago, 1985), 8. The author wishes to acknowledge the importance of this publication, particularly its descriptions of each of the artist's projects.

2. Gordon Matta-Clark in Donald Wall, "Gordon Matta-Clark's Building Dissections," *Arts Magazine* 50, no. 9 (May 1976): 77.

3. Dan Graham, "Gordon Matta-Clark," in *Gordon-Matta Clark,* exh. cat. (Marseille: Musée Cantini, 1993), 380.

4. Matta-Clark in Wall, "Gordon Matta-Clark's Building Dissections," 76.

SPLITTING (1974)
Black-and-white photo collage. 40 x 30 in. Collection Jane Crawford, Courtesy
Rhona Hoffman Gallery, Chicago.

SPLITTING: EXTERIOR (c. 1974)
Six black-and-white photographs. Two at 12 1/2 x 8 1/4 in. (31.8 x 21.0 cm); four
at 16 x 20 in. (40.6 x 50.8 cm). Collection Eileen and Michael Cohen, New York.
Photo Adam Reich.

SPLITTING: FOUR CORNERS, (1974)
Four building fragments. 52 3/4 x 40 1/2 x 44 in. (134.0 x 102.9 x 111.8 cm);
54 x 43 3/4 x 42 1/2 in. (137.2 x 136.5 x 108.0 cm); 54 1/2 x 42 x 42 in.
(138.4 x 106.7 x 106.7 cm); 56 x 43 1/2 x 42 3/4 in. (142.2 x 113.5 x 108.9 cm).
Courtesy Gordon-Matta-Clark Trust. Installation view, "Gordon Matta-Clark:
Splitting: Four Corners," Holly Solomon Gallery, New York, November–December 1990.

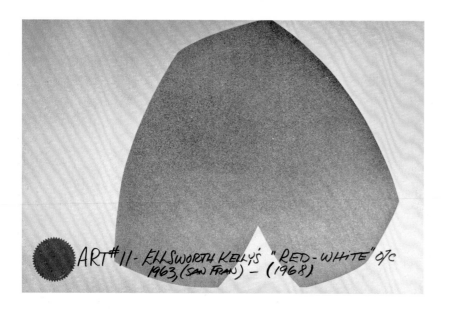

ART #11 — ELLSWORTH KELLY'S "RED-WHITE" O/C 1963, (SAN FRAN) — (1968)

N.E. THING CO.

(Iain Baxter, b. 16
November 1936,
Middlesborough, England;
lives in Windsor,
Ontario
Ingrid Baxter,
b. 10 February 1938,
Spokane, Washington;
active 1966-78)

N.E. Thing Company (NETCO) is the name of a collaborative venture formed by Iain and Ingrid Baxter. Developing out of an earlier collaborative, "IT," formed in 1966, NETCO was founded in Vancouver in 1966 as N. E. Baxter Thing Co., renamed in 1967, formally incorporated as a business in 1969, and dissolved in 1978, when the Baxters divorced. As an enterprise, NETCO "sought to dissolve the boundaries between art and life through interdisciplinary, collaborative activities carried out under the rubric of an umbrella organization."[1] NETCO blurred the distinctions between family, life, art, and business as it worked within and outside the conventions of all three.

Above all it sought to reconsider and redefine in a cross-disciplinary manner the role of the artist and the terminology of art, locating both within the broad realm of information. When the Baxters officially registered NETCO as a corporation, they defined the following objectives:

i *To produce sensitivity information:*
ii *To provide a consultation and evaluation service with respect to things:*
iii *To produce, manufacture, import, export, buy, sell, and otherwise deal in things of all kinds.*[2]

In a 1969-70 statement, NETCO elaborated upon this union of art and business:

Business is interested in pushing information around so that the keenest of its character, the practicality of its energy, results in profit and goods flow. This is what we call Practical Information. This is where the artist enters and with his sense of play and pureness of vision is able to take all this practical information and handle it sensitively and end up with Sensitivity Information *(regardless of his sense form).*[3]

According to NETCO's glossary (as included in the 1971 work ART IS ALL OVER), the artist is redesignated a "Visual Informer" ("as someone who knows how to handle visual information sensitively"); "Visual Sensitivity Information" replaces the terms "art," "fine art," or "visual art"; "Sound Sensitivity Information" replaces "music, poetry (read), singing, oratory"; and "Moving Sensitivity Information" replaces movies, dance, mountain climbing, track, etc." NETCO had eleven departments (Research, Thing, Accounting, ACT, ART, Photography, Printing, COP, Movie, Project, and Consulting) and used conventional vehicles of communication and certification (photography, telex transmissions, preprinted "Information" forms, certificates, seals of approval, and signs) to authorize, identify, and distribute its production.

Its early work developed from Baxter's activity as a solo artist, which included bagging and heat-sealing "landscapes" in plastic. This concept was further elaborated upon in BAGGED PLACE (1966), an installation at the University of British Columbia Fine Arts Gallery that consisted of the furnishings for a four-room apartment set up in the gallery space, with each object—from furniture and appliances to food and trash—individually sealed in plastic. NETCO not only relocated the domestic setting into the exhibition space, but also invoked the strategies of a commercial enterprise by transforming the domestic objects into packaged commodities.

Many of NETCO's projects were derived from or took place in the landscape. As Nancy Shaw has written,

Like typical West Coast and Canadian artists, the Baxters made landscapes, though theirs were expanded to include the sites of work and leisure, and urban and suburban spaces....[T]he Company's landscapes investigated how information technologies, corporate relations and institutions such as the art world and the nuclear family interact to redefine "landscape" as a product of human interest, an element of subjectivity and charted its rela-

ACT 107 *TRIANGULAR-SHAPED (VSI) VISUAL SENSITIVITY INFORMATION, TELE-CASTED VIEW OF MOON'S SURFACE FROM INSIDE APPOLO 8 SPACECRAFT THROUGH WINDOW AS SEEN ON CANADIAN NATIONAL C.B.C. T.V. OVER SANYO T.V. SET, 9", IN NORTH 25, 1968 (1968)*

tionship to forms of identity and national positioning.[4]
In its ACT (Aesthetically Claimed Things) and ART (Aesthetically Rejected Things) works NETCO produced photographs and certificates marking its claims. The ACT works identified elements of domestic or industrialized architecture, or other interventions into the North American landscape, while the ART works focused on works of art, most often made by artists associated with the center of the art world. As William Wood observed, in these works, NETCO specifically considered its geographic location in relation to the prevailing power relations of the art world:

> *Though not forming a consistent pattern, the ART and ACT works do tend to reject "activities" at the centre, and we can view the project as motivated and sustained by the perceived distance of NETCO from the centre of art world designation. The peripheral parodies the centre's claim of authority by assuming that power for itself. As well, the works can be said to recognize and celebrate the local landscape as product of a culture of logging and colonization and as distinctively different from the "sensitivity information" produced as art by the centres of artistic culture and power.*[5]

1/4 MILE LANDSCAPE (1968), first made for an exhibition at the Newport Harbor Art Museum in Newport Beach, California, comprises three signs located at equal distances apart from each other that read as follows: "You Will Soon Pass By a 1/4 Mile N.E. Thing Co. Landscape," "Start Viewing," and "Stop Viewing." Like the ACT pieces, the 1/4 MILE LANDSCAPE literally appropriates a section of roadside landscape. — AG

Notes

1. Nancy Shaw, "Expanded Consciousness and Company Types: Collaboration Since Intermedia and the N. E. Thing Company," in ed. Stan Douglas, *Vancouver Anthology: The Institutional Politics of Art* (Vancouver: Talonbooks, 1991), 91.

2. N.E. Thing Co., cited in William Wood, "Capital and Subsidiary: The N. E. Thing Co. and the Revision of Conceptual Art," in *You Are Now in the Middle of a N. E. Thing Co. Landscape: Works by Iain and Ingrid Baxter, 1965-1971*, exh. cat. (Vancouver: UBC Fine Arts Gallery, 1993), 13.

3. N.E. Thing Co., "Some Thoughts re: Communications and Concepts," 1969-70, as cited in *You Are Now in the Middle*, 42.

4. Nancy Shaw, "Siting the Banal: The Expanded Landscapes of the N.E. Thing Co.," in *You are Now in the Middle*, 25.

5. William Wood, "Capital and Subsidiary: The N.E. Thing Company and Conceptual Art," *Parachute* (Montreal), no. 67 (July-August-September 1992): 15.

ACT #107 TRIANGULAR-SHAPED (VSI) VISUAL SENSITIVITY INFORMATION, TELECASTED VIEW OF MOON'S SURFACE FROM INSIDE APOLLO 8 SPACECRAFT THROUGH WINDOW AS SEEN ON CANADIAN NATIONAL C.B.C. T.V. OVER SANYO T.V. SET, 9", IN NORTH VANCOUVER, B.C., CANADA, DECEMBER 25, 1968 (1969)
Felt pen and collage on gelatin-silver print. 27 x 39 in. (70.3 x 100.4 cm).
National Gallery of Canada, Ottawa. Photo © NGC/MBAC.

1/4 MILE LANDSCAPE (detail) (1968)
Hand-tinted gelatin-silver prints, printed map, and watercolor and graphite on
paper. Five parts: drawing, 12 x 18 in. (30.4 x 45.8 cm); photograph 1: 24 x 35
7/8 in. (60.9 x 91.1 cm) (sheet), photograph 2: 24 x 36 in. (60.9 x 91.5 cm)
(sheet), photograph 3: 24 1/8 x 36 in. (61.2 x 91.3 cm) (sheet), map, 25 7/8 x 31
in. (65.7 x 78.8 cm) (sheet). Art Gallery of Toronto.

ACT #53 SASKATCHEWAN PRAIRIE, WHEAT HARVEST SEASON, NEAR REGINA SASKATCHEWAN, 1968 (1968)
Felt pen on gelatin-silver print. 13 x 20 in. (33.0 x 50.8 cm).
Collection Ian and Charlotte Townsend-Gault.

BRUCE NAUMAN

(b. 6 December 1940,
Fort Wayne, Indiana;
lives in New Mexico)

The continuing search for methods of creating meaningful form underlies the diversity of Bruce Nauman's work. In the interest of absolving himself from conventional methods of making art, he has embraced a wide range of media, including photography, film, and video, in order to investigate alternatives to painting and, quite literally, to reform sculpture. Early fiberglass works of 1965 re-evaluate previous approaches to sculpture insofar as their elongated shapes that lean or appear to push themselves against the wall question the traditional, free-standing, volumetric nature of figurative or abstract sculpture.

Language has played a dominant role in Nauman's re-evaluation of pictorial and sculptural form, as has the artist's use of his own bodily presence. ELEVEN COLOR PHOTOGRAPHS (1966-67/70), a portfolio of eleven color photographs, synthesizes many aspects of Nauman's underlying aesthetic concerns. Through linguistic and visual double entendres they comment on—and reject—the usual materials, processes, and forms of art production, bringing them down from their lofty, serious heights through humor. Thus, the title of one of the photographs, BOUND TO FAIL, and the photographed enactment of being tied up, refers to the presupposed goal of success that, even if unspoken, motivates an artist. In another photograph, SELF PORTRAIT AS A FOUNTAIN, Nauman embodies and wittily debunks the tradition of self-portraiture and outdoor garden sculpture all at once. At the same time he pays homage to Marcel Duchamp, who questioned the nature of the traditional art object with his Readymades, which include an ordinary urinal he rotated, signed "R. Mutt," and entitled FOUNTAIN (1917).

EATING MY WORDS and WAXING HOT, from the same portfolio, literally speak about how language, with its potential for double meanings, need not only represent *something* but can also be the thing or subject being represented. In the former, the artist sits at a table actually eating the word "words," and in the latter, the word "hot" takes the form of a red, painted, wooden sculpture that is being polished. In these photographs, sculpture and enacted idioms, as in a game of charades, are fused when plays on words and the playing with words materialize as objects and ultimately turn the traditional sculptural object into an object of inquiry. By thus acting out abstract phrases to the letter, so to say, Nauman infuses them with physicality. Paradoxically, by objectively observing himself, he succeeds, moreover, in distancing himself from acts of personal expression.

COMPOSITE PHOTO OF TWO MESSES ON THE STUDIO FLOOR (1967) also utilizes photography in its documentary capacity to record. In this work, Nauman similarly explores alternatives to conventional sculpture by featuring the residue of fabrication—the leftover materials that haphazardly fall by the wayside in the process of making a work—as the work itself. Bearing a fundamental relationship to an earlier fiberglass floor piece entitled PLATFORM MADE UP OF THE SPACE BETWEEN TWO RECTILINEAR BOXES ON THE FLOOR (1966), in which Nauman had explicitly represented negative, nonmaterial space in positive, material terms, COMPOSITE PHOTO turns its attention toward the non-art "side" of aesthetic production—toward what is left over. Because they have not been arranged by the artist, the actual messes escape the manipulation traditionally associated with art.

Paradoxically, the literally untouched debris on the studio floor, with its inherent randomness thus highlighted as subject matter, exempts the artist from arbitrary improvisations not based in reality.

Since 1967, Nauman has intermittently also used neon as a medium to translate verbal form and expression into sculpture. His neon pieces are based on the phonetic, phonemic, figurative, and referential properties of words. Minor changes in the positioning/repositioning, or the addition/subtraction, of single letters in works such as RAW WAR (1970) or DEATH EAT (1972) cause major changes in meaning. Illuminating each word in alternating succession, these works often touch on the human and social condition. Sometimes treading the thin line between sense and non-sense, they explore elements that render verbal meaning. Resembling anonymous advertising signs that serve to draw attention, they confer material form on signification and, in this way, alternatively bestow signification on material form.[1] — AR

Notes
1. See Brenda Richardson, *Bruce Nauman: Neons*, exh. cat. (Baltimore: The Baltimore Museum of Art, 1982-83), 20.

COMPOSITE PHOTO OF TWO MESSES ON THE STUDIO FLOOR, (1967)
Gelatin-silver print. 40 1/2 x 123 in. (102.9 x 312.4 cm). The Museum of Modern Art, New York, Gift of Philip Johnson 1984. Copy print © 1995 The Museum of Modern Art, New York.

WAXING HOT. From ELEVEN COLOR PHOTOGRAPHS (1966-67/70)
Portfolio of eleven color photographs published by Leo Castelli Gallery, New York. Sheet and image, 20 1/16 x 20 1/4 in. (51 x 51.4 cm). Whitney Museum of American Art, New York, Purchase. Photo Geoffrey Clements.

MARIA NORDMAN

(b. 1943, Goerlitz, Silesia; lives in the cities of her works and Los Angeles)

Since 1967, initially in various locations in and around Los Angeles and later around the world, Maria Nordman began to work directly with the city. Using the given materials of everyday existence, including sun, shadow, time, and ambient sounds, Nordman's work uses the conditions of experience and place within the specific urban contexts and social situations of the city. Early on, her work proposed as important elements for art an invisibility as it participates within a specific place and indivisibility from the conditions of life. The work is there and not there. As she has written, "It is not a subject. It is not an object. It is not passive. It is not finished."[1]

Conjoining architecture and illumination, image and frame, inside and outside, Nordman cites the importance of the film director Josef von Sternberg, who was teaching at the University of California in Los Angeles in the 1960s when she was a student there and at the time making films. In 1969-70 she worked as an editorial assistant to architect Richard Neutra, whose architecture integrated aspects of inside and outside.

Nordman's method of working with place and illumination developed out of her work in still and motion-picture photography. As she has stated, referring to her work of 1966, "the choice of place is within the image of the urban landscape. The camera is at that time for me an active place of hesitation—whatever is external appears internal."[2]

Nordman's early work in still photography developed into works that, using the moving image of film projection, incorporated the place in which one experienced the work. In her silent film EAT (1966-67), two people sit down at table and eat a meal. The film is made with two cameras: a stationary one records the overall scene, including the floor and walls of the room; the other pans to selected details of the actions of the two people seated at the table. The film is projected onto the setting in which it was made, the projectors taking the place of the two cameras. The wall behind the table is used as the screen and is divided by an additionally constructed wall that separates the two images and creates three contiguous rooms. The table, now just set with a white tablecloth, also receives part of the image. The film integrates the overall scene with random details within the image—as well as with those present in the room itself—with the left side receiving the entire image and the right side the details of the participants' actions, such as picking up a piece of bread or lifting a glass. Its ideal audience is the two actors or two other persons who can, in effect, take their places.

After the film projections, Nordman began to produce works not made public that involved projections of coherent light into rooms. These pieces were followed by works in which she intended to "find a way of working that would be open to any person of any personal, interpersonal, or societal background."[3] As Nordman has noted, these works directly employ the light of the sun: "I open the door and start to work with the sun and the people walking by on the street, and the sound in the city."[4]

WORKROOM, an ongoing work since 1969, is situated in a storefront room on Pico Boulevard in Santa Monica, California. The room is entered through a door directly from the sidewalk. Three steps lead up to a wooden seating platform, which is at the base of a large window glazed with a two-way mirror filter. The fixtures of electrical illumination have been removed. From the outside in daytime, the window reflects the passersby in the mirrored surface. From the inside, the window frames the image and sounds of the street. In the nighttime, the illumination from an adjacent room reverses the position of the image. A passerby would see an image of the room, and the person inside would see him- or herself reflected in the window.

In 1973 Nordman was invited to make a work for an exhibition at the Newport Harbor Art Museum in Newport Beach, California, which, at the time, was located in a warehouse located between Pacific Coast Highway and the ocean.[5] She selected a loading door that opened to the alley at the rear of the museum—and a time, 12:30 p.m., 26 February 1973, the date of the exhibition's opening. For exactly that moment, a wood and drywall structure was built inside the door at the angle of incidence of the sunlight passing through it at the specified time. Nordman has described the possibilities of encountering the work: "A person could go into the museum and find the outside of the construction, or leave the museum, and go into the alley to find the work. The work could also be encountered by chance by a passer-by while walking down the street to the ocean."[6] — AG

Notes

1. Maria Nordman, *De Sculptura: Works in the City: Some Ongoing Questions* (Munich: Schirmer/Mosel, 1986), 10.

2. Conversation with the artist, 3 February 1995.

3. Ibid.

4. Ibid.

5. The source for this description is Maria Nordman, *De Musica: New Conjunct City Proposals,* exh. cat. (Münster: Westfälisches Landesmuseum, Lucerne: Kunstmuseum Luzern, New York: Public Art Fund Inc. and Dia Center for the Arts, Hamburg: Kulturbehörde, and Rennes: FRAC Bretagne, 1993), 44.

6. Ibid.

2/26/1973 12:30PM (1973)
Door construction and alley to Pacific Ocean in
Newport Beach, Newport Harbor Art Museum.

UNTITLED (1973-)
Exterior construction inside the Newport Harbor Art Museum,
Newport Beach, California.

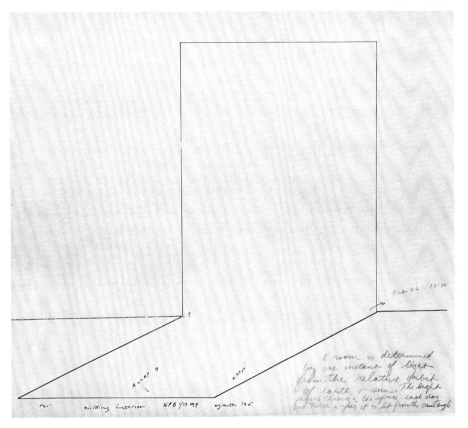

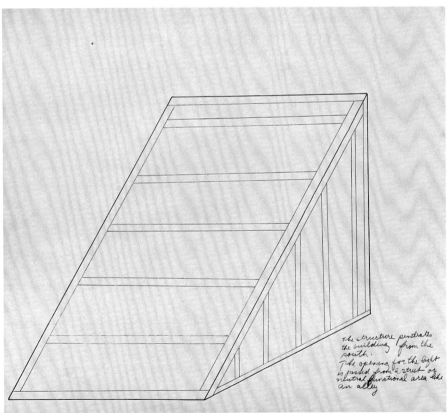

NEWPORT PLAN (a particular realization of UNTITLED (1973–))
Pencil on vellum. Solomon R. Guggenheim Museum, New York,
Panza Collection, Gift.

DENNIS OPPENHEIM

(b. 6 September 1938, Mason City [now Electric City], Washington; lives in New York City) Since 1967, Dennis Oppenheim's works have encompassed performance, land-based projects, interior installations, body-related activities, time-based projects, photography, film, and video. Moving to New York in 1960 following the conclusion of his graduate studies in art at Stanford University, Oppenheim worked in reaction to the object-bound aspects of Minimalism, challenging the conventional subject/object relationships of works of art in an attempt erase the distinctions. The emphasis on process that emerged in his work of the late 1960s is suggested by a lexicon of such action-oriented words as claiming, imprinting, transferring, depleting, exchanging, excavating, and displacing. Reflecting upon the transition, Oppenheim has remarked:

> One replaced making with thinking. It was muting manual production and opting for an art of mental activation. There are various examples of why one would believe this, just by looking at the sterile pursuits of the Minimalists in 1965 and 1966, and pushing these things to the zero point. So the alternatives were obvious in terms of physicality. You would either go down below the ground or you would deal with more horizontal, ground related situations. The whole notion of horizontality seemed to conjure up aspects of distance that were never allowed sculpture. Once we consider the alternatives that were being called for because of the stagnation of Minimalism, we can't help but find ourselves calling upon energies that were never really considered in art making before. These energies were partly in the form of conceptual distance, the activation of things through another agent.[1]

Oppenheim's earliest works reflect his attempt to explore alternatives to traditional gallery objects. In SITE MARKERS (1967), ten numbered, cast-iron stakes designed to resemble those used by land surveyors were employed to indicate specific locations, most often indicating fragments of architecture. The works, which ultimately included photographic documentation and a certificate describing the site, constituted themselves through the act of claiming.

THE VIEWING SYSTEM FOR GALLERY SPACE of the same year comprised wooden platforms or "viewing stations" that Oppenheim designed as devices on which the viewer would stand to survey a space. The VIEWING STATIONS foreground the activity of looking and mitigate the separation between a work and the space in which it is experienced. When located within an interior gallery space, they emphasized the activity of "viewing from" over that of "looking at."

Oppenheim's works of the late 1960s evolved from a focus on claiming to one on transfers of energy and material. In several GALLERY TRANSPLANTS (1969), he transferred the floorplan, actual-size, of an institutional gallery space onto a new site. For example, he transplanted a gallery of the Andrew Dickson White Museum of Art at Cornell University in Ithaca, New York, to a frozen pond in a bird sanctuary and a gallery of the Stedelijk Museum in Amsterdam to a site in Jersey City, New Jersey. His STERILIZED SURFACE. GLASS. of the same year consisted of applying and removing glass cleaner to the windows of Galerie Yvon Lambert in Paris, thus representing the process of addition and removal, as well as the transfer of energy.

In later works Oppenheim's body became the site of his actions. He described this transition in an interview with Allan Schwartzman:

> After coming from large scale land-based pieces and retracting into the body...came an attempt to find out if this preoccupation with external works was going to hold up. Body related works became a profound alternative. It was a rich area. The works dealt with getting close to the material, becoming the material, becoming the object.[2]

In READING POSITION FOR SECOND DEGREE BURN (1970) Oppenheim slept on Jones Beach on Long Island with an open copy of a red, hardcover book entitled Tactics on his chest. The five-hour exposure left him sunburned except for the area covered by the book:

> That was a kind of inversion or reversal of energy expenditure. The body was placed in the position of recipient, exposed plane, a captive surface. The piece has its roots in the notion of colour change. Painters have always artificially instigated colour activity. I allowed myself to be painted, my skin became pigment. I could regulate its intensity through control of the exposure time. Not only would my skin tones change, but its change registered on a sensory level as well—I could feel the act of becoming red. I was tattooed by the sun.[3]

At the time that Oppenheim produced these land- and body-related works, he made photodocumentation of them. These large-scale pieces comprise photographs that record aspects of the pieces, along with descriptive texts. They raise questions about the nature of documentation to the original, ephemeral work of art. Oppenheim used the medium of photography casually (many of the photographs were not taken by the artist and were printed by commercial labs), and specifically for its documentary properties: "They were there simply to indicate a radical art that had already vanished. The photograph was necessary only as a residue for communication."[4] — AG

Notes

1. "Dennis Oppenheim: An Interview with Allan Schwartzman," in Early Work by Five Contemporary Artists, exh. cat. (New York: The New Museum, 1977), unpag.

2. Ibid.

3. Dennis Oppenheim, "Dennis Oppenheim Interviewed by Willoughby Sharp," Studio International (London) 182, no. 938 (November 1971): 188.

4. Dennis Oppenheim, cited in Alison de Lima Greene, "Dennis Oppenheim: No Photography," Spot (Houston) 12, no. 1 (Spring 1993): 5.

READING POSITION FOR SECOND DEGREE BURN.
Stage I, Stage II. Book, skin, solar energy.
Exposure time: 5 hours. Jones Beach, 1970.

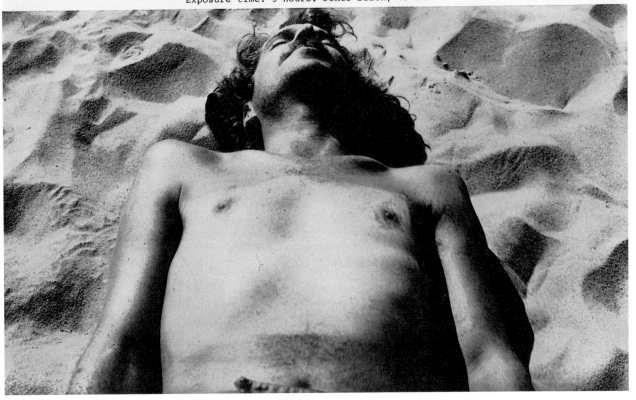

READING POSITION FOR SECOND DEGREE BURN (1970)
Stage #1 and Stage #2. Skin, book, solar energy. Exposure time: 5 hours. Jones
Beach, 1970. Two color photographs and black-and-white photographic text dry-
mounted on museum board. Three panels: two at 40 x 60 in. (101.6 x 152.4 cm);
one at 6 x 60 in. (15.2 x 152.4 cm). Collection the artist.

BLINKY PALERMO

(b. Peter Schwarze, 2 June 1943, Leipzig; last name changed to Heisterkamp after adoption in 1943; assumed artist pseudonym Blinky Palermo in 1964; d. 17 February 1977, Iles Maldives)

When Blinky Palermo died in 1977 at the age of thirty-four, he left behind a highly significant body of work.[1] During the late 1960s and early 1970s, Palermo's ideas resulted in distinct and separate, yet overlapping series, including the OBJEKTEN (Objects, 1964-79) and STOFFBILDER (Textile Pictures, 1966-72). At the end of 1968 Palermo realized the earliest of his WANDZEICHNUNGEN and WANDMALEREI (Wall Drawings and Wall Paintings); HIMMELSRICHTUNGEN (Cardinal Points, 1976), his last work relating to the walls of an architectural space, was presented at the Venice Biennale of 1976.[2] By 1974 Palermo had begun the series of metal paintings that would concern him in the last years of his life.

The Wall Drawings and Paintings were conceived in several different ways. Those made for the Galerie Ernst in Hannover (1969), the Lisson Gallery in London (1970), the Atelier in Mönchengladbach (1970-71), and for the house of Franz Dahlem in Darmstadt (1971) resulted from a similar approach. Palermo's written proposal for the Lisson Gallery stipulates: "A white wall with a door at any place surrounded by a white line of a hand's breadth. The wall must have right angles. The definite form of the line is directed to the form of the wall." In each instance the formerly blank wall areas acquired independent form. Following the same principle, Palermo painted the identical, opposite walls of the Galerie Heiner Friedrich in Munich in 1971 by following the outline of the rectangular wall elevation and door. One wall was painted white, outlined by a strip the width of a hand in ochre, while the other, in reverse, was painted ochre and outlined in white. The surface of the wall clearly functioned as the support for the painting since the white/ochre outlines took their shape from—and gave shape to—their architectural setting.

If form coincided with the walls of an existing structure in certain works, in others, Palermo transposed the formal properties of a particular architectural element for representation elsewhere. For a piece entitled TREPPENHAUS (Stairwell, 1970), realized in the Galerie Konrad Fischer in Düsseldorf, Palermo painted the profile of the staircase from his home in Düsseldorf onto one of the gallery's walls in a suitable, relatively narrow area. In this way the surface of the wall became the supporting ground for an abstract shape derived from the actuality of found architectural form. Employing the same principle, he produced FENSTER I (Window I, 1970) and FENSTER II (Window II, 1971), both executed in Bremerhaven, by copying the structural outline of the mullions from the glass entranceway to the Kabinett für aktuelle Kunst, where the exhibition was held, onto the surface of the wall inside.

For DOCUMENTA 5 in Kassel in 1972, Palermo painted the space of the first-floor landing of the staircase of the Museum Friedricianum with Bleimennige, a deep orange, rust-preventative lead undercoating. The emphatic orange color suffused the towering stair-landing and set the enclosed wall area off as a large rectangle that, when viewed from various vantage points, took the form of an irregular polygon. By thus covering an existing area of the given architecture with paint, Palermo succeeded in "uncovering" a pre-existing form rather than arbitrarily inventing a new one.

Palermo often took advantage of the full context of a space. In the large exhibition room of the Kunsthalle Baden-Baden, for example, in 1970, he painted a thin encircling blue stripe beneath an ornate molding on the wall just below the ceiling; the surrounding space as a whole, therefore, joined with the encircling painted form. In an isolated instance Palermo enlisted a predetermined shape for a Wall Painting of 1972 made for an exhibition at the Palais des Beaux-Arts in Brussels. Rather than highlighting specific aspects of the architectural space, he painted blue isosceles triangles directly on the wall, at its center, in a continuous row around the rectangular room. Placed at regular intervals, the triangles themselves bore no reference to any previously existing structural element, but nonetheless fused independent form and architectural space. — AR

Notes

1. Blinky Palermo, the name he assumed in 1964, was the name of the manager of the boxer Sonny Liston. Joseph Beuys, with whom Palermo studied at the Staatliche Kunstakademie in Düsseldorf, is said to have told Palermo that he looked like him when wearing a certain hat.

2. See Germano Celant, *Ambiente/arte dal futurismo alla body art* (Venice: Edizioni La Biennale di Venezia, 1977), 119, 219. For photographic documentation of this and the artist's other works, see Thordis Moeller, ed., *Palermo*, 2 vols. (Bonn: Kunstmuseum in association with Stuttgart: Oktagon, 1994).

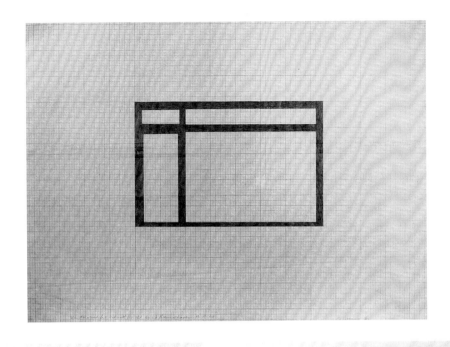

ZU "FENSTER I" WANDMALEREI IM KABINETT FÜR AKTUELLE KUNST, BREMERHAVEN
(Documentation of FENSTER I Wall Painting for Kabinett für aktuelle Kunst,
Bremerhaven, 1970)
Collection Kunstmuseum Bonn.
TOP: Pencil on graph paper. 23 1/8 x 32 3/4 in. (58.7 x 83.3 cm). LEFT BOTTOM:
Pencil on imitation parchment and color photograph mounted on board. One panel,
35 3/8 x 26 in. (90 x 66 cm). RIGHT BOTTOM: Black paint on brown paper and
color photograph mounted on board. One panel, 35 3/8 x 26 in. (90 x 66 cm).

192

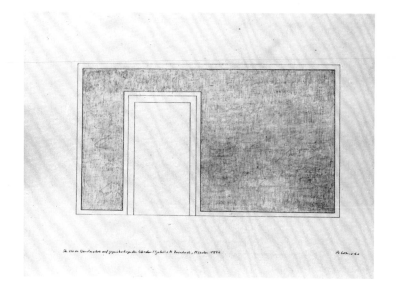

ZU WANDMALEREI AUF GEGENÜBERLIEGENDEN WÄNDEN IN DER GALERIE HEINER FRIEDRICH,
MÜNCHEN (Documentation of Wall Painting on Opposite Walls in the Galerie Heiner
Friedrich, Munich, 1971)
Collection Kunstmuseum Bonn.
TOP: Black-and-white photographs and pencil and gouache on paper mounted on board.
One panel, 36 1/2 x 29 in. (93 x 73.7 cm). BOTTOM: Gouache and pen and pencil on
paper, with black-and-white photograph. 15 3/4 x 17 3/4 in. (40 x 45 cm).

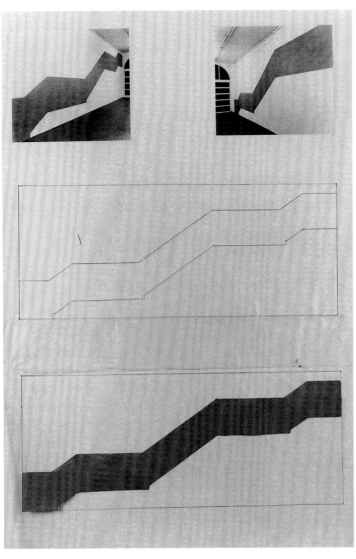

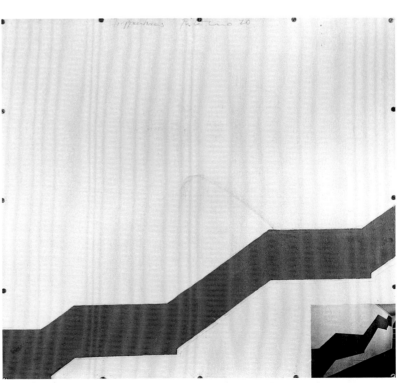

ZU "TREPPENHAUS," GALERIE KONRAD FISCHER, DÜSSELDORF (Documentation of STAIRWELL,
Galerie Konrad Fischer, Düsseldorf, 1970) (detail)
Collection Kunstmuseum Bonn.
TOP: Pencil on paper mounted on board. One panel, 26 x 35 3/8 in. (66 x 90 cm).
BOTTOM: Two color photographs. One panel, 26 x 35 3/8 in. (66 x 90 cm).

GIULIO PAOLINI

(b. 5 November 1940, Genoa, Italy; lives in Turin)

Giulio Paolini has made the material, authorial, contextual, and historical prerequisites of painting and sculpture the specific thematic subject of his work. Since 1960, he has made self-reflective works that comment on these conventions as historically validated categories of aesthetic production.

During the first half of the 1960s, Paolini formulated his approach to the fundamental practice of creating an image on the canvas surface. His early paintings exhibit the preliminary methods or particular materials that precede the traditional construction of a final image rather than providing a "finished" representation of a subject external to the concerns of the work. He has explained that his aim was "to free the picture from its function as a vehicle for images" to the extent that "the picture is none other than the very elements which go to make it up."[1] In this regard, SENZA TITOLO (Untitled, 1961) consists of an actual can of paint displayed behind a sheet of transparent plastic stretched on a supporting wooden frame. The can of paint is not a representation on a canvas surface, but a presentation of an actual object that contains the material—paint—necessary to produce an image. Standing in for the usually opaque canvas surface, the transparent plastic allows the viewing of something real in lieu of an illusionistic image.

From the mid-1960s on, paintings by Paolini propose an aesthetic agenda in which the canvas surface provides a forum for painting to examine itself in terms of its existence as an image-bearing, rectangular object that, having issued from the mind of a creator, takes its place in the historical continuum on the walls of designated exhibition spaces with others of its kind. Seeking from this time to acknowledge the authorial role of the artist while simultaneously declaring that his work is not about the artist on any individual or subjective level, Paolini demonstrates how he is a part of the process of implementation—a tool for engendering representation.

Paolini's APOTESI DI OMERO (Apotheosis of Homer, 1970-71), is meant to be an homage to authorship in general as opposed to a paean to any one individual. It is an installation consisting of numerous music stands, each with a different score presenting a photograph of a living actor. Modeled in concept on Ingres' painting APOTHEOSIS OF HOMER (1827), the actors photographed in the scores represent historical figures, which a key of paired names on one of the stands makes explicit. Those represented in Paolini's work include Socrates and Jesus Christ, Arthur Rimbaud and Queen Elizabeth I. Like the ancient and modern historical figures in Ingres' painting, such as Pheidias or Poussin, all have had a major impact on their culture. Paolini's actors, moreover, similarly pay homage to Homer as an "emblem of classical inspiration" according to the artist, who has noted further that the "spectator can feel himself reflected in each of the actors, and thus in each of the historical characters."[2] The viewer is thus given the opportunity to assume the role of one or many characters through identification with the actors. The artist himself, however, in an act of self-banishment, has vanished from the scene for which he is the impresario. — AR

Notes

1. Giulio Paolini, in *Giulio Paolini: Survey of Works 1960-1980*, exh. cat. (Amsterdam: Stedelijk Museum and Oxford: The Museum of Modern Art, 1980), 12.

2. Ibid., 28.

APOTESI D'OMERO (Apotheosis of Homer, 1970-71)
Thirty-three music stands, thirty folders with black-and-white photographs, two folders with color photographs, and one folder with two pages of text. Each folder, 11 7/8 x 13 3/8 in. (30 x 34 cm). Installation dimensions variable. Herbert collection, Ghent.

Antoine-Laurent Lavoisier	Antonio Pierfederici	Giulio Cesare	Rino Sudano
Beatrice d'Este	Ottavia Piccolo	Isabella d'Aragona	Martha Fisher
Giovanna d'Arco	Teresa Martin	Atahualpa	Christopher Plummer
Leone Trotzkij	Richard Munch	Vladimir Majakowskij	Dimitrij Cerkassov
Paul Verlaine	Jean Claude Brialy	Luigi XIV	Jean Marie Patte
Lawrence d'Arabia	Peter O'Toole	Gerolamo Savonarola	Antonio Battistella
Paolo	Edoardo Torricella	Francisco Pizarro	Robert Shaw
Raffaello Sanzio	Giuseppe Scarcella	Sophia Scholl	Nicoletta Rizzi
Oliver Cromwell	Richard Harris	Elisabetta I	Flora Robson
Camille Desmoulins	Paolo Graziosi	Attila	Jack Palance
Socrate	Jean Sylver	Isabella d'Este	Bianca Toccafondi
Socrate bambino	Jaime Moraleda	Caligola	Carmelo Bene
Paolo Casaroli	Renato Salvatori	Gesù Cristo	Giacomo Balla
Giovanni	Mohamed Kouka	Arthur Rimbaud	Terence Stamp
Alessandro Magno	Alfredo Bianchini	Emiliano Zapata	Marlon Brando
Isabella la Cattolica	Aurora Bautista	Henry Van Meegeren	Riccardo Cucciolla
Perugino	Diego Della Valle	Maria Waleska	Greta Garbo
Nicolaj Lenin	Kurt Bech	Enrico Mattei	Gian Maria Volonté
Marchese Joseph de La Fayette	Dario Penne	Bernadette Soubirous	Jennifer Jones
Leonardo da Vinci	Philippe Leroy	Blaise Pascal	Pierre Artidi
Leonardo da Vinci bambino	Gianluca Cicalè	Vittorio Emanuele III	Giulio Girola
Leonardo da Vinci giovinetto	Arduino Paolini	George Christine Jorgensen	John Hansen
Marchese di Posa	Massimo De Francovich		

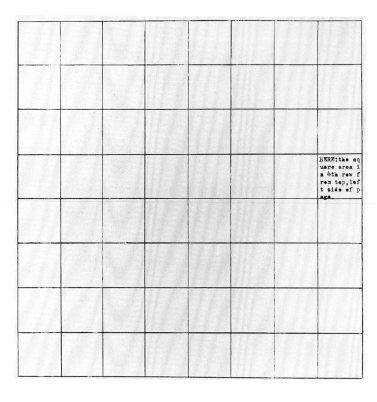

HERE:the sq
uare area i
n 4th row f
rom top,lef
t side of p
age.

ADRIAN PIPER

(b. 20 September 1948, New York City; lives in Wellesley, Massachusetts)

In November 1968, Adrian Piper produced a work entitled HERE AND NOW. This work consists of a title and "systems" page and a portfolio of sixty-four loose sheets of paper mimeographed with a one-inch square grid. One square of each sheet contains a self-descriptive text that identifies its position within the grid. The work was constructed to refer concretely to itself, and through the activity of examining the sheets, the self-referential aspect of the work remains indexed to the present as it incorporates the participation of the viewer. This aspect of the "here and now" as it is constructed through a self-reflexive object is not only key to Piper's early work, but also forms a critical link to her later work dealing with objectification related to race, gender, identity, and xenophobia.

While studying at the School of Visual Arts in New York, Piper began to redirect the course of her work away from the production of Minimalist objects to the self-reflexive exploration of ideas of space, time, form, dimension, language, and "objects qua objects." She has written about this transition in her work:

I made another small hop, this time to the level of abstract thought about space, time, and the objects within it; their materiality, concreteness, their infinite divisibility and variability, their indefinite serial progression through states; their status as instances of abstract concepts. Sol LeWitt's work and writings offered me the tools and encouragement to pursue this line, against the disapproval of some of my teachers at SVA. [1]

In the late 1960s, Piper began to reconsider "the difference between the object and the conceptual framework in which it is embedded." [2] More recently, she has traced her self-awareness through LeWitt's development of a self-reflective content that shifts primacy from the object to the

conceptual system it self-reflexively generates…. For Joseph Kosuth and the Art & Language group, this natural progression was from linguistic analysis of the concept of art to discursive Marxist critique of the means of art production; for Hans Haacke, it was from self-sustaining material systems to self-sustaining political systems; in my own work, it was from my body as a conceptually and spatio-temporally immediate art object to my person as a gendered and ethnically stereotyped art commodity. [3]

In March 1969, Piper's 3 UNTITLED PROJECTS (0 TO 9 PROJECT) was published by Vito Acconci and distributed as an exhibition through the mail by his 0 to 9 Press. This work comprises an advertisement in *The Village Voice* and a list of the "exhibition" locations (the addresses of the mailing list), as well as the three projects, each of which makes reference to its own concrete reality and existence in space and time. The first project consists of a text, a map of New York, and nineteen blank pages.

The Hypothesis series (1968-70) comprises twenty works or "Situations" that document what Piper saw through the viewfinder of a camera, with accompanying graphs locating herself in a coordinate system of time and space. The photographs document what she was looking at at a particular moment, such

HERE AND NOW (November 1968)
Portfolio of sixty-four loose sheets of typewritten mimeographed paper, with one sheet of typewritten paper and one sheet of graph paper, in cardboard folder. Folder, 9 x 9 1/8 x 1/2 in. (22.9 x 23.2 x 1.3 cm); each sheet, 8 1/4 x 8 1/4 in. (21.0 x 21.0 cm). Courtesy John Weber Gallery, New York. Photo Paula Goldman.

196

as the space of her loft, the television, or the view through her window as she was meditating. As she has written,

> I was investigating myself as equally an object in space and time, an object that moves through space and time just like any other object; but unlike other specific three-dimensional objects, this one has a peculiar capacity: namely the capacity to register self-consciously the space and time I am moving through, to actually represent that consciousness symbolically—in photographs—and abstractly—in a coordinate grid, and communicate it.[4]

Piper's use of self-referentiality is also manifested in the notebooks CONTEXT #7 (June-September 1970), CONTEXT #8 (June 1970), and CONTEXT #9 (May-June 1970), all of which reflect her growing political awareness. CONTEXT #7 was Piper's contribution to the "Information" exhibition at The Museum of Modern Art in New York. During the exhibition, notebooks, filled with blank pages, were placed on a base in front of a wall on which the following statement was posted:

> You (the viewer) are requested to write, draw, or otherwise indicate any response suggested by this situation (this statement, the blank notebook and pen, the museum context, your immediate state of mind, etc.) in the pages of the notebook beneath this sign. The information entered in the notebook will not be altered or utilized in any way.

Visitors filled the blank pages of the notebooks with comments that range from doodles, to criticism of the exhibition, to anti-war slogans.

CONTEXT #8 consists of "Written Information Voluntarily Supplied to Me During the Period of April 30 to May 30, 1970." Collected in it are gallery announcements, flyers for anti-war protests and peace rallies, a text by Jean Genet on freeing Bobby Seale, and the loan form for the work Piper contributed to "Information," among other materials. CONTEXT #9, "Written Information Ellicited From Me During the Period of May 15 to June 15, 1970," contains information produced by Piper, such as notes, lists, and drafts of texts, including several drafts and a final copy of a letter explaining the of withdrawal of her work "Hypothesis" from "Conceptual Art and Conceptual Aspects," an exhibition presented at The New York City Cultural Center in 1970, in protest of the United States' invasion of Cambodia and the Kent State massacre:

> The decision to withdraw has been taken as a protective measure against the increasingly pervasive conditions of fear, repression, hatred, hypocrisy, and murder which have come to characterize this country.
> Rather than submit the work to the deadly and poisoning influence of these conditions, I submit its absence as evidence of the inability of art expression to have meaningful existence under conditions other than those of peace, equality, truth, trust, and freedom.

Piper produced FOOD FOR THE SPIRIT (1971) "while

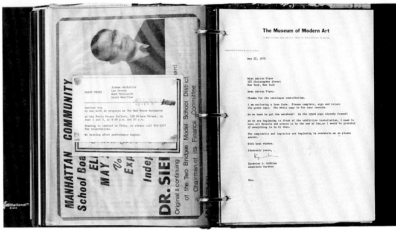

reading and writing a paper on Kant's *Critique of Pure Reason*, fasting, doing yoga, and isolating myself socially." It comprises a notebook containing annotated pages from the *Critique of Pure Reason* interspersed with fourteen photographs in which Piper, in a private loft performance, photographed herself naked before a mirror. FOOD FOR THE SPIRIT parallels Kant's discussion of space, time, and perception and documents Piper's objectification of herself as the subject of her work. In this work and the earlier Catalysis series (1970) of situations and actions, Piper relocated the self-referential object of her work from the piece of paper of the earlier works to herself: "I experimented with my own objecthood, transforming it sculpturally as I had other objects, took it into the street, confronted others with the end products, and watched the effects on my social relations."[5] — AG

Notes

1. Adrian Piper, "Flying," in *Adrian Piper*, exh. cat. (Birmingham: Ikon Gallery and Manchester: Cornerhouse, 1991), 23.

2. Conversation with the artist, 29 November 1993.

3. Adrian Piper, "The Logic of Modernism," *Callaloo* 16, no. 3 (Summer 1993): 577-578.

4. Adrian Piper, artist's statement, 20 January 1994.

5. Piper, "Flying," 24.

Pages from CONTEXT #8 (June 1970)
Three-ring binder filled with printed, photocopied, and mimeographed pages encased in plastic sleeves. Binder, 11 3/4 x 10 1/2 x 3 in. (29.8 x 26.7 x 7.6 cm) (closed); sleeves, 11 x 8 1/2 in. (27.9 x 21.6 cm); pages, various dimensions. Courtesy John Weber Gallery, New York. Photo Paula Goldman.

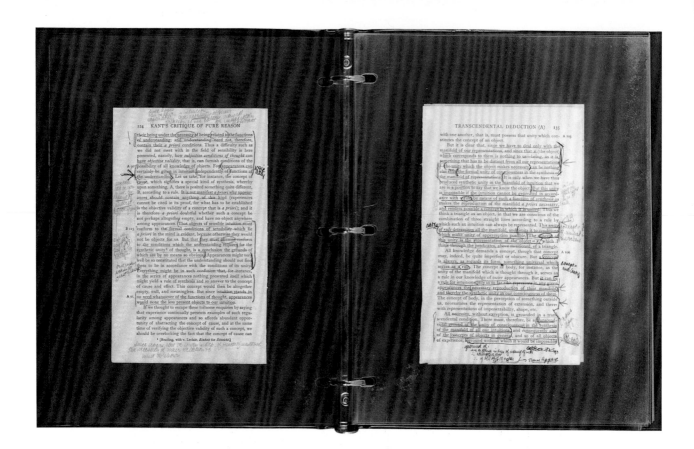

Pages from FOOD FOR THE SPIRIT (1971)
Three-ring binder filled with pages torn from Immanuel Kant, *Critique of Pure Reason,* annotated by the artist, and with black-and-white photographic self-portraits of the artist, each encased in plastic sleeves.
Binder, 11 3/4 x 10 1/2 x 1 1/2 in. (29.8 x 26.7 x 3.8 cm) (closed); sleeves, 11 x 8 1/2 in. (27.9 x 21.6 cm); pages, 7 1/4 x 4 1/2 in. (18.4 x 11.4 cm); photographs, 3 5/8 x 3 5/8 in. (3.6 x 3.6 cm).
Collection Thomas Erben, New York. Photo Paula Goldman.

Adrian Piper

FOOD FOR THE SPIRIT (1971) (detail)
Black-and-white photograph. 20 x 16 in. (50.8 x 40.6 cm).
Courtesy John Weber Gallery, New York. Photo Paula Goldman.

YVONNE RAINER

(b. 24 November 1934, San Francisco; lives in New York City)

Yvonne Rainer's highly influential work in dance, choreography, and performance developed in the milieu of choreographers such as Merce Cunningham, Simone Forti, Ann Halprin, Trisha Brown, Steve Paxton, and Lucinda Childs; composers such as John Cage, La Monte Young, and Philip Corner; and artists such as Carolee Schneemann, Alex Hay, Robert Morris, and Robert Rauschenberg. Her early performances in the Concerts of Dance at the Judson Memorial Church in New York were among the first works cooperatively organized at that site. Rainer has recalled that someone once described her early dance performances by saying, "But she walks as though she's in the street."[1] Among those early performances is ORDINARY DANCE, first performed at Judson Church in 1962. This work consisted of a "solo accompanied by an autobiographical monologue spoken by the performer," a rambling, fragmented narrative in which Rainer interspersed dates and events in her life with nonsensical phrases.[2] It marked an early stage of her ongoing exploration of language, autobiography, and narrative form, which she would develop further in her later work, particularly that in film.[3]

Rainer's four and one half minute performance, TRIO A, was first performed at the Judson Church in 1966 as THE MIND IS A MUSCLE, PART I. Involving three performers, this work was developed in a parallel text by Rainer entitled, "A Quasi Survey of Some 'Minimalist' Tendencies in the Quantitatively Minimal Dance Activity Midst the Plethora, or an Analysis of TRIO A," which proposed a direct relationship between Minimalist objects and dance.[4] Addressing her work in relation to the polemics of Minimalism, Rainer devised companion lists tailored to "objects" and "dances" according to that which should be eliminated or minimized, and that which should be substituted. For example, just as, for objects, "literalness" replaces "illusionism," the parallel in dance replaces "performance" with "task or tasklike activity."

Starting in 1967, Rainer began to incorporate projected texts and images and films in her performances. In 1971 she made film the primary focus of her work. All her performances subsequent to GRAND UNION DREAMS (1971) have been developed in relation to specific film projects. Her first feature-length film, LIVES OF PERFORMERS (1972), which developed from and incorporated GRAND UNION DREAMS, is the story of a man who cannot choose between two women. The film's examination of gender and relationships uses distinct cinematic devices such as voice-over, synchronized sound, direct address, audience response, and intertitles to elaborate upon or disrupt the narrative and the play between the real and fictive roles of Rainer as director and choreographer, as well as those of the performers.

In 1973, in an exchange of letters with Nan Piene following a screening of LIVES OF PERFORMERS, Rainer wrote about the transition from dance to film:

I had started to talk about how as a dancer the unique nature of my body and movement makes a personal statement, but how dancing could no longer encompass or "express" the new content in my work, i.e., the emotions…. Dance is ipso facto about me (the so-called kinesthetic response of the spectator notwithstanding, it only rarely transcends that narcissistic-voyeuristic duality of doer and looker); whereas the area of the emotions must necessarily directly concern both of us. This is what allowed me permission to start manipulating what at first seemed like blatantly personal and private material. But the more I get into it the more I see how such things as rage, terror, desire, conflict, et al., are not unique to my experience the way my body and its functioning are. I now—as a consequence—feel much more connected to my audience, and that gives me great comfort.[5]

FILM ABOUT A WOMAN WHO… (1974), which developed out of the performance, THIS IS THE STORY OF A WOMAN WHO… (1973), is also the story of the conflicts and power relations between men and women. Rainer has commented:

> For me the story is an empty frame on which to hang
> images and thoughts which need support. I feel no
> obligation to flesh out this armature with credible
> details of location and time. LIVES OF PERFORMERS
> tried to do this to a greater extent than WOMAN WHO....
> In WOMAN WHO... I was much more concerned with
> interweaving psychological and formal content, i.e. with
> images being "filled up" or "emptied" by readings or
> their absence, with text and speech being "illustrated"
> to varying degrees by images. This made for a situation
> where the story came and went, sometimes disappear-
> ing altogether as in the extreme prolongation of certain
> soundless images. [6]

Autobiography remains a major aspect of these works, as Rainer has commented:

> Autobiography, as I use it, is a rich source of material,
> and like all material, can be manipulated: fragmented,
> redistributed, magnified, analyzed, juxtaposed. I am a
> performer, a dancer, a director, a person who has been
> through shit and come up smiling, etc. The actuality of
> these roles lends a credibility to what otherwise I would
> have to invent totally from my imagination, which I'm
> not prepared to do. Autobiography saves me needless
> work. When it is distributed among a number of people,
> as in LIVES OF PERFORMERS, or depersonalized by the
> use of the third person pronoun, as in THIS IS THE
> STORY OF A WOMAN WHO..., it has the possibility of
> becoming more objectively biographical, and finally,
> fictional. [7]

Rainer's experimentations in the early 1970s with film narrative and the relationship between word and image were among the earliest explorations of issues of representation in terms of gender and power, and they prove highly influential later in the decade. Reflecting upon the initial emergence of her work in relationship to the developments in feminism at that time,

Rainer has stated:

> Feminist responses to my films in the early 70s had a
> much simpler view of what positive heroines should be
> like. They complained: "Can't there be a positive way to
> create images of women without all this irony and
> ambivalence?" But irony is a way of revealing the pres-
> sure points in an unjust society—for instance, depicting
> the female self trapped between habitual modes of
> behaviour and new knowledge of social strictures. True,
> irony is only a first step, a tearing of a hole in the fabric
> and peeking through. [8] — AG

Notes

1. Yvonne Rainer, *Work 1961-73* (Halifax: The Press of the Nova Scotia College of Art and Design and New York: New York University Press, 1974), vii.

2. Ibid., 288.

3. See "Yvonne Rainer: An Introduction," *Camera Obscura* (Berkeley), no. 1 (Fall 1976): 56, for a discussion of this work and its relation to the films.

4. This essay is reprinted in Gregory Battcock, ed., *Minimal Art: A Critical Anthology* (New York: E. P. Dutton and Co., 1968), 263-273, and in Rainer, *Work 1961-73*, 63-69.

5. Yvonne Rainer, letter to Nan Piene, 27 January 1973, in Rainer, *Work 1961-73*, 238.

6. Yvonne Rainer, in "Yvonne Rainer: Interview," *Camera Obscura* (Berkeley), no. 1 (Fall 1976): 89.

7. Rainer, *Work 1961-73*, 275.

8. Yvonne Rainer, in Laleen Jayamanne, Geeta Kapur, and Rainer, "Discussing Modernity, 'Third World,' and *The Man Who Envied Women*, in *Art and Text* (Melbourne) 23, no. 4 (March-May 1987): 50.

TRIO A (THE MIND IS A MUSCLE, PART I)
Choreographed 1966; filmed in 16 mm 14 August 1978.
Videotape: 10 min., b/w, silent. Courtesy the artist.

TOP: FILM ABOUT A WOMAN WHO…(1974)
Still from film (16mm, 105 min., b/w and color, sound), showing Dempster Leech
and Renfreu Neff. Courtesy the artist and Zeitgeist Films.

MIDDLE AND BOTTOM: LIVES OF PERFORMERS (1972)
Stills from film (16mm, 90 min., b/w, sound), respectively showing Shirley
Soffer, Fernando Torm, Valda Setterfield, and John Erdman; and Soffer,
Setterfield, and Torm.
Courtesy the artist and Zeitgeist Films.

LIVES OF PERFORMERS (1972).

ALLEN RUPPERSBERG

(b. 5 January 1944, Cleveland; lives in New York City and Santa Monica, California)

Since the late 1970s, Allen Ruppersberg has produced works in numerous media, including drawing, painting, sculpture, photography, video, film, slide projection, installation, and books. As he stated in his text "Fifty Helpful Hints on the Art of the Everyday" (1984), his practice is grounded in everyday life, in the "ordinary and the rare, their interconnectedness and interchangeability." Drawing from film, literature, advertising, and the experiences of his life, Ruppersberg enters into and plays with the spectrum of representations that construct reality. In particular, he incorporates the "reality of impressions and the impression of reality," the influences and intersections of illusionism and concrete banality, that can be found in contemporary Los Angeles.[1]

In 1968 Ruppersberg published his first book, 23 PIECES. This small, spiral-bound, offset book includes photographs of twenty-three locations in Los Angeles, such as the window display of the Liberty Lighting and Lamps store in Studio City and the house phones at the Ambassador Hotel. It and its sequel, 24 LOCATIONS (1970), which features interventions into hotel rooms in Los Angeles, as well as the unpublished 25 LOCATIONS (1972), are, as Howard Singerman has written, "all overloaded on the side of place. But repeated generic, typical, more like others like themselves than their locations, they are isolated and sectioned off, placeless, as well. Ruppersberg's sites are always the sites of fictions."[2]

In 1969, for his first one-person exhibition at Eugenia Butler Gallery in Los Angeles, Ruppersberg made LOCATION PIECE. For that exhibition, the gallery was empty, except for the address of an office on Sunset Boulevard where Ruppersberg installed large, set-like sculptures using theatrical backdrops and objects from the desert that recalled the mixed-media aquarium still-life sculptures he had begun to make in 1968.

He also explored the concept of the alternative setting in two major projects, "Al's Cafe" (1969) and "Al's Grand Hotel" (1971). In "Al's Cafe," an installation in a storefront at 1913 West Sixth Street, near downtown Los Angeles, Ruppersberg constructed a menu based on a Hollywood diner. "Al's Cafe" featured such specialties as the "Patti Melt" ($2.00) consisting of a "Patti Page photo (or reasonable facsimile) covered with toasted marshmallows" and the "Angeles National Forest Special" ($3.00), which included tree bark, assorted twigs and rocks, and a pine cone.

"Al's Grand Hotel," located in a two-story, craftsman-style house at 7175 Sunset Boulevard in Hollywood, was a fully operational hotel open Friday and Saturday nights from 7 May to 12 June 1971. Each room featured a double bed and daily maid service; room rates ranged from fifteen to thirty dollars per night. The seven guest rooms included The Breakfast Room (restaurant booths and halved furniture and pictures), The Al Room (seven different life-size, freestanding photographic cut-outs of Ruppersberg holding up his left hand in a peace symbol, along with party decorations), The Ultra Violet Room (nine signed and dated framed sheets of notebook paper, each bearing the title of a film in which the Warhol superstar Ultra Violet appeared), The Day Room (166

paper pails containing cereal boxes, canned food, comic books, and tabloid newspapers), The Jesus Room (furnished with rented motel furniture and a fifteen foot-long wooden cross that extended diagonally across the room), The "B" Room (126 *Life* magazines on the walls and a picnic set-up on the floor), and The Bridal Suite (plastic ivy and flowers over the bed, a pillowcase embroidered with the name "Wanda," seven framed wedding photographs surrounding a pink mirrored dressing table, ten wedding presents and cards, and a three-tier wedding cake). All items in the house were for sale and listed in the accompanying catalogue.

In addition to exploring location as an aspect of representation and the integration of art into everyday life, Ruppersberg's work has consistently incorporated language, as well as the subject of reading. His sources range from detective novels and newspapers, to the works of literary figures such as Henry David Thoreau, Oscar Wilde, and William Butler Yeats. In 1973 he made HENRY DAVID THOREAU'S WALDEN BY ALLEN RUPPERSBERG, in which he transcribed Thoreau's book by hand onto sheets of paper. Widely read by young people during the late 1960s and early 1970s, *Walden* documents Thoreau's embrace of the primacy of direct individual experience. In Ruppersberg's work, *Walden* becomes a source for the ironic *re-presentation* of such experience. As Singerman has observed, "Ruppersberg's paradoxical authorship recalls, or rewrites not only Thoreau, but another author as well: Borges' 'Pierre Menard, Author of Quixote.'...Despite their disparate methods, Ruppersberg and Menard and their texts bear the same relationship to their originals: they are different."[3]

In "Fifty Helpful Hints" Ruppersberg wrote: "The act of copying something allows the use of things as they are, without altering their original nature. They can then be used with ideas about art on a fifty-fifty basis, and create something entirely new."[4] In THE PICTURE OF DORIAN GRAY (1974), he transcribed Wilde's novel free-hand with a Pentel marker onto twenty six-foot square, unprimed, stretched canvases. When the work was first exhibited at Claire Copley Gallery in Los Angeles in 1974, Ruppersberg used the architecture of the gallery to give it form. As the wall space could not accommodate all twenty canvases, some were stacked against one of the hanging panels (notably not the last), breaking the continuity of the story and treating the objects like casual commodities. This transformation of a novel about a painting into a painting to be read is, as Peter Plagens has observed, "an alleged work of painting that is really literature about a work about literature which is about a painting."[5] — AG

Notes

1. Allen Ruppersberg, "Fifty Helpful Hints on the Art of the Everyday," in *Allen Ruppersberg: The Secret of Life and Death, Volume 1 1969-1984*, exh. cat. (Los Angeles: The Museum of Contemporary Art and Santa Barbara: Black Sparrow Press, 1985), 111.

2. Howard Singerman, "Allen Ruppersberg: Drawn from Life," in *Allen Ruppersberg*, 22.

3. Ibid., 31.

4. Ruppersberg, "Fifty Helpful Hints," 112.

5. Peter Plagens, "Ruppersberg's Encyclopedia," *Art in America* 73, no. 12 (December 1985): 90.

AL'S GRAND HOTEL, 7175 Sunset Boulevard, Los Angeles (7 May-12 June 1971).
Top to bottom: "The Al Room," "The 'B' Room," "The Day Room," "The Jesus Room."

206

Interior view of AL'S CAFE, 1913 West Sixth Street, Los Angeles (1969).

"Sandwiches: "Patti Melt — Patti Page Photo (or Reasonable Facsimile)
Covered with Toasted Marshmellows: $2.00." From AL'S CAFE

THE PICTURE OF DORIAN GRAY (1974)
Pentel on canvas. Twenty panels: each, 72 x 72 in. (182.9 x 182.9 cm).
Collection Stuart and Judy Spence, South Pasadena, California. Installation
view, Claire Copley Gallery, Los Angeles, 9 April–4 May 1974.

EDWARD RUSCHA

(b. 16 December 1937,
Omaha, Nebraska; lives
in Los Angeles)

In an interview published in 1972, Edward Ruscha recalled recording a daydream about an imaginary person he called THE INFORMATION MAN:

The INFORMATION MAN *is someone who comes up to you and begins telling you stories and related facts about a particular subject in your life. He came up to me and said, 'Of all the books of yours that are out in the public, only 171 are placed face up with nothing covering them; 2,026 are in vertical positions in libraries, and 2,715 are under books in stacks. The most weight on a single book is 68 pounds, and that is in the city of Cologne, Germany, in a bookstore. Fifty-eight have been lost; 14 have been totally destroyed by water or fire; 216 books could be considered badly worn. Three hundred and nineteen books are in positions between 40 and 50 degrees. Eighteen of the books have been deliberately thrown away or destroyed. Fifty-three books have never been opened, most of these being newly purchased and put aside momentarily... Of the approximately 5,000 books of Ed Ruscha that have been purchased, only 32 have been used in a directly functional manner. Thirteen of these have been used as weights for paper or other small things, seven have been used as swatters to kill small insects such as flies and mosquitoes, two were used as a device to nudge open a door, six have been used to transport foods like peanuts to a coffee table, and four*

208

The artist covered with a selection of his books (c. 1969).

have been used to nudge wall pictures to their correct levels. Two hundred and twenty-one people have smelled pages of the books. Three of the books have been in continual motion since their purchase; all three of these on a boat near Seattle, Washington. Now wouldn't it be nice to know these things?[1]

Ruscha produced seventeen books between 1962 and 1972. The first, conceived in 1962 and published in January 1963, is TWENTYSIX GASOLINE STATIONS, which consists of photographs of gas stations on Route 66 between Los Angeles and Oklahoma City:

I wanted to make a book of some kind. And at the same time, I—my whole attitude about everything came out in this one phrase that I made up for myself, which was 'twentysix gasoline stations.' I worked on that in my mind for a long time and I knew that title before the book had even come about. And then, paradoxically, the idea of the photographs of the gas stations came around, so it's an idea first—and then I kind of worked it down.[2]

Many of Ruscha's subsequent books, including VARIOUS SMALL FIRES AND MILK (1964), SOME LOS ANGELES APARTMENTS (1965), EVERY BUILDING ON THE SUNSET STRIP (1966), THIRTYFOUR PARKING LOTS IN LOS ANGELES (1967), NINE SWIMMING POOLS AND A BROKEN GLASS (1968), and A FEW PALM TREES (1971), were inspired by the vernacular architecture and culture of Los Angeles.

Ruscha's books are self-published, unsigned, offset-printed paperbacks; with the exception of the first printing of his first book, they are unnumbered. Until recently they have been periodically reprinted. Moving away from the notion of the precious, limited edition livre d'artiste, Ruscha's books may be regarded as among the earliest artists' books that sought alternative forms and spaces for the production and distribution of art. As Clive Phillpot has written,

This was a radical break with the nature of previous interactions between artists and books. The customary aura of artworks was instantly dispelled. These were no precious objects to be locked away and protected from inquisitive viewers. They were obviously for use, and intended to be handled and enjoyed. Thus, Ruscha created the paradigm for artists' books.[3]

Equal in importance to the form of the book is Ruscha's functional, rather than aestheticized, use of photography. As he has stated, "I never take pictures just for the taking of pictures; I'm not interested in that at all. I'm not intrigued *that* much with the medium. ...I want the end product; that's what I'm really interested in. It's strictly a medium to use or to not use, and I use it only when I have to. I use it to do a job, which is to make a book."[4]

Ruscha's book/portfolio STAINS (1969) is the artist's first work to use organic materials as the medium. STAINS is a portfolio of seventy-five loose sheets of paper, each of which has been

209

stained with an organic substance ranging from Los Angeles tap water to Coca-Cola to semen. Ruscha's investigation of these materials then led to the use of vegetable matter and organic materials in silkscreen prints and later as a kind of paint on such surfaces as silk and taffeta.

In the summer of 1970 Ruscha was invited to participate in the Venice Biennale. Several artists, including Robert Rauschenberg, boycotted the Biennale in protest of the United States' participation in the Vietnam war. Although Ruscha also considered boycotting, and in fact wrote a fictitious letter from his mother to excuse him from participating, he ultimately did participate in what was a summer-long experimental graphic workshop: CHOCOLATE ROOM. For this work the walls of the galleries of the American Pavilion were hung with 360 sheets of paper silkscreened with chocolate paste. Henry Hopkins, who coordinated the United States' representation in that year's Biennale, described the work's impact:

The visual experience and odor were quite overwhelming. Whether planned or not, the work became a protest of its own, since visitors found that they could moisten their fingers and write into the chocolate surface. Many antiwar statements were made. The piece came to an end when the Venetian ants invaded and set up incredible patterns on the surface. Such is justice.[5] — AG

Notes

1. Edward Ruscha in A. D. Coleman, "My Books End Up in the Trash," *The New York Times*, 27 August 1972, 2:12.

2. Edward Ruscha in A. D. Coleman, "I'm Not Really a Photographer," *The New York Times*, 10 September 1972, 2:35.

3. Clive Phillpot, "Some Contemporary Artists and Their Books," in *Artists' Books: A Critical Anthology and Sourcebook*, ed. Joan Lyons (Rochester; Visual Studies Workshop Press, 1985), 97.

4. Edward Ruscha in Coleman, "I'm Not Really a Photographer," 2:35.

5. Henry T. Hopkins, "Director's Foreword: Ed Ruscha: Three Contact Points," in *The Works of Edward Ruscha*, exh. cat. (San Francisco: San Francisco Museum of Modern Art and New York: Hudson Hills Press, 1982), 11.

CHOCOLATE ROOM (1970)
Chocolate silkscreened on paper and hung on walls. Installation view, Venice Biennale, 1970.

VARIOUS SMALL FIRES AND MILK (1964)
Bound artist's book printed by Anderson, Ritchie & Simon, Los Angeles
(48 pp. with 16 offset photographs). 7 x 5 1/2 in. (17.8 x 14 cm). First ed.: 400;
second ed. (1970): 3,000. Photo Paula Goldman.

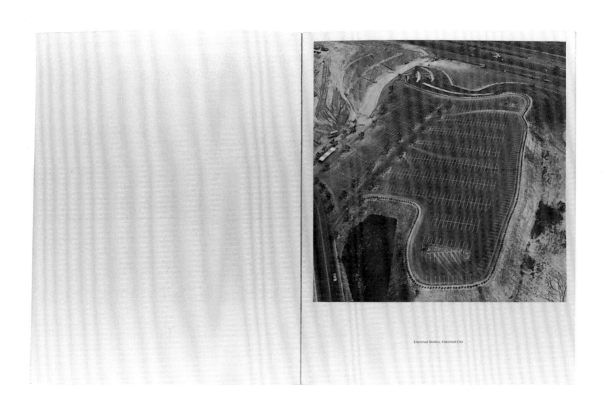

THIRTYFOUR PARKING LOTS IN LOS ANGELES (1967)
Bound artist's book (46 pp. with 31 offset halftone reproductions). 10 x 8 in. (25.4 x 20.3
cm). First ed.: 2,413; second ed.: 2,000 (1974). Photo Paula Goldman.

Edward Ruscha's (left) left hand being examined by Mason Williams' (right) right hand over what's left of the typewriter. right?

(Left) Edward Ruscha (left) and Mason Williams (right) examining main body of typewriter.

ROYAL ROAD TEST (1967)
Spiral—bound artist's book (62 pp. with 36 offset halftone reproductions). 9 1/2 x 6 5/16 in. (24.1 x 16.0 cm). First ed.: 1,000; Second ed. (1969): 1,000; third ed. (1971): 2,000; fourth ed. (1980): 1,500. Text and photographs by Mason Williams, Edward Ruscha, and Patrick Blackwell. Photo Paula Goldman.

N.W. corner of Doheny Dr. & Elevado Ave.

A FEW PALM TREES (1971)
Bound artist's book published by Heavy Industry Publications, Hollywood (64pp. with 14 offset halftone reproductions). 7 x 5 1/2 in. (17.8 x 14 cm). Photo Paula Goldman.

ROBERT SMITHSON

(b. 2 January 1938, Passaic, New Jersey; d. 20 July 1973, Tecovas Lake, Texas)

A small-scale, pencil drawing entitled A HEAP OF LANGUAGE (1966) predates the large-scale outdoor earthworks proposed or realized by Robert Smithson in the early 1970s. In this small drawing sequentially penciled words relating to language, such as "phraseology," "speech," "tongue," "lingo," "English," "dialect," "brogue," or "cipher," have been amassed and layered next to and above one another to form a pyramidal shape. The words fill up the piece of graph paper on which they are written and suggest an analogy between themselves and materials heaped up to form a monumental mound. The individual words that give rise to this work function both as piled objects and as nouns that deal linguistically with structures built of words.

Smithson's unique drawing is hinged between his work as a sculptor and his work as a writer. Although these two modes of endeavor, sculpture and writing, stem from the two different but related activities pursued by Smithson until his early death in 1973, he taunted the hard and fast nature of their separation. Although leaving them more or less intact, Smithson's work signaled the potential porousness of the linguistic category of literature versus the material categories of painting and sculpture. Just as words perform as both objects and abstractions in A HEAP OF LANGUAGE, so in writings by Smithson, words are often employed to create analogies between the metaphoric and the material, between the mental and the physical, and between language, art, and the materiality of the earth.

Although they are information-bearing, printed, textual documents, Smithson's published pieces present themselves as a form of hybrid between an artwork and a standard, published article. Thus, "The Domain of the Great Bear," written in collaboration with Mel Bochner and published in the magazine *Art Voices* in February 1966, successfully eludes typecasting. An essay on the American Museum of Natural History and Hayden Planetarium in New York, it is an illustrated exegesis that carries the reader from the cosmic heights of planetary movements to the bathos of institutional settings and presents an unusual design (including a reproduction of a sign with a hand pointing to "SOLAR SYSTEM & REST ROOM"). This work strikes a different note from the more typical expository contributions to the magazine without, however, forfeiting its discursive character as an essay.

Smithson developed the sculptures he called Nonsites in 1968. A typed description, in combination with a map, figures as a crucial element in these works, which bring materials such as rocks, sand, or cinders directly into the exhibition space without transforming them. Geometrically-shaped, painted metal bins, alone or in a series depending upon the particular work, contain industrial or natural debris, while the map and accompanying textual documentation locate and detail the surrounding nature of the site where the Nonsites originated. Framed descriptive texts reconnect the Nonsite to their original sites by recontextualizing their former environment within the new context of an exhibition. Through linguistic as well as cartographic representation Smithson was able to join art contexts with non-art contexts that exist on the industrial fringes of civilization. The Nonsites divorce sculptural practice from its associations with hand- or man-made, three-dimensional objects. At the same time, they unite the object on view with its place of origin and undermine its autonomy, otherwise taken for granted, within a gallery space. — AR

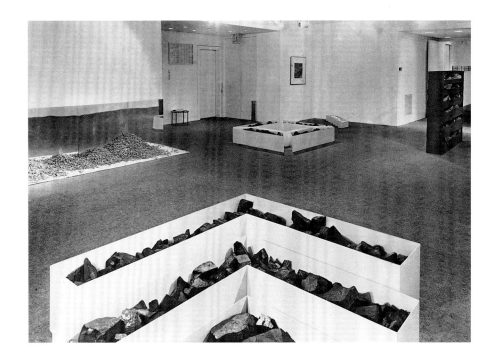

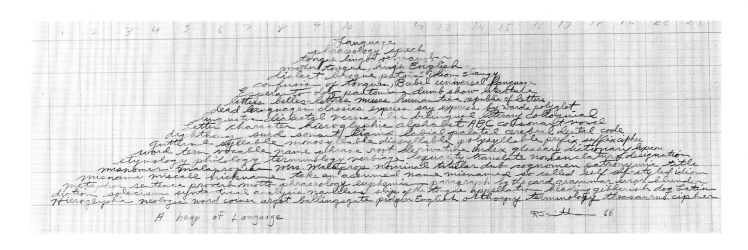

Installation view, "Robert Smithson," Dwan Gallery, New York, 1–26 February 1969.
Courtesy Silent Partners Consulting, Brooklyn, New York.

A HEAP OF LANGUAGE (1966)
Pencil on graph paper. 6 1/2 x 22 in. (16.5 x 55.9 cm).
Courtesy Estate of Robert Smithson and John Weber Gallery, New York.

MICHAEL SNOW

(b. 10 December 1929, Toronto, Ontario; lives in Toronto)

Michael Snow's work since the early 1950s has been distinguished by a remarkable diversity, including painting, drawing, sculpture, music, film, photography, sound, books, and writings. Addressing the relationship between representation and reality, Snow's self-reflexive work encompasses and exhibits the apparatus and conditions of its production, function, physical manifestation, and perception. Writing about Snow's work in 1971, Annette Michelson described the course of the artist's career as "an inquiry into the modes of seeing, recording, reflecting, composing, remembering and projecting."[1]

Snow's Walking Woman series (1961-67) consists of various manifestations of an idealized profile silhouette of a woman in stride. Realized as positive and negative life-size cut-outs, paintings, drawings, sculptures, and decals, and placed within numerous contexts, the Walking Woman series exhaustively explores the process of representation as the re-representation and the reconstruction of meaning.

Snow's landmark forty-five minute 16mm film WAVELENGTH (1966-67) marks a significant transition in his work. Filmed with a stationery camera in a continuous zoom across the artist's eighty-foot long loft, it commences with a wide-angle shot and concludes with a close-up of a photograph of the surface of the sea. The progression of the zoom is interrupted by the sounds of the movement of a bookcase, a Beatles song, a death and its report on the telephone, as well as physical manipulations of and superimpositions on the film stock itself, which draw attention to the spatial, temporal, and dimensional aspects of the image, the apparatus of its construction, and the process of seeing. The spatial and temporal play between two and three dimensions is further explored in such films as ↔ (1968-69) and LA REGION CENTRALE (1970-71).

Philip Monk has termed the work in film, sculpture, and photography that Snow produced from 1967 to 1969 as a specific period "around Wavelength."[2] He has stated that "[t]hese works concentrated their apparatus on the function of viewing in order to make sight visible."[3] TAP (1969), for example, comprises a dispersed composition of five parts, as listed in the text that constitutes Part Three: "1. a sound, 2. an image, 3. a text, 4. an object, 5. a line, which would be unified but the parts of which would be of interest in themselves if the connections between them were not seen (but better if seen)." The "image" in the work is a large photograph of Snow tapping his fingers against the microphone of a reel-to-reel tape recorder, the "sound" of which is audible on a speaker (the "object") and echoed in the production of the typewritten, self-describing "text," which together produce a line of connection looping between the dispersed elements of the work. Presented simultaneously, the various elements of TAP cohere into what Snow describes in the final paragraph of Part Three as

> a kind of still sound movie. The ways in which the different elements occupy space are interesting: the sound filling it, having a source but no definite 'edges', the line, reading backwards, threading and carrying the sound and have an unseen end, the image flat, two

214

TAP (1969-72)
Framed black-and-white photographs, framed typewritten texts on paper, tape
player, speaker, wire, and audiotape. Photograph with frame, 42 x 61 1/2 in.
(106.8 x 156.3 cm); typewritten text with frame: 25 5/8 x 15 3/4 in.
(65.1 x 40.0 cm); speaker: 19 x 15 x 10 in. (48.3 x 38.1 x 25.4 cm).
National Gallery of Canada, Ottawa. Photo © NGC/MBAC.

dimensional, this flat, black, linear, small, in your eyes
and in your mind.

Regina Cornwell has described the relationship of this work to
Conceptual art:

Characterizing the line of wire as an "object" recalls
conceptual art's antithetical concern with the demateri-
alization of art. TAP *becomes almost a parody of fram-*
ing in which the speaker frames the sound, the brown
colour of the speaker is used on frames for the image
and the text, and the image is of one of hands framed
on a tape recorder making sound. Once again as in
Snow's other photographic works the references are
internal, falling back on themselves. [4]

Snow's book COVER TO COVER (1975) comprises 360
photographs that show two sides of each object photographed. As
the actions of Snow are recorded, the images also reflect the production, documentation, and examination of the book itself, thus
bringing the process of production and representation into a self-

reflexive circle. As Snow has stated, "There are 360 pages—360
photos—and the whole thing is basically built on this recto-verso
principle, that the other side of the page is the other side of what
is being photographed. Also it is built of sequences of varying
lengths so that while individual photos are, I hope, very interesting alone, they are always part of a sequence which is itself part
of a large 'narrative' which is itself about the book." [5] — AG

Notes

1. Annette Michelson, "Toward Snow: Part I," *Artforum* 9, no. 10 (June 1971): 37.

2. See Philip Monk, "Around Wavelength," in *The Michael Snow Project: Visual Art:
1951-1993*, exh. cat. (Toronto: Art Gallery of Ontario, The Power Plant, and Alfred A.
Knopf Canada, 1993), 293-385.

3. Monk, "Around Wavelength," 294.

4. Regina Cornwell, *Snow Seen: The Films and Photographs of Michael Snow* (Toronto:
PMA Books, 1980), 49.

5. Michael Snow, statement in Tim Guest, ed. *Books by Artists* (Toronto: Art Metropole,
1981), 79.

NIELE TORONI

(b. 15 March 1937,
Locarno-Muralto,
Switzerland; lives in
Paris)

From his first public exhibition at the beginning of 1967 to the present, Niele Toroni has given the same title to all of his works: IMPRINTS OF A NO. 50 BRUSH REPEATED AT REGULAR INTERVALS OF 30 CM. As this title makes clear, his working method consistently involves the placement of the same-sized, 50 mm, rectangular brushmark on a specified surface at the same distance of 30 cm (nearly one foot) apart. Plotting this constantly maintained interval in advance and proceeding from left to right, Toroni does not diverge from his approach of setting each brushmark down at an identical distance from both the previous one and from the line of brushmarks above it.

The paint color used for an individually defined surface area of brushmarks does not vary within a particular sequence. Generally, although not always, Toroni uses black or primary colors. Color functions as a factual component of the work as a whole, one hue being equal in importance to any other; series of brushmarks are always identical in color.

Toroni has encapsulated the important aspects of his approach to painting in a formulaic statement describing his "Method of Work":

> On the given support a no. 50 brush is applied at regular intervals of 30 cm.
> Support: canvas, cloth, paper, oil-cloth, wall, ground... , generally white surfaces.
> To apply: "to place a thing upon another one so as to cover it and stick on it, or leave an imprint.
> Brush no. 50: flat paintbrush 50 mm. wide.
> Interval: "...distance from one point to another"

As his statement specifically notes, a given support—normally white—may consist of any material or surface.

The artist installing a work outside his studio.

The significance of the imprint, derived from the controlled manipulation of a standard brush filled with enough liquid paint to be pressed against a surface without dripping, rests in the fact that the artist obtains only the image left by the bristles of his brush. No one imprint takes precedence over another as there is no differentiation between them in color, in their hierarchical status within the structure of an overall grid, or in their size. Slight, if barely noticeable, variations among the individual imprints preserve the singularity of each brushstroke. The consistent repetition of the imprints bears witness to the irregularities of hand production, while mimicking the mechanical aspects of reproduction.

Toroni arrived at the decision to generate equidistant and repeated imprints systematically in the latter months of 1966 and first exhibited the results publicly in Paris in January 1967. Serving first and foremost as an anonymous sign for the painted surface par excellence, the brushstroke as imprint has come to be exclusively associated with Toroni. From the beginning of his career to the present, his method of working has remained the same with each work being differentiated by its material support.—AR

Installation view, "Travail/Peinture de Niele Toroni," Wide White Space, Antwerp, 26 February 1975.

WILLIAM WEGMAN

(b. 2 December 1943, Holyoke, Massachusetts; lives in New York City) William Wegman's photographs, videotapes, and drawings of the late 1960s to mid-1970s engage in an exchange of signs and pictures, reading and looking, and fiction and truth, through the play of visual and verbal language. As Martin Kunz has written, "Words are vital and sometimes dominant in Wegman's art, and not only as captions for images or voice-over narration in videos; they also figure actively in thoughtfully conceived photographs, pictures, or drawings. Sometimes Wegman will cite words in his pictures; sometimes words ARE the picture."[1] Wegman's straightforward use of conventional form and narrative sequence is visible in the construction of his visual puns, manipulated consequences, and disrupted logic. His work, often discussed in terms of a deadpan, Keaton-esque humor, also reflects the inspiration of Jorge Luis Borges's "parables of circular time."[2]

Wegman began working in video in 1969 while teaching sculpture at the University of Wisconsin in Madison. Up to that point, his work in sculpture had involved actions, such as tossing radios from buildings or floating words in the water, that were documented through photography and 8mm films. Wegman eventually began to construct images intended specifically to be recorded by the camera. He has described a key moment that developed from this early use of photography and video, as well as from his desire to distance himself from the Minimalist and Conceptualist practices of artists like Sol LeWitt, Carl Andre, and Robert Smithson[3]:

I had a "Eureka" type experience. Both video and photography contributed to that moment. I remember one photo in particular—COTTO [1970]. I had drawn little rings—little circles on my left hand on my fingers with my ring on my index finger and I went to a party....Well, a plate of salami was on the table and reaching in I was struck by the peculiar relationship of these little rings with the little rings in the salami—the peppercorns. Anyway I rushed home with the salami, set up my camera and photographed it with my own hand reaching in. I developed the negative and printed it and..."Eureka."...Meaning I could construct a picture and that way directly produce a work—not a secondary record of it. The "construction" existed only for that purpose.[4]

In the late 1960s Wegman developed an interest in the work of the Southern Californian artists Edward Ruscha, Bruce Nauman, and Allen Ruppersberg.[5] In 1970 he moved to California to accept a teaching position at California State University in Long Beach; he would live in the Los Angeles area until late 1972. Also in 1970 Wegman began producing works featuring his newly acquired Weimeraner puppy Man Ray (a practice he continued until Man Ray's death in 1982). In an interview published in 1973, Wegman commented that

I had no idea I was going to be using him in the pieces. ...I didn't get him for that reason. He was brought up under the camera all along because he'd be around

COTTO (1969)
Gelatin-silver print. 10 1/8 x 10 1/4 in. (25.7 x 26.0 cm).
Collection Edward Ruscha.

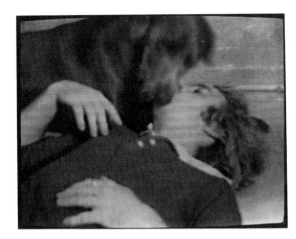

while I was working and get into some photographs and tapes accidentally, so it became very matter of fact to use him. [6]

Although Wegman is now closely identified with Man Ray, he notes that he used the dog in only ten percent of his photographs and videotapes. [7]

In a text on the artist's photographs, Frédéric Paul described two major themes that traverse the work: perception and identity. [8] CROW (1970), for example, plays with the act of the double take required to distinguish the parrot from the cast shadow, and the systematized positions of Man Ray's incremental ascent and descent in RAY-O-VAC (1973) has been seen as playing with the serial forms of Minimalism. [9]

Unlike the photographs, in which he depicted objects in different states simultaneously, Wegman used video for its ability to record the passage of real time. The videotapes he produced between 1970 and 1977 comprise seven reels of approximately twenty to thirty minutes each. Wegman describes the tapes as "brief vignettes involving studio and familiar household props." [10] The visual puns of such REEL 1 (1970-72) vignettes as "Hot Sake" or "Nosy" recall the plays with language explored by Bruce Nauman in such works as EATING MY WORDS, FEET OF CLAY, and WAXING HOT, from his series of eleven color photographs of 1966-67/70. The tapes that comprise REEL 2 (1972), REEL 3 (1972-73), and REEL 4 (1973-74), as Wegman has written, are "more audio oriented than the earlier works, given somewhat to a fascination with narrative. Usually the image came first and a narrative

was thought up to accomodate it." [11]

In 1972 Wegman began to make pencil and pen drawings on typing paper. Like the photographs and videos, they incorporate visual puns, banal speculations (NEIGHBOR'S BALL BOUNCES OVER HOUSE, 1973), plays of logic against nonsense (PERCENTAGE PROBLEM, 1973), and rebuses (OWN YOUR OWN, 1975). As Wegman commented, their sketch-like simplicity of form and content contributes to their ambiguity of meaning: "Those first drawings were more about form—lists and statistical info. How to dot i's. Then later how to gouge them out with a bird beak." [12] — AG

Notes

1. Martin Kunz, "Drawings: Conceptual Pivot of Wegman's Artistic Worlds," in *William Wegman: Paintings, Drawings, Photographs, Videotapes*, exh. cat. (Lucerne: Kunstmuseum Luzern and New York: Harry N. Abrams, Inc., 1990), 133.

2. William Wegman, in Peter Schjeldahl, "The Faith of Daydreams," in *William Wegman*, exh. cat. (Monterrey: Museo de Monterrey, 1993), 12.

3. See William Wegman's text "Eureka" in *William Wegman Photographic Works/L'oeuvre photographique 1969-1976*, exh. cat. (Limoges: F.R.A.C. Limousin, 1991), 9-14.

4. William Wegman in David Ross, "An Interview with William Wegman," in *William Wegman: Paintings, Drawings, Photographs, Videotapes*, 15.

5. Conversation with the artist, 23 November 1993.

6. William Wegman in Liza Béar, "Man Ray, Do You Want To . . . : An Interview with William Wegman," *Avalanche*, no. 7 (Winter-Spring 1973): 40.

7. William Wegman in Ross, "An Interview with William Wegman," 19 (note).

8. Frédéric Paul, "Bill, William & Prof. Wegman: Fundamental Works: 1969-1976," in *William Wegman Photographic Works*, 19.

9. See Alain Sayag, "Photographs: The Invention of an Art," in *William Wegman: Paintings, Drawings, Photographs, Videotapes*, 49.

10. William Wegman, "Videotapes: Seven Reels," in *William Wegman: Paintings, Drawings, Photographs, Videotapes*, 25.

11. Ibid.

12. William Wegman in David Ross, "An Interview with William Wegman," 21.

"The Kiss." Still from Reel 2 (1972) of SELECTED WORKS Videotape: 14 min. 9 sec., b/w, sound.

"Man Ray, Do You Want To?" Still from Reel 3 (1972-73) of SELECTED WORKS Videotape: 17 min. 54 sec., b/w, sound.

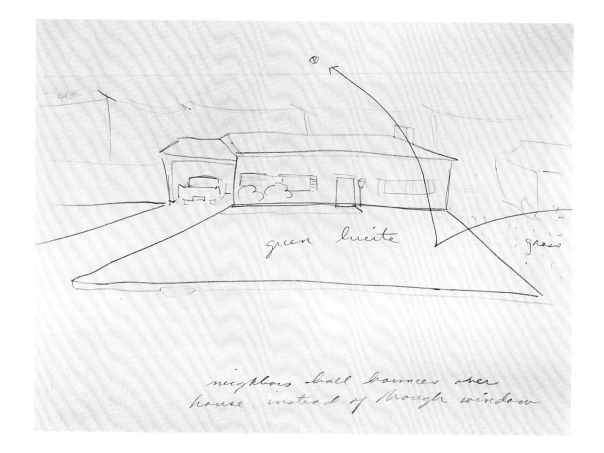

green lucite   grass

neighbors ball bounces over house instead of through window

NEIGHBOR'S BALL BOUNCES OVER HOUSE (1973)
Pencil on paper. 8 1/2 x 11 in. (21.6 x 27.9 cm). Courtesy the artist.

RAY-O-VAC (1973)
Six photographs mounted on board. Overall, 25 3/4 x 44 1/4 in. (65.4 x 112.3 cm).
The Museum of Modern Art, New York. Given anonymously, 1981.
Copy print © 1995 The Museum of Modern Art, New York.

LAWRENCE WEINER

(b. 10 February 1942,
Bronx, New York City; lives
in New York City
and Amsterdam)

In the spring of 1968 Lawrence Weiner reached the conclusion that it might be possible to forego the physical construction of a work. Until this moment sculptural works he had "drawn up" in advance as descriptive phrases were meant to be built according to their verbally-stated elements. Weiner has recounted that what might be considered the definitive turning point in his approach to sculpture occurred when he was in the process of installing a piece for the now historic outdoor exhibition, "Carl Andre, Robert Barry, Lawrence Weiner," conceived by Chuck Ginnever and organized by Seth Siegelaub, which was held on the grounds of Windham College in Putney, Vermont, in 1968. Having placed his work, entitled A SERIES OF STAKES SET IN THE GROUND AT REGULAR INTERVALS TO FORM A RECTANGLE—TWINE STRUNG FROM STAKE TO STAKE TO DEMARK A GRID—A RECTANGLE REMOVED FROM THIS RECTANGLE, in a vulnerable location, he later found it damaged.[1] Because the sculpture had been initially formulated in language, Weiner determined that, paradoxically, its permanence was ensured. Despite the physical damage it suffered, the sculpture remained intact as testimony to a material object, for which, as a linguistic construction, it could stand in at any time.

Soon thereafter, in the fall of 1968, Weiner devised the statement that has accompanied presentations of his work since 1969.[2] It reads:

1. The artist may construct the piece.

2. The piece may be fabricated.

3. The piece need not be built.

Each being equal and consistent with the intent of the artist, the decision as to condition rests with the receiver upon the occasion of receivership.

By means of this statement, the artist stipulates that the actual,

physical realization of any one of his works is not a requirement but, instead, an option left open to the discretion of any perceiving subject, Weiner himself included. A 36" x 36" REMOVAL TO THE LATHING OR SUPPORT WALL OF PLASTER OR WALLBOARD FROM A WALL (1968), for example, was realized for the Kunsthalle Bern's exhibition "When Attitudes Become Form: Works—Concepts—Processes—Situations—Information: Live in Your Head." The same year, A SQUARE REMOVAL FROM A RUG IN USE (1969) was physically realized in the home of collectors who had purchased the piece. At their request, Weiner came to their residence in Cologne and cut a square section out of the rug. He thereby created a lacuna, not an additional *objet d'art*, to their collection.

Although all works by Weiner may, in principle, be materially constructed, they must first be registered in the mind's eye and grasped with respect to their linguistic specifications. Because of the manner in which they are embodied in language, they are never conclusive descriptions subject to one static mode of interpretation. Infinitely open-ended, they have the potential for being visualized and/or realized in countless ways and contexts. Unlike a traditional painting or sculpture, they may be presented on a wall, or in a book, or they may simply be spoken. They are not, furthermore, limited to being shown in any one place at any one time and may take an indefinite number of presentational forms either within or outside of conventional exhibition spaces. — AR

Notes

1. See Weiner's account in Lynn Gumpert's interview with the artist in *Early Work: Lynda Benglis, Joan Brown, Luis Jimenez, Gary Stephan, Lawrene Weiner*, exh. cat. (New York: The New Museum of Contemporary Art, 1982), 48.

2. See Benjamin H. D. Buchloh, ed., *Lawrence Weiner: Posters November 1965-April 1986* (Halifax: The Press of the Nova Scotia College of Art and Design and Toronto: Art Metropole, 1987), 173. As Buchloh specifies, Weiner's so-called "declaration of intent" was published for the first time in *Art News* in fall 1968 before being published again in the catalogue for Seth Siegelaub's group exhibition, "January 5-31, 1969."

Lawrence Weiner preparing flare for THE RESIDUE OF A FLARE IGNITED UPON A BOUNDARY (1969), for "Op Losse Schroeven: Situaties en Cryptostructuren (Square Pegs in Round Holes)," Stedelijk Museum, Amsterdam, 15 March-27 April 1969. Courtesy the artist.

ONE QUART GREEN EXTERIOR INDUSTRIAL ENAMEL THROWN ON A BRICK WALL (1968)
Collection Alice Zimmerman Weiner, New York. This view, June 1969.

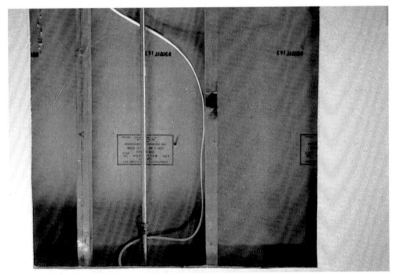

A 36" X 36" REMOVAL TO THE LATHING OR SUPPORT WALL OF PLASTER OR WALLBOARD FROM A WALL (1968)
The Siegelaub Collection and Archives. Installation views of this work in venues for the traveling exhibition, "The Presence of Absence," organized by Nina Felshin for Independent Curators Incorporated (1989–90). Photos courtesy The Seth Siegelaub Collection and Archives.

IAN WILSON

(b. 17 January 1940,
Durban, South Africa;
lives in New York)

In 1968 Ian Wilson began his search for an art in which no evidence of physicality would intrude. Touch an end he supplanted traditional visual representation with language, operating only through the channels of speech until the 1980s, when he turned to the production of books.

Wilson began with the idea of taking the word "time" as a point of departure for making works without a visible object. Within the course of casual conversation, he would bring up "time" as a subject, thereby allowing a single word/concept to serve as a focal point for possible discussion.

Wilson's Time work lasted for about a year and led to a subsequent, ongoing work that would occupy him for several years thereafter. Under the descriptive term "Oral Communication," he sought to examine, also by means of casual dialogue, the specific methodology that he had begun to develop with his study of the word "time." Throughout the 1970s he limited his work to the activity of speech and, pursuant to his later, more formalized "Discussions," referred to his art practice as Oral Communication.

As in the case of the Time work, Oral Communication was presented in the course of the artist's daily life and social encounters with people. Instead of bringing up "time" as a subject, as he had before, Wilson would say that he was interested in "oral communication." Whereas his Time work stemmed from his understanding that a word might represent a concept, Oral Communication grew out of his realization that the Time project principally concerned the process of communication. The designation Oral Communication, he decided, more pertinently served to characterize an endeavor whose ultimate subject and object, he once stated, "is speech itself," or "art spoken."[1]

During the period he was exploring Oral Communication and developing his investigation into the idea of using spoken language as an art form, Wilson was invited to participate in a number of major group exhibitions. He included his name in the official listing of artists in the catalogue, or in its checklist, as the means of acknowledging that his work was "in" the exhibition, although there was no physical object to be seen or had. The catalogue for the exhibition, "18 Paris IV. 70," presented in a space at 66, rue Mouffetard, in Paris in April 1970, for example, explicitly spells out in English, French, and German—in accordance with the guidelines for submission given to each participating artist—Wilson's proposed work, as well as the work he actually exhibited:

I. My project will be to visit you in Paris in April 1970 and there make clear the idea of oral communication as artform.

II. Ian Wilson came to Paris in January 1970 and talked about the idea of oral communication as artform.[2]

Wilson's participation in exhibitions at the end of the 1960s and the beginning of the 1970s did not demand a mandatory appearance on the part of the artist for his Oral Communication to be operative. However, as the Paris exhibition catalogue entry suggests, Oral Communication lent itself to various occasions for gathering and discussion. A specific invitation to include work in an exhibition might inspire such an occasion or such might occur—spontaneously or by prearrangement—independently of a particular group exhibition.[3]

The first Discussion took place at the John Weber Gallery in New York on 29 November 1972 and was officially announced in advance by a mailed announcement card. Since then Wilson has engaged in numerous Discussions at museums, galleries, and with private individuals. Wilson's Discussions evolved gradually from his meditation on how to define a course within the context of art unhampered by the perceptual and conceptual limits of the visible, concrete world or by the material(istic) confines of an object.
— AR

Notes

1. In Tommaso Trini, "Intervista con Ian Wilson/Ian Wilson, An Interview," Data, 1, no. 1 (September 1971): 32.

2. Ian Wilson, in 18 Paris IV. 70, exh. cat. (Paris: Seth Siegelaub), 1.

3. See Trini, "Intervista."

STEPHEN MELVILLE

ASPECTS *(1)* Teaching a ten-week survey of American art since 1945 has perhaps the virtue of imposing certain economies, so allowing one to discover, in ways that more expansive formats do not, what one can and cannot live without. My experience has been that I can more or less live without the terms "Conceptualism" or "Conceptual" art. I do not mean that I can live without much of the work that often figures under these labels and in this exhibition, or even that I can live without the adjective "conceptual," a word that comes in for quite heavy use as I work my way through the material. So it seems to be the case that I find myself without any need to take up that work in relation to a general name; this is, by contrast, strikingly not true of my relation to a term like "Minimalism." In practice this means that I am, in the classroom context, more or less likely to let the labels dwindle to something that approaches a mere excursus on the work and writing of Joseph Kosuth, perhaps set about with brief invocations of, say, Lawrence Weiner or Robert Barry.

In reflecting on this practice, shoddy as it may be, two things seem worth noting: (1) an evident sense that "Conceptual" art does not play a determinative role in the narrative shape my course gives to recent American art and (2) an equally evident sense that the emergence of the "conceptual" in contemporary art is an important, perhaps even distinguishing, feature of it.

I do not pretend that my treatment of Conceptual art is fair, and I certainly do not imagine this is how everyone chooses with respect to it under such straitened circumstances; indeed, that it clearly is not universally the case is a way of beginning to elaborate the stakes around Conceptual art (a term that I am, after all, perfectly happy to use and explore when I am free of the imposed choices of the classroom).

Taking up simply the first issue—the place of Conceptual art in narratives of postwar American art—I imagine that those who try to teach such courses as a matter in need of argument and not simply enumeration are almost inevitably forced to the determination of a crux. There are a limited number of candidates for that position available; among the most prominent of these would be Pop, Minimalism, Conceptualism, and Fluxus. It seems right to say, speaking only very roughly and intuitively, that the choice between Minimalism and Pop reflects a deeper difference between a critical and theoretical orientation toward the nature or naturalness of art and one toward its social and cultural circulation or construction; that the choice between either of these and Fluxus represents a difference in imaginations of the continuing power of avant-gardism; and that the choice between these three and Conceptualism reflects a difference in how one conceives the depth and nature of a break between "modernism" and "postmodernism."[1] To the extent that any narratively structured account of the period is obliged to order itself to the emergence of something that calls itself "postmodern," this last will, of course, be true of all the candidates I have proposed—that is what it would mean to nominate one or another of them as "crucial." So the stake of this essay must ultimately lie in its ability to deliver on the particular difference Conceptualism makes in this position. If we turn to the second point of practice, is seems likely that this should play out as an elaboration of the difference between taking up "Conceptualism" and confining one's self more nearly to speaking of "the conceptual."

All of this is, of course, approximate—a confession of what I extracted on the rack of teaching, and, like any forced confession, it is the assumption of a position. A position is, we might say, that from which something is seen or not seen, from which something is visible in whole or in part. It is clear enough that the work we tend to call "conceptual" places a certain premium on questions of position and has played a large role in determining the apparent centrality of such questions in contemporary art and criticism. So it is at least generally appropriate that this essay open with such a confession, as well as a certain remarking of resistance to the assumption of position it entails. Whatever else the comments that follow may be, they can at least be taken as an effort to understand my own apparently unstable relation to a certain number of works and a general label under which they appear to be gathered. Because such claims as I will advance in the pages that follow are not so much accounts as propositions to be tested against one's experience of the works on exhibit—attempts to say what is to be seen—the essay will proceed, by and large, without offering specific examples.

(2) The labels art history uses are, for the most part, intended to work as style names, although they are often taken to have a deep enough relation to the broader terms of culture to do double-duty as period names as well, and often enough they slide still further, toward something that we are more likely to imagine as a school or, more recently, a movement. Perhaps because we tend to take "modernism" itself as the relevant period name, the labels commonly used in speaking of twentieth-century art tend to move back and forth between some stylistic ground (as with "Cubism") and something like a movement name ("Surrealism"). Sometimes (as with "De Stijl") they function both ways. "Cubism" is far from a neutral example; it is perhaps the last fully secure style name in the current history of art. For "Abstract Expressionism" and "Minimalism" we have available fairly strong stylistic descriptions, but they are troubled, in a way "Cubism" is not, by alternative descriptions that strongly resist reduction to questions of style. That such descriptions are at least not clearly style names seems to me to point toward an important shift in the work of art-historical labels in the late modern period—say, a new or exacerbated uncertainty about just how they mean (what they mean, what they point to, is pretty much always clear enough—it's not that they don't succeed in classifying but just that the grounds of the sorting remain significantly opaque. From account to account, there is an ungraspable and shifting margin within which particular names, of works and of artists, are in constant transit—as, for example, between "Abstract Expressionism," "Action Painting," "Color Field Painting," and so on).

If "Cubism" is taken as the last fully secure style name, "Fluxus" would appear to be that last of the movement names bound in its inner logic to the aspiration of the traditional avant-garde (except perhaps for the Situationist International, which was clear enough about the impossibility of avant-garde art to make the cessation of art-making a condition of its continuation as a movement). And if "Minimalism" is not quite a style name, this is perhaps because the shift it marks seems deeper (at least, to those of us who take it as a crux) than can be taken account of from within the matrix in which the notion of style is formed; we are inclined to take it as marking a "paradigm shift" that calls for a very different kind of accounting. It is this sense of paradigmatic, rather than stylistic, shift that presumably underlies the desire to speak of some "postmodernism."[2]

One might, then, see Conceptualism as a label deployed uneasily across the gap between Minimalism and Fluxus. To the extent that it means or has meant something like a movement, it is hardly surprising that Henry Flynt was the first to, as it were, float a recognizable form of the term within the context of Fluxus. Nor is it surprising that Conceptualism should find one important expression through an explicit group formation like Art & Language (although the more pertinent comparison, given the group's willingness to engage in direct theoretical and historical reflection, is perhaps to the Situationists). One's sense in thinking about this version of the conceptual is likely to be of a group or movement whose unity lies in a commitment to rendering "the aesthetic" answerable to principles that lie beyond it or of which it is at best a partial and mystified embodiment, so that if the impact of both Situationism and Art & Language Conceptualism on contemporary British art appears to remain limited, contemporary British theory, art history, and cultural studies cannot be fully understood without reference to them. The connection here to certain understandings of "postmodernism" appears quite strong.[3]

Most discussions of Conceptual art nonetheless do not start with Art & Language but with the work of Kosuth, and here, despite moments of overlap and mutual interest and support, there is not the same sense of an explicit group or movement, although Kosuth's theoretical writings do in many ways look like manifestoes for such a movement, and the efforts to assert his historical priority in the emergence of Conceptual art suggest a much diminished version of the kind of proprietary interest one associates with, say, André Breton in relation to Surrealism or George Maciunas with regard to Fluxus.[4] What may make the difference here is Kosuth's determination, especially in his early work, that "the aesthetic" be shown to be tautologically linked to its own propositional content rather than to a body of propositions grounded beyond it in some larger world. That is, if at the core of the idea of a "movement" as opposed to a "style" is some strong sense that the principles at stake in artistic work cannot simply be displayed as the work but must, in order that they be done justice, be enunciated in broader social or cultural terms, Kosuth's work seems to want to split the difference, both demanding the recognition of principles enunciated beyond the series, in essays like "Art after Philosophy," and the recognition of them as analytically embedded in and as the work, as in the work ART AS IDEA AS IDEA. Kosuth's work is in this sense finally deeply ambiguous with respect to what I have been trying to distinguish as "style labels" and "movement labels." I take this ambiguity to underlie both the political claims that inform his work, as well as his tendency to extend the weight of his crucial early theoretical and organizing work toward a relation to Conceptualism that seem in certain respects to repeat those associated with leadership within a movement.

To take up Conceptualism, as an historical or critical object or as one's own practice, as a movement of sorts is to understand it as moved by a broadly political desire—a desire for a renegotiation or overcoming of a presumed gap between art and life, and a desire for a community or socius not ordered by the terms and practices that currently govern our practices. It

231

Andy Warhol
BRILLO BOXES (1964)
Painted wood. Each box, 17 x 17 x 14 in. (43.2 x 43.2 x 35.6 cm). Installation view. Courtesy Leo Castelli Gallery, New York.

is in these terms that one will then be inclined to understand the non-availability of much conceptual work—either its appearance only through the detour of documentation or its absolute non-appearance—as a resistance to or refusal of current conditions of visibility. This same understanding can generate criteria for such visibility as conceptual work might aspire to—a visibility that would refuse to detach itself from an engagement with the conditions of its appearance. Locating the political desire of Conceptualism in this way allows one, I think, to see how the underlying political fantasy dreams of a telepathic community—say, a community that is not riven by the fact of beholding and so one in which work is not defined by its ability to engender an audience. Telepathy is a way of sharing privacy apart from the mediations of language and institution that con-

stitute the public sphere in general, as well as its uneasy division into such separable spheres as, for example, the political, the technical, the aesthetic, and the intellectual. Conceived as a movement, Conceptualism appears obliged to intend itself as a secret history—that is, one whose very visibility and historical success is a measure of a certain kind of failure when measured against the inner standard of an impossible and an invisible performance. Telling its history would entail consolidating that failure just in order to renew the ambition.[5]

It should not be surprising, then, that whatever light it may shed on certain strands both within the work and within the historical discussions of it, the idea of Conceptual art as a movement has proven incapable of containing the range of practices and understandings that traverse the work we are now inclined to recognize as "conceptual." One is thus inevitably led to explore the other side of the rough distinction from which I set out—the side that understands "Conceptualism" to name something that floats between a "style" and a "paradigm." On this side, the essential unavailability of much conceptual work appears less as a social fact or aspiration than as a formal one presumably bound to the issues of vision and opticality that are brought to crisis by Minimalism in the early and mid-1960s. The leading questions here will be about the nature and relevance of some notion of medium in addressing conceptual work and about whether and how the developments so conceived are to be understood as participating in or transforming or refusing the apparent logic of modernist art. In particular, one will have the question of whether conceptual work is to be understood as some kind of deep turn within a continuing modernism (call this Conceptualism as something like a style) or as some still deeper rupture with modernism altogether (in which case one might be drawn to invoke some notion of paradigm shift or epistemological rupture).[6] If the picture of Conceptualism as an avant-garde movement leads one to find its leading alliances and filiations within the history of anti-art from Dada through the Situationist International, this interest will more naturally focus on the interplay between an apparently central line of modernist developments and those that appear to contest it more or less from within—as, for example, the Duchamp of precision optics and the LARGE GLASS rather than the apparent Dadaist of the readymades. The emergence of Conceptualism may even seem to lay the groundwork for the renewed and extended visibility of Duchamp registered in the work of such writers as Thierry de Duve, Rosalind Krauss, and Jean-François Lyotard.[7]

Marcel Duchamp
REVOLVING GLASS PLATES (PRECISION OPTICS) (1920)
Five glass plates painted with segments of black and white circles, turning on a metal axis powered by an electric motor, supported by frame of metal and wood. To top of largest blade, 5 ft. 5 in. (166.3 cm); to top of axial shaft, 3 ft. 9 in. (117.8 cm); largest glass blade, 5 1/4 x 39 in. (14.2 x 99.3 cm); wooden base at floor, 4 ft. x 4 ft. 8 in. (120.8 x 145.8 cm). Yale University Art Gallery, New Haven. Gift of Collection Société Anonyme. Photo Jospeh Szasfai.

Lawrence Weiner
A 36" X 36" REMOVAL TO THE LATHING OR SUPPORT WALL OF PLASTER OR WALLBOARD FROM A WALL (1969)
Installation view, "January 5-31, 1969," rented office space at 44 East 52nd Street, New York. Courtesy The Siegelaub Collection & Archives. Photo Seth Siegelaub.

Joseph Kosuth
CLEAR SQUARE GLASS LEANING (1965)
Four glass plates with black lettering. Each plate, 36 x 60 in. (91.4 x 152.4 cm). Solomon R. Guggenheim Museum, New York, Panza Collection. Extended loan.

To address conceptual work in terms like these is to want to speak of a certain dematerialization of the object; of the emergence of ideas or language or systematicity as a medium for advanced art; of a new relation to philosophy or theory or criticism. All of these will be ways to account for the emergence of an art of invisible features or an art that presents the invisible as something like a dimension of the visible. As one moves through these various particular descriptions, different figures offer themselves as central—for example Sol LeWitt or Robert Smithson or Dan Graham—and familiar ones show themselves in a new light. One can come to see Kosuth holding a complex double position—polemically contesting Greenberg even as his own practice seems to reinscribe Greenbergian theory into a new and different key, so that one comes to imagine Kosuth engaged in a struggle with Greenberg oddly like the struggle with artistic predecessors Greenberg would ascribe to Pollock. We know, or think we know, what it means to say that modernist art is obliged to defeat or take over the work that has enabled it and set its condi-

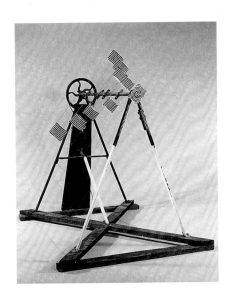

tions; it is, I think, considerably less clear what it might mean for art to feel compelled to defeat or take over the work of criticism, although it is perhaps clear enough that the effect of such a move is to enforce a certain silence on the work's audience—as if the work's volubility were a form not of communication but of radical reserve.

It is clear, however, that Conceptual art has hardly confined itself within these narrow strictures, and equally that it has found other ways of engaging criticism and theory. Perhaps the most important of these other routes (at least in the United States and in retrospect) are those traced by LeWitt and Smithson. That both of these are perhaps most readily understood as interpretations, extensions, or revisions of Minimalism will be important to the general drift of these remarks, but for the moment it seems appropriate to stress the way in which LeWitt's work stages a certain Conceptualism through the analytic exhaustion of a given situation, dissolving the distinction between work and series (and with that, the presumption of a distinction between a work and a separable style which it instances or in which it participates), thus rendering the work

CLEAR   **SQUARE**   **GLASS**   **LEANING**

wholly responsible for the display of its conceptual parameters. Smithson's work also turns on a reimagining of the relation between work and the conditions of its appearance or display, but now by presenting the work itself as a movement of displacement that cannot recover its conditions of possibility except through their further transformation. What Smithson, LeWitt, and Kosuth might all be said to share is an orientation to repetition that can be read as a response to the Minimalist interest in repetition; what would divide them is the way they take the force of repetition, and so also the way they understand what it is that is open to or realized in repetition.

(3) The current view of Conceptual art from 1965 to 1975 appears to be importantly conditioned by two subsequent developments—the neo-Conceptualism of the 1980s, and the full emergence of structuralist and post-structuralist theory in both art and criticism. The first of these can be said to revise the terms of conceptual practice back toward a certain objectivity and visibility; the second marks, and to a degree conceals, a radical shift in interpretive mood or orientation that is perhaps most readily tracked by noting the recession of the Wittgensteinian appeals so central to the writings of both Kosuth and Art & Language. Such appeals were hardly confined to the art world in the early and mid-sixties (just as their subsequent recession is not the art world's fact alone). The attraction exercised by Ludwig Wittgenstein's writings is, I think, a complex matter. Certainly one would have to speak of Jasper Johns's pictorial exploitations of the linguistic thought experiments of the *Philosophical Investigations* and the consequent awareness that painting, for example, could no longer assume its sensory availability without also assuming the linguistic mediation of that experience and so also the possibility that language and sensation might diverge or collide in any number of ways (much the same, of course, can be said of Edward Ruscha's work).

But in order to cross the bridge from Johns's work to Kosuth's we have to recognize the way in which such particular possibilities were themselves embedded in a broader intellectual and cultural context in which "positivism" still powerfully named both a potential threat to and promise for the making of art. Wittgenstein's early work was, in its historical moment, taken as the foundation for what came to be called "logical positivism," while the later work appeared as a repudiation of the earlier; but there are also themes and formulations within the early work that complicate this division and force a more difficult imagination of Wittgenstein's philosophic enterprise. The result is that Wittgenstein, both early and late, offered ambiguous resources for imagining art's place between the promise and threat of positivism, while the propositional style of the early work and the aphoristic or experimental style of the later seemed to give permission to take one's Wittgenstein as one found (or wanted to find)

it, rendering fluid the distinction between the logical concerns of the early work and the grammatical focus of the later.

Given these broad readerly permissions and uncertainties, what Wittgenstein seemed to license was a certain practice of self-reference that could nonetheless count as rigorous, as measuring up to a certain (albeit obscure) standard of objectivity that would let art count as a mode of investigation more or less on par with—say, sharing a certain spirit with—modern science. It would be important that although an ambition outlined in these terms seems naturally opposed to the mystifications seeming to inhere in appeals to quality and value, the notion that modern art shares its procedures and standards with modern science runs fairly deep in Greenberg's writings (often at some cost to the coherence of his apparently foundational references to Kant's aesthetics).[8] At this level Greenberg and many of his artistic and critical detractors can be said to have shared to a surprising degree a general picture of the situation of art that makes it difficult to draw clean lines between them; the native ground of this confusion is, I would suggest, the extraordinary epistemologism of the sixties—the general belief that art was a mode of knowledge and that its particularity as such lay in its self-reference. This last point would be a particular interpretation of the more general Greenbergian orientation to what he called "radical self-criticism"—and its specificity becomes salient if one considers all the ways in which it does not appear to make sense to think of Pollock's painting as self-referential or to imagine Greenberg as claiming that it is. Its plausibility, by contrast, becomes clear if one thinks of the ways in which it does appear to make sense to speak of Frank Stella's early work as self-referential and so to conflate that self-referentiality with the "self-criticism" attributed to advanced art by Greenberg and others.

I would not want to inflate the importance of Wittgenstein as active and explicit influence or resource (although I also would not want to surrender easily my sense of a certain widespread resonance between his ways of presenting his work and the quasi-propositional modes through which much early conceptual work presents itself). In any case, I am clearly taking explicit appeals to Wittgenstein as symptomatic of a broader tendency to conceive of art as engaged essentially with issues of knowledge, and particularly self-knowledge. If I think that the invocation of Wittgenstein is a particularly interesting symptom, it is because that invocation seems, like the Freudian symptom, distinctly double-edged, traversed by conflicting desires and points of identification that make its work one of simultaneous concealment and betrayal.

There are several ways to phrase the ambiguity of Wittgenstein's presence in and to the art world.

Robert Smithson
MIRROR DISPLACEMENTS
From Incidents of Travel in the Yucatan, 1969. Nine chromogenic-development prints. Each, 10 x 10 in. (25.4 x 25.4 cm). Estate of Robert Smithson, courtesy John Weber Gallery, New York.

235

Perhaps the most direct is to say that there are in Wittgenstein—for reasons deeply linked to his understanding of his own procedures—all the resources for renewing the very dream of a private language his work seems determined to undo, with the result that appeals to his work can seem to offer ways of at once acknowledging and bypassing the conventions that structure our exchanges with art, of imagining the language of art as at once private and publicly accessible. Arguably, Michael Fried's essay "Art and Objecthood" was as controversial as it was because—beneath the explicit references to Kant and Greenberg and Jonathan Edwards—it was above all aimed at diagnosing and overcoming this too easy settlement with Wittgenstein.[9] This would be a way of thinking about what was at stake for Fried in the contrast he drew between Tony Smith's sense that he had discovered something crucial for artmaking in an experience that essentially refused convention and language, on the one hand, and Anthony Caro's insistence on articulation and grammar, on the other.

The mid-to-late sixties saw this epistemologism increasingly complicated and modified by the emergence of a rather different philosophical temper. Its specific difference from the mood I have been exploring lies in its refusal of this fundamentally epistemological orientation (a refusal, then, to identify self-criticism with self-reference) in favor of a different imagination of how language matters for an apprehension of the visual: language is more nearly taken as a condition of a thing or a work's appearing (its being what it is) than as the screen, transparent or opaque, that stands between us and things, even threatening to supplant them (as well as more simply standing between us as the limit of our communication). To the extent that this appears as a reading of Wittgenstein, it is one that opens in a very different direction—toward, in the first instance, the work of such European philosophers as Martin Heidegger and, more pointedly, Maurice Merleau-Ponty. That the various writers who came to take an interest in Merleau-Ponty in particular (I think most prominently of Annette Michelson, Rosalind Krauss, and Michael Fried) were riven by their own internal differences and disputes over priority is abundantly evident, and yet it seems to me that it is right and important to group them together in this respect. Given the shift in interest or mood I have tied to the name of Merleau-Ponty and would gloss more generally as a move from epistemological concerns to ones that are more nearly ontological and phenomenological, what often appears as the core of Conceptual art in Kosuth, Weiner, Art & Language, and so on will be of at best peripheral interest. What will be more central is the less clearly categorizable work of figures like Robert Morris or Dan Graham or Robert Smithson—work that is conceptual in the broad sense of having something like invisible features but that cannot be easily addressed within the picture of knowledge and communication I have suggested is central to presumably purer forms of Conceptualism.

One way to put this might be to say that this work is resolutely anti-telepathic; it needs its material existence and refuses any imagination of its own transparency. A more theoretical way to put it would be to say that it reads identity propositions—as, for example, "art is art"—as transformations rather than fixations or enclosures (as, that is, more nearly synthetic than analytic). Such propositions are taken as if they were not literal but importantly rhetorical, so that one might want to compare the implied (and presumably "formalist") assertion that "art is (as) art" with the conceptual quasi-proposition "art as idea." The obvious difference is in the work the two phrases open toward: in the one case a work of ongoing transgression, art passing always beyond itself into itself, and in the other a work of purification, art moving always inward toward an internal vanishing point that is both the completion of its identity and its passage out of visibility altogether. A less obvious but crucial difference lies in the understanding of

rhetoric more generally and so of the force to be attributed to the "as" both propositions share: "art as idea" seems to grant the "as" the force of metaphor and to understand metaphor as the substituting of one name for another; "art is (as) art" seems to take the "as" as metonymic, displacing a name within itself and prolonging it into new regions. And this is probably sufficient to make clear the ways in which the two propositions offer very different understandings of the work of repetition: in the one case, art's repetitions, within a work or within a history, are the way to secure an underlying identity ever more surely; in the other these same repetitions are the means of its ongoing alteration and transformation.

237

It is, I would suggest, this transformative and metonymical orientation, more nearly ontological than epistemological in its emphases, that becomes particularly explicit with the neo-Conceptualism of the late seventies and early eighties, both renewing and complicating the question of the conceptual in art; but of course by this time whatever Wittgensteinian roots or resonances it might have had have been occluded under the newer wave of French structuralist and poststructuralist theory (a transition enabled at least to some degree by the introduction of Merleau-Ponty's work). Metaphor and metonymy taken together constitute the actual weave of any text, orienting it in their shifting emphases toward the play of presence and absence or toward the play of presence and representation; in the context of late modernist or emergent postmodernist art they also offer resources for thinking or working through the relative weight of opposed tendencies toward repetition as a means of securing identity through a, so to speak, centripetal work of purification or through an outward spiral of ongoing displacement. It can at times be tempting to let this distinction settle as if it simply were the difference between Conceptualism and neoConceptualism (this essay is inclined this way), but to do so too simply is to ignore the ways in which the one not only repeats the other but in which both are, in themselves, exposed to repetition. History—the kind of history modernist art makes—is always both purification and alteration or transformation.

This is, of course, to say that these reflections are themselves theoretical and indulge the luxuries of distinction and simple opposition that are the privileges of such an approach. It is, for example, important that the French theory I have been valorizing here is also received within the epistemological framework to which I have opposed it, so that the tension I have been trying to explore is continued, in new ways, within its reception and so is still very much a part of the contemporary terrain (one might note, for example, that Jean-François Lyotard provided the foreword to Kosuth's *Art After Philosophy and*

Jasper Johns
JUBILEE (1959)
Oil and collage on canvas. 60 x 44 in. (152.4 x 111.8 cm).
Collection David H. Steinmetz.
Photo courtesy Leo Castelli Gallery, New York.

Sherrie Levine
AFTER WALKER EVANS: 7 (1981)
Black-and-white photograph. 8 x 10 in. (20.3 x 25.4 cm).
Courtesy Marian Goodman Gallery, New York.

Robert Morris
UNTITLED (MIRRORED CUBES) (1971)
Refabrication of a 1965 original. Plexiglas mirrors on wood.
Four units, each 21 x 21 x 21 in. (53.3 x 53.3 x 53.3 cm).
Courtesy Solomon R. Guggenheim Foundation, New York.

After).[10] These distinctions cannot—any more than the similar distinctions posed in the previous section—offer a means of simply disposing of any particular works or of creating clean breaks within a history; their use, if they are found useful, will lie in opening up the tensions that organize both works and histories; and some part of their pertinence is itself historical insofar as they mean to at least roughly map something of the terrain in which various configurations of Conceptualism and the conceptual are sometimes visible and sometimes obscured.

(4)   In his 1990 essay for *L'art conceptuel, une perspective*, Benjamin Buchloh is led to argue that "The visual forms corresponding most accurately (or preparing the transition) to the linguistic form of the tautology are the square and its stereometric rotation, the cube."[11]   His larger argumentative interest, which this statement means to enable, lies in making out the difference between "modernist self-referentiality" and a "self-reflexivity" that transcends it. It is what he takes to be the Conceptualist impulse toward such a self-reflexivity that makes it "the most significant paradigmatic change of post World War II artistic production."[12] This last claim is, however, crucially qualified: if Conceptual art successfully strips modernist self-referentiality of all its apparent aesthetic supports, it will in its reduced form remain little more than a pale echo of the social order in which it now nakedly finds itself (an order of self-reference, self-surveillance, and administration) until and unless it finds ways to make that situation itself the object of its analysis—as, Buchloh argues, it does in the cases of Hans Haacke, Daniel Buren, Marcel Broodthaers, and Michael Asher. Conceptual art so conceived is—or should be—an unstable and vanishing moment, that of the passage from traditional aesthetic production (painting and sculpture) to institutional critique, and it is importantly prepared by what Buchloh calls the irreversible proto-Conceptual passage from painting to sculpture, a passage that he emblematically orders to the appearance of the square canvas that "inevitably assumes the character of a relief/object situated in actual space."[13]

There is, I think, a good deal of common ground between this account and the one I have less directly sketched in these pages—in terms both of a certain failure of social imagination and an allied theoretical expediency. But the path I have tried to take here also diverges from Buchloh's in important respects, and one way to see that divergence is to return to Buchloh's remark about the square and the cube.

This is a statement that does not lend itself to any simple verification; there appears, for example, to be no compelling barrier to imagining a history in which the circle or sphere presented itself as corresponding to or preparing a way toward the tautology. But that would be a different history, and Buchloh's remark seems profoundly right for the one we have—so much so that the question that follows seems to me to be about the nature of a history in which this finally rather odd equation could appear to be (more or less) natural.

Heidegger sometimes seems to write out of a sort of deep metaphor in which Being is indeed imagined as a kind of sphere on which things are inscribed and so raised into light or cast into darkness by its rotation. This image, or quasi-image, is in service to his broader insistence that Being—the obscure and central hinge on which any tautology turns—because it is sheltered in language, is always relational and aspectual: there is no thing except through its relation to other things that are not; every world in which things appear happens as a double process of bringing into light and casting into shadow, and that process is what or how a world is. Any particular patterning of light and shadow cannot be thought apart from the language grace of which there is anything at all; if we did not have language, we would not have a world (would not have that structure of light and shadow, distance and proximity, horizon and orientation). That is one way of imagining a relation between logic and geometry over and against the one Buchloh picks out.

Michael Asher
Project for Claire Copley Gallery, Inc., Los Angeles,
California, 21 September–12 October 1974. Viewing through
gallery toward office and storage areas; viewing through
gallery toward entry/exit and street. Photo Gary Kruger.

Stéphane Mallarmé seems to offer another such image. It is more difficult to make out, but the thought that ramifies across his writing suggests repeatedly that an achieved poem—a poem that is fully itself—is something at once wholly contingent and entirely absolute and self-justifying. One line of imagery that answers to this ambition gives the poem as a block—of ice or of stone or of text—embedded in or as a page, and finding its ultimate expression in a book, a volume, that is at once utterly mobile and unbound, and entirely dense and solid.

These examples are, as presented, historically arbitrary and find their specific purchase within significantly different practices and concerns, but if we nonetheless set these imaginations against the one historically instantiated in Buchloh's proto-Conceptualism, certain features of his square and cube stand out in a new way. Against the Heideggerean imagination, for example, one sees the importance of squares and cubes as things possessed of faces or aspects that are importantly recognized as such because there are other aspects that do not face us or are not immediately accessible to us. On Heidegger's sphere there is nothing that is not accessible to us—what is there is all there is and there is nothing we cannot know, even as our knowing cannot make any claim to be total or transparent (it has error and shadow as its condition, just as the world has a horizon as its limit). And against the Mallarméan example, one sees that this thought of facing (toward or away, visible or concealed) is bound up with a certain imagination of hollowness that Mallarmé's version of poetic ambition precludes: the identity of the work as he understands it would be an instance of self-consciousness (having, that is, the shape or integrity of a self as opposed to that of a thing) without containing within itself the empty space that would permit a reflection on itself (the kind of self-consciousness we associate with having a view of the self from some further or higher position that is also within it).

These contrasts not only help to pin down the specificity of the equation Buchloh proposes; they also, I think, make it clear that he is able to take this equation or correspondence between cube or square and tautology over as directly as he does because he is already committed to the general picture of modernist self-criticism as dependent on, or derivative from, self-reference and self-reflexivity. Fried, to take a sharply contrasting critic, is clearly more at home with something close to Mallarmé's imaginative geometry—so that one can, for example, trace what would seem a fairly clear line from his invocations of Mallarmé in the context of Morris Louis through his critique of the "hollowness" of Minimalist work (most notably Tony Smith's cube DIE) to his difficult essay on the role of shape in Frank Stella's painting; along this line it matters crucially that self-criticism and self-reference not be conflated.[14]

But now my imaginative exercise has become concrete and pertinent: as a contrast between Fried and Buchloh, it represents a particular historical and critical dispute, the central stake of which can be put in terms of the status and prospects of sculpture. For Buchloh the Conceptualist aesthetic of admin-

Marcel Broodthaers
UN COUP DE DES N'ABOLIRA LE HASARD (IMAGE), BY STEPHANE MALLARME
Antwerp: Galerie Wide White Space; Cologne: Galerie Michael
Werner, 1969. Photolithograph, printed in black on transparent
paper. Page, 12 13/16 x 9 13/16 in. (32.5 x 24.9 cm). The
Museum of Modern Art, New York. Purchased with funds given by
Howard B. Johnson in honor of Riva Castleman.
Photograph © 1995 The Museum of Modern Art, New York.

Tony Smith
DIE (1962)
Steel, ed. 3. 72 x 72 x 72 in. (182.9 x 182.9 x 182.9 cm).
Courtesy Paula Cooper Gallery, New York. Photo
Geoffrey Clements.

240

istration is the logical outcome of the complete collapse of the idea of a medium: painting, exhausted in its reduction to the square canvas, passes over into sculpture, and the cube, in its exhaustion, passes over into architecture, which politically construed, is the native ground of institutional critique. For Fried, the passage from the square to the cube is not, finally, a passage from painting to sculpture at all (it is a passage into what he calls theater), and the possibilities of sculpture are understood to be elsewhere, most notably in the work of David Smith and Anthony Caro. What matters in their work is its essential openness and refusal of containment (and so also of hollowness) in favor of a mode of articulation and relation that establishes the unity of the work as a unity of surface or aspect independent of any expression of an inner core.[15] There are a number of ways to phrase this achievement; one that matters in this context would be, say, that Smith and Caro find a way to make work that is fully publicly available even as it also explicitly acknowledges and indeed foregrounds the necessary contingency of that availability.

The possibility or impossibility of sculpture is, I would suggest, the central buried issue of sixties art, and the one on which its deepest formal and, eventually, political issues turn and continue to turn in large measure today.[16] If painting is always touched with the hint of a certain reservation or limitation—say, the sense that there is something behind the painting's face to which we do not have access— sculpture traditionally figures for us as essentially public, open from all sides and graspable in its integrity at every moment. This is and is not true of the constructed sculpture of Smith and Caro: it remains open and available as a whole at every moment, explicitly refusing even the prospect that it might be the outward expression of some hidden internal core[17]; and yet it also admits or makes explicit that the whole so apprehended, just because it expresses no interiority, will shift with the viewer's position and will thus also be always partial, finite, or contingent. It is, in this sense, all aspect—and yet there is nothing behind the aspects themselves in which they can be grounded or assembled, or to which they can be reduced. Aspectuality is not a contingent feature of a work that in its essence lies beyond such partiality; rather, it is the very stuff of its being.[18]

Abstraction in painting was felt by its strongest formalist champions in the fifties and sixties to entail severe limitations on the public role of art, so that in Greenberg's writing, to take the central instance, that valorization is repeatedly qualified by wishes either that painting find some way back through abstraction to something like representation, or that sculpture find some way to supply the deficit of painting. The first disqualifies itself as nostalgic almost as soon as it is spoken,[19] but the second becomes the bearer of a real, if repeatedly frustrated, hope— one that is keyed to Smith and Caro, and one that comes, for Greenberg and Fried, to apparent ruin in Minimalism with its reduction of sculptural aspectuality to the condition of painterly facing and reservation—that is, to sculptural work that gives itself as merely the face or aspect of something presented only as unreachably beyond, behind, or within the work (and so presented only as withdrawn).

It is against this larger historical field that I think it matters to see the various works we call "conceptual." That is, I want to suggest

the possibility and importance of seeing such work as arising in the wake of Minimalism and as such responsive to what one might call a certain impossibility of sculpture—an impossibility inscribed as a particular intersection of concerns with transparency and opacity, interiority and exteriority, surface and depth, and deployed as a material grammar offering to figure our our mutual exposure and hiddenness. The point of seeing things this way would, of course, be to insert questions of aspectuality and publicness at the heart of the Conceptualist withdrawal from visibility so as to be able to ask how far the presumed unity of Conceptualism is worked by a radical dif-

ference between that work which, as if baffled by the apparent inaccessibility of interiority, realizes itself as a refusal of aspect altogether (a refusal I would link closely to Buchloh's notion of an aesthetic of administration) and that other work which realizes itself as an extraordinary extension beyond the terms of mere perceptual visibility of an aspectuality it knows to have no ground beyond itself.

I suppose that I am inclined to think of this contrast as the one that gets into my own tendency to separate Conceptualism, understood as something like the name of a movement, and "conceptual" as a qualification or aspect of the conditions for a wide range of post-Minimal artistic production that nonetheless does not offer to summarize that range. I imagine also that the distinction I have been exploring offers a way to think about the relations between Conceptualism and its later repetition or renewal, about what does and does not pass between them, and about the histories they do and do not share. Putting these two thoughts together amounts to further suggesting that the later work plays a role in bringing to visibility the distinction I have put as between Conceptualism and "the conceptual." On this view, the work of Sherrie Levine or Cindy Sherman or any number of others who emerge in the early 1980s appears as a strong reading of the earlier moment that, like any strong reading, forces new distinctions within its object and revises its history.

If this roughly sketched history of moods and figures informing our continuing, post-Greenbergian interest in such terms as "self-reference," "self-reflexivity," and "self-criticism" is persuasive, it seems possible to draw one further consequence from it: we can perhaps begin to read what Buchloh takes as a passage beyond the constraints of medium as more nearly a reinterpretation of the logic of those constraints. In doing this we would no longer take the square as self-evidently the form of self-containment, but as a system of relations that necessarily includes within its dynamic the terms of its own surpassing, toward, for example, the cube—but also toward more abstract figures like the "Greimasian Square" Rosalind Krauss has variously employed to explore both the dispersion of sculpture as a post-Minimal medium and the terms of closure of (and so also the terms of resistance to) modernist visuality or visibility.[20] Much of the interest, and difficulty, of her efforts here lie in what seems to me her clear sense

Anthony Caro
EARLY ONE MORNING (1962)
Steel and aluminum, painted red. 114 x 244 x 131 in. (290 x 620 x 333 cm). Tate Gallery, London. Photo John Riddy.

that she is appealing not simply to a useful model but to something that has some internal connection with the objects of her concern—a sense, perhaps, that it is not so much a model for as a figure of (belonging to, effected by) the work itself. This is, in a sense, an attempt to continue the impulse to grasp a work as an exhibition of its medium within the transformed terms imposed by Minimalism, and something of its difficulty is perhaps apparent in the way that attempt continues to be divided within her work by the line between painting and sculpture.[21]

What I take to be promising in such an effort is the way it can lead one to think that the question of aspect within the work, as it arises in the early and mid-sixties, ultimately plays out in a view of the notion of medium as itself significantly aspectual. One would then understand "art" not as what is left when painting, sculpture, and so on have exhausted themselves (as if "art" were the name of the core—empty or solid, real or illusory—concealed behind the limitations of particular media), but as the general name of what happens only in and as particular moments within the play of relations that constitute its having media. "Art," on such a view, would be an ungrounded system of aspects that (like David Smith's sculpture, but perhaps also like Stella's painting) is all surface, wholly visible, and yet not without concealment.[22] And, extending oneself out the full length of this particular limb, one might go on to say that "Conceptualism" names the wish to take this fact as itself being appropriable in the shape of a medium, and that "the conceptual" names the attempt to register such play as an internal condition of any medium and so also of any work.

243

(5) One does not speak of Conceptual art without invoking, at one level or another, some imagination of the end of art. The shape of that imagination is, I think, almost always implicitly Hegelian—at least insofar as for Hegel "art" could never be more than the name for a passing moment in the larger history of Spirit, a history that finds its ultimate fulfillment in the concept made wholly visible and transparent to itself. This moment of art's passage over into philosophy is also the moment of its passage over into life—which is also, in Hegel's fuller narrative, the moment of life's overcoming of its self-alienation into or as art.

Hegel is interesting in this context on several accounts. He is, for example, a sort of phantom presence in Greenberg's criticism and theoretical reflection, hovering, nearly invisible, between the references to Kant and those to Marx (or between the practice of judgment and the terms of historical reflection on those judgments).[23]

More interesting, from the present vantage, is Hegel's way of tying his imagination of the history and end of art to a view of its media. Given that art is not, as he understands it, a self-supporting subject, Hegel's history of it plots its movement from a certain embeddedness in the world toward its appearance as an autonomous subject and its subsequent fall away from that finally illusory appearance. Hegel argues that each of the three moments in this narrative has also its own dominant medium (a proposition of a kind that much interested the young Greenberg[24])—so that its beginning and end are dominated, respectively, by architecture and painting, each of which is understood as a moment in which art makes itself out of its own internal disparities. These two moments are juxtaposed with the the the third, middle moment of sculpture—in which art claims to have overcome its internal disparities and to have achieved a non-contradictory identity of form and content. Historically, sculpture's moment is Classicism and socially or politically it is the idealized Greek polis. Painting's moment is Romanticism and its world an extended version of the one we

Diagram by Rosalind Krauss in her essay "Toward Postmodernism," in *The Originality of the Avant-Garde and Other Modernist Myths* (Cambridge: The MIT Press, 1986), 284.

call modern. Post-Romantic or postmodern art would, in Hegel's view, be art for which anything is possible and nothing is consequential (that is, new art is merely chronologically new and cannot discover new possibilities of meaning or social being). For it there is no favored or dominant medium outside the general and transparent prose of the world. Perhaps curiously, one consequence of Hegel's view is that everything we call "art," as well as our desire that some things should be singled out as "art," is already a sign of art's decline from itself, its fall into Romanticism (into painting, into irony, and finally into prose). And this can be put the other way around as well: our desire that "art" should cease, that its name should no longer be a way of distinguishing some things from others, would read as a desire to enter finally into a world become conceptually, if not yet practically, transparent to itself (a world, we might say, that does not block its own view).

So Hegel perhaps provides one last surface on which Conceptualism, or the conceptual, in recent art can seem to divide from itself: on the one hand, it appears as a peculiarly Hegelian outcome to the story of art (and Buchloh appears, loosely, as its young Marx, asking practical fulfillment of what has been achieved as theory); on the other hand, the conceptual also appears within the history I have tried to sketch as a peculiar claimant to the title of sculpture in its late impossibility.

The works—objects, propositions, performances, films, documents, alterations, instructions, and residues—that this exhibition asks us to reconsider would then be understood as holding themselves uneasily between a passage into regions where they can no longer allow themselves the name of art (or can allow themselves only that name) and a return through that name back into the specificity of a sculpture, dismembered but not wholly defaced, that can realize its claims only in inevitable displacement from itself and can assert its continuing presence only as the abstract model of its scattered aspects.

(6) These tracings of the uneasy bonding of Conceptualism with what I have been calling "the conceptual" have, I suppose, been an attempt to understand the happiness and unhappiness those terms provoke in me. I hope that they are more generally serviceable as a way of understanding the work's simultaneous desire and inability either to fully embrace or fully disavow the unities of style or movement or medium that are inevitably borne in our desire to speak of or reflect upon it. But of course if they are useful that way, one of the things they will point to is our current inability to exist—to desire, to speak, to experience—as the unified subject Hegel imagined to have found or affirmed itself in the face of classical sculpture. We would find ourselves instead torn between a dream of telepathy darkly doubled by surveillance and some other social fact or imagination in which what we might call community can no longer stand apart from or above its own scattering and aspectuality.[25] If the first of these appears to be what is left to us now of the ideal of the Greek polis, the second dreams of something worth calling postmodern.

André Cadere carrying one of his BAR-RES DE BOIS during the exhibition "Galerie Yvon Lambert at Fine Arts Building Gallery," New York, 6–30 November 1976. Courtesy Galerie Yvon Lambert. Photo Harry Shunk.

Notes

1. This last characterization is one I will be concerned to flesh out further in the body of this essay, but I should note here that my awareness of it has been forced by the work of Thomas Crow. Although I do not know of any one place where what I take to be his argument is fully and explicitly fleshed out, its general lines seem to be visible in his recent work on Christopher Williams and to gain a certain historical anchorage in his account of the arguments at the foundation of the French academy. See "The Simple Life: Pastoralism and the Persistence of Genre in Recent Art," October, no. 63 (Winter 1993): 41-67 and "Unwritten Histories of Conceptual Art" in Oehlen Williams 95, exh. cat. (Columbus, Ohio: Wexner Center for the Arts, 1995), 86-101.

2. But it would be important that the notion of a paradigm shift is itself initially elaborated, within the context of the history of science, in partial dependence on the notion of stylistic transformation. For an instance of "a different kind of accounting," see Rosalind E. Krauss, "Sculpture in the Expanded Field," in The Originality of the Avant-Garde and Other Modernist Myths (Cambridge: The MIT Press, 1985), 276-290

3. See, for example, the continuing series of art history and theory anthologies edited by Charles Harrison and others.

4. See, for example, the exchanges around Benjamin H. D. Buchloh's 1990 essay "Conceptual Art 1962-1969: From the Aesthetic of Administration to the Critique of Institutions," October, no. 55 (Winter 1990): 105-143. Joseph Kosuth and Seth Siegelaub, "Replies to Benjamin Buchloh on Conceptual Art," October, no. 57 (Summer 1991): 152-157 and Benjamin H. D. Buchloh, "Reply to Joseph Kosuth and Seth Siegelaub," 158-161. I should be clear that I have neither any interest in nor the scholarly competence adequate to joining in the particular argument about priority so prominent in these exchanges. Joseph Kosuth's early and continuing centrality to Conceptual art seems to me abundantly clear. It is the particular difficulty of characterizing this centrality and the way in which one's choice of characterization opens into the question of Conceptual art itself that seems to me to bear remarking.

5. See, for example, Michael Asher's contribution to L'art conceptuel, une perspective, exh. cat. (Paris: Musée d'art moderne de la Ville de Paris, 1989), 112, which reads in part: "Historical objectification ought to be accelerated while there is still a collective experience and memory which can assist in the clarity of an analysis simultaneously, opening up a space to ask fundamental questions regarding history making," as well as Crow's essay (which takes Asher's remark for its epigraph) in Oehlen Williams 95.

6. If I follow the drift of Crow's work correctly, he is working toward a case of this kind, seeing in Conceptualism an overcoming of the radical cultural dislocation concealed with the Rubéniste triumph in the French academy.

7. One measure of the complex play between Duchamp and conceptual work can perhaps be found in the recently published round-table discussion, "Conceptual Art and the Reception of Duchamp," October, no. 70 (Fall 1994): 127-146. Among the participants were Benjamin H. D. Buchloh, Rosalind E. Krauss, and Thierry de Duve; the discussion—complex, frustrating, and at points deeply interesting—appeared while the present essay was in its final revisions, and so I can do no more than direct the reader's attention to it.

8. Greenberg's remarks about the convergence between positivism and modern art are scattered throughout his postwar writings, but one might particularly note the interesting remark in "Modernist Painting" that "Kantian self-criticism, as it now turns out, has found its fullest expression in science rather than in philosophy." See Clement Greenberg, "Modernist Painting," in The Collected Essays and Criticism, vol. 4: Modernism with a Vengeance, 1957-1969, ed. John O'Brian (Chicago: University of Chicago Press, 1993), 90.

9. This would be a way of thinking about the force of the conversations with the philosopher Stanley Cavell that inform so much of Fried's critical writing.

10. Particularly important in this context has been the work of the literary theorist Frederic Jameson and the late Craig Owens. In the present context it is perhaps particularly useful to point to the connection between Jameson's early appreciation of structuralist and poststructuralist theory in terms of a "prison house of language" and his later work on, for example, Hans Haacke. A selection of Owens's writings is now available as Beyond Recognition: Representation, Power, and Culture, eds. Scott Bryson, Barbara Kruger, Lynne Tillman, and Jane Weinstock (Berkeley: University of California Press, 1992).

11. Benjamin H. D. Buchloh, "From the Aesthetic of Administration to Institutional Critique," in L'art conceptuel, une perspective, exh. cat. (Paris: Musée d'art moderne de la Ville de Paris, 1989), 48. By contrast, Christian Schlatter appeals not to geometry but to color, finding his natural equivalent in the monochrome and, more particularly the black monochrome (Reinhardt and then Stella), which he ties to Hegel's figure of philosophical belatedness and exhaustion. See "L'art conceptuel dans son geste," in Art conceptuel, formes conceptuelles/Conceptual Art, Conceptual Forms, exh. cat. (Paris:

Galerie 1900Δ2000, 1990). This seems to me a weaker view, but interesting in its urge to connect up with Hegelian issues.

12. Buchloh, "From the Aesthetic of Administration" (Paris), 53.

13. Ibid., 49. This is the self-referential reading of Stella that opens the passage to Minimalism.

14. But Mallarmé is hardly a stable term; one might note, for example, his invocatory presence in Brian O'Doherty's guest-edited issue of Aspen magazine, no. 5-6 (Fall-Winter 1967), a collection that I take to be an important token of how particular writings and works could hang together and apart in 1967.

15. For a strong account of this in relation to David Smith (and despite a number of points of substantial disagreement with Fried's general terms of appreciation), see Rosalind E. Krauss, Terminal Iron Works: The Sculpture of David Smith (Cambridge: The MIT Press, 1971).

16. For a different way of exploring this connection, see Benjamin H. D. Buchloh, "Michael Asher and the Conclusion of Modernist Sculpture" in C. Pontbriand, Performance Text(e)s & Documents (Montréal: Parachute, 1981).

17. Where a sculpture strikes us as the outward expression of an essentially hidden (as opposed to merely inward) core, it will appear to approach the condition of an automaton. I take this to be a gloss on Fried's remarks about anthropomorphism and its hiddenness in "Art and Objecthood," in Minimalism: A Critical Anthology, ed. Gregory Battcock (New York: E. P. Dutton and Co., 1968), 116-147. See also Stanley Cavell's sustained examination of humans and automatons in The Claim of Reason: Wittgenstein, Skepticism, Morality, and Tragedy (Oxford: Oxford University Press, 1979).

18. It is in this sense purely visible and does not present itself as the object of any imaginative grasp.

19. Conceptualism—I take this to be part of the interest of Crow's work—has clearly shifted this in ways whose possibilities remain hard to calculate.

20. In addition to "Sculpture in the Expanded Field," see Krauss's The Optical Unconscious (Cambridge: The MIT Press, 1993), as well as "Une note sur l'inconscient optique," Les cahiers du Musée national d'art moderne, no. 37 (Autumn 1991): 61-77.

21. This line in Krauss's work is everywhere traversed and complicated by an engagement with photography, and this complication is in its turn very closely linked to the emergence of photography as a medium capable of carrying the force of language in much recent and contemporary conceptual work. There seems to be a generally good fit between a claim couched in the terms of this essay that photography can be discovered to give us things in their aspectuality and Krauss's claim, in the very different context of Surrealist photographic practice, that "Surreality is, we could say, nature convulsed into a kind of writing. The special access that photography, as a medium, has to this experience is photography's privileged connection to the real. . . . The experience of nature as sign or representation comes naturally, then, to photography." See Rosalind E. Krauss, "Photography in the Service of Surrealism," in Krauss and Jane Livingston, L'amour fou, exh. cat. (Washington, D.C.: The Corcoran Gallery of Art, 1985), 35.

22. If one hears the spatial accent in "without" that makes it name the place where visibility is, one may also see the pertinence of the Heideggerean imagination invoked earlier.

23. It is perhaps not entirely surprising that Greenberg's place has now to a degree been taken up by the explicitly Hegelian philosopher and critic, Arthur Danto. Danto's own stance toward Conceptualism and related tendencies seems to me interestingly unclear.

24. See, for example, "Towards a Newer Laocoon" in Clement Greenberg, The Collected Essays and Criticism, vol. 1: Perceptions and Judgments, 1939-1944, ed. John O'Brian (Chicago: University of Chicago Press, 1986), 23-37. This essay is usually taken, correctly, as an early assertion of the principle of medium specificity that comes to play such a large role in Greenberg's criticism, but it is worth noting that its first argumentative section begins "There can be, I believe, such a thing as a dominant art form," 24. The effects of this belief are, I think, palpable in Greenberg's later attempts to negotiate his way between painting and sculpture.

25. For explorations of community in these terms, see Maurice Blanchot, The Unavowable Community, trans. Pierre Joris (Barrytown, New York: Station Hill Press, 1988); Jean-Luc Nancy, The Inoperative Community, ed. Peter Connor and trans. Connor, Lisa Garbus, Michael Holland, and Simona Sawhney (Minneapolis: University of Minnesota Press, 1991); Community at Loose Ends, ed. Miami Theory Collective (Minneapolis: University of Minnesota Press, 1991); Giorgio Agamben, The Coming Community, trans. Michael Hardt (Minneapolis: University of Minnesota Press, 1993).

1555 ARTESIA BLVD.

6565 FOUNTAIN AVE.

JEFF WALL

"MARKS OF INDIFFERENCE": ASPECTS OF PHO-TOGRAPHY IN, OR AS, CONCEPTUAL ART *(Preface)* This

essay is a sketch, an attempt to study the ways that photography occupied Conceptual artists, the ways that pho-tography decisively realized itself as a modernist art in the experiments of the 1960s and 1970s. Conceptual art played an important role in the transformation of the terms and conditions within which art-photography defined itself and its relationships with the other arts, a transformation which established photography as an institutionalized modernist form evolving explicitly through the dynamics of its auto-critique.

Photography's implication with modernist painting and sculpture was not, of course, developed in the 1960s; it was central to the work and discourse of the art of the 1920s. But, for the sixties generation, art-photography remained too comfortably rooted in the pictorial traditions of modern art; it had an irritatingly serene, marginal existence, a way of holding itself at a distance from the intellectual drama of avant-gardism while claiming a prominent, even definitive place within it. The younger artists wanted to disturb that, to uproot and radicalize the medium, and they did so with the most sophisticated means they had in hand at the time, the auto-critique of art identified with the tradition of the avant-garde. Their approach implied that photography had not yet become "avant-garde" in 1960 or 1965, despite the epithets being casually applied to it. It had not yet accomplished the preliminary auto-dethronement, or deconstruction, which the other arts had established as fundamental to their development and their *amour-propre*.

Through that auto-critique, painting and sculpture had moved away from the practice of depiction, which had historically been the foundation of their social and aesthetic value. Although we may no longer accept the claim that abstract art had gone "beyond" representation or depiction, it is certain that such developments added something new to the corpus of possible artistic forms in Western culture. In the first half of the 1960s, Minimalism was decisive in bringing back into sharp focus, for the first time since the 1930s, the general problem of how a work of art could validate itself as an object among all other objects in the world. Under the regime of depiction, that is, in the history of Western art before 1910, a work of art was an object whose validity as art was constituted by its being, or bearing, a depiction. In the process of developing alternative proposals for art "beyond" depiction, art had to reply to the suspicion that, without their depictive, or representational function, art objects were art in name only, not in body, form, or function.¹ Art projected itself forward bearing only its glamorous traditional name, thereby entering a troubled phase of restless searching for an alternative ground of validity. This phase continues, and must continue.

Photography cannot find alternatives to depiction, as could the other fine arts. It is in the physical nature of the medium to depict things. In order to participate in the kind of reflexivity made mandatory

Edward Ruscha
From SOME LOS ANGELES APARTMENTS (1965) Bound artist's book.
Photo Paula Goldman.

for modernist art, photography can put into play only its own necessary condition of being a depiction-which-constitutes-an-object.

In its attempts to make visible this condition, Conceptual art hoped to reconnect the medium to the world in a new, fresh way, beyond the worn-out criteria for photography as sheer picture-making. Several important directions emerged in this process. In this essay I will examine only two. The first involves the rethinking and "refunctioning" of *reportage*, the dominant type of art-photography as it existed at the beginning of the 1960s. The second is related to the first, and to a certain extent emerges from it. This is the issue of the de-skilling and re-skilling of the artist in a context defined by the culture industry, and made controversial by aspects of Pop art.

(I. From Reportage to Photodocumentation)   Photography entered its post-Pictorialist phase (one might say its "post-Stieglitzian" phase) in an exploration of the border-territories of the utilitarian picture.   In this phase, which began around 1920, important work was made by those who rejected the Pictorialist enterprise and turned toward immediacy, instantaneity, and the evanescent moment of the emergence of pictorial value out of a practice of reportage of one kind or another. A new version of what could be called the "Western Picture," or the "Western Concept of the Picture," appears in this process.

The Western Picture is, of course, that *tableau*, that independently beautiful depiction and composition that derives from the institutionalization of perspective and dramatic figuration at the origins of modern Western art, with Raphael, Dürer, Bellini and the other familiar *maestri*. It is known as a product of divine gift, high skill, deep emotion, and crafty planning. It plays with the notion of the spontaneous, the unanticipated. The master picture-maker prepares everything in advance, yet trusts that all the planning in the world will lead only to something fresh, mobile, light and fascinating. The soft body of the brush, the way it constantly changes shape as it is used, was the primary means by which the genius of composition was placed at risk at each moment, and recovered, transcendent, in the shimmering surfaces of magical feats of figuration.

Pictorialist photography was dazzled by the spectacle of Western painting and attempted, to some extent, to imitate it in acts of pure composition. Lacking the means to make the surface of its pictures unpredictable and important, the first phase of Pictorialism, Stieglitz's phase, emulated the fine graphic arts, re-invented the beautiful book, set standards for gorgeousness of composition, and faded. Without a dialectical conception of its own surface, it could not achieve the kind of planned spontaneity painting had put before the eyes of the world as a universal norm of art. By 1920, photographers interested in art had begun to look away from painting, even from modern painting, toward the vernacular of their own medium, and toward the cinema, to discover their own principle of spontaneity, to discover once again, for themselves, that unanticipated appearance of the Picture demanded by modern aesthetics.

At this moment the art-concept of photojournalism appears, the notion that art can be created by imitating photojournalism. This imitation was made necessary by the dialectics of avant-garde experimentation. Non-autonomous art-forms, like architecture, and new phenomena such as mass communications, became paradigmatic in the 1920s and 1930s because the avant-gardes were so involved in a critique of the autonomous work of art,

248

so intrigued by the possibility of going beyond it into a utopian revision of society and consciousness. Photojournalism was created in the framework of the new publishing and communications industries, and it elaborated a new kind of picture, utilitarian in its determination by editorial assignment and novel in its seizure of the instantaneous, of the "news event" as it happened. For both these reasons, it seems to have occurred to a number of photographers (Paul Strand, Walker Evans, Brassaï, Henri Cartier-Bresson) that a new art could be made by means of a mimesis of these aims and aspects of photography as it really existed in the world of the new culture industries.

This mimesis led to transformations in the concept of the Picture that had consequences for the whole notion of modern art, and that therefore stand as preconditions for the kind of critique proposed by the Conceptual artists after 1965. Post-pictorialist photography is elaborated in the working out of a demand that the Picture make an appearance in a practice which, having already largely relinquished the sensuousness of the surface, must also relinquish any explicit preparatory process of composition. Acts of composition are the property of the tableau. In reportage, the sovereign place of composition is retained only as a sort of dynamic of anticipatory framing, a "hunter's consciousness," the nervous looking of a "one-eyed cat," as Lee Friedlander put it. Every picture-constructing advantage accumulated over centuries is given up to the jittery flow of events as they unfold. The rectangle of the viewfinder and the speed of the shutter, photography's "window of equipment," is all that remains of the great craft-complex of composition. The art-concept of photojournalism began to force photography into what appears to be a modernist dialectic. By divesting itself of the encumbrances and advantages inherited from older art forms, reportage pushes toward a discovery of qualities apparently intrinsic to the medi-

um, qualities that must necessarily distinguish the medium from others, and through the self-examination of which it can emerge as a modernist art on a plane with the others.

This force, or pressure, is not simply social. Reportage is not a photographic type brought into existence by the requirements of social institutions as such, even though institutions like the press played a central part in defining photojournalism. The press had some role in shaping the new equipment of the 1920s and 1930s, particularly the smaller, faster cameras and film stock. But reportage is inherent in the nature of the medium, and the evolution of equipment reflects this. Reportage, or the spontaneous, fleeting aspect of the photographic image, appears simultaneously with the pictorial, tableau-like aspect at the origins of photography; its traces can be seen in the blurred elements of Daguerre's first street scenes. Reportage evolves in the pursuit of the blurred parts of pictures.

In this process, photography elaborates its version of the Picture, and it is the first new version since the onset of modern painting in the 1860s, or, possibly, since the emergence of abstract art, if one considers abstract paintings to be, in fact, pictures anymore. A new version of the Picture implies necessarily a turn-

ing-point in the development of modernist art. Problems are raised which will constitute the intellectual content of Conceptual art, or at least significant aspects of that content.

One of the most important critiques opened up in Conceptual art was that of art-photography's achieved or perceived "aestheticism." The revival of interest in the radical theories and methods of the politicized and objectivistic avant-garde of the 1920s and 1930s has long been recognized as one of the most significant contributions of the art of the 1960s, particularly in America. Productivism, "factography," and Bauhaus concepts were turned against the apparently "depoliticized" and resubjectivized art of the 1940s and 1950s. Thus, we have seen that the kind of formalistic and "re-subjectivized" art-photography that developed around Edward Weston and Ansel Adams on the West Coast, or Harry Callahan and Aaron Siskind in Chicago in those years (to use only American examples) attempted to leave behind *not only* any *link* with agit-prop, but even any connection with the nervous surfaces of social life, and to resume a stately modernist pictorialism. This work has been greeted with opprobrium from radical critics since the beginnings of the new debates in the 1960s. The orthodox view is that Cold War pressures compelled socially-conscious photographers away from the borderline forms of art-photojournalism toward the more subjectivistic versions of *art informel*. In this process, the more explosive and problematic forms and concepts of radical avant-gardism were driven from view, until they made a return in the activistic neo-avant-gardism of the 1960s. There is much truth in this construction, but it is flawed in that it draws too sharp a line between the methods and approaches of politicized avant-gardism and those of the more subjectivistic and formalistic trends in art-photography.

The situation is more complex because the possibilities for autonomous formal composition in photography were themselves refined and brought onto the historical and social agenda by the medium's evolution in the context of vanguardist art. The art-concept of photojournalism is a theoretical formalization of the ambiguous condition of the most problematic kind of photograph. That photograph emerges on the wing, out of a photographer's complex social engagement (his or her assignment); it records something significant in the event, in the engagement, and gains some validity from that. But this validity alone is only a social validity—the picture's success as reportage *per se*. The entire avant-garde of the 1920s and 1930s was aware that validity as reportage *per se* was insufficient for the most radical of purposes. What was necessary was that the picture not only succeed as reportage and be socially effective, but that it succeed in putting forward a new proposition or model of the Picture. Only in doing both these things simultaneously could photography realize itself as a modernist art form, and participate in the radical and revolutionary cultural projects of that era. In this context, rejection of a classicizing aesthetic of the picture—in the name of proletarian amateurism, for example—must be seen as a claim to a new level of pictorial consciousness.

Thus, art-photography was compelled to be both anti-aestheticist and aesthetically significant, albeit in a new "negative" sense, at the same moment. Here, it is important to recognize that it was the content of the avant-garde dialogue itself that was central in creating the demand for an aestheticism which was the object of critique by that same avant-garde. In *Theory of the Avant-Garde* (1974) Peter Bürger argued that the avant-garde emerged historically in a critique of the completed aestheticism of nineteenth-century modern art.[2] He suggests that, around 1900, the avant-garde generation, confronted with the social and institutional fact of the separation between art and the other autonomous domains of life felt compelled to attempt to leap over that separation and reconnect high art and the conduct of affairs in the world in order to save the aesthetic dimension by transcending it. Bürger's emphasis on this drive to transcend Aestheticism and autonomous art neglects the fact that the obsession with the aesthetic, now transformed into a sort of taboo, was carried over into the center of every possible artistic thought or critical idea developed by vanguardism. Thus, to a certain extent, one can invert Bürger's thesis and say that avant-garde art not only constituted a critique of Aestheticism, but also re-established Aestheticism as a permanent issue through its intense problematization of it. This thesis corresponds especially closely to the situation of photography within vanguardism. Photography had no history of autonomous status perfected over time into an imposing institution. It emerged too late for that. Its aestheticizing thus was not, and could not be, simply an object for an avant-gardist critique, since it was brought into existence by that same critique.

In this sense, there cannot be a clear demarcation between aestheticist formalism and various modes of engaged photography. Subjectivism could become the foundation for radical practices in photography just as easily as neo-factography, and both are often present in much work of the 1960s.

The peculiar, yet familiar, political ambiguity *as art* of the experimental forms in and around Conceptualism, particularly in the context of 1968, is the result of the fusion, or even confusion, of tropes of art-photography with aspects of its critique. Far from being anomalous, this fusion reflects precisely the inner structure of photography as potentially avant-garde or even neo-avant-garde art. This implies that the new forms of photographic practice and experiment in the sixties and seventies did not derive exclusively from a revival of anti-subjectivist and anti-formalist tendencies. Rather, the work of figures like Douglas Huebler, Robert Smithson, Bruce Nauman, Richard

Long, or Joseph Kosuth emerge from a space constituted by the already-matured transformations of both types of approach—factographic and subjectivist, activist and formalist, "Marxian" and "Kantian"—present in the work of their precursors in the 1940s and 1950s, in the intricacies of the dialectic of "reportage as art-photography," as art-photography *par excellence*. The radical critiques of art-photography inaugurated and occasionally realized in Conceptual art can be seen as both an overturning of academicized approaches to these issues, and as an extrapolation of existing tensions inside that academicism, a new critical phase of academicism and not simply a renunciation of it. Photoconceptualism was able to bring new energies from the other fine arts into the problematic of art-photojournalism, and this has tended to obscure the ways in which it was rooted in the unresolved but well-established aesthetic issues of the photography of the 1940s and 1950s.

Intellectually, the stage was thus set for a revival of the whole drama of reportage within avant-gardism. The peculiar situation of art-photography in the art market at the beginning of the 1960s is another precondition, whose consequences are not simply sociological. It is almost astonishing to remember that important art-photographs could be purchased for under $100 not only in 1950 but in 1960. This suggests that, despite the internal complexity of the aesthetic structure of art-photography, its moment of recognition as art in capitalist societies had not yet occurred. All the aesthetic precondi-

Richard Long
ENGLAND 1968 (1968)
Gelatin-silver photographic print mounted on Fome-Cor.
30 x 40 in. (76.2 x 101.6 cm). The Dorothy and Herbert Vogel
Collection.

tions for its emergence as a major form of modernist art had come into being, but it took the new critiques and transformations of the sixties and seventies to actualize these socially. It could be said that the very absence of a market in photography at the moment of a rapidly booming one for painting drew two kinds of energy toward the medium.

The first is a speculative and inquisitive energy, one which circulates everywhere things appear to be "undervalued." Undervaluation implies the future, opportunity, and the sudden appearance of something forgotten. The undervalued is a category akin to Benjaminian ones like the "just past," or the "recently forgotten."

The second is a sort of negative version of the first. In the light of the new critical skepticism toward "high art" that began to surface in the intellectual glimmerings around Pop art and its mythologies, the lack of interest of art marketeers and collectors marked photography with a utopian potential. Thus, the thought occurred that a photograph might be the Picture which could not be integrated into "the regime," the commercial-bureaucratic-discursive order which was rapidly becoming the object of criticisms animated by the attitudes of the Student Movement and the New Left. Naive as such thoughts might seem today, they were valuable in turning serious attention toward the ways in which art-photography had not yet become Art. Until it became Art, with a big A, photographs could not be *experienced* in terms of the dialectic of validity which marks all modernist aesthetic enterprises.

Paradoxically, this could only happen in reverse. Photography could emerge socially as art only at the moment when its aesthetic presuppositions seemed to be undergoing a withering radical critique, a critique apparently aimed at foreclosing any further aestheticization or "artification" of the medium. Photoconceptualism led the way toward the complete acceptance of photography as art—autonomous, bourgeois, collectible art—by virtue of insisting that this medium might be privileged to be the negation of that whole idea. In being that negation, the last barriers were broken. Inscribed in a new avant-gardism, and blended with elements of text, sculpture, painting, or drawing, photography became the quintessential "anti-object." As the neo- avant-gardes re-examined and unravelled the orthodoxies of the 1920s and 1930s, the boundaries of the domain of autonomous art were unexpectedly widened, not narrowed. In the explosion of post-autonomous models of practice which characterized the discourse of the seventies, we can detect, maybe only with hindsight, the extension of avant-garde aestheticism. As with the first avant-garde, post-autonomous, "post-studio" art required its double legitimation—first, its legitimation as having transcended—or at least having authentically tested—the boundaries of autonomous art and having become functional in some real way; and then, secondly, that this test, this new utility, result in works or forms which proposed compelling models of art as such, at the same time that they seemed to dissolve, abandon, or negate it. I propose the following characterization of this process: autonomous art had reached a state where it appeared that it could only validly be made by means of the strictest imitation of the non-autonomous. This heteronomy might take the form of direct critical commentary, as with Art & Language; with the production of political propaganda, so common in the 1970s; or with the many varieties of "intervention" or appropriation practiced more recently. But, in all these procedures, an autonomous work of art is still necessarily created. The innovation is that the content of the work is the validity of the model or hypothesis of non-autonomy it creates.

This complex game of mimesis has been, of course, the foundation for all "endgame" strategies within avant-gardism. The profusion of new forms, processes, materials and subjects which characterizes the art of the 1970s was to a great extent stimulated by mimetic relationships with other social production processes: industrial, academic, commercial, cinematic, etc. Art-photography, as we have seen, had already evolved an intricate mimetic structure, in which artists imitated photojournalists in order to create Pictures. This elaborate, mature mimetic order of production brought photography to the forefront of the new pseudo-heteronomy, and permitted it to become a paradigm for all aesthetically-critical, model-constructing thought about art. Photoconceptualism worked out many of the implications of this, so much so that it may begin to seem that many of Conceptual art's essential achievements are either created in the form of photographs or are otherwise mediated by them.

Reportage is introverted and parodied, manneristically, in aspects of photoconceptualism. The notion that an artistically significant photograph can any longer be made in a direct imitation of photojournalism is rejected as having been historically completed by the earlier avant-garde and by the lyrical subjectivism of 1950s art-photography. The gesture of reportage is withdrawn from the social field and attached to a putative theatrical event. The social field tends to be abandoned to professional photojournalism proper, as if the aesthetic problems associated with depicting it were no longer of any consequence, and photojournalism had entered not so much a postmodernist phase as a "post-aesthetic" one in which it was excluded from aesthetic evolution for a time. This, by the way, suited the sensibilities of those political activists who attempted a new version of proletarian photography in the period.

This introversion, or subjectivization, of reportage was manifested in two important directions. First, it brought photography into a new relationship with the problematics of the staged, or posed, picture, through new concepts of performance. Second, the inscription of photography into a nexus of experimental practices led to a direct but distantiated and parodic relationship with the art-concept of photojournalism. Although the work of many artists could be discussed in this context, for the sake of brevity I will discuss the photographic work of Richard Long and Bruce Nauman as representative of the first issue, that of Dan Graham, Douglas Huebler, and Robert Smithson of the second.

Long's and Nauman's photographs document already-conceived artistic gestures, actions, or "studio events"—things that stand self-consciously as conceptual, aesthetic models for states of affairs in the world, which, as such, need no longer appear directly in the picture. Long's ENGLAND 1968 (1968) documents an action or gesture, made by the artist alone, out in the countryside, away from the normal environs of art or performance. Generically, his pictures are landscapes, and their mood is rather different from the typologies and intentions of reportage. Conventional artistic landscape photography might feature a foreground motif, such as a curious heap of stones or a gnarled tree, and counterpoint it to the rest of the scene, showing it to be singular, differentiated from its surroundings, and yet existing by means of those surroundings. In such ways, a landscape picture can be thought to report on a state of affairs, and therefore be consistent with an art-concept of reportage. Long's walked line in the grass substitutes itself for the foreground motif. It is a gesture akin to Barnett Newman's notion of the establishment of a "Here" in the void of a primeval terrain. It is simultaneously agriculture, religion,

253

urbanism, and theater, an intervention in a lonely, picturesque spot which becomes a setting completed artistically by the gesture and the photograph for which the gesture was enacted. Long does not photograph events in the process of their occurrence, but stages an event for the benefit of a preconceived photographic rendering. The picture is presented as the subsidiary form of an act, as "photo-documentation." It has become that, however, by means of a new kind of photographic mise-en-scène. That is, it exists and is legitimated as continuous with the project of reportage by moving in precisely the opposite direction, toward a completely designed pictorial method, an introverted masquerade that plays games with the inherited aesthetic proclivities of art-photography-as-reportage.

Many of the same elements, moved indoors, characterize Nauman's studio photographs, such as FAILING TO LEVITATE IN THE STUDIO (1966) or SELF-PORTRAIT AS A FOUNTAIN (1966-67/70). The photographer's studio, and the generic complex of "studio photography," was the Pictorialist antithesis against which the aesthetics of reportage were elaborated. Nauman changes the terms. Working within the experimental framework of what was beginning at the time to be called "performance art," he carries out photographic acts of reportage whose subject-matter is the self-conscious, self-centered "play" taking place in the studios of artists who have moved "beyond" the modern fine arts into the new hybridities. Studio photography is no longer isolated from reportage: it is reduced analytically to coverage of whatever is happening in the studio, that place once so rigorously controlled by precedent and

254

formula, but which was in the process of being reinvented once more as theater, factory, reading room, meeting place, gallery, museum, and many other things.

Nauman's photographs, films, and videos of this period are done in two modes or styles. The first, that of FAILING TO LEVITATE, is "direct," rough, and shot in black and white. The other is based on studio lighting effects—multiple sources, colored gels, emphatic contrasts—and is of course done in color. The two styles, reduced to a set of basic formulae and effects, are signifiers for the new co-existence of species of photography which had seemed ontologically separated and even opposed in the art history of photography up to that time. It is as if the reportage works go back to Muybridge and the sources of all traditional concepts of photographic documentary, and the color pictures to the early "gags" and jokes, to Man Ray and Moholy-Nagy, to the birthplace of effects used for their own sake. The two reigning myths of photography—the one that claims that photographs are "true" and the one that claims they are not—are shown to be grounded in the same praxis, available in the same place, the studio, at that place's moment of historical transformation.

These practices, or strategies, are extremely common by about 1969, so common as to be *de rigueur* across the horizon of performance art, earth art, Arte Povera, and Conceptualism, and it can be said that these new methodologies of photographic practice are the strongest factor linking together the experimental forms of the period, which can seem so disparate and irreconcilable.

This integration or fusion of reportage and performance, its manneristic introversion, can be seen as an implicitly parodic critique of the concepts of art-photography. Smithson and Graham, in part because they were active as writers, were able to provide a more explicit parody of photojournalism than Nauman or Long.

Photojournalism as a social institution can be defined most simply as a collaboration between a writer and a photographer. Conceptual art's intellectualism was engendered by young, aspiring artists

Cover of *Artforum* 8, no. 1 (September 1969), with photograph
of *Robert Smithson's* FIRST MIRROR DISPLACEMENT (1969)

Robert Smithson
"The Bridge Monument Showing Sidewalks" as reproduced in his
essay "The Monuments of Passaic," *Artforum* 6, no. 4
(December 1967): 49.

for whom critical writing was an important practice of self-definition. The example of Donald Judd's criticism for *Arts Magazine* was decisive here, and essays like "Specific Objects" (1964) had the impact, almost, of literary works of art. The interplay between a veteran littérateur, Clement Greenberg; a young academic art critic, Michael Fried; and Judd, a talented stylist, is one of the richest episodes in the history of American criticism, and had much to do with igniting the idea of a written critique standing as a work of art. Smithson's "The Crystal Land," published in *Harper's Bazaar* in 1966, is an homage to Judd as a creator of both visual and literary forms. Smithson's innovation, however, is to avoid the genre of art criticism, writing a mock-travelogue instead. He plays the part of the inquisitive, belletristic journalist, accompanying and interpreting his subject. He narrativizes his account of Judd's art, moves from critical commentary to storytelling and re-invents the relationships between visual art and literature. Smithson's most important published works, such as "The Monuments of Passaic," and "Incidents of Mirror-Travel in the Yucatan" are "auto-accompaniments." Smithson the journalist-photographer accompanies Smithson the artist-experimenter and is able to produce a sophisticated apologia for his sculptural work in the guise of popular entertainment. His essays do not make the Conceptualist claim to be works of visual art, but appear to remain content with being works of literature. The photographs included in them purport to illustrate the narrative or commentary. The narratives, in turn, describe the event of making the photographs. "One never knew what side of the mirror one was on," he mused in "Passaic," as if reflecting on the parody of photojournalism he was in the process of enacting. Smithson's parody was a way of dissolving, or softening, the objectivistic and positivistic tone of Minimalism, of subjectivizing it by associating its reductive formal language with intricate, drifting, even delirious moods or states of mind.

The Minimalist sculptural forms to which Smithson's texts constantly allude appeared to erase the associative chain of experience, the interior monologue of creativity, insisting on the pure immediacy of the product itself, the work as such, as "specific object." Smithson's exposure of what he saw as Minimalism's emotional interior depends on the return of ideas of time and process, of narrative and enactment, of experience, memory, and allusion, to the artistic forefront, against the rhetoric of both Greenberg and Judd. His photojournalism is at once self-portraiture—that is, performance—and reportage about what was hidden and even repressed in the art he most admired. It located the impulse toward self-sufficient and non-objective forms of art in concrete, personal responses to real-life, social experiences, thereby contributing to the new critiques of formalism which were so central to Conceptual art's project.

Dan Graham's involvement with the classical traditions of reportage is unique among the artists usually identified with Conceptual art, and his architectural photographs continue some aspects of Walker Evans's project. In this, Graham locates his practice at the boundary of photojournalism, participating in it, while at the same time placing it at the service of other aspects of his oeuvre. His architectural photographs provide a social grounding for the structural models of intersubjective experience he elaborated in text, video, performance and sculptural environmental pieces. His

nected Bergen County with Passaic County. Noonday sunshine cinema-ized the site, turning the bridge and the river into an over-exposed *picture*. Photographing it with my Instamatic 400 was like photographing a photograph. The sun became a monstrous light-bulb that projected a detached series of "stills" through my Instamatic into my eye. When I walked on the bridge, it was as though I was walking on an enormous photograph that was made of wood and steel, and underneath the river existed as an enormous movie film that showed nothing but a continuous blank.

The steel road that passed over the water was in part an open grating flanked by wooden sidewalks, held up by a heavy set of beams, while above, a ramshackle network hung in the air. A rusty sign glared in the sharp atmosphere, making it hard to read. A date flashed in the sunshine . . . 1899 . . . No . . . 1896 . . . maybe (at the bottom of the rust and glare was the name Dean & Westbrook Contractors, N.Y.). I was completely controlled by the Instamatic (or what the rationalists call a camera). The glassy air of New Jersey defined the structural parts of the monument as I took snapshot after snapshot. A barge seemed fixed to the surface of the water as it came toward the bridge, and caused the bridge-keeper to close the gates. From the banks of Passaic I watched the bridge rotate on a central axis in order to allow an inert rectangular shape to pass with its unknown cargo. The Passaic (West) end of the bridge rotated south, while the Rutherford (East) end of the bridge rotated north; such rotations suggested the limited movements of an outmoded world. "North" and "South" hung over the static river in a bi-polar manner. One could refer to this bridge as the "Monument of Dislocated Directions."

Along the Passaic River banks were many minor monuments such as concrete abutments that supported the shoulders of a new highway in the process of being built. River Drive was in part bulldozed and in part intact. It was hard to tell the new highway from the old road; they were both confounded into a unitary chaos. Since it was Saturday, many machines were not working, and this caused them to resemble prehistoric creatures trapped in the mud, or, better, extinct machines—mechanical dinosaurs stripped of their skin. On the edge of this prehistoric Machine Age were pre- and post-World War II suburban houses. The houses mirrored themselves into colorlessness. A group of children were throwing rocks at each other near a ditch. "From now on you're not going to come to our hide-out. And I mean it!" said a little blonde girl who had been hit with a rock.

As I walked north along what was left of River Drive, I saw a monument in the middle of the river — it was a pumping derrick with a long pipe attached to it. The pipe was supported in part by a set of pontoons, while the rest of it extended about three blocks along the river bank till it disappeared into the earth. One could hear

The Bridge Monument Showing Wooden Sidewalks. (Photo: Robert Smithson)

fornia Method' consisted simply of determining in advance the exact amount and lengths of pieces of lumber and multiplying them by the number of standardized houses to be built. A cutting yard was set up near the site of the project to saw rough lumber into those sizes. By mass buying, greater use of machines and factory produced parts, assembly line standardization, multiple units were easily fabricated.

Each house in a development is a lightly constrected 'shell' although this fact is often concealed by fake (half-stone) brick walls. Shells can be added or subtracted easily. The standard unit is a box or a series of boxes, sometimes contemptuously called 'pillboxes.' When the box has a sharply oblique roof it is called a Cape Cod. When it is longer than wide it is a 'ranch.' A two-story house is usually called 'colonial.' If it consists of contiguous boxes with one slightly higher elevation it is a 'split level.' Such stylistic differentiation is advantagous to the basic structure (with the possible exception of the split level whose plan simplifies construction on discontinuous ground levels). There is a recent trend toward 'two home homes' which are two boxes split by adjoining walls and having separate entrances. The left and right hand units are mirror reproductions of each other. Often sold as private units are strings of apartment-like, quasi-discrete cells formed by subdividing laterally an extended rectangular parallelopiped into as many as ten or twelve separate dwellings.

Developers usually build large groups of individual homes sharing similar floor plans and whose overall grouping possesses a discrete flow plan. Regional shopping centers and industrial parks are sometimes integrated as well into the general scheme. Each development is sectioned into blocked-out areas containing a series of identical or sequentially related types of houses all of which have uniform or staggered set-backs and land plots.

The logic relating each sectioned part to the entire plan follows a systematic plan. A development contains a limited, set number of house models. For instance, Cape Coral, a Florida project, advertises eight different models:

A The Sonata
B The Concerto
C The Overture
D The Ballet
E The Prelude
F The Serenade
G The Noctune
H The Rhapsody

In addition, there is a choice of eight exterior colors:

1 White
2 Moonstone Grey
3 Nickle
4 Seafoam Green
5 Lawn Green
6 Bamboo
7 Coral Pink
8 Colonial Red

Each block of houses is a self-contained sequence—there is no development—selected from the possible acceptable arrangements. As an example, if a section was to contain eight houses of which four model types were to be used, any of these permutational possibilities could be used:

AABBCCDD	ABCDABCD
AABBDDCC	ABDCABDC
AACCBBDD	ACBDACBD
AACCDDBB	ACDBACDB
AADDCCBB	ADBCADBC
AADDBBCC	ADCBADCB
BBAACCDD	BADCBADC
BBAADDCC	BACDBACD
BBCCAADD	BCADBCAD
BBCCDDAA	BCDABCDA
BBDDAACC	BDACBDAC
BBDDCCAA	BDCABDCA
CCAABBDD	CABDCABD
CCAADDBB	CADBCADB
CCBBDDAA	CBADCBAD
CCBBAADD	CBDACBDA
CCDDAABB	CDABCDAB
CCDDBBAA	CDBACDBA
DDAABBCC	DACBDACB
DDAACCBB	DABCDABC
DDBBAACC	DBACDBAC
DDBBCCAA	DBCADBCA
DDCCAABB	DCABDCAB
DDCCBBAA	DCBADCBA

As the color series usually varies [illegible] pendently of the model series, a block [illegible] eight houses utilizing four models and [illegible] colors might have forty-eight times [illegible] eight or 2,304 possible arrangements.

A given development might use, [illegible] *four* of these possibilities as an [illegible] scheme for different sectors; then [illegible] four from another scheme which [illegible] the remaining four unused models [illegible] colors; then select four from another [illegible] which utilizes all eight models and [illegible] colors; then four from another scheme [illegible] utilizes a single model and all eight [illegible] (or four or two colors); and finally [illegible] that single scheme for one model and [illegible] color. This serial logic might follow [illegible] sistently until, at the edges, it is [illegible] terminated by pre-existent highways, [illegible] ing alleys, shopping plazas, car hops, [illegible] count houses, lumber yards or factories.

Although there is perhaps some [illegible] precedence in the row houses which [illegible] indigenous to many older cities along [illegible] east coast, and built with uniform [illegible] and set-backs early this century, [illegible] developments as an architectural [illegible] non seem peculiarly gratuitous. They [illegible] apart from prior standards of 'good' [illegible] ture. They were not built to satisfy [illegible] needs or tastes. The owner is [illegible] tangential to the product's completion. [illegible] home isn't really possessable in the [illegible] sense; it wasn't designed to 'last for generations'; and outside of its [illegible] 'here and now' context it is useless, [illegible] to be thrown away. Both architecture [illegible] craftsmanship as values are subverted [illegible] dependence on simplified and easily [illegible] cated techniques of fabrication and [illegible] ized modular plans. Contingencies [illegible] mass production technology and land [illegible] economics make the final decisions, [illegible] the architect his former 'unique' role. [illegible] velopments stand in an altered relationship to their environment. Designed to fill [illegible] 'dead' land areas, the houses needn't [illegible] to or attempt to withstand Nature. [illegible] is no organic unity connecting the land [illegible] and the home. Both are without roots [illegible] separate parts in a larger, predetermined synthetic order.

"Contingencies such as mass production technology and land use economics make the final decisions, denying the architect his former 'unique' role." Above: Wooden Houses, Boston, 1930, from *American Photographs* by Walker Evans, published by The Museum of Modern Art. Below: house plan courtesy Cape Coral Homes.

The SERENADE
Three Bedrooms, Two Baths, Enclosed Garage, Screened Porch

22

ARTS MAGAZINE/December 1966-January 19[illegible]

Armory '66

Not Quite What We Had in Mind

ERICA ABEEL

In 1926, Martha Graham's first recital inaugurated the search for a movement system at once indigenous and universal. Eugene O'Neill's grown-up dramas were galvanizing a moribund American theater. It was only a year from Movietone News' sound coverage of Charles Lindbergh's solo trans-Atlantic flight to the unguentine warblings of the first dramatic talkie, Al Jolson's The Jazz Singer. *Picasso was painting his first composite-form figures; Surrealism was asserting the primacy of the unconscious.*

Now who, forty years ago, could have conjured up in some far-out thought-bubble of the imagination the newest *(at press-time) breakthrough in the arts,* Nine Evenings of Theater and Engineering? *Marcel Duchamp? Possibly. One suspects he knew about it all along.*

They promised the New Art of the Future. 1913 all over again. Barnum & Bailey thrills 'n chills. A cast of thousands. Human dirigibles. Jet-propelled vacuum cleaners. UFO's. The Colossus of the Armory. The world will never be the same again. Forget Vietnam.

It was the next logical step. At some point in the 'fifties a number of artists started playing around with the demarcations between painting, sculpture, dance and music. Out of these experiments emerged a new intermedia genre, variously designated as the Theater Piece, the Happening, Action Theater, Dance, take your pick. The old Theater Piece had this hand-sewn, unique, made-on-West-Broadway look. And although it utilized props, people-as-props and an environment, it was scaled to the limitations of the naked human body. One night in a Washington rink Bob Rauschenberg took to roller skates, an extension of the motion of feet. But why stop there? Why not make all of electronic technology available to the artist, and, by extending the means he has at his disposal, greatly magnify the range of what he is able to express? Swell, said Billy Kluver of Bell Labs, and put the artists and the engineers in a room together.

The products of this were on view in *Nine Evenings of Theater and Engineering* at the 25th Street Armory from October 13-23. The press proclaimed it a colossal bust. The audience emitted static; or vacated the premises mid-way, noses pointing self-righteously toward the Exit.

An artist creating an art-object is involved in a relatively limited manipulation of materials. It is essentially a one-man operation, even though the sculptor may send his 'plans' off to the factory to be manufactured. A theatrical medium is another matter. A single piece in *Nine Evenings* tended to be operatic in scope, requiring the coordination of performers reaching, in some instances, Caracallan proportions, technicians and, what may have proved to be the most capricious diva in all theatrical history, TEEM (Theater Electronic Environment Modular System). The one-man operation permits testing, discarding, new testing. But can you just scrap thousands of dollars of equipment, the product of nine months of work if, after its completion, it turns out to be not quite what the artist had in mind? John Cage characteristically courts the failure of the original *intention:* "The technical problems involved in any single project tend to reduce the impact of the original idea, but in being solved they produce a situation different than anyone could have pre-imagined."

The concert, for Cage, is no longer just a matter of listening to music (music = any sound including 'silence,' which is non-existent) but a visual experience as well. The concert is a theatrical performance. In Cage's *Variations VII*, the audience is bombarded by a symphony of sounds present in the air at the moment of the performance, some of which are phoned in, live, from the ASPCA, a garbage disposal works and Luchow's. Into this cacaphonous mix are tossed the amplified sounds of 'instruments' such as fans, eggbeaters and blenders. Not only are you hearing (a lady next to me remarked she'd paid three dollars, plus baby sitter, to come listen to sounds that ordinarily she does everything in her power to avoid) but seeing. Art, says John Cage, is an enactment of a life situation, but 'framed' by the theater at a 'special occasion.'

While a fortuitous pigeon or two may roost comfortably in the Cageian scheme of things, the Lady of Aleatory is not equally kind to everyone. Something was definitely mucking up the first performance of David Tudor's *Bandoneon! (a combine)*. Second time around it was the best piece in the series. This was the real thing. The quantities and qualities of sound unleashed by a bandoneon, a crazy, multi-bagged accordion which creates signals activating programmed audio circuits, moving loud-speakers, TV images and lighting are not to be believed. "*Bandoneon* uses no composing means; when activated it composes itself out of its own composite instrumental nature."

Alex Hay's *Grass Field* also suffered from mechanical difficulties at the first performance and, I hear, at the second as well, but the real problem does not lie with the nuts and bolts. *Grass Field* is a victim of the new work or task aesthetic. Long after Marcel Duchamp's signed comb and urinal found movement, the kinetic equivalent found its way into dance. It's all there in the Judson Theater where sneakered cuties stack mattresses, unstack mattresses. Forget the 'how' of movement (the trained dancers, as it turned out, were poor stackers) and concentrate instead on the 'what' of the activity at hand. I don't mean to write off found movement. Maybe it's a question of who does the finding and in what context it is presented. In *Grass Field* the amplification of body sounds—pulse,' eye movements, other muscle changes, brain waves—*to fill an entire Armory* is a spectacular notion.

Straddling the work school and traditional dance is Debbie Hays. She has resolved the contradiction in *Solo*, a work for twenty-four performers, by having non-

". . . but the real problem does not lie with the nuts and bolts." Photo by Peter Moore.

Installation of the 1913 Armory Show.

23

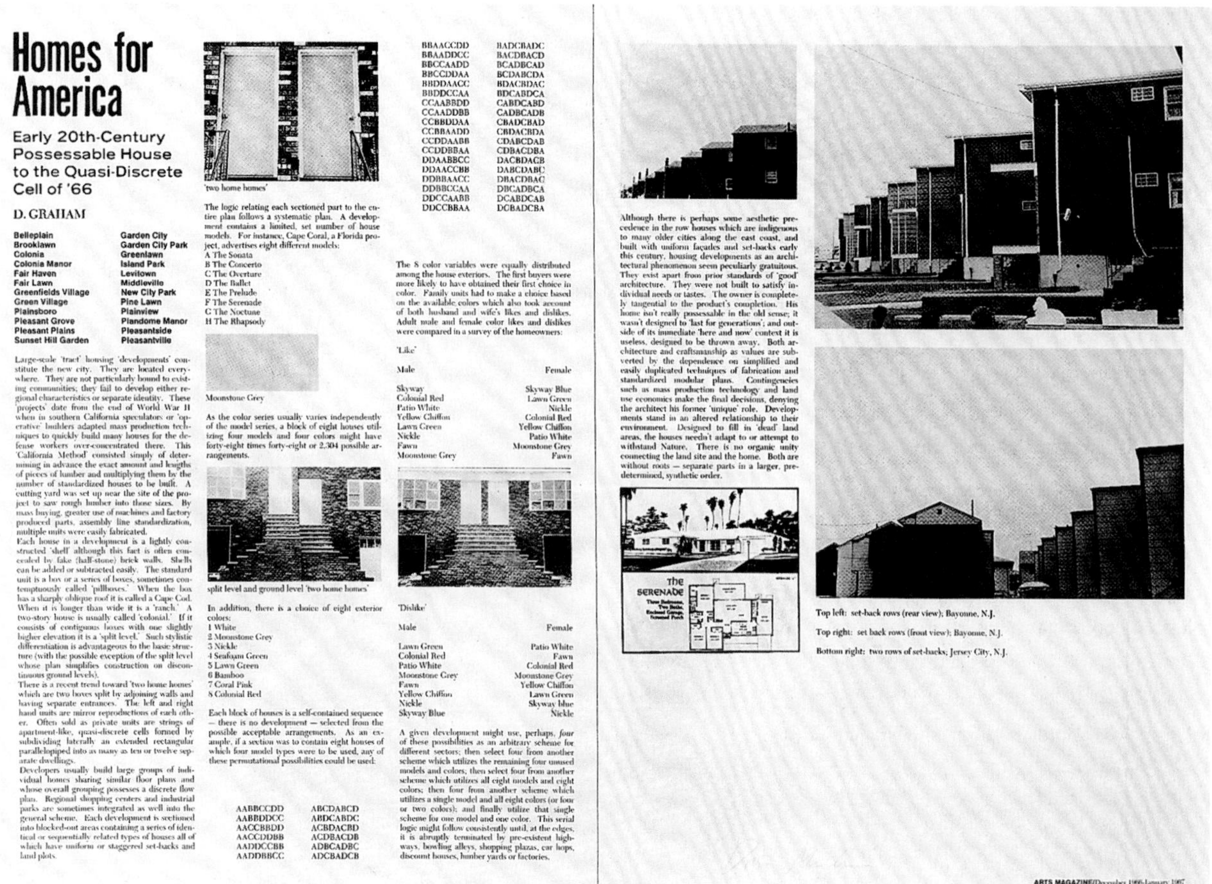

Homes for America

Early 20th-Century Possessable House to the Quasi-Discrete Cell of '66

D. GRAHAM

Belleplain	Garden City
Brooklawn	Garden City Park
Colonia	Greenlawn
Colonia Manor	Island Park
Fair Haven	Levittown
Fair Lawn	Middleville
Greenfields Village	New City Park
Green Village	Pine Lawn
Plainsboro	Plainview
Pleasant Grove	Plandome Manor
Pleasant Plains	Pleasantside
Sunset Hill Garden	Pleasantville

Large-scale 'tract' housing 'developments' constitute the new city. They are located everywhere. They are not particularly bound to existing communities; they fail to develop either regional characteristics or separate identity. These 'projects' date from the end of World War II when in southern California speculators or 'operative' builders adapted mass production techniques to quickly build many houses for the defense workers over-concentrated there. This 'California Method' consisted simply of determining in advance the exact amount and lengths of pieces of lumber and multiplying them by the number of standardized houses to be built. A cutting yard was set up near the site of the project to saw rough lumber into those sizes. By mass buying, greater use of machines and factory produced parts, assembly line standardization, multiple units were easily fabricated.

Each house in a development is a lightly constructed 'shell' although this fact is often concealed by fake (half-stone) brick walls. Shells can be added or subtracted easily. The standard unit is a box or a series of boxes, sometimes contemptuously called 'pillboxes.' When the box has a sharply oblique roof it is called a Cape Cod. When it is longer than wide it is a 'ranch.' A two-story house is usually called 'colonial.' If it consists of contiguous boxes with one slightly higher elevation it is a 'split level.' Such stylistic differentiation is advantageous to the basic structure (with the possible exception of the split level whose plan simplifies construction on discontinuous ground levels).

There is a recent trend toward 'two home homes' which are two boxes split by adjoining walls and having separate entrances. The left and right hand units are mirror reproductions of each other. Often sold as private units are strings of apartment-like, quasi-discrete cells formed by subdividing laterally an extended rectangular parallelopiped into as many as ten or twelve separate dwellings.

Developers usually build large groups of individual homes sharing similar floor plans and whose overall grouping possesses a discrete flow plan. Regional shopping centers and industrial parks are sometimes integrated as well into the general scheme. Each development is sectioned into blocked-out areas containing a series of identical or sequentially related types of houses all of which have uniform or staggered set-backs and land plots.

'two home homes'

The logic relating each sectioned part to the entire plan follows a systematic plan. A development contains a limited, set number of house models. For instance, Cape Coral, a Florida project, advertises eight different models:

A The Sonata
B The Concerto
C The Overture
D The Ballet
E The Prelude
F The Serenade
G The Noctune
H The Rhapsody

Moonstone Grey

As the color series usually varies independently of the model series, a block of eight houses utilizing four models and four colors might have forty-eight times forty-eight or 2,304 possible arrangements.

split level and ground level 'two home homes'

In addition, there is a choice of eight exterior colors:

1 White
2 Moonstone Grey
3 Nickle
4 Seafoam Green
5 Lawn Green
6 Bamboo
7 Coral Pink
8 Colonial Red

Each block of houses is a self-contained sequence — there is no development — selected from the possible acceptable arrangements. As an example, if a section was to contain eight houses of which four model types were to be used, any of these permutational possibilities could be used:

AABBCCDD	ABCDABCD
AABBDDCC	ABDCABDC
AACCBBDD	ACBDACBD
AACCDDBB	ACDBACDB
AADDCCBB	ADBCADBC
AADDBBCC	ADCBADCB
BBAACCDD	BADCBADC
BBAADDCC	BACDBACD
BBCCAADD	BCADBCAD
BBCCDDAA	BCDABCDA
BBDDAACC	BDACBDAC
BBDDCCAA	BDCABDCA
CCAABBDD	CABDCABD
CCAADDBB	CADBCADB
CCBBDDAA	CBADCBAD
CCBBAADD	CBDACBDA
CCDDAABB	CDABCDAB
CCDDBBAA	CDBACDBA
DDAABBCC	DACBDACB
DDAACCBB	DABCDABC
DDBBAACC	DBACDBAC
DDBBCCAA	DBCADBCA
DDCCAABB	DCABDCAB
DDCCBBAA	DCBADCBA

The 8 color variables were equally distributed among the house exteriors. The first buyers were more likely to have obtained their first choice in color. Family units had to make a choice based on the available colors which also took account of both husband and wife's likes and dislikes. Adult male and female color likes and dislikes were compared in a survey of the homeowners:

'Like'

Male	Female
Skyway	Skyway Blue
Colonial Red	Lawn Green
Patio White	Nickle
Yellow Chiffon	Colonial Red
Lawn Green	Yellow Chiffon
Nickle	Patio White
Fawn	Moonstone Grey
Moonstone Grey	Fawn

'Dislike'

Male	Female
Lawn Green	Patio White
Colonial Red	Fawn
Patio White	Colonial Red
Moonstone Grey	Moonstone Grey
Fawn	Yellow Chiffon
Yellow Chiffon	Lawn Green
Nickle	Skyway blue
Skyway Blue	Nickle

A given development might use, perhaps, *four* of these possibilities as an arbitrary scheme for different sectors; then select four from another scheme which utilizes the remaining four unused models and colors; then select four from another scheme which utilizes all eight models and eight colors; then four from another scheme which utilizes a single model and all eight colors (or four or two colors); and finally utilize that single scheme for one model and one color. This serial logic might follow consistently until, at the edges, it is abruptly terminated by pre-existent highways, bowling alleys, shopping plazas, car hops, discount houses, lumber yards or factories.

Although there is perhaps some aesthetic precedence in the row houses which are indigenous to many older cities along the east coast, and built with uniform façades and set-backs early this century, housing developments as an architectural phenomenon seem peculiarly gratuitous. They exist apart from prior standards of 'good' architecture. They were not built to satisfy individual needs or tastes. The owner is completely tangential to the product's completion. His home isn't really possessable in the old sense; it wasn't designed to 'last for generations'; and outside of its immediate 'here and now' context it is useless, designed to be thrown away. Both architecture and craftsmanship as values are subverted by the dependence on simplified and easily duplicated techniques of fabrication and standardized modular plans. Contingencies such as mass production technology and land use economics make the final decisions, denying the architect his former 'unique' role. Developments stand in an altered relationship to their environment. Designed to fill in 'dead' land areas, the houses needn't adapt to or attempt to withstand Nature. There is no organic unity connecting the land site and the home. Both are without roots — separate parts in a larger, predetermined, synthetic order.

Top left: set-back rows (rear view); Bayonne, N.J.

Top right: set back rows (front view); Bayonne, N.J.

Bottom right: two rows of set-backs; Jersey City, N.J.

ARTS MAGAZINE/December 1966-January 1967

works do not simply make reference to the larger social world in the manner of photojournalism; rather, they refer to Graham's own other projects, which, true to Conceptual form, are models of the social, not depictions of it.

Graham's HOMES FOR AMERICA (1966-67) has taken on canonical status in this regard. Here the photo-essay format so familiar to the history of photography has been meticulously replicated as a model of the institution of photojournalism. Like Walker Evans at *Fortune*, Graham writes the text and supplies the pictures to go along with it. HOMES was actually planned as an essay on suburban architecture for an art magazine, and could certainly stand unproblematically on its own as such. By chance, it was never actually published as Graham had intended it. Thereby, it migrated to the form of a lithographic print of an apocryphal two-page spread.[3] The print, and the original photos included in it, do not constitute an act or practice of reportage so much as a model of it. This model is a parody, a meticulous and detached imitation whose aim is to interrogate the legitimacy (and the processes of legitimation) of its original, and thereby (and only thereby) to legitimate itself as art.

The photographs included in the work are among Graham's most well-known and have established important precedents for his subsequent photographic work. In initiating his project in photography in terms of a parodic model of the photo-essay, Graham positions all his picture-making as art in a very precise, yet very conditional, sense. Each photograph may be—or, must be considered as possibly being—no more than an illustration to an essay, and therefore not an autonomous work of art. Thus, they appear to satisfy, as do Smithson's photographs, the demand for an imitation of the non-autonomous. HOMES FOR AMERICA, in being both really just an essay on the suburbs and, as well, an artist's print, constituted itself explicitly as a canonical instance of the new kind of anti-autonomous yet autonomous work of art. The photographs in it oscillate at the threshold of the autonomous work, crossing and recrossing it, refusing to depart from the artistic dilemma of reportage and thereby establishing an aesthetic model of just that threshold condition.

Huebler's work is also engaged with creating and examining the effect photographs have when they masquerade as part of some extraneous project, in which they appear to be means and not ends. Unlike Smithson or Graham, though, Huebler makes no literary claims for the textual part of his works, the "programs" in which his photographs are utilized. His works approach Conceptual art per se in that they eschew literary status and make claims only as visual art objects. Nevertheless, his renunciation of the literary is a language-act, an act enunciated as a manoeuvre of writing. Huebler's "pieces" involve the appropriation, utilization and mimesis of various "systems of documentation," of which photography is only one. It is positioned within the works by a group of generically related protocols, defined in writing, and it is strictly within these parameters that the images have meaning and artistic status. Where Graham and Smithson make their works through mimesis and parody of the forms of photojournalism, its published product, Huebler parodies the assignment, the "project" or enterprise that sets the whole process into motion to begin with. The seemingly pointless and even trivial procedures that constitute works like DURATION PIECE #5, AMSTERDAM, HOLLAND (1970) or DURATION PIECE # 7, ROME (1973) function as models for that verbal or written construction which, in the working world, causes photographs to be made. The more the assignment is emptied of what could normatively considered to be compelling social subject matter, the more visible it is simply as an instance of a structure, an order, and the more clearly it can be experienced as a model of relationships between writing and photography. By emptying subject matter from his practice of photography, Huebler recapitulates important aspects of the development of modernist painting. Mondrian, for example, moved away from depictions of the landscape, to experimental patterns with only a residual depictive value, to abstract works which analyze and model relationships but do not depict or represent them. The idea of an art which provides a direct experience of situations or relationships, not a secondary, representational one, is one of abstract art's most

257

Dan Graham
HOMES FOR AMERICA
Arts Magazine 41 (December 1966-January 1967): 21-22. Part of
HOMES FOR AMERICA as it was published in *Arts Magazine* contrary to the artist's intentions.
Photo David Sundberg.

Dan Graham
HOMES FOR AMERICA (1966-67)
Lithograph of artist's original lay-out for project for *Arts Magazine* (December 1966-January 1967).

powerful creations. The viewer does not experience the "re-representation" of absent things, but the presence of a thing, the work of art itself, with all of its indwelling dynamism, tension and complexity. The experience is more like an encounter with an entity than with a mere picture. The entity does not bear a depiction of another entity, more important than it; rather, it appears and is experienced in the way objects and entities are experienced in the emotionally-charged contexts of social life.

Huebler's mimesis of the model-constructive aspects of modernist abstract art contradicts, of course, the natural depictive qualities of photography. This contradiction is the necessary center of these works. By making photography's inescapable depictive character continue even where it has been decreed that there is nothing of significance to depict, Huebler aims to make visible something essential about the medium's nature. The artistic, creative part of this work is obviously not the photography, the picture-making. This displays all the limited qualities identified with photoconceptualism's de-skilled, amateurist sense of itself. What is creative in these works are the written assignments, or programs. Every element that could make the pictures "interesting" or "good" in terms derived from art-photography is systematically and rigorously excluded. At the same time, Huebler eliminates all conventional "literary" characteristics from his written statements. The work is comprised of these two simultaneous negations, which produce a "reportage" without event, and a writing without narrative, commentary, or opinion. This double negation imitates the criteria for radical abstract painting and sculpture, and pushes thinking about photography toward an awareness of the dialectics of its inherent depictive qualities. Huebler's works allow us to contemplate the condition of "depictivity" itself and imply that it is this contradiction between the unavoidable process of depicting appearances, and the equally unavoidable process of making objects, that permits photography to become a model of an art whose subject matter is the idea of art.

(II. Amateurization) Photography, like all the arts that preceded it, is founded on the skill, craft, and imagination of its practitioners. It was, however, the fate of all the arts to become modernist through a critique of their own legitimacy, in which the techniques and abilities most intimately identified with them were placed in question. The wave of reductivism that broke in the 1960s had, of course, been gathering during the preceding half-century, and it was the maturing (one could almost say, the totalizing) of that idea that brought into focus the explicit possibility of a "conceptual art," an art whose content was none other than its own idea of itself, and the history of such an idea's becoming respectable.

Painters and sculptors worked their way into this problem by scrutinizing and repudiating—if only experimentally—their own abilities, the special capacities that had historically distinguished them from other people—non-artists, unskilled or untalented people. This act of renunciation had moral and utopian implications. For the painter, a radical repudiation of complicity with Western traditions was a powerful new mark of distinction in a new era of what Nietzsche called "a revaluation of all values."[4] Moreover, the significance of the repudiation was almost immediately apparent to people with even a passing awareness of art, though apparent in a negative way. "What! You don't want things to look three-dimensional? Ridiculous!" It is easy to experience the fact that something usually considered essential to art has been removed from it. Whatever the thing the artist has thereby created might appear to be, it is first and foremost that which results from the absence of elements which have hitherto always been there. The reception, if not the production, of modernist art has been consistently formed by this phenomenon, and the idea of modernism as such is inseparable from it. The historical process of critical reflexivity derives its structure and identity from the movements possible in, and characteristic of, the older fine arts, like painting. The drama of modernization, in which artists cast off the antiquated characteristics of their *métiers*, is a compelling one, and has become the conceptual model for mod-

Douglas Huebler
DURATION PIECE #7, ROME (1973)
Fourteen black-and-white photographs and statement. Overall,
39 1/4 x 32 1/4 in. (99.7 x 81.9 cm) (framed). Courtesy the
artist and Leo Castelli Gallery, New York.

Duration Piece #7
Rome

*Fourteen photographs were made, at exact 30
second intervals, in order to document specific
changes in the relationship between two aspects of
the water falling from the rocks in one area at the
base of the Fountain of Trevi.*

*The photographs, undesignated by the sequence in
which they were made, join with this statement to
constitute the form of this work.*

March, 1973   Douglas Huebler

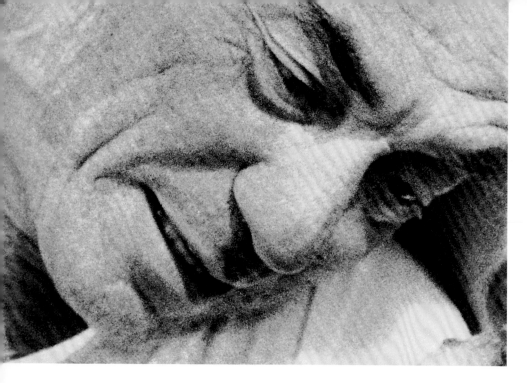

ernism as a whole. Clement Greenberg wrote: "Certain factors we used to think essential to the making and experiencing of art are shown not to be so by the fact that Modernist painting has been able to dispense with them and yet continue to offer the experience of art in all its essentials."[5]

Abstract and experimental art begins its revolution and continues its evolution with the rejection of depiction, of its own history as limning and picturing, and then with the deconsecration of the institution which came to be known as Representation. Painting finds a new *telos*, a new identity and a new glory in being the site upon which this transformation works itself out.

It is a commonplace to note that it was the appearance of photography which, as the representative of the Industrial Revolution in the realm of the image, set the historical process of modernism in motion. Yet photography's own historical evolution into modernist discourse has been determined by the fact that, unlike the older arts, it cannot dispense with depiction and so, apparently, cannot participate in the adventure it might be said to have suggested in the first place.

The dilemma, then, in the process of legitimating photography as a modernist art is that the medium has virtually no dispensable characteristics, the way painting, for example, does, and therefore cannot conform to the ethos of reductivism, so succinctly formulated by Greenberg in these lines, also from "Modernist Painting": "What had to be exhibited was not only that which was unique and irreducible in art in general, but also that which was unique and irreducible in each particular art. Each art had to determine, through its own operations and works, the effects exclusive to itself. By doing so it would, to be sure, narrow its area of competence, but at the same time it would make its possession of that area all the more certain."[6]

The essence of the modernist deconstruction of painting as picture-making was not realized in abstract art as such; it was realized in emphasizing the distinction between the institution of the Picture and the necessary structure of the depiction itself. It was physically possible to separate the actions of the painter—those touches of the brush which had historically always, in the West at least, led to a depiction—from depiction, and abstract art was the most conclusive evidence for this.

Photography constitutes a depiction not by the accumulation of individual marks, but by the instantaneous operation of an integrated mechanism. All the rays permitted to pass through the lens form an image immediately, and the lens, by definition, creates a focused image at its correct focal length. Depiction is the only possible result of the camera system, and the kind of image formed by a lens is the only image possible in photography. Thus, no matter how impressed photographers may have been by the analytical rigor of modernist critical discourse, they could not participate in it directly in their practice because the specificities of their medium did not permit it. This physical barrier has a lot to do with the distanced relationship between painting and photography in the era of art-photography, the first sixty or so years of this century.

Despite the barrier, around the middle of the 1960s, numerous young artists and art students appropriated photography, turned their attention away from *auteurist* versions of its practice, and forcibly subjected the medium to a full-scale immersion in the logic of reductivism. The essential reduction came on the level of skill. Photography could be integrated into the new radical logics by eliminating all the pictorial suavity and technical sophistication it had accumulated in the process of its own imitation of the Great Picture. It was possible, therefore, to test the medium for its indispensable elements, without abandoning depiction, by finding ways to legitimate pictures that demonstrated the absence of the conventional marks of pictorial distinction developed by the great auteurs, from Atget to Arbus.

Already by around 1955, the revalorization and reassessment of vernacular idioms of popular culture had emerged as part of a new "new objectivity," an objectivism bred by the limitations of lyrical *art informel*, the introverted and self-righteously lofty art forms of the 1940s and 1950s. This new critical trend had sources in high art and high academe, as the names Jasper Johns and Piero Manzoni, Roland Barthes and Leslie Fiedler, indicate. It continues a fundamental project of the earlier avant-garde—the transgression of the boundaries between "high" and "low" art, between artists and the rest of the people, between "art" and "life." Although Pop art in the late fifties and early sixties seemed to concentrate on bringing mass-culture elements into high-culture forms, already by the 1920s the situation had become far more complex and reciprocal than that, and motifs and styles from avant-garde and high-culture sources were circulating extensively in the various new Culture Industries in Europe, the United States, the Soviet Union, and elsewhere. This transit between "high" and "low" had become the central problematic for the avant-garde because it reflected so decisively the process of modernization of all cultures. The great question was whether or not art as it had emerged from the past would be "modernized" by being dissolved into the new mass-cultural structures.

Hovering behind all tendencies toward reductivism was the shadow of this great "reduction." The experimentation with the "anaesthetic," with "the look of non-art," "the condition of no-art," or with "the loss of the visual," is in this light a kind of tempting of fate. Behind the Greenbergian formulae, first elaborated in the late 1930s, lies the fear that there may be, finally, no indispensable characteristics that distinguish the arts, and that art as it has come down to us is very dispensable indeed. Gaming with the anaesthetic was both an intellectual necessity in the context of modernism, and at the same time the release of social and psychic energies which had a stake in the "liquidation" of bourgeois "high art." By 1960 there was pleasure to be had in this experimentation, a pleasure, moreover, which had been fully sanctioned by the aggressivity of the first avant-garde or, at least, important parts of it.

Radical deconstructions therefore took the form of searches for models of "the anaesthetic." Duchamp had charted this territory before 1920, and his influence was the decisive one for the new critical objectivisms surfacing forty years later with Gerhard Richter, Andy Warhol, Manzoni, John Cage, and the rest. The anaesthetic found its emblem in the Readymade, the commodity in all its guises, forms, and traces. Working-class, lower-middle class, suburbanite, and underclass milieux were expertly scoured for the relevant utilitarian images, depictions, figurations, and objects that violated all the criteria of canonical modernist taste, style, and technique. Sometimes the early years of Pop art seem like a race to find the most perfect, metaphysically banal image, that cipher that demonstrates the ability of culture to continue when every aspect of what had been known in modern art as seriousness, expertise, and reflexiveness had been dropped. The empty, the counterfeit, the functional, and the brutal themselves were of course nothing new as art in 1960, having all become tropes of the avant-garde via Surrealism. From the viewpoint created by Pop art, though, earlier treatments of this problem seem emphatic in their adherence to the Romantic idea of the transformative power of authentic art. The anaesthetic is transformed as art, but along the fracture-line of shock. The shock caused by the appearance of the anaesthetic in a serious work is calmed by the aura of seriousness itself. It is this aura which becomes the

John Cassavetes
FACES (filmed 1965/released 1968)
Publicity still. Photo courtesy The Museum of Modern Art, New York.

target of the new wave of critical play. Avant-garde art had held the anesthetic in place by a web of sophisticated manoeuvres, calculated transgressive gestures, which always paused on the threshold of real abandonment. Remember Bellmer's pornography, Heartfield's propaganda, Mayakovsky's advertising. Except for the Readymade, there was no complete mimesis or appropriation of the anaesthetic, and it may be that the Readymade, that thing that had indeed crossed the line, provided a sort of fulcrum upon which, between 1920 and 1960, everything else could remain balanced.

The unprecedented mimesis of "the condition of no art" on the part of the artists of the early sixties seems to be an instinctive reflection of these lines from Theodor Adorno's *Aesthetic Theory*, which was being composed in that same period: "Aesthetics, or what is left of it, seems to assume tacitly that the survival of art is unproblematic. Central for this kind of aesthetics therefore is the question of how art survives, not whether it will survive at all. This view has little credibility today. Aesthetics can no longer rely on art as a fact. If art is to remain faithful to its concept, it must pass over into anti-art, or it must develop a sense of self-doubt which is born of the moral gap between its continued existence and mankind's catastrophes, past and future," and "At the present time significant modern art is entirely unimportant in a society that only tolerates it. This situation affects art itself, causing it to bear the marks of indifference: there is the disturbing sense that this art might just as well be different or might not exist at all."[7]

The pure appropriation of the anaesthetic, the imagined completion of the gesture of passing over into anti-art, or non-art, is the act of internalization of society's indifference to the happiness and seriousness of art. It is also, therefore, an expression of the artist's own identification with baleful social forces. This identification may be, as always in modernism, experimental, but the experiment must be carried out in actuality, with the risk that an "identification with the aggressor" will really occur and will be so successful socially as art that it becomes inescapable and permanent. Duchamp gingerly seemed to avoid this; Warhol perhaps did not. In not doing so, he helped make explicit some of the hidden energies of reductivism. Warhol made his taboo-breaking work by subjecting photography to reductivist methodology, both in his silkscreen paintings and in his films. The paintings reiterated or appropriated photojournalism and glamour photography and claimed that picture-making skills were of minor importance in making significant pictorial art. The films extended the argument directly into the regime of the photographic, and established an aesthetic of the amateurish which tapped into New York traditions going back via the Beats and independents to the late 1930s and the film experiments of James Agee and Helen Levitt. To the tradition of independent, intimate, and naturalistic filmmaking, as practiced by Robert Frank, John Cassavetes, or Frederick Wiseman, Warhol added (perhaps "subtracted" would be the better word) the agony of reductivism. Cassavetes fused the documentary tradition with method acting in films like FACES (1968), with the intention of getting close to people. The rough photography and lighting drew attention to itself, but the style signified a moral decision to forego technical finish in the name of emotional truth. Warhol reversed this in films like EAT, KISS, or SLEEP (all 1963), separating the picture-style from its radical humanist content-types, in effect using it to place people at a peculiar distance, in a new relationship with the spectator. Thus a methodological model is constructed: the nonprofessional or amateurist camera technique, conventionally associated with anti-commercial naturalism and existential, if not political, commitment, is separated from those associations and turned toward new psycho-social subjects, including a new version of the glamour it wanted to leave behind. In this process, amateurism as such becomes visible as the photographic modality or style which, in itself, signifies the detachment of photography from three great norms of the Western pictorial tradition—the formal, the technical, and the one relating to the range of subject-matter. Warhol violates all these norms simultaneously, as Duchamp had done before him with the Readymade. Duchamp managed to separate his work as an object from the dominant traditions, but not until Warhol had the picture been

262

accorded the same treatment.[8] Warhol's replacement of the notion of the artist as a skilled producer with that of the artist as a consumer of new picture-making gadgets was only the most obvious and striking enactment of what could be called a new amateurism, which marks so much of the art of the 1960s and earlier 1970s.

Amateurish film and photographic images and styles of course related to the documentary tradition, but their deepest resonance is with the work of actual amateurs—the general population, the "people." To begin with, we must recognize a conscious utopianism in this turn toward the technological vernacular: Joseph Beuys's slogan "every man is an artist," or Lawrence Weiner's diffident conditions for the realization and possession of his works reflect with particular clarity the idealistic side of the claim that the *making* of artworks needs to be, and in fact has become, a lot easier than it was in the past. These artists argued that the great mass of the people had been excluded from art by social barriers and had internalized an identity as "untalented," and "inartistic" and so were resentful of the high art that the dominant institutions unsuccessfully compelled them to venerate. This resentment was the moving force of philistine mass culture and kitsch, as well as of repressive social and legislative attitudes toward the arts. Continuation of the regime of specialized high art intensified the alienation of both the people and the specialized, talented artists who, as the objects of resentment, developed elitist antipathy toward "the rabble" and identified with the ruling classes as their only possible patrons. This vicious circle of "avant-garde and kitsch" could be broken only by a radical transformation and negation of high art. These arguments repeat those of the earlier Constructivists, Dadaists, and Surrealists almost word for word, nowhere more consciously than in Guy Debord's *The Society of the Spectacle* (1967): "Art in the period of its dissolution, as a movement of negation in pursuit of its own transcendence in a historical society where history is not directly lived, is at once an art of change and a pure expression of the impossibility of change. The more grandiose its demands, the further from its grasp is true self-realization. This is an art that is necessarily *avant-garde*; and it is an art that *is not*. Its vanguard is its own disappearance."[9]

The practical transformation of art (as opposed to the idea of it) implies the transformation of the practices of both artists and their audiences, the aim being to obliterate or dissolve both categories into a kind of dialectical synthesis of them, a Schiller-like category of emancipated humanity which needs neither Representation nor Spectatorship. These ideals were an important aspect of the movement for the transformation of artistry, which opened up the question of skill. The utopian project of rediscovering the roots of creativity in a spontaneity and intersubjectivity freed from all specialization and spectacularized expertise combined with the actual profusion of light consumer technologies to legitimate a widespread "de-skilling" and "re-skilling" of art and art education. The slogan "painting is dead" had been heard from the avant-garde since 1920; it meant that it was no longer necessary to separate oneself from the people through the acquisition of skills and sensibilities rooted in craft-guild exclusivity and secrecy; in fact, it was absolutely necessary not to do so, but rather to animate with radical imagination those common techniques and abilities made available by modernity itself. First among these was photography.

The radicals' problem with photography was, as we have seen, its evolution into an art-photography. Unable to imagine anything better, photography lapsed into an imitation of high art and uncritically recreated its esoteric worlds of technique and "quality." The instability of the concept of art-photography, its tendency to become reflexive and to exist at the boundary-line of the utilitarian, was muffled in the process of its "artification." The criteria of deconstructive radicalism—expressed in ideas like "the conditions of no art," and "every man is an artist"—could be applied to photography primarily, if not exclusively, through the imitation of amateur picture-making. This was no arbitrary decision. A popular system of photography based on a minimal level of skill was instituted by George Eastman in 1888, with the Kodak slogan, "you push the button; we do the rest." In the 1960s, Jean-Luc Godard debunked his own creativity with the comment that "Kodak does 98 percent." The means by which photography could join and contribute to the movement of the modernist autocritique was the user-friendly mass-market gadget-camera. The Brownie, with its small-gauge roll-film and quick shutter was also, of course, the prototype for the equipment of the photojournalist, and therefore is present, as a historical shadow, in the evolution of art-photography as it emerged in its dialectic with photojournalism. But the process of professionalization of photography led to technical transformations of small-scale cameras, which, until the more recent proliferation of mass-produced SLRs, reinstituted an economic barrier for the amateur that became a social and cultural one as well. Not until the 1960s did we see tourists and picnickers sporting Pentaxes and Nikons; before then they used the various Kodak or Kodak-like products, such as the Hawkeye, or the Instamatic, which were little different from a 1925-model Brownie.[10]

It is significant, then, that the mimesis of amateurism began around 1966; that is, at the last moment of the "Eastman era" of amateur photography, at the moment when Nikon and Polaroid were revolutionizing it. The mimesis takes place at the threshold of a new technological situation, one in which the image-producing capacity of the average citizen was about to make a quantum leap. It is thus, historically speaking, really the last moment of "amateur photography" as such, as a social category established and maintained by custom and technique. Conceptualism turns toward the past just as the

UNION, NEEDLES, CALIFORNIA

past darts by into the future; it elegizes something at the same instant that it points toward the glimmering actualization of avant-garde utopianism through technological progress.

If "every man is an artist," and that artist is a photographer, he will become so also in the process in which high-resolution photographic equipment is released from its cultish possession by specialists and is made available to all in a cresting wave of consumerism. The worlds of Beuys and McLuhan mingle as average citizens come into possession of "professional-class" equipment. At this moment, then, amateurism cease to be a technical category; it is revealed as a mobile social category in which limited competence becomes an open field for investigation.

"Great art" established the idea (or ideal) of unbounded competence, the wizardry of continually-evolving talent. This ideal became negative, or at least seriously uninteresting, in the context of reductivism, and the notion of limits to competence, imposed by oppressive social relationships, became charged with exciting implications. It became a subversive creative act for a talented and skilled artist to imitate a person of limited abilities. It was a new experience, one which ran counter to all accepted ideas and standards of art, and was one of the last gestures which could produce avant-gardist shock. This mimesis signified, or expressed, the vanishing of the great traditions of Western art into the new cultural structures established by the mass media, credit financing, suburbanization, and reflexive bureaucracy. The act of renunciation required for a skilled artist to enact this mimesis, and construct works as models of its consequences, is a scandal typical of avant-garde desire, the desire to occupy the threshold of the aesthetic, its vanishing-point.

Many examples of such amateurist mimesis can be drawn from the corpus of photoconceptualism, and it could probably be said that almost all photoconceptualists indulged in it to some degree. But one of the purest and most exemplary instances is the group of books published by Edward Ruscha between 1963 and 1970.

For all the familiar reasons, Los Angeles was perhaps the best setting for the complex of reflections and crossovers between Pop art, reductivism, and their mediating middle term, mass culture, and Ruscha for biographical reasons may inhabit the persona of the American Everyman particularly easily. The photographs in SOME LOS ANGELES APARTMENTS (1965), for example, synthesize the brutalism of Pop art with the low-contrast monochromaticism of the most utilitarian and perfunctory photographs (which could be imputed to have been taken by the owners, managers, or residents of the buildings in question). Although one or two pictures suggest some recognition of the criteria of art-photography, or even architectural photography (e.g. "2014 S. Beverly Glen Blvd."), the majority seem to take pleasure in a rigorous display of generic lapses: improper relation of lenses to subject distances, insensitivity to time of day and quality of light, excessively functional cropping, with abrupt excisions of peripheral objects, lack of attention to the specific character of the moment being depicted—all in all a hilarious performance, an almost sinister mimicry of the way "people" make images of the dwellings with which they are involved. Ruscha's impersonation of such an Everyperson obviously draws attention to the alienated relationships people have with their built environment, but his pictures do not in any way stage or dramatize that alienation the way that Walker Evans did, or that Lee Friedlander was doing at that moment. Nor do they offer a transcendent experience of a building that pierces the alienation usually felt in life, as with Atget, for example. The pictures are, as reductivist works, models of our actual relations with their subjects, rather than dramatized representations that transfigure those relations by making it impossible for us to have such relations with *them*.

Ruscha's books ruin the genre of the "book of photographs," that classical form in which art-photography declares its independence. TWENTYSIX GASOLINE STATIONS (1963) may depict the service stations along Ruscha's route between Los Angeles and his family home in Oklahoma, but it derives its artistic significance from the fact that at a moment when "The Road" and roadside life had already become an auteurist cliché in the hands of Robert Frank's epigones, it resolutely denies any representation of its theme, seeing the road as a system and an economy mirrored in the structure of both the pictures he took and the publication in which they appear. Only an idiot would take pictures of nothing but the filling stations, and the existence of a book of just those pictures is a kind of proof of the existence of such a person. But the person, the asocial cipher who cannot connect with the others around him, is an abstraction, a phantom conjured up by the construction, the structure of the product said to be by his hand. The anaesthetic, the edge or boundary of the artistic, emerges through the construction of this phantom producer, who is unable to avoid bringing into visibility the "marks of indifference" with which modernity expresses itself in or as a "free society."

Amateurism is a radical reductivist methodology insofar as it is the form of an *impersonation*. In photoconceptualism, photography posits its escape from the criteria of art-photography through the artist's performance as a non-artist who, despite being a non-artist, is nevertheless compelled to make photographs. These photographs lose their status as Representations before the eyes of their audience: they are "dull," "boring," and "insignificant." Only by being so could they accomplish the intellectual mandate of reductivism at the heart of the enterprise of Conceptual art. The reduction of art to the condition of an intellectual concept of itself was an aim which cast doubt upon any given notion of the sensuous experience of art. Yet the loss of the sensuous was a state which itself had to be experienced. Replacing a work with a theoretical essay which could hang in its place was the most direct means toward this end; it was Conceptualism's most celebrated action, a gesture of usurpation of the predominant position of all the intellectual organizers who controlled and defined the Institution of Art. But, more importantly, it was the proposal of the final and definitive negation of art as depiction, a negation which, as we've seen, is the *telos* of experimental, reductivist modernism. And it can still be claimed that Conceptual art actually accomplished this negation. In consenting to read the essay that takes a work of art's place, spectators are presumed to continue the process of their own redefinition, and thus to participate in a utopian project of transformative, speculative self-reinvention: an avant-garde project. Linguistic conceptualism takes art as close to the boundary of its own self-overcoming, or self-dissolution, as it is likely to get, leaving its audience with only the task of rediscovering legitimations for works of art as they had existed, and might continue to exist. This was, and remains, a revolutionary way of thinking about art, in which its right to exist is rethought in the place or moment traditionally reserved for the enjoyment of art's actual existence, in the encounter with a work of art. In true modernist fashion it establishes the dynamic in which the intellectual legitimation of art as such—that is, the philosophical content of aesthetics—is experienced as the content of any particular moment of enjoyment.

But, dragging its heavy burden of depiction, photography could not follow pure, or linguistic, Conceptualism all the way to the frontier. It cannot provide the experience of the negation of experience, but must continue to provide the experience of depiction, of the Picture. It is possible that the fundamental shock that photography caused was to have provided a depiction which could be experienced more the way the visible world is experienced than had ever been possible previously. A photograph therefore shows its subject by means of showing what experience is like; in that sense it provides "an experience of experience," and it defines this as the significance of depiction.

In this light, it could be said that it was photography's role and task to turn away from Conceptual art, away from reductivism and its aggressions. Photoconceptualism was then the last moment of the prehistory of photography as art, the end of the Old Regime, the most sustained and sophisticated attempt to free the medium from its peculiar distanced relationship with artistic radicalism and from its ties to the Western Picture. In its failure to do so, it revolutionized our concept of the Picture and created the conditions for the restoration of that concept as a central category of contemporary art by around 1974.

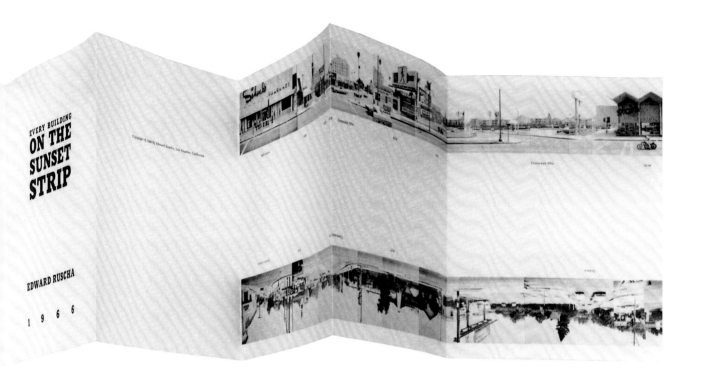

NOTES

1. Cf. Thierry de Duve's discussion of nominalism, in *Pictorial Nominalism: On Marcel Duchamp's Passage from Painting to the Readymade*, trans. Dana Polan with the author (Minneapolis: University of Minnesota Press, 1991).

2. Peter Bürger, *Theory of the Avant-Garde*, trans. Michael Shaw (Minneapolis: University of Minnesota Press, 1984).

3. A variant, made as a collage, is in the Daled Collection, Brussels.

4. Friedrich Nietzsche, "Ecce Homo," in *On the Genealogy of Morals and Ecce Homo*, ed. Walter Kaufmann and trans. Kaufmann and R. J. Hollingdale (New York: Vintage Books, 1967), 290.

5. Clement Greenberg, "Modernist Painting," in *Clement Greenberg: The Collected Essays and Criticism*, vol. 4: *Modernism with a Vengeance, 1957-1969*, ed. John O'Brian (Chicago: University of Chicago Press, 1993), 92.

6. Ibid., 86.

7. Theodor Adorno, *Aesthetic Theory*, trans. C. Lenhardt (London: Routledge & Kegan Paul, 1984), 464, 470.

8. Cf. de Duve's argument that the Readymade can/should be nominated as painting.

9. Guy Debord, *The Society of the Spectacle*, trans. Donald Nicholson-Smith (New York: Zone Books, 1994), 135 (thesis 190).

10. Robert A. Sobieszek discusses Robert Smithson's use of the Instamatic camera in his essay, "Robert Smithson: Photo Works," in *Robert Smithson: Photo Works*, exh. cat. (Los Angeles: Los Angeles County Museum of Art and Albuquerque: University of New Mexico Press, 1993), 16, 17 (note 24), 25 (note 61).

Edward Ruscha
EVERY BUILDING ON THE SUNSET STRIP (1966)
Nine joined sheets folded fifty-three times vertically, with offset halftone reproductions. Folded, 7 x 5 1/2 in. (17.8 x 14.0 cm); unfolded, 7 x 294 1/2 in. (17.8 x 748 cm). Photo Paula Goldman.

Douglas Huebler
HAVERHILL-WINDHAM-NEW YORK MARKER PIECE, 1968
Private collection. Installation view, "January 5–31, 1969," rented office space at
44 East 52nd Street, New York, organized by Seth Siegelaub. Courtesy The Siegelaub
Collection & Archives. Photo Seth Siegelaub.

SUSAN L. JENKINS

**INFORMATION, COMMUNICATION, DOCUMENTA-
TION: AN INTRODUCTION TO THE CHRONOLOGY OF
GROUP EXHIBITIONS AND BIBLIOGRAPHIES** Exhibition
chronologies and bibliographies are integral components of the defining apparatus of Conceptual art. Thus, the diverse approaches to artistic
production and the prevailing concern with the institutionalization of
art that are associated with this movement must be considered along
with the means through which they were disseminated. The information
contained in the following lists evinces the variety of attempts made to
capture and convey the often complex nature of this work, especially as
manifested by the development of expanded or alternative exhibition
and publication formats. Although the problem of categorization is
inherent in a project such as this, an attempt has been made within the
Chronology of Group Exhibitions to produce a comprehensive record of
the most important group exhibitions associated with the formation
and representation of Conceptual art. The *General Bibliography* ranges
from seminal to lesser-known texts, while the individual artists' bibliographies include more widely available texts along with comprehensive publications which, in many cases, serve as references for more
complete sources of information. Together, these records offer a sense
of the substantive issues, extensive experimentation, epistemological
investigation, and international scope that characterize Conceptual art.

The unorthodox character of much Conceptual art—including the
use of ephemeral materials and situations; the emphasis on documentation; and the incorporation of mediums such as video, film, television,
the body, audio-recordings, photography, and natural elements, among
others—often led to then-unorthodox methods of presentation that
obscured the boundaries between work and text, exhibition and catalogue. Among the more significant developments associated with the
movement were attempts made by some exhibition organizers to create
display situations that would convey the subversive or radical nature of
this new art. As artists began to question just what art was, and what
it could or should be in the midst of the social and political crises of the
mid-to-late 1960s, they rejected traditional categories of artistic production in favor of work that could be less easily commodified within
the institutions of the art world, more democratic in its accessibility to
a broadly conceived audience, and ultimately less adherent to notions
of preciousness, uniqueness, and genius. In response to this environment and the work produced within it, organizers like Seth Siegelaub
and Lucy R. Lippard experimented with various exhibition and publication strategies to offer alternative possibilities of reception.

Siegelaub organized numerous exhibitions that were among the
first to emphasize ideas rather than objects. Siegelaub had directed a
conventional art gallery from 1964 to 1966. In 1968, however, he began
to implement situations that responded directly to the linguistic, docu-

mentary, and dematerialized work being produced by Robert Barry,
Douglas Huebler, Joseph Kosuth, and Lawrence Weiner—the artists with
whom he is most closely associated. No longer attached to a specific
gallery, Siegelaub found exhibition spaces when he needed them, as he
did for "January 5-31, 1969."[1] This exhibition, presented in a rented office
at 44 East 52nd Street, included two works by each of the above artists,
although Siegelaub clarified the relationship between the physical
object and its visual representation in a panel displayed in the exhibition space: "The exhibition consists of (the ideas communicated in) the
catalog; the physical presence (of the work) is supplementary to the catalog."[2] Unlike traditional catalogues, *January 5-31, 1969* functioned as
the most important source of information about the works included in
the exhibition, exemplifying Siegelaub's belief that "when art concerns
itself with things not germane to physical presence, its intrinsic (com-
municative) value is not altered by its presentation in printed media....
The catalogue can now act as primary information for the exhibition, as
opposed to secondary information about art in magazines, catalogues,
etc."[3] Perhaps even more radically, Siegelaub also published catalogues
that functioned as exhibitions, such as *Douglas Huebler: November
1968*, in which the artist's works—typewritten statements, maps, and
photographs—appeared in catalogue form alone. Similarly, Lawrence
Weiner's *Statements* (1968) eliminated the need for an exhibition altogether, since there was nothing that necessarily needed to be displayed
beyond the texts printed in the book.

Siegelaub extended the catalogue-only exhibition format to several significant group exhibitions. *Carl Andre, Robert Barry, Douglas
Huebler, Joseph Kosuth, Sol Le Witt, Robert Morris, Lawrence Weiner*
(1968), more commonly known as the *Xeroxbook*, is a publication for
which each of the invited artists contributed a project that consisted of
twenty-five consecutive photocopied pages. Similarly, *July-August 1970*,
originally accessible only in the volume of the same date of the British

270

> This ¼ page advertisement (4½″ x 4¾″),
> appearing in the November 1968 issue of
> ARTFORUM magazine, on page 8, in the
> lower left corner, is one form of
> documentation for the November 1968
> exhibition of DOUGLAS HUEBLER.
>
> *(Seth Siegelaub, 1100 Madison
> Avenue, New York, N.Y. 10028)*

Advertisement for "Douglas Huebler: November 1968," organized by Seth Siegelaub,
in *Artforum* 7, no. 3 (November 1968): 8.

periodical *Studio International*, is a forty-eight page exhibition for which Siegelaub respectively requested six critics to "edit an 8-page section of the magazine, and in turn, to make available their section to the artist(s) that interest them."[4] Unencumbered by the commodity-oriented atmosphere of the gallery space and the mediating effects of subjectively formulated titles (which were always taken from the dates of or artists in each exhibition), as well as from accompanying critical or explanatory texts (which were never included in his publications), Siegelaub's exhibitions/catalogues presented the work of Conceptual artists in as straightforward a manner as possible. Yet, ironically, as Conceptual art became integrated into the narrative of art history, the objects associated with it assumed a comparable status. Hence, the fetishistic and monetary value of Siegelaub's and other cheaply produced publications from the period has greatly risen, ultimately belying the purpose of their original creation.

Lippard's extensive connections to Conceptual art include her role as an organizer of innovative exhibitions and catalogues. In 1969 she organized a traveling exhibition whose title changed according to the population of the city in which it was held; in Seattle it was known as "557,087" and in Vancouver as "955,000." Artworks were located both inside the museums and in a wide radius beyond them; some were constructed or implemented by Lippard and her staff based on instructions received from the artists.[5] The catalogue consists of randomly arranged 4 x 6 inch index cards, forty-six of which were designed by the artists. Replacing the traditional critical essays are twenty cards containing quotations and texts by various philosophers, theorists, and others. Lippard's effort to efface the often authoritarian and hierarchical organizing principles of exhibitions and catalogues was perceived by one critic as a projection of her own aesthetic sensibility, compelling him to state that "there is a total style to the show, a style so pervasive as to invite the conclusion that Lucy Lippard is in fact the artist and that her

medium is other artists."[6]

Lippard applied these same organizing principles to two other exhibitions: "2,972,453," presented at the Centro de Arte y Comunicación in Buenos Aires in 1970, and "C. 7500," which originated in 1973 at the California Institute of the Arts in Valencia and then traveled throughout the United States and Great Britain. Noteworthy for its inclusion of only women Conceptual artists, as well as for its innovative logistics, the latter gathered together the work of twenty-six artists which, though continuing to fit within the parameters of Conceptual art, conveyed the experiences of women who were also inspired by the growing Feminist Art Movement. Many of these works—photographs, texts, charts, photocopies—were pinned directly to the wall, while cassette tapes and spiral-bound books were made available on tables. The entire exhibition fit into one packing case that was inexpensively mailed from venue to venue so that the cost of mounting the show also remained minimal.

Though not nearly as radical as Siegelaub's or Lippard's exhibitions, of greater importance for the dissemination of Conceptual art into a broad, public consciousness were the survey exhibitions organized by major museums in Europe and the United States in the late 1960s and early 1970s. These large exhibitions abandoned traditional formats to grapple with the often unconventional forms of what was generically referred to as "the new art" (which at the time often meant works associated with Conceptual art, along with others now distinguished as Arte Povera, Process Art, Anti-Form, and Earth or Land Art).

Among the earliest of these exhibitions is "When Attitudes Become Form: Works—Concepts—Processes—Situations," organized by Harald Szeemann in 1969 for the Kunsthalle Bern. To emphasize the importance of artistic process over object, Szeemann converted the museum into a giant studio in which an international group of radical artists could produce works and from which they could extend their

activities outside of the museum and into the city.[7] Extending this emphasis on process and informality is the catalogue, a paperboard binder (rather than a traditional bound book) that includes an alphabetical index of the artists and a photographic reproduction of the address book Szeeman used during a research trip to New York.

In the United States, perhaps the most noteworthy of the large group exhibitions of Conceptual art is "Information." Organized by Kynaston McShine for The Museum of Modern Art in 1970, "Information" is one of the most unconventional exhibitions ever presented by this institution. McShine described it as "an international report" of the activities of younger artists from fifteen countries, including such "peripheral" nations as Argentina, Yugoslavia, and Brazil, who were "broadening artistic definitions" and "generating pertinent issues" in their efforts to communicate with a general audience.[8] The rather unorthodox publication that accompanied the exhibition contains pages designed by each of the artists; a recommended reading list that includes texts on philosophy, new technologies, ecology, information systems, and Marxism, among other subjects of interest to artists at the time; and blank pages for the reader's own images or texts. Through the inclusion of photographs of political events, such as demonstrations and protest marches, as well as reprints of newspaper articles about cur-

rent events, including the Vietnam war, this catalogue situates contemporary art within the context of current social and political crises and concerns more explicitly than any other of the period. In his essay, McShine reiterated this connection:

> It may seem too inappropriate, if not absurd, to
> get up in the morning, walk into a room, and
> apply dabs of paint from a little tube to a square
> of canvas. What can you as a young artist do that
> seems relevant and meaningful?[9]

While it has been suggested that "Information" was organized to appease organizations such as the Art Workers Coalition, which had protested the actions and policies of The Museum of Modern Art,[10] this exhibition nevertheless reveals how traditional institutions could present—or accommodate—art that contested the cultural and political values that such institutions were chartered to uphold.

More modest exhibitions redefined the concept of the exhibition in equally innovative ways. The presentation of documentary material —diagrams, proposals, propositions, programs, signs, photocopies, photographs—rather than objects as an exhibition's sole content was a curatorial principle that guided the organization of several important projects. "Conceptual Art and Conceptual Aspects," presented at the

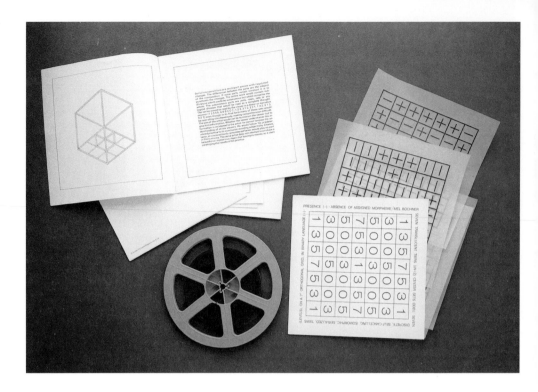

New York Cultural Center in 1970, was the first large-scale exhibition to incorporate the term "Conceptual art" into its title and to focus upon what Donald Karshan referred to in the accompanying catalogue as "Post-Object Art."[11] Comprised primarily of printed texts and photographs, the exhibition is reprised in the catalogue, which includes artists' texts and statements but no images.

Incorporating the typed or photocopied descriptions of works sent to the curator by the invited artists, "Art in the Mind" was organized by Athena Tacha Spear for the Allen Memorial Art Museum at Oberlin College in Oberlin, Ohio, in 1970. This project is described in the catalogue's introduction as an "imaginary" exhibition that dealt with form through the creation of "thought structures" rather than physical objects. Tacha Spear believed that presenting Conceptual art in a museum or gallery context was an artificial situation that put the viewer at a disadvantage. As she stated, "the interested spectator is not given the best chance to absorb new complex thoughts by standing in front of a wall covered with endless typed or hand-scribbled pages; and the space of art museums and galleries is wasted when filled with documents. Such material belongs to publications and libraries."[12] Following Siegelaub's example, Tacha Spear presented "Art in the Mind" in catalogue form, although some of the works were executed by students at Oberlin College, while all of the pages of an unbound copy of the catalogue were displayed in a well-frequented corridor of Oberlin's Art Building.

Other exhibitions, organized in response to the growing interest in mass media and technological advances in communication, focused on specific modes of conveying information that further extended the concept of art and its exhibition. "Art by Telephone," organized by Jan van der Marck for the Museum of Contemporary Art in Chicago in 1969, included thirty-seven artists from the United States and Europe who were asked to relay instructions by phone to the staff of the museum for an idea to be executed by an intermediary.[13] The results of these interchanges, which favored intellectual premise over visual result and were sometimes accessible only through verbal description, were then exhibited in the museum. The catalogue, which was released as a record album, includes the recordings of the telephone conversations between the curator and the artists in which instructions for the works were given.

"Prospect '71: Projection," presented at the Städtisches Kunsthalle in Düsseldorf in 1971, likewise rejected the display of traditional objects in favor of the projection of videotapes, slides, and films throughout the exhibition space in an ever-changing program. Similarly, "Sonsbeek '71: Buiten de perken/Beyond Lawn and Order," an exhibition organized by Wim Beeren and a working committee that was presented at Park Sonsbeek in Arnhem, Holland, and throughout The Netherlands, utilized various modes of communication, including a film and television program, texts and concepts published in local newspapers, and "information centers" installed in five cities connected by telex with the central pavilion in Sonsbeek—technologies designed to encourage artists to actualize their art outside the conditions of the museum.[14]

In a related project, Gerry Schum established the Fernsehgalerie or Television Gallery in 1969 in Berlin, where he organized "exhibitions" broadcast nationwide over German television. The first of these was "Land Art," a film shot on location while each of the eight artists made works set in or using the land. Conceived specifically for presentation on television, these works were presented without commentary, although an accompanying catalogue was published.[15] Besides television's ability to reach a much larger audience, Schum believed it to be "eminently suited to serve visual art in the same way the press and publishing serve literature and the gramaphone industry serves music."[16]

Extending the anti-institutional attitude at the heart of much Conceptual art production was the establishment of alternative or artist-controlled exhibition spaces. Among those founded by Conceptual artists are the important, though short-lived, Lannis Gallery

Aspen, no. 5-6 (Fall-Winter 1966-67). Photo David Sundberg.

in New York and the Museum of Conceptual Art (MOCA) in San Francisco. The former, established in 1967 by Joseph Kosuth, Christine Kozlov, Michael Rinaldi, and Ernest Rossi, was named after Kosuth's cousin Lannis Spencer, who paid the rent. This space, which was renamed the Museum of Normal Art after its first month of operation, provided the earliest opportunities for viewing the work of many Conceptual artists and also presented unconventional exhibitions, including "Non-Anthropomorphic Art by Four Young Artists: Joseph Kosuth, Christine Kozlov, Michael Rinaldi, Ernest Rossi" and "Fifteen People Present Their Favorite Book."[17] On the West Coast, Tom Marioni established MOCA in 1970. Though intended primarily as a performance space, exhibitions organized around a variety of themes—including sound, time, radio, television, and the body—were also held there. Breen's Bar, a saloon downstairs from MOCA, served as a gathering place for artists under the museum's auspices on Wednesday afternoons—a practice continued by the artist to this day.

In addition to redefining the concept of the exhibition, curators, critics, and artists themselves developed innovative strategies for presenting and distributing work that bypassed the museum altogether. In this regard, art periodicals provided an especially important forum. The periodical *Aspen* was a multi-media magazine contained in a box whose contents were realized in media that suited the theme of each issue, two of which could conceivably function as Conceptual-art exhibitions. The first, issue no. 5-6 (Fall-Winter 1967), compiled by Brian O'Doherty, is a collection of works, several original, that includes five records, four films, artists' projects by Sol LeWitt and Mel Bochner, and a sculpture by Tony Smith to be fabricated by the reader, as well as the first publication of Roland Barthes' "The Death of the Author." In addition, the "magazine" includes the first realization of Dan Graham's work POEM (SCHEMA) (1966). SCHEMA, like many of Graham's other works, is an "interrogation not only of the formal and material aspects of an art

work, but also its social conditions of production and reproduction."[18] Similarly, his HOMES FOR AMERICA (1966) functions simultaneously as artwork and article, original and reproduction, acknowledging the collapsing of boundaries that typified much Conceptual-art production.

Several other periodicals founded during the period were designed specifically to present Conceptually-oriented art. *Avalanche*, established in New York in 1970, was described by its publishers Willoughby Sharp and Liza Béar as "an artist's art magazine" intended to facilitate direct communication between artists and their audiences.[19] As such, most of its pages were devoted to artist-designed sections and interviews, as well as an informational bulletin-board called "Rumbles." Providing another alternative exhibition forum for Conceptual artists was *Interfunktionen*, published and edited by Friedrich Wolfram Heubach in Cologne from 1968 to 1974, when these responsibilities were taken over by Benjamin H. D. Buchloh. Issues contained sections devoted to various aspects of the movement, including Body Art, Story Art, and the Book as Art Work.

Periodicals also provided an important forum for the dissemination of artists' texts, in addition to their works. Seeming to supersede the need for interpretative criticism, some of the most influential texts on Conceptual art were originally published by artists in art periodicals. *Art-Language*, published from 1969 to 1985, was the primary critical organ for the artists associated with the Art & Language collective and included the texts which were the mainstay of their artistic production. The first issue includes a reprint of Sol LeWitt's "Sentences on Conceptual Art," a follow-up to the artist's seminal "Paragraphs on Conceptual Art," which appeared in *Artforum* in 1967. Joseph Kosuth, who for a time was the American editor of *Art-Language*, first published his seminal essay "Art after Philosophy," in *Studio International* in 1969.[20] Other artists contributed texts that introduced many of the philosophical and theoretical ideas that evolved throughout their artis-

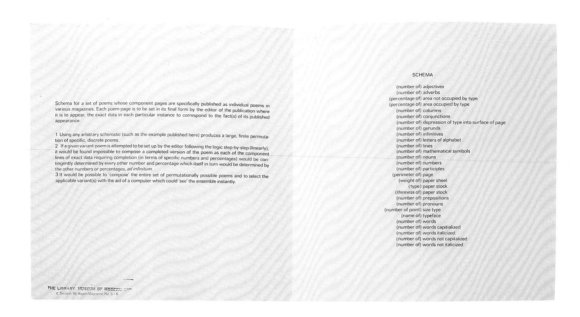

tic output. This was particularly true for Robert Smithson, who published numerous critical essays from 1966 until his death in 1973 in many of the major art magazines, including *Artforum, Art News,* and *Arts Magazine,*[21] essays which established him as a serious writer and intellect.

Among the more enduring attempts to elucidate the complex nature of Conceptual art by critics is Lucy Lippard's *Six Years: The Dematerialization of the Art Object from 1966 to 1972* (1973), an annotated chronological record of the publications, events, exhibitions, and individual works associated with Conceptual art. As such, it provides the most thorough attempt to understand what Lippard considered at the time to be a "chaotic network of ideas in the air, in America and abroad," through the reconstruction of the above-mentioned activities and the inclusion of previously unpublished artists' texts and symposia transcripts.[22] Ursula Meyer's *Conceptual Art* (1972) is a survey of forty-five Conceptual artists' work that incorporates texts, documentation, and interviews of and by a number of artists as a means of providing an overview of Conceptual art but which functions in a manner similar to the "unmediated" presentation of artists' works in the catalogues-as-exhibitions discussed above. Finally, *Idea Art*, edited by Gregory Battcock and published in 1973, is a collection of the more significant essays of the time by many of the critics and artists most closely associated with the formation and critical explanation of the movement.

Many of the exhibitions and publications associated with Conceptual art granted artists an unprecedented degree of control over the presentation and distribution of their work. As artists mailed, telexed, telegrammed, or telephoned their work, as they submitted texts and photographic documentation, as they performed actions inside and outside of the museum, and as their photocopies, photographs, postcards, verbal messages, and other unorthodox materials were accepted for installation or inclusion, they redefined the notion of art and threat-

ened the boundaries that separated it from other systems of information distribution. Conceptual artists also challenged the role of the critic by providing their own explanations and interpretations of their work as part of their total artistic output. While the more utopian aspects of the movement (the refusal of commodification, the commitment to more inexpensive and democratic modes of distribution, and the elimination of uniqueness and genius as the arbitrating factors of quality) may have been largely unsustainable, many of these ideas and strategies of Conceptual art have infiltrated to varying degrees much of the art produced today.

Dan Graham
SCHEMA
As published in *Konzeption-Conception: Dokumentation einer heutigen Kunstrichtung/Documentation of Today's Art Tendency,* exh. cat. (Leverkusen: Staedtisches Museum), unpag.

Notes

1. See Bruce Altshuler, "Dematerialization: The Voice of the Sixties," in *The Avant-Garde in Exhibition: New Art in the Twentieth Century* (New York: Harry N. Abrams, 1994) for a thorough discussion of this and other Siegelaub exhibitions, 236-255.

2. Reprinted in Lucy R. Lippard, ed., *Six Years: The Dematerialization of the Art Object from 1966 to 1972* (New York: Praeger, 1973), 71.

3. Seth Siegelaub, "On Exhibitions and the World at Large: Seth Siegelaub in Conversation with Charles Harrison," *Studio International* (London) 178, no. 917 (December 1969): 202.

4. Seth Siegelaub, "July-August 1970," *Studio International* (London) 180, no. 924 (July-August 1970): table of contents.

5. See Lippard, *Six Years*, 111-113, for a description of the exhibition.

6. Peter Plagens, "557,087," *Artforum* 8, no. 3 (November 1969): 64.

7. Altshuler, "Dematerialization," 245.

8. Kynaston L. McShine, *Information*, exh. cat. (New York: The Museum of Modern Art, 1970), 1.

9. McShine, *Information* 138.

10. Les Levine, "The Information Fall-out," *Studio International* (London) 181, no. 934 (June 1971), 266. For an idea of the issues involved see Lucy R. Lippard, "The Art Workers' Coalition: Not a History," *Studio International* (London) 180, no. 927 (November 1970): 171-174.

11. See reprint of essay in *Studio International* (London) 180, no. 925 (September 1970): 69-70.

12. Athena Tacha Spear, *Art in the Mind*, exh. cat. (Oberlin, Ohio: Allen Memorial Art Museum, 1970), unpag.

13. "Art by Telephone," press release (Chicago: Museum of Contemporary Art, 1969).

14. For a more complete description of this exhibition see Bruce Kurtz, "Sonsbeek 71: Beyond Lawn and Order," *Arts Magazine* 46, no. 1 (September-October 1971): 50-52.

15. See Charles Harrison, "Art on TV," *Studio International* (London) 181, no. 929 (January 1971): 30-31.

16. Cited in Martha Fleming, "Gerry Schum, A Space Gallery," *Artforum* 19, no. 8 (April 1981): 75.

17. Joseph Kosuth, "Replies to Benjamin Buchloh on Conceptual Art," *October* (New York), no. 57 (Summer 1991): 152.

18. Alexander Alberro, "Reductivism in Reverse," in *Tracing Cultures: Art History, Criticism, Critical Fiction*, ed. Miwon Kwon (New York: Whitney Museum of American Art, 1994), 11.

19. See questionnaire and response in "A Survey of Contemporary Art Magazines," *Studio International* (London) 193, no. 983 (September-October 1976): 145, 157-158.

20. For further discussion of this essay see Gabriele Guerico, "Introduction," in Joseph Kosuth, *Art after Philosophy and After: Collected Writings, 1966-1990* (Cambridge: The MIT Press, 1991), xxi-xlii. Kosuth's essay is included in this book, 13-32.

21. See Robert Smithson, *The Writings of Robert Smithson*, ed. Nancy Holt (New York: New York University Press, 1979).

22. Lippard, *Six Years*, 5.

PRIMARY STRUCTURES: YOUNGER AMERICAN AND BRITISH SCULPTORS. The Jewish Museum, New York. 27 April-12 June. Organized by Kynaston L. McShine. Artists: Carl Andre, David Annesley, Richard Artschwager, Larry Bell, Ronald Bladen, Michael Bolus, Anthony Caro, Tony DeLap, Walter de Maria, Tom Doyle, Dan Flavin, Peter Forakis, Paul Frazier, Judy Gerowitz, Daniel Gorski, David Gray, Robert Grosvenor, David Hall, Douglas Huebler, Donald Judd, Ellsworth Kelly, Phillip King, Lyman Kipp, Gerald Laing, Sol LeWitt, Tina Matkovic, John McCracken, Robert Morris, Forrest Myers, Peter Phillips, Peter Pinchbeck, Salvatore Romano, Tim Scott, Anthony Smith, Robert Smithson, Michael Todd, Anne Truitt, William Tucker, Richard Van Buren, David von Schlegell, Isaac Witkin, and Derrick Woodham. Catalogue.

ART IN PROCESS: THE VISUAL DEVELOPMENT OF A STRUCTURE. Finch College Museum of Art, New York. 11 May-30 June. Organized by Elayne H. Varian. Artists: Stephen Antonakos, Richard Artschwager, Richard Baringer, Mary Bauermeister, Chryssa, Dan Flavin, Paul Frazier, Charles Hinman, Will Insley, Donald Judd, Lyman Kipp, Sol LeWitt, Sven Lukin, Victor Millonzi, Robert Morris, Otto Piene, Robert Smithson, and John Willenbecher. Catalogue.

> Mel Bochner, "Art in Process — Structures," Arts Magazine 40, no. 9 (September-October 1966): 38-39.

SYSTEMIC PAINTING. Solomon R. Guggenheim Museum, New York. 21 September-27 November. Organized by Lawrence Alloway. Artists: Jo Baer, Robert Barry, Al Brunelle, Thomas Downing, Paul Feeley, Dean Fleming, Peter Gourfain, Al Held, Ralph Humphrey, Robert Huot, Will Insley, Ellsworth Kelly, Nicholas Krushenick, Tadaaki Kuwayama, David Lee, Robert Mangold, Agnes Martin, Howard Mehring, Kenneth Noland, David Novros, Larry Poons, Edwin Ruda, Robert Ryman, Leon Polk Smith, Frank Stella, Neil Williams, Jack Youngerman, and Lawrence Zox. Catalogue.

> Robert Pincus-Witten, "Systemic Painting," Artforum 5, no. 3 (November 1966): 42-45.

NON-ANTHROPOMORPHIC ART BY FOUR YOUNG ARTISTS: JOSEPH KOSUTH, CHRISTINE KOZLOV, MICHAEL RINALDI, ERNEST ROSSI. Lannis Gallery, New York. 19 February-May. Catalogue.
Gordon D. Brown, "Kosuth, Kozlov, Rinaldi, Rossi," Arts Magazine 41, no. 7 (May 1967): 61.

FIFTEEN PEOPLE PRESENT THEIR FAVORITE BOOK. Lannis Gallery, New York. 7 May-7 June. Organized by Joseph Kosuth. Artists: Carl Andre, Jo Baer, Mel Bochner, Dan Graham, Joseph Kosuth, Christine Kozlov, Sol LeWitt, Robert Mangold, Robert Morris, Ad Reinhardt, Michael Rinaldi, Ernest Rossi, Robert Ryman, Robert Smithson, and Sinan Tanju.
Joseph Kosuth, "15 People Present Their Favorite Book," Arts Magazine 42, no. 1 (September-October 1967): 61.

SERIELLE FORMATIONEN. Studio Galerie, Johann Wolfgang Goethe Universität, Frankfurt. 22 May-30 June. Organized by Peter Roehr and Paul Maenz. Artists: Carl Andre, Arman, Thomas Bayrle, Ronald Bladen, Hans Breder, Enrico Castellani, Christo, Herman de Vries, Jan Dibbets, May Fasnacht, Eberhard Fiebig, Dan Flavin, Raimund Girke, Hermann Goepfert, Kuno Gonschior, Gruppe X, Hans Haacke, Jan Henderikse, Ewerdt Hilgemann, Bernhard Höke, Donald Judd, Jiří Kolář, Yayoi Kusama, Walter LeBlanc, Kaspar Thomas Lenk, Sol LeWitt, Konrad Lueg, Adolf Luther, Piero Manzoni, Agnes Martin, Almir Mavignier, Henk Peeters, Larry Poons, Charlotte Posenenske, Markus Raetz, Bridget Riley, Peter Roehr, Diter Rot, Felix Schlenker, Wolfgang Schmidt, Jan Schoonhoven, Klaus Staudt, Michael Steiner, Frank Stella, Paul Talman, Günther Uecker, Victor Vasarely, and Andy Warhol. Catalogue.

LANGUAGE TO BE LOOKED AT AND/OR THINGS TO BE READ. Dwan Gallery, New York. 3-28 June. Artists: Carl Andre, Arakawa, Barry Bryant, Walter de Maria, Marcel Duchamp, Dan Flavin, Dan Graham, Robert Indiana, Jasper Johns, On Kawara, Edward Kienholz, Sol LeWitt, Roy Lichtenstein, René Magritte, Filippo Marinetti, Robert Morris, Claes Oldenburg, Francis Picabia, Ad Reinhardt, Robert Smithson, and Kenneth Snelson. Press release by Eton Corrasable (Robert Smithson).

19:45-21:55: SEPTEMBER 9TH, 1967: FRANKFURT, GERMANY: DIES ALLES HERZCHEN WIRD EINMAL DIR GEHÖREN. Galerie Loehr, Frankfurt. 9 September. Organized by Paul Maenz. Artists: Jan Dibbets, Barry Flanagan, Bernhard Höke, John Johnson, Richard Long, Konrad Lueg, Charlotte Posenenske, and Peter Roehr. Catalogue.

NORMAL ART. The Museum of Normal Art, New York. Opened 12 November. Organized by Joseph Kosuth. Artists: Carl Andre, Jo Baer, Sandy Balboza, Frederick Barthelme, Mel Bochner, Dan Christensen, Hanne Darboven, Walter de Maria, Dan Flavin, Ernest Frasier, Dan Graham, Eva Hesse, Donald Judd, On Kawara, Joseph Kosuth, Christine Kozlov, Kuwayama, Sol LeWitt, Douglas Lichter, Lee Lozano, Robert Mangold, Robert Morris, Claes Oldenburg, Michael Rinaldi, Dorothea Rockburne, Ernest Rossi, Robert Ryman, Ken Showell, Robert Smithson, Frank Stella, Sinan Tanju, Tom Trengove, Richard Van Buren, and Frank Lincoln Viner.

ART IN SERIES. Finch College Museum of Art, New York. 22 November-6 January 1968. Organized by Elayne H. Varian and Mel Bochner. Artists include: Carl Andre, Mel Bochner, William Bollinger, Al Brunelle, Hanne Darboven, Dan Flavin, Dan Graham, Eva Hesse, Donald Judd, David Lee, Sol LeWitt, Charles Ross, and Robert Smithson. Catalogue.
David Lee, "Serial Rights," Art News 66, no. 8 (December 1967): 42-45, 68.

"Language to Be Looked at and/or Things to Be Read."
Dwan Gallery, New York. 3-28 June 1967
Courtesy Silent Partner Consulting, Brooklyn, New York.

CARL ANDRE, ROBERT BARRY, LAWRENCE WEINER. Bradford Junior College, Bradford, Massachusetts. 4 February-2 March. Organized by Seth Siegelaub.

AIR ART. Arts Council, YM/YWHA, Philadelphia. 13-31 March. Traveled to Contemporary Arts Center, Cincinnati, 25 April-19 May; Lakeview Center for the Arts and Sciences, Peoria, Illinois, 7-28 June; University Art Museum, University of California, Berkeley, 13 January-16 February 1969; Lamont Gallery, The Phillips Exeter Academy, Exeter, New Hampshire, 25 February-18 March 1969. Organized by Willoughby Sharp. Artists: Architectural Association Group (Simon Conolly, Jonny Devas, David Harrison, and David Martin), Hans Haacke, Akira Kanayama, Les Levine, Preston McClanahan, David Medalla, Robert Morris, Marcello Salvadori, Graham Stevens, John Van Saun, and Andy Warhol. Catalogue.

> Willoughby Sharp, "Air Art," Studio International (London) 175, no. 900 (May 1968): 262-265.

CARL ANDRE, ROBERT BARRY, LAWRENCE WEINER. Windham College, Putnam, Vermont. May. Organized by Seth Siegelaub at the suggestion of Chuck Ginnever.

LANGUAGE II. Dwan Gallery, New York. 25 May-22 June. Artists: William Anastasi, Carl Andre, Arakawa, Art & Language, Mel Bochner, James Lee Byars, Rosemarie Castoro, William Copley, Hanne Darboven, Walter de Maria, Marcel Duchamp, R. Denis Dunn, Dan Flavin, Freifeld, Dan Graham, Michael Heizer, Bici Hendricks, Dick Higgins, Peter Hutchinson, Robert Indiana, Ray Johnson, Allan Kaprow, Steve Katz, Lila Katzen, On Kawara, Edward Kienholz, Joseph Kosuth, Christine Kozlov, Sol LeWitt, Jackson MacLow, Ed Meeneley, Robert Morris, Dennis Oppenheim, Robert Rauschenberg, Carl Frederick Rentersward, Robert Smithson, Elaine Sturtevant, Bernar Venet, Hannah Weiner, Lawrence Weiner, H. C. Westermann, and William T. Wiley.

> John Chandler, "The Last Word in Graphic Art," Art International 12, no. 9 (20 November 1968): 25-28.

PROSPEKT 68. Städtische Kunsthalle, Düsseldorf. 20-29 September. Organized by Konrad Fischer and Hans Strelow. Artists include: Giovanni Anselmo, Joseph Beuys, Alighiero e Boetti, Marcel Broodthaers, Daniel Buren, Pier Paolo Calzolari, Mario Ceroli, Mario Merz, Robert Morris, Bruce Nauman, Panamarenko, Primi, Reiner Ruthenbeck, Richard Serra, Bernar Venet, and Gilberto Zorio. Catalogue.

> Charles Harrison, "Prospect '68 – An International Showcase," Studio International (London) 176, no. 905 (November 1968): 204.

> Pierre Restany, "Prospect '68 ou l'esprit de l'escalier," Domus (Milan) 467, no. 10 (October 1968): 53-54.

> Ed Sommer, "Prospect 68 and Kunstmarkt 68," Art International 13, no. 2 (February 1969): 32-36.

EARTHWORKS. Dwan Gallery, New York. 5-30 October. Artists: Carl Andre, Herbert Bayer, Walter de Maria, Michael Heizer, Stephen J. Kaltenbach, Sol LeWitt, Robert Morris, Claes Oldenburg, Dennis Oppenheim, and Robert Smithson.

> John Perreault, "Long Live Earth!," The Village Voice, 17 October 1968, 17.

> Sidney Tillim, "Earthworks and the New Picturesque," Artforum 7, no. 4 (December 1968): 42-45.

CARL ANDRE, ROBERT BARRY, DOUGLAS HUEBLER, JOSEPH KOSUTH, SOL LEWITT, ROBERT MORRIS, LAWRENCE WEINER. Also known as "Xeroxbook." December. Organized by Seth Siegelaub and John W. Wendler. Catalogue. Exhibition existed in catalogue format only.

NINE AT LEO CASTELLI. Leo Castelli Warehouse, New York. 4-28 December. Organized by Robert Morris. Artists: Giovanni Anselmo, William Bollinger, Eva Hesse, Stephen J. Kaltenbach, Bruce Nauman, Alan Saret, Richard Serra, Keith Sonnier, and Gilberto Zorio.

> Max Kozloff, "Nine in a Warehouse: An 'Attack on the Status of the Object,'" Artforum 7, no. 6 (February 1969): 38-42.

> Philip Leider, "'The Properties of Materials': In the Shadow of Robert Morris," The New York Times, 22 December 1968, D31.

> Gregoire Müller, "Robert Morris Presents Anti-form: The Castelli Warehouse Show," Arts Magazine 43, no. 4 (February 1969): 29-30.

> John Perreault, "Art: A Test," The Village Voice, 19 December 1968, 19.

"Nine at Leo Castelli." Leo Castelli Warehouse, New York. 4-28 December 1968. Photo Harry Shunk.

Lawrence Weiner
STAPLES, STAKES, TWINE, TURF, 1968
34 stakes, staples, and 510 yeds. of heap twine. 70 x 100 ft. (with a 10 x 20 ft. notch removed) 6 ft. off the ground; topoliogically variable. Made for "Carl Andre, Robert Barry, Lawrence Weiner." Windham College, Putnam, Vermont. May 1968. Courtesy The Siegelaub Collection & Archives. Photo Seth Siegelaub.

JANUARY 5-31, 1969. Rented office space at 44 East 52nd Street, New York. Organized by Seth Siegelaub. Artists: Robert Barry, Douglas Huebler, Joseph Kosuth, and Lawrence Weiner. Catalogue. Exhibition intended to serve only as supplementary material to the catalogue.

> *Dore Ashton, "New York Commentary," Studio International (London) 177, no. 909 (March 1969): 136.*

> *John Perreault, "Art: Disturbances," The Village Voice, 23 January 1969, 14, 18.*

ELECTRIC ART. UCLA Art Galleries, University of California, Los Angeles. 19 January-23 March. Traveled to Phoenix Art Museum, 15 April-15 June. Organized by Oliver Andrews. Artists: Oliver Andrews, Stephen Antonakas, Fletcher Benton, Zbigniew Blazeje, Robert Breer, Jack Burnham, Eugenia Butler, James Lee Byars, Enrique Castro-Cid, Chryssa, Mike Cooper, Mary Corse, François Dallegret, Dana Draper, Dan Flavin, William Grover, Intersystems (Michael Hayden, John Mills-Cockell, Blake Parker, and Dick Zander), Joseph Kosuth, Stanley Landsman, Linda Levi, Les Levine, "Su Li" (Eric Orr), Tom Lloyd, Ronald Mallory, Boyd Mefferd, Pat O'Neill, Nam June Paik, Chuck Prentiss, Earl Reiback, Joseph Riccio, John Rosenbaum, Morio Shinoda, Takis, Jean Tinguely, Sy Weisman, and Thomas Wilfred. Catalogue.

EARTH ART. Andrew Dickson White Museum of Art, Cornell University, Ithaca, New York. 11 February-16 March. Organized by Willoughby Sharp. Artists: Jan Dibbets, Hans Haacke, Neil Jenney, Richard Long, David Medalla, Robert Morris, Dennis Oppenheim, Robert Smithson, and Günther Uecker. Catalogue.

> *Dore Ashton, "Exercises in Anti-Style: Six Ways of Regarding Un, In and Anti-Form." Arts Magazine 43, no. 6 (April 1969): 45-47.*

> *Howard Junker, "Down to Earth," Newsweek, 24 March 1969, 101.*

BLOCKADE '69. Galerie René Block, Berlin. 28 February-22 November. Artists: Joseph Beuys, Giese, K. H. Hödicke, Bernd Lohaus, Wolf Knoebel, Blinky Palermo, Panamarenko, Sigmar Polke, and Reiner Ruthenbeck. Catalogue.

JOSEPH KOSUTH, ROBERT MORRIS. Laura Knott Gallery, Bradford Junior College, Bradford, Massachusetts. March. Organized by Seth Siegelaub. Catalogue.

ONE MONTH. Also known as "March 1969." Various locations throughout the world. Organized by Seth Siegelaub. Each invited artist made a work on an assigned day during the month of March. Artists and their dates: 1. Carl Andre, 2. Michael Asher, 3. Terry Atkinson, 4. Michael Baldwin, 5. Robert Barry, 6. Frederick Barthelme, 7. Iain Baxter, 8. James Lee Byars, 9. John Chamberlain, 10. Ron Cooper, 11. Barry Flanagan, 12. Dan Flavin, 13. Alex Hay, 14. Douglas Huebler, 15. Robert Huot, 16. Stephen J. Kaltenbach, 17. On Kawara, 18. Joseph Kosuth, 19. Christine Kozlov, 20. Sol LeWitt, 21. Richard Long, 22. Robert Morris, 23. Bruce Nauman, 24. Claes Oldenburg, 25. Dennis Oppenheim, 26. Allen Ruppersberg, 27. Edward Ruscha, 28. Robert Smithson, 29. De Wain Valentine, 30. Lawrence Weiner, 31. Ian Wilson. Catalogue.

> *Lawrence Alloway, "Art," The Nation, 7 April 1969, 446.*

> *Grace Glueck, "Art Notes: Venice, Anyone?" The New York Times, 16 March 1969, D23.*

> *John Perreault, "Art: Off the Wall," The Village Voice, 13 March 1969, 13-14.*

SAMMLUNG 1968: KARL STRÖHER. Kunstverein and Neue Nationalgalerie, Berlin. 1 March-14 April. Traveled to Städtische Kunsthalle, Düsseldorf, 25 April-17 June; Kunsthalle, Bern, 12 July-17 August and 23 August-28 September. Artists include: Carl Andre, Georg Baselitz, Hanne Darboven, Walter de Maria, Dan Flavin, Erwin Heerich, Donald Judd, Markus Lüpertz, Blinky Palermo, Gerhard Richter, Reiner Ruthenbeck, Eugen Schönebeck, Norbert Tadeusz, and Franz Erhard Walther. Catalogue.

OP LOSSE SCHROEVEN: SITUATIES EN CRYPTOSTRUCTUREN (SQUARE PEGS IN ROUND HOLES). Stedelijk Museum, Amsterdam. 15 March-27 April. Traveled to Museum Folkwang, Essen, as "Verborgene Strukturen," 9 May-22 June. Organized by Wim Beeren. Artists: Carl Andre, Giovanni Anselmo, Joseph Beuys, Marinus Boezem, William Bollinger, Pier Paolo Calzolari, Walter de Maria, Jan Dibbets, Ger van Elk, Rafael Ferrer, Barry Flanagan, Michael Heizer, Douglas Huebler, Paolo Icaro, Neil Jenney, Olle Kaks, Jannis Kounellis, Richard Long, Mario Merz, Marisa Merz, Robert Morris, Bruce Nauman, Dennis Oppenheim, Panamarenko, Emilio Prini, Reiner Ruthenbeck, Robert Ryman, Alan Saret, Richard Serra, Robert Smithson, Keith Sonnier, Frank Lincoln Viner, Lawrence Weiner, and Gilberto Zorio. Catalogue.

> *Cor Blok, "Letter from Holland," Art International 13, no. 5 (20 May 1969): 52-53.*

> *Klaus Honnef, "Op Losse Schroeven: Situaties en Cryptostructuren," Das Kunstwerk (Stuttgart) 22, no. 9-10 (June-July 1969): 62-63.*

> *Tommaso Trini, "The Prodigal Maker's Trilogy: Op Losse Schroeven," Domus (Milan) 478, no. 9 (September 1969): 47-48.*

279

"January 5-31, 1969." Rented office space at 44 East 52nd Street, New York. Installation view showing works by Douglas Huebler (books on window sill), Lawrence Weiner (rug stain), Robert Barry (labels), and Joseph Kosuth (newspapers). Courtesy The Siegelaub Collection & Archives. Photo Seth Siegelaub.

WHEN ATTITUDES BECOME FORM: WORKS — CONCEPTS — PROCESSES — SITUATIONS — INFORMATION: LIVE IN YOUR HEAD. Kunsthalle, Bern. 22 March–27 April. Traveled to Museum Folkwang, Essen, and as a revised version to Museum Haus Lange, Krefeld, 10 May–15 June, and to the Institute of Contemporary Art, London, 28 August–27 September. Organized by Harald Szeemann (London exhibition organized by Charles Harrison). Artists: Carl Andre, Giovanni Anselmo, Richard Artschwager, Thomas Bang, Jared Bark, Robert Barry, Joseph Beuys, Mel Bochner, Alighiero e Boetti, Marinus Boezem, William Bollinger, Victor Burgin (London only), Michael Buthe, Pier Paolo Calzolari, Paul Cotton, Hanne Darboven, Walter de Maria, Jan Dibbets, Ger van Elk, Rafael Ferrer, Barry Flanagan, Ted Glass, Hans Haacke, Michael Heizer, Eva Hesse, Douglas Huebler, Paolo Icaro, Alain Jacquet, Neil Jenney, Stephen J. Kaltenbach, Jo Ann Kaplan, Edward Kienholz, Yves Klein, Joseph Kosuth, Jannis Kounellis, Gary B. Kuehn, Sol LeWitt, Bernd Lohaus, Richard Long (Bern only), Roelof Louw, Bruce McLean, David Medalla, Mario Merz, Robert Morris, Bruce Nauman, Claes Oldenburg, Dennis Oppenheim, Panamarenko, Pino Pascali, Paul Pechter, Michelangelo Pistoletto, Emilio Prini, Markus Raetz, Allen Ruppersberg, Reiner Ruthenbeck, Robert Ryman, Fred Sandback, Alan Saret, Sarkis, Jean-Frédéric Schnyder, Richard Serra, Robert Smithson, Keith Sonnier, Richard Tuttle, Frank Lincoln Viner, Franz Erhard Walther, William Wegman, Lawrence Weiner, William T. Wiley, and Gilberto Zorio. Catalogue.

Jean-Christophe Ammann, "Schweizer Brief," Art International 13, no. 5 (20 May 1969): 47-50.

Cor Blok, "Letter from Holland," Art International 13, no. 5 (20 May 1969): 52-53.

Tommaso Trini, "The Prodigal Maker's Trilogy: When Attitudes Become Form," Domus (Milan) 478, no. 9 (September 1969): 47-48.

ARTISTS AND PHOTOGRAPHS. Multiples Gallery, New York. 28 March–5 April. Artists: Mel Bochner, Christo, Jan Dibbets, Tom Gormley, Dan Graham, Douglas Huebler, Allan Kaprow, Michael Kirby, Joseph Kosuth, Sol LeWitt, Richard Long, Robert Morris, Bruce Nauman, Dennis Oppenheim, Robert Rauschenberg, Edward Ruscha, Robert Smithson, Bernar Venet, and Andy Warhol. Catalogue.

Nicolas Calas, "Documentizing," Arts Magazine 44, no. 7 (May 1970): 30-32.

"When Attitudes Become Form." Kunsthalle, Bern.
22 March–27 April 1969.
Photo Harry Shunk.

18'6" x 6'9" x 11'2 1/2" x 47' x 11'3/16" x 29'8 1/2" x 31'9 3/16". San Francisco Art Institute. 11 April–3 May. Traveled to Centre for Communications and the Arts, Simon Fraser University, Burnaby, British Columbia, 7 July–1 August. Organized by Eugenia Butler. Artists: Michael Asher, Robert Barry, Iain Baxter, Eugenia Butler, James Lee Byars, Douglas Huebler, Stephen J. Kaltenbach, Edward Kienholz, Joseph Kosuth, Barry Le Va, Dennis Oppenheim, Eric Orr, Tim Rudnick, Robert Watts, and Lawrence Weiner.

LAND ART. Fernsehgalerie Gerry Schum, Hanover, and TV Germany Chanel 1, Berlin. 15 April. Organized by Gerry Schum. Artists: Marinus Boezem, Walter de Maria, Jan Dibbets, Barry Flanagan, Michael Heizer, Richard Long, Dennis Oppenheim, and Robert Smithson. Exhibition consisted of a thirty-minute film of eight outdoor sculptural projects broadcast on German television. Catalogue.

Charles Harrison, "Art on TV," Studio International (London) 181, no. 929 (January 1971): 30-31.

J. Leering, "Televisie galerie," Museumjournaal (London) 14, no. 3 (June 1969): 138-140.

INVISIBLE PAINTING AND SCULPTURE. Richmond Art Center, Richmond, California. 24 April–1 June. Organized by Tom Marioni. Artists: Jerry Ballaine, Larry Bell, Bruce Conner, Albert Fisher, Lloyd Hamrol, Wally Hedrick, Warner Jepson, Harry Lum, George Neubert, Harold Paris, Michelangelo Pistoletto, David R. Smith, and William T. Wiley. Catalogue.

THE APPEARING/DISAPPEARING IMAGE/OBJECT. Newport Harbor Art Museum, Newport Beach, California. 11 May–28 June. Organized by Tom Garver. Artists: Michael Asher, John Baldessari, Ron Cooper, Doug Edge, Barry Le Va, Tim Rudnick, and Allen Ruppersberg. Brochure.

ECOLOGIC ART. John Gibson Gallery, New York, 17 May–28 June. Artists: Carl Andre, Christo, Jan Dibbets, Peter Hutchinson, Will Insley, Richard Long, Robert Morris, Claes Oldenburg, Dennis Oppenheim, and Robert Smithson.

NUMBER 7. Paula Cooper Gallery, New York. 18 May–15 June. Organized by Lucy R. Lippard. Artists: Carl Andre, Richard Artschwager, Terry Atkinson, Michael Baldwin, Robert Barry, Frederick Barthelme, Iain Baxter, Gene Beery, Mel Bochner, William Bollinger, Jonathan Borofsky, Donald Burgy, Luis Camnitzer, Rosemarie Castoro, Hanne Darboven, Walter de Maria, Jan Dibbets, Dan Graham, Hans Haacke, Douglas Huebler, Robert Huot, Stephen J. Kaltenbach, On Kawara, Michael Kirby, Joseph Kosuth, Christine Kozlov, Sol LeWitt, Richard Long, Duane Lunden, Robert Morris, Bruce Nauman, Adrian Piper, Allen Ruppersberg, Edward Ruscha, Richard Serra, Robert Smithson, Bernar Venet, Lawrence Weiner, and Ian Wilson. Benefit for the Art Workers Coalition.

John Perreault, "Para-Visual," The Village Voice, 5 June 1969, 16-17.

SIMON FRASER EXHIBITION. Centre for Communications and the Arts, Simon Fraser University, Burnaby, British Columbia. 19 May–19 June. Organized by Seth Siegelaub. Artists: Art & Language, Robert Barry, Jan Dibbets, Douglas Huebler, Stephen J. Kaltenbach, Joseph Kosuth, Sol LeWitt, N. E. Thing Co., and Lawrence Weiner. Symposium held on 17 June 1969 at Simon Fraser University Theatre via telephone hookup between New York, Ottawa, and Burnaby. Catalogue entitled *Catalogue for the Exhibition.*

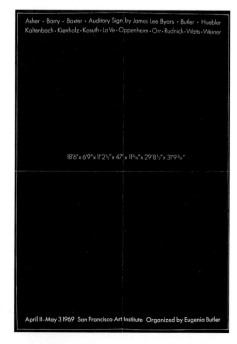

"18'6" x 6'9" x 11'2 1/2" x 47' x 11'3/16" x 29'8 1/2 'x 31'9 3/16"."
San Francisco Art Institute. 11 April–3 May 1969.
Photo Paula Goldman.

ANTI-ILLUSION: PROCEDURES/MATERIALS. Whitney Museum of American Art, New York. 19 May-6 July. Organized by James Monte and Marcia Tucker. Artists: Carl Andre, Michael Asher, Lynda Benglis, William Bollinger, John Duff, Rafael Ferrer, Robert Fiore, Philip Glass, Eva Hesse, Neil Jenney, Barry Le Va, Robert Lobe, Robert Morris, Bruce Nauman, Steve Reich, Robert Rohm, Robert Ryman, Richard Serra, Joel Shapiro, Michael Snow, Keith Sonnier, and Richard Tuttle. Catalogue.

Scott Burton, "Time on Their Hands," Art News 68, no. 4 (Summer 1969): 40-43.

Grace Glueck, "Air, Hay, and Money," The New York Times, 25 May 1969, 2:42.

J. Patrice Marandel, "Lettre de New York," Art International 14, no. 9 (November 1970): 66-68.

Peter Schjeldahl, "New York Letter," Art International 13, no. 7 (September 1969): 70-71.

Emily Wasserman, "Process," Artforum 8, no. 1 (September 1969): 57-58.

LANGUAGE III. Dwan Gallery, New York. 24 May-18 June. Artists: Vito Acconci, William Anastasi, Terence Anderson, Carl Andre, Eleanor Antin, Arakawa, Terry Atkinson, John Baldessari, Frederick Barthelme, Iain Baxter, Gene Beery, Marcel Broodthaers, Donald Burgy, Luis Camnitzer, Rosemarie Castoro, Roger Cutforth, Hanne Darboven, Naomi Dash, Walter de Maria, Marcel Duchamp, Carl Fernbach-Flarsheim, Charles Frazier in collaboration with Michael Benedikt, Madeline Gins, John Giorno, Ted Glass, Dan Graham, Ronald Gross, Michael Heizer, Bici Hendricks, Douglas Huebler, Ruth Jacoby, Stephen J. Kaltenbach, On Kawara, Edward Kienholz, Joseph Kosuth, Christine Kozlov, Sol LeWitt, Lee Lozano, Robert Morris, David Nelson, Robert Newman, Les Packer, Paul Pechter, John Perreault, Adrian Piper, Mel Ramsden, Ad Reinhardt, Richmond, Charles Ross, Fred Sandback, John Seery, Schuldt, Kurt Schwitters, Robert Smithson, Kenneth Snelson, Marjorie Strider, Bernar Venet, and Hannah Weiner. Catalogue.

John Perreault, "Para-Visual," The Village Voice, 5 June 1969, 16-17.

Peter Schjeldahl, "New York Letter," Art International 13, no. 8 (October 1969): 75-76.

CONCEPTION-PERCEPTION. Eugenia Butler Gallery, Los Angeles. 1-25 July. Artists include: John Baldessari, Douglas Huebler, Joseph Kosuth, Barry Le Va, and Lawrence Weiner.

JULY, AUGUST, SEPTEMBER 1969. Various locations throughout the world. 1 July-30 September. Organized by Seth Siegelaub. Artists: Carl Andre (The Hague, The Netherlands), Robert Barry (Baltimore), Daniel Buren (Paris), Jan Dibbets (Amsterdam), Douglas Huebler (Los Angeles), Joseph Kosuth (Portales, New Mexico), Sol LeWitt (Düsseldorf), Richard Long (Clifton Down, Bristol, England), N. E. Thing Co. (Vancouver), Robert Smithson (Uxmal, Yucatan, Mexico), and Lawrence Weiner (Niagara Falls, New York and Ontario). Catalogue.

Howard Junker, "Idea as Art," Newsweek, 11 August 1969, 81.

LETTERS. Long Beach Island, New Jersey. 11-31 July. Organized by Phillips M. Simkin. Artists: William Bollinger, Christo, Rafael Ferrer, Hamish Fulton, Michael Heizer, Peter Hutchinson, Will Insley, Sol LeWitt, Robert Morris, Dennis Oppenheim, Reiner Ruthenbeck, Richard Serra and Philip Glass, Robert Smithson, Keith Sonnier and Richard Landry, and Tina. Catalogue.

WALL SHOW. Ace Gallery, Los Angeles. 5 August-20 September. Artists: Mel Bochner, Douglas Huebler, Robert Huot, Sol LeWitt, Robert Ryman, and Lawrence Weiner.

PLACE AND PROCESS. Edmonton Art Gallery, Alberta. 4 September-26 October. Traveled to Kineticism Press, New York, 1-28 November. Organized by Willoughby Sharp. Artists include: Carl Andre, Iain Baxter, Joseph Beuys, Walter de Maria, Jan Dibbets, Barry Flanagan, Hans Haacke, Michael Heizer, David Latham, Les Levine, Richard Long, Preston McClanahan, Bruce McLean, David Medalla, Robert Morris, Dennis Oppenheim, Klaus Rinke, Robert Smithson, John Van Saun, William Wegman, and Lawrence Weiner; film by Evander D. Schley and Robert Fiore.

William Kirby, "Place and Process," Artscanada (Toronto) 26, no. 5 (October 1969): 38-39.

Willoughby Sharp, "Place and Process," Artforum 8, no. 3 (November 1969): 46-49.

557,087. Seattle Art Museum Pavilion, Seattle Art Museum. 5 September-5 October 1969. Traveled as "955,000" to Vancouver Art Gallery, University of British Columbia, 13 January-8 February 1970. Organized by Lucy R. Lippard. Artists: Vito Acconci, Morrie Alhadeff (Seattle only), Carl Andre, Keith Arnatt, Richard Artschwager, Michael Asher (Seattle only), Terry Atkinson, John Baldessari, Michael Baldwin, Robert Barry, Frederick Barthelme, Iain Baxter (Seattle only), Gene Beery, Mel Bochner, William Bollinger, Jonathan Borofsky, Daniel Buren, Donald Burgy, Rosemarie Castoro, Greg Curnoe (Vancouver only), Hanne Darboven, Walter de Maria, Jan Dibbets, Christos Dikeakos (Vancouver only), Robert Dootson (Seattle only), Rafael Ferrer, Barry Flanagan (Seattle only), Anne Gerber (Seattle only), Dan Graham, Hans Haacke, Alex Hay (Vancouver only), Michael Heizer, Eva Hesse, Douglas Huebler, Robert Huot, Stephen Kaltenbach, On Kawara, Edward Kienholz, Robert Kinmont, Joseph Kosuth, Christine Kozlov, John Latham, Barry Le Va, Sol LeWitt, Lucy R. Lippard (Seattle only), Roelof Louw, Duane Lunden, Thomas Maythem (Seattle only), Bruce McLean, Robert Morris, Bruce Nauman, N. E. Thing Co. (Vancouver only), New York Graphic Workshop (Luis Camnitzer, José Guillermo Castillo, and Liliana Porter), George Nicolaidis (Vancouver only), Dennis Oppenheim, John Perreault, Adrian Piper, Polly Rawn (Seattle only), Robert Rohm, Allen Ruppersberg, Edward Ruscha, Robert Ryman, Fred Sandback, Alan Saret, George Sawchuk, Richard Serra, Randy Sims, Robert Smithson, Keith Sonnier, Frank Lincoln Viner (Seattle only), Jeff Wall, Lawrence Weiner, Ian Wilson, and Jinny Wright (Seattle only). Films by Robert Barry, Hollis Frampton, Ernie Gehr, Robert Huot, Ken Jacobs, George Landow, Claes Oldenburg, Richard Serra, Paul Sharits, Michael Snow, and Joyce Wieland, as well as the film Land Art, produced by Gerry Schum. Catalogue.

Tim Lindberg, "955,000: An Exhibition Organized by Lucy Lippard," Artscanada (Toronto) 27, no. 3 (June 1970): 50.

Peter Plagens, "557,087," Artforum 8, no. 3 (November 1969): 64-67.

William Wilson, "Seattle Celebrates Concept Style," Los Angeles Times Calendar, 21 September 1969, 52, 63.

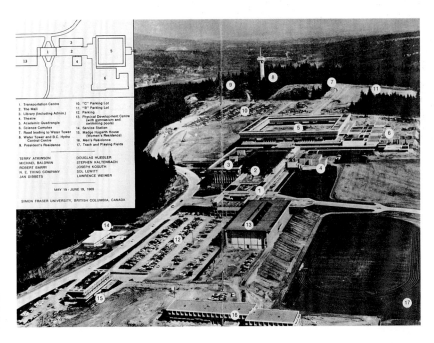

"Simon Fraser Exhibition." Centre for Communications and the Arts, Simon Fraser University, Burnaby, British Columbia. 19 May-19 June 1969. Photo Paula Goldman.

OTHER IDEAS. The Detroit Institute of Arts. 10 September-19 October. Organized by Samuel J. Wagstaff, Jr. Artists: Cecile Abish, Peter Alexander, Carl Andre, Jo Baer, Lynda Benglis, William Bollinger, Robert Bücker, Robert Cumming, Walter de Maria, Susan Deming, Royce Dendler, Jean Dupuy, William Dutterer, George Ettl, Dan Flavin, Sam Gilliam, Hans Haacke, Michael Heizer, Robert Huot, Sheldon Iden, Neil Jenney, Shlomo Koren, Aris Koutroulis, Robert Lobe, Edward McGowin, Nam June Paik, David Prentice, Fred Sandback, Charles Santon, Thomas Shannon, Robert Stalkhouse, James Storey, Richard Tuttle, and William Wegman. Catalogue.

THE RETURN OF ABSTRACT EXPRESSIONISM. Richmond Art Center, Richmond, California. 25 September-2 November. Organized by Tom Marioni. Artists: Bob Anderson, Paul Crowley, Allan Fish (Tom Marioni), Terry Fox, Ron Goldstein, Mel Henderson, Paul Kos, Phil Linhares, N. E. Thing Co., Dennis Oppenheim, Sherry Stewart, Jo Ann TeSelle, Peter Veres and Tony Gnazzo, and John Woodall. Catalogue.

NEW ALCHEMY: ELEMENTS, SYSTEMS, FORCES/NOUVELLE ALCHIMIE: ELEMENTS, SYSTEMES, FORCES. Art Gallery of Ontario, Toronto. 27 September-26 October. Traveled to Musée d'art contemporain, Montreal, 5 November-14 December. Organized by Dennis Young. Artists: Hans Haacke, Charles Ross, Takis, and John Van Saun. Catalogue.

PROSPECT 69. Städtische Kunsthalle, Düsseldorf. 30 September-12 October. Organized by Konrad Fischer and Hans Strelow. Artists: Bernd and Hilla Becher, Joseph Beuys, Alighiero e Boetti, Marcel Broodthaers, Stanley Brouwn, Daniel Buren, Eugenia Butler, James Lee Byars, Pier Paolo Calzolari, Paul Cotton, Hanne Darboven, Ben d'Armagnac, Gerrit Dekker, Jan Dibbets, Hans Haacke, Michael Heizer, Jannis Kounellis, Sol LeWitt, Richard Long, Eliseo Mattiacci, Dennis Oppenheim, Eric Orr, Giuseppe Penone, Emilio Prini, Markus Raetz, Reiner Ruthenbeck, Robert Ryman, Jean-Frédéric Schnyder, Robert Smithson, Niele Toroni, and Zaj (Walther Marchetti). Catalogue.

> R. G. Dienst, "Prospect 69," Das Kunstwerk (Stuttgart) 23, no. 1-2 (October-November 1969): 59-60.

> Margit Staber, "Prospecta — Kunstmarkt 1969." Art International 14, no. 1 (20 January 1970): 65-70.

KONZEPTION-CONCEPTION: DOKUMENTATION EINER HEUTIGEN KUNSTRICHTUNG/DOCUMEN-TATION OF TODAY'S ART TENDENCY. Städtisches Museum, Leverkusen. October-November. Organized by Rolf Wedewer. Artists: Keith Arnatt, John Baldessari, Robert Barry, Iain Baxter, Bernd and Hilla Becher, Mel Bochner, Alighiero e Boetti, Marcel Broodthaers, Stanley Brouwn, Daniel Buren, Victor Burgin, Donald Burgy, Eugenia Butler, Pier Paolo Calzolari, Paul Cotton, Hanne Darboven, Jan Dibbets, Hamish Fulton, Gilbert & George, Dan Graham, Douglas Huebler, Richard Jackson, Stephen J. Kaltenbach, On Kawara, Michael Kirby, Joseph Kosuth, David Lamelas, Sol LeWitt, Bruce McLean, Bruce Nauman, Giuseppe Penone, Adrian Piper, Sigmar Polke, Emilio Prini, Markus Raetz, Allen Ruppersberg, Edward Ruscha, Fred Sandback, Richard Sladden, Robert Smithson, Timm Ulrichs, Bernar Venet, Lawrence Weiner, and Zaj (Walther Marchetti). Catalogue.

> Catherine Millet, "L'art conceptuel," Chroniques de l'art vivant (Paris), no. 7 (January 1970): 26-27.

A REPORT — TWO OCEAN PROJECTS. The Museum of Modern Art, New York. 20 October-30 November. Artists: Peter Hutchinson and Dennis Oppenheim. Documentation of works made by the artists in the waters off Tobago in August 1969.

> William Johnson, "Scuba Sculpture," Art News 68, no. 7 (November 1969): 52-53, 81.

> Anthony Robbin, "Two Ocean Projects at the MOMA," Arts Magazine 44, no. 2 (November 1969): 24-25.

ART BY TELEPHONE. Museum of Contemporary Art, Chicago. 1 November-14 December. Organized by Jan van der Marck. Artists: Siah Armajani, Arman, Richard Artschwager, John Baldessari, Iain Baxter, Mel Bochner, George Brecht, Jack Burnham, James Lee Byars, Robert Cumming, François Dallegret, Jan Dibbets, John Giorno, Robert Grosvenor, Hans Haacke, Richard Hamilton, Dick Higgins, Davi Det Hompson, Robert Huot, Alain Jacquet, Edward Kienholz, Joseph Kosuth, Les Levine, Sol LeWitt, Robert Morris, Bruce Nauman, Claes Oldenburg, Dennis Oppenheim, Richard Serra, Robert Smithson, Günther Uecker, Stan VanDerBeek, Bernar Venet, Frank Lincoln Viner, Wolf Vostell, William Wegman, and William T. Wiley. Catalogue. Artists' projects were recorded as telephone instructions on a 12-inch LP record that serves as the catalogue for the exhibition.

GROUPS. The Visual Arts Gallery, School of Visual Arts, New York. 3-20 November. Organized by Lucy R. Lippard. Artists: Robert Barry, Iain Baxter, Mel Bochner, Jonathan Borofsky, Martin Bressler, Frazier Dougherty, Stylianos Gianakos, Gloria Greenberg, Alex Hay, Douglas Huebler, Robert Huot, Alex Katz, Christine Kozlov, June Leaf, Leslie Miller, Francis Moyer, Henry Pearson, Adrian Piper, Alejandro Puente, Peter Robbins, Peter Tangen, Joyce Wieland, Lawrence Weiner, Kestus Zapkus, and various students of the School of Visual Arts.

> Lucy R. Lippard, "Groups," Studio International (London) 179, no. 920 (March 1970): 93-99.

PLÄNE UND PROJEKTE ALS KUNST/PLANS AND PROJECTS AS ART. Kunsthalle, Bern. 8 November-7 December. Organized by Harald Szeemann. Artists include: Mel Bochner, Daniel Buren, Antonio Dias, Jan Dibbets, Gilbert & George, Joseph Kosuth, Sol LeWitt, and Lawrence Weiner. Catalogue.

ART IN PROCESS IV. Finch College Museum of Art, New York. 11 December-26 January 1970. Artists: Carl Andre, Lynda Benglis, Mel Bochner, William Bollinger, Rafael Ferrer, Barry Flanagan, Eva Hesse, Robert Morris, Bruce Nauman, Robert Ryman, Richard Van Buren, and Lawrence Weiner. Catalogue.

> Philip Leider, "Art in Process IV," Artforum 8, no. 6 (February 1970): 70.

> Bitite Vinklers, "New York," Art International 14, no. 3 (March 1970): 91-92.

SPACES. The Museum of Modern Art, New York. 30 December-1 March 1970. Organized by Jennifer Licht. Artists: Michael Asher, Larry Bell, Dan Flavin, Robert Morris, Pulsa (Michael Cain, Patrick Clancy, William Crosby, William Duesing, Paul Fuge, Peter Kindlmann, and David Rumsey), and Franz Erhard Walther. Catalogue.

> Gregory Battcock, "The Politics of Space," Arts Magazine 44, no. 4 (February 1970): 40-43.

> Philip Leider, "Spaces," Artforum 8, no. 6 (February 1970): 69-70.

"Language III." Dwan Gallery, New York.
24 May-18 June 1969.
Courtesy Silent Partner Consulting, Brooklyn, New York.

"18 Paris IV. 70." 66, rue Mouffetard, Paris.
April 1970, organized by Michel Claura.
Courtesy The Siegelaub Collection & Archives.
Photo Seth Siegelaub.

ART CONCEPTS FROM EUROPE. Bonino Gallery, New York. 10-28 March. Organized by Pierre Restany. Artists: Martin Barré, Marinus Boezem, Christian Boltanski, Bernard Borgeaud, Marcel Broodthaers, Peter Brüning, Pier Paolo Calzolari, Eugenio Carmi, Gianni Colombo, Contenotte, Robert Cyprich, Danil, Hanne Darboven, Antonio Dias, Jan Dibbets, Erik Dietmann, Dymny, Stano Filko, Barry Flanagan, Paolo Icaro, Alain Jacquet, Michael Journiac, Karahalios, Alain Kirili, Hans Koetsier, Jannis Kounellis, Piotr Kowalski, David Lamelas, Jean Legac, Richard Long, Elio Marchegiani, Enzo Mari, Mario Merz, Alex Mlynarcik, Tania Mouraud, Krzysztof Niemczyk, Nikos, Lev Nusberg, Panamerenko, Gina Pane, Luca Patella, Gianni Pisani, Emilio Prini, Eliane Radigue, K. F. Reuterswärd, Marc de Rosny, Reiner Ruthenbeck, Jean-Michel Sanejouand, Jean-Frédéric Schnyder, Gianni Emilio Simonetti, Alina Szapocznikow, Szczepanski, Timm Ulrichs, and Nicolás García Uriburu.

> Pierre Restany, "Art Concepts from Europe," Domus (Milan) 487, no. 6 (June 1970): 48.

EVIDENCE ON THE FLIGHT OF SIX FUGITIVES. Museum of Contemporary Art, Chicago. 28 March-10 May. Organized by Jan van der Marck. Artists: Walter de Maria, Michael Heizer, Peter Hutchinson, Richard Long, Dennis Oppenheim, and Robert Smithson. Exhibition consisted of photographic and film documentation of artists' projects.

18 PARIS IV. 70. 66, rue Mouffetard, Paris. April. Organized by Michel Claura. Artists: Robert Barry, Marcel Broodthaers, Stanley Brouwn, Daniel Buren, Jan Dibbets, Jean-Pierre Djian, Gilbert & George, François Guinochet, Douglas Huebler, On Kawara, David Lamelas, Sol LeWitt, Richard Long, Edward Ruscha, Robert Ryman, Niele Toroni, Lawrence Weiner, and Ian Wilson. Catalogue.

> Michel Claura and René Denizot, "18 Paris IV. 70," Studio International (London) 179, no. 921 (April 1970): 179.

> Gérald Gassiot-Talabot, "Concept non concept," La quinzane littéraire (Paris), 1-15 May 1970, 16-17.

CONCEPTUAL ART AND CONCEPTUAL ASPECTS. The New York Cultural Center, New York, in association with Fairleigh Dickinson University, Madison, New Jersey. 10 April-25 August. Organized by Donald Karshan. Artists: Art & Language (Terry Atkinson, David Bainbridge, Michael Baldwin, and Harold Hurrell), Robert Barry, Frederick Barthelme, Iain Baxter, Mel Bochner, Daniel Buren, Donald Burgy, Ian Burn, James Lee Byars, Roger Cutforth, Jan Dibbets, Hans Haacke, Douglas Huebler, Stephen J. Kaltenbach, On Kawara, Joseph Kosuth, Christine Kozlov, Bruce Nauman, Dennis Oppenheim, Saul Ostrow, Adrian Piper, Mel Ramsden, Edward Ruscha, Bernar Venet, Lawrence Weiner, and Ian Wilson. Catalogue.

> Willis Domingo, "In the Museums: Conceptual Art," Arts Magazine 44, no. 7 (May 1970): 54-56.

> Donald Karshan, "The Seventies: Post-Object Art," Studio International (London) 180, no. 925 (September 1970): 69-70. Reprint of introduction to exhibition catalogue.

> Carter Ratcliff, "New York," Art International 14, no. 6 (Summer 1970): 133-134.

> Peter Schjeldahl, "Don't Just Stand There — Read!" The New York Times, 9 August 1970, D17.

ART IN THE MIND. Allen Memorial Art Museum, Oberlin College, Oberlin, Ohio. 17 April-12 May. Organized by Athena Tacha Spear. Artists: Vito Acconci, Siah Armajani, Michael Asher, John Baldessari, Robert Barry, Frederick Barthelme, Bill Beckley, Mel Bochner, Jonathan Borofsky, George Brecht, Victor Burgin, Donald Burgy, Scott Burton, James Lee Byars, Luis Camnitzer, Rosemarie Castoro, Don Celender, Fred Cornell Cone, Christopher Cook, Eduardo Costa, Robert Cumming, Royce Dendler, David Dunlap, David Eisler, Robert Feke, Rafael Ferrer, George Gladstone, Dan Graham, Ira Joel Haber, Richards Jarden, On Kawara, Michael Kirby, Paul Kos, Joseph Kosuth, R. Rexinger Lau, Barry Le Va, Les Levine, Glenn Lewis, Sol LeWitt, Martin Maloney, Bruce McLean, Bruce Nauman, David Nelson, N. E. Thing Co., Claes Oldenburg, Saul Ostrow, Paul Pechter, John Perreault, Adrian Piper, Glenn Rea, Allen Ruppersberg, Thomas Duncan Shannon, Society for Theoretical Art and Analyses (Ian Burn, Roger Cutforth, and Mel Ramsden), Marjorie Strider, John Van Saun, Bernar Venet, Jeff Wall, William Wegman, Hannah Weiner, and Lawrence Weiner. Catalogue.

SOUND SCULPTURE AS. Museum of Conceptual Art, San Francisco. 30 April. Performances with sound by Arlo Acton, Allan Fish (Tom Marioni), Terry Fox, Mel Henderson, Paul Kos and Richard Beggs, Peter McCann, Jim McCready, Jim Melchert, and Herb Yarno.

> Brenda Richardson, "Bay Area Survey: The Myth of Neo-Dada," Arts Magazine 44, no. 8 (Summer 1970): 46-49.

> "Sound Sculpture Event," Artweek (San Jose, California) 1, no. 17 (25 April 1970): 2.

> Jerome Tarshis, "San Francisco," Artforum 9, no. 1 (September 1970): 90-93.

BETWEEN MAN AND MATTER: TOKYO BIENNALE '70. Tokyo Metropolitan Art Gallery. 10-30 May. Traveled to Kyoto Municipal Art Museum, 6-28 June; Aichi Prefectural Art Gallery, Nagoya, 15-26 July. Organized by Yusuke Nakahara. Artists: Dietrich Albrecht, Carl Andre, Marinus Boezem, Daniel Buren, Christo, Jan Dibbets, Ger van Elk, Koji Enokura, Luciano Fabro, Barry Flanagan, Hans Haacke, Michio Horikawa, Kenji Inumaki, Stephen J. Kaltenbach, Tatsuo Kawaguchi, On Kawara, Kazushige Koike, Stanislav Kolibal, Susumu Koshimizu, Jannis Kounellis, Edward Krasinski, Sol LeWitt, Roelof Louw, Yutaka Matsuzawa, Mario Merz, Katsuhiko Narita, Bruce Nauman, Hitoshi Nomura, Panamarenko, Giuseppe Penone, Markus Raetz, Klaus Rinke, Reiner Ruthenbeck, Jean-Frédéric Schnyder, Richard Serra, Satoru Shoji, Keith Sonnier, Jiro Takamatsu, Shintaro Tanaka, and Gilberto Zorio. Catalogue.

> Joseph P. Love, "The Tenth Tokyo Biennale of Contemporary Art," Art International 14, no. 6 (Summer 1970): 70-74.

PROJECTIONS: ANTI-MATERIALISM. La Jolla Museum of Art, La Jolla, California. 15 May-5 July. Organized by Lawrence Urrutia. Artists: Robert Barry, David Deutsch, Charles Emerson, Barry Le Va, Sol LeWitt, and David Thompson. Catalogue.

CONCEPTUAL ART, ARTE POVERA, LAND ART. Galleria Civica d'Arte Moderna, Turin. June-July. Organized by Germano Celant. Artists: Carl Andre, Giovanni Anselmo, John Baldessari, Robert Barry, Joseph Beuys, Mel Bochner, Alighiero e Boetti, Pier Paolo Calzolari, Christo, Hanne Darboven, Walter de Maria, Jan Dibbets, Luciano Fabro, Dan Flavin, Hamish Fulton, Gilbert & George, Hans Haacke, Michael Heizer, Douglas Huebler, Stephen J. Kaltenbach, On Kawara, Yves Klein, Joseph Kosuth, Jannis Kounellis, Sol LeWitt, Piero Manzoni, Mario Merz, Robert Morris, Bruce Nauman, Dennis Oppenheim, Giulio Paolini, Pino Pascali, Giuseppe Penone, Michelangelo Pistoletto, Emilio Prini, Robert Ryman, Fred Sandback, Richard Serra, Robert Smithson, Keith Sonnier, Bernar Venet, Lawrence Weiner, and Gilberto Zorio. Catalogue.

> Tommaso Trini, "Conceptual Art, Arte Povera, Land Art: The Eclipse and Diffusion of the Work of Art," Arte illustrata (Milan) 3, no. 34-36 (October-December 1970): 105-107.

LANGUAGE IV. Dwan Gallery, New York. 2-25 June. Artists: William Anastasi, Carl Andre, Arakawa, Art & Language, Mel Bochner, Jonathan Borofsky, Barry Bryant, Walter de Maria, Agnes Denes, Marcel Duchamp, Terry Fugate-Wilcox, Madeline Gins, Michael Heizer, HoJo, Jasper Johns, Ray Johnson, Edward Kienholz, Joseph Kosuth, Filippo Marinetti, Robert Morris, Giora Novak, Claes Oldenburg, Francis Picabia, Adrian Piper, Ad Reinhardt, Dorothea Rockburne, Charles Ross, Robert Smithson, Kenneth Snelson, Bernar Venet, Hannah Weiner, and Ian Wilson.

> Robert Pincus-Witten, "New York," Artforum 9, no. 1 (September 1970): 75-76.

IDEA STRUCTURES: SURVEY '70. Camden Arts Centre and Central Library, Swiss Cottage, London. 24 June-19 July. Organized by Peter Carey and Charles Harrison. Artists: Keith Arnatt, Terry Atkinson, David Bainbridge, Michael Baldwin, Victor Burgin, Ed Herring, Harold Hurrell, and Joseph Kosuth. Catalogue.

JULY-AUGUST 1970. Organized by Seth Siegelaub. An exhibition that existed in catalogue format only, in which six critics were each asked to select artists for an eight-page section of the magazine *Studio International*: David Antin (Eleanor Antin, John Baldessari, Harold Cohen, Dan Graham, Fred Lonidier, George Nicolaidis, Richard Serra, and Keith Sonnier); Germano Celant (Giovanni Anselmo, Alighiero e Boetti, Pier Paolo Calzolari, Mario Merz, Giuseppe Penone, Michelangelo Pistoletto, Emilio Prini, and Gilberto Zorio); Michel Claura (Daniel Buren); Charles Harrison (Keith Arnatt, Art & Language [Terry Atkinson, David Bainbridge, Michael Baldwin, and Harold Hurrell], Victor Burgin, Barry Flanagan, Joseph Kosuth, John Latham, and Roelof Louw); Lucy R. Lippard (Robert Barry, Frederick Barthelme, Douglas Huebler, Stephen J. Kaltenbach, On Kawara, Sol LeWitt, N. E. Thing Co., and Lawrence Weiner); Hans Strelow (Hanne Darboven and Jan Dibbets). Catalogue (*Studio International* 180, no. 924 (July-August 1970): 1-48).

INFORMATION. The Museum of Modern Art, New York. 2 July-20 September. Organized by Kynaston L. McShine. Artists: Vito Acconci, Carl Andre, Siah Armajani, Keith Arnatt, Art & Language (Terry Atkinson, David Bainbridge, and Michael Baldwin), Art & Project, Richard Artschwager, David Askevold, John Baldessari, Barrio, Robert Barry, Frederick Barthelme, Bernd and Hilla Becher, Joseph Beuys, Mel Bochner, William Bollinger, George Brecht, Stig Brøgger, Stanley Brouwn, Daniel Buren, Victor Burgin, Donald Burgy, Ian Burn and Mel Ramsden, James Lee Byars, Jorge Luis Carballa, Christopher Cook, Roger Cutforth, Carlos D'Alessio, Hanne Darboven, Walter de Maria, Jan Dibbets, Gerald Ferguson, Rafael Ferrer, Barry Flanagan, Group Frontera (Adolfo Bronowski, Carlos Espartaco, Mercedes Esteves, and Ines Gross), Hamish Fulton, Gilbert & George, Giorno Poetry Systems, Dan Graham, Hans Haacke, Ira Joel Haber, Randy Hardy, Michael Heizer, Hans Hollein, Douglas Huebler, Robert Huot, Peter Hutchinson, Richards Jarden, Stephen J. Kaltenbach, On Kawara, Joseph Kosuth, Christine Kozlov, John Latham, Barry Le Va, Sol LeWitt, Lucy R. Lippard, Richard Long, Guilherme Magalães Vaz, Bruce McLean, Cildo Meireles, Marta Minujin, Robert Morris, N. E. Thing Co., Bruce Nauman, New York Graphic Workshop (Luis Camnitzer, José Guillermo Castillo, and Liliana Porter), Newspaper, Group OHO (Milenko Matanović, David George Nez, Marko Pogačnik, Andraž Šalamun, and Tomaž Šalamun), Hélio Oiticica, Yoko Ono, Dennis Oppenheim, Panamarenko, Giulio Paolini, Paul Pechter, Giuseppe Penone, Adrian Piper, Michelangelo Pistoletto, Emilio Prini, Alejandro Puente, Markus Raetz, Yvonne Rainer, Klaus Rinke, Edward Ruscha, Jean-Michel Sanejouand, Richard Sladden, Robert Smithson, Keith Sonnier, Ettore Sottsass Jr., Erik Thygesen, John Van Saun, Bernar Venet, Jeff Wall, Lawrence Weiner, and Ian Wilson. Catalogue.

Gregory Battcock, "Information Exhibition at the Museum of Modern Art," Arts Magazine 44, no. 8 (Summer 1970): 24-27.

R. G. Dienst, "Information," Das Kunstwerk (Stuttgart) 23, no. 11-12 (October-November 1970): 66-67.

Hilton Kramer, "Miracles, 'Information,' 'Recommended Reading,'" The New York Times, 12 July 1970, D19.

Les Levine, "The Information Fall-Out," Studio International (London) 181, no. 934 (June 1971): 264-267.

J. Patrice Marandel, "Lettre de New York," Art International 14, no. 9 (November 1970): 66-68.

Carter Ratcliff, "New York Letter," Art International 14, no. 7 (September 1970): 95.

NOTTINGHAM FESTIVAL 1970: VISIONS, PROJECTS, PROPOSALS. Midland Group Gallery, Nottingham, England. 11 July-2 August. Artists include: Jan Dibbets, Donald Judd, Sol LeWitt, Richard Long, and Robert Morris. Catalogue.

SOFTWARE: INFORMATION TECHNOLOGY: ITS MEANING FOR ART. The Jewish Museum, New York. 16 September-8 November. Traveled to Smithsonian Institution, Washington, D.C., 16 December-14 February 1971. Organized by Jack Burnham. Artists: Vito Acconci, David Antin, John Baldessari, Robert Barry, Scott Bradner, Donald Burgy, Paul F. Conley, Agnes Denes, Robert Duncan Enzmann, Carl Fernbach-Flarsheim, Giorno Poetry Systems, John Goodyear, Hans Haacke, Douglas Huebler, Allan Kaprow, Joseph Kosuth, Les Levine, Theodor H. Nelson, Jack Nolan, R.E.S.I.S.T.O.R.S. (Radically Emphatic Students Interested in Science, Technology, and Other Research Studies), Allen M. Razdow, Evander D. Schley, Sonia Sheridan, Theodosius W. Victoria, Lawrence Weiner, and Ned Woodman. Catalogue.

Dore Ashton, "New York Commentary," Studio International (London) 180, no. 927 (November 1970): 200-202.

Kenneth Baker, "New York," Artforum 9, no. 4 (December 1970): 79-81.

J. Patrice Marandel, "Lettre de New York," Art International 14, no. 9 (November 1970): 66-68.

Carter Ratcliff, "New York Letter: Software," Art International 15, no. 1 (20 January 1971): 29-30.

Bitite Vinklers, "Art and Information: 'Software' at the Jewish Museum," Arts Magazine 45, no. 1 (September-October 1970): 46-49.

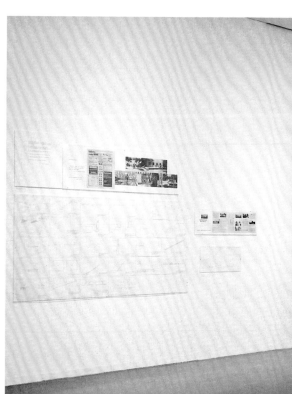

```
"Conceptual Art and Conceptual Aspects."
The New York Cultural Center, New York, in association with
Fairleigh Dickinson University, Madison, New Jersey.
10 April-25 August 1970.

"Information." The Museum of Modern Art, New York.
2 July-20 September 1970.
Photo ©1995 The Museum of Modern Art, New York
```

RECORDED ACTIVITIES. Moore College of Art, Philadelphia. 16 October-19 November. Organized by Diane Vanderlip. Artists: Vito Acconci, John Baldessari, Mel Bochner, Michael Findlay, Dan Graham, Peter Hutchinson, Ray Johnson, Joseph Kosuth, Les Levine, Bruce Nauman, Dennis Oppenheim, Michael Snow, Telethon (Billy Adler and John Margolies), John Van Saun, Bernar Venet, and Robert Smithson. Catalogue.

BODY WORKS. Museum of Conceptual Art, San Francisco. 18 October. Organized by Willoughby Sharp. Artists: Vito Acconci, Terry Fox, Bruce Nauman, Dennis Oppenheim, Keith Sonnier, and William Wegman. Exhibition consisted of the screening of a videotape of the participating artists using their own bodies as sculptural expression.

"Body Works at MOCA," Artweek (San Jose, California), 1, no. 34 (10 October 1970): 2.

Jerome Tarshis, "San Francisco," Artforum 9, no. 6 (February 1971): 85.

CONCEPT-THÉORIE. Galerie Daniel Templon, Paris. 3-21 November. Artists: Art & Language (Terry Atkinson, David Bainbridge, Michael Baldwin, and Harold Hurrell), Victor Burgin, Ian Burn, Alain Kirili, Joseph Kosuth, Christine Kozlov, Emilio Prini, Mel Ramsden, and Bernar Venet. Catalogue.

Jacques Henric, "Lettre de Paris: Scientisme et/ou esthétisme," Art International 15, no. 3 (March 1971): 58.

PUBLICATION. Nigel Greenwood, London. 23 November-6 December. Organized by David Lamelas. Participants: Keith Arnatt, Robert Barry, Stanley Brouwn, Daniel Buren, Victor Burgin, Michel Claura, Gilbert & George, John Latham, Lucy R. Lippard, Martin Maloney, Barbara M. Reise, Lawrence Weiner, and Ian Wilson. Catalogue.

"IDENTIFICATIONS." Fernsehgalerie Gerry Schum, Düsseldorf. 30 November. Organized by Gerry Schum. Artists include: Walter de Maria, Jan Dibbets, Hamish Fulton, Gilbert & George, Michael Heizer, and Lawrence Weiner. Exhibition broadcast by SudWestFunk TV.

Charles Harrison, "Art on TV," Studio International (London) 181, no. 929 (January 1971): 30-31.

2,972,453. Centro de Arte y Comunicación, Buenos Aires. Opened 4 December. Traveled to Museo de Bellas Artes, Montevideo, May 1971. Organized by Lucy R. Lippard as an unofficial continuation of "557,087" and "955,000." Artists: Eleanor Antin, Siah Armajani, David Askevold, Stanley Brouwn, Victor Burgin, Pier Paolo Calzolari, Don Celender, James Collins, Christopher Cook, Gilbert & George, Ira Joel Haber, and Richards Jarden. Catalogue.

WALL SHOW. Lisson Gallery, London. January. Artists: Keith Arnatt, Sue Arrowsmith, Tom Edmonds, Barry Flanagan, Michael Ginsberg, Gerald Hemsworth, John Hilliard, John Latham, Bob Law, Sol LeWitt, Roelof Louw, Ian Munro, Gerald Newman, Blinky Palermo, Klaus Rinke, Ed Sirrs, John Stezaker, David Tremlett, and Richard Wentworth. Catalogue.

FORMULATION. Addison Gallery of American Art, Phillips Academy, Andover, Massachusetts. 8 January-14 February. Organized by Konrad Fischer and Gian Enzo Sperone. Artists: Alighiero e Boetti, Stanley Brouwn, Daniel Buren, Hanne Darboven, Jan Dibbets, Hamish Fulton, Giulio Paolini, Giuseppe Penone, and Salvo. Catalogue.

CONCEPTS AND INFORMATION. Israel Museum, Jerusalem. February. Artists: Georgette Batlle, Yitzhak Danziger, Michael Druks, Benni Efrat, Moshe Gershuni, Avital Geva, Yossi Mar-Chaim, Gerard Marx, Joshua Neustein, and Yohanan Zarai. Catalogue.

PIER 18. An abandoned pier on the Hudson River, New York, February-March. Organized by Willoughby Sharp. Artists: Vito Acconci, David Askevold, John Baldessari, Robert Barry, Bill Beckley, Mel Bochner, Daniel Buren, Jan Dibbets, Terry Fox, Dan Graham, Douglas Huebler, Lee Jaffe, Richards Jarden, Gordon Matta-Clark, Mario Merz, Robert Morris, Dennis Oppenheim, Allen Ruppersberg, Italo Scanga, Richard Serra, Michael Snow, Keith Sonnier, Wolfgang Stoerchle, George Trakas, John Van Saun, William Wegman, and Lawrence Weiner. Photographic documentation of works, all of which used the pier, by Shunk-Kender exhibited as "Projects: Pier 18" at The Museum of Modern Art, New York, 18 June-2 August (installed by Jennifer Licht). Press release. (Catalogue published for exhibition of the photographs entitled Harry Shunk: Projects — Pier 18, presented at the Musée d'art moderne et d'art contemporain, Nice, 3 July-6 September 1992; includes interview with Shunk by Loïc Mallé.)

EARTH, AIR, FIRE, WATER: ELEMENTS OF ART. Museum of Fine Arts, Boston. 4 February-4 April. Organized by Virginia Gunter. Artists: Rachel Bas-Cohain, William Bollinger, Stan Brain, Richard Budelis, Lowry Burgess, Donald Burgy, Christo, François Dallegret, Geny Dignac, Edward Franklin, John Goodyear, Dan Graham, Laura Grisi, Hans Haacke, Newton Harrison, Gerald Hayes, Michael Heizer, Douglas Huebler, Peter Hutchinson, Neil Jenney, Allan Kaprow, Gyula Kosice, Richard Long, Joshua Neustein and Georgette Batlle and Gerard Marx, Dean Nimmer, Dennis Oppenheim, James Piatt, Otto Piene, Ravio Puusemp, Gary Rieveschl, Charles Ross, Richard Serra, Vera Simons and Fred Hartman, Robert Smithson, Alan Sonfist, Christopher Sproat and Elizabeth Clark and Jay Jaroslav, Marvin Torrfield, Nicolás García Uriburu, John Van Saun, Andy Warhol, William Wegman, and Scott Wixon. Catalogue.

David Antin, "It Reaches a Desert in Which Nothing Can Be Perceived but Feeling," Art News 70, no. 1 (March 1971): 38-41, 66-71. Reprint of catalogue essay.

Kenneth Baker, "Boston," Artforum 9, no. 7 (March 1971): 72-74.

285

"Pier 18." An abandoned pier on the Hudson River, New York. February–March 1971.

SITUATION CONCEPTS. Galerie im Taxispalais, Innsbruck. 9 February-4 March. Traveled to Galerie Nächst St. Stephan, Vienna, 15 March-3 April. Organized by Peter Weiermair. Artists include: Arakawa, Arts Agency (Klaus Groh), John Baldessari, Mel Bochner, Daniel Buren, Gino De Dominicis, Wolfgang Ernst, Luciano Fabro, Gianpietro Fazion, Gilbert & George, Mimmo Germanà, Jochen Gerz, Hans Haacke, Michael Heizer, Hans Hollein, Michio Horikawa, Douglas Huebler, Hans Werner Kalkmann, Tatsuo Kawaguchi, Joseph Kosuth, Richard Kriesche, Allesandro Jasci, Sol LeWitt, Lindow, Yutaka Matsuzawa, Eliseo Mattiacci, Eckart Moshammer, Mario Merz, N. E. Thing Co., Nagasawa, George Nicolaidis, Oswald Oberhuber, Masaro Ohmyia, Dennis Oppenheim, Giulio Paolini, Vettor Pisani, Markus Raetz, H. A. Schult, Richard Serra, Robert Smithson, Shintaro Tanaka, Timm Ulrichs, and Lawrence Weiner. Catalogue.

GUGGENHEIM INTERNATIONAL EXHIBITION. Exh. cat. Solomon R. Guggenheim Museum, New York. 12 February-11 April. Organized by Diane Waldman and Edward F. Fry. Artists: Carl Andre, Victor Burgin, Hanne Darboven, Walter de Maria, Antonio Dias, Jan Dibbets, Dan Flavin, Michael Heizer, Donald Judd, On Kawara, Joseph Kosuth, Sol LeWitt, Richard Long, Mario Merz, Robert Morris, Bruce Nauman, Robert Ryman, Richard Serra, Jiro Takamatsu, and Lawrence Weiner. Catalogue.

> Gerrit Henry, "New York Letter," Art International 15, no. 5 (20 May 1971): 73-74, 84.

> Carter Ratcliff, "New York Letter, Spring, Part 2," Art International 15, no. 5 (May 1971): 38-39, 45.

> Barbara Rose, "Gobbledygook at the Guggenheim," New York, 8 March 1971, 48-50.

EIGHT PROPOSALS. Galleria Françoise Lambert, Milan. Opened 26 February. Artists: Robert Barry, Daniel Buren, Donald Burgy, Jan Dibbets, Douglas Huebler, Edward Kienholz, Hidetoshi, Nagasawa, and Lawrence Weiner.

AT THE MOMENT. Doorway-Hall, Zagreb, Yugoslavia. March-April. Artists: Giovanni Anselmo, Robert Barry, Stanley Brouwn, Daniel Buren, Victor Burgin, Jan Dibbets, Braco Dimitrijević, Barry Flanagan, Eventstructure, Douglas Huebler, Alain Kirili, Jannis Kounellis, John Latham, Sol LeWitt, Milenko Matanović, David Nez, Marko Pogačnik, Anraž Šalamun (Group OHO), Goran Trbuljak, Lawrence Weiner, and Ian Wilson. Poster-catalogue.

ENTWÜRFE, PARTITUREN, PROJEKTE: ZEICHNUNGEN. Galerie René Block, Berlin. 5-31 March. Artists: Joseph Beuys, Claus Böhmler, George Brecht, K. P. Brehmer, Michael Buthe, Stanley Brouwn, Hanne Darboven, Jan Dibbets, Hansjoachim Dietrich, Bensu Erdem, Robert Filliou, Ludwig Gosewitz, Robert Graham, Erwin Heerich, K. H. Hödicke, Arthur Köpcke, Wolf Knoebel, Sol LeWitt, Markus Lüpertz, Piero Manzoni, Gislind Nabakowski, Panamarenko, Blinky Palermo, Sigmar Polke, Gerhard Richter, Diter Rot, Gerhard Rühm, Reiner Ruthenbeck, Tomas Schmit, Emil Schult, Jürgen Vallen, Ben Vautier, Young Voss, Wolf Vostell, and Rudolf Weiher. Catalogue.

"WAS DIE SCHÖNHEIT SEI, DAS WEISS ICH NICHT": KÜNSTLER, THEORIE, WERK: ZWEITEN BIENNALE NÜRNBERG. Kunsthalle, Nuremberg. 30 April-1 August. Organized by Jürgen Harten et al. Artists in "Concept-Konzept" section: Robert Barry, Bernd and Hilla Becher, Marcel Broodthaers, Hanne Darboven, Gilbert & George, Joseph Kosuth, John Latham, Robert Smithson, and Lawrence Weiner. Catalogue.

EL ARTE COMO IDEA EN INGLATERRA. Centro de Arte y Comunicación, Buenos Aires. May. Organized by Charles Harrison. Artists: Keith Arnatt, Sue Arrowsmith, Art & Language (Terry Atkinson, David Bainbridge, Michael Baldwin, and Harold Hurrell), Victor Burgin, David Dye, and William Woodrow. Catalogue.

THE BRITISH AVANT-GARDE. The New York Cultural Center, New York, in association with Fairleigh Dickinson University, Madison, New Jersey. 19 May-29 August. Organized by Charles Harrison. Artists: Keith Arnatt, Sue Arrowsmith, Terry Atkinson, David Bainbridge, Michael Baldwin, Victor Burgin, Colin Crumplin, Andrew Dipper, David Dye, Barry Flanagan, Gilbert & George, Harold Hurrell, Richard Long, Roelof Louw, Bruce McLean, Gerald Newman, and David Tremlett. Catalogue.

> Donald Karshan, "Acquisition versus Exhibition," Studio International (London) 181, no. 933 (May 1971): 200. Reprint of introduction to exhibition catalogue.

> Robert Pincus-Witten, "Anglo-American Standard Reference Works: Acute Conceptualism," Artforum 10, no. 2 (October 1971): 82-85.

SONSBEEK 71: BUITEN DE PERKEN. Park Sonsbeek, Arnhem, The Netherlands. 19 June-15 August. Organized by Wim Beeren et al. Artists: Vito Acconci, Bas Jan Ader, Carl Andre, Richard Artschwager, Bruce Baillie, Douwe Jan Bakker, Joseph Beuys, Ronald Bladen, Marinus Boezem, Stanley Brouwn, Daniel Buren, Christo, Tony Conrad, Hanne Darboven, Ben d'Armagnac, Walter de Maria, Hans de Vries, Ad Dekkers, Ger Dekkers, Jan Dibbets, Ger van Elk, Pieter Engels, Groep Enschede (Nico van den Berg, Sake de Boer, Pier van Dijk, Dries Ringenier, and Wim van Stek), E.R.G. (Eventstructure Research Group: Theo Botschuijver and Jeffrey Shaw), Hans Eykelboom, Barry Flanagan, Fluxus, Hollis Frampton, Ernie Gehr, Dan Graham, Robert Grosvenor, Michael Heizer, Douglas Huebler, I.C.W. (Institut voor Creatif Werk, Finsterwolde), Ken Jacobs, joepat, Donald Judd, On Kawara, Wolf Knoebel, Hans Koetsier, Peter Kubelka, George Landow, Standish Dyer Lawder, Sol LeWitt, Richard Long, Mass Moving (Fons van Assche, Jef de Groote, Bernard Delville, Vincent Loute, Elisabeth Magis, Raphaël Opstaël, and Helen Pink), Yutaka Matsuzawa, Mario Merz, Robert Morris, Bruce Nauman, Robert Nelson, Groep Noord-Brabant (Theo Besemer, Cees Gubbels, Hub Hendrickx, J. C. J. van der Heyden, Johan Lennarts, Hub Leyendeckers, Pieter Laurens Mol, and Rolf Weber), Claes Oldenburg, Dennis Oppenheim, Nam June Paik, Panamarenko, E. Philips, Emilio Prini, Klaus Rinke, Peter Roehr, Ulrich Rückreim, Edward Ruscha, Fred Sandback, Jean-Michel Sanejouand, Wim T. Schippers, Richard Serra, Paul Sharits, Eric Siegel, Tony Smith, Robert Smithson, Kenneth Snelson, Michael Snow, Koert Stuyf, Shinkichi Tajiri, Tenjo Sajiki (Shuji Terayama, et al.), Axel van der Kraan, Carel Visser, André Volten, Lex Wechgelaar, Lawrence Weiner, Joyce Wieland, and Yokoyama. Catalogue.

> Carel Blotkamp, "Sculpture at Sonsbeek," Studio International (London) 183, no. 936 (September 1971): 70.

> Bruce Kurtz, "Sonsbeek 71: Beyond Lawn and Order," Arts Magazine 46, no. 1 (September-October 1971): 50-52.

> Kasha Linville, "Sonsbeek: Speculations, Impressions," Artforum 10, no. 2 (October 1971): 54-61.

ARTE DE SISTEMAS. Centro de Arte y Comunicación, Buenos Aires. July. Organized by Jorge Glusberg. Artists: Vito Acconci, Eleanor Antin, Arakawa, Sue Arrowsmith, David Askevold, Walter Aue, John Baldessari, Manuel Barbadillo, Robert Barry, Otto Beckmann, Luis Benedit, Mel Bochner, Christian Boltanski, Ian Breakwell, Eugen Brikcius, Stuart Brisley, Stanley Brouwn, Donald Burgy, Don Celender, Christo, Jürgen Claus, James Collins, Agnes Denes, Mirtha Dermisache, Antonio Dias, Geniy Dignac, Gregorio Dujovny, David Dye, Stano Filko, Barry Flanagan, Terry Fox, Herbert Franke, Ken Friedman, Hamish Fulton, Nicolás García Uriburu, Jochen Gerz, Gilbert & George, Carlos Ginzburg, Jorge González Mir, Dan Graham, Víctor Grippo, Klaus Groh, Hans Haacke, Olaf Hanel, Rafael Hastings, Douglas Huebler, Peter Hutchinson, Alain Jacquet, Richards Jarden, Allan Kaprow, On Kawara, Michael Kirby, Alain Kirili, Dusan Klimes, J. H. Kocman, Joseph Kosuth, Uzi Kotler, Christine Kozlov, Alexis Rafael Krasilovsky, Josef Kroutvor, Peter Kuttner, David Lamelas, John Latham, Auro Lecci, Les Levine, Richard Long, Lea Lublin, Jorge de Luján Gutiérrez, Mario Mariño, Vicente Marotta, Charles Mattox, Mario Merz, Mauricio Nannucci, Georg Nees, Dennis Oppenheim, Marie Orensanz, Luis Pazos, Alberto Pellegrino, Alfredo Portillos, Juan Pablo Renzi, Dorothea Rockburne, Juan Carlos Romero, Edward Ruscha, Bernardo Salcedo, Jean-Michel Sanejouand, Richard Serra, Petr Stembera, Clorindo Testa, Antonio Trotta, Timm Ulrichs, Franco Vaccari, Jiri Valoch, John Van Saun, Bernar Venet, Edgardo Antonio Vigo, Lawrence Weiner, Ian Wilson, Robert Wittmann, William Woodrow, and Gilberto Zorio. Catalogue.

Dore Ashton, "New York Commentary: Abracadabrizing Art," Studio International (London) 183, no. 940 (January 1972): 38-39.

PERSONA. International Theatre Festival, Belgrade. 10 September. Organized by Achille Bonito Oliva. Artists: Alighiero e Boetti, Pier Paolo Calzolari, Gino De Dominicis, Luciano Fabro, Mimmo Germanà, Jannis Kounellis, Mario Merz, Giulio Paolini, Giuseppe Penone, Vettor Pisani, Michelangelo Pistoletto, and Emilio Prini. Catalogue.

SEPTIÈME BIENNALE DE PARIS. Parc Floral de Paris. 24 September-1 November. "Concept" section organized by Nathalie Aubergé, Catherine Millet, and Alfred Pacquement. Artists: Art & Language (Terry Atkinson, David Bainbridge, Michael Baldwin, and Harold Hurrell), Robert Barry, Stig Brøgger, Victor Burgin, Ian Burn, J. Charlier and Cl. Delfosse (Bernd Lohaus, Guy Mees, and Panamarenko), James Collins, Roger Cutforth, Hanne Darboven, Braco Dimitrijević, Group/E (Čedomir Drča, Vladmir Kopicl, Ana Raković, and Misa Zivanović), Dan Graham, Ed Herring, Group KOD (Slavko Bogdanovic, Miroslav Mandic, Mirko Radojčić, Slobodan Tisma, and Pedja Vranešević), Joseph Kosuth, Christine Kozlov, David Lamelas, Group OHO (Milenko Matanović, David Nez, Marko Pogačnik, and Andraž Šalamun), Paul Ostrow, Giulio Paolini, Philip Pilkington, Adrian Piper, Emilio Prini, Mel Ramsden, Groupe Le Retraite Tihomir Simcic (Slovodan Dimitrijević and Goran Trbuljak), David Rushton, and Bernar Venet. "Film" section organized by Alfred Pacquement. Artists: Vito Acconci, Christian Boltanski, Achille Bonito Oliva, Robert Breer, K. P. Brehmer, Gino De Dominicis, Serban Epure, Mimmo Germanà, Dan Graham, Nancy Graves, K. H. Hödicke, Lee Jaffe, Jannis Kounellis, David Lamelas, Jean Le Gac, Bruce Nauman, Dennis Oppenheim, Vettor Pisani, Sarkis, Richard Serra, Keith Sonnier, Peter Stampfli, and Lawrence Weiner, as well as the films *Land Art* and *Identifications*, produced by Gerry Schum. Catalogue.

Gilbert Gatellier, "L'art conceptuel," Opus International (Paris), no. 28 (November 1971): 50.

Alfred Pacquement, "L'art conceptuel," Connaissance des arts (Paris), no. 236 (October 1971): 100-104.

Ellen Schwartz, "Paris in September," Art International 15, no. 9 (20 November 1971): 63-64.

Virginia Whiles-Serreau, "Paris Biennale," Studio International (London) 182, no. 939 (December 1971): 256.

ARTE CONCETTUALE. Galleria Daniel Templon, Milan. October. Artists: Art & Language (Terry Atkinson, David Bainbridge, Michael Baldwin, and Harold Hurrell), Victor Burgin, Ian Burn, Joseph Kosuth, Mel Ramsden, and Bernar Venet.

PROSPECT 71: PROJECTION. Städtische Kunsthalle, Düsseldorf. 8-17 October. Organized by Konrad Fischer, Jürgen Harten, and Hans Strelow. Traveled as "Projektion: Udstilling på Louisiana" to Louisiana Museum, Humlebaek, Denmark, 22 January-14 February 1972. Artists: Vito Acconci, Bas Jan Ader, John Baldessari, Robert Barry, Bernd and Hilla Becher, Joseph Beuys, Claus Böhmler, Christian Boltanski, Ian Breakwell, K. P. Brehmer, Stig Brøgger, Marcel Broodthaers, Stanley Brouwn, Victor Burgin, John Chamberlain, Chuck Close, Roger Cutforth, Hanne Darboven, Gino De Dominicis, Walter de Maria, Jan Dibbets, Ger van Elk, Barry Flanagan, Terry Fox, Hollis Frampton, Howard Fried, Hamish Fulton, Gilbert & George, Dan Graham, Nancy Graves, Hans Haacke, David Hall, Richard Hamilton, Michael Heizer, John Hilliard, K. H. Hödicke, Robert Huot, Lee Jaffee, Wolf Knoebel, Ferdinand Kriwet, David Lamelas, John Latham, Barry Le Va, Les Levine, Bruce McLean, Mario Merz, Tony Morgan, Robert Morris, Bruce Nauman, Claes Oldenburg, Dennis Oppenheim, A. R. Penck, Marinella Pirelli Lotte, Brigid Polk, Sigmar Polke, Carl Frederik Reutersward, Gerhard Richter, Klaus Rinke, Peter Roehr, Charles Ross, Ulrich Rückriem, Salvo, Richard Serra, Robert Smithson, Michael Snow, Keith Sonnier, Petr Stembera, David Tremlett, Günter Uecker, Ben Vautier, Wolf Vostell, Franz Erhard Walther, Andy Warhol, William Wegman, and Lawrence Weiner. Catalogue.

Georg Jappe, "Projection: The New Trend at Prospect 71," Studio International (London) 182, no. 939 (December 1971): 258-259.

John Anthony Thwaites, "Cologne," Art and Artists (London) 6, no. 10 (January 1972): 52-53.

CHANGING TERMS. Museum School Gallery, Museum of Fine Arts, Boston. 3 December-14 January 1972. Artists: Mel Bochner, Rosemarie Castoro, Elizabeth Clark, Eva Hesse, Sol LeWitt, Gordon Matta-Clark, Dorothea Rockburne, Fred Sandback, Christopher Sproat, Marjorie Strider, Jon Swan, and Lawrence Weiner. Catalogue.

287

Daniel Buren
INSIDE (CENTER OF GUGGENHEIM), 1971
Acrylic on cloth. 65 ft. 7 1/2 in. x 29 ft. 9 3/4 in. (20 x 9.1 m).
Collection the artist. Photo/souvenir installed at the Solomon
R. Guggenheim Museum for one day before the opening of the
"Guggenheim International Exhibition," 1971.

"KONZEPT"-KUNST. Kunstmuseum, Basel. 18 March-23 April. Organized by Konrad Fischer. Artists: Art & Language, John Baldessari, Robert Barry, Mel Bochner, Stanley Brouwn, Daniel Buren, Victor Burgin, Hanne Darboven, Jan Dibbets, Gilbert & George, Hans Haacke, Douglas Huebler, On Kawara, and Lawrence Weiner. Catalogue.

DAS KONZEPT IST DIE FORM. Westfälischer Kunstverein, Münster. 25 March. Artists include: Robert Barry, Stanley Brouwn, Daniel Buren, Hanne Darboven, Jan Dibbets, Gilbert & George, Douglas Huebler, Joseph Kosuth, Sol LeWitt, Emilio Prini, Lawrence Weiner, and Ian Wilson.

DE EUROPA. John Weber Gallery, New York. 29 April-24 May. Artists: Giovanni Anselmo, Art & Language (Terry Atkinson, David Bainbridge, Michael Baldwin, and Harold Hurrell), Alighiero e Boetti, Daniel Buren, Hanne Darboven, Jan Dibbets, Hamish Fulton, Richard Long, Mario Merz, Giulio Paolini, Reiner Ruthenbeck, Salvo, and Gilberto Zorio. Catalogue.

ENCUENTROS 1972 PAMPLONA. Museo de Navarro, Pamplona, Spain, and other locations. 26 June-3 July. Organized by Luis de Pablo and José Luis Alexanco. Artists include: Vito Acconci, Art & Language, John Baldessari, Robert Barry, Mel Bochner, Victor Burgin, Ian Burn, Jan Dibbets, On Kawara, Joseph Kosuth, Richard Long, Bruce Nauman, Dennis Oppenheim, Mel Ramsden, Edward Ruscha, Robert Smithson, and Lawrence Weiner. Catalogue.

DOCUMENTA 5: BEFRAGUNG DER REALITÄT: BILDWELTEN HEUTE. Neue Galerie and Museum Fridericianum, Kassel. 30 June-8 October. "Idee" section organized by Konrad Fischer and Klaus Honnef. Artists: Vincenzo Agnetti, Art & Language (Terry Atkinson, David Bainbridge, Michael Baldwin, Ian Burn, Harold Hurrell, Joseph Kosuth, and Mel Ramsden), John Baldessari, Robert Barry, Bernd and Hilla Becher, Mel Bochner, Stanley Brouwn, Daniel Buren, Victor Burgin, Hanne Darboven, Jan Dibbets, Hamish Fulton, Michael Harvey, Douglas Huebler, Wolf Knoebel, Sol LeWitt, Richard Long, Robert Mangold, Brice Marden, Agnes Martin, Blinky Palermo, Peter Roehr, Allen Ruppersberg, Edward Ruscha, Robert Ryman, David Tremlett, Richard Tuttle, William Wegman, and Lawrence Weiner. Catalogue.

> Lawrence Alloway, "'Reality': Ideology at D5," Artforum 11, no. 2 (October 1972): 30-36.
>
> Lizzie Borden, "Cosmologies," Artforum 11, no. 2 (October 1972): 45-50.
>
> Bruce Kurtz, "Documenta 5: A Critical Preview," Arts Magazine 46, no. 8 (Summer 1972): 30-43.

THE NEW ART. Hayward Gallery, London. 17 August-24 September. Organized by Anne Seymour. Artists: Keith Arnatt, Art & Language, Victor Burgin, Michael Craig-Martin, David Dye, Barry Flanagan, Hamish Fulton, Gilbert & George, John Hilliard, Richard Long, Keith Milow, Gerald Newman, John Stezaker, and David Tremlett. Catalogue.

> Rosetta Brooks, "The New Art," Studio International (London) 184, no. 948 (October 1972): 152-153.
>
> William Feaver, "London Letter: Summer," Art International 16, no. 9 (November 1972): 38-39.
>
> R. H. Fuchs, "More on 'The New Art,'" Studio International (London) 184, no. 949 (November 1972): 194-195.
>
> Robert Melville, "Making It New," The Architectural Review (London) 152, no. 908 (October 1972): 247-248.

BOOK AS ARTWORK 1960/72. Nigel Greenwood, London. 20 September-14 October. Organized by Germano Celant. Artists include: Vito Acconci, Vincenzo Agnetti, Carl Andre, Giovanni Anselmo, Terry Atkinson and Michael Baldwin, David Bainbridge, John Baldessari, Robert Barry, Gianfranco Baruchello, Bernd and Hilla Becher, Joseph Beuys, E. Blackwell, J. Blake, Mel Bochner, Derek Boshier, Mark Boyle, George Brecht, Stig Brøgger, Marcel Broodthaers, Stanley Brouwn, Daniel Buren, Victor Burgin, Donald Burgy, Ian Burn, James Lee Byars, John Cage, A. Carlin, José Luis Castillejo, Giuseppe Chiari, James Collins, Philip Corner, Claudio Costa, Giancarlo Croce, Merce Cunningham, Roger Cutforth, Hanne Darboven, Walter de Maria, Jan Dibbets, Ger van Elk, G. Fabbris, Gerald Ferguson, Robert Filliou, Joel Fisher, Fluxus, Henry Flynt, Simone Forti, Hamish Fulton, Gilbert & George, Dan Graham, Robert Graham, S. Greco, Richard Hamilton, Michael Harvey, G. Hemsworth, J. Hidalgo, Dick Higgins, Douglas Huebler, Harold Hurrell, Ray Johnson, Stephen J. Kaltenbach, Allan Kaprow, Alison Knowles, Joseph Kosuth, David Lamelas, K. Lang, John Latham, Bob Law, Sol LeWitt, K. Lole, Richard Long, M. Maloney, Piero Manzoni, Walter Marchetti, Bruce McLean, Mario Merz, Robert Morris, Bruce Nauman, N. E. Thing Co., Claes Oldenburg, Yoko Ono, Dennis Oppenheim, Nam June Paik, Eduardo Paolozzi, Giulio Paolini, Giuseppe Penone, Tom Phillips, Philip Pilkington, Michelangelo Pistoletto, Emilio Prini, Mel Ramsden, Peter Roehr, Diter Rot, Allen Ruppersberg, Edward Ruscha, David Rushton, P. Smith, Keith Sonnier, G. Spiller, Daniel Spoerri, Klaus Staeck, John Stezaker, Athena Tacha, Gerard Titus-Carmel, Richard Tuttle, Ben Vautier, Bernar Venet, Franz Erhard Walther, Andy Warhol, Lawrence Weiner, Emmett Williams, La Monte Young, and Michele Zazeela. Catalogue.

ACTUALITÉ D'UN BILAN. Galerie Yvon Lambert, Paris. October. Organized by Michel Claura. Artists: Carl Andre, Arakawa, David Askevold, Robert Barry, Bill Beckley, Marcel Broodthaers, Daniel Buren, Christo, Daniel Dezeuze, Jan Dibbets, Hamish Fulton, Douglas Huebler, On Kawara, Edward Kienholz, David Lamelas, Sol LeWitt, Richard Long, Robert Mangold, Brice Marden, Dennis Oppenheim, Edda Renouf, François Ristori, Robert Ryman, Salvo, Fred Sandback, Niele Toroni, Richard Tuttle, Cy Twombly, and Lawrence Weiner. Catalogue.

ARTISTS BOOKS. Moore College of Art, Philadelphia. 23 March-20 April. Traveled to University Art Museum, University of California, Berkeley, 16 January-24 February 1974. Organized by Dianne Perry Vanderlip. Artists: Bas Jan Ader, Harry Anderson, Carl Andre, Karl Ardo, Robert Arneson, Dana Atchley, Terry Atkinson, Dottie Attie, John Baldessari, Michael Baldwin, Robert Barry, Bernd and Hilla Becher, Larry Becker, John Benson, Ted Berrigan, Mel Bochner, Victor Bockris, Joe Brainard, George Brecht, A. A. Bronson, Stanley Brouwn, Kathan Brown, Robert Delford Brown, Robert E. Brown, Donald Burgy, James Lee Byars, John Cage, Luis Camnitzer, Eugenio Carmi, Neke Carson, Don Celender, Tom Clark, Fellows of C/one, Philip Corner, Gerald Crimmins, Merce Cunningham, Lucio DelPezzo, Jan Dibbets, Eleanor Dickinson, Jim Dine, Peter Downsbrough, Fred Escher, Sorel Etrog, Charles Fahlen, John Fawcett, Eugene Feldman, Hans-Peter Feldmann, Lynn Fernald, Robert Filliou, Ian Hamilton Finlay, Hugh Fox, Walter Gabrielson, Gilbert & George, Andrew Ginzel, David Gray, Derrick Greaves, Art Green, Scott Grieger, Mimi Gross, Red Grooms, Melissa Gurdus, Ira Joel Haber, Marcia Hafif, Richard Hamilton, Al Hansen, Robert Heinecken, Dick Higgins, David Hockney, Nelson Howe, Eleanor Hubbard, Lydia Hunn, Gordon Huntly, Ray Johnson, Tim Johnson, Ynez Johnston, Lynda S. Kahn, Allan Kaprow, William Katz, Alison Knowles, Joseph Kosuth, Jack Krueger, David Lamelas, Ellen Lanyon, Leandro, Seaver W. Leslie, Sol LeWitt, Jackson MacLow, Gerard Malanga, Cynthia Marsh, Gordon Matta-Clark, Mario Merz, Michael Metz, Gilbert Miller, Bruce Nauman, James Neitt, Gladys Nillson, Richard Nonas, Arthur Okamura, Claes Oldenburg, Dennis O'Leary, Ron Padgett, Eduardo Paolozzi, Mike Parr, Tom Phillips, Brigid Polk, Bern Porter, Liliana Porter, Arnulf Rainer, Steve Reich, Suellen Rocca, Diter Rot, Allen Ruppersberg, Edward Ruscha, Lucas Samaras, Aram Saroyan, Alfonse Schilling, Willoughby Sharp, Seth Siegelaub, Alison Sky, Alan Sondheim, John Sparks, Daniel Spoerri, Saul Steinberg, Antonio Tàpies, Wayne Thiebaud, Walasse Ting, Richard O. Tyler, Ian Tyson, Van Schley, Lester Van Winkle, William Vazan, Bernar Venet, Wolf Vostell, Keith Waldrop, Tom Weatherly, Lawrence Weiner, Robert Whitman, William T. Wiley, Emmett Williams, Jonathan Williams, Karl Wirsum, Viky Wulff, Andrew Wylie, and Terry Yoshida. Catalogue.

BILDER — OBJEKTE — FILME — KONZEPTE. Städtische Galerie im Lenbachhaus, Munich. 3 April-13 May. Artists: Carl Andre, Georg Baselitz, Joseph Beuys, Claus Böhmler, Marcel Broodthaers, Daniel Buren, James Lee Byars, Ron Cooper, Hanne Darboven, Walter de Maria, Franz Eggenschwiler, Dan Flavin, Gilbert & George, Erwin Heerich, Douglas Huebler, Jörg Immendorff, On Kawara, Imi W. Knoebel, Bruce Nauman, Claes Oldenburg, Blinky Palermo, Panamarenko, A. R. Penck, Sigmar Polke, Gerhard Richter, Diter Rot, Robert Ryman, Richard Tuttle, Lawrence Weiner, and Stefan Wewerka. Catalogue.

STORY. John Gibson Gallery, New York. 7 April-3 May. Artists: David Askevold, John Baldessari, Bill Beckley, Ger van Elk, Peter Hutchinson, Jean Le Gac, Bernadette Mayer, Italo Scanga, David Tremlett, William Wegman, and Roger Welch.

James Collins, "Story," Artforum 12, no. 1 (September 1973): 83-85.

c. 7,500. Gallery A-402, California Institute of the Arts, Valencia. 14-18 May. Traveled to Wadsworth Atheneum, Hartford, 19 June-31 July; Moore College of Art, Philadelphia, 21 September-19 October; Walker Art Center, Minneapolis, 16 November-16 December; Institute of Contemporary Art, Boston; Smith College Museum of Art, Northampton, Massachusetts, 17 January-10 February 1974; Garage or 48 Earlham Street, London, 8-26 April 1974; A.I.R. Gallery, New York, 1-15 June 1974; And/Or, Seattle, 17 September-6 October 1974. Organized by Lucy R. Lippard in response to belief that there were no women Conceptual artists. Artists: Renate Altenrath, Laurie Anderson, Eleanor Antin, Jacki Apple, Alice Aycock, Jennifer Bartlett, Hanne Darboven, Agnes Denes, Doree Dunlap, Nancy Holt, Poppy Johnson, Nancy Kitchel, Christine Kozlov, Suzanne Kuffler, Pat Lasch, Bernadette Mayer, Christiane Möbus, Rita Myers, Renee Nahum, N. E. Thing Co. (Ingrid Baxter), Ulrike Nolden, Adrian Piper, Judith Stein, Athena Tacha, Mierle Laderman Ukeles, and Martha Wilson.

Florence Berkman, "The Idea is All, but Is It Enough?," Hartford Sunday Times, 24 January 1973.

Su Braden, "Politics in Art," Studio International (London) 187, no. 967 (June 1974): 272-274.

Nessa Foreman, "Do Women Make Conceptual Art?" The Philadelphia Inquirer, 30 September 1973.

Peter Frank, "Philadelphia: Focus on the Contemporary," Art News 72, no. 9 (November 1973).

Jolene Goldenthal, "Idea Is All in 'C. 7500' Show, Hartford Current, 24 June 1973.

Roszika Parker, "Art of Course Has No Sex, but Artists Do," Spare Rib (London) 25 (July 1974): 34-35.

Lee Sheridan, "Conceptual Art Discussed," Daily News (Springfield, Massachusetts), 6 February 1974.

DOKUMENTI O POST-OBJEKTNIM POJAVAMA U JUGOSLOVENSKOJ UMETNOSTI, 1968-1973/DOCUMENTS OF POST-OBJECT TRENDS IN YUGOSLAV ART, 1968-1973. Salon Muzeja Savremene Umetnosti/Gallery of the Museum of Modern Art, Belgrade. June-July. Artists: Ekipa A³ (Marina Abramović, Rista Banić, Radomir Damnjanović-Damnjan, Mladen Jevdović, Slobodan Milivojević-Era, Zoran Popović, Slavko Timotjević, Dragoljub Todosijević-Raša, Gergelj Urkom, and Jugoslav Vlahović), Group Bosch + Bosch (Laszlo Kerekes, Slavko Matković, Laszlo Szalma, and Balint Szombathy), Group KOD (Čedomir Drča, Vladimir Kopicl, Mirko Radojičić, Ana Raković, and Peda Vranešević), Group OHO (Boris Bućan, Slobodan Dimitrijević-Braco, Nuša Dragan, Srečo Dragan, Sanja Iveković, Jagoda Kaloper, Dalibor Martinis, Milenko Matanović, David Nez, Marko Pogačnik, Andraž Šalamun, Tomaž Šalamun, Davor Tomičić, Goran Trbuljak, and Gorki Žuvela). Catalogue.

DEURLE 11/7/73. Museum Dhont-Dhaernens, Deurle, Belgium. 11 July-8 August. Organized by Galerie MTL, Brussels. Artists: Carl Andre, John Baldessari, Robert Barry, Marcel Broodthaers, Victor Burgin, Ian Burn and Mel Ramsden, André Cadere, Dan Graham, Douglas Huebler, Joseph Kosuth, Sol LeWitt, Robert Ryman, Joost A. Romeu, Lawrence Weiner, and Ian Wilson. Catalogue.

100 AVANT-GARDE PUBLICATIONS. Galerie Paul Maenz, Brussels. 13-29 July 1973. Artists: Carl Andre, Art & Language, Robert Barry, Mark Boyle, Marcel Broodthaers, Stanley Brouwn, Daniel Buren, Hanne Darboven, Jan Dibbets, Hans-Peter Feldmann, Gilbert & George, Hans Haacke, Douglas Huebler, Donald Judd, Joseph Kosuth, Sol LeWitt, Richard Long, Robert Morris, Bruce Nauman, Giulio Paolini, Giuseppe Penone, Anne and Patrick Poirier, Klaus Rinke, Peter Roehr, Ulrich Rückriem, Reiner Ruthenbeck, Edward Ruscha, Salvo, Keith Sonnier, Niele Toroni, Carel Visser, Franz Erhard Walther, and Lawrence Weiner.

FESTIVAL D'AUTOMNE À PARIS: ASPECTS DE L'ART ACTUEL. Galerie Sonnabend au Musée Galliéra, Paris. 14 September-25 October. Artists: Vito Acconci, John Baldessari, Bernd and Hilla Becher, Mel Bochner, Christian Boltanski, Trisha Brown, Pier Paolo Calzolari, Jim Dine, Joel Fisher, Simone Forti, Gilbert & George, Philip Glass, Hisashika, Joan Jonas, Alain Kirili, Jannis Kounellis, Robert Morris, Bruce Nauman, Dennis Oppenheim, Charlemagne Palestine, Giulio Paolini, Robert Peterson, Anne and Patrick Poirier, Robert Rauschenberg, James Rosenquist, Sarkis, Richard Serra, David Tremlett, William Wegman, and Robert Whitman. Catalogue.

CONTEMPORANEA. Parcheggio di Villa Borghese, Rome. November-February 1974. Organized by Incontri Internazionali d'Arte, Rome. "Art" section organized by Achille Bonito Oliva. Artists: Vito Acconci, Vincenzo Agnetti, Carl Andre, Giovanni Anselmo, Arman, Art & Language, John Baldessari, Robert Barry, Lothar Baumgarten, Bernd and Hilla Becher, Joseph Beuys, Mel Bochner, Alighiero e Boetti, George Brecht, Marcel Broodthaers, Daniel Buren, Victor Burgin, Fred Cane, Castellani, Giuseppe Chiari, Christo, Hanne Darboven, Gino De Dominicis, Walter de Maria, Jan Dibbets, Jim Dine, Luciano Fabro, Robert Filliou, Dan Flavin, Hamish Fulton, Gilbert & George, Giorgio Griffa, Hans Haacke, Richard Hamilton, Michael Heizer, Douglas Huebler, Jasper Johns, Donald Judd, Allan Kaprow, On Kawara, Ellsworth Kelly, Yves Klein, Joseph Kosuth, Jannis Kounellis, Sol LeWitt, Roy Lichtenstein, Richard Long, Lo Savio, Urs Lüthi, George Maciunas, Robert Mangold, Piero Manzoni, Brice Marden, Martin, Mario Merz, Robert Morris, Bruce Nauman, Barnett Newman, Kenneth Noland, Claes Oldenburg, Roman Opalka, Blinky Palermo, Giulio Paolini, Pino Pascali, Vettor Pisani, Michelangelo Pistoletto, Emilio Prini, Robert Rauschenberg, Ad Reinhardt, Gerhard Richter, Dorothea Rockburne, James Rosenquist, Rotella, Robert Ryman, Mario Schifano, George Segal, Richard Serra, Simonetti, Keith Sonnier, Daniel Spoerri, Frank Stella, Testa, Jean Tinguely, Richard Tuttle, Cy Twombly, Ben Vautier, Wolf Vostell, Andy Warhol, Robert Watts, Lawrence Weiner, Robert Whitman, and Ian Wilson. "Artists' books" section organized by Michel Claura and Yvon Lambert. Artists: Vito Acconci, Vincenzo Agnetti, Carl Andre, Laurie Anderson, Giovanni Anselmo, Arakawa, Terry Atkinson and Michael Baldwin, Bruce Babbitt, David Bainbridge, Michael Baldwin, Robert Barry, Gianfranco Baruchello, Bernd and Hilla Becher, Gottfried Bechtold, Sirio Bellucci, Duccio Berti, Jean Pierro Bertrand, Ida Biard, J. Blake, Mel Bochner, Christian Boltanski, Derek Boshier, Mark Boyle, Angelo Bozzolla, George Brecht, Stanley Brouwn, Daniel Buren, Stig Brøgger, Marcel Broodthaers, Donald Burgy, Ian Burn, James Lee Byars, Andre Cadere, A. Carlin and K. Lang, José Luis Castillejo, Tullio Catalano, Sandro Chia, Giuseppe Chiari, Claudio Cintoli, Jean Clareboudt, James Collins, Jack Collom, Philip Corner, Claudio Costa, Giancarlo Croce, Roger Cutforth, Werner Cuvelier, Hanne Darboven, Ferruccio De Filippi, Shilla Decker Dernd, Jan Dibbets, Erik Dietmann, Peter Downsbrough, Ger van Elk, G. Fabbris and G. Spiller, Hans-Peter Feldmann, Gerald Ferguson, Stano Filko, Robert Filliou, Joel Fisher, Jochen Gerz, Gilbert & George, Zbigniew Gostomski, Dan Graham, Robert Graham, S. Greco, Laura Grisi, Hans Haacke, Richard Hamilton, Michael Harvey, Robert Hebert, Gerard Hemsworth, Juan Hidalgo, Dick Higgins, Hans Rudolph Huber, Douglas Huebler, Harold Hurrell, Emilio Isgrò, Stephen Kaltenbach, Ray Johnson, Tadeusz Kantor, Allan Kaprow, Alain Kirili, Alison Knowles, Joseph Kosuth, Jannis Kounellis, Jaroslaw Kozlowski, David Lamelas, K. Lang, John Latham, Bernt Lauter, Bob Law, Jean Le Gac, Leandro, Sol

LeWitt, Kevin Lole and Peter Smith, Alfonso Lopez Gradoli, Martin Maloney, Piero Manzoni, Walter Marchetti, Francesco Matarrese, Anthony McCall's, Bruce McLean, Mario Merz, Verena Moser, Ian Murray, N. E. Thing Co., Maurizio Nannucci, Bruce Nauman, Gianfranco Notargiacomo, Claes Oldenburg, Yoko Ono, Gina Pane, Giulio Paolini, Eduardo Paolozzi, Luca Patella, Giuseppe Penone, Tom Phillips, Philip Pilkington and David Rushton, Pineau, Bernard Plossu, Anne and Patrick Poirier, Mel Ramsden, Klaus Rinke, Peter Roehr, Diter Rot, Allen Ruppersberg, Edward Ruscha, Salvo, Sarkis, Van Schley, Lievens Somerlinck van Snick, Allan Sondheim, Keith Sonnier, Daniel Spoerri, Klaus Staeck, Judith Stein, John Stezaker, Athena Tacha, Gérard Titus-Carmel, Medina Valcarcel, Ben Vautier, Franz Erhard Walther, Andy Warhol, Lawrence Weiner, Emmet Williams, Steve Willats, Hiroshi Yokoyama, La Monte Young and Marian Zazeela, Michele Zaza, and Valentino Zini. Catalogue.

ITALY TWO: ART AROUND '70. Museum of the Philadephia Civic Center, Philadephia. 2 November-16 December. Artists: Vincenzo Agnetti, Carlo Alfano, Arcelli e Comini, Nanni Balestrini, Gianfranco Baruchello, Carlo Battaglia, Maurizio Benveduti, Bureau for a Preventive Imagination, S.p.A., Pier Paolo Calzolari, Tullio Catalano, Sandro Chia, Claudio Cintoli, Francesco Clemente, Mariateresa Corvino, Paolo Cotani, Giancarlo Croce, Gino De Dominicis, Ferruccio De Filippi, Giuseppe Del Franco, Bruno Di Bello, Diego Esposito, Luciano Fabro, Marco Gastini, Giorgio Griffa, Laura Grisi, Jannis Kounellis, Ketty La Rocca, Sergio Lombardo, Enzo Mari, Plinio Martelli, Eliseo Mattiacci, Fabio Mauri, Mario Merz, Marisa Merz, Maurizio Mochetti, Carmengloria Morales, Gianfranco Notargiacomo, Palamara e Fiorentino, Giulio Paolini, Pino Pascali, Luca Patella, Luca Piffero, Vettor Pisani, Michelangelo Pistoletto, Emilio Prini, Cloti Ricciardi, Remo Salvadori, Aldo Spinelli, Ernesto Tatafiore, Claudio Verna, Michele Zaza, and Valentino Zini. Catalogue.

ARTE CONCEPTUAL FRENTE AL PROBLEMA LATINOAMERICANO. Museo Universitario de Ciencias y Arte, Ciudad Universitaria, Buenos Aires. January-February. Artists: Marcel Alocco, Siah Armajani, Alvaro Barrios, Jacques Bendel, Luis Benedit, Juan Bercetche, Sheila Berkley, Antonio Berni, César Bolaños, Lawry Burgess, Antonio José Caro Lopera, Elda Cerrato, Jaime Davidovich, Guillermo Deisler, Agnes Denes, Ken Friedman, Nicolás García Uriburu, Jochen Gerz, Carlos Ginzburg, Jorge Glusberg, Haroldo González, Jorge González Mir, Víctor Grippo, Klaus Groh, GAAG (Jon Hendricks and Jean Toche), Rafael Hastings, Mariano Hernández Ossorno, Dick Higgins, Fernando Huici, Peter Kennedy and Mike Parr, Michael Kenny, Richard Kostelanetz, Uzi Kotler, Bernardo Krasniansky, Auro Lecci, Francisco Mariotti, Oscar Maxera, Julian Mereutza, Carlos Mills, Victor Mira, Abraham Moles, Ion Muresanu, Maurizio Nannucci, Marie Orensanz, Luis Pazos, Alberto Pellegrino, Alfredo Portillos, Alejandro Puente, Gomersindo Quevado, Osvaldo Romberg, Juan Carlos Romero, Ricardo Roux, Javier Ruiz, Bernado Salcedo, Máximo Soto, Julio Teich, Clorindo Testa, Enrique Torroja, Horts Tress, Jiri Valoch, Constantín Xenabis, Horacio Zàbala. Catalogue.

CARL ANDRE, MARCEL BROODTHAERS, DANIEL BUREN, VICTOR BURGIN, GILBERT & GEORGE, ON KAWARA, RICHARD LONG, GERHARD RICHTER. Palais des Beaux-Arts, Brussels. 9 January-3 February. Organized by Yves Gevaert. Catalogue.

IDEA AND IMAGE IN RECENT ART. The Art Institute of Chicago. 23 March-5 May. Organized by Anne Rorimer. Artists: Vito Acconci, Giovanni Anselmo, John Baldessari, Bernd and Hilla Becher, Joseph Beuys, Mel Bochner, Christian Boltanski, John Cage, Michael Craig-Martin, Hanne Darboven, Jim Dine, Douglas Huebler, Jasper Johns, Edward Kienholz, Joseph Kosuth, Roy Lichtenstein, Robert Morris, Bruce Nauman, Robert Rauschenberg, Andy Warhol, William Wegman, Lawrence Weiner, and William T. Wiley. Catalogue.

DELLA FALSITÀ. Istituto di Storia dell'arte Università di Parma. April. Organized by committee under direction of Arturo Carlo Quintavalle. Artists: Adriano Altamira, Luciano Fabro, Emilio Isgro, Elio Marchegiani, Plinio Martelli, Idetoshi Nagasawa, Ferdinando Tonello, and Antonio Trotto. Catalogue.

KUNST — ÜBER KUNST: WERKE UND THEORIEN: EINE AUSSTELLUNG IN DREI TEILEN. Kunstverein, Cologne. 11 April-26 May. Part 3: "Nach 1965." Organized by Paul Maenz. Artists: Carl Andre, Art & Language (Terry Atkinson, David Bainbridge, Michael Baldwin, Harold Hurrell, Philip Pilkington, and David Rushton), Daniel Buren, Victor Burgin, Ian Burn and Mel Ramsden, Douglas Huebler, Donald Judd, Joseph Kosuth, Sol LeWitt, Robert Morris, Peter Roehr, and Lawrence Weiner. Catalogue.

Barbara Catoir, "Kunst — über Kunst," Das Kunstwerk (Stuttgart) 27, no. 4 (July 1974): 42-43.

ART NOW '74: A CELEBRATION OF THE AMERICAN ARTS. John F. Kennedy Center for the Performing Arts, Washington, D.C. 30 May-16 June. Artists: Vito Acconci, Carl Andre, Arakawa, John Baldessari, Lewis Baltz, Robert Barry, Larry Bell, Lynda Benglis, Robert Breer, Trisha Brown, Harry Callahan, Peter Campus, Christo, Mark Cohen, Douglas Davis, Gene Davis, Willem de Looper, Maya Deren, Juan Downey, William Eggleston, Ed Emshwiller, Rafael Ferrer, Dan Flavin, Laura Foreman and John Watts, Richard Foreman, Terry Fox, Hermine Freed, Lee Friedlander, Frank Gillette, Sam Gilliam, Philip Glass, Joel Glassman, Emmet Gowin, Nancy Graves, Michael Heizer, Jerome Hill, Nancy Holt, Douglas Huebler, Will Insley, Robert Irwin, Ken Jacobs, Joan Jonas, Donald Judd, Beryl Korot, Paul Kos, Joseph Kosuth, Rockne Krebs, Shigeko Kubota, Richard Landry, Barry Le Va, Sol LeWitt, Robert Mangold, Andy Mann, Robert Morris, Ed Moses, Bruce Nauman, Dennis Oppenheim, Nam June Paik, Anthony Ramos, Robert Rauschenberg, Steve Reich, Nancy Rexroth, Ira Schneider, Richard Serra, Paul Sharits, Keith Sonnier, Alan Shields, Stephen Shore, Harry Smith, Keith Smith, Michael Snow, Gary Stephan, Richard Tuttle, Richard Van Buren, Bill Viola, Andy Warhol, William Wegman, Roger Welch, Robert Whitman, William T. Wiley, Robert Wilson, and Garry Winogrand. Catalogue.

KUNST BLEIBT KUNST: PROJEKT '74: ASPEKTE INTERNATIONALER KUNST AM ANFANG DER 70ER JAHRE. Wallraf-Richardtz Museum, Kölnischer Kunstverein, and Kunsthalle, Cologne. 6 July-8 September. Artists include: Vito Acconci, Giovanni Anselmo, Arakawa, David Askevold, Alice Aycock, Robert Barry, Larry Bell, Mel Bochner, Claus Böhmler, Christian Boltanski, Mark Boyle, Marcel Broodthaers, Daniel Buren, Victor Burgin, Hanne Darboven, Jan Dibbets, David Dye, Murray Favro, Hans-Peter Feldmann, Robert Filliou, Terry Fox, Howard Fried, Hamish Fulton, Dan Graham, Gilbert & George, Hans Haacke, Joan Jonas, Joseph Kosuth, Jean Le Gac, Helen Mayer and Newton Harrison, Mario Merz, Bruce Nauman, Dennis Oppenheim, Giulio Paolini, A. R. Penck, Giuseppe Penone, Anne and Patrick Poirier, Gerhard Richter, Klaus Rinke, Ulrich Ruckreim, Reiner Ruthenbeck, H. A. Schult, Alan Sonfist, Timm Ulrichs, Bernar Venet, Lawrence Weiner, Roger Welch, and Gilberto Zorio. Catalogue.

Charles Harrison, "Projekt '74," Studio International (London) 188, no. 969 (September 1974): 102-103.

Klaus Honnef, "Projekt '74: A Colonia," Domus (Milan) 538, no. 9 (September 1974): 41-43.

Lynda Morris, "Projekt '74," Studio International (London) 188, no. 969 (September 1974): 103-104.

Antje Von Graeventiz, "Kunst bleibt Kunst: Projekt '74," Pantheon (Munich) 32, no. 4 (October-December 1974): 413-416.

NARRATIVE ART. Palais des Beaux-Arts, Brussels. 26 September-3 November. Artists: David Askevold, Didier Bay, Bill Beckley, Robert Cumming, Peter Hutchinson, Jean Le Gac, and Roger Welch. Catalogue.

L'ART AU PRESENT. Palais Galliéra, Paris. 2 October-10 November. Organized by Daniel Templon. Artists: Arman, Art & Language (Terry Atkinson and Michael Baldwin), Martin Barré, Victor Burgin, Louis Cane, Marc Devade, Dan Flavin, Giorgio Griffa, Donald Judd, Ellsworth Kelly, Joseph Kosuth, Jean Le Gac, Jacques Martinez, Jean-Michel Meurice, Olivier Mosset, Robert Motherwell, Kenneth Noland, Jules Olitski, Frank Stella, Gérard Titus-Carmel, Andre Valensi, Ben Vautier, and Bernar Venet. Catalogue.

EIGHT CONTEMPORARY ARTISTS. The Museum of Modern Art, New York. 9 October-5 January 1975. Organized by Jennifer Licht. Artists: Vito Acconci, Alighiero e Boetti, Daniel Buren, Hanne Darboven, Jan Dibbets, Robert Hunter, Brice Marden, and Dorothea Rockburne. Catalogue.

Max Kozloff, "Traversing the Field ... 'Eight Contemporary Artists' at MOMA," Artforum 13, no. 4 (December 1974): 44-49.

13 "PROJEKT '74" ARTISTS. Internationaler Kunstmarkt, Cologne. 19-24 October. Organized by Paul Maenz. Artists: Hans Haacke, Joseph Kosuth, Giulio Paolini, Anne and Patrick Poirier, Ulrich Rückriem, and Salvo.

ART AS THOUGHT PROCESS: WORKS BOUGHT FOR THE ARTS COUNCIL BY MICHAEL COMPTON. The Art Gallery, Huddersfield, England. November. Traveled to Serpentine Gallery, London, 14 December-12 January 1975; exhibited in various galleries in Great Britain, 18 January-12 October 1975. Organized by Michael Compton. Artists: Art & Language (Terry Atkinson and Michael Baldwin), Victor Burgin, Judy Clark, Michael Craig-Martin, John Hilliard, Malcolm Hughes, Mark Lancaster, Kenneth Martin, Keith Milow, Tom Phillips, Bridget Riley, Richard Smith, and Stephen Willats. Catalogue.

Tony Del Renzio, "London Exhibition Reviews," Art and Artists (London) 9, no. 12 (March 1975): 42-43.

Peter Fuller, "Art as Thought Process," Connoisseur (New York) 188, no. 757 (March 1975): 242-243.

Peter Smith, "Art as Thought Process," Studio International (London) 189, no. 973 (January-February 1975): 11.

VIDEO ART. Institute of Contemporary Art, University of Pennsylvania, Philadelphia. 17 January-28 February. Traveled to The Contemporary Arts Center, Cincinnati, 22 March-30 May; Museum of Contemporary Art, Chicago, 28 June-31 August; Wadsworth Atheneum, Hartford, 17 September-2 November. Organized by Suzanne Delehanty. Artists: Vito Acconci, Sonia Andrade, Ant Farm (Chip Lord, Hudson Marquez, Doug Michels, and Curtis Schreier), Eleanor Antin, David Askevold, John Baldessari, Lynda Benglis, Jim Byrne, Pier Paolo Calzolari, Colin Campbell, Peter Campus, Giuseppe Chiari, Fernando França Cocchiarale, Andrea Daninos, Douglas Davis, Antonio Dias, Juan Downey, Ed Emshwiller, Valie Export, Terry Fox, Howard Fried, Seiichi Fujii, Anna Bella Geiger, Michael Geissler and Video Audio Medien (Dörte Vötz and Lena Conradt), General Idea (Ron Gabe, Jorge Saia, and Michael Tims), Frank Gillette, Dan Graham, Sakumi Hagiwara, Martha Haslanger, Michael Hayden, K. H. Hödicke, Nancy Holt, Rebecca Horn, Mako Idemitsu, Taka Iimura, Joan Jonas, Allan Kaprow, Nobuhiro Kawanaka, Hakudo Kobayashi, Masao Komura, Beryl Korot and Ira Schneider, Paul Kos, Ernie Kovacs, Shigeko Kubota, Richard Landry, Les Levine, Alvin Lucier, Urs Lüthi, Ivens Olinto Machado, Andy Mann, Toshio Matsumoto, Kyoko Michishita, Robert Morris, Philip Morton, Fujiko Nakaya, Bruce Nauman, Dennis Oppenheim, Jean Otth, Nam June Paik, Giulio Paolini, Ulrike Rosenbach, Reiner Ruthenbeck, Daniel Sandin, Ira Schneider, Eric Siegel, Richard Serra, Nina Sobel, Keith Sonnier, Lisa Steele, Skip Sweeney, Telethon (Billy Adler and John Margolies), Top Value Television (Michael Couzens, Betsy Grigon, Hudson Marquez, Allen Rocher, Michael Shamberg, Tom Weinberg, and Megan William), Steina Vasulka and Woody Vasulka, Bill Viola, Wolf Vostell, Morihiro Wada, Andy Warhol, William Wegman, Peter Weibel, Katsuhiro Yamaguchi, and Keigo Yamamoto. Catalogue.

PAINTING, DRAWING, AND SCULPTURE OF THE '60S AND THE '70S FROM THE DOROTHY AND HERBERT VOGEL COLLECTION. Institute of Contemporary Art, University of Pennsylvania, Philadelphia. 7 October-18 November. Traveled to The Contemporary Arts Center, Cincinnati, 17 December-15 February 1976. Organized by Suzanne Delehanty. Artists: Vito Acconci, Carl Andre, Stephan Antonakos, Richard Artschwager, Jo Baer, Jared Bark, Robert Barry, Bernd and Hilla Becher, Lynda Benglis, Jake Berthot, Joseph Beuys, James Bishop, Ronald Bladen, Mel Bochner, William Bollinger, Bower, Daniel Buren, Peter Campus, John Chamberlain, Christo, Michael Clark, Chuck Close, Cooke, Hanne Darboven, Davis, Ad Dekkers, Agnes Denes, Jan Dibbets, Mark di Suvero, Benni Efrat, Erdman, Paul Feeley, Janet Fish, Dan Flavin, Richard Francisco, Michael Goldberg, Ronald Gorchov, Dan Graham, Nancy Graves, Robert Grosvenor, Eva Hesse, Douglas Huebler, Ralph Humphrey, Peter Hutchinson, Will Insley, Patrick Ireland, Jensen, Donald Judd, Stephen J. Kaltenbach, Joseph Kosuth, Sol LeWitt, Robert Lobe, Richard Long, Robert Mangold, Sylvia Plimack Mangold, Andy Mann, Brice Marden, Miralda, Robert Morris, Robert Motherwell, Forrest Myers, Bruce Nauman, Richard Nonas, David Novros, Claes Oldenburg, Dennis Oppenheim, Nam June Paik, Parker, Betty Parsons, Philip Pearlstein, Pearson, Pettibone, Picard, Howardena Pindell, Larry Poons, Porter, Lucio Pozzi, Rabinowitch, Edda Renouf, Judy Rifka, Klaus Rinke, Dorothea Rockburne, Rosenthal, Diter Rot, Robert Ryman, Salt, Lucas Samaras, Alan Saret, Richard Serra, Joel Shapiro, Shields, Robert Smithson, Eve Sonneman, Stanley, Gary Stephan, Richard Tuttle, Vallador, Richard Van Buren, Ruth Vollmer, Andy Warhol, Lawrence Weiner, Jack Youngerman, and Mario Yrissary. Catalogue.

ANTI-OBJECT ART. *Triquarterly* (Evanston, Illinois), no. 32 (Winter 1975). Organized by Lawrence Levy and John Perreault. Artists: Vito Acconci, Eleanor Antin, Alice Aycock, John Baldessari, Robert Barry, Phil Berkman, Joseph Beuys, Daniel Buren, Scott Burton, Christo, Michael Crane, Agnes Denes, Rafael Ferrer, Gilbert & George, Hans Haacke, Ira Joel Haber, Nancy Holt, Douglas Huebler, Will Insley, Michael Kirby, Joseph Kosuth, Les Levine, Sol LeWitt, Richard Long, Brenda Miller, John Perreault, Adrian Piper, Gregg Powell, A. Ribé, Richard Serra, Robert Smithson, Marjorie Strider, Jan Sullivan, Lawrence Weiner, LeAnn Bartok Wilchusky, and Stephen Zaima. Exhibition existed only as a publication.

"Artists and Photographs." Multiples Gallery, New York. 28 March–5 April 1969.

A

Actualité d'un bilan. Exh. cat. Paris: Galerie Yvon Lambert, 1972. Acknowledgments and preface by Yvon Lambert and essay by Michel Claura.

Air Art. Exh. cat. Philadelphia: Arts Council, YM/YWHA, 1968. Acknowledgments by Willoughby Sharp, Peter Selz, and Evar Miller; introduction by Mrs. William Wolgin, William A. Leonard, and Gary E. Whitbeck; essay by Sharp; artists' biographies and bibliographies.

Alloway, Lawrence. "Artists as Writers, Part Two: The Realm of Language." *Artforum* 12, no. 8 (April 1974): 30-31.

————. "The Expanding and Disappearing Work of Art: Notes on Changing American Esthetics." *Auction* (New York) 3, no. 2 (October 1969): 34-37. Reprint of a lecture given on 7 December 1968 at Parke-Bernet Galleries, New York.

————. "Network: The Art World Described as a System." *Artforum* 11, no. 1 (September 1972): 28-32.

Altamira, Adriano. "Concettuali giapponesi." *Notiziario arte contemporanea* (Rome), no. 12 (December 1972): 25-26.

Altshuler, Bruce J. "Dematerialization: The Voice of the Sixties: January 5-31, 1969, 44 East 52nd Street, New York; When Attitudes Become Form: Works-Processes-Concepts-Situations-Information (Live in Your Head), Kunsthalle Bern, March 22-April 27, 1969." In *The Avant-Garde in Exhibition: New Art in the Twentieth Century*, 236-255. New York: Harry N. Abrams, 1994.

American Narrative/Story Art: 1967-1977. Exh. cat. Houston: Contemporary Arts Museum, 1978. Preface by James Harithas; introduction by Paul Schimmel; essays by Alan Sondheim and Marc Freidus; artists' biographies; bibliography; list of artists' books and recordings.

Analytical Art, no. 1 (July 1971). Introduction by Philip Pilkington and David Rushton; essays by Rushton, Pilkington, Kevin Lole, Terry Atkinson and Michael Baldwin, Graham Howard, Ian Burn and Mel Ramsden, Peter Smith, and Christopher Willsmore.

Analytical Art, no. 2 (June 1972). Introduction by Philip Pilkington and David Rushton; essays by Kevin Lole, Peter Smith, I. Johnson, and P. Tate.

Anti-Illusion: Procedures/Materials. Exh. cat. New York: Whitney Museum of American Art, 1969. Essays by James Monte and Marcia Tucker; bibliography; artists' bibliographies and exhibition chronologies.

Antin, David. "Talking at Pomona." *Artforum* 11, no. 1 (September 1972): 38-47.

Arnaudet, Didier. "Art conceptuel: Le tigre dans la bibliothèque." *Colóquio artes* (Lisbon) 31, no. 81 (June 1989): 50-53. Exh. review of "Art conceptuel I."

Art as Thought Process: Works Bought for the Arts Council by Michael Compton. Exh. cat. London: Arts Council of Great Britain, 1974. Preface by Norbert Lynton; essay by Michael Compton; artists' biographies.

L'art au présent. Exh. cat. Paris: Galerie Daniel Templon in association with Palais Galliéra, 1974. Artists' exhibition chronologies.

Art by Telephone. Exh. cat. Chicago: Museum of Contemporary Art, 1969. LP-record with jacket text by Jan van der Marck.

"L'art conceptuel." *VH 101* (Paris), no. 3 (Autumn 1970): 1-53. Essay by Catherine Millet and artists' projects by Robert Barry, Douglas Huebler, David Lamelas, Victor Burgin, Lawrence Weiner, Alain Kirili, Mel Bochner, and Joseph Kosuth.

Art conceptuel, formes conceptuelles/Conceptual Art, Conceptual Forms. Exh. cat. Paris: Galerie 1900△2000 and Galerie de Poche, 1990. Acknowledgments by Marcel Fleiss and Christian Schlatter; essay by Schlatter; texts by the artists and various authors.

Art conceptuel I. Exh. cat. Bordeaux: Centre d'art plastique contemporain, Musée d'art contemporain, 1988. Essays by Michel Bourel, Jean-Marc Poinsot, Robert C. Morgan, Lucy R. Lippard, and Benjamin H. D. Buchloh; interviews by Jeanne Siegel and Arthur R. Rose [pseud.]; exhibition chronology; bibliography.

L'art conceptuel, une perspective. Exh. cat. Paris: Musée d'art moderne de la Ville de Paris, 1989. Preface by Suzanne Pagé; essays by Claude Gintz, Benjamin H. D. Buchloh, Charles Harrison, Gabriele Guercio, Seth Siegelaub, and Robert C. Morgan; reprinted texts by Joseph Kosuth and Daniel Buren; exhibition chronology; bibliography.

Art in the Mind. Exh. cat. Oberlin, Ohio: Allen Memorial Art Museum, Oberlin College, 1970. Introduction by Athena Tacha Spear.

Art in Process IV. Exh. cat. New York: Finch College Museum of Art, 1969. Foreword and acknowledgments by Elayne H. Varian; artists' statements.

Art in Process: The Visual Development of a Structure. Exh. cat. New York: Finch College Museum of Art, 1966. Foreword by Elayne H. Varian; artists' statements.

Art in Series. Exh. cat. New York: Finch College Museum of Art, 1968. Foreword by Elayne H. Varian.

Art Now '74: A Celebration of the American Arts. Exh. cat. Washington, D.C.: John F. Kennedy Center for the Performing Arts in association with Artrend Foundation, 1974.

Forewords by Jocelyn Kress and by Henry T. Hopkins and Maurice Tuchman; texts by Nina Sundell, Jaromir Stephany, and David A. Ross.

El arte como idea en Inglaterra. Exh. cat. Buenos Aires: Centro de Arte y Comunicación, 1971. Essay by Jorge Glusberg; artists' biographies.

Arte conceptual frente al problema latinoamericano. Exh. cat. Buenos Aires: Museo Universitario de Ciencias y Arte, Ciudad Universitaria, 1974. Prefaces by Helen Escobedo and Jorge Glusberg; essay by Glusberg.

Arte concettuale. Exh. cat. Milan: Galleria Daniel Templon, 1971. Essay by Catherine Millet.

Arte de sistemas. Exh. cat. Buenos Aires: Centro de Arte y Comunicación, 1971. Essay by Jorge Glusberg; artists' biographies, museum collections, and exhibition chronologies.

Arte inglese oggi 1960-1976: Parte seconda. Exh. cat. Milan: Palazzo Reale and British Council, Comune di Milano in association with Electa Editrice, 1976. Essay by Richard Cork; artists' statements, biographies, bibliographies, and exhibition chronologies.

Arte italiana 1960-1982. Exh. cat. London: Arts Council of Great Britain in association with Electa Editrice, 1982. Foreword by Carlo Tognoli, Guido Aghina, Joanna Drew, and Andrew Dempsey; essays by Caroline Tisdall, Guido Balla, Vittorio Fagone, Robert Sanesi, Renato Barilli, Flavio Caroli, and Luciano Giaccari; chronology by Loredana Parmesani; artists' biographies.

Arte Povera, Antiform: Sculptures 1966-1969. Exh. cat. Bordeaux: Centre d'arts plastiques contemporains, 1982. Acknowledgments by Jean-Louis Froment; essay by Germano Celant; exhibition chronology; bibliography; artists' biographies.

Artists and Photographs. Exh. cat. New York: Multiples Gallery, 1969. Boxed collection of artists' books and projects. Essay by Lawrence Alloway. Reprinted in *Studio International* 179, no. 921 (April 1970): 162-164.

Artists' Books. Exh. cat. London: Arts Council of Great Britain, 1976. Foreword by Joanna Drew; essays by Richard Francis and Martin Attwood, Clive Phillpot, and Brandon Taylor; list of artists' publications; list of anthologies, catalogues, magazines, and periodicals; list of reference books and bibliographies; list of suppliers.

Artists Books. Exh. cat. Philadelphia: Moore College of Art, 1973. Foreword by Dianne Perry Vanderlip; essays by Lynn Hershman and John Perreault.

Art-Language (Coventry, England) 1, no. 1 (May 1969)-5, no. 3 (March 1985). First issue only subtitled "The Journal of Conceptual Art."

Artstudio (Paris), no. 15 (Winter 1989). Special issue: Des mots. Editorial by Ann Hindry; essays by Nicolaus Borriaud, Christophe Domino, Jean-Michel Foray, Claude Frontisi, André Gunthert, Luc Lang, Jacques Lepage, Robert Mahoney, Bernard Marcadé, and Jean-Marc Poinsot.

Aspen (New York), no. 5-6 (Fall-Winter 1967). Guest edited by Brian O'Doherty. Boxed collection of essays by Roland Barthes, George Kubler, and Susan Sontag; recorded works by Samuel Beckett, Naum Gabo and Antoine Pevsner, William Burroughs, Alain Robbe-Grillet, Morton Feldman, John Cage, Merce Cunningham, Marcel Duchamp, and Richard Huelsenbeck; texts and projects by Tony Smith, Douglas McAgy, Michael Butor, Dan Graham, Sol LeWitt, Mel Bochner, O'Doherty, and Cage and Max Neuhaus; musical score by Feldman; films by Hans Richter, László Moholy-Nagy, Robert Morris, Stan VanDerBeek, and Robert Rauschenberg.

Aspen, no. 8 (Fall-Winter 1970-71). Guest edited by Dan Graham. Boxed collection of texts and projects by David Antin, Terry Atkinson and Michael Baldwin, Philip Glass, Richard Serra and Steve Reich, La Monte Young, Yvonne Rainer, Jo Baer, Jackson MacLow, Robert Morris and Dennis Oppenheim, Robert Smithson, and Edward Ruscha; recordings by MacLow and Young.

"Attualità internazionali '72-76." In *La Biennale di Venezia: Ambiente, partecipazione, strutture culturali.* Exh. cat. Vol. 2, *Catalogo generale*, 289-385. Venice: Biennale di Venezia, 1976. Texts by Eduardo Arroyo, Enrico Crispolti, Raffaele De Grada, Pontus Hulten, Tommaso Trini, and Olle Granath.

Aue, Walter, ed. *P. C. A. — Projekte, Conzepte, und Actionen.* Cologne: M. Dumont Schauberg, 1971.

Avalanche, no. 1 (Fall 1970). Includes contributions by Carl Andre, Jan Dibbets, Richard Long, Robert Morris, Joseph Beuys, Michael Heizer, Dennis Oppenheim, and Robert Smithson.

Avalanche, no. 2 (Winter 1971). Includes contributions by Bruce Nauman, Terry Atkinson, Klaus Rinke, John Van Saun, Dennis Oppenheim, Richard Serra, Yves Klein, Bruce McLean, William Wegman, and Vito Acconci.

Avalanche (New York), no. 3 (Fall 1971). Includes contributions by David Tremlett, Bill Beckley, Joel Fisher, Gordon Matta-Clark, Robert Morris, Italo Scanga, Ulrich Rückreim, George Trakas, and Barry Le Va.

Avalanche, no. 4 (Spring 1972). Includes contributions by Jackie Windsor, Sol LeWitt, Howard Fried, Alice Aycock, Stanley Brouwn, Franz Erhard Walther, Hanne Darboven, Walter de Maria, and Lawrence Weiner.

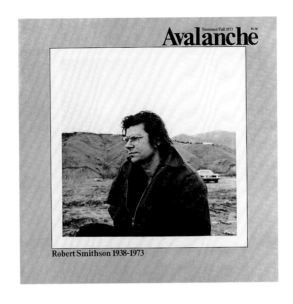

Avalanche Summer/Fall 1973 $2.50

Robert Smithson 1938-1973

Avalanche, no. 5 (Summer 1972). Includes contributions by Braco Dimitrijević, Joseph Beuys, Jannis Kounellis, Philip Glass, Keith Sonnier, and Yvonne Rainer.

Avalanche, no. 6 (Fall 1972). Special issue: Vito Acconci. Documentation of artist's projects; interview by Liza Béar; biography; bibliography.

Avalanche, no. 7 (Winter-Spring 1973). Includes contributions by General Idea, Van Schley, Lowell Darling, Edward Ruscha, and William Wegman.

Avalanche, no. 8 (Summer-Fall 1973). Includes contributions by Robert Smithson, Robert Morris, Gilbert & George, The Grand Union, Tina Girouard, and Chris Burden.

Avalanche, no. 9 (May 1974). Special issue: Video Performance. Includes contributions by Joseph Beuys, William Wegman, Ulrike Rosenbach, Chris Burden, Dennis Oppenheim, Willoughby Sharp, Vito Acconci, Keith Sonnier, and Richard Serra.

Avalanche, no. 10 (December 1974). Includes contributions by Hans Haacke, Daniel Buren, Simone Forti, Stephen Laub, Jack Smith, Joel Fisher, Terry Fox, Gordon Matta-Clark, and The Phil Glass Ensemble.

Avalanche, no. 11 (Summer 1975). Includes contributions by Alan Saret, Darcy Lange, Joel Shapiro, On Kawara, Laurie Anderson, and Steve Paxton.

Avalanche, no. 12 (Winter 1975). Includes contributions by Robin Winters, Christopher Knowles, Robert Wilson, Alexis Smith, Rita Myers, Michael McClard, and Barbara Dilley.

Avalanche, no. 13 (Summer 1976). Includes contributions by Colleen Fitzgibbon, Jim Roche, Reiner Ruthenbeck, Bas Jan Ader, Meredith Monk, and Diego Cortez.

Avanguardia transavanguardia 68-77. Exh. cat. Milan: Mura Aureliane da Porta Metronia a Porta Latina in association with Gruppo Editorale Electa, 1982. Texts by Pierluigi Severi, Renato Nicolini, Achille Bonito Oliva, Alberto Arbasino, Giulio Carlo Argan, Paolo Bertetto, Massimo Cacciari, Enrico Filippini, Ruggero Guarini, Alberto Moravia, Beniamino Placido, Paolo Portoghesi, Anne Marie Sauleau-Boetti, and Gianni Vattimo.

B

Baker, Elizabeth C. "Traveling Ideas: Germany, England." *Art News* 69, no. 4 (Summer 1970): 38-40, 70-72.

Barnitz, Jacqueline. "Conceptual Art and Latin America: A Natural Alliance." In *Encounters/Displacements: Luis Camnitzer, Alfredo Jaar, Cildo Meireles,* exh. cat., 35-48. Austin: Archer M. Huntington Art Gallery, College of Fine Arts, The University of Texas at Austin, 1992.

Battcock, Gregory. "Marcuse and Anti-Art." *Arts Magazine* 43, no. 8 (Summer 1969): 17-19; part 2: 44, no. 2 (November 1969): 20-22.

_____, ed. "Documentation in Conceptual Art: Weiner, Buren, Bochner, LeWitt." *Arts Magazine* 44, no. 6 (April 1970): 42-45.

_____, ed. *Idea Art: A Critical Anthology.* New York: E. P. Dutton and Co., 1973. Essays by Dore Ashton, Gregory Battcock, Jonathan Benthall, Cheryl Bernstein, Jack Burnham, Robert Hughes, Joseph Kosuth, Lucy R. Lippard, Ursula Meyer, John Perreault, Arthur R. Rose [pseud.], Harold Rosenberg, Seth Siegelaub, Lawrence Weiner, Daniel Buren, Mel Bochner, and Sol LeWitt.

Benezra, Neal. "'To Speak Another Language': The Critique of Painting and the Beginnings of Minimal and Conceptual Art." In *American Art in the 20th Century: Painting and Sculpture 1913-1993,* exh. cat., edited by Christos M. Joachimedes and Norman Rosenthal, 117-124. London: Royal Academy of Arts in association with Munich: Prestel, 1993.

Berleant, Arnold. "The Visual Arts and the Art of the Unseen." *Leonardo* (Oxford) 12, no. 1 (Winter 1979): 231-235.

Between Man and Matter: Tokyo Biennale '70. Exh. cat. Tokyo: Mainichi Newspapers and Japan International Art Promotion Association, 1970. Text by Yusuke Nakahara; artists' biographies; bibliographies; exhibition chronologies.

Between Spring and Summer: Soviet Conceptual Art in the Era of Late Communism. Exh. cat. Tacoma, Washington: Tacoma Art Museum and Boston: The Institute of Contemporary Art, 1990. Preface by David A. Ross; essays by Ross, Richard Lourie, Margarita Tupitsyn, Ilya Kabakov, Elisabeth Sussman, Joseph Bakshtein, Victor Tupitsyn, Peter Wollen, Alexander Rappaport, Mikhail Ryklin, and Dmitri Prigov; artists' chronologies; bibliography.

Beyond Painting and Sculpture: Works Bought for the Arts Council by Richard Cork. Exh. cat. London: Arts Council of Great Britain, 1973. Preface by Norbert Lynton; introduction by Richard Cork; artists' biographies and bibliographies.

Carl Andre   Georg Baselitz   Joseph Beuys   Claus Böhmler
Marcel Broodthaers   Daniel Buren   James Lee Byars
Ron Cooper   Hanne Darboven   Walter de Maria
Franz Eggenschwiler   Dan Flavin   Gilbert & George
Erwin Heerich   Douglas Huebler   Jörg Immendorff
On Kawara   Imi W. Knoebel   Bruce Nauman   Claes Oldenburg
Palermo   Panamarenko   A. R. Penck   Sigmar Polke
Gerhard Richter   Diter Rot   Robert Ryman   Richard Tuttle
Lawrence Weiner   Stefan Wewerka

Bilder · Objekte · Filme · Konzepte

Das Bild einer Geschichte 1956/1976: Die Sammlung Panza di Biumo: Die Geschichte eines Bildes: Action Painting, New Dada, Pop Art, Minimal, Conceptual, Environmental Art. Düsseldorf: Kunstsammlung, Kunstmuseum, and Kunsthalle, in association with Milan: Electa International, 1980. Foreword by Jürgen Harten, Hans Albert Peters, and Werner Schmalenbach; texts by Germano Celant; artists' biographies and bibliographies; bibliography.

Bilder – Objekte – Filme – Konzepte. Exh. cat. Munich: Städtische Galerie im Lenbachhaus, 1973. Preface by Michael Petzet; acknowledgments by Barbara Herbig and Jost Herbig.

Binkley, Timothy. Review of *Six Years: The Dematerialization of the Art Object from 1966 to 1972*, by Lucy R. Lippard; *Idea Art: A Critical Anthology*, edited by Gregory Battcock; and *Art & Language*, by Terry Atkinson et al. *The Journal of Aesthetics and Art Criticism* (Madison, Wisconsin) 33, no. 1 (Fall 1974): 109-111.

Blockade '69. Exh. cat. Berlin: Galerie René Block, 1969. Artists' biographies and exhibition chronologies.

Boice, Bruce. "The Quality Problem." *Artforum* 11, no. 2 (October 1972): 68-70.

Bonito Oliva, Achille. "America antiforma: Un viaggio negli Stati Uniti d'America, nell'estate 1969." *Domus* (Milan) 478, no. 9 (September 1969): 32.

_____. *Dialoghi d'artista: Incontri con l'arte contemporanea 1970-1984.* Milan: Electa, c. 1984. Includes interviews with Bruce Nauman, Sol LeWitt, Robert Smithson, Vito Acconci, Gilbert & George, Joseph Kosuth, Daniel Buren, Robert Barry, Ian Wilson, Lawrence Weiner, Giulio Paolini, and Niele Toroni.

_____. "Process, Concept, and Behavior in Italian Art." *Studio International* (London) 191, no. 979 (January-February 1976): 3-5.

Book as Artwork 1960/72. Exh. cat. London: Nigel Greenwood, 1972. Essay by Germano Celant; chronological list of artists' books compiled by Celant and Lynda Morris.

Borden, Lizzie. "Three Modes of Conceptual Art." *Artforum* 10, no. 10 (June 1972): 68-71.

Borgeaud, Bernard. "Body Art." *Chroniques de l'art vivant* (Paris), no. 22 (July-August 1971): 20.

The British Avant-Garde. Exh. cat. New York: The New York Cultural Center in association with Madison, New Jersey: Fairleigh Dickinson University, 1971. Essays by Terry Atkinson and Michael Baldwin, Victor Burgin, Andrew Dipper, Charles Harrison, and Donald Karshan; artists' biographies and bibliographies. Also published in *Studio International* (London) 181, no. 933 (May 1971): 201-239.

Bronson, A. A., and Peggy Gale, eds. *Museums by Artists.* Toronto: Art Metropole, 1983. Introduction by Gale; essays by Jean-Christophe Ammann, Michael Asher, Bronson, Marcel Broodthaers, Benjamin H. D. Buchloh, Daniel Buren, Marcel Duchamp, Robert Filliou, Vera Frenkel, General Idea, Walter Grasskamp, Hans Haacke, Wulf Herzogenrath, Donald Judd, On Kawara, Garry Neill Kennedy, Joseph Kosuth, Les Levine, Glenn Lewis, George Maciunas, Piero Manzoni, Museum of Conceptual Art, N. E. Thing Co., Claes Oldenburg, Harald Szeemann, and Ursula Wevers; dialogue between Tom Marioni and Carl Loeffler.

Brook, Donald. "Toward a Definition of 'Conceptual Art.'" *Leonardo* (Oxford) 5, no. 1 (Winter 1972): 49-50.

Brown, Gordon D. "The Dematerialization of the Object." *Arts Magazine* 43, no. 1 (September-October 1968): 56.

Buchloh, Benjamin H. D. "Conceptual Art 1962-1969: From the Aesthetic of Administration to the Critique of Institutions." *October*, no. 55 (Winter 1990): 105-143. (Original version published in *L'art conceptuel, une perspective.*) See also Joseph Kosuth and Seth Siegelaub, "Replies to Benjamin Buchloh on Conceptual Art," *October*, no. 57 (Summer 1991): 152-157, and Benjamin H. D. Buchloh, "Reply to Joseph Kosuth and Seth Siegelaub," *October*, no. 57 (Summer 1991): 158-161.

Burn, Ian. "Conceptual Art as Art." *Art and Australia* (Sydney) 8, no. 2 (September 1970): 167-170.

_____. "The Sixties: Crisis and Aftermath (Or the Memoirs of an Ex-Conceptual Artist)." *Art and Text* (Melbourne), no. 1 (1981): 49-65.

Burnham, Jack. "Alice's Head: Reflections on Conceptual Art." *Artforum* 8, no. 6 (February 1970): 37-43.

_____. "Problems of Criticism, IX." *Artforum* 9, no. 5 (January 1971): 40-45.

_____. "Real Time Systems." *Artforum* 8, no. 1 (September 1969): 49-55.

_____. "Systems Esthetics." *Artforum* 7, no. 1 (September 1968): 31-35.

C

C. 7,500. Exh. cat. Valencia: California Institute of the Arts, 1973. Introduction by Lucy R. Lippard. Catalogue comprised of randomly ordered index cards designed by the artists.

Carl Andre, Marcel Broodthaers, Daniel Buren, Victor Burgin, Gilbert & George, On Kawara, Richard Long, Gerhard Richter. Exh. cat. Brussels: Palais des Beaux-Arts, 1974. Acknowledgments by Yves Gevaert; artists' biographies and bibliographies.

Carl Andre, Robert Barry, Douglas Huebler, Joseph Kosuth, Sol LeWitt, Robert Morris, Lawrence Weiner. Also known as *Xeroxbook.* Exh. cat. New York: Seth Siegelaub and John W. Wendler, 1968.

Catalogue for the Exhibition. Exh. cat. for "Simon Fraser Exhibition." Burnaby, British Columbia: Centre for Communications and the Arts, Simon Fraser University, 1969.

Celant, Germano. *Arte Povera: Earthworks, Impossible Art, Actual Art, Conceptual Art.* New York: Praeger, 1969. Revised edition published as *Arte Povera.* Translated by Anne Machet, Jean-Georges d'Hostes, and Fabian Palmiri. Paris: Centre national des arts plastiques, 1989. Exhibition chronology by Ida Gianelli; artists' exhibition chronologies and bibliographies.

_____. "Book as Artwork, 1960/70." *Data* (Milan) 1, no. 1 (September 1971): 35-49.

_____. "Conceptual Art, Part One." *Casabella* (Milan) 34, no. 347 (April 1970): 42-49.

_____. *Precronistoria 1966-69: Minimal art, pittura sistemica, arte povera, land art, conceptual art, body art, arte ambientale e nuovi media.* Florence: Centro Di, 1976.

Chandler, John, and Lucy R. Lippard. "Visual Art and the Invisible World." *Studio International* (London) 11, no. 5 (20 May 1967): 27-30.

Changing Terms. Exh. cat. Boston: Museum School Gallery, Museum of Fine Arts, 1971.

Claura, Michel. "Actualité." *VH 101* (Paris), no. 5 (Spring 1971): 40-47.

_____, and Seth Siegelaub. "L'art conceptuel." *XXe siècle* (Paris) 35, no. 41 (December 1973): 156-159. Interview.

Collection: Christian Boltanski, Daniel Buren, Gilbert & George, Jannis Kounellis, Sol LeWitt, Richard Long, Mario Merz. Exh. cat. Bordeaux: Centre d'art plastique contemporain, Musée d'art contemporain, 1990. Preface by Jean-Louis Froment; essays by Michel Bourel, Sylvie Couderc, Jean-Marc Poinsot, Didier Semin, Sami-Ali, Luc Lang, Wolf Jahn, Renaud Camus, Bruno Cora, Christine Buci-Glucksmann, Bernard Marcadé, Pascal Dusapin, Paco Calvo Serraller, Marcel Cohen, Marlis Grüterich, and Sylvie Vauclair.

Collins, James. "Things and Theories." *Artforum* 11, no. 9 (May 1973): 32-36. See also Rosetta Brooks, "Letters," *Artforum* 12, no. 3 (November 1973): 9, and James Collins, "Letters," *Artforum* 12, no. 3 (November 1973): 9, 11.

Colpitt, Frances. "The Photograph and the Photographed." *Journal: Southern California Art Magazine* (Los Angeles), no. 24 (September-October 1979): 46-51.

Combalía Dexeus, Victoria. *La poética de lo neutro: Análisis y crítica del arte conceptual.* Barcelona: Editorial Anagrama, 1975.

Concept Art. Exh. cat. Copenhagen: Stalke Galleri, 1988. Preface by Yves Michel Bernard and Brigitte March; essays by Evelyn Weiss, Vincenzo Agnetti, and Jan Foncé; artists' exhibition chronologies.

Concept Art, Minimal Art, Arte Povera, Land Art: Sammlung Marzona. Exh. cat. Bielefeld: Kunsthalle in association with Stuttgart: Edition Cantz, 1990. Foreword by Ulrich Weisner; essays by Werner Lippert and Erich Franz; artists' biographies and exhibition chronologies; glossary; bibliography.

Concept—Décoratif: Anti-Formalist Art of the 70s. Exh. cat. New York: Nahan Contemporary, 1990. Essay by Robert C. Morgan.

Concept, Narrative, Document: Recent Photographic Works from the Morton Neumann Family Collection. Exh. cat. Chicago: Museum of Contemporary Art, 1979. Introduction by Judith Tannenbaum.

Concept-Théorie. Exh. cat. Paris: Galerie Daniel Templon, 1970. Introduction by Catherine Millet.

Concepts and Information. Exh. cat. Jerusalem: Israel Museum, 1971. Foreword; artists' biographies.

Conceptual Art, Arte Povera, Land Art. Exh. cat. Turin: Galleria Civica d'Arte Moderna, 1970. Texts by Germano Celant, Lucy R. Lippard, Luigi Mallé, Aldo Passoni, and the artists; bibliography.

Conceptual Art and Conceptual Aspects. Exh. cat. New York: The New York Cultural Center in association with Madison, New Jersey: Fairleigh Dickinson University, 1970. Artists' texts, statements, biographies, and bibliographies.

"Conceptual Art and the Reception of Duchamp." *October*, no. 70 (Fall 1994): 127-146. Round table discussion with Alexander Alberro, Yve-Alain Bois, Benjamin H. D. Buchloh, Martha Buskirk, Thierry de Duve, and Rosalind E. Krauss.

Contemporanea. Exh. cat. Rome: Parcheggio di Villa Borghese in association with Florence: Centro Di, 1973. Foreword by Graziella Lonardi; "Art" section text by Achille Bonita Oliva; "Artists' Books and Records" section text by Michel Claura.

Cork, Richard. "UK Commentary." *Studio International* (London) 183, no. 942 (March 1972): 118-121.

Corradini, Nicola. *Dal concettualismo alla nuova pittura: Arte, mercato, e critica in Italia 1970-1973.* Pisa: Ets Editrice, 1973.

Crow, Thomas. "Unwritten Histories of Conceptual Art." In *Oehlen Williams 95*, exh. cat., 86-101. Columbus, Ohio: Wexner Center for the Arts, 1995.

Cummins, Louise. "L'art conceptuel: Peut-il guérir de la philosophie?" *Parachute* (Montreal), no. 61 (January-February-March 1991): 37-42.

Czartoryska, Urszula. *Od Pop-Artu do szutki konceptualnej.* Warsaw: Wydawnictwa Artystyczne i Filmowe, 1973.

D

Davis, Douglas. "The Size of Non-Size." *Artforum* 15, no. 4 (December 1976): 46-51.

_____. "What is Content? Notes Toward an Answer." *Artforum* 12, no. 2 (October 1973): 59-63.

De Europa. Exh. cat. New York: John Weber Gallery, 1972.

De Vries, Gerd, ed. *On Art: Artists' Writings on the Changed Notion of Art after 1965/Über Kunst: Künstlertexte zum veränderten Kunstverständnis nach 1965.* Cologne: M. DuMont Schauberg, 1974. Texts by Carl Andre, Art & Language, Daniel Buren, Victor Burgin, Ian Burn and Mel Ramsden, Douglas Huebler, Donald Judd, Joseph Kosuth, Sol LeWitt, Robert Morris, Peter Roehr, and Lawrence Weiner; artists' bibliographies.

_____. *Paul Maenz Köln: 1970-1980-1990: Eine Avantgarde-Galerie und die Kunst unserer Zeit.* Cologne: DuMont, 1991. Essays by Donald Kuspit, Wolfgang Max Faust, and Paul Maenz; exhibition chronology; bibliography.

De Vries Robbé, Lon. "Het kunstconcept van concept kunst." *Museumjournal* (Otterloo) 20, no. 6 (December 1975): 241-250.

Della falsità. Exh. cat. Parma: Istituto di Storia dell'Arte, Università di Parma, 1974. Introduction by Arturo Carlo Quintavalle; texts on artists by Adriano Altamira, Gillo Flores, Luciano Fabro, Idetoshi Nagasawa, Ferdinando Tonello, and Antonio Trotto; artists' exhibition chronologies and bibliographies.

Denizot, René. "De l'art, du pouvoir, de l'image, de l'histoire et de deux artists: Lawrence Weiner, On Kawara." *Art Press* (Paris), no. 54 (December 1981): 12-15.

_____. "La limite du concept." *Opus International* (Paris), no. 17 (April 1970): 14-16.

Deurle 11/7/73. Exh. cat. Deurle, Belgium: Museum Dhont-Dhaernens in association with Oostende: Publigrafik, 1973. Texts by artists.

Documenta 5: Befragung der Realität: Bildwelten heute. Exh. cat. 3 vols. Kassel: Neue Galerie and Museum Fridericianum in association with Documenta GmbH and C. Bertelsmann, 1972. Introduction by Klaus Honnef and Gisela Kaminski; artists' biographies, bibliographies, exhibition chronologies, and statements.

Documenta 6: Malerei, Plastik, Performance. Exh. cat. 3 vols. Kassel: Paul Dierichs KG and Co., 1977. Forewords by Hans Eichel, Arnold Bode, Gerhard Bott, and Manfred Schneckenburger; texts by Lothar Romain, Bazon Brock, Karl Oskar Blase, Klaus Honnef, Lothar Lang, Schneckenburger, Günter Metken, Joachim Diederichs, David A. Ross, Wieland Schmied, Peter W. Jansen, Ulrich Gregor, Birgit Hein, Wulf Herzogenrath, Bott, Michael Maek-Gérard, Rolf Dittmar, and Evelyn Weiss.

Dokumenti o post-objektnim pojavama u jugoslavenskoj umetnosti 1968-1973. Exh. cat. Belgrade: Salon Muzej Savremene Umetnosti/Gallery of the Museum of Modern Art, 1973. Introduction by Ješa Denegri; exhibition chronology; bibliography.

Dorfles, Gillo. "Arte concettuale o arte povera?" *Art International* 13, no. 3 (20 March 1969): 35-38.

Dreher, Thomas. *Konzeptuelle Kunst in Amerika und England zwischen 1963 und 1976.* Frankfurt: Peter Lang, 1992. Includes reprints of texts by Mel Bochner, Sol LeWitt, Joseph Kosuth, and Art & Language; artists' biographies; bibliography.

Dusinberre, Deke. "Working with Shadows, Working with Words." *Art Monthly* (London), no. 12 (December 1988-January 1989): 3-6. Interview with Daniel Buren, Michel Claura, and Seth Siegelaub.

E

Earth, Air, Fire, Water: Elements of Art. Exh. cat. 2 vols. Boston: Museum of Fine Arts, 1971. Foreword by Perry T. Rathbone; acknowledgments and introduction by Virginia Gunter; essay by David Antin; bibliography.

Earth Art. Exh. cat. Ithaca, New York: Andrew Dickson White Museum of Art, Cornell University, 1969. Foreword by Thomas W. Leavitt; essays by Willoughby Sharp and William C. Lipke; excerpts from transcript of symposium held on 6 February 1969 at Cornell University (moderator: Leavitt; panelists: Dennis Oppenheim, Robert Smithson, Günther Uecker, Hans Haacke, Neil Jenney, and Richard Long); bibliography; artists' bibliographies and exhibition chronologies.

557,087

an exhibition organized by lucy r. lippard for the contemporary

art council of the seattle art museum at the seattle art museum

pavilion from september 5 to october 5 1969; version titled

955,000 to vancouver art gallery 1970.

Eight Contemporary Artists. Exh. cat. New York: The Museum of Modern Art, 1974. Acknowledgments by Jennifer Licht; artists' statements.

18 Paris IV. 70. Exh. cat. Paris: Seth Siegelaub, 1970. Acknowledgments and introduction by Michel Claura.

Electric Art. Exh. cat. Los Angeles: UCLA Art Galleries, University of California, 1969. Foreword by Oliver Andrews; essay by Jack Burnham; artists' biographies and exhibition chronologies.

Encuentros 1972 Pamplona. Exh. cat. Pamplona: Museo de Navarra in association with Madrid: Grupo Alea, 1972. Includes original and reprinted texts by various authors.

Entwürfe, Partituren, Projekte: Zeichnungen. Berlin: Galerie René Block, 1971. Introduction by René Block.

Erhard, Ernst Otto. *Pop, Kitsch, Concept-Art: Aufsätze zur gegenwärtigen Situation der Kunst.* Ravensburg: Otto Maier, 1974.

Europe in the Seventies: Aspects of Recent Art. Exh. cat. Chicago: The Art Institute of Chicago, 1977. Introduction by A. James Speyer and Anne Rorimer; essays by Jean-Christophe Ammann, David Brown, R. H. Fuchs, and Benjamin H. D. Buchloh; bibliography; artists' biographies.

F

Festival d'automne à Paris: Aspects de l'art actuel. Exh. cat. Paris: Galerie Sonnabend au Musée Galliera in association with Florence: Centro Di, 1973. Artists' texts and reprints of texts on artists by various authors.

557,087. Seattle: Seattle Art Museum, 1969. *955,000.* Vancouver: Vancouver Art Gallery, 1970. Exh. cat. Foreword by Morrie J. Alhadeff; acknowledgments by Lucy R. Lippard; texts by various authors; bibliography; film list; installation photographs. Catalogue comprised of randomly ordered index cards.

Flynt, Henry. "Concept Art." In *An Anthology*, edited by Jackson MacLow and La Monte Young, unpag. New York: La Monte Young and Jackson MacLow, 1963. Also in *Esthetics Contemporary*, edited by Richard Kostelanetz, 329-331. Buffalo, New York: Prometheus Books, 1989.

Foote, Nancy. "The Anti-Photographers." *Artforum* 15, no. 1 (September 1976): 46-54.

Foray, Jean-Michel. "Art conceptuel: Une possibilité de rien." *Artstudio* (Paris), no. 15 (Winter 1989): 44-55.

Formulation. Exh. cat. Andover, Massachusetts: Addison Gallery of American Art, Phillips Academy, 1971.

Fowkes, William. "A Hegelian Critique of Found Art and Conceptual Art." *The Journal of Aesthetics and Art Criticism* (Madison, Wisconsin) 37, no. 2 (Winter 1978): 157-168.

The Fox, no. 1 (1975). Includes contributions by Sarah Charlesworth, Michael Baldwin and Philip Pilkington, Joseph Kosuth, Andrew Menard, Zoran Popovic and Jasna Tijardovic, Ian Burn, Adrian Piper, Mel Ramsden, Michael Corris, David Rushton and Paul Wood, Preston Heller, Lynn Lemaster, and Terry Atkinson.

The Fox, no. 2 (1975). Includes contributions by Eunice Lipton, Mel Ramsden, Terry Smith, Lizzie Borden, Sarah Charlesworth, Mark Klienberg, Adrian Piper, Andrew Menard, Michael Corris, Ian Burn, Bruce Kurtz, Stefan Morawski, David Rushton and Paul Wood, Joseph Kosuth, Ron White, Terry Atkinson, Karl Beveridge and Burn, and Trevor Pateman.

The Fox, no. 3 (1976). Includes contributions by Peter Benchley, Kathryn Bigelow, Sarah Charlesworth, Martha Rosler, Mel Ramsden, Art & Language, Carole Condé and Karl Beveridge, Steve Lockard, Christine Kozlov and Mayo Thompson, Sharlene Spingler, Ian Burn, Jasna Tijardovic, Ross Neher, Nigel Lendon, Joseph Kosuth, Fern Tiger and Edward Robbins, Michael Corris and Preston Heller and Andrew Menard, David Rushton and Paul Wood, Goran Djordjevic, and Hervé Fischer.

Francblin, Catherine. "L'art conceptuel entre les actes." *Art Press* (Paris), no. 139 (September 1989): 45-47.

From the Collection of Dorothy and Herbert Vogel. Exh. cat. Elmira, New York: Arnot Art Museum and Exhibits USA Mid America Arts Alliances, 1988. Introduction and texts by Pamela Becher.

From the Collection of Sol LeWitt. Exh. cat. New York: Independent Curators Incorporated in association with Hartford: Wadsworth Atheneum, 1984. Acknowledgments by Susan Sollins; essay by Andrea Miller-Keller.

From Concept to Context: Robert Barry, Stanley Brouwn, Daniel Buren, Lawrence Weiner. Exh. cat. Toronto: Art Gallery of York University, 1989. Foreword by Loretta Yarlow; essay by David Bellman.

From Minimal to Conceptual Art: Works from The Dorothy and Herbert Vogel Collection. Exh. cat. Washington, D.C.: National Gallery of Art, 1994. Essay by John T. Paoletti; interview by Ruth E. Fine; artists' writings; bibliography and exhibition chronology of Vogel Collection.

G

Gerry Schum. Exh. cat. Amsterdam: Stedelijk Museum, 1979. Foreword by Edy de Wilde; introduction by Dorine Mignot; texts by Gerry Schum and Ursula Wevers; artists' statements; biography; bibliography.

Glusberg, Jorge. *Arte en la Argentina: Del pop-art a la nueva imagen.* Buenos Aires: Ediciones de Arte Gaglianone, 1985.

Goldin, Amy. "The Post-Perceptual Portrait." *Art in America* 63, no. 1 (January-February 1975): 79-82.

_____, and Robert Kushner. "Conceptual Art as Opera." *Art News* 69, no. 2 (April 1970): 40-43.

Goldsmith, Barbara. "Where Is the Art? Join the Concept of the Month Club and Find Out." *Harper's Bazaar*, May 1970, 144-147.

Gravity and Grace: The Changing Condition of Sculpture 1965-1975. Exh. cat. London: Hayward Gallery, The South Bank Centre, 1993. Essays by Jon Thompson, William Tucker, and Yehuda Safran.

Groh, Klaus, ed. *If I Had a Mind .../(Ich stelle mir vor ...): Concept-Art, Project-Art.* Cologne: M. Dumont Schauberg, 1971. Artists' projects; bibliography.

Grundberg, Andy. "Conceptual Art and the Photography of Ideas." In *Photography and Art: Interactions Since 1946*, edited by Andy Grundberg and Kathleen McCarthy Gauss, 133-168. New York: Abbeville Press, 1987.

Guest, Tim, ed. *Books by Artists.* Toronto: Art Metropole, 1981. Acknowledgments, preface, and essay by Guest; essay by Germano Celant; bibliography.

Guggenheim International Exhibition. Exh. cat. New York: Solomon R. Guggenheim Museum, 1971. Preface by Thomas M. Messer; acknowledgments by Edward F. Fry and Diane Waldman; essays by Waldman and Fry; artists' bibliographies and exhibition chronologies; bibliography; exhibition chronology.

H

Hapgood, Susan. "Remaking Art History." *Art in America* 78, no. 7 (July 1990): 114-122, 181.

Harrison, Charles. "Conceptual Art: Myths and Scandals." *Artscribe International* (London), no. 80 (March-April 1990): 15-16. Exh. review of "L'art conceptuel, une perspective."

_____. "The Legacy of Conceptual Art." In *Place, Position, Presentation, Public*, edited by Ine Gevers, 42-59. Maastricht: Jan Van Eyck Akademie and Amsterdam: De Balie, 1993.

_____. "Notes Towards Art Work." *Studio International* (London) 179, no. 919 (February 1970): 42-43.

_____. "On Exhibitions and the World at Large: Seth Siegelaub in Conversation with Charles Harrison." *Studio International* (London) 178, no. 917 (December 1969): 202-203. Interview.

_____. "'A Very Abstract Context.'" *Studio International* (London) 180, no. 927 (November 1970): 194-197.

Harry Shunk: Projects — Pier 18. Exh. cat. Nice: Musée d'art moderne et d'art contemporain, 1992. Includes interview with Shunk by Loïc Mallé.

Heath, Adrian. "Concerning Conceptualism." *Art Monthly* (London), no. 113 (February 1988): 4-6.

Helgadottir, Laufey. "Photography and Conceptual Art in Iceland." *Siksi: Nordic Art Review*, pt. 2 (1988): 7-13.

Heller, Preston, and Andrew Menard. "Kozloff: Criticism in Absentia." *Artforum* 11, no. 6 (February 1973): 32-36.

Henning, Edward B. "The Trouble with Conceptualism." *Art International* 22, no. 8 (January 1979): 53-59.

Hernández, Maria José. "El 'conceptual' y el objeto artistico." *Cimál*, no. 21 (September 1983): 9-12.

Hier et Après/Yesterday and After. Exh. cat. Montreal: The Montreal Museum of Fine Arts, 1980. Acnowledgments by Jean Trudel; texts by Jean-Christophe Ammann, Diana Nemiroff, and Normand Thériault; artists' bibliographies and exhibition chronologies.

Hoffmann, Klaus. *Kunst-im-Kopf: Aspekte der Realismus.* Cologne: M. Dumont Schauberg, 1972.

Honnef, Klaus. *Concept Art*. Cologne: Phaidon, 1971. Exhibition chronology; bibliography; artists' bibliographies.

_____. "Concept Art." *Kunst* (Mainz) 10, no. 38 (1970): 1759-1767. Includes bibliography and exhibition chronology.

_____. "Conceptual-Art." *Kunst-Bulletin* (Zurich), no. 4 (April 1972): 1-6.

Hugunin, James. "Warp and Woof: Structure and Context in Recent Art." *The Dumb Ox*, no. 2 (Fall 1976): 5-7.

Idea and Image in Recent Art. Exh. cat. Chicago: The Art Institute of Chicago, 1974. Foreword by A. James Speyer; introduction by Anne Rorimer; artists' bibliographies.

Idea Structures: Survey '70. Exh. cat. London: Camden Arts Centre and Central Library in association with London Borough of Camden, Libraries, Arts, and Amenities Committee, 1970.

Idees i actituds: Entorn de l'art conceptual a Catalunya, 1964-1980. Exh. cat. Barcelona: Centre d'Art Santa Mònica, 1992. Essays by Pilar Parcerisas, Alícia Suàrez and Mercè Vidal, Glòria Picazo, Teresa Camps, Annemieke van de Pas, Carles Hac Mor, Antoni Mercader, Eugeni Bonet, and Joaquim Dols; interview with Simón Marchán Fiz by Parcerisas and interviews with various artists by Alvert Macìa; artists' bibliographies and general bibliography by Montse Badia and Parcerisas; chronology.

In Other Words: Wort und Schrift in Bildern der konzeptuellen Kunst. Exh. cat. Dortmund: Museum am Ostwall, 1989. Foreword by Ingo Bartsch; essays by Anna Meseure and Dietmar Elger; artists' biographies and bibliographies.

In Site: Five Conceptual Artists from the Bay Area. Exh. cat. Amherst: University Gallery, Fine Arts Center, University of Massachusetts at Amherst, 1990. Acknowledgments by Betsy Siersma; essay by Regina Coppola; bibliography; artists' biographies and bibliographies.

Information. Exh. cat. New York: The Museum of Modern Art, 1970. Acknowledgments and essay by Kynaston L. McShine; artists' projects; film program; bibliography.

Inquiries: Language in Art. Exh. cat. Toronto: Art Gallery of Ontario, 1990. Acknowledgments and essay by Christina Ritchie.

Interfunktionen (Cologne), no. 1. Includes contributions by Friedrich Wolfram Heubach, Karolus, G. Altorjay, K. P. Brehmer, W. Reinecke, Jörg Immendorff, and Wolf Vostell.

Interfunktionen, no. 2. Includes contributions by Mauricio Kagel, Joseph Beuys, Wolf Vostell, Feussner, Friedrich Wolfram Heubach, Jörg Immendorff, and Burghardt.

Interfunktionen, no. 3. Includes contributions by L. Schirmer, Friedrich Wolfram Heubach, H. Lieberknecht, Wolf Vostell, Diter Rot, Joseph Beuys, Johannes Stüttgen, M. Schäffer, Günter Brus, H. Stumpfl, and G. Altorjay.

Interfunktionen, no. 4 (March 1970). Includes contributions by Panamarenko, Dennis Oppenheim, Keith Arnatt, Joseph Beuys, Daniel Buren, Friedrich Wolfram Heubach, Diter Rot, Mauricio Kagel, Claus Böhmler, Jörg Immendorff and W. Reinicke and B. Hein, Günter Brus, Gilbert & George, Dieter Meier, and Jan Dibbets.

Interfunktionen, no. 5 (November 1970). Includes contributions by Dennis Oppenheim, Robert Smithson, Peter Hutchinson, Weibel, Valie Export, Jan Dibbets, Gilbert & George, John Baldessari, Schuldt, Brecht, Nemetschek, Hamish Fulton, Pulsa, Ehrenberg, Christo, Will Insley, Michael Oppitz, Keith Arnatt, Joseph Beuys, Johannes Stüttgen, Friedrich Wolfram Heubach, Oswald Weiner, Claus Böhmler, Tomas Schmidt, Lothar Baumgarten, Giuseppe Penone, and Dan Graham.

Interfunktionen, no. 6 (1971). Includes contributions by Bruce Nauman, Dennis Oppenheim, Vito Acconci, Arnulf Rainer, Joseph Beuys and Terry Fox, Friedrich Wolfram Heubach, Hamish Fulton, Heinz Frank, Michael Heizer, Johannes Stüttgen, Robert Morris, Rob Can, Richard Budelis, and Peter Weibel.

Interfunktionen, no. 7 (1971). Special issue: Joseph Beuys and Land Art/Earth Works. Includes contributions by Joseph Beuys, Michael Heizer, Peter Hutchinson, Dennis Oppenheim, Richard Long, Robert Smithson, Buckminster Fuller, Nam June Paik, Dan Graham, Lothar Baumgarten, Will Insley, Jürgen Kramer, and Panamarenko.

Interfunktionen, no. 8 (January 1972). Includes contributions by Sigmar Polke, Vito Acconci, Dan Graham, Arnulf Rainer, Günter Brus, Bazon Brock, Friedrich Wolfram Heubach, Peter Hutchinson, Richard Budelis, Rebecca Horn, Terry Fox, Roger Welch, Will Insley, Wagner & Weyhing, Bruce Nauman, John Baldessari, Peter Weibel, and Matthias Schäffer.

Interfunktionen, no. 9. Includes contributions by Dennis Oppenheim, Lothar Baumgarten, Friedrich Wolfram Heubach, Dan Graham, John Baldessari, Roger Welch, Didier Bay, Hans Haacke, Feely McCann, Horst Schmidt-Brümmer, Terry Fox, William Wegman, Steve Reich, Gufo Reale, Will Insley, Ernst Mitzka, Doug Waterman, Mark Oppitz, Adler Pfeife Urinoir, Jürgen Kramer, Ulrich Meister, Joseph Beuys, and Sigmar Polke.

Interfunktionen, no. 10. Includes contributions by Bill Beckley, Sigmar Polke, Reiner Ruthenbeck, Didier Bay, Vito Acconci, Roger Welch, Marcel Broodthaers, Will Insley, Tadeusz, Gufo Reale, Johannes Brus, William Wegman, John Baldessari, Philip Glass, Jon Gibson, Laura Dean, Friedrich Wolfram Heubach, Ulrich Meister, and Rainer Geise.

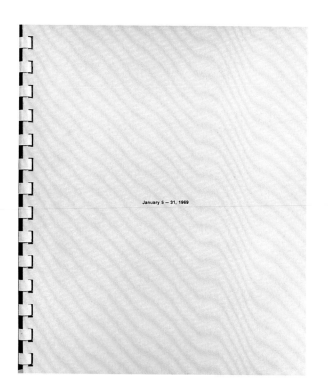

January 5 — 31, 1969

Interfunktionen, no. 11 (1974). Includes contributions by Marcel Broodthaers, Jörg Immendorff, A. R. Penck, Roman Jakobson, Lawrence Weiner, Michel Claura, Germano Celant, Dan Graham, Daniel Buren, Bruce Nauman, Italo Scanga, and Bill Beckley; list of books as art, 1960-74.

Interfunktionen, no. 12 (1975). Special issue: Films by Artists. Includes contributions by Daniel Buren, Yvonne Rainer, David Lamelas, Maria Nordman, Roman Jakobson, Antonius Höckelmann, and Anselm Kiefer; dialogue between Carl Andre and Hollis Frampton; list of artists' films, 1960-74.

Interfunktionen, no. 13. Special issue: Documentation of Artists' Works in/as Architectonic Space. Includes contributions by Michael Asher, Daniel Buren, Dan Graham, Bruce Nauman, Maria Nordman, Blinky Palermo, Niele Toroni, Richard Tuttle.

Interventions. Exh. cat. Toronto: Art Gallery of Ontario, 1992. Acknowledgments by Roald Nasgaard; essay by Christina Ritchie; excerpts of articles and interviews on the artists by various authors.

Invisible Painting and Sculpture. Exh. cat. Richmond, California: Richmond Art Center, 1969. Introduction by Tom Marioni.

Italy Two: Art around '70. Exh. cat. Philadephia: Museum of the Philadephia Civic Center, 1973. Acknowledgments by Frank L. Rizzo and John Pierron; texts by Furio Colombo, Alberto Boatto, and Filberto Menna.

J

Jamieson, Dale. "The Importance of Being Conceptual." *The Journal of Aesthetics and Art Criticism* (Madison, Wisconsin) 45, no. 2 (Winter 1986): 117-123.

January 5-31, 1969. Exh. cat. New York: Seth Siegelaub, 1969.

Jappe, Georg. "Interview with Konrad Fischer." *Studio International* (London) 181, no. 930 (February 1971): 68-71.

Jeffery, Ian. "Art Theory and the Decline of the Art Object." *Studio International* (London) 186, no. 961 (December 1973): 267-271.

Jochimsen, Margarethe. "Story Art: Text-Foto-Synthesen." *Magazine Kunst* (February 1974): 43-73.

Joseph Beuys, Daniel Buren, Dan Graham, Bruce McLean, Giulio Paolini. Exh. cat. Tokyo: The Japan Foundation, The Tokyo Metropolitan Art Museum, and Laforet Harajuku in association with Flex Co., 1982. Introduction by Nobuo Nakamura; texts by Nina Dimitrijević, Giorgio de Marchis, Nakamura, and Caroline Tisdall; artists' biographies and exhibition chronologies.

Joseph Kosuth, Robert Morris. Exh. cat. Bradford, Massachusetts: Laura Knott Gallery, Bradford Junior College, 1969.

July, August, September 1969. Exh. cat. New York: Seth Siegelaub, 1969. Acknowledgments by Seth Siegelaub.

July 1969. New York: Art Press, 1969. Includes contributions by Ian Burn, Adrian Piper, Mel Ramsden, Roger Cutforth, Stephen J. Kaltenbach, Sol LeWitt, and David Nelson.

K

Kaprow, Allan. "The Education of the Un-Artist, Part III." *Art in America* 62, no. 1 (January-February 1974): 85-91.

Karshan, Donald H. "The End of 'the Cult of the Unique.'" *Studio International* (London) 181, no. 934 (June 1971): 285-288.

Knowledge: Aspects of Conceptual Art. Exh. cat. Santa Barbara: University Art Museum, University of California at Santa Barbara, 1992. Foreword by Marla C. Berns; essays by Frances Colpitt and Phyllis Plous; exhibition chronology; artists' biographies and bibliographies.

"Konzept"-Kunst. Exh. cat. Basel: Kunstmuseum, 1972. Texts by Zdenek Felix and Klaus Honnef; exhibition chronology; artists' biographies and bibliographies by Erika Fischer.

Konzeption-Conception: Dokumentation einer heutigen Kunstrichtung/Documentation of Today's Art Tendency. Exh. cat. Leverkusen: Städtisches Museum in association with Cologne and Opladen: Westdeutscher, 1969. Foreword by Rolf Wedewer; introduction by Sol LeWitt; artists' bibliographies and exhibition chronologies.

Kozloff, Max. "Pygmalion Reversed." *Artforum* 14, no. 3 (November 1975): 30-37.

_____. "The Trouble with Art-as-Idea." *Artforum* 11, no. 1 (September 1972): 33-37.

Kunst bleibt Kunst: Projekt '74: Aspekte internationaler Kunst am Anfang der 70er Jahre. Exh. cat. Cologne: Kunsthalle and Wallraf-Richardtz Museum, 1974. Introduction by Dieter Ronte; texts by Evelyn Weiss, Manfred Schneckenberger, Albert Schug, Marlis Grüterich, Wulf Herzogenrath, David A. Ross, and Birgit Hein; artists' projects.

Kunst in Europa na '68. Exh. cat. Ghent: Museum van Hedendaagse Kunst and Centrum voor Kunst en Cultur, 1980. Essays by Jan Hoet, Germano Celant, Johannes Cladders, K. J. Geirlandt, Sandy Nairne, Piet Vandaalen, and Koenraad De Wolf; bibliography.

Kunst – über Kunst: Werke und Theorien: Eine Ausstellung in drei Teilen. Exh. cat. Cologne: Kölnischer Kunstverein, 1974. Introduction by Wulf Herzogenrath; essay in

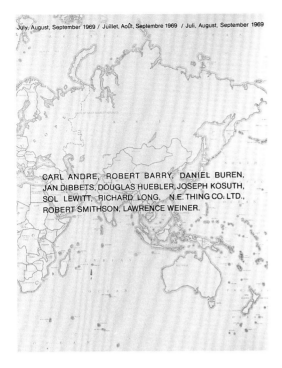

July, August, September 1969 / Juillet, Août, Septembre 1969 / Juli, August, September 1969

CARL ANDRE, ROBERT BARRY, DANIEL BUREN, JAN DIBBETS, DOUGLAS HUEBLER, JOSEPH KOSUTH, SOL LEWITT, RICHARD LONG, N.E. THING CO. LTD., ROBERT SMITHSON, LAWRENCE WEINER.

"Nach 1965" section by Paul Maenz; artists' biographies, bibliographies, and exhibition chronologies.

Künstler Bücher 1. Exh. cat. Krefeld: Kunstmuseum, 1993. Essay by Eva Meyer-Hermann; artists' bibliographies.

Kurtz, Bruce D. *Contemporary Art: 1965-1990.* Englewood Cliffs, New Jersey: Prentice Hall, 1992.

L

Lamelas, David, ed. *Publication.* London: Nigel Greenwood, 1970. Statements and texts by Keith Arnatt, Robert Barry, Stanley Brouwn, Daniel Buren, Victor Burgin, Michel Claura, Gilbert & George, John Latham, Lucy R. Lippard, Martin Maloney, Barbara M. Reise, Lawrence Weiner, and Ian Wilson.

Lamy, Laurent. "L'art conceptuel." *Vie des arts* (Montreal), no. 64 (Autumn 1971): 30-33; English translation, 87-88.

Land Art. Exh. cat. Hanover: Fernsehgalerie Gerry Schum, 1970. Texts by Gerry Schum and Jean Leering; exhibition reviews.

Leen, Frederik. "Seth Siegelaub: Conceptual Art; Exhibitions." *Forum International* 2, no. 9 (September 1991): 64-72.

Letters. Exh. cat. Long Beach Island, New Jersey, 1969. Introduction by Phillips M. Simkin; essay by Lenore Malen.

Lévêque, Jean-Jacques. "Art conceptuel." *Galerie-Jardin des arts* (Paris), no. 134 (February 1974): 44-46.

Linker, Kate. "The Artist's Book as an Alternative Space." *Studio International* (London) 195, no. 990 (1/1980): 75-79.

Lippard, Lucy R. "The Artist's Book Goes Public." *Art in America* 65, no. 1 (January-February 1977): 40-41.

_____. "Time: A Panel Discussion." *Art International* 13, no. 9 (November 1969): 20-23, 39. Transcript of panel discussion held at the New York Shakespeare Festival Theatre on 17 March 1969 (moderator: Seth Siegelaub; panelists: Carl Andre, Michael Cain, Douglas Huebler, and Ian Wilson).

_____. *Six Years: The Dematerialization of the Art Object from 1966 to 1972.* New York: Praeger, 1973. A chronological reconstruction of publications, events, and exhibitions.

_____. "Some of 1968." *Arts Magazine* 47, no. 3 (December 1972-January 1973): 45-47. Excerpts from *Six Years: The Dematerialization of the Art Object from 1966 to 1972,* 36-45.

_____, and John Chandler. "The Dematerialization of Art." *Art International* 12, no. 2 (20 February 1968): 31-36.

Llorens, Tomàs. "Arte concettuale in Spagna." *Notiziario arte contemporanea,* no. 10 (October 1972): 30.

Louw, Roelof. "Judd and After." *Studio International* (London) 184, no. 949 (November 1972): 171-175.

Lyons, Joan, ed. *Artists' Books: A Critical Anthology and Sourcebook.* Rochester, New York: Visual Studies Workshop Press, 1985. Essays by Richard Kostelanetz, Ulises Carrión, Lucy R. Lippard, Shelley Rice, Barbara Moore and Jon Hendricks, Clive Phillpot, Susi R. Bloch, Betsy Davids and Jim Petrillo, Felipe Ehrenberg and Magali Lara and Javier Cadena, Alex Sweetman, and Robert C. Morgan; artists' books collections; bibliography.

M

Maenz, Paul, and Gerd De Vries. *1970-1975: Paul Maenz Köln.* Cologne: Paul Maenz, 1975. Acknowledgments by Maenz and De Vries; essay by Germano Celant; texts by various authors.

Mahoney, Robert. "Une contrée inexplorée: La Logos dans l'espace." *Artstudio* (Paris), no. 15 (Winter 1989): 104-113.

Mallander, J.O. "Konst och identitet 1-3." *Paletten* (Göteborg), pt. 4 (1972): 10-23.

Marchán Fiz, Simón. *Del arte objetual al arte de concepto: Las artes plásticas desde 1960.* Madrid: Ediciones Akal, 1988.

Mastai, Judith, ed. *An Evening Forum at the Vancouver Art Gallery with Terry Atkinson, Jeff Wall, Ian Wallace, and Lawrence Weiner, February 1990.* Vancouver: Vancouver Art Gallery, 1992. Transcript of interview with the artists.

Master Works of Conceptual Art. Exh. cat. Cologne: Galerie Maenz, 1983. Introduction by Paul Maenz and Gerd de Vries.

McEvilley, Thomas. "I Think Therefore I Art." *Artforum* 23, no. 10 (Summer 1985): 74-84.

Meehan, Thomas. "'Non-art,' 'anti-art,' 'non-art art,' and 'anti-art art' are useless. If someone says his work is art, it's art: A non-art article on art." *Horizon* (New York) 13, no. 4 (Autumn 1971): 4-15.

Mellow, James R. "Art beyond Art." *The New Leader* 52, no. 12 (23 June 1969): 29-30.

Messer, Thomas M. "Impossible Art — Why It Is." *Art in America* 57, no. 3 (May-June 1969): 30-31.

Meyer, Ursula. *Conceptual Art.* New York: E. P. Dutton and Co., 1972. Artists' texts, works, and interviews.

_____."De-Objectification of the Object." *Arts Magazine* 43, no. 8 (Summer 1969): 20-22.

Migliorini, Ermanno. *Conceptual Art.* Florence: D'Arte Il Fiorino, 1972.

Millet, Catherine. "L'art conceptuel." *Opus International* (Paris), no. 15 (December 1969): 20-23.

_____. "L'art de la fin de l'art … 10 ans après." *Art Press* (Paris), no. 54 (December 1981): 6-9.

_____. "Le montant de la rançon." *Art Press* (Paris), no. 139 (September 1989): 36-41.

_____. *Textes sur l'art conceptuel.* Paris: Daniel Templon, 1972.

Minimal + Conceptual Art aus der Sammlung Panza. Exh. cat. Basel: Museum für Gegenwartskunst, 1980. Acknowledgments, essay, and artists' texts by Franz Mayer; artists' bibliographies.

Modes of Address: Language in Art Since 1960. Exh. cat. New York: Whitney Museum of American Art, 1988. Essays by Michael Waldron and Amy Heard, Tom Hardy, and Ingrid Periz.

Morawski, Stefan. "Nie wykorzystana szansa polskiego konceptualizmu." *Sztuka* (Warsaw), no. 4 (1975): 37-39.

Morgan, Robert C. "Beyond Formalism: Language Models, Conceptual Art, and Environmental Art." In *An American Renaissance: Painting and Sculpture Since 1940*, edited by Sam Hunter, 148-157. New York: Abbeville Press, 1986.

_____. *Commentaries on the New Media Arts: Fluxus and Conceptual Art, Artists' Books, Correspondence Art, Audio and Video Art.* Pasadena, California: Umbrella Associates, 1992.

_____. *Conceptual Art: An American Perspective.* Jefferson, North Carolina: McFarland and Co., 1994. Foreword by Michael Kirby; interviews with Hans Haacke, Lawrence Weiner, and Allan Kaprow.

_____. "Conceptual Art and the Continuing Quest for a New Social Context." *Journal: Southern California Art Magazine* (Los Angeles), no. 21 (June-July 1979): 30-36.

_____. "Conceptual Art and Photographic Installations: The Recent Outlook." *Afterimage* (Rochester, New York) 9, no. 5 (December 1981): 8-11.

_____. "Fables, Grids, and Swimming Pools: Phototexts in Perspective." *Journal: Southern California Art Magazine* (Los Angeles), no. 24 (September-October 1979): 39-43.

_____. "Idea, Concept, System." *Arts Magazine* 64, no. 1 (September 1989): 61-65.

_____. "The Role of Documentation in Conceptual Art: An Aesthetic Inquiry." Ph.D. diss., New York University, 1978.

_____. "The Situation of Conceptual Art: The 'January Show' and After." *Arts Magazine* 63, no. 6 (February 1989): 40-43.

_____. "Word, Document, Installation: Recent Developments in Conceptual Art." *Arts Magazine* 65, no. 9 (May 1991): 65-69.

Morgan, Stuart. "A Rhetoric of Silence: Redefinitions of Sculpture in the 1960s and 1970s." In *British Sculpture in the Twentieth Century*, edited by Sandy Nairne and Nicholas Serota, 197-208. Exh. cat. London: Whitechapel Art Gallery, 1981.

Morris, Robert. "Notes on Sculpture, Part 4: Beyond Objects." *Artforum* 7, no. 8 (April 1969): 50-54.

Morton, Luise H. "Theories of Three Conceptual Artists: A Critique and Comparison [Kosuth, LeWitt, Atkinson]." Ph.D. diss., Ball State University, Muncie, Indiana, 1985.

Music, Sound, Language, Theater: John Cage, Tom Marioni, Robert Barry, Joan Jonas. Exh. cat. Oakland, California: Crown Point Press, 1980. Essays by Kathan Brown, Jackson MacLow, William Spurlock, Peter Frank, and Douglas Crimp; artists' biographies and exhibition chronologies.

N

Nemser, Cindy. "Subject-Object: Body Art." *Arts Magazine* 46, no. 1 (September-October 1971): 38-42.

New Alchemy: Elements, Systems, Forces／Nouvelle alchimie: Elements, systèmes, forces. Exh. cat. Toronto: Art Gallery of Ontario, 1969. Foreword by Antonio Toledo; acknowledgments by W. J. Withrow; introduction by Dennis Young; artists' biographies, bibliographies, and exhibition chronologies.

The New Art. Exh. cat. London: Hayward Gallery in association with Arts Council of Great Britain, 1972. Preface by Robin Campbell and Norbert Lynton; introduction by Anne Seymour; exhibition chronology.

The New Art Practice in Yugoslavia 1966-1978. Exh. cat. Zagreb: Galerije Grada Zagreba, 1978. Foreword by Marijan Susovski; texts by Ješa Denegri, Tomaž Brejc, Davor Matičević, Nena Baljković, Ida Biard, Mirko Radojičić, Bálint Szombathy, Vladan Radovanović, Jasna Tijardović, Slavko Timotijević, Ratomir Kulić and Vladimir Mattioni, and Group 143.

19:45-21:55: September 9th, 1967: Frankfurt, Germany: Dies alles Herzchen wird einmal Dir gehören. Exh. cat. Frankfurt: Paul Maenz, 1967.

1977 Biennial Exhibition: Contemporary American Art. Exh. cat. New York: Whitney Museum of American Art, 1977. Foreword by Tom Armstrong; introduction by Barbara Haskell, Marcia Tucker, and Patterson Sims; essay by John G. Hanhardt and Mark Segal.

1965 to 1972: When Attitudes Became Form. Exh. cat. Cambridge: Kettle's Yard Gallery and Edinburgh: Fruitmarket Gallery, 1984. Introduction by Hilary Gresty; essays by Charles Harrison and Victor Burgin; exhibition chronology; bibliography.

1967: At the Crossroads. Exh. cat. Philadelphia: Institute of Contemporary Art, University of Pennsylvania, 1987. Essays by Janet Kardon, Hal Foster, Lucy R. Lippard, Barbara Rose, and Irving Sandler; art activities and time line by Kardon; bibliography.

No Title: The Collection of Sol LeWitt. Exh. cat. Middletown, Connecticut: Wesleyan University Art Gallery and the Davison Art Center at Wesleyan University, 1981. Preface by Andrea Miller-Keller and Tracy Atkinson; introduction and texts by John T. Paoletti; bibliography.

Non-Anthropomorphic Art by Four Young Artists: Joseph Kosuth, Christine Kozlov, Michael Rinaldi, Ernest Rossi. New York: Lannis Gallery, 1966.

"A Note on Conceptual Art." In *The Tate Gallery 1972-74: Biennial Report and Illustrated Catalogue of Acquisitions,* 29-33. London: Tate Gallery, 1975.

Nottingham Festival 1970: Visions, Projects, Proposals. Exh. cat. Nottingham, England: Midland Group Gallery, 1970. Essay by Tim Threefall.

Nye, Timothy. "Conceptual Art: A Spatial Perspective." In *The Power of the City/The City of Power,* exh. cat., 11-23. New York: Whitney Museum of American Art, New York, 1992.

O

O'Doherty, Brian. "The Gallery as a Gesture." *Artforum* 20, no. 4 (December 1981): 25-34.

_____. *Inside the White Cube: The Ideology of the Gallery Space.* Santa Monica, California: Lapis Press, 1986. Introduction by Thomas McEvilley.

Olek, Jerzy. "Cielesność konceptualizmu"?/"Tangibility of Conceptualism?" *Projektu* 2 (1988): 66-69, 77, 86.

One Month (also known as *March 1969*). Exh. cat. New York: Seth Siegelaub, 1969.

Op Losse Schroeven: Situaties en Cryptostructuren (Square Pegs in Round Holes). Exh. cat. Amsterdam: Stedelijk Museum, 1969. In two parts: Part 1 includes preface by Edy de Wilde; essay by Wim Beeren; artists' exhibition chronologies and bibliographies. Part 2 contains a "page project" by each artist. Also published as *Verborgene Strukturen.* Exh. cat. Essen: Museum Folkwang, 1969. Preface by Dieter Honisch; introduction by Wim Beeren; artists' bibliographies and exhibition chronologies.

Other Ideas. Exh. cat. Detroit: The Detroit Institute of Arts, 1969. Introduction by Samuel J. Wagstaff, Jr.

"Out of Sight, Out of Mind." Exh. brochure. London: Lisson Gallery, 1993. Text by Nicholas Logsdail.

P

Painting, Drawing, and Sculpture of the '60s and the '70s from the Dorothy and Herbert Vogel Collection. Exh. cat. Philadelphia: Institute of Contemporary Art, University of Pennsylvania, 1975. Foreword by Suzanne Delehanty.

Perreault, John. "False Objects: Duplicates, Replicas, and Types." *Artforum* 16, no. 6 (February 1978): 24-27.

Persona. Exh. cat. Belgrade: International Theatre Festival in association with Florence: Centro Di, 1971.

Phillpot, Clive. "Art Magazines and Magazine Art." *Artforum* 18, no. 6 (February 1980): 52-54.

_____, comp. "Art Works in Print." *Studio International* (London) 193, no. 983 (September-October 1976): 126-131.

Pier + Ocean: Construction in the Art of the Seventies. Exh. cat. London: Hayward Gallery in association with Arts Council of Great Britain, 1980. Acknowledgments by Joanna Drew and Andrew Dempsey; introduction by Gerhard von Graevenitz; text by Samuel Beckett; selected texts compiled by Barry Barker; artists' exhibition chronologies.

Pincus-Witten, Robert. "Theater of the Conceptual: Autobiography and Myth." *Artforum* 12, no. 2 (October 1973): 40-46.

Pläne und Projekte als Kunst/Plans and Projects as Art. Exh. cat. Bern: Kunsthalle, 1969. Introduction by P. F. Althaus.

Popper, Frank. *Art — Action and Participation.* New York: New York University Press, 1975.

The Presence of Absence: New Installations. Exh. cat. New York: Independent Curators Incorporated, 1989. Essay by Nina Felshin.

Primary Structures: Younger American and British Sculptors. Exh. cat. New York: The Jewish Museum, 1966. Acknowledgments and introduction by Kynaston L. McShine; artists' biographies and exhibition chronologies; bibliography.

Projections: Anti-Materialism. Exh. cat. La Jolla, California: La Jolla Museum of Art, 1970. Foreword by Buckminster Fuller; introduction by Lawrence Urrutia; artists' exhibition chronologies.

Prospect 71: Projection. Exh. cat. Düsseldorf: Städtische Kunsthalle in association with Art-Press, 1971. Foreword by Hans Strelow; artists' biographies.

ProspectRetrospect: Europa 1946-1976. Exh. cat. Düsseldorf: Städtische Kunsthalle in association with Cologne: Buchhandlung Walther König, 1976. Texts by Benjamin H. D. Buchloh, R. H. Fuchs, Konrad Fischer, Jürgen Harten, John Matheson, and Hans Strelow; chronology of exhibitions organized by Städtische Kunsthalle Düsseldorf, 1946-1976.

R

Ramírez, Mari Carmen. "Blueprint Circuits: Conceptual Art and Politics in Latin America." In *Latin American Artists of the Twentieth Century*, exh. cat., edited by Waldo Rasmussen with Fatima Bercht and Elizabeth Ferrer, 156-167. New York: The Museum of Modern Art, 1993.

Ravicz, Marilyn Ekdahl. "Aesthetic Anthropology: Theory and Analysis of Pop and Conceptual Art in America." Ph.D. diss., University of California, Los Angeles, 1974.

The Record as Artwork: From Futurism to Conceptual Art. Exh. cat. Fort Worth, Texas: The Fort Worth Art Museum, 1977. Acknowledgments and essay by Germano Celant; introduction by Anne Livet; discography; list of record producers; Celant biography. Essay is a revised version of "Record as Artwork," *Studio International* (London) 192, no. 984 (November-December 1976): 267-273.

Recorded Activities. Exh. cat. Philadelphia: Moore College of Art, 1970. Preface by Lucy R. Lippard.

Reise, Barbara M. "Art et langage (verbal)." *Chroniques de l'art vivant* (Paris), no. 29 (April 1972): 4-6.

————. "Spinofferie." Review of *Idea Art: A Critical Anthology*, edited by Gregory Battcock. *Studio International* (London) 187, no. 964 (March 1974): 149-150.

The Return of Abstract Expressionism. Exh. cat. Richmond, California: Richmond Art Center, 1969. Introduction by Tom Marioni.

Richard, Nelly. *Art and Text* (Melbourne), no. 21 (May-July 1986). Special issue: Margins and Institutions: Art in Chile Since 1973.

Ridgeway, Sally Ormiston. "When Object Becomes Idea: The Social History of an Avant-Garde Art Movement." Ph.D. diss., The City University of New York, 1975.

Robert Barry, Victor Burgin, Hamish Fulton, Gilbert & George, Hans Haacke, John Hilliard, Joseph Kosuth/Sarah Charlesworth, David Tremlett, Lawrence Weiner. Exh. cat. Edinburgh: Fruit Market Gallery in association with Scottish Arts Council, 1976. Foreword by Robert Breen; introduction by Barry Barker; artists' biographies, bibliographies, and exhibition chronologies; exhibition chronology.

Rorimer, Anne. "Photography — Language — Context: Prelude to the 1980s." In *A Forest of Signs: Art in the Crisis of Representation*, exh. cat., edited by Catherine Gudis, 129-153. Los Angeles: The Museum of Contemporary Art in association with Cambridge: The MIT Press, 1989.

Rose, Arthur R. [pseud.]. "Four Interviews with Barry, Huebler, Kosuth, Weiner." *Arts Magazine* 43, no. 4 (February 1969): 22-23.

————. "The Return of Arthur R. Rose." *Arts Magazine* 63, no. 6 (February 1989): 46-50. Interviews with Robert Barry, Douglas Huebler, Joseph Kosuth, and Lawrence Weiner.

Rose, Barbara. "Problems of Criticism, VI: The Politics of Art, Part III." *Artforum* 7, no. 9 (May 1969): 46-51.

Russell, Charles. "Toward Tautology: The 'Nouveau Roman' and Conceptual Art." *MLN* (Baltimore) 91, no. 5 (October 1976): 1044-1060.

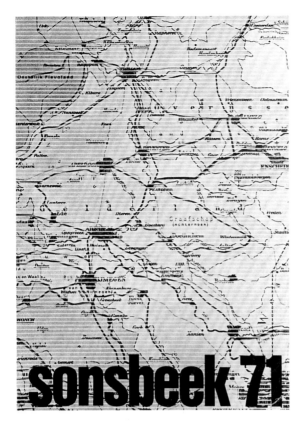

sonsbeek 71

s

Sammlung 1968: Karl Ströher. Exh. cat. Berlin: Kunstverein and Neue Nationalgalerie, 1969. Essay by Hans Strelow.

Sandler, Irving. *American Art of the 1960s*. New York: Harper and Row, 1988.

Schmalriede, Manfred. "Konzeptkunst und Semiotik." *Kunstforum International* (Mainz) 42, no. 6 (1980): 35-47.

Schneider, Ira, and Beryl Korot, eds. *Video Art: An Anthology*. New York: Harcourt Brace Jovanovich, 1976. Acknowledgments and introduction by Schneider and Korot; essays by Shigeko Kubota, Rebecca Lawrence, George Bolling, Robert Stearns, James Beck, Russell Connor, David Antin, Stephen Beck, Eric Cameron, Douglas Davis, Anne Focke, Peter Frank, Hermine Freed, Davidson Gigliotti, Frank Gillette, John G. Hanhardt, Wulf Herzogenrath, Bruce Kurtz, David A. Ross, Willoughby Sharp, Bill Viola, and Ingrid Wiegand.

Schwarz, Michael. "Über den Realismus politischer Konzeptkunst." *Kunstforum International* (Stuttgart) 42, no. 6 (1980): 14-34.

Sclafani, Richard J. Review of *Conceptual Art*, by Ursula Meyer. *The Journal of Aesthetics and Art Criticism* (Madison, Wisconsin) 32, no. 3 (Spring 1974): 443-444.

_____. "What Kind of Nonsense Is This?" *The Journal of Aesthetics and Art Criticism* (Madison, Wisconsin) 33, no. 4 (Summer 1975): 455-458.

A Selection of Conceptual Works by Eight Americans. Exh. cat. New York: Julian Pretto Gallery, 1978. Artists' texts.

Septième Biennale de Paris. Exh. cat. Paris: Parc Floral de Paris, Bois de Vincennes, Manifestation Biennale and Internationale des Jeunes Artistes, 1971. Essays in "Concept" section by Catherine Millet and Alfred Pacquement.

Serielle Formationen. Exh. cat. Frankfurt: Studio Galerie, Johann Wolfgang Goethe Universität, 1967. Acknowledgments by Siegfried Bartels; introduction by Paul Maenz and Peter Roehr; artists' texts.

73-74: An Annual of New Art and Artists. New York: Harry N. Abrams, 1974. Foreword by Willem Sandberg; introduction by Sam Hunter.

Shirey, David L. "Impossible Art — What It Is." *Art in America* 57, no. 3 (May-June 1969): 32-47.

Siegelaub, Seth, ed. "July-August 1970." *Studio International* (London) 180, no. 924 (July-August 1970): 1-48. Also published as *July/August Exhibition Book*. London: Studio International and Seth Siegelaub, 1970.

Situation Concepts. Exh. cat. Innsbruck: Galerie im Taxispalais, 1971. Texts by Mel Bochner, Joseph Kosuth, Sol LeWitt, Bruce Nauman, and Ricky Comi.

'60 '80: Attitudes/Concepts/Images. Exh. cat. Amsterdam: Stedelijk Museum in association with Van Gennep, 1982. Forewords by Edy de Wilde and George Weissman; introduction by Ad Petersen; essays by de Wilde, Gijs van Tuyl, Wim Beeren, Antje von Graevenitz, and Cor Blok; list of exhibitions at the Stedelijk Museum, 1960-1980; artists' bibliographies, exhibition chronologies, and statements. Catalogue supplement introduction by Ad Petersen; essays by Dorine Mignot, Frans van Rossum, and Petersen; calendar and documentation of events.

65-75: Aspetti e pratiche dell'arte europea. Exh. cat. Turin: Castello di Rivara, 1990. Essay by Gregorio Magnani.

Smith, Roberta. "Conceptual Art." In *Concepts of Modern Art*, edited by Nikos Stangos, 256-272. London: Thames and Hudson, 1989.

Software: Information Technology: Its New Meaning for Art. Exh. cat. New York: The Jewish Museum, 1970. Preface by Roy D. Chapin, Jr.; introduction by Karl Katz; essay by Jack Burnham; texts by James A. Mahoney, Ned Woodman and Theodor Nelson, and the artists.

Sonsbeek 71: Buiten de perken. Exh. cat. 2 vols. Arnhem, The Netherlands: Sonsbeek 71 Foundation, 1971. Preface by P. Sanders; introduction by Wim Beeren; bibliography; exhibition chronology; documentation of events.

Soundings. Exh. cat. Purchase, New York: Neuberger Museum, State University of New York at Purchase, 1981. Acknowledgments and essay by Suzanne Delehanty; essays by Delehanty, Dore Ashton, Germano Celant, and Lucy Fischer; bibliography.

Space/Time/Sound: Conceptual Art in the San Francisco Bay Area: The 1970s. Exh. cat. San Francisco: San Francisco Museum of Modern Art, 1979. Texts by Suzanne Foley; chronology by Constance Lewallen.

Spaces. Exh. cat. New York: The Museum of Modern Art, 1969. Acknowledgments and essay by Jennifer Licht.

Stainback, Charles. "Special Collections: The Photographic Order from Pop to Now." In *Special Collections: The Photographic Order from Pop to Now*, exh. cat., 5-15. New York: International Center for Photography, 1992.

Staniszewski, Mary Anne, ed. "Conceptual Supplement." *Flash Art*, no. 143 (November-December 1988): 88-117. Texts by Michael Baldwin, Robert Barry, Victor Burgin, Ian Burn, Clegg & Guttmann, General Idea, Dan Graham, Jenny Holzer, Harold Hurrell, Alfredo Jaar,

Silvia Kolbowski, Joseph Kosuth, Barbara Kruger, Muntadas, and Adrian Piper; interviews with Mary Kelly, Jeff Koons, and Mel Ramsden.

Stellweg, Carla. "'Magnet-New York': Conceptual, Performance, Environmental, and Installation Art." In *The Latin American Spirit: Art and Artists in the United States, 1920-1970*, exh. cat., 284-311. The Bronx, New York: The Bronx Museum of the Arts in association with Harry N. Abrams, Inc., 1989.

Sterckx, P., and V. Baudoux. "Concept and cie." *Clés pour les arts*, no. 44 (June 1974): 26-27.

Stezaker, John. "Conceptual Documentation." *Studio International* (London) 184, no. 946 (July-August 1972): 51-52. Review of *Conceptual Art*, by Ursula Meyer.

Stimson, Paul. "Between the Signs." *Art in America* 67, no. 6 (October 1979): 80-81.

Subotic, Irina. "Jugoslavia: Arte concettuale." *D'Are* 13, no. 58-59 (February-March 1972): 66-71.

A Survey of the Avant-Garde in Britain. Exh. cat. London: Gallery House, 1972. Introduction by Rosetta Brooks.

Systemic Painting. Exh. cat. New York: The Solomon R. Guggenheim Foundation, 1966. Preface by Thomas M. Messer; acknowledgments and introduction by Lawrence Alloway; bibliography; artists' statements and bibliographies.

Szeemann, Harald. *Dokumente zur aktuellen Kunst 1967-1970: Material aus dem Archiv Szeemann*. Lucerne: Kunstkreis, 1972. Texts by Georg Jappe, Aurel Schmidt, and Szeemann.

T

The Third Biennale of Sydney. Exh. cat. Sidney: The Art Gallery of New South Wales and The Australian Centre for Photography, 1979. Section introductions by Nick Waterlow, Wieland Schmied, and Béatrice Parent; essays by George Boudaille and Karl Ruhrberg; artists' exhibition chronologies.

Tomassoni, Italo. "Dall'oggetto al concetto: Elogia della tautologia." *Flash Art*, no. 28-29 (December 1971-January 1972): 14-15.

Trini, Tommaso. "Neoclassicism in Black and White with Notes on Neoconceptualism." *Domus* (Milan) 495, no. 2 (February 1971): 52-54; English translation between 54 and 55.

Triquarterly (Evanston, Illinois), no. 32 (Winter 1975). Special issue: Anti-Object Art. Edited by Lawrence Levy and John Perreault. Introduction by Perreault; artists' projects.

The Turning Point: Art and Politics in 1968. Exh. cat. Cleveland: Cleveland Center for Contemporary Art, 1988. Preface and acknowledgments by Nina Castelli Sundell and Marjorie Talalay; essays by Sundell and Irwin Unger; chronology of art activities, exhibitions, and events; bibliography.

2,972,453. Exh. cat. Buenos Aires: Centro de Arte y Comunicación. Exh. cat. Texts by Lucy R. Lippard and Jorge Glusberg. Catalogue comprised of randomly ordered index cards.

V

Van der Marck, Jan. "Inside Europe Outside Europe." *Artforum* 16, no. 5 (January 1978): 49-55. Exh. review of "Europe in the Seventies: Aspects of Recent Art."

Van Mechelen, Marga. "Language as Art, Art as Language: A Study on the Journals *Art-Language* and *The Fox*." Ph.D. diss., Arnhem, The Netherlands, 1978.

Van Tuyl, Gijs. "Informatie en/of Interpretie." *Museumjournaal* (Otterloo) 18, no. 4 (September 1973): 163-169.

Vergine, Lea. "Arte concettuale." In *Dall'informale alla body art: Dieci voci dell'arte contemporanea: 1960/1970*, 100-109. Turin: Cooperativa Editoriale Studio Forma, 1976. Bibliography.

_____. "Arte concettuale." *Notiziario arte contemporanea* (Rome), no. 11 (November 1973): 23-24.

Vicente Aliaga, Juan. "Conceptual Art in Spain: Traditionalism Subtly Undermined." *Art International*, no. 6 (Spring 1989): 28-31.

_____, and José Miguel G. Cortés. *Arte conceptual revisado/Conceptual Art Revisited*. Valencia: Departamento de Escultura, Facultad de Bellas Artes, Universidad Politecnica de Valencia, 1990. Texts by Vicente Aliaga and Cortés, Catherine Millet, and Robert C. Morgan; interviews with Art & Language (Michael Baldwin and Mel Ramsden), John Baldessari, Simón Marchán Fiz, Millet, Stuart Morgan, and Robert Barry/Douglas Huebler/Joseph Kosuth/Lawrence Weiner by Arthur R. Rose [pseud.].

Video Art. Exh. cat. Philadelphia: Institute of Contemporary Art, University of Pennsylvania, 1975. Acknowledgments by Suzanne Delehanty; essays by David Antin, Lizzie Borden, Jack Burnham, and John McHale; artists' biographies and exhibition chronologies; bibliography.

Virginia Dwan: Art minimal — art conceptuel — earthworks: New York, les années 60-70. Exh. cat. Paris: Galerie Montaigne, 1991. Foreword by Loïc Mallé; essay by Jan van der Marck; reprint of oral history by Virginia Dwan; statements by Dwan and Charles Stuckey; Dwan Gallery exhibition chronology.

LIVE IN YOUR HEAD

WHEN ATTITUDES BECOME FORM
WORKS · CONCEPTS · PROCESSES · SITUATIONS · INFORMATION

WENN ATTITÜDEN FORM WERDEN
WERKE · KONZEPTE · PROZESSE · SITUATIONEN · INFORMATION

QUAND LES ATTITUDES DEVIENNENT FORME
OEUVRES · CONCEPTS · PROCESSUS · SITUATIONS · INFORMATION

QUANDO ATTITUDINI DIVENTANO FORMA
OPERE · CONCETTI · PROCESSI · SITUAZIONI · INFORMAZIONE

AN EXHIBITION SPONSORED BY PHILIP MORRIS EUROPE

Vision (Oakland, California), no. 1 (September 1975). Special issue: California. Essays by Claes Oldenburg and Tom Marioni; other contributions by Wayne Thiebaud, Fred Martin, Bruce Conner, William T. Wiley, Tom Marioni, Terry Fox, Paul Kos, Jim Melchert, Paul Cotton, Howard Fried, Bonnie Sherk, Linda Montano, Larry Bell, Robert Irwin, Doug Wheeler, Michael Asher, Bruce Nauman, Edward Ruscha, Allen Ruppersberg, Chris Burden, Eleanor Antin, Barbara Smith, and Charles Hill.

Vision, no. 2 (January 1976). Special issue: Eastern Europe. Essay by Tom Marioni; other contributions by Radomir Damnjan, Mića Popović, Julije Knifer, Zoran Popovicević, Braco Dimirijević, Marina Abramović, Raša Todosijević, Gabor Attalai, Endre Tot, Visy László, Petr Stembera, Jan Mlćoch, Karel Miller, Milan Grygar, Miloslav Moucha, Peter Bartos, Tadeusz Kantor, Druga Grupa, Roman Opalka, Andrzej Lachowicz, and Krzysztof Wodiczko.

Vision, no. 3 (November 1976). Special issue: New York. Essay by Tom Marioni; other contributions by Claes Oldenburg, Allan Kaprow, Les Levine, Walter de Maria, Daniel Buren, George Maciunas, Carl Andre, Sol LeWitt, Hans Haacke, Lawrence Weiner, Robert Barry, Chuck Close, and Vito Acconci.

W

"Was die Schönheit sei, das weiss ich nicht": Künstler, Theorie, Werk: Katalog zur zweiten Biennale Nürnberg. Exh. cat. Nuremberg: Kunsthalle and Cologne: M. Dumont Schauberg, 1971. Artists' biographies, bibliographies, and exhibition chronologies.

West Coast Conceptual Photography. Exh. cat. San Francisco: La Mamelle, 1976. Introduction by Carl Loeffler; essays by Lew Thomas and James Richard Hugunin; history of Conceptual photography by Mary Stofflet.

When Attitudes Become Form: Works — Concepts — Processes — Situations — Information: Live in Your Head. Exh. cat. Bern: Kunsthalle, 1969. Acknowledgments and introduction by Harald Szeemann; essays by Scott Burton, Gregoire Müller, and Tommaso Trini; artists' biographies; bibliography. "Against Precendents" by Charles Harrison published for London exhibition catalogue (reprinted in *Studio International* (London) 178, no. 914 (September 1969): 90-93).

White, Robert, and Gary Michael Dault. "Word Art and Art Word." *Artscanada* (Toronto), no. 118-119 (June 1968): 17-20.

Wolfe, Clair. "On Art Writing, Part II: A Conceptual Criticism." *Journal: Southern California Art Magazine* (Los Angeles), no. 24 (September-October 1979): 56-59.

SPECIAL COLLECTIONS

The library of The Museum of Modern Art in New York has perhaps the largest single collection of artists' books and exhibition catalogues related to Conceptual art. Seth Siegelaub's archive of material from his work as an art dealer and exhibition organizer between 1964 and 1971 has been catalogued by Alexander Alberro and is in his care in Brooklyn, New York. Many of Lucy R. Lippard's notes, papers, collection of exhibition ephemera, and artists' files have been deposited with the Archives of American Art in Washington, D.C. The records for Virginia Dwan's gallery, including the four exhibitions on language she organized, can be accessed through Silent Partners Consulting, located in Brooklyn, New York, while documentation of exhibitions for the now defunct New York Cultural Center can be found at Farleigh Dickinson University in Morristown, New Jersey. The Conceptual Art Study Center at the University Art Museum and Pacific Film Archive of the University of California at Berkeley houses Conceptual art works, archival documents, books, exhibition catalogues, videotapes and sound recordings, including the archives of Tom Marioni's San Francisco–based Museum of Conceptual Art, and the "Konzeption-Conception" exhibition held in Leverkusen, West Germany, in 1969. And finally, the Research Center of the J. Paul Getty Museum in Santa Monica, California, recently purchased the complete archives and exhibition photographic documentation of the Paul Maenz Gallery.

310

Edward Ruscha
EVERY BUILDING ON THE SUNSET STRIP, (1966)
Installation view, "18 Paris IV.70," 66 rue Mouffetard, Paris, April 1970
(organized by Michel Claura). Photo courtesy The Siegelaub Collection & Archives.

VITO ACCONCI

Avalanche (New York), no. 6 (Fall 1972). Special issue: Vito Acconci. Documentation of artist's projects; interview by Liza Béar; biography; bibliography.

Diacono, Mario. *Vito Acconci: Dal testo-azione al corpo come testo.* New York: Out of London Press, 1975. Includes artist's texts; chronology of works.

Kunz, Martin. "Interview with Vito Acconci about the Development of His Work Since 1966." In *Vito Acconci: Cultural Space Pieces 1974-1978,* unpag. Exh. cat. Lucerne: Kunstmuseum Luzern, 1978. Includes biography; bibliography.

Linker, Kate. *Vito Acconci.* New York: Rizzoli, 1994. Biography; exhibition chronology; bibliography.

Pincus-Witten, Robert. "Vito Acconci and the Conceptual Performance." *Artforum* 10, no. 8 (April 1972): 47-49.

Sondheim, Alan. "Vito Acconci: Work, 1973-1974." *Arts Magazine* 49, no. 7 (March 1975): 49-52.

Vito Acconci: Photographic Works 1969-70. Exh. cat. Chicago: Rhona Hoffman Gallery, 1988. Essays by Kate Linker and Acconci; biography; exhibition chronology.

Vito Acconci: A Retrospective: 1969-1980. Exh. cat. Chicago: Museum of Contemporary Art, 1980. Essay by Judith Russi Kirshner; exhibition chronology; bibliography.

BAS JAN ADER

Ader, Bas Jan. "'In Search of the Miraculous' (Songs for the North Atlantic: July 1975)." *Art & Project Bulletin* (Amsterdam), no. 89 (July 1975): unpag.

_____. *What Makes Me So Pure, Almost Holy? And More + What Does it Mean? Cheep Cheep.* Claremont, California: Claremont Colleges Printing Service, 1967.

Bas Jan Ader: Kunstenaar/Artist. Exh. cat. Amsterdam: Stedelijk Museum, 1988. Foreword by Rini Dippel; essays by Paul Andriesse, Ger van Elk, and William Leavitt; biography; exhibition chronology; bibliography.

Béar, Liza, and Willoughby Sharp. "A Telephone Conversation with Mary Sue Ader, Los Angeles, May 28th, 1976." *Avalanche* (New York), no. 13 (Summer 1976): 26-27.

Roberts, James. "Bas Jan Ader: The Artist Who Fell from Grace with the Sea." *Frieze* (London), no. 17 (June-July-August 1994): 32-35.

GIOVANNI ANSELMO

Giovanni Anselmo. Exh. cat. Basel: Kunsthalle and Eindhoven: Stedelijk Van Abbemuseum, 1979. Texts by Jean-Christophe Ammann, R. H. Fuchs, Anselmo, and M. Suter.

Giovanni Anselmo. Exh. cat. Grenoble: Musée de Grenoble, 1980. Introduction by Thierry Raspail; essay by Jean-Christophe Ammann; text by R. H. Fuchs; exhibition chronology; bibliography.

Giovanni Anselmo. Exh. cat. Lucerne: Kunstmuseum Luzern, 1973. Text by Jean-Christophe Ammann; exhibition chronology; bibliography.

Giovanni Anselmo. Exh. cat. Modena: Galleria Civica, Florence: Hopeful Monster, and Lyon: Musée d'art contemporain, 1989. Text by B. Merz; bibliography.

Giovanni Anselmo. Exh. cat. Paris: Les Amis du Musée d'art moderne de la Ville de Paris, 1985. Introduction by Suzanne Pagé; essay by Daniel Soutif; exhibition chronology; bibliography.

Giovanni Anselmo. Exh. cat. Turin: Galleria Sperone, 1968. Texts by Germano Celant and Maurizio Fagiolo.

ELEANOR ANTIN

Antin, Eleanor. "An Autobiography of the Artist as an Autobiographer." *Journal* (Los Angeles), no. 2 (October 1974): 18-20.

_____. "Out of the Box." *The Art Gallery* (Ivoryton, Connecticut) 15, no. 9 (June 1972): 26-27, 88.

Bowen, Nancy. "On Art and Artists: Eleanor Antin." *Profile* (Chicago) 1, no. 4 (July 1981): 1-22. Introduction by Arlene Raven; interview; bibliography.

Eleanor Antin: The Angel of Mercy. Exh. cat. La Jolla, California: La Jolla Museum of Contemporary Art, 1977. Acknowledgments by Christopher Knight and Antin; essays by Jonathan Crary and Kim Levin; biography; exhibition chronology; bibliography.

Nemser, Cindy. "Eleanor Antin." In *Art Talk: Conversations with 12 Women Artists,* 266-294. New York: Charles Scribner's Sons, 1975.

Portner, Dinah. "Interview with Eleanor Antin." *Journal: Southern California Art Magazine* (Los Angeles), no. 26 (February-March 1980): 34-37.

Raven, Arlene, and Deborah Marrow. "Eleanor Antin: What's Your Story?" *Chrysalis* (Los Angeles), no. 8 (Summer 1979): 43-51.

ART & LANGUAGE

Aliaga, Juan Vicente, and José Miguel García Cortés. "Michael Baldwin and Mel Ramsden on Art & Language." *Art and Text* (Melbourne), no. 35 (Summer 1990): 23-37.

Art & Language. Exh. cat. Eindhoven: Stedelijk Van Abbemuseum, 1980. Artists' texts; bibliography.

Art & Language. Exh. cat. Paris: Galerie nationale du Jeu de Paume, 1993. Foreword by Alfred Pacquement and Catherine David; essays by Paul Wood, Art & Language, and Charles Harrison; exhibition chronology; bibliography.

Art & Language 1966-1975. Exh. cat. Oxford: Museum of Modern Art, 1975. Artists' texts.

Art & Language: Proceedings I-IV. Exh. cat. Lucerne: Kunstmuseum Luzern, 1974. Introduction by Jean-Christophe Ammann; biographies.

Atkinson, Terry et al. "Status and Priority." *Studio International* (London) 179, no. 918 (January 1970): 28-31.

Harrison, Charles. *Essays on Art & Language.* Cambridge, Massachusetts: Basil Blackwell, 1991. Foreword by Thomas Crow.

_____, and Fred Orton. *A Provisional History of Art & Language.* Paris: Editions Eric Fabre, 1982.

Maenz, Paul, and Gerd de Vries, comps. *Art & Language: Texte zum Phänomen Kunst und Sprache.* Cologne: Dumont-Schauberg, 1972.

Smith, Terry. "Art and Art & Language." *Artforum* 12, no. 6 (February 1974): 49-52.

MICHAEL ASHER

Asher, Michael. *Writings 1973-1983 on Works 1969-1979.* Edited by Benjamin H. D. Buchloh. Halifax: The Press of the Nova Scotia College of Art and Design and Los Angeles: The Museum of Contemporary Art, 1983. Includes editor's note by Buchloh; exhibition chronology; bibliography.

Michael Asher. Exh. cat. Villeurbanne: Le Nouveau Musée, 1991. Introduction by Asher; essay by Frederik Leen; exhibition chronology; bibliography.

Michael Asher: Exhibitions in Europe 1972-1977. Exh. cat. Eindhoven: Stedelijk Van Abbemuseum, 1980. Essays by Benjamin H. D. Buchloh and R. H. Fuchs.

Rorimer, Anne. "Michael Asher: Recent Work." *Artforum* 18, no. 8 (April 1980): 46-50.

DAVID ASKEVOLD

David Askevold. Exh. cat. Eindhoven: Stedelijk Van Abbemuseum, 1981. Preface by Frederick Dolan; essays by Peggy Gale and Alan Sondheim; texts by Askevold.

Extra (Cologne), no. 4 (April 1975). Special issue: David Askevold. Bibliography; exhibition chronology; documentation of works.

JOHN BALDESSARI

John Baldessari. Exh. cat. Eindhoven: Stedelijk Van Abbemuseum and Essen: Museum Folkwang, 1981. Acknowledgments by Zdenek Felix and R. H. Fuchs; preface by Fuchs; artist's texts; exhibition chronology; bibliography.

John Baldessari. Exh. cat. New York: The New Museum of Contemporary Art and Dayton, Ohio: University Art Galleries, Wright State University, 1981. Essays by Marcia Tucker and Robert Pincus-Witten; interview by Nancy Drew; exhibition chronology.

van Bruggen, Coosje. *John Baldessari.* Exh. cat. Los Angeles: The Museum of Contemporary Art and New York: Rizzoli, 1990. Includes foreword and acknowledgments by Richard Koshalek; biography, exhibition chronology, and bibliography by David Platzker.

ROBERT BARRY

Denizot, René. *Word for Word: It's about Time/Mot pour mot: Il est temps.* Paris: Yvon Lambert, 1980.

Franz, Erich, ed. *Robert Barry.* Bielefeld: Karl Kerber, 1986. Interview and essay by Robert Morgan; biography.

Nickas, Robert. "Robert Barry." *Journal of Contemporary Art* (New York) 5, no. 1 (Spring 1992): 5-15.

Robert Barry. Exh. cat. Amsterdam: Stedelijk Museum, 1974. Includes review by Lucy R. Lippard.

Robert Barry. Exh. cat. Eindhoven: Stedelijk Van Abbemuseum, 1977. Essays by Jan Debbaut and R. H. Fuchs.

Robert Barry. Exh. cat. Lucerne: Kunstmuseum Luzern, 1974. Introduction by Jean-Christophe Ammann; exhibition chronology; bibliography.

LOTHAR BAUMGARTEN

Brayer, Marie-Ange. "Lothar Baumgarten." *Forum International* 4, no. 19 (October-November 1993): 103-111.

Gale, Peggy. "The Origin of the Night." *Parachute* (Montreal), no. 43 (June-July-August 1986): 5-9.

Lothar Baumgarten: Unsettled Objects. Exh. cat. for "America Invention." New York: Solomon R. Guggenheim Museum, 1993. Introduction by Michael Govan; essays by N. Scott Momaday, Hal Foster, Robert S. Grumet, Govan, Vincent Crapanzano, and Craig Owens; bibliography; exhibition chronology.

Owens, Craig. "Improper Names." *Art in America* 74, no. 10 (October 1986): 126-134, 187.

BERND AND HILLA BECHER

Andre, Carl. "A Note on Bernhard and Hilla Becher." *Artforum* 11, no. 4 (December 1972): 59.

Becher, Bernd and Hilla. *Anonyme Skulpturen: A Typology of Technical Constructions.* New York: Wittenborn and Co., 1970.

_____. *Blast Furnaces.* Cambridge: The MIT Press, 1990.

_____. *Gas Tanks.* Cambridge: The MIT Press, 1993.

_____. *Industrial Façades.* Cambridge: The MIT Press, 1994.

_____. *Water Towers.* Cambridge: The MIT Press, 1988. Essays by Reyner Banham, Weston J. Naef, and the Bechers.

Bernd and Hilla Becher. Exh. cat. La Jolla, California: La Jolla Museum of Contemporary Art, 1974. Acknowledgments and preface by Sebastian Adler; essay by Germano Celant; biography; exhibition chronology; bibliography.

Bernd und Hilla Becher. Exh. cat. Aachen: Gegenverkehr e.V. Zentrum für aktuelle Kunst, 1971. Artists' texts; biographies; exhibition chronology; bibliography.

Bernd und Hilla Becher. Exh. cat. Eindhoven: Stedelijk Van Abbemuseum, 1981. Introduction by R. H. Fuchs; essay by Bernhard Kerber; biography; exhibition chronology; bibliography.

Bernd und Hilla Becher: Fotografien 1957 bis 1975. Exh. cat. Bonn: Rheinisches Landesmuseum, 1975. Foreword by Christoph B. Rüger and Götz Adriani; essay by Klaus Honnef; exhibition chronology.

MEL BOCHNER

Mel Bochner: Number and Shape. Exh. cat. Baltimore: Baltimore Museum of Art, 1976. Foreword by Tom L. Freudenheim; essay by Brenda Richardson; biography; exhibition chronology; bibliography.

Mel Bochner: Photo-Pieces 1966-1967. Exh. cat. New York: David Nolan Gallery, 1990. Excerpts of artist's texts; exhibition chronology and bibliography of photographic works.

Mel Bochner: Thought Made Visible (1966-1973). Exh. cat. New Haven: Yale University Art Gallery, 1995. Essays by Richard Field, Sasha Newman, Yve-Alain Bois, Rosalind E. Krauss, Frederik Leen, James Meyer, Jessica Prinz, Ulrich Wilmes, and Bill Wilson; bibliography; exhibition chronology.

Mel Bochner (toward) Axiom of Indifference: 1971-1973. Exh. cat. New York: Sonnabend Gallery, 1973. Essay by Bruce Boice; reprint from *Arts Magazine* 47, no. 6 (April 1973): 66-68.

Pincus-Witten, Robert. "Bochner at MOMA: Three Ideas and Seven Procedures." *Artforum* 10, no. 4 (December 1971): 28-30.

_____. "Mel Bochner: The Constant as Variable." *Artforum* 11, no. 4 (December 1972): 28-34.

Schwabsky, Barry. "Mel Bochner: Gravats: Représentation des premières oeuvres." *Exposé* (Paris), no. 2 (1995): 134-143.

MARCEL BROODTHAERS

Buchloh, Benjamin H. D., ed. *Marcel Broodthaers: Writings, Interviews, Photographs.* Cambridge: The MIT Press, 1988. Introduction by Buchloh; texts by Broodthaers; essays by Dieter Schwarz, Buchloh, Anne Rorimer, Dirk Snauwaert, Rainer Borgemeister, Michael Oppitz, Birgit Pelzer, and Yves Gevaert; bibliography by Marie-Pascale Gildemyn. Originally published in *October*, no. 42 (Fall 1987).

Marcel Broodthaers. Exh. cat. London: Tate Gallery, 1980. Foreword by Alan Bowness; preface by Pontus Hulten and Maria Gilissen Broodthaers; essays by Marcel Broodthaers, Michael Compton, and Barbara M. Reise; exhibition chronology; film list; bibliography by Marie-Pascale Gildemyn.

Marcel Broodthaers. Exh. cat. Minneapolis: Walker Art Center in association with New York: Rizzoli, 1989. Introduction by Marge Goldwater; essays by Michael Compton, Douglas Crimp, Bruce Jenkins, and Martin Mosebach; exhibition chronology; bibliography.

Marcel Broodthaers. Exh. cat. Paris: Galerie nationale du Jeu de Paume, 1991. Foreword by Alfred Pacquement; preface by Maria Gilissen; essays by Catherine David and Birgit Pelzer; biography by Michael Compton; exhibition chronology; bibliography.

Marcel Broodthaers: Der Adler vom Oligozän bis Heute. 2 vols. Exh. cat. Düsseldorf: Städtische Kunsthalle, 1972. Prefaces by Broodthaers, Jürgen Harten, and Karl Ruhrberg; introduction by Harten; texts by Broodthaers, Michael Oppitz, and Harten; reprints of reviews by various critics; encyclopedia by Harten; bibliography.

Marcel Broodthaers: Catalogue des livres/Catalogue of Books/Katalog der Bücher 1957-1975. Exh. cat. Cologne: Galerie Michael Werner, New York: Marian Goodman Gallery, and Paris: Galerie Gillespie, Laage, Salomon, 1982.

STANLEY BROUWN

Bibliographical information on the artist has not been included at his request.

DANIEL BUREN

Buren, Daniel. *Les couleurs: sculptures/Les formes: peintures.* Edited by Benjamin H. D. Buchloh. Halifax: The Press of the Nova Scotia College of Art and Design in association with Paris: Musée national d'art moderne, Centre Georges Pompidou, 1981. Essays by Buren, Buchloh, Jean-François Lyotard, and Jean-Hubert Martin.

_____. *Les écrits (1965-1990).* 3 vols. Edited by Jean-Marc Poinsot. Bordeaux: Centre d'art plastique contemporain, Musée d'art contemporain, 1991.

_____. *Entrevue: Conversations avec Anne Baldassari.* Paris: Flammarion, 1987. Includes forewords by Robert Bordaz and Henri Martre; introduction by Pontus Hulten; essay by François Mathey.

Daniel Buren. Exh. cat. Mönchengladbach: Städisches Museum, 1971. Essay by Johannes Cladders; texts by Buren.

Daniel Buren: Metamorphoses — Works in Situ. Exh. cat. Amherst: University Gallery, Fine Arts Center, University of Massachusetts, 1987. Introduction by Helaine Posner; essay by Buren; bibliography.

Daniel Buren: Photos–Souvenirs 1965-88. Villeurbanne: Art Edition, 1988.

Francblin, Catherine. *Daniel Buren.* France: Artpress, 1987. Biography; exhibition chronology; bibliography.

Rorimer, Anne. "*Up and Down, In and Out, Step by Step, a Sculpture,* a Work by Daniel Buren." *Museum Studies* (Chicago) 11, no. 2 (Spring 1985): 140-155.

White, Robin. *View* (Oakland, California) 1, no. 9 (February 1979). Special issue: Daniel Buren. Interview; bibliography.

VICTOR BURGIN

Burgin, Victor. *Between.* London: Basil Blackwell and Institute of Contemporary Arts, 1986.

_____. *The End of Art Theory: Criticism and Postmodernity.* Atlantic Highlands, New Jersey: The Humanities Press International, 1986.

_____. "Situational Aesthetics." *Studio International* (London) 178, no. 915 (October 1969): 118-121.

_____. *Thinking Photography.* London: Macmillan, 1982.

_____. *Work and Commentary.* London: Latimer New Dimensions, 1973.

Godfrey, Tony. "Sex, Text, Politics: An Interview with Victor Burgin." *Block* (East Barnet, Hertfordshire, England), no. 7 (1982): 2-26.

Louw, Roelof. "Victor Burgin: Language and Perception." *Artforum* 12, no. 6 (February 1974): 53-55.

Millet, Catherine. "Victor Burgin: Linguaggio, percezione, e funzione, rappresentativa." *Data* (Milan) 2, no. 3 (April 1972): 35-38; English translation, 73-74.

Victor Burgin: Passages. Exh. cat. Villeneuve d'Ascq: Musée d'art moderne de la Communauté Urbaine de Lille, 1991. Essays by Joëlle Pijauder, Régis Durand, and Burgin; excerpts from previously published interviews, exhibition notes, and lectures; biography; bilbiography; exhibition chronology.

ANDRE CADERE

André Cadere: All Walks of Life. Exh. cat. New York: P.S. 1 Museum, The Institute for Contemporary Art, 1989. Forewords by Suzanne Pagé and Alanna Heiss; essays by Bernard Marcelis, Cornelia Lauf, and Jean-Pierre Criqui; biography; bibliography. Also published as *Collections permanente: Hommage à André Cadere* (Paris: Musée d'art moderne de la Ville de Paris, 1992).

Bourdon, David. "André Cadere, 1934-1978." *Arts Magazine* 53, no. 3 (November 1978): 102-103.

Cadere, André. *Histoire d'un travail.* Ghent: Herbert-Gewad, 1982. Documentation of public events, November 1971-November 1977.

Lotringer, Sylvère. "André Cadere: Boy with Stick." *Semiotext(e)* (New York) 3, no. 2 (1979): 140-142. Interview.

Présentation d'un travail/Utilisation d'un travail. Hamburg: Hossmann and Brussels: MTL Gallery, 1975. Lecture given 10 December 1974 at Faculté de Philosophie et Lettres de l'Université Catholique de Louvain, Belgium. Also published as *Presentazione di un lavoro/Utilizzione di un lavoro* (Genoa: Saman Edizione, 1975).

JAMES COLEMAN

James Coleman. Exh. cat. Belfast: Ulster Museum, 1974. Essay by Achille Bonito Oliva.

James Coleman. Exh. cat. Dublin: Douglas Hyde Gallery, 1982. Essay by Jean Fisher; bibliography; exhibition chronology; biography.

James Coleman. Exh. cat. Milan: Studio Marconi, 1970. Texts by Cyril Barret and James Coleman; biography.

James Coleman. Exh. cat. Milan: Studio Marconi, 1973. Essay by Gillo Dorfles; biography; exhibitions.

James Coleman. Exh. cat. Milan: Studio Marconi, 1975. Essay by Riccardo Lucio; exhibition chronology.

James Coleman: Projected Images: 1972-1994. Exh. cat. New York: Dia Center for the Arts, 1995. Preface and acknowledgments by Michael Govan; introduction by Lynne Cooke; essays by Jean Fisher and Benjamin H.D. Buchloh; exhibition chronology; bibliography.

James Coleman: Selected Works. Exh. cat. Chicago: The Renaissance Society at The University of Chicago, 1985. Essays by Anne Rorimer and Michael Newman; biography; bibliography.

HANNE DARBOVEN

Graw, Isabelle. "Marking Time: Time and Writing in the Work of Hanne Darboven." *Artscribe International* (London), no. 79 (January-February 1990): 68-71.

Hanne Darboven. Exh. cat. Münster: Westfälischer Kunstverein, 1971. Introduction by Klaus Honnef; essays by Honnef and Johannes Cladders; exhibition chronology; bibliography.

Hanne Darboven: Ein Monat, ein Jahr, ein Jahrhundert: Arbeiten von 1968 bis 1974. Exh. cat. Basel: Kunstmuseum, 1974. Essay by Franz Meyer; exhibition chronology; bibliography. Also published as *Hanne Darboven: Een maand, een jaar, een eeuw: Werken van 1968 tot en met 1974* (Amsterdam: Stedelijk Museum, 1975).

Hanne Darboven: Primitive Zeit/Uhr Seit/Primitive Time/Clock Time. Exh. cat. Philadelphia: Goldie Paley Gallery, Moore College of Art and Design, 1990. Foreword by Elsa Longhauser; afterword by Coosje van Bruggen; essay by Klaus Honnef; interview; biography; bibliography.

Lippard, Lucy R. "Deep in Numbers." *Artforum* 12, no. 2 (October 1973): 35-39.

Thwaites, John Anthony. "The Numbers Game." *Art and Artists* (London) 6, no. 10 (January 1972): 24-25.

JAN DIBBETS

Boice, Bruce. "Jan Dibbets: The Photograph and the Photographed." *Artforum* 11, no. 8 (April 1973): 45-49.

Fuchs, R. H., and Gloria Moure. *Jan Dibbets: Interior Light, Works on Architecture 1969-1990.* New York: Rizzoli, 1991. Includes artist's statements; biography; bibliography.

Jan Dibbets. Exh. cat. Edinburgh: Scottish Arts Council and Welsh Arts Council, 1976. Acknowledgments by Francis Pugh and Robert Breen; essays by Barbara M. Reise and M. M. M. Vos; exhibition chronology; bibliography.

Jan Dibbets. Exh. cat. Eindhoven: Stedelijk Van Abbemuseum, 1980. Essay by R. H. Fuchs; exhibition chronology; bibliography.

Jan Dibbets. Exh. cat. Minneapolis: Walker Art Center, 1987. Introduction by Martin Friedman; essays by M. M. M. Vos and R. H. Fuchs; biography; exhibition chronology; bibliography.

Reise, Barbara M. "Jan Dibbets: A Perspective Correction." *Art News* 71, no. 4 (Summer 1972): 38-41.

_____. "Notes[1] on Jan Dibbets's[2] Contemporary[3] Nature[4] of Realistic[5] Classicism[6] in the Dutch[7] Tradition[8]." *Studio International* (London) 183, no. 945 (June 1972): 248-255.

Sharp, Willoughby. "Interview with Jan Dibbets." *Avalanche* (New York), no. 1 (Fall 1970): 33-39.

PETER DOWNSBROUGH

Hoang-Gia, Bruno. "Le mot et son usage dans l'oeuvre de Peter Downsbrough." Ph.D. diss., Université de Paris I, Pantheon-Sorbonne, 1993.

Peter Downsbrough. Exh. cat. Eindhoven: Stedelijk Van Abbemuseum, 1977. Texts by R. H. Fuchs and Downsbrough.

Peter Downsbrough: Bücher/Books. Exh. cat. Bremen: Neue Museum Weserburg, 1993. Essay by Guy Schraenen; exhibition chronology; bibliography.

GER VAN ELK

Ger van Elk. Exh. cat. Amsterdam: Stedelijk Museum, 1974. Essay by R. H. Fuchs; biography; exhibition chronology; bibliography.

Ger van Elk. Exh. cat. Basel: Kunsthalle, Paris: Musée d'art moderne de la Ville de Paris, and Rotterdam: Museum Boymans-van Beuningen, 1980. Acknowledgments by Suzanne Pagé, Jean-Christophe Ammann, and Wim Beeren; foreword by Ammann; essay by Beeren; biography; exhibition chronology; bibliography.

Ger van Elk. Exh. cat. Eindhoven: Stedelijk Van Abbemuseum, 1973. Introduction by Jan Leering; interview by Ron Kaal; essay by R. H. Fuchs; biography; exhibition chronology; bibliography.

Ger van Elk. Exh. cat. Karlsruhe: Bädischer Kunstverein, 1977. Preface by Bernhard Holeczek, Klaus Honnef, and Michael Schwarz; essays by R. H. Fuchs and Schwarz; interview by Antje von Graevenitz; biography; exhibitions.

MORGAN FISHER

Andersen, Thom. "Films by Morgan Fisher." Los Angeles: Theatre Vanguard, 1974. Mimeographed program note for screening of 12 February.

_____. "Morgan Fisher." Columbus: Department of Photography and Cinema, Ohio State University, 1979. Mimeographed program note for screening of 4 May in series "Independent Film Makers in Columbus."

Hoberman, J. "After Avant-Garde Film." in *Art after Modernism: Rethinking Representation,* edited by Brian Wallis, 58-73. New York: The New Museum of Contemporary Art and Boston: David R. Godine Publisher, 1984.

James, David. "Morgan Fisher's *Production Stills.*" In *Allegories of Cinema: American Film in the Sixties,* 249-252. Princeton: Princeton University Press, 1989.

MacDonald, Scott. "Morgan Fisher." In *A Critical Cinema: Interviews with Independent Filmmakers,* 353-374. Berkeley: University of California Press, 1988.

_____. "Morgan Fisher: Film on Film." *Cinema Journal* (Lawrence, Kansas) 28, no. 2 (Winter 1989): 13-27.

Sitney, P. Adams. "The Achievement of the American Avant-Garde Cinema, 1960-1979." In *"The Pleasure Dome": Amerikansk Experimentfilm 1939-1979/American Experimental Film 1939-1979,* 21-35. Exh. cat. Stockholm: Moderna Museet, 1980.

Williams, Alan. "Evenings for New Film: Morgan Fisher." Buffalo: Albright Knox Gallery in collaboration with Media Study/Buffalo and Center for Media Study, State University of New York, 1976. Photocopied program note for screening of 15 January.

GILBERT & GEORGE

Gilbert & George: The Complete Pictures 1971-1985. New York: Rizzoli, 1986. Text by Gilbert & George; essay by Carter Ratcliff; documentation of works, 1971-85; biographies; exhibition chronology; bibliography.

Gilbert & George 1968 to 1980. Exh. cat. Eindhoven: Stedelijk Van Abbemuseum, 1980. Essay by Carter Ratcliff; biography; exhibition chronology; bibliography.

Gilbert & George: Post-Card Sculptures and Ephemera, 1969-1981. Exh. cat. New York: Hirschl & Adler Modern, 1990. Introduction by Carter Ratcliff; biography; exhibition chronology; list of postal sculptures, works in edition, film and video, and living sculpture presentations; bibliography.

Jahn, Wolf. *The Art of Gilbert & George, or An Aesthetic of Existence.* Translated by David Britt. New York: Thames and Hudson, 1989. Biography; exhibition chronology; bibliography.

Ratcliff, Carter, and Robert Rosenblum. *Gilbert & George: The Singing Sculpture.* New York: Anthony McCall, 1993. Documentation of performances of *The Singing Sculpture,* 1969-73; chronology; bibliography.

DAN GRAHAM

Alberro, Alexander. "Reductivism in Reverse." In *Tracing Cultures: Art History, Criticism, Critical Fiction*, edited by Miwon Kwon, 7-27. New York: Whitney Museum of American Art, 1994.

Dan Graham. Exh. cat. Perth: The Art Gallery of Western Australia, 1985. Acknowledgments and introduction by Gary Dufour; essays by Graham and Jeff Wall; exhibition chronology.

Dan Graham: Buildings and Signs. Exh. cat. Chicago: The Renaissance Society at The University of Chicago and Oxford: Museum of Modern Art, 1981. Acknowledgments by Susanne Ghez; essay by Anne Rorimer; texts by Graham; bio-bibliographical notes.

Dan Graham: For Publication. Exh. cat. Los Angeles: Otis Art Institute, 1975. Documentation of works made for publication.

Dan Graham: Video-Architecture-Television: Writings on Video and Video Works 1970-1978. Edited by Benjamin H. D. Buchloh. Halifax: The Press of the Nova Scotia College of Art and Design and New York: New York University Press, 1979. Introduction by Graham; texts by Michael Asher and Dara Birnbaum; exhibition chronology; bibliography.

Graham, Dan. *Articles.* Edited by R. H. Fuchs. Eindhoven: Stedelijk Van Abbemuseum, 1978. Includes texts by Fuchs and Anton Herbert.

_____. *Rock My Religion: Writings and Art Projects 1965-1990.* Edited by Brian Wallis. Cambridge: The MIT Press, 1993. Includes essay by Wallis.

_____. *Selected Work, 1965-1972.* Cologne: Koenig Publishing and London: Lisson Publications, 1972.

HANS HAACKE

Burnham, Jack. "Hans Haacke: Wind and Water Sculpture." *Tri-Quarterly Supplement*, no. 1 (Spring 1967): 1-24.

_____. "Hans Haacke's Cancelled Show at the Guggenheim." *Artforum* 9, no. 10 (June 1971): 67-71.

Fry, Edward F., ed. *Hans Haacke: Werkmonographie.* Cologne: DuMont Schauberg, 1972. Essay by Fry; texts by Haacke; interviews by Jack Burnham and Jeanne Siegel; documentation of cancelled exhibition at the Solomon R. Guggenheim Museum; biography; exhibition chronology; bibliography.

Hans Haacke. Vol. 1. Exh. cat. Oxford: Museum of Modern Art, 1978 and Eindhoven: Stedelijk Van Abbemuseum, 1979. Interview by Margaret Sheffield; texts by Haacke.

Hans Haacke. Vol. 2, *Works 1978-1983.* Exh. cat. Eindhoven: Stedelijk Van Abbemuseum and London: Tate Gallery, 1984. Texts by Haacke; essays by Tony Brown and Water Grasskamp.

Hans Haacke: Framing and Being Framed: 7 Works 1970-1975. Halifax: The Press of the Nova Scotia College of Art and Design and New York: New York University Press, 1975. Editor's note by Kaspar Koenig; texts by Haacke; essays by Jack Burnham and by Howard S. Becker and John Walton.

Hans Haacke: Unfinished Business. Exh. cat. New York: The New Museum of Contemporary Art and Cambridge: The MIT Press, 1986. Foreword by Marcia Tucker; acknowledgments by Brian Wallis; essays by Leo Steinberg, Rosalyn Deutsche, Fredric Jameson, Wallis, and Haacke; catalogue of works, 1969-86; bibliography.

Siegel, Jeanne. "An Interview with Hans Haacke." *Arts Magazine* 45, no. 7 (May 1971): 18-21.

DOUGLAS HUEBLER

Auping, Michael. "Talking with Douglas Huebler." *Journal* (Los Angeles), no. 15 (July-August 1977): 37-44.

Douglas Huebler. Exh. cat. Eindhoven: Stedelijk Van Abbemuseum, 1979. Essays by Lucy R. Lippard, Jack Burnham, April Kingsley, Jeremy Gilbert-Rolfe, and René Denizot.

Douglas Huebler. Exh. cat. Münster: Westfälischer Kunstverein, 1972. Introduction by Klaus Honnef; biography; exhibition chronology; bibliography.

Douglas Huebler: Location Pieces, Site Sculpture, Duration Works, Drawings, Variable Pieces. Exh. cat. Boston: Museum of Fine Arts and Institute of Contemporary Art, 1972. Preface by Kenworth Moffett; afterword by Christopher Cook; biography; exhibition chronology; bibliography.

Douglas Huebler: November 1968. Exh. cat. New York: Seth Siegelaub, 1968.

Douglas Huebler: Selected Drawings, 1968-1973. Exh. cat. Turin: Sperone, 1975.

Douglas Huebler: «Variable», etc. Exh. cat. Limoges: F.R.A.C. Limousin, 1992. Essays by Frédéric Paul, René Denizot, and Robert C. Morgan; interviews by Paul; artist's statements; biography; exhibition chronology; bibliography.

Honnef, Klaus. "Douglas Huebler." *Art and Artists* (London) 7, no. 10 (January 1973): 22-25.

Kingsley, April. "Douglas Huebler." *Artforum* 10, no. 9 (May 1972): 74-78.

JOAN JONAS

De Jong, Constance. "Joan Jonas: Organic Honey's Vertical Roll." *Arts Magazine* 47, no. 5 (March 1973): 27-29.

_____. "Organic Honey's Visual Telepathy." *The Drama Review* (New York) 16, no. 2 (June 1972): 66-74.

Joan Jonas: Scripts and Descriptions, 1968-1982. Berkeley: University Art Museum, University of California and Eindhoven: Stedelijk Van Abbemuseum, 1983. Edited by Douglas Crimp. Acknowledgments and closing statement by Jonas; foreword by James Elliott; introduction by Crimp; essay by David Ross; list of performances, videotapes, and films; biography; bibliography; exhibition chronology.

Joan Jonas: Works 1968-1994. Exh. cat. Amsterdam: Stedelijk Museum, 1994. Introduction by R. H. Fuchs; essays by Dorine Mignot and Bruce Ferguson; texts by Lawrence Weiner, Susan Rothenberg, Mary Heilmann, Richard Serra, Alvin Curran, Simone Forti, Robin Winters, and Alice Weiner; performers' biographies; biography; bibliography.

Jonas, Joan (with Rosalind Krauss). "Seven Years." *The Drama Review* (New York) 19, no. 1 (March 1975): 13-16.

Kaye, Nick. "Mask, Role, Narrative: An Interview with Joan Jonas." *Performance* (New York), no. 65-66 (Spring 1992): 48-59.

STEPHEN J. KALTENBACH

Nemser, Cindy. "An Interview with Stephen Kaltenbach." *Artforum* 9, no. 3 (November 1970): 47-53.

Steven [Stephen] Kaltenbach: Portrait of My Father: A Painting in Progress. Exh. cat. Sacramento, California: E. B. Crocker Art Gallery, 1979. Essay by Roger D. Clisby.

ON KAWARA

Denizot, René. *Mot pour mot: Les images quotidiennes du pouvoir: On Kawara au jour le jour / Word for Word: The Daily Images of Power: On Kawara from Day to Day*. Paris: Yvon Lambert, 1979.

On Kawara. Exh. cat. Dijon: Le Consortium, 1985. Introduction by Xavier Douroux and Franck Gautherot; essays by Sunkichi Baba, David Higginbotham, Jörg Johnen, Seigou Matsuoka, and Anne Rorimer; biography by Jean-Hubert Martin.

On Kawara: Continuity / Discontinuity, 1963-1979. Exh. cat. Stockholm: Moderna Museet, 1980. Acknowledgments by Olle Granath, Zdenek Felix, R. H. Fuchs, and Keinosuke Murata; essays by Granath and Peter Nilson; text by Kawara; biography; chronological documentation of works and exhibitions, 1963-79, including journals and subtitles.

On Kawara 1967. Exh. cat. Los Angeles: Otis Art Institute Gallery, 1977. Essay by Lucy R. Lippard.

On Kawara: 1973 – Produktion eines Jahres / One Year's Production. Exh. cat. Bern: Kunsthalle, 1974. Preface by Johannes Gachnang; texts by Marianne Schmidt and Kasper Koenig. Also published as *On Kawara: Production de l'année 1973 / Produktie van het jaar 1973* (Brussels: Palais des Beaux-Arts, 1975).

Rorimer, Anne. "The Date Paintings of On Kawara." *Museum Studies* (Chicago) 17, no. 2 (1991): 120-137.

JOHN KNIGHT

Campagne. Exh. cat. Brussels: One Five, 1995. Texts by Lily van Ginneken and by Gina Rey and Mario Coyula; essay by Birgit Pelzer; bibliography.

Dillon, Kurt. "The Site of the Bicycle." *Archis* (Amsterdam) (May 1993): 12-13. Interview.

"John Knight: A Catalogue for Exhibition." *Journal: A Contemporary Art Magazine* (Los Angeles) 4, no. 40 (Fall 1984): 104-111. Introduction by Daniel Alexander Wasil; essays by Kim Gordon and Dan Graham.

John Knight. Exh. cat. Chicago: The Renaissance Society at The University of Chicago, 1983. Acknowledgments by Susanne Ghez; essay by Anne Rorimer; bibliography.

John Knight-Haim Steinbach. Exh. cat. Brussels: Palais des Beaux-Arts, 1991. Interviews by Joel Benzakin with Benjamin H. D. Buchloh, Germano Celant, Knight, Dirk Snauwaert, and Steinbach.

Leen, Frederik. "Unfinished: John Knight and the Position of the Proper Name in the Negotiation between the Structural and Historical Moments of the Linguistic and Aesthetic Process." *Exposé* (Paris), no. 1 (1994): 48-53.

MCMLXXXVI. Exh. cat. New York: Marian Goodman Gallery, 1986. Essay by Benjamin H. D. Buchloh; bibliography.

Treize travaux. Exh. cat. Villeurbanne: Le Nouveau Musée and Rotterdam: Witte de With, centre for contemporary art, 1989. Essays by Anne Rorimer and Benjamin H. D. Buchloh; bibliography.

Une vue culturelle. Saint Etienne: Maison de la culture et de la communication, 1987. Introduction by Yves Aupetitallot; essay by Claude Gintz; bibliography.

JOSEPH KOSUTH

Joseph Kosuth, l'art de les idees: Una visió de trenta anys, 1965-1995. Exh. cat. Mallorca: Fundació Pilar i Joan Miró, 1995. Essays by Pablo Rico, Amada Cruz, Francisco Jarauta, and Kosuth.

Joseph Kosuth: Bedeutung von Bedeutung: Texte und Dokumentation der Investigation en über Kunst seit 1965 in Auswahl / Joseph Kosuth: The Making of Meaning: Selected Writings and Documentation of Investigations on Art Since 1965. Stuttgart: Staatsgalerie, 1981. Biography, exhibition chronology, and bibliography by Charles Le Vine.

Joseph Kosuth: (Eine grammatische Bemerkung) / (A Grammatical Remark). Stuttgart: Württembergischer Kunstverein and Edition Cantz, 1993. Essays by Eva Meyer and Stefan Schmidt-Wulffen; exhibition chronology; bibliography; list of recent architectural and public projects.

Joseph Kosuth: Investigationen über Kunst und 'Problemkreise' seit 1965. 5 vols. Exh. cat. Lucerne: Kunstmuseum Luzern, 1973. Texts by Terry Atkinson, Michael Baldwin, Philip Pilkington, Mel Ramsden, Davie Rushton, and Terry Smith.

Kosuth, Joseph. *Art after Philosophy and After: Collected Writings, 1966-1990*. Edited by Gabriele Guercio. Cambridge: The MIT Press, 1991. Includes foreword by Jean-François Lyotard; bibliography; exhibition chronology.

_____. *Function Funzione Fonction Funktion*. Turin: Sperone Editore, 1970. Essays by Germano Celant and Pierluigi Pero.

CHRISTINE KOZLOV

"Christine Kozlov." In *Art conceptuel, formes conceptuelles / Conceptual Art, Conceptual Forms*, 268-270. Exh. cat. Paris: Galerie 1900Δ2000 and Galerie de Poche, 1990.

Kozlov, Christine. Artist's card. In *C. 7,500*, unpag. Exh. cat. Valencia: California Institute of the Arts, 1973.

_____. Artist's statement. In *Conceptual Art and Conceptual Aspects*, 9. Exh. cat. New York: The New York Cultural Center in association with Madison, New Jersey: Fairleigh Dickinson University, 1970.

DAVID LAMELAS

Arthur, Paul. "Some Notes around a Film by David Lamelas." *Journal: Southern California Art Magazine* (Los Angeles), no. 28 (September-October 1980): 71-81.

David Lamelas: Fifteen Years. Exh. cat. Buenos Aires: Centro de Arte y Comunicación, 1978. Essay by Jorge Glusberg.

Jouffroy, Alain. "David Lamelas." *Opus International* (Paris), no. 17 (April 1970): 17-19.

Lamelas, David. "The Desert People: Filmscript." *Interfunktionen* (Cologne), no. 12 (1975): 50-83.

_____. "La lecture d'un film." *Art Press* (Paris), no. 3 (March-April 1973): 16.

Morris, Lynda. "David Lamelas: An Introduction to the Structural Development." *Studio International* (London) 187, no. 962 (January 1974): 44-45.

WILLIAM LEAVITT

Lawson, Thomas. "Every Picture Tells a Story, Don't It?" *Real Life Magazine* (New York), no. 2 (October 1979): 10-12.

Winer, Helene. "Scenarios / Documents / Images 1." *Art in America* 61, no. 2 (March-April 1973): 42-47.

Young, Joseph. "William Leavitt." *Art International* 15, no. 1 (January 1970): 84.

SOL LEWITT

Alloway, Lawrence. "Sol LeWitt: Modules, Walls, Books." *Artforum* 13, no. 8 (April 1975): 38-44.

Krauss, Rosalind E. "LeWitt in Progress." In *The Originality of the Avant-Garde and Other Modernist Myths*, 244-258. Cambridge: The MIT Press, 1987.

Kuspit, Donald. "Sol LeWitt: The Look of Thought." *Art in America* 63, no. 5 (September-October 1975): 43-49.

LeWitt, Sol. "Paragraphs on Conceptual Art." *Artforum* 5, no. 10 (June 1967): 79-81.

_____. "Sentences on Conceptual Art." *Art-Language* (Coventry, England) 1, no. 1 (May 1969): 11-13.

Lippard, Lucy R. "Sol LeWitt: Non-Visual Structures." *Artforum* 5, no. 8 (April 1967): 42-46.

Sol LeWitt. Exh. cat. The Hague: Gemeentemuseum, 1970. Acknowledgments by L. I. F. W.; texts by John N. Chandler, Carl Andre, Terry Atkinson, Mel Bochner, Enno Develing, Dan Flavin, Dan Graham, Eva Hesse, Coosje van Bruggen, Michael Kirby, LeWitt, Ira Licht, Lucy R. Lippard, Barbara M. Reise, Hans Strelow, Dick Van der Net, and Lawrence Weiner; biography; bibliography; exhibition chronology.

Sol LeWitt. Exh. cat. New York: The Museum of Modern Art, 1978. Introduction by Alicia Legg; chronology; essays by Robert Rosenblum, Lucy R. Lippard, and Bernice Rose; texts by LeWitt; bibliography; exhibition chronology.

Sol LeWitt: Drawings 1958-1992. Exh. cat. The Hague: Haags Gemeentemuseum, 1992. Acknowledgments by LeWitt and Susanna Singer; foreword by R. H. Fuchs; essays by Franz W. Kaiser.

Sol LeWitt: Wall Drawings 1968-1984. Exh. cat. and catalogue raisonne. Amsterdam: Stedelijk Museum, 1984. Acknowledgments by Susanna Singer and LeWitt; preface by Edy de Wilde and R. H. Fuchs; essays by Alexander van Grevenstein and Jan Debbaut; interview by Andrea Miller-Keller; texts by David Shulman and Michael Harvey.

RICHARD LONG

"Richard Long." *Avalanche* (New York), no. 1 (Fall 1970): 40-47.

Richard Long. Exh. cat. New York: Solomon R. Guggenheim Museum and Thames and Hudson, 1986. Acknowledgments by Diane Waldman; text by R. H. Fuchs; artist's statements; chronology; list of artist's publications.

Richard Long: Land Art im Museum Haus Lange Krefeld. Exh. cat. Krefeld: Museum Haus Lange, 1970. Essay by Paul Wember.

Richard Long: Skulpturen. Exh. cat. Mönchengladbach: Stadtisches Museum, 1970. Statements by Johannes Cladder and the artist.

Richard Long: Walking in Circles. New York: George Braziller, 1993. Acknowledgments by Joanna Drew and Susan Ferleger Brades; essay by Anne Seymour; interview by Seymour; transcript of 1988 radio interview by Richard Cork; text by Hamish Fulton; exhibition chronology; bibliography.

TOM MARIONI

Futterman, Hilla. "Activity as Sculpture: Tom Marioni Discusses His Work with Hilla Futterman. *Art and Artists* (London) 8, no. 5 (August 1973): 18-21.

Marioni, Tom. "The Newer Art: Tom Marioni in Conversation with Prudence Juris." *Studio International* (London) 183, no. 944 (May 1972): 191.

Smith, Barbara T. "Tom Marioni: A Conversation with San Francisco's Premier Conceptual Artist." *High Performance* (Los Angeles) 8, no. 4 (1985): 27-33.

The Sound of Flight: Tom Marioni. San Francisco: M. H. De Young Memorial Museum, 1977. Essay by Thomas H. Garver.

White, Robin. *View* (Oakland, California) 1, no. 5 (October 1978, updated January 1981). Special issue: Tom Marioni. Interview; exhibition chronology.

GORDON MATTA-CLARK

Gordon Matta-Clark. Exh. cat. Marseille: Musée Cantini, 1993. Acknowledgments by Corinne Diserens; preface by Carmen Alborch, Bernard Blistène, and Julia Peyton-Jones; essays by Diserens, Mariane Brouwer, Judith Russi Kirshner, Liza Béar, Dan Graham, and Eugenio Trias; documentation of projects, 1969-78; texts by Matta-Clark; interview by Kirshner with Matta-Clark; interviews by Richard Armstrong with Anne Alpert, Roberto Matta, Tina Girouard, Mary Heilmann, Keith Sonnier, Carol Goodden, Richard Nonas, Jene Highstein, Jackie Winsor, Ted Greenwald, Joseph Kosuth, Horace Solomon, Jeffrey Lew, Joan Simon, and Jane Crawford; biography; chronology of exhibitions, projects, and performances; filmography; bibliography.

Gordon Matta-Clark: A Retrospective. Exh. cat. Chicago: Museum of Contemporary Art, 1985. Foreword by I. Michael Danoff; introduction, acknowledgments, and catalogue of works by Mary Jane Jacob; essay by Robert Pincus-Witten; interviews by Joan Simon; chronology, exhibition chronology, and bibliography by Carrie Przybilla.

Gordon Matta-Clark: Splitting: Four Corners. Exh. cat. New York: Holly Solomon Gallery, 1990. Introduction by Mary Jane Jacob.

N. E. THING CO.

Baxter²: Any Choice Works 1965-1970. Exh. cat. Toronto: Art Gallery of Ontario, 1982. Preface by William J. Withrow; acknowledgments and essay by Marie L. Fleming; texts by N. E. Thing Co.; exhibition chronology to 1970; bibliography.

"N. E. Thing Co. Section." *Capilano Review* (North Vancouver, British Columbia), no. 8-9 (Fall 1975-Spring 1976): 135-167. Introduction by Ann Rosenberg; interview; statements on Conceptual art by various artists.

Report on the Activities of the N. E. Thing Co. at the National Gallery of Canada, Ottawa, and Other Locations, June 4-July 6. Ottawa: National Gallery of Canada, 1969. Exhibition chronology.

Trans VSI Connection NSCAD-NETCO: September 15-October 5, 1969. Exh. cat. Halifax: The Press of the Nova Scotia College of Art and Design, 1970. Includes the chronologically arranged exchanges of information between the Nova Scotia College of Art and Design and N. E. Thing Co. via telex, telecopier, and telephone that constituted the exhibition.

White, Robin. *View* (Oakland, California) 2, no. 4 (September 1979). Special issue: Iain Baxter/N. E. Thing Co. Interview.

You Are Now in the Middle of a N. E. Thing Co. Landscape: Works by Iain and Ingrid Baxter, 1965-1971. Exh. cat. Vancouver: University of British Columbia Fine Arts Gallery, 1993. Introduction by Scott Watson; essays and texts by William Wood, Nancy Shaw, N. E. Thing Co., Greg Curnoe, Joan Lowndes, Germano Celant, Alvin Balkind, Paul Grescoe, Lucy R. Lippard, David P. Silcox, Pierre Théberge, and Charlotte Townsend-Gault.

BRUCE NAUMAN

Bruce Nauman. Exh. cat. London: Whitechapel, 1986. Acknowledgments by Nicholas Serota, Jean-Christophe Ammann, and Suzanne Pagé; essays by Joan Simon and Ammann; biography; bibliography. Also published as *Bruce Nauman: Werken von 1965 bis 1986* (Basel: Kunsthalle, 1986).

Bruce Nauman. Exh. cat. New York: Leo Castelli Gallery, 1968. Text by David Whitney.

Bruce Nauman. Exh. cat. and catalogue raisonne. Minneapolis: Walker Art Center and Washington, D.C.: Hirshhorn Museum and Sculpture Garden, 1994. Preface and acknowledgments by Neal Benezra and Kathy Halbreich; essays by Benezra, Halbreich, Paul Schimmel, and Robert Storr; catalogue raisonne; chronology; exhibition history; bibliography.

Bruce Nauman: Drawings/Zeichnungen 1965-1986. Exh. cat. Basel: Museum für Gegenwartkunst, 1986. Biography; introduction by Dieter Koepplin; essays by Coosje van Bruggen, Koepplin, and Franz Meyer; bibliography.

Bruce Nauman: Work from 1965 to 1972. Exh. cat. Los Angeles: Los Angeles County Museum of Art and New York: Praeger, 1972. Preface, acknowledgments, and essays by Jane Livingston and Marcia Tucker; biography; exhibition chronology; lists of editions, films, and videotapes; bibliography.

Sharp, Willoughby. "Bruce Nauman." *Avalanche* (New York), no. 2 (Winter 1971): 23-35. Interview.

van Bruggen, Coosje. *Bruce Nauman*. New York: Rizzoli, 1988. Bibliography; chronology of films and videos.

MARIA NORDMAN

Celant, Germano. "Urban Nature: The Work of Maria Nordman." *Artforum* 18, no. 7 (March 1980): 62-67.

Maria Nordman: Poeima, Notizen / Notes 1970-. Cologne: Walther König, 1982.

Maria Nordman: Saddleback Mountain. Exh. cat. Irvine: Irvine Art Gallery, University of California, 1973. Interview by Barbara Haskell.

Nordman, Maria. *De Musica: New Conjunct City Proposals.* Münster: Westfälisches Landesmuseum, 1993.

————. *De Sculptura: Works in the City: Some Ongoing Questions.* Munich: Schirmer/Mosel, 1986.

Plagens, Peter. "Maria Nordman." *Artforum* 12, no. 6 (February 1974): 40-41.

DENNIS OPPENHEIM

Bourgeois, Jean-Louis. "Dennis Oppenheim." *Artforum* 8, no. 2 (October 1969): 34-38.

Dennis Oppenheim. Exh. cat. Brussels: Société des Expositions du Palais des Beaux-Arts, 1975. Essays by Jean-Pierre van Tieghem and Vincent Baudoux.

Dennis Oppenheim: Rétrospective de l'oeuvre 1967-1977. Exh. cat. Montreal: Musée d'art contemporain, 1978. Foreword by Louise Letocha; introductions by Alain Parent and Peter Frank and Lisa Kahane; interview by Parent; biography; bibliography.

Dennis Oppenheim: Selected Works, 1967-90: And the Mind Grew Fingers. Exh. cat. New York: P.S. 1 Museum, Institute for Contemporary Art and Harry N. Abrams, 1992. Introduction and interview by Alanna Heiss; essay by Thomas McEvilley; chronology; exhibition chronology; bibliography.

Sharp, Willoughby. "An Interview with Dennis Oppenheim." *Studio International* (London) 182, no. 983 (November 1971): 186-193.

BLINKY PALERMO

Glozer, Laszlo. "On Blinky Palermo: A Conversation with Joseph Beuys." *Arts Magazine* 64, no. 7 (March 1990): 60-65.

Palermo. Exh. cat. and catalogue raisonne. Vol. 1, *Bilder und Objekte.* Vol. 2, *Zeichnungen.* Bonn: Kunstmuseum in association with Stuttgart: Oktagon, 1994. Acknowledgments and preface by Thordis Moeller; essays by Klaus Schrenk and Christoph Schreier; biography; exhibition chronology; bibliography.

Palermo: Druckgraphik 1970-1974. Exh. cat. Leverkusen: Städtisches Museum Schloss Morsbroich, 1975. Text by Walter Ehrmann and Rolf Wedewer.

Palermo: Stoffbilder 1966-1972. Exh. cat. Krefeld: Museum Haus Lange, 1977. Essay by Gerhard Storck; exhibition chronology.

Palermo: Werke 1963-1977. Exh. cat. Winterthur, Switzerland: Kunstmuseum and Munich: Schirmer/Mosel, 1984. Essays by Bernhard Bürgi, Erich Franz, and Max Wechsler; dialogue between Laszlo Glozer and Joseph Beuys; biography; bibliography. Also published as *Palermo: Oeuvres 1963-1977* (Paris: Musée national d'art moderne, Centre Georges Pompidou, 1985). Preface by Dominique Bozo; additional essays by Bernard Blistène and Laura Arici.

Rorimer, Anne. "Blinky Palermo: Objects, 'Stoffbilder,' Wall Paintings." *Artforum* 17, no. 3 (November 1978): 28-35.

GIULIO PAOLINI

Giulio Paolini. Exh. cat. Bern: Kunsthalle, 1974. Essay by Carlo Huber; exhibition chronology.

Giulio Paolini. Exh. cat. Milan: Galleria dell'Ariete, 1966. Text by Carla Lonzi.

Giulio Paolini. Exh. cat. New York: Sonnabend Press, 1972. Text and interview by Germano Celant; exhibition chronology; bibliography.

Giulio Paolini. Exh. cat. Parma: Istituto di Storia dell'Arte, Università di Parma. 1976. Essays by Maurizio Fagiolo, Arturo Carlo Quintavalle, Mirella Bandini, Renato Barilli, Achille Bonito Oliva, Maurizio Calvesi, Giorgio de Marchis, Paolo Fossati, Carlo Huber, Carla Lonzi, Henry Martin, Filiberto Menna, Nello Ponente, Giovan Battista Salerno, Jr., Claudia Terenzi, Tommaso Trini, and Marisa Volpi Orlandini; exhibition chronology; bibliography.

Giulio Paolini. 4 vols. Exh. cat. Stuttgart: Staatsgalerie, 1986. Foreword by Gudrun Inbodin; essays by Inbodin, Michael Scholz-Hänsel, Mirella Bandini, and Johannes Meinhardt; artist's statements; interviews; exhibition chronology; bibliography.

Giulio Paolini: Werke und Schriften 1960-1980. 2 vols. Exh. cat. Lucerne: Kunstmuseum Luzern, 1981. Introduction and essay by Max Wechsler; exhibition chronology; bibliography.

ADRIAN PIPER

Adrian Piper. Exh. cat. Birmingham: Ikon Gallery and Manchester: Cornerhouse, 1991. Essay by Claudia Barrow; biography; bibliography; exhibition chronology; artist's writings; collections.

Adrian Piper, Reflections 1967-1987. Exh. cat. New York: Alternative Museum, 1987. Introduction by Jane Farver; essays by Lowery S. Sims and John T. Paoletti; chronology by Piper; biography; exhibition and performance chronology; bibliography.

Cottingham, Laura. "Adrian Piper." *Journal of Contemporary Art* (New York) 5, no. 1 (Spring 1992): 88-136. Interview.

Lippard, Lucy R. "Catalysis: An Interview with Adrian Piper." *The Drama Review* (New York) 16, no. 1 (March 1972): 76-78.

Piper, Adrian. *Out of Order, Out of Sight.* Vol. 1, *Selected Writings in Meta-Art, 1968-1992.* Vol. 2, *Selected Writings in Art Criticism, 1967-1992.* Cambridge: The MIT Press, 1995.

YVONNE RAINER

Blumenthal, Lyn. "On Art and Artists: Yvonne Rainer." *Profile* (Chicago) 4, no. 5 (1984): 2-48. Interview; bibliography.

Green, Shelley. *Radical Juxtaposition: The Films of Yvonne Rainer.* Metuchen, New Jersey: The Scarecrow Press, 1994. Filmography; bibliography.

Lippard, Lucy R. "Yvonne Rainer on Feminism and Her Film." In Lippard, *From the Center: Feminist Essays on Womens' Art,* 265-279. New York: E. P. Dutton, 1976.

Michelson, Annette. "Yvonne Rainer, Part One: The Dancer and the Dance." *Artforum* 12, no. 5 (January 1974): 57-63.

————. "Yvonne Rainer, Part Two: 'Lives of Performers.'" *Artforum* 12, no. 6 (February 1974): 30-35.

Rainer, Yvonne. *The Films of Yvonne Rainer.* Bloomington: Indiana University Press, 1989. Foreword by Teresa de Lauretis; introduction by B. Ruby Rich; essay by Bérénice Reynaud; interview by Mitchell Rosenbaum; film scripts; filmography; bibliography by Patricia White.

————. *Work 1961-73.* Halifax: The Press of the Nova Scotia College of Art and Design and New York: New York University Press, 1974. Film scripts; chronology of work; bibliography.

"Yvonne Rainer: An Introduction." *Camera Obscura* (Berkeley), no. 1 (Fall 1976): 53-70. See also "Appendix: Rainer's Descriptions of Her Films": 71-75 and "Yvonne Rainer: Interview": 76-96.

ALLEN RUPPERSBERG

Allen Ruppersberg. Exh. cat. Claremont, California: Pomona College Gallery, Montgomery Art Center, 1972. Introduction by Helene Winer; exhibition chronology; bibliography.

Allen Ruppersberg: The Secret of Life and Death, Volume 1 1969-1984. Exh. cat. Los Angeles: The Museum of Contemporary Art and Santa Barbara: Black Sparrow Press, 1985. Acknowledgments by Richard Koshalek; introduction by Julia Brown; essay by Howard Singerman; exhibition chronology; bibliography.

Levin, Daniel. "Allen Ruppersberg." *Journal of Contemporary Art* (New York) 5, no. 2 (Fall 1992): 68-77. Interview.

EDWARD RUSCHA

Antin, Eleanor. "Reading Ruscha." *Art in America* 61, no. 6 (November-December 1973): 64-71.

Bourdon, David. "Ruscha as Publisher (Or All Booked Up)." *Art News* 71, no. 2 (April 1972): 32-36, 68-69.

Edward Ruscha: Books and Prints. Exh. cat. Santa Cruz: Mary Porter Senson Gallery, College V, University of California, 1972. Essays by Nan R. Piene and Marcia R. McGrath; biography; exhibition chronology; list of books and prints.

Edward Ruscha (Ed-werd Rew-shay) Young Artist. Exh. cat. Minneapolis: The Minnesota Institute of Arts, 1972. Biography.

Edward Ruscha: Paintings / Schilderijen. Exh. cat. Rotterdam: Museum Boymans-van Beuningen, London: Serpentine Gallery, and Los Angeles: The Museum of Contemporary Art, 1989. Acknowledgments by Jean-Hubert Martin, Wim Crouwel, Maria Corral, Alister Warman, and Richard Koshalek; preface by Elbrig de Groot; essays by Dan Cameron and Pontus Hulten; interview with Bernard Blistène; biography; exhibition chronology; list of artist's books and films; bibliography.

Paintings, Drawings and Other Works by Edward Ruscha. Exh. cat. Buffalo: Albright-Knox Art Gallery, 1976. Foreword by Robert T. Buck; acknowledgments and essay by Linda Cathcart; exhibition chronology; list of artist's books.

Sharp, Willoughby. "'A Kind of HUH?' An Interview with Edward Ruscha . . . ." *Avalanche* (New York), no. 7 (Winter-Spring 1973): 30-39.

The Works of Edward Ruscha. Exh. cat. San Francisco: San Francisco Museum of Modern Art in association with New York: Hudson Hills Press: 1982. Foreword by Henry T. Hopkins; acknowledgments and introduction by Anne Livet; essays by Dave Hickey and Peter Plagens; chronology by Miriam Roberts; exhibition chronology by Karen Lee; bibliography by Eugenie Candau.

ROBERT SMITHSON

Arts Magazine 52, no. 9 (May 1978). Special section on Smithson. Articles by Philip Leider, Will Insley, Carl Andre, Ted Castle, William S. Wilson, Rolf-Dieter Hermann, Thomas A. Zaniello, Alex Gildzen, Stuart Morgan, David Bellman, Howard Junker, John Beardsley, Kim Levin, Valentin Tatransky, and Nancy Holt.

Owens, Craig. "Earthwords." In *Beyond Recognition: Representation, Power, and Culture*, edited by Scott Bryson, Barbara Kruger, Lynne Tillman, and Jane Weinstock, 40-51. Berkeley: University of California Press, 1992.

Robert Smithson: El paisaje entrópico: Una retrospectiva 1960-1973. Exh. cat. Valencia: IVAM Centre Julio González, 1993. Foreword by Carmen Alborch and Bernard Blistène; essays by Maggie Gilchrist, James Lingwood, and Kay Larson; artist's texts; biography; exhibition chronology; bibliography.

Robert Smithson: Photo Works. Exh. cat. Los Angeles: Los Angeles County Museum of Art and Albuquerque: University of New Mexico Press, 1993. Foreword by Michael E. Shapiro; acknowledgments and essay by Robert A. Sobieszek; bibliography.

Robert Smithson: Sculpture. Exh. cat. Ithaca, New York: Herbert F. Johnson Museum of Art, Cornell University, 1980. Foreword by Thomas W. Leavitt; introduction by Robert Hobbs; essays by Lucy R. Lippard, Lawrence Alloway, and John Coplans. Also published as a book by Cornell University Press in 1981 with additional essay by Hobbs, chronology, and bibliography by Peter Chametzky.

Robert Smithson Unearthed: Drawings, Collages, Writings. Exh. cat. New York: Miriam and Ira D. Wallach Art Gallery, Columbia University and Columbia University Press, 1991. Foreword by David Rosand; introduction by Johanna Drucker; essay by Eugenie Tsai; previously unpublished artist's texts.

Robert Smithson: Zeichnungen aus dem Nachlass / Drawings from the Estate. Exh. cat. Münster: Westfälisches Landesmuseum für Kunst und Kulturgeschichte, 1989. Preface by Klaus Bussmann and Christian Gether and Michael Tacke; interview with Dan Graham by Eugenie Tsai; essays by Tsai, Eva Schmidt, Dieter Meschede, and Friedrich Meschede.

Smithson, Robert. *The Writings of Robert Smithson*. Edited by Nancy Holt. New York: New York University Press, 1979. Introduction by Philip Leider; biographical note.

MICHAEL SNOW

Afterimage (Rochester, New York), no. 11 (Winter 1982-83). Special issue: Sighting Snow. Includes essays by Nicky Hamlyn, Michael O'Pray, and Jonathan Rosenbaum; Bruce Elder in conversation with Snow.

Cornwell, Regina. *Snow Seen: The Films and Photographs of Michael Snow*. Toronto: PMA Books, 1979. Filmography; list of photographic works; bibliography.

Michael Snow. Exh. cat. Paris: Musée national d'art moderne, Centre Georges Pompidou, 1978. Preface by Pontus Hulten; essays by Pierre Théberge, Alain Sayag, and Dominique Noguez; conversation with Théberge; texts by Snow; exhibition chronology; bibliography; discography. Also published as *Michael Snow: Werke 1969-1978, Filme 1964-1976* (Lucerne: Kunstmuseum Luzern, 1979).

Michael Snow: Cover to Cover. Halifax: The Press of the Nova Scotia College of Art and Design and New York: New York University Press, 1975.

The Michael Snow Project: Visual Art 1951-1993. Exh. cat. Toronto: Art Gallery of Ontario and The Power Plant, 1994. Essays by Dennis Reid, Philip Monk, Louise Dompierre, Richard Rhodes, and Derrick de Kerckhove; chronology; bibliography.

Michael Snow: A Survey. Toronto: Art Gallery of Ontario in collaboration with The Isaacs Gallery, 1970. Essays by Robert Fulford, Dennis Young, Richard Foreman, and P. Adams Sitney; biography; exhibition chronology.

Michelson, Annette. "Toward Snow." *Artforum* 9, no. 10 (June 1971): 30-37.

Snow, Michael. *The Michael Snow Project: The Collected Writings of Michael Snow*. Waterloo, Ontario: Wilfred Laurier University Press, 1994. Foreword by Louise Dompierre.

_____, ed. *The Michael Snow Project: Music / Sound 1948-1993*. Exh. cat. Toronto: Art Gallery of Ontario and The Power Plant, 1994. Essays by Snow; David Lancashire; Nubota Kubota, Alan Mattes, and Snow; Paul Dutton; John Kamevaar; Raymond Gervais; and Bruce Elder and Snow; discography.

NIELE TORONI

Buchloh, Benjamin H. D. *L'index de la peinture.* Brussels: Editions Daled, 1985.

Niele Toroni: Catalogue raisonnable 1967-1987, 20 ans d'empreintes. Exh. cat. Nice: Villa Arson and Grenoble: Musée de peinture et de sculpture, 1987. Biography by Toroni; exhibition chronology; bibliography; essays by Christian Besson, Eric Colliard and Xavier Douroux and France Gautherot, Alain Coulange, René Denizot, Jean-Michel Foray, R. H. Fuchs, Johannes Gachnang, Jean-Hubert Martin, Jean-Paul Monery, Joseph Mouton, and Michel Verjux.

Niele Toroni: 52 pages/52 pagine/52 Seiten. Exh. cat. Bern: Kunsthalle, 1978. Texts by Toroni; epilogue by Johannes Gachnang.

Niele Toroni: Une empreinte n'est jamais seule. Exh. cat. Paris: Galerie Yvon Lambert, 1975. Essay by René Denizot.

Siegel, Jeanne. "Real Paintings: A Conversation with Niele Toroni." *Arts Magazine* 64, no. 2 (October 1989): 47-51.

WILLIAM WEGMAN

Béar, Liza. "Man Ray, Do You Want To . . .: An Interview with William Wegman." *Avalanche* (New York), no. 7 (Winter-Spring 1973): 40-52.

Lavin, Maud. "Notes on William Wegman." *Artforum* 13, no. 7 (March 1975): 44-47.

Wegman's World. Exh. cat. Minneapolis: Walker Art Center, 1982. Essays by Lisa Lyons and Kim Levin; biography; exhibition chronology; bibliography.

Wegman, William. "Shocked and Outraged as I Was, It Was Nice Seeing You Again, or Mrs. Burke, I Thought You Were Dead." *Avalanche* (New York), no. 2 (Winter 1971): 58-69.

William Wegman. Exh. cat. Los Angeles: Los Angeles County Museum of Art, 1973. Introduction by Jane Livingston.

William Wegman: Paintings, Drawings, Photographs, Videotapes. New York: Whitney Museum of American Art in association with Harry N. Abrams, 1990. Essays by Martin Kunz, Alain Sayag, Peter Schjeldahl, and Peter Weiermair; interview by David Ross.

William Wegman: Photographic Works/L'oeuvre photographique, 1969-1976. Exh. cat. Limoges: F.R.A.C. Limousin, 1991. Texts by Wegman; essays by Frédéric Paul; biography; exhibition chronology; bibliography.

William Wegman: Videotapes, Photographic Works, Arrangements. Exh. cat. Claremont, California: Pomona College Art Gallery, 1971. Introduction by Helene Winer; exhibition chronology.

LAWRENCE WEINER

Claura, Michel. "Entretien de Lawrence Weiner." *VH 101* (Paris), no. 5 (Spring 1971): 64-65.

Lawrence Weiner: Posters November 1965-April 1986. Halifax: The Press of the Nova Scotia School of Art and Design and Toronto: Art Metropole, 1986. Essay by Benjamin H. D. Buchloh.

Lawrence Weiner: Sculpture. Exh. cat. Paris: Musée d'art moderne de la Ville de Paris, 1985. Interview by Suzanne Pagé.

Lawrence Weiner: A Selection of Works with Commentary by Rudi Fuchs. Exh. cat. Eindhoven: Stedelijk Van Abbemuseum, 1976. Exhibition chronology.

Lawrence Weiner: Specific and General Works. Exh. cat. Villeurbanne: Le Nouveau Musée/Institut d'art contemporain, 1993.

Lawrence Weiner: Werken vanaf het begin van de jaren zestig tot aan het einde van de jaren tachtig/Lawrence Weiner: Works from the Beginning of the Sixties Towards the End of the Eighties. Exh. cat. Amsterdam: Stedelijk Museum, 1988. Preface and introduction by Wim Beeren; essays by Anne Rorimer, Edward G. Leffingwell, Marja Bloem, and R. H. Fuchs; exhibition chronology; bibliography.

Mari, Bartomeu, ed. *Show (&) Tell: The Films and Videos of Lawrence Weiner: A Catalogue Raisonné.* Ghent: Imschoot, 1992. Preface by R. H. Fuchs; essays by Alice Wiener, Dieter Schwarz, Mari, and Weiner; interview by Mari; documentation; bibliography.

Rorimer, Anne. "Sculpture: Figures of Structure: The Work of Lawrence Weiner." In *5 Figures of Structures.* Exh. cat. Chicago: The Arts Club of Chicago, 1987.

Schwarz, Dieter. *Lawrence Weiner: Books 1968-1989: Catalogue Raisonné.* Cologne: Walter König and Villeurbanne: Le Nouveau Musée, 1989.

Sharp, Willoughby. "Lawrence Weiner at Amsterdam." *Avalanche* (New York), no. 4 (Spring 1972): 64-73. Interview.

Weiner, Lawrence. *Works.* Hamburg: Anatol AV und Filmproduktion, 1977.

Werke und Rekonstruktionen/Works and Reconstructions: Lawrence Weiner. Exh. cat. Bern: Kunsthalle, 1983. Essay by Jean-Hubert Martin; exhibition chronology; bibliography of artist's publications.

IAN WILSON

Bonito Oliva, Achille. "Ian Wilson." In *Dialoghi d'artista: Incontri con l'arte contemporanea 1970-1984*, 196-203. Milan: Electa, 1984. Interview.

Denizot, René. "Ian Wilson, For Example: Texts on Words." *Artforum* 18, no. 7 (March 1980): 68-70.

Trini, Tommaso. "Intervista con Ian Wilson/Ian Wilson, an Interview." *Data* (Milan), 1, no. 1 (September 1971): 32-34.

Wilson, Ian. "Conceptual Art." *Artforum* 22, no. 6 (February 1984): 60-61.

CHECKLIST OF THE EXHIBITION

This checklist consists of the works that constitute the primary representation of each artist in the exhibition. For the exhibition, these works have been supplemented by additional films and videotapes, as well as artists' books, original manuscripts, publications, and archival materials.

Dates separated by a hyphen indicate that the work was produced between the years listed. Dates separated by a slash indicate that the first date is the year of the work's original execution; the second, the year of execution of the version included in this exhibition.

Height precedes width precedes depth.

VITO ACCONCI

Selected photo-activities, audiotapes, and documentation of performances, installations, and activities from 1969-71, including:

Following Piece (3–25 October 1969)

"Street Works IV," sponsored by the Architectural League of New York
Activity: various locations in New York City; twenty-three days, varying times each day
Courtesy the artist and Barbara Gladstone Gallery, New York

Service Area (June–September 1970)

"Information," The Museum of Modern Art, New York
Installation/activity
Dimensions: 6 x 3 x 3 ft. (182.9 x 91.4 x 91.4 cm); three months, varying days, varying times each day
Courtesy the artist and Barbara Gladstone Gallery, New York

Proximity Piece (16 September–8 November 1970)

"Software," The Jewish Museum, New York
Activity
Varying times over fifty-two days
Courtesy the artist and Barbara Gladstone Gallery, New York

Untitled Project for Pier 17 (27 March–24 April 1971)

West Street and Park Place, New York
Activity/performance
Dimensions: approx. 25 x 75 x 300 ft. (7.62 x 22.86 x 91.44 m); twenty-nine days, one hour each night
Courtesy the artist and Barbara Gladstone Gallery, New York

BAS JAN ADER

On the Road to a New Neo Plasticism Westkapelle Holland (1971)

Four color photographs (ed. 3/3)
Each, 11 x 11 in. (28 x 28 cm)
Collection Bas Jan Ader Estate, Courtesy Patrick Painter Editions, Inc., Vancouver/Hong Kong

Farewell to Faraway Friends (1971)

Color photograph (ed. 3/3)
19 5/8 x 23 5/8 in. (50 x 60 cm)
Collection Bas Jan Ader Estate, Courtesy Patrick Painter Editions, Inc., Vancouver/Hong Kong

In Search of the Miraculous (One Night in Los Angeles) (1973)

Eighteen black-and-white photographs with handwritten text in white ink
Each, 8 x 10 in. (20.3 x 25.4 cm)
Private Collection, London

Untitled (Flower Work) (1974)

Twenty-one color photographs (ed. 1/3)
Each photograph, 11 x 14 in. (27.8 x 36 cm)
Collection Bas Jan Ader Estate, Courtesy Patrick Painter Editions, Inc., Vancouver/Hong Kong

I'm Too Sad to Tell You (1971)

Film: 16mm, 3 min. 8 sec., b/w, silent
Collection Bas Jan Ader Estate, Courtesy Patrick Painter Editions, Inc., Vancouver/Hong Kong

Broken Fall (Geometric) (1971)
Westkapelle, Holland
Film: 16mm, 1 min. 50 sec., b/w, silent
Collection Bas Jan Ader Estate, Courtesy
Patrick Painter Editions, Inc.,
Vancouver/Hong Kong

Broken Fall (Organic) (1971)
Amsterdamse Bos, Amsterdam, Holland
Film: 16mm, 2 min., b/w, silent
Collection Bas Jan Ader Estate, Courtesy
Patrick Painter Editions, Inc.,
Vancouver/Hong Kong

Nightfall (1971)
Film: 16mm, 4 min. 10 sec., b/w, silent
Collection Bas Jan Ader Estate, Courtesy
Patrick Painter Editions, Inc.,
Vancouver/Hong Kong

Primary Time (1974)
Videotape: 26 min., color, silent
Collection Bas Jan Ader Estate, Courtesy
Patrick Painter Editions, Inc.,
Vancouver/Hong Kong

GIOVANNI ANSELMO
Particolare (Detail, 1972/95)
Slide projections
Dimensions variable
Courtesy the artist and Marian Goodman
Gallery, New York

ELEANOR ANTIN
Blood of a Poet Box (1965–68)
Box with one hundred glass slides of poets'
blood specimens
11 1/2 x 7 3/4 x 1 1/2 in. (29.2 x 19.7 x 3.8 cm)
Courtesy Ronald Feldman Fine Arts, New
York

Carving: A Traditional Sculpture
(1972)
148 black-and-white photographs and text
panel
Each photograph, 7 x 5 in. (17.8 x 12.7 cm);
text panel, 15 1/2 x 10 1/4 in. (39.4 x 26 cm)
Courtesy Ronald Feldman Fine Arts, New
York

ART & LANGUAGE
Index 01 (1972)
Eight file cabinets, text, and photostats
Each cabinet, 9 x 11 3/8 x 24 5/8 in. (23 x
29 x 62.5 cm)
Private Collection
Participating members for this work: Terry
Atkinson, David Bainbridge, Michael
Baldwin, Ian Burn, Charles Harrison, Harold
Hurrell, Joseph Kosuth, and Mel Ramsden

MICHAEL ASHER
Vertical column of accelerated air (adapted from
1966-67 projects utilizing pressured air)
Courtesy the artist

DAVID ASKEVOLD
Shoot Don't Shoot (A Sum Zero
Game Matrix) (1970)
Text and color photographs
19 x 20 in. (48.3 x 50.8 cm)
Courtesy the artist

Making Connections (Dashiell
Hammett & Martin Shubik) (1970)
Black-and-white print
18 x 24 in. (45.7 x 61 cm)
Courtesy the artist

Andromeda Strain (1971)
Black-and-white print
18 x 24 in. (45.7 x 61 cm)
Courtesy the artist

Taming Expansion (1971)
Silkscreen on paper (trial proof)
25 x 33 in. (63.5 x 83.8 cm)
Courtesy the artist

The Ambit (Nine Clauses and Their
Allocations) (1975–76)
Nine color photographs with text
Each, 40 x 60 in. (101.6 x 152.4 cm)
Stedelijk Van Abbemuseum, Eindhoven, The
Netherlands

JOHN BALDESSARI
A Work with Only One Property
(1967–68)
Acrylic on canvas
45 x 45 in. (114.3 x 114.3 cm)
The Grinstein Family, Los Angeles

Composing on a Canvas (1967–68)
Acrylic on canvas
114 x 96 in. (289.6 x 243.8 cm)
Museum of Contemporary Art, San Diego,
Gift of the Artist

Clement Greenberg (1967–68)
Acrylic on canvas
65 x 57 in. (165.1 x 144.8 cm)
Collection Craig Robins, Miami Beach

Painting for Kubler (1967–68)
Acrylic on canvas
68 x 56 1/2 in. (172.7 x 143.5 cm)
Collection Stuart and Judy Spence, South
Pasadena, California

The Spectator is Compelled . . .
(1967-68)
> Acrylic and photoemulsion on canvas
> 59 x 45 in. (149.9 x 114.3 cm)
> Collection Robert Shapazian, Los Angeles

This Is Not To Be Looked At
(1968)
> Acrylic and photoemulsion on canvas
> 59 x 45 in. (149.9 x 114.3 cm)
> Collection Councilman Joel Wachs, Los
> Angeles

A Painting That Is Its Own
Documentation (1968-present)
> Acrylic on canvas
> 102 x 56 1/2 in. (259.1 x 143.5 cm)
> Collection Norah and Norman Stone, San
> Francisco

ROBERT BARRY
90 mc Carrier Wave (FM) (October
1968)
> FM radio carrier wave
> Dimensions variable
> The Siegelaub Collection & Archives

FM Carrier Wave (Approx. 98 mc)
(1968)
> FM radio carrier wave
> Dimensions variable
> Solomon R. Guggenheim Museum, New
> York, Panza Collection, Extended Loan

Closed Gallery (1969)
> Four announcement cards
> 13 3/4 x 33 1/4 in. (34.9 x 84.5 cm)
> The Dorothy and Herbert Vogel Collection

Inert Gas Series: Krypton (1969)
(From a measured volume to indefinite
expansion. On March 3, 1969 in Beverly Hills,
Califonia, one liter of Krypton was returned
to the atmosphere.)
> Documentation: three color photographs
> and typewritten text
> Overall, 11 3/4 x 15 3/4 in. (30 x 40 cm)
> FER Collection, Laupheim, Germany

Inert Gas Series: Xenon (1969)
(From a measured volume to indefinite
expansion. On March 4, 1969 on U.S. Route
5 in the Tehachapi Mountains in California,
one quarter liter of Xenon was returned to
the atmosphere.)
> Documentation: color photograph and
> typewritten text
> Photograph, 8 x 10 in. (20.3 x 25.4 cm); text,
> 11 x 8 1/2 in. (29.1 x 20.3 cm)
> Courtesy the artist and Holly Solomon
> Gallery, New York

Radiation Piece, Cesium 137
(1969)
> Cesium
> Solomon R. Guggenheim Museum, New
> York, Panza Collection, Extended Loan

Telepathic Piece (1969)
> Pages from catalogue for "Simon Fraser
> Exhibition," Centre for Communications and
> the Arts, Simon Fraser University, Burnaby,
> British Columbia, 19 May-19 June 1969
> Each page, 9 x 6 in. (22.9 x 15.2 cm)
> Courtesy the artist and Holly Solomon
> Gallery, New York

27 Pieces (1969-71)
> Twenty-seven black-and-white slides
> Dimensions variable
> Courtesy the artist

Marcuse Piece (1970-71)
> Text on wall
> Dimensions variable
> Courtesy the artist and Holly Solomon
> Gallery, New York

Invitation Piece (1972-73)
> Invitation cards (set 2 of 8)
> Eight parts: each individually framed, 9 1/4
> x 12 in. (23.5 x 30.5 cm)
> Herbert Collection, Ghent, Belgium

LOTHAR BAUMGARTEN
Eine Reise oder "Mit der MS
Remscheid auf dem Amazonas": Der
Bericht einer Reise unter den
Sternen des Kühlschranks (A
Voyage or "With the MS Remscheid
on the Amazon": The Account of a
Voyage under the Stars of the
Refrigerator, 1968-70)
> Projection of eighty-one slides
> Projected image, 35 x 24 in. (90 x 60 cm)
> Courtesy the artist and Marian Goodman
> Gallery, New York

Projektion (Projection, 1971)
> Projection of one slide combined with real
> objects
> 118 x 197 in. (300 x 500 cm)
> Stedelijk Van Abbemuseum, Eindhoven, The
> Netherlands

BERND AND HILLA BECHER
Typology of Water Towers (1972)
Six suites of nine photographs each
Each photograph, 15 3/4 x 11 3/4 in. (40.0 x
29.8 cm); each panel overall, 52 1/8 x
40 1/16 in. (132.4 x 101.8 cm)
The Eli and Edythe L. Broad Collection

MEL BOCHNER
Language is Not Transparent (1970)
Chalk on paint on wall
Dimensions variable
Courtesy the artist and Sonnabend Gallery,
New York

Five Sculptures (From a Theory
of Sculpture) (1969-72)
Chalk and stones on floor
Dimensions variable
Courtesy the artist and Sonnabend Gallery,
New York

MARCEL BROODTHAERS
Un jardin d'hiver (A Winter
Garden, 1974)
Two vitrines with four copies of the
catalogue for the exhibition "Carl Andre,
Marcel Broodthaers, Daniel Buren, Victor
Burgin, Gilbert & George, On Kawara,
Richard Long, Gerhard Richter," Palais des
Beaux-Arts, Brussels (1974); two copies of the
artist's book Un jardin d'hiver, twenty-six
engravings; six framed black-and-white
photographic enlargements of engravings;
thirty-six potted palm trees; sixteen garden
chairs; rolled red sisal carpet; black-and-
white closed circuit video camera/monitor
Courtesy Michael Werner Gallery, New York
and Cologne

Un jardin d'hiver (A Winter
Garden, 1974)
Film: 16mm, color, 7 min., sound
Collection Maria Gilissen, Brussels

STANLEY BROUWN
This Way Brouwn (1962-64)
Four drawings on paper
Each, 9 5/8 x 12 1/2 in. (24.5 x 31.8 cm)
Herbert Collection, Ghent, Belgium

DANIEL BUREN
Bus Benches (1970/82/95)
A work in situ consisting of fifty bus
benches, located throughout Los Angeles,
silkscreened with 8.7 cm (3 1/2 in.) white
and colored vertical stripes.
Courtesy the artist

VICTOR BURGIN
All Criteria . . . (1970)
Printed text on paper
Two sheets: each, 11 11/16 x 8 1/4 in. (29.7 x
21 cm)
Courtesy the artist, John Weber Gallery, New
York, and Galerie Liliane & Michel Durand-
Dessert, Paris

Performative/Narrative (1971)
Black-and-white photographs and printed
text in sixteen parts
Each, 18 x 34 in. (45.7 x 86.4 cm)
Courtesy the artist, John Weber Gallery, New
York, and Galerie Liliane & Michel Durand-
Dessert, Paris

VI (1973)
Offset lithography and printed text in ten
parts
Each, 18 x 24 in.(45.7 x 70 cm)
Courtesy the artist, John Weber Gallery, New
York, and Galerie Liliane & Michel Durand-
Dessert, Paris

ANDRÉ CADERE
Quatre barres de bois ronds
(Four Round Bars of Wood)
Painted wooden segments (black, white,
blue, yellow, red, orange, green)
Four parts: each, 32 1/4 x 1 1/2 in. (82.5 x
3.8 cm)
Collection Yvon Lambert, Paris

Barre de bois rond (Round Bar of
Wood)
Painted wooden segments (red, yellow,
white, black)
73 1/4 x 3 3/4 in. (186 x 9.5 cm)
Collection Yvon Lambert, Paris

Barre de bois rond (Round Bar of
Wood)
Painted wooden segments (red, white, black)
77 1/4 in. x 3 3/4 in. (198 x 9.5 cm)
Courtesy Galerie Liliane & Michel Durand-
Dessert, Paris

JAMES COLEMAN
Slide Piece (1972-73)
Projected images with synchronized audio
narration
Courtesy the artist

HANNE DARBOVEN
24 Gesänge — B. Form (24 Songs —
B. Form, 1974)
Ink on paper
120 parts: 48 at 50 5/8 x 12 in. (128.6 x 30.5
cm); 72 at 17 x 70 3/8 in. (43.2 x 178.8 cm)
Stedelijk Museum, Amsterdam

JAN DIBBETS
The Shadows in My Studio as They
Were at 27-7-69 from 8:40 —
14:10 Photographed Every 10
Minutes (1969)
Thirty-four black-and-white photographs
mounted on cardboard
Overall, 9 1/8 x 407 1/2 in. (23.2 x 1035 cm)
Herbert Collection, Ghent, Belgium

PETER DOWNSBROUGH
Two pole piece, one suspended from the
ceiling, the other implanted in the floor,
according to the constructs for these pieces
established in 1970
Courtesy the artist

Neon 54″/27″ — one piece from a series of
work with neon begun in 1970.

GER VAN ELK
Paul Klee — Um den Fisch, 1926
(1970)
Nine color slides projected on table with
white tablecloth
Stedelijk Museum, Amsterdam

The Rose More Beautiful than
Art, but Difficult, therefore
Art is Splendid (1972)
Color slides projected on framed watercolor
on paper
Collection Liliane and Michel Durand-
Dessert, Paris

The Adieu, III (1974)
Gouache and ink on color photograph
mounted on aluminum
39 1/8 x 36 3/8 in. (99.2 x 92.3 cm) (in
trapezoidal frame)
The Museum of Modern Art, New York,
Hedwig van Amerigen Foundation Fund,
1975

MORGAN FISHER
Score for Picture and Sound Rushes
(1972)
Typewritten on paper
8 1/2 x 11 in. (21.6 x 27.9 cm)
Courtesy the artist

Diagram for an unproduced film (1972)
Typewritten on paper
8 1/2 x 11 in. (21.6 x 27.9 cm)
Courtesy the artist

The Director and His Actor Look
at Footage Showing Preparations
for an Unmade Film (2) (1968)
Film: 16mm, 15 min., b/w, sound
Courtesy the artist

Screening Room (1968/95)
State for the Ahmanson Auditorium, The
Museum of Contemporary Art, Los Angeles
Film: 16 mm, 6 min., b/w, silent
Courtesy the artist

Production Stills (1970)
Film: 16mm, 11 min., color, sound
Courtesy the artist

Picture and Sound Rushes (1973)
Film: 16mm, 11 min., b/w, sound
Courtesy the artist

Cue Rolls (1974)
Film: 16mm, 5 1/2 min., color, sound
Courtesy the artist

GILBERT & GEORGE
Smashed (1972)
Ten black-and-white photographs
Overall, 75 x 52 in. (190.5 x 132.1 cm)
Collection Ileana Sonnabend, New York

Muscadet (1973)
Twenty-nine black-and-white photographs
Overall, 49 x 27 in. (124.5 x 68.6 cm)
Courtesy Anthony d'Offay Gallery, London

Raining Gin (1973)
Forty-four black-and-white photographs
Overall, 78 x 45 in. (198.1 x 114.3 cm)
Courtesy Sonnabend Gallery, New York

DAN GRAHAM
Figurative (1965)
Original source materials and publication
documentation
Source materials, 24 x 24 1/2 in. (61 x 62.2
cm); publication documentation, 15 x 22 in.
(38 x 56 cm)
Herbert Collection, Ghent, Belgium

Detumescence (1966)
Original source materials and publication documentation
28 x 27 in. (71.1 x 68.6 cm)
Courtesy the artist and Marian Goodman Gallery, New York

March 31, 1966 (1966)
Typewritten paper
3 1/8 x 9 in. (7.9 x 22.9 cm)
Daled Collection, Brussels

Schema (1966)
Printed text and handwriting on paper
Fifteen parts: each individually framed, 20 1/2 x 16 1/2 in. (52.1 x 41.9 cm)
Daled Collection, Brussels

Homes for America (1966–67)
Written and printed texts and black-and-white and color photographs mounted on illustration board
Two panels: each, 40 x 30 in. (101.6 x 76.2 cm)
Daled Collection, Brussels

Side Effect/Common Drug (1966–67)
Offset on paper
46 x 29 7/8 in. (117 x 76 cm)
Daled Collection, Brussels

HANS HAACKE
Shapolsky et al. Manhattan Real Estate Holdings, a Real-Time Social System, as of May 1, 1971 (1971)
Two maps, 142 black-and-white photographs with typewritten data sheets framed in 23 sets of 6 per frame and 1 set of 4 per frame, 6 charts, and explanatory panel (ed. 2)
Maps: each, 24 x 20 in. (61.0 x 50.8 cm); photographs and data sheets: each, 20 x 7 1/2 in. (50.8 x 19.1 cm) (framed sets, 23 at 21 x 43 1/2 [53.3 x 110.5 cm] and 1 at 21 1/2 x 30 in. [54.6 x 76.2 cm]; charts: each, 24 x 20 in. (61.0 x 25.4 cm); panel, 24 x 20 in. (61.0 x 50.8 cm)
Collection the artist

DOUGLAS HUEBLER
Site Sculpture Project – 42° Parallel Piece (1968)
Photocopies, typewritten texts, and postal receipts
Panel, 17 3/4 x 38 in. (45.1 x 96.5 cm); vitrine, 11 1/2 x 23 x 39 in. (29.2 x 58.4 x 99.1 cm)
Courtesy the artist and Holly Solomon Gallery, New York

Location Piece #13, Kern County, California (1969)
Three color photographs, California Section Map No. 66, general map of California, and statement
Each photograph, two at 10 x 8 in. (25.4 x 20.3 cm) and one at 8 x 10 in. (20.3 x 25.4 cm); section map, 10 3/8 x 8 1/2 in (26.4 x 21.6 cm); general map, 25 x 14 in. (63.5 x 35.6 cm); statement, 11 x 8 1/2 in. (27.9 x 21.6 cm); overall, 32 x 38 in. (81.3 x 96.5 cm)
Private Collection

Duration Piece #5, New York City (1969)
Ten black-and-white photographs and statement
Each photograph, 9 1/4 x 7 1/2 in. (23.5 x 19.1 cm); statement, 11 x 8 1/2 in. (27.9 x 21.6 cm); overall, 48 x 42 in. (121.9 x 106.7 cm)
Collection Lucy R. Lippard

Location Piece #7, New York City, Pier 18 (1971)
Four black-and-white photographs by Shunk-Kender, four black-and-white photographs by the artist, and statement
Each photograph, 6 5/8 x 9 1/4 in. (16.8 x 23.5 cm); statement, 11 x 8 1/2 in. (27.9 x 21.6 cm); 40 x 36 in. (101.6 x 91.4 cm)
Collection Jack and Nell Wendler, London

Duration Piece #7, Rome (1973)
Fourteen black-and-white photographs and statement
Overall, 39 1/4 x 32 1/4 in. (99.7 x 81.9 cm)
Courtesy the artist and Leo Castelli Gallery, New York

81/Variable Piece #70: 1971, Rome (1973)
Twenty-five black-and-white photographs, twenty-four hand-painted acrylic portrait renderings, and statement mounted on board
Overall, 48 3/4 x 45 3/4 in. (123.8 x 116.2 cm)
Courtesy the artist and Holly Solomon Gallery, New York

Variable Piece #101, West Germany (1973)
    Ten black-and-white photographs and statement
    Each photograph, 6 1/2 x 4 1/2 in. (16.5 x 11.4 cm); statement, 11 x 8 1/2 in. (27.9 x 21.6 cm); overall, 32 x 38 in. (81.3 x 96.5 cm)
    Collection the artist

Untitled (1969)
    Wall drawing
    Courtesy the artist, Collection Gian Enzo Sperone, Turin

JOAN JONAS

Organic Honey's Visual Telepathy/Organic Honey's Vertical Roll (1972/94)
    Mirror Check (1971)
        Videotape: 6 min., b/w, silent
    Organic Honey's Visual Telepathy (1972)
        Videotape: 23 min., b/w, sound
        Camera by Joan Jonas, assisted by Linda Patton
    Vertical Roll (1972)
        Videotape: 20 min., b/w, sound
        Camera by Roberta Nieman
    Anxious Automation (1972)
        by Richard Serra
        Videotape: 3 min., b/w, sound
        Choreography by Joan Jonas, sound by Philip Glass
    Thirty-seven slides of original performance
    Closed-circuit cameras
    Blackboard with drawing
    Original props on table: two fans, doll, silver spoon, knotted wood, brass plate, rock
    Three costumes
    Reconstructed mirror on wheels
    Selection of original drawings and photographs
    Paper wall
    Photographs: Organic Honey (three details), costume (detail), dog
    Fan
    Original posters: Organic Honey's Vertical Roll and Organic Honey's Visual Telepathy
    Stedelijk Museum, Amsterdam, except **Mirror Check**, Courtesy the artist

STEPHEN J. KALTENBACH

Urn (1967)
    Ceramic pot glazed with ashes from second toe of artist's left foot
    4 x 7 in. (10.2 x 17.8 cm)
    Collection the artist

Time Capsule for Bruce Nauman (1968)
    Stainless steel cylinder
    Collection Bruce Nauman

Time Capsule Series (1968)
    Two stainless steel cylinders
    Length: each, 7 7/8 in. (20 cm); diam., 2 7/8 in. (7.3 cm)
    Courtesy the artist and John Natsoulas Gallery, Davis, California

Time Capsule for The Museum of Modern Art (1968)
    Stainless steel cylinder and ink on paper
    Cylinder: length, 12 1/16 in. (30.6 cm) ; diam., 3 in. (7.6 cm); text, 3 7/8 x 11 1/8 in. (9.8 x 28.3 cm)
    Library of The Museum of Modern Art, New York

Kiss (Graffiti Stamp: Lips of the Artist) (1968)
    Rubber stamp and red ink
    Image size, 7/8 x 1 3/4 in. (2.2 x 4.4 cm)
    Courtesy the artist and John Natsoulas Gallery, Davis, California

Sidewalk Plaques (1968)
    Cast bronze plaques to be set in concrete
    "Art Works": 5 x 8 1/8 x 5/8 in. (12.7 x 20.6 x 1.6 cm)
    "Earth": 3 3/4 x 10 11/16 x 1/4 in. (9.5 x 27.1 x 0.6 cm)
    "Air": 3 3/4 x 6 5/8 x 1/4 in. (9.5 x 16.8 x 0.6 cm)
    "Fire": 3 3/4 x 7 3/4 x 1/4 in. (9.5 x 19.7 x 0.6 cm)
    "Water": 3 3/4 x 11 x 1/4 in. (9.5 x 27.9 x 0.6 cm)
    "Blood": 4 x 10 1/2 x 1/4 in. (10.2 x 26.7 x 0.6 cm)
    "Flesh": 4 x 10 1/2 x 1/4 in. (10.2 x 26.7 x 0.6 cm)
    "Skin": 4 x 8 1/2 x 1/4 in. (10.2 x 21.6 x 0.6 cm)
    "Bone": 4 x 9 x 1/4 in. (10.2 x 22.9 x 0.6 x cm)
    Courtesy the artist and John Natsoulas Gallery, Davis, California

Artforum Ads (November 1968-December 1969)
Texts placed as advertisments in twelve
issues of *Artforum*
Page size: each, 10 1/2 x 10 1/2 in. (26.7 x
26.7 cm)
"Art Works": 7, no. 3 (November 1968):
72
"Johnny Appleseed": 7, no. 4 (December
1968): 74
"Art": 7, no. 5 (January 1969): 15
"Tell a lie": 7, no. 6 (February 1969): 71
"Start a rumor": 7, no. 7 (March 1969):
96
"Perpetrate a hoax": 7, no. 8 (April
1969): 80
"Build a reputation": 7, no. 9 (May
1969): 73
"Become a legend": 7, no. 10 (Summer
1969): 11
"Teach Art": 8, no. 1 (September 1969):
69
"Smoke": 8, no. 2 (October 1969): 79
"Trip.": 8, no. 3 (November 1969): 85
"You are me.": 8, no. 4 (December
1969): 75
Courtesy the artist

Slant Step (c. 1969)
Fiberglass and rubber mat
Approx. 18 x 18 x 18 in. (45.7 x 45.7 x 45.7
cm)
Private Collection

Design for Neil Armstrong's Left Boot Tread
(1969)
Drawing and letter
Drawing, 18 x 24 in. (45.7 x 60.9 cm); letter,
11 x 8 1/2 in. (27.9 x 21.6 cm)
Collection the artist

Blood Money (c. 1968)
Artist's blood mixed with acrylic medium on
gauze
2 7/8 x 2 7/8 in. (7.3 x 7.3 cm)
Courtesy the artist

ON KAWARA
Title (1965)
Liquitex on canvas
Three panels: two at 46 1/2 x 51 1/2 in. (118.1
x 130.8 cm); one at 51 1/2 x 63 in. (130.8 x
160 cm)
Collection the artist

JOHN KNIGHT
One in a series of closed-circuit video projects
produced between early 1969 through 1971
Courtesy the artist

JOSEPH KOSUTH
Leaning Glass (1965)
Glass and metal plaque
72 x 72 in. (182.9 x 182.9 cm)
Courtesy Margo Leavin Gallery, Los Angeles

Clear Square Glass Leaning
(1965)
Four glass plates with black lettering
Each plate, 36 x 36 in. (91.4 x 91.4 cm)
Solomon R. Guggenheim Museum, New
York, Panza Collection, Extended Loan

One and Three Chairs (1965)
Photographic enlargement and chair
Dimensions variable
Private Collection

One and Three Photographs (1965)
Photographic enlargements
Dimensions variable
Collection the artist

Wall – One and Five (1965)
Photographic enlargements and wall
Dimensions variable
Courtesy Leo Castelli Gallery, New York

One and Eight – A Description
(1965)
Blue neon tubing
4 x 153 1/2 in. (10.2 x 389.9 cm)
Solomon R. Guggenheim Museum, New
York, Panza Collection, Extended Loan

Self-Described and Self-Defined
(1965)
White neon tubing
Approx. 5 x 48 in. (12.7 x 121.9 cm)
Courtesy Margo Leavin Gallery, Los Angeles

Three Titled Meanings (Art as
Idea as Idea) (1966)
Three black-and-white mounted
photographs
Each, 48 x 48 in. (121.9 x 121.9 cm)
Courtesy Leo Castelli Gallery, New York

The Second Investigation (Art as
Idea as Idea) (1968-69)
Photographic documentation presented
through projected slides
Stedelijk Van Abbemuseum, Eindhoven, The
Netherlands

CHRISTINE KOZLOV

No Title (Black Film #1) (1965)
Film in canister
Canister: 3 3/4 in. (9.5 cm) diam.
Private Collection

No Title (Transparent Film #2)
(1967)
Leader tape in canister
Canister: 7 in. (17.8 cm) diam.
Private Collection

Neurological Compilation (c.
1967)
Nine notebooks
Each, 11 x 8 1/2 in. (27.9 x 21.6 cm)
Private Collection

Information Drift (1968)
Documentation and recorded audiotape
14 3/4 x 12 in. (37.5 x 30.4 cm)
Private Collection

271 Sheets of Blank Paper
Corresponding to 271 Days of
Concepts Rejected (1968)
Sheets of blank paper with typewritten top
sheet
11 x 8 1/2 x 1 in. (27.9 x 21.6 x 2.5 cm)
Private Collection

This Is Not Art (1969)
Ink and pencil on paper
21 1/2 x 17 in. (54.6 x 43.2 cm)
Private Collection

Eating Piece (Figurative Work
#1) (1969)
Twelve typewritten sheets of paper
11 x 8 1/2 in. (27.9 x 21.6 cm)
Collection Eric Fabre, Paris

A Mostly Painting (Red) (1969)
Acrylic on canvas
9 1/4 x 12 1/8 in. (23.5 x 30.6 cm)
Private Collection

Information: No Theory (1970)
Documentation for tape recorder with loop
tape
10 1/4 x 9 3/4 in. (26.0 x 24.8 cm)
Private Collection

DAVID LAMELAS

Film Script (The Manipulation of
Meaning) (1972)
Four projections: Super-8 color film
(transferred to 16mm) and three 35mm slide
projections
Projection one: film (16 mm, 10 min., color,
silent); projection two: sixty-nine color slides;
projection three: sixty-nine color slides;
projection four: fifty-nine color slides
Collection Anny de Decker and Bernd
Lohaus, Antwerp, Belgium

WILLIAM LEAVITT

California Patio (1972)
Mixed-media
Dimensions variable
Courtesy Margo Leavin Gallery, Los Angeles

SOL LEWITT

Wall Drawing #153 (1973)
The Location of a Circle

*A circle whose radius is equal to half the
distance between two points, the first point
is found where two lines would cross if the
first line were drawn from a point halfway
between a point halfway between the center
of the wall and the upper right corner and
the midpoint of the top side to a point
halfway between a point halfway between
the center of the wall and the midpoint of
the right side, and a point halfway between
the midpoint of the right side and the lower
right corner, the second line of the first set is
drawn from a point halfway between a point
halfway between the center of the wall and
a point halfway between the midpoint of the
left side and the upper left corner and the
midpoint of the left side to a point halfway
between a point halfway between the center
of the wall and the upper right corner and a
point halfway between the midpoint of the
right side and the upper right corner; the
second point is found where two lines would
cross if the first line is drawn from a point
halfway between a point halfway between
the center of the wall and the midpoint of
the bottom side and a point halfway
between the center of the wall and the lower
left corner to a point halfway between the
end of the first line of the first set and the
end of the second line of the first set, the
second line of the second set is drawn from
a point halfway between the point where
the first two lines have crossed and a point
halfway between the start of the first line of
the first set and a point halfway between the
midpoint of the left side and the upper left*

corner to a point halfway between the end of the first line of the second set and the midpoint of the bottom side; and whose center is located equidistant to three points, the first of which is located at the center of the wall, the second point is located at a point halfway between a point halfway between the center of the wall and the upper left corner, the third point is located halfway between the start of the first line of the first set and the end of the first line of the second set.

Black pencil, black crayon circle
First drawn by: Peter Forde, James Hoffman, Mike Lawrence, Lois Leckman, Sol LeWitt, Gifford Myers, Ruth May Russell
First installation: The University of California, Irvine, California, March, 1973
Courtesy of the artist

Paragraphs on Conceptual Art (first published 1967)
Original manuscript (four handwritten pages)
Each, 11 11/16 x 8 1/4 in. (29.7 x 21 cm)
Daled Collection, Brussels

Sentences on Conceptual Art (first published 1969)
Original manuscript (four handwritten pages)
Each, 11 11/16 x 8 1/4 in. (29.7 x 21 cm)
Daled Collection, Brussels

RICHARD LONG
Untitled-England (1967)
Two black-and-white photographs
20 x 40 in. (51 x 101 cm)
Solomon R. Guggenheim Museum, New York, Panza Collection, 1991

Untitled (1967)
Black-and-white photographs and mixed media on board
Overall, 24 x 32 in. (61.1 x 81.9 cm)
Tate Gallery, London, Purchased 1976

England 1968 (1968)
Gelatin-silver print mounted on Fome-Cor
30 x 40 in. (76.2 x 101.6 cm)
The Dorothy and Herbert Vogel Collection

A 2 1/2 Mile Walk Sculpture (1969)
Black-and-white photograph and text on paper
7 x 8 in. (18 x 20 cm)
Solomon R. Guggenheim Museum, New York, Panza Collection, 1991

Wiltshire (1969)
Map with text
14 x 13 in. (35 x 33 cm)
Solomon R. Guggenheim Museum, New York, Panza Collection, 1991

5 Fifteen Minute Even Walks on Dartmoor, MOORLAND, MARSH, WOODS, ROAD (27 March 1971)
Map and typewritten text
16 x 16 in. (40.6 x 40.6 cm)
Collection Angela Westwater, New York, Courtesy Sperone Westwater, New York

Walking a Line in Peru (1972)
Black-and-white photograph and text on board
25 x 35 in. (64 x 88.7 cm)
Courtesy Lisson Gallery, London

TOM MARIONI
The Act of Drinking Beer with Friends Is the Highest Form of Art (1970-95)
Recreation of an ongoing installation: table and chairs, bar, refrigerator, wooden shelves, free beer, full and empty bottles, framed documentation, and yellow light
Courtesy the artist and Galerie Paule Anglim, San Francisco

GORDON MATTA-CLARK
Splitting (1974)
Black-and-white photo-collage
40 x 30 in. (10.2 x 76.2 cm)
Collection Jane Crawford, Courtesy Rhona Hoffman Gallery, Chicago

Splitting: Four Corners (1974)
Four color photographs
Each, 16 x 20 in. (40.6 x 50.8 cm); overall, 32 x 40 in. (81.3 x 101.6 cm)
Courtesy Gordon Matta-Clark Trust and Rhona Hoffman Gallery, Chicago

Splitting: Four Corners (1974)
Four building fragments
52 3/4 x 40 1/2 x 44 in. (134.0 x 102.9 x 111.8 cm); 54 x 43 3/4 x 42 1/2 in. (137.2 x 136.5 x 108 cm); 54 1/2 x 42 x 42 in. (138.4 x 106.7 x 106.7 cm); 56 x 43 1/2 x 42 3/4 in. (142.2 x 113.5 x 108.9 cm)
Courtesy Gordon Matta-Clark Trust

Splitting: Exterior (c. 1974)
    Six black-and-white photographs
    Two at 12 1/2 x 8 1/4 in. (31.8 x 21 cm); four
    at 16 x 20 in. (40.6 x 50.8 cm)
    Collection Eileen and Michael Cohen, New
    York

N. E. THING CO.
(Iain Baxter and Ingrid Baxter)

1/4 Mile Landscape (1968/95)
    Reconstruction in the spirit of a work from
    1968 comprised of three signs and 1/4 mile
    of landscape
    Courtesy N. E. Thing Co., Vancouver

ACT #111 Ellsworth Kelly's
Painting Blue and White
(Toronto) (1968)
    Felt pen on gelatin-silver print
    13 x 20 in. (33.0 x 49.5 cm)
    University of British Columbia, Courtesy
    Morris and Helen Belkin Art Gallery,
    Vancouver

ART #16 Robert Smithson's "Non-
Sites" (1968) (1968-69)
    Felt pen on gelatin-silver print
    27 x 39 in. (70.5 x 100.3 cm)
    National Gallery of Canada, Ottawa

ART #19 Marcel Duchamp's Total
Art Production Except His Total
Readymade Production (1968)
    Felt pen on gelatin-silver print
    27 x 39 in. (70.5 x 100.3 cm)
    Collection N. E. Thing Co., Vancouver

ACT #25 Three Orange Columns,
Fairfield & Hartford Place,
Seymour Heights, North
Vancouver, B.C. Canada. 1967-68
(1967-68)
    Felt pen on gelatin-silver print
    27 x 39 in. (70.5 x 100.3 cm)
    Collection N. E. Thing Co., Vancouver

ACT #53 Saskatchewan Prairie,
Wheat Harvest Season, Near
Regina Saskatchewan, 1968 (1968)
    Felt pen on gelatin-silver print
    13 x 20 in. (33 x 49.5 cm)
    Collection Ian and Charlotte Townsend-
    Gault

ACT #58 Get It at Woodward's
Garage, Free Parking and Two
Arrows Woodward's Shopping
Centre, Cambie and Cordova
Corner, 1967 (1967)
    Felt pen on gelatin-silver print
    13 x 20 in. (33 x 49.5 cm)
    Collection N. E. Thing Co., Vancouver

ACT #102 Back of Outdoor Movie
"Drive In" Screen, 60 Miles East
of Toronto on Highway 401, 1968
(1968)
    Felt pen on gelatin-silver print
    13 x 20 in. (33 x 49.5 cm)
    University of British Columbia, Courtesy
    Morris and Helen Belkin Art Gallery,
    Vancouver

ACT #107 Triangular-Shaped (VSI)
Visual Sensitivity Information,
Telecasted View of Moon's
Surface from inside Apollo 8
Spacecraft through Window as
Seen on Canadian National C.B.C.

T.V. over Sanyo T.V. Set, 9", in
North Vancouver, B.C., Canada,
December 25, 1968 (1968) (1969)
    Felt pen and collage on gelatin-silver print
    27 x 39 in. (70.3 x 100.4 cm)
    National Gallery of Canada, Ottawa

BRUCE NAUMAN
Eleven Color Photographs (1966-
67/70)
    Portfolio of eleven color photographs
    published by Leo Castelli Gallery, New York
    (ed. 6/8)
        "Bound to Fail"
        19 3/4 x 23 1/2 in. (50.2 x 59.7 cm)
        "Coffee Spilled Because the Cup Was
    Too Hot"
        19 3/8 x 23 in. (49.2 x 58.4 cm)
        "Coffee Thrown Away Because It Was
    Too Cold"
        19 7/8 x 23 5/8 in. (50.5 x 60 cm)
        "Drill Team"
        19 7/8 x 23 3/4 in. (50.5 x 60.3 cm)
        "Eating My Words"
        9 3/8 x 23 1/8 in. (49.2 x 58.7 cm)
        "Feet of Clay"
        23 3/8 x 22 3/8 in. (59.4 x 56.8 cm)
        "Finger Touch No. 1"
        19 5/8 x 23 1/2 in. (49.8 x 59.7 cm)
        "Finger Touch with Mirrors"
        19 7/8 x 23 3/4 in. (50.5 x 60.3 cm)
        "Self-Portrait as a Fountain"
        19 5/8 x 23 1/2 in. (49.8 x 59.7 cm)
        "Untitled (Potholder)"
        19 3/4 x 23 3/4 in. (50. 2 x 60.3 cm)
        "Waxing Hot"
        19 7/8 x 19 3/8 in. (50.5 x 49.2 cm)
    Heithoff Family Collection

Composite Photo of Two Messes on
the Studio Floor (1967)
  Gelatin-silver print
  40 1/2 x 123 in. (102.9 x 312.4 cm)
  The Museum of Modern Art, New York, Gift
  of Philip Johnson, 1984

MARIA NORDMAN
Untitled (1973-)
150 N. Alameda 11:15 am October 12, 1995
Open through October 12-29, 1995, Tues. - Sun.
11 am - 5 pm;
October 31, 1995 - February 4, 1996, 10 am - 5 pm
With opening time continuously adjusted as to
coordinate time of construction.
Unlimited as to form.
The choice of place in the city is the work already.
The chance presence of the passersby constructs
the coordinates of meaning (naming–not naming).
The choice of time determines the emplacement
of materials.
A loading door onto a sidewalk used by persons
working in the center of Los Angeles or going to
the train station south of Temple on the warehouse side of the Temporary Contemporary that
has never been used for a work of art or as an
entrance.

Choice of site and first preparation details in the
presence of the artist.

DENNIS OPPENHEIM
Gallery Transplant, 1969
  Floor specifications of Gallery #3, Stedelijk
  Museum, Amsterdam, transplanted to Jersey
  City, New Jersey. Surface: snow, dirt, and
  gravel. Duration: 4 weeks.
  Black-and-white photograph, stamped black-
  and-white photographic topographic map,

black-and-white floor plan, black-and-white
photographic texts dry-mounted on museum
board.
Four panels: two at 40 x 60 in. (101.6 x 152.4
cm); one at 60 x 40 in. (152.4 x 101.6 cm);
one at 16 x 60 in. (40.6 x 152.4 cm); overall,
160 x 75 in. (406.4 x 127 cm)
Collection the artist

Sterilized Surface. Glass.
(1969)
  Galerie Yvon Lambert, Paris
  Stage #1. Application of commercial glass
  cleaner.
  Stage #2. Removal of cleaner.
  Stage #3. Sterilized surface.
  The residual film produced a surface only
  1/4" from the gallery interior.
  Black-and-white photographs and black-and-
  white photographic texts dry-mounted on
  museum board
  Four panels: each, 30 x 40 in. (76.2 x 101.6
  cm) (overall, 160 x 30 in. [406.4 x 76.2 cm])
  Collection the artist

Reading Position for Second
Degree Burn (1970)
  Stage #1 and Stage #2. Skin, book, solar
  energy.
  Exposure time: 5 hours.
  Jones Beach, 1970.
  Two color photographs and black-and-white
  photographic text dry-mounted on museum
  board
  Three panels: two at 40 x 60 in. (101.6 x
  152.4 cm); one at 6 x 60 in. (15.2 x 152.4 cm)
  Collection the artist

BLINKY PALERMO
Zu "Treppenhaus," Galerie Konrad
Fischer, Düsseldorf
(Documentation of "Stairwell,"
Galerie Konrad Fischer,
Düsseldorf, 1970)
  Black-and-white photographs and pencil and
  gouache on paper
  One panel, 36 1/2 x 29 in. (93 x 73.7 cm)
  Kunstmuseum, Bonn

Zu "Fenster I" Wandmalerei im
Kabinett für aktuelle Kunst,
Bremerhaven (Documentation of
"Fenster I" Wall Painting for
Kabinett für aktuelle Kunst,
Bremerhaven, 1970/71)
  Color photographs and pencil on paper
  Two panels: each, 35 3/8 x 26 in. (90 x 66 cm)
  Kunstmuseum, Bonn

Zu Wandmalerei auf gegenüber-
liegenden Wänden in der Galerie
Heiner Friedrich, München
(Documentation of Wall Painting
on Opposite Walls in the Galerie
Heiner Friedrich, Munich, 1971)
  Color photographs and pencil on paper
  Three panels: each, 26 x 35 3/8 in. (66 x 90
  cm)
  Kunstmuseum, Bonn

Zu Wandmalerei "Treppenhaus"
documenta 5, Kassel, 1972
(Documentation of Wall Painting
"Stairwell" Documenta 5, Kassel,
1972, 1972)
  Color plate and black-and-white photograph
  on paper
  One panel, 26 x 35 3/8 in. (66 x 90 cm)
  Kunstmuseum, Bonn

Zu "Blaue Dreiecke" Palais des
Beaux-Arts, Brüssel
(Documentation of "Three Blue
Corners," Palais des Beaux-Arts,
Brussels, 1972)
Color photograph and pencil on paper
One panel, 35 3/8 x 26 in. (90 x 66 cm)
Kunstmuseum, Bonn

GIULIO PAOLINI
Apoteosi d'Omero (Apotheosis of
Homer, 1970-71)
Thirty-three music stands, thirty folders with
black-and-white photographs, two folders
with color photographs, and one folder with
two pages of text
Each folder, 11 7/8 x 13 3/8 in. (30 x 34 cm)
Installation dimensions variable
Herbert Collection, Ghent, Belgium

ADRIAN PIPER
Here and Now (November 1968)
Portfolio of sixty-four loose sheets of typewritten mimeographed paper, with one
sheet of typewritten paper and one sheet of
graph paper, in cardboard folder
Folder, 9 x 9 1/8 x 1/2 in. (22.9 x 23.2 x 1.3
cm); each sheet, 8 1/4 x 8 1/4 in. (21 x 21 cm)
Courtesy John Weber Gallery, New York

Utah-Manhattan Transfer (1968)
United States Department of the Interior
Geological Survey map, Camel's Back Ridge,
Northeast Quadrangle, Utah, with square
removal from New York City subway map
taped onto surface; New York City subway
map with square removal from Geological
Survey glued onto surface
Geological Survey map, 13 1/2 x 14 1/2 in.
(34.3 x 36.8 cm); New York City subway map,
12 1/8 x 12 1/4 in. (30.8 x 31.1 cm)
Courtesy John Weber Gallery, New York

Hypothesis: Situation #4
(September 1969-March 1970)
Black-and-white photographs collaged to
graph paper, photocopy, and typewritten
paper
11 x 17 in. (27.9 x 43.1 cm), 11 x 8 1/2 in. (27.9
x 21.6 cm), 11 x 41 in. (27.9 x 104.1 cm)
Courtesy Paula Cooper Gallery, New York

3 Untitled Projects (0 to 9
Project) (March 1969)
Three-ring binder filled with pages from 13
March 1969 issue of *The Village Voice*, typewritten pages, blank pages, photocopy of
map, and graph paper, each encased in plastic sleeves
Binder, 11 3/4 x 10 1/2 x 3 in. (29.8 x 26.7 x
7.6 cm); sleeves, 11 x 8 1/2 in. (27.9 x
21.6 cm); sheets, various dimensions
Courtesy John Weber Gallery, New York

Hypothesis: Situation #5
(September 1969-March 1970)
Black-and-white photographs and ink on
paper, photocopy, and typewritten paper
10 7/8 x 29 1/2 in. (27.6 x 74.9 cm) and 11 x
17 in. (27.6 x 74.9 cm), and 11 x 8 1/2 (27.9 x
21.6 cm)
Courtesy Paula Cooper Gallery, New York

Hypothesis: Situation #10
(September 1969-March 1970)
Black-and-white photographs and ink on
paper, photocopy, and typewritten paper
10 7/8 x 18 1/8 in. (27.6 x 46 cm), 11 x 17 in.
(27.6 x 74.9 cm), and 11 x 8 1/2 (27.9 x 21.6
cm)
Courtesy Paula Cooper Gallery, New York

Context #7 (June-September 1970)
Seven three-ring binders labeled "i"-"vii" and
filled with blank pages written and drawn on
by visitors to "Information," The Museum of
Modern Art, New York, 2 July-20 September
1970
Each binder, 11 3/4 x 10 1/2 x 3 in. (29.8 x
26.7 x 7.6 cm) (closed); each page, 11 x 8 1/2
in. (27.9 x 21.6 cm)
Courtesy John Weber Gallery, New York

Context #8 (June 1970)
Three-ring binder filled with printed, photocopied, and mimeographed pages encased
in plastic sleeves
Binder, 11 3/4 x 10 1/2 x 3 in. (29.8 x 26.7 x
7.6 cm) (closed); sleeves, 11 x 8 1/2 in. (27.9 x
21.6 cm); pages, various dimensions
Courtesy John Weber Gallery, New York

Context #9 (May-June 1970)
Three-ring binder filled with handwritten
and typed pages by the artist encased in
plastic sleeves
Binder, 11 3/4 x 10 1/2 x 1 3/4 in.; (29.8 x
26.7 x 4.4 cm) (closed); sleeves, 11 x 8 1/2 in.
(27.9 x 21.6 cm); pages, various dimensions
Courtesy John Weber Gallery, New York

Food for the Spirit (1971)
Three-ring binder filled with pages torn from
Immanuel Kant, *Critique of Pure Reason*,
annotated by the artist, and with black-and-
white photographic self-portraits of the
artist, each encased in plastic sleeves; twelve
black-and-white photographs
Binder, 11 3/4 x 10 1/2 x 1 1/2 in. (29.8 x
26.7 x 3.8 cm) (closed); sleeves, 11 x 8 1/2 in.
(27.9 x 21.6 cm); pages, 7 1/4 x 4 1/2 in.
(18.4 x 11.4 cm); photographs in binder,
3 5/8 x 3 5/8 in. (3.6 x 3.6 cm); photographs, 24 x 24 in. (61 x 61 cm)
Collection Thomas Erben, New York

YVONNE RAINER
Trio A (The Mind Is a Muscle,
Part I) (1966)
Choreographed 1966; filmed in 16mm, 14
August 1978
Videotape: 10 min., b/w, silent
Courtesy the artist

Lives of Performers (1972)
Film: 16mm, 90 min., b/w, sound
Courtesy the artist and Zeitgeist Films

Film About a Woman Who . . .
(1974)
Film: 16mm, 105 min., b/w, sound
Courtesy the artist and Zeitgeist Films

ALLEN RUPPERSBERG
The Picture of Dorian Gray
(1974)
Pentel on canvas
Twenty panels: each, 72 x 72 in. (182.9 x
182.9 cm)
Collection Stuart and Judy Spence, South
Pasadena, California

EDWARD RUSCHA
Chocolate Room (1970/95)
360 sheets of paper silkscreened with
chocolate
Installation dimensions variable
Courtesy the artist

ROBERT SMITHSON
Mono Lake Non-Site (Cinders near
Black Point) (1968)
Painted steel container, cinders, and site map
Container, 7 x 39 3/4 x 39 3/4 in. (17.8 x
101.0 x 101 cm); map, 40 1/4 x 40 1/4 in.
(102.2 x 102.2 cm)
Museum of Contemporary Art, San Diego,
Museum Purchase

Nonsite: Line of Wreckage,
(Bayonne, New Jersey) (1968)
Painted aluminum and broken concrete,
photodocumentation, and map
Aluminum and concrete, 59 x 70 x 12 1/2 in.
(149.9 x 177.8 x 31.8 cm); photodocumenta-
tion: three panels: each, 3 3/4 x 49 in. (9.5 x
124.5 cm); map, 3 3/4 x 49 in. (9.5 x 124.5 cm)
Milwaukee Art Museum, Purchase, National
Endowment for the Arts Matching Funds

MICHAEL SNOW
Tap (1969–72)
Framed black-and-white photographs,
framed typewritten texts on paper, tape
player, speaker, wire, and audiotape
Photograph with frame, 42 x 61 1/2 in.
(106.8 x 156.3 cm); typewritten text with
frame, 25 5/8 x 15 3/4 in. (65.1 x 40 cm);
speaker, 19 x 15 x 10 in. (48.3 x 38.1 x 25.4 cm)
National Gallery of Canada, Ottawa

NIELE TORONI
Imprints of a No. 50 Brush
Repeated at Regular Intervals of
30 cm (1966/95)
Courtesy the artist

WILLIAM WEGMAN
Cotto (1969)
Gelatin-silver print
10 1/8 x 10 1/4 in. (25.7 x 26 cm)
Collection Edward Ruscha

Duck/Crow (1970)
Gelatin-silver print
10 1/4 x 10 1/4 in. (26 x 26 cm)
Collection Edward Ruscha

Dog/Milk (1970)
Two gelatin-silver prints
Each, 13 1/2 x 10 1/2 in. (34.3 x 26.7 cm)
Collection Edward Ruscha

Family Combinations (1972)
Six gelatin-silver prints
Each, 12 1/2 10 5/16 in. (31.7 x 26.2 cm)
Collection Edward Ruscha

Ray-o-vac (1973)
Six photographs mounted on board
Overall, 25 3/4 x 44 1/4 in.
The Museum of Modern Art, New York, Given
anonymously, 1981

16 Es and 16 Ls (1972)
Ink on paper
11 x 8 1/2 in. (27.9 x 21.6 cm)
Courtesy the artist

4 Hairpins; 4 Paper Clips (1973)
Pencil on paper
8 1/2 x 11 in. (21.6 x 27.9 cm)
Courtesy the artist

Percentage Problem (1973)
  Pencil on paper
  8 1/2 x 11 in. (21.6 x 27.9 cm)
  Courtesy the artist

Neighbor's Ball Bounces over
House (1973)
  Pencil on paper
  8 1/2 x 11 in. (21.6 x 27.9 cm)
  Courtesy the artist

Own Your Own (1975)
  Ink on paper
  12 x 9 in. (9.5 x 22.9 cm)
  Courtesy Sperone Westwater, New York

Selected Works
  Videotapes
    Reel 1 (1970-72)
    30 min. 8 sec., b/w, sound
    Reel 2 (1972)
    14 min. 9 sec., b/w, sound
    Reel 3 (1972-73)
    17 min. 54 sec., b/w, sound
    Reel 4 (1973-74)
    20 min. 57 sec., b/w, sound
    Reel 5 (1975)
    26 min. 38 sec., b/w, sound
    Reel 6 (1975, dated 1976)
    18 min. 35 sec., b/w and color, sound
  Courtesy the artist

LAWRENCE WEINER

ONE QUART GREEN EXTERIOR INDUS-
TRIAL ENAMEL THROWN ON A BRICK
WALL (cat. 002/1968)
  Collection Alice Zimmerman Weiner, New
  York

A 36" X 36" REMOVAL TO THE LATHING
OR SUPPORT WALL OF PLASTER OR
WALLBOARD FROM A WALL (cat.
021/1968)
  The Siegelaub Collection & Archives

FIRECRACKER RESIDUE OF EXPLO-
SIONS AT EACH CORNER OF THE
EXHIBITION AREA (cat. 027/1968)
  The Siegelaub Collection & Archives

AN OBJECT TOSSED FROM ONE
COUNTRY TO ANOTHER (cat. 028/1968)
  Collection Public Freehold

A SQUARE REMOVAL FROM RUG IN USE
(cat. 054/1969)
  Museum Moderner Kunst, Stiftung Ludwig,
  Vienna, Collection Hahn, Cologne

A TRANSLATION FROM ONE LANGUAGE
TO ANOTHER (cat. 071/1969)
  Collection Public Freehold

MIDDLE OF THE ROAD (cat. 224/1970)
  Daled Collection, Brussels

LEFT OF CENTER (cat. 225/1970)
  Daled Collection, Brussels

RIGHT OF CENTER (cat. 226/1970)
  Daled Collection, Brussels

IAN WILSON

See pp. 226 of this publication